The Sacred Willow

*Four Generations
in the Life
of a Vietnamese Family*

Duong Van Mai Elliott

OXFORD
UNIVERSITY PRESS

OXFORD

UNIVERSITY PRESS

Oxford New York
Athens Auckland Bangkok Bogotá Buenos Aires
Calcutta Cape Town Chennai Dar es Salaam Delhi Florence
Hong Kong Istanbul Karachi Kuala Lumpur Madrid
Melbourne Mexico City Mumbai Nairobi Paris São Paulo
Singapore Taipei Tokyo Toronto Warsaw

and associated companies in
Berlin Ibadan

First published by Oxford University Press, Inc., 1999
198 Madison Avenue, New York, New York 10016 .

First issued as an Oxford University Press paperback, 2000

Oxford is a registered trademark of Oxford University Press

Library of Congress Cataloging-in-Publication Data
Elliott, Duong Van Mai, 1941
The sacred willow : four generations in the life of a Vietnamese family / by Duong Van Mai Elliott.
p. cm.
Includes bibliographical references and index.
ISBN 0-19-512434-0 (Cloth)
ISBN 0-19-513787-6 (Pbk.)
1. Vietnam--History--19th century. 2. Vietnam--History--20th century.
3. Elliott, Duong Van Mai, 1941- --Family. 4. Duong family.
5. Van Dinh (Vietnam)--Genealogy. 6. Vietnam--Genealogy.
I. Title.
DS556.8.E44 1999
959.704--dc21
98-14204

10 9 8 7 6 5 4 3 2 1
Printed in the United States of America
on acid-free paper

The Sacred Willow

Dedicated to my family

THE LEGEND OF THE SACRED WILLOW

Long ago, a king's son became sick
and fell unconscious. A holy man
from India broke off a branch from
the Duong willow tree, dipped it
in water, and sprinkled the water
on the prince, who immediately
revived and was cured. From then
on, the Duong willow was said to
be a sacred tree.

Contents

Preface

Growing up in Hanoi, Haiphong, and Saigon, I loved listening to the stories told by my parents and other relatives about *their* parents and grandparents. I found these tales fascinating—some funny, some tragic—but although I knew that they spoke of family continuity, values, and Vietnamese traditions, they did not, at first, coalesce in my mind into a narrative larger than the individual parts. It was when I was in my late teens that I began to see how these anecdotes merged into a whole—a tale that reflected, in miniature, the history of Vietnam in the modern era. Still later, I began to see the common threads that ran through the lives of my great-grandfather, grandfather, parents, and siblings: the struggle to adapt and survive in the face of upheavals that more than once turned their world upside down, and the attempt to make the right choices for their families, for themselves, and for their country, often in very confusing circumstances. Someday, I told myself, I would write that story. In this book, *The Sacred Willow*, I hope I have done it justice.

The work that follows is based on dozens of interviews that I conducted with my relatives over the years, on family records, on archive documents, on research done on-site in Vietnam, and on information from existing works in English, French, and Vietnamese. It traces the social, cultural, and political events that have shaped the men and women of our family over four generations—the scholars and mandarins, the silk merchants, the military officers, and the revolutionaries—who were witnesses as well as participants at many of the key moments. These events, beginning in the late nineteenth century, include the French conquest of Vietnam, the war against French colonial rule, the brief years of peace, the socialist transformation of the north, the resumption of fighting in the south with American involvement until the communist victory in 1975, the evacuation of refugees from Saigon, and the effect of the communist victory on my relatives who remained in Vietnam. *The Sacred Willow* is also my story, from my childhood in northern Vietnam to my adolescence in Saigon, my student days in the United States, my meeting and falling in love with my American husband, my life and work in South Vietnam during some of the fiercest years of the war in the 1960s, and my evolution from hawk to dove.

I have chosen to tell my family's story in a scope and depth that, as far as I know, have not been attempted by a narrative work written by a Vietnamese in English. I believe that this provides a continuity that allows readers to see the chain of events unfold from the beginning and follow their impact on my family until the final resolution of the conflict and its aftermath. My purpose is to show Vietnam in all its complexities at peace and at war, good and bad, traditional and transformed. I have elected to tell a story, rather than write an academic analysis, because I believe that a personal narrative can render history more immediate to readers and make them empathize better with the people who lived through the events. Other works published in the West have focused on the French and Americans and have relegated the Vietnamese to the background, but I have shown them—as they saw themselves—as the central players in their own history.

The Vietnamese who appear in American writing (and film) about the war are most often either villagers in combat areas or Saigonese soldiers or bar girls, yet Vietnam had a substantial population of educated, urban, middle-class families, including mine. As the reader will see, this did not mean they were untouched by war and turbulence. I have attempted, above all, to evoke the intense and conflicting feelings of each generation of my family, and others like them. I have presented the dilemma confronting the Duong in choosing sides in the internecine conflicts unleashed by the French conquest, and have shown those conflicts through the eyes of relatives on opposing sides. While most of my relatives threw in their lot with the French and, later on, with the Americans, others went against personal and family interests to join the communist-led resistance and revolution. These divisions were not unique to my family, and actually extended throughout the middle class, dating from the watershed years of 1945-46, when hundreds of thousands of patriotic Vietnamese joined the communist resistance to fight the French, who were trying to reimpose their colonial rule after Ho Chi Minh had declared independence.

Looking back over this narrative, one of the themes I see in it is the irony and unpredictability of history. The choices each person made had unforeseen consequences that, at times, made losers out of winners. I see also the tenacity of family bonds that, though strained, were ultimately stronger than any political differences. I find it heartening that the Duong, and the Vietnamese people, have survived through the turmoil. Like the willow, they have bent with the wind, but remain unbroken.

Acknowledgments

A book of this scope could not have been written without the generous help of many people. First, I express my gratitude to my parents, especially my mother, who became my main source of information on the family after my father's death in 1979. Second, I thank all my siblings who shared their remembrances with me, in particular my sister Thang, her husband Hau, my brothers Giu, Xuong, Luong, and Tuan, and my sisters Yen, Tuyet, and Loan. I also convey my appreciation to my cousins, nephews, and nieces, especially Phi, Luc, Thuc, Trung, An, Minh, Lap, Hien, Lan, and Nam, for the information they provided. I want to emphasize that none of my relatives should be held accountable for anything that appears in this book. They supplied the stories, but the interpretation and analysis is mine, and I take full responsibility for it. I am also indebted to many relatives for the family photos, documents, and other information that they gave me, especially my brother-in-law Khiet, my nephew Bao and his father Chuong, and my uncle Tong, who wrote an erudite book about my great-grandfather Duong Lam.

This book would not have been as historically insightful and accurate without my husband David's suggestions. I feel I can never thank him enough for his love, unflagging interest, and enthusiastic support.

Without the grant from the National Endowment for the Humanities, it would have taken me longer to complete this book: I would have had to wait until I could save enough money to undertake the many research trips I ended up making. But more important than speeding up the process, the NEH support put the imprimatur of a prestigious institution on my book and gave it more credibility. I am certain that the grant opened doors for me and allowed me to eventually get my manuscript into print. For this invaluable backing, I thank the NEH and its staff who helped steer my application through to approval.

I am also indebted to the numerous authors—Vietnamese, French, and American—whose books I have relied on to describe the historical background and validate the dates and events in my family story. They can take comfort in the fact that their scholarship has been put to good use. Finally, I could not have gotten this book published without the dedication and commitment of the Wylie Agency, in particular of Jin Auh and Sarah Chalfant, and without the support of Oxford University Press, especially Peter Ginna, who edited my manuscript with great skill and sensitivity. Last, but not least, I thank the numerous relatives and friends who gave me constant encouragement and showed intense interest in my project, and, above all, I express my gratitude to my mother-in-law Louise for her loving support.

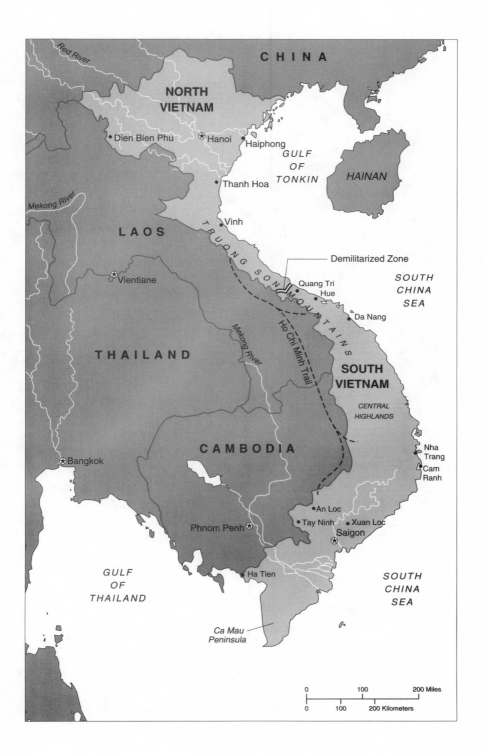

CHINA

NORTH
VIETNAM

Red River

• Dien Bien Phu   ⊛ Hanoi
        • Haiphong   *GULF*
                     OF
                     TONKIN   *HAINAN*

Mekong River   • Thanh Hoa

                • Vinh

LAOS

                              Demilitarized Zone

⊛ Vientiane   *SOUTH*
                      Quang Tri   *CHINA*
                      Hue   *SEA*

                             • Da Nang

THAILAND

Mekong River

                    SOUTH
                    VIETNAM

                    CENTRAL
                    HIGHLANDS

CAMBODIA   Nha
                              Trang
                              Cam
⊛ Bangkok   Ranh

              • An Loc
Phnom Penh ⊛ • Tay Ninh   • Xuan Loc
                      Saigon ⊛

GULF   • Ha Tien   *SOUTH*
OF   *CHINA*
THAILAND   *SEA*

Ca Mau
Peninsula

0   100   200 Miles
0   100   200 Kilometers

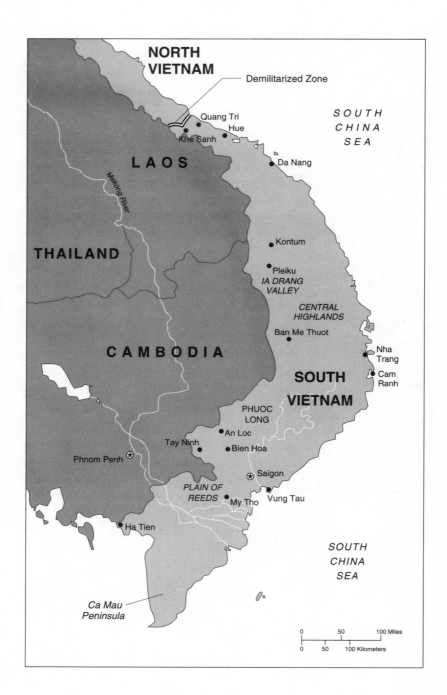

NORTH VIETNAM

Demilitarized Zone

Quang Tri
Hue
Khe Sanh

Da Nang

LAOS

Mekong River

THAILAND

Kontum

Pleiku
*IA DRANG
VALLEY*

*CENTRAL
HIGHLANDS*

Ban Me Thuot

*SOUTH
CHINA
SEA*

Nha
Trang

Cam
Ranh

CAMBODIA

**SOUTH
VIETNAM**

PHUOC
LONG

An Loc

Tay Ninh

Bien Hoa

Phnom Penh

Saigon

*PLAIN OF
REEDS*

My Tho

Vung Tau

Ha Tien

*SOUTH
CHINA
SEA*

*Ca Mau
Peninsula*

| 0 | 50 | 100 Miles |
| 0 | 50 | 100 Kilometers |

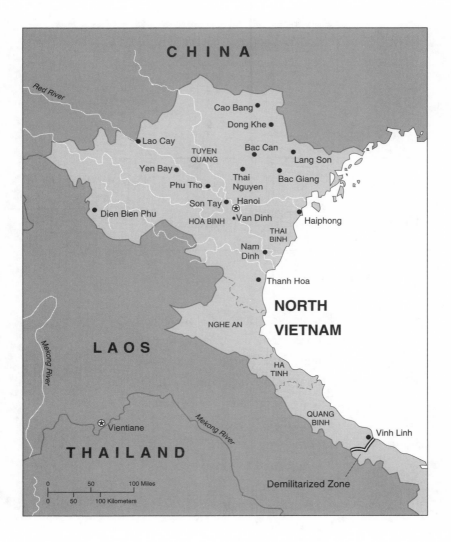

CHINA

Red River

Cao Bang
Dong Khe
Lao Cay
TUYEN QUANG
Bac Can
Lang Son
Yen Bay
Thai Nguyen
Bac Giang
Phu Tho
Son Tay
Hanoi
Dien Bien Phu
HOA BINH
Van Dinh
Haiphong
THAI BINH
Nam Dinh
Thanh Hoa

NORTH VIETNAM

NGHE AN

LAOS

Mekong River

HA TINH

QUANG BINH

Vientiane

Vinh Linh

THAILAND

Mekong River

Demilitarized Zone

0   50   100 Miles
0   50   100 Kilometers

Family Tree

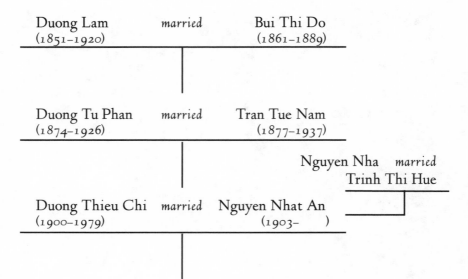

Duong Lam   *married*   Bui Thi Do
(1851–1920)   (1861–1889)

Duong Tu Phan   *married*   Tran Tue Nam
(1874–1926)   (1877–1937)

Nguyen Nha   *married*
Trinh Thi Hue

Duong Thieu Chi   *married*   Nguyen Nhat An
(1900–1979)   (1903–   )

Duong Van Luat (*died in infancy*)
Duong Hong Ta (*died in infancy*)
Duong Van Thang
Duong Van Mao (*died in 1969*)
Duong Hong Hung (*died in infancy*)
Duong Hong Giu
Duong Hong Xuong
Duong Van Phu (*died 1984*)
Duong Hong Luong
Duong Hong Tuan
Duong Van Binh
Duong Van Yen
Duong Hong Nam (*died in infancy*)
Duong Van Mai
Duong Van Cuc (*died in childhood*)
Duong Van Loan
Duong Van Tuyet

The Sacred Willow

1

≡

A Burial in the Night

My family owes its good fortune to
a mysterious man. What he did one
night changed my ancestors' destiny, leading them from poverty to
social prominence.

When this enigmatic figure
appeared in my family's story
toward the end of the eighteenth
century, Vietnam was still in the
throes of a civil war that would
erupt intermittently and last over
200 years. It was an unsettled time,
with several clans backed by armies
vying for domination. After their
province in the central region of the
country had turned into a raging
battlefield, my ancestors fled. But
there was no safe haven in the next
province, or the next, as the opposing armies swept back and forth

destroying everything in their path. So, along with thousands of other desperate peasants, my ancestors kept moving further and further north, trying to escape warfare, drought, and hunger. The trek finally took them to Van Dinh, where they settled down. This village is located on the bank of the Day River, about forty kilometers south of Hanoi. People here earned their livelihood by growing rice. They also grew vegetables in the soil along the bank of the river and sugarcane on higher ground. For extra food, they caught fish, shrimp, and freshwater clams, as well as crabs and snails that became plentiful in the flooded rice fields during the rainy season. The industrious villagers also sold bricks, cooking pots, and toys that they made by using clay scooped from the riverbank.

The Day is a branch of the mighty Red River, which irrigates and nourishes the delta of northern Vietnam with its rich silt. From its source in the mountain range in southern China, the Red River flows for hundreds of miles before pouring into the sea. As it penetrated into the flat delta, this river, enlarged by tributaries, began to course in a bed that was higher than the surrounding plain. During the monsoon, especially in July and August, the river would become menacing. Swollen by the incessant and torrential rainfall, it raged its way to the sea, frequently overflowing its banks and threatening to drown the surrounding land. To tame the floodwaters, an elaborate network of dikes had been constructed centuries before. But the dikes, built with wooden pillars, bamboo poles, and compacted earth, could not always contain the river and its branches. Inundations continued to occur almost every year, killing people and animals, and destroying crops and houses. Bandits usually emerged after the most disastrous inundations, as destitute peasants resorted to armed robbery for survival.

For villages like Van Dinh, the Day River was both a blessing and a bane, providing water to irrigate their lands, but also threatening them with flooding. The river drew the villagers to its rich alluvial soil, but also compelled them to keep their distance, shielded by the dike or safely perched on the higher ground near the market place. The thirteen-foot-tall dike, whose flat and wide top also served as the main road into the village, dominated Van Dinh's landscape. When my ancestors arrived, all the desirable housing spots had been taken, so they built their hut near the river's edge, on the "wrong side" of the dike. Whenever the water level rose, the river overflowed into their back yard and occasionally even into their house. As outsiders, my ancestors were viewed with suspicion and discriminated against by the clannish villagers. Most of the rice fields were the communal property of the village and were distributed only to the indigenous residents for cultivation. Migrants who came to settle like my ancestors were not entitled to a part of the land, and so were deprived of this main source of income. Some of the migrants earned their living by making clay pots, while others survived by doing odd jobs, fishing in the river, and by catching crabs and snails in the rice fields. The only hope for them to escape their lowly status and poverty was to produce sons who could become mandarins—officials in the imperial bureaucracy and the elite of society at the time.

Scholars who aspired to become mandarins had to spend years mastering classical Chinese, introduced when China ruled the country from 111 B.C. to A.D. 939, and thereafter retained by the royal court, even after independence had been achieved, as the official language for all its documents. In addition, these scholars had to digest a daunting body of Chinese writings, learn how to compose elegant prose and poetry, and memorize Vietnamese and Chinese history, in order to pass a series of progressively more difficult exams. The goal of this education was not to encourage original thinking, but to produce men of culture who could master the wisdom of Confucius and his disciples and apply it to protect the welfare of the people. The higher the degree earned, the higher the potential appointment would be within the imperial bureaucracy and the faster the rise to the top. Only a relatively small number of people had the ambition and the persistence to pursue this career path.

My ancestors, who descended from scholars, were determined to continue their family's tradition, in spite of their poverty. The men focused on their studies and did odd jobs on the side. They survived mainly because their wives were able to contribute to the meager income by buying and selling goods at the various local markets. Every three years, the men tried their chances at the civil service exams, hoping to pass and to earn a position in the bureaucracy. If they succeeded, they would have power and prestige, though they certainly would not become rich, as the court paid mandarins only a low salary, supplemented with a rice ration sufficient to feed their families. Joining the imperial bureaucracy meant joining a select group whose members were expected to dedicate themselves to a life of virtue and duty and to accept a standard of living that was only slightly above that of the people they governed. In the view of the court, when it made a scholar a mandarin, it gave him such an honor—anointing him as one of the country's most wise, most educated, and most virtuous men—that it did not need to pay him generously as well.

The mysterious man's connection with my family began with his friendship with Duc Thang, my ancestor of six generations ago. By this time, my family had lived in Van Dinh for about a hundred years. Three generations had come and gone, without achieving any noticeable success. The family had escaped poverty at one point, when one of the men married into a rich household. But by Duc Thang's generation, the family had once again fallen into abject poverty, victimized by the bandits that were taking advantage of the unsettled situation in the countryside. In their forays into Van Dinh, they had ransacked and burned down Duc Thang's hut—not once, but several times. Instead of destroying his spirit, this motivated him to study harder to pass his exam and escape his predicament.

At this time, most people could not read or write. Whenever illiterate people needed to have something recorded, they would go to students, scholars, or retired mandarins for help. In exchange, they would pay them a small sum or, since barter was common, give them betel leaves, areca nuts, rice wine, tea, or a combination of these. Duc Thang used to sit outside the gate of a pagoda near his village and hire himself out to the faithful, writing prayers in Chinese characters in exchange for a small fee. When worshipers had a big favor to ask of the deities, they would burn such messages in a special trough inside the pagoda courtyard to convey their pleas to the gods.

It was at this pagoda that the mysterious man met Duc Thang, and liked him immediately. They became friends, but after Duc Thang stopped visiting the pagoda, the man lost contact with him. Several years later, he decided to look for him in Van Dinh. When he arrived, disguised as a poor traveler, he learned that the scholar had been dead for many years. He found Duc Thang's house as evening fell. The poverty he saw was appalling. Without telling her who he was, he asked Duc Thang's widow for some water to wash his dusty feet. Although he looked poor, she greeted him with kindness and hospitality. He thought she was worthy of help and revealed that he was a geomancer, someone who could read signs in the earth and identify auspicious spots for burial sites to ensure the good fortune of future generations. He said, "I can show you where to put your husband's grave so that your descendants will have a better life. But you must tell me first whether you want them to be rich or to become successful scholars and mandarins." She answered, "I want them to have success and prestige, not wealth." Her choice made sense because, during the time in which she lived, scholars and mandarins were the most respected social classes. The wealthy, on the other hand, were despised because people believed that commerce, the usual source of money for the rich, was a parasitic—if not dishonest—occupation. Over time, as social values changed, my relatives would come to regret the widow's selection. In my generation, many of my relatives would rather have traded their academic successes and poorly paid government jobs for wealth. And in my family, whenever we had money problems, my siblings and I would half-jokingly condemn Duc Thang's widow for her bad judgment.

After the widow told him what she wanted, the man said, "I'll help you get your wish. I know of a very good location for a grave in the village. I want you to dig up your husband's bones and rebury them there." But she protested. Exhumation was out of the question: she did not have the money to buy a clay pot in which to put the bones for reburial, as required by custom. The stranger reassured her, "Don't worry, just use a bamboo basket, if you can't afford to buy a clay pot." At exactly midnight, the man asked Duc Thang's widow and son to take him to the grave. After the bones had been dug up and placed in the basket, he told them to follow him. Guided only by starlight, they made their way to the new site the man had chosen. It turned out to be located in the middle of a common graveyard, where only wretched people without relatives or descendants to take care of their graves were buried. Wandering souls resided here, forever disconsolate because no one was burning joss sticks or making offerings to their spirits. Duc Thang's widow wept with disappointment and clung to the basket, refusing to bury the bones here. The stranger soothed her, "Don't worry. This is an auspicious site. In three years, all the other graves will be relocated. With them gone, the earth's currents will be unblocked and will flow directly into your husband's grave." Before leaving, he told the widow not to build a tomb over the grave. He also wrote a cryptic poem predicting the successes of future generations:

> First, a member of the Royal Academy
> Second, two governors
> Every twenty years, a generation of scholars
> Every twenty years, a generation of mandarins

Earth termites later built up the mound so that the grave, unrestricted by construction, kept growing year by year, an encouraging sign that it had been placed in powerful earth currents. It is said that if you stood on high ground and looked down at the grave, you would see that the contours of the earth around it formed the shape of an ink slab and a brush, the writing implements used by a scholar. You would also see the shape of a horse, the animal that a scholar rode on his triumphant return to his village, after winning the *tien si*, or doctorate degree—the pinnacle of academic achievement and a door-opener to a high position in the government. When I visited Duc Thang's grave in October 1993, I was astonished to find that, after almost 200 years, the mound had not been leveled by the passage of time. While all the old graves in the vicinity had disappeared, Duc Thang's burial site could still be seen protruding over the rice fields surrounding it. The ink slab and the brush had, unfortunately, been turned into rice fields, and the horse had had his left foot clipped when a nearby road was built. Because of this injury to the horse's left foot, people in my clan have become prone to accidents involving the left leg. When I fell and broke my left kneecap in 1981, I became another casualty of the carelessness of those road builders.

For about a hundred years after he first appeared in our history, we did not know who the mysterious stranger was. Then, one night, my great-grandfather spoke to the god of Tan Vien Mountain, Vietnam's most sacred peak, through a medium. This spirit, a mythical figure associated with the origins of our people, told him that this enigmatic person was a monk who had taken the ordained name of Thanh Tinh Thien Su, or Master of Purity and Serenity. From that day onward, my great-grandfather began to worship the monk as if he were one of our ancestors. On the anniversaries of their deaths and at Tet, our lunar new year, when he prayed to their departed souls, he would also thank this holy man for his deed. This became a tradition for my clan. The predictions came true one by one. Duc Thang's son received the honorific title of royal academician upon his retirement as the mandarin in charge of education for Son Tay Province, and launched the family on the path of success and better fortune. The two governors foretold by the monk, Duong Lam and Duong Khue, my great-grandfather and great-granduncle, did not appear until three generations later. Every twenty years—or so runs my family's belief—one or several relatives should achieve prominence in government service or as scholars, just as the monk predicted.

Duong Lam, my great-grandfather, was born in 1851, the third year of Emperor Tu Duc's reign during the Nguyen dynasty, the one that had emerged triumphant from the long civil war and that would be the last to exist. Considering the tradition in Duong Lam's family, there was no question that he would train to become a scholar and an official. So he immersed himself for years in the study of philosophy, history, and poet-

ry, under his father's tutelage. He wanted success for himself, to earn
fame as a scholar and prestige as a mandarin. But he also wanted success
for his parents, who had great hopes for him, and whom he wanted to
repay with the honor that society would bestow on them if he tri-
umphed. He excelled in his studies, and mastered the art of writing
prose and poetry. But scholastic brilliance could not always guarantee
success. As is the case with any exam anywhere in the world, luck—or
fate—has much to do with passing or failing. The Vietnamese also
believed that justice beyond the grave was at work during exams. The
souls of those that had been wronged would come back to seek revenge
against the perpetrators, while those that owed a debt to those still living would return to help their benefactors.

The first-level examination consisted of three to four sessions.
Candidates who passed all of them received what can be called a master's degree—or *cu nhan*—and those who passed all but one earned a *tu
tai*—or a bachelor's degree—the lowest in the system. The examination
was extremely competitive, and only a few candidates were chosen out
of a field of thousands, with usually twenty to twenty-five master's
degrees and seventy to seventy-five bachelor's degrees at each site.
Seven major categories of complex if not incomprehensible rules governed all the exams, and an infraction could result in disqualification or
even imprisonment, depending on the seriousness of the oversight or
offense. A careless juxtaposition of words unintentionally implying a
criticism of the throne was considered *lèse-majesté* and could land the
candidate in jail.

The exam tested not only a candidate's intellect, but also his mental
and physical endurance. Due to the huge number of candidates at each
site, there were no permanent exam rooms. Instead, each candidate had
to bring his own tent, a portable bamboo couch that also served as a
writing table, paper, brushes, ink, water, and food, as each session lasted all day and candidates were not allowed to leave the site. On exam
day, the candidates had to arrive before daybreak and submit themselves
to a thorough search by the guards before being allowed inside, to make
sure they were not smuggling in any written materials along with their
paraphernalia.

Strict measures were taken to prevent cheating. Sentinels standing
guard in watchtowers and soldiers patrolling on horseback kept vigil to
prevent candidates from sneaking into one another's tent and offering
help. To make sure that the papers submitted by the candidate had been
composed at the site and not prepared beforehand and smuggled in, the

first ten or so pages used by each candidate were stamped with an official seal, and the manuscript had to be stamped again at noon on the exam day. An elaborate procedure for selecting the examiners and for grading was observed to prevent cheating. Mandarins appointed as examiners were chosen from outside the region where the exam was to be held. At the site, they were put in cramped quarters, and held virtually like prisoners until the sessions were over, completely cut off from the outside world, and even unable to communicate among themselves. The manuscripts submitted to them for grading were anonymous, with the candidates' names removed and bearing only coded numbers. Two sets of examiners independently graded each manuscript, and the cumulative grade stood as the final grade, to ensure objectivity and avoid favoritism or cheating. As an added precaution, a military mandarin with no ties to the examiners was put in charge of keeping watch over them and enforcing order at the site.

In his first try at the regional examination, in 1867 at age sixteen, my great-grandfather did not succeed completely, getting only the bachelor's degree. If he was disappointed, he would also have felt comforted by the fact that he had done better than thousands of other scholars who never managed to earn even this degree, and spent their youth making repeated but fruitless attempts. Brilliant scholars who failed were not despised but simply pitied because fate did not reward their talent, and *hoc tai thi phan*—"learning depends on one's ability, but succeeding at the exams depends on one's fate"—became the common lament for those cursed with bad luck at the exam site.

In normal times, my great-grandfather would have focused his energy only on succeeding in the next exam. But he was not living in normal times. In 1873, French troops bombarded and stormed Hanoi's citadel. This attack was France's first salvo in its war to take over the northern part of Vietnam following its conquest of the southern region in 1867. Outgunned, the governor of Hanoi felt he had only one honorable response. Wounded and taken prisoner, he ripped off his bandages and committed suicide by starving himself to death. After taking over Hanoi, French forces moved out to conquer the surrounding area. The campaign gave my great-grandfather the opportunity to prove himself. He recruited and trained militiamen to defend a citadel in his native district that stood in the way of the French advance. Under his leadership, the citadel resisted the enemy siege for two months. It was ultimately spared when the invaders withdrew from the north following their commander's death in a skirmish in Hanoi. For his achievement, Duong Lam was later cited by the court in its official account of those events.

With the departure of the French, things returned to normal. In 1878, Duong Lam took the mandarin exam again and not only earned the *cu nhan* degree, but took the highest honor as the valedictorian. In a country that revered learning, Duong Lam's success won him instant fame. After that, there was only one thing left for him to do: pursue the most prized degree—the *tien si*, equivalent to the doctorate. But first, he would have to make the arduous trip to Hue, the imperial capital, where this series of exams was held. Hundreds of miles lay between Van Dinh and Hue. He would have to get there and back on foot and by boat, sailing along the shore of the South China Sea, then making his way by land through jungles and mountains. The trip took over a month.

The imperial exam, held every three years, was extremely competitive. Each time, only ten scholars out of a field of 150 to 200 candidates would be chosen. The exam would begin with three rigorous sessions. Those that passed would sit for a fourth, held in the Imperial Palace, with subjects chosen by the emperor himself. Sometimes, an emperor would even grade the exams personally. If the candidates succeeded, they would earn the doctorate degree. If not, they would become "candidate doctors." My great-grandfather entered the first round of exams with great confidence. But although he turned in brilliant papers, he was disqualified because of a minor infraction. For the rest of his life, this twist of fate would nag at him. When his oldest son, my grandfather, also failed the same exam years later, it was like rubbing salt in the wound. The family was finally vindicated in 1919 when my oldest uncle Tuong earned the doctorate degree, in the last *tien si* exam to be held in Vietnam.

The failure rankled even more because Duong Lam's older brother Duong Khue, whom he measured himself against, had taken and passed this exam in 1868, and had received many honors. My great-granduncle could easily have failed as well. When Duong Khue sat for the palace exam, he and the other candidates were asked to write an essay on a topic Emperor Tu Duc had chosen himself: "Make War or Make Peace." The imperial Council of Ministers was then hotly debating this issue. The court was split. On one side were those that wanted to make peace with the French. On the other side were those that wanted to go to war to get back the southern provinces that the emperor had been forced to cede to France. The emperor took the opportunity of the exam to test the best minds in the country on this issue. For the candidates, it was a loaded topic, because they had no way of knowing what the emperor himself was thinking. However they came down on the issue, they might run the risk of offending the throne.

Duong Khue couched his essay in such diplomatic language that the emperor did not take offense. In it, my great-granduncle opposed the concession the emperor had made, but avoided criticizing the throne directly. He said simply that as a loyal subject he had wept upon reading the royal edict announcing the loss of territory to the French. Then he went on to recommend that the court go to war to expel the foreigners. The emperor liked the composition, but did not agree with this suggestion, and wrote the comment "Not appropriate to the situation" in vermillion ink in the margin. That was not the last time my great-granduncle recommended going to war. He would do this two more times in petitions he addressed to the throne. This audacity could have cost him his career, if not his freedom or even his head.

If my great-grandfather had passed the *tien si* exam, he would have enjoyed the many honors that his older brother had experienced. After earning the doctorate degree, Duong Khue was granted an audience with the emperor, entertained at a royal banquet, given a robe and a hat adorned with a silver flower design of his own choosing, and invited to stroll the imperial garden. The emperor also gave Duong Khue a gift of precious cinnamon bark that had been presented to the court as tribute, observing, "We notice that *tien si* Duong Khue does not look well. We instruct him to take care of his health so that he can serve the country." This was a great honor, since this cinnamon—a kind found on only a few trees out of thousands growing in a cinnamon forest—was believed to be a wonder drug, capable of curing innumerable diseases, and even of bringing the dying back to life.

My great-grandfather, however, did not have the luxury of indulging in anger and disappointment. The French were back. After a third attempt, they occupied Hanoi in 1883. Although it would take France twelve years to pacify the north, this date marked the end of Vietnamese independence. Sporadic and localized armed resistance against French domination would continue until the last band of rebels was subdued in 1913. But it had become clear to most people after 1883 that military struggle would be futile and would bring only further death and destruction to the people. For the mandarins, the choice was either to accept the situation and collaborate, or to resist passively by resigning or refusing to take up their posts when appointed. Most had to adapt and to cooperate, to avoid retaliation against themselves and their families. Most were also driven to cooperation because government work, the only career they were trained for, was the most viable means for them to support their families.

Following the conquest, the north became a French protectorate and assumed the name of Tonkin. The emperor would continue to rule this region through a viceroy, but all the latter's decisions had to be presented to and approved by the French official representative, called a *résident supérieur*. In addition, French officials were placed at the head of each province to oversee the mandarins who, however, were allowed to retain most of their autonomy. From that date onward, my great-grandfather's life and career would be drastically changed by the French presence.

In 1884, when the French consolidated their hold over the north, my great-grandfather had just begun his mandarin career, having become district magistrate in Ha Dong province in 1883. The goal he had struggled for was finally within his grasp. Yet, as fate would have it, the moment of triumph would become clouded only months later by the loss of independence. He stayed in this position for three years, but his heart was not in it. He resigned in 1886, using his mother's illness as an excuse, the first of many resignations during his career. Although he was forced to resume government service time and again, either in response to official summonses that he could not turn down, to meet his family's heavy financial burdens, or to do whatever good he could as a mandarin for a country in its hour of need, my great-grandfather did so with reluctance.

For the rest of his life, until his retirement, he would feel the conflicting pull of what scholars at the time called "engagement" and "withdrawal." Should he, as a scholar trained to serve the court and the country, join the government and risk getting stigmatized by collaborating with the French? Or should he abstain from dealing with affairs of state, even if he could make some difference, and keep his reputation intact? He would also struggle with the issue of loyalty, a value that scholars considered central to their lives. Could he, in "engaging," separate loyalty to the court from loyalty to France, which controlled it? And could he, as a mandarin, be loyal to the people and their welfare, without also furthering the interests of France? Despite his frequent discomfort and discouragement at "engaging" himself, he always met his mandarin responsibilities head-on, for he was a man of honor and took his duties seriously. He knew he could not singlehandedly change the situation, so he carried on as best he could and bided his time, waiting for the opportunity to reverse his country's fate. Unfortunately, this opportunity never came during his lifetime.

A year after he resigned as district magistrate, the dilemma presented itself in the form of a summons. Nguyen Huu Do, the first viceroy of Tonkin following the French conquest, appointed my great-grandfather as his assistant. It was an honor and a demand that Duong Lam could not have rejected. If he had refused, the court and the French would have viewed his decision as an act of opposition. Besides, by this time, he had a large family to support: a wife, three children, and two parents without an income of their own. So this appointment, giving him a sizable salary, was too attractive to turn down. Thus began a long period of "engagement" for my great-grandfather, one that would last for ten years.

His new position was a double-edged sword. The viceroy admired and trusted him, but Duong Lam's power created enemies. Complaints that he was using his influence to put his friends in key positions soon reached the ears of the French. They became alarmed and suspected that my great-grandfather was trying to create a political network. There was perhaps some substance to the charges. But more probably Duong Lam was simply fulfilling his personal obligations. In Vietnam there was a saying that "when one man becomes a mandarin, the whole clan can benefit from his position." So my great-grandfather must have been under intense pressure from relatives as well as friends to give them jobs in the government. If he had refused to help, he would have been accused of failing to meet his obligations—a serious criticism in a society that prized good personal relationships.

Duong Lam's influence continued to rise even after the death of the viceroy at the end of 1888. Tran Luu Hue, the new viceroy, admired and trusted him as much as the previous one, and even promoted him to a higher grade. This official came to rely on my great-grandfather so much that Duong Lam's jealous colleagues began to complain that he was the real viceroy of Tonkin. Hanoi, as the seat of power for north Vietnam, was full of intrigues, where the more unscrupulous mandarins jockeyed for positions and influence, tried to curry favors with the new French masters, and did not hesitate to resort to slander and anonymous denunciations to bring down their rivals. Even jealous relatives could turn into enemies, such as the one in Van Dinh who denounced Duong Lam and his older brother to the French in 1888, accusing them of seditious activities. This was a serious allegation that could have cost Duong Lam and his brother their freedom, if not their lives, and ruined their families.

Duong Lam's colleagues' complaints about him became more vociferous. This time, the French reaction was more serious. One high-ranking official, a member of the *résident supérieur*'s cabinet, expressed his uneasiness over Duong Lam in a memo, in which he called my great-grandfather brilliant but too arrogant, and advocated removing him from the viceroy's circle. When the viceroy and Duong Lam became personally linked by the marriage of their children—my grandfather and grandmother—they had to inform the authorities of this relationship, in conformity with a law that the French had established to prevent collusion among high officials. My great-grandfather had to request a transfer, and the French gladly complied, transferring him in 1889 to Hung Hoa, a distant province.

The year 1889 was a trying one for my great-grandfather. His first wife died, and he had to pull up stakes and move from the capital of Hanoi to a trouble spot. Duong Lam had married his first wife, the daughter of a governor, when she was thirteen years old, a very acceptable age considering that girls past the age of sixteen were already considered too old to marry. My family's chronicle did not say much about my great-grandmother (or any of my female ancestors, for that matter) except to praise her virtues, in particular her filial piety, her devotion to her husband and children, and her harmonious relationship with everyone. Family records were not written to reveal the truth, but to inspire awe and respect for ancestors. So my great-grandmother was held up as the model of a "great and virtuous lady."

When she fell ill, my great-grandfather took a month-long leave of absence to care for her at their residence in Hanoi. But his ministrations and those of the doctor failed. At her death, my great-grandmother left five children, the youngest newly born. Still reeling from this tragedy, my great-grandfather received the order to leave the comfort and security of Hanoi for troubled Hung Hoa province, where he had been appointed judge, one of several assistants to the mandarin in charge of a province, called a governor in the case of a small province, or a governor general in the case of a large one. Hung Hoa was located in the hilly region above the flat delta plain, and its main town, bearing the same name, controlled navigation on the Red River. Occupying such a strategic point on the water route leading into the vital delta, the town was a fortified citadel topped with an observation tower famous for its attractive design. The province of Hung Hoa at this time was plagued by the Black Flags, members of the T'aiping Rebellion in China who had fled to Vietnam. For a while, the Vietnamese court had used them to fight the French. But like guests that refuse to leave after a party, the Black Flags stayed on when they were no longer needed and began to resort to banditry. They were reinforced by Vietnamese bandits who joined them to pillage, kidnap, and sow terror among the villages.

There were daring attacks on the Hung Hoa citadel during the time my great-grandfather served as judge in this province. Most nights, the citadel echoed with the sound of cannon fire, rifle shots, and war drums, as the government forces fought these roving bands. After such assaults, government troops would launch counter-expeditions, returning with captured suspects to throw into the provincial jail. As the judge, my great-grandfather had to try each case. He believed in justice and in the ideal that mandarins should be humane toward their subjects. During his tenure, he ordered the release of hundreds of these prisoners once he determined they were innocent. His performance impressed the French official overseeing the province, who gave him a flattering annual appraisal, calling him an "active, intelligent, and erudite man" and observing that he "appeared" loyal. It also earned him a promotion three months later, as chief judge and chief administrator of another important province closer to the delta. But his rejoicing was cut short. Hoang Cao Khai, the new viceroy and a former colleague who had watched Duong Lam's swift rise with resentment, now used his power to banish my great-grandfather to Luc Nam, a province tucked deeper into the mountains near the border with China.

In this posting, he would have to display the conflicting qualities that the court looked for in its mandarins: He would have to be a ruthless military commander to maintain law and order, and he would have to be a benign administrator, a "father and mother" figure, that the people he governed aspired to have. Luc Nam was a pestilential region surrounded by thick forests and plagued by Chinese and Vietnamese bandits who engaged in pillage and in opium and arms smuggling. The night after he assumed his position, he heard explosions around the citadel and, looking out from his window, he saw the sky aflame. He could hear the yells of the bandits, who fought their way to the gate of the citadel before the defenders' cannon fire and bullets drove them away.

As the mandarin in charge of the province, my great-grandfather was responsible for maintaining peace and security within his territory. So, after this brazen attack, he began leading expeditions against the Chinese bandits and their Vietnamese allies. The rugged territory favored the bandits, who were encamped on the high points controlling the passes. Logistics and troop movements were slow and arduous. In this terrain where soldiers had to scale cliffs or march single file, hacking their way through the forest's thick growth, my great-grandfather could not deploy massive forces to overwhelm the bandits or take them by surprise. The French later would face the same problem here against the Communists and their allies, as would the Americans in similar rugged terrain in South Vietnam.

Once, the bandits came close to capturing and killing my great-grandfather. They had routed his forces and surrounded him in a forest clearing. Duong Lam jumped on his horse, tugged at the reins, and shouted, "Don't fail me now!" The horse took off instantly, scattering the bandits. Duong Lam knew they could track him from the hoofprints, so when he approached his residence, he dismounted and set the animal loose to return to the stable on its own. Then he smeared his face and clothes with mud and hid in a culvert under the road. From his hiding place, he could hear the bandits' feet thundering over his head as they charged headlong in pursuit.

That experience did not deter my great-grandfather from continuing his operations. He eventually succeeded in subduing the bandits, capturing their leaders—one of whom he beheaded—and destroying their lair. Peace would finally come to the border region when the Chinese bandits retreated back into their country. During his expeditions, my great-grandfather also released a large number of women that the bandits had kidnapped and held in their stronghold. At the end of his life, he would look back on this liberation of innocent villagers with pride, as an example of the good that he was able to achieve as a mandarin. His success in ridding the villages of the bandits' scourge earned him the gratitude of the local people, who built a small temple in Quynh Village to worship him. Although the temple was later destroyed by the French during 1945 to 1954, two pillars praising Duong Lam's accomplishment are still standing.

My great-grandfather knew that Hoang Cao Khai, his enemy in Hanoi who had dispatched him to Luc Nam, expected him to be ravaged physically and mentally by the experience. So he wrote a poem, ostensibly to give news of himself, but in fact to mock this mandarin. In it, he said that, far from being destroyed, he—a good man enjoying divine protection—had prevailed. He also painted the picture of himself as a man who refused to let the stress unnerve him and who could still take his ease amidst the turbulence to enjoy music and an occasional cup of wine, relaxations that scholars considered refined and worthy of their time.

> As I look up at the blue Tan Mountain
> I send you, my friends, my best wishes.
> These mountains and rivers are all part of our country.

Wherever I go, heaven protects me.
My confidence sustains me as I strike.

In 1891, Hoang Cao Khai acknowledged Duong Lam's competence
by summoning him back to Hanoi to serve as his assistant. The viceroy,
who had resented Duong Lam's rising star, now realized he needed my
great-grandfather's literary talent to fulfill a task the French had given
him: to start an official journal that would disseminate news and communicate official policies to the mandarins. Being a scholar known for
his learning and writing style, my great-grandfather was considered the
most qualified man to serve as editor of this journal. With its elegant
and erudite writing, the journal quickly became a favorite among scholars and mandarins. Khai was a learned and very capable man, but also a
ruthless and authoritarian mandarin who did not hesitate to use his
power to crush those that dared to defy him. He enjoyed the complete
confidence of the French, which he had earned after quelling the last
armed resistance movement in the delta of Tonkin. This suppression
made him the most controversial figure in Tonkin at the time. But he was
such a dangerous man that no one dared to cross or oppose him openly.
And so began my great-grandfather's uneasy relationship with the
viceroy, whom he feared—as did everyone else at that time—but did
not admire. Duong Lam tarried in Luc Nam after his appointment and
did not report immediately to Hanoi, until the viceroy sent him a
peremptory cable commanding him to do so.

To reward him for the success of the journal, the viceroy appointed
Duong Lam governor of Thai Binh province in 1892, when this position
became vacant. Thai Binh was an important province and the home of
many scholars. The viceroy knew that my great-grandfather, with his
reputation as both a brilliant scholar and an able mandarin, would be
not only accepted but also respected by the local population. The year
my great-grandfather assumed his new function, the Tonkin delta was
flooded when the Red River overflowed its banks. The maintenance of
the dike network was one of the most critical duties of the mandarins,
and required enormous expenses of money and labor. Each year, mandarins had to conduct frequent inspections and supervise the maintenance work performed by conscripted villagers, who lived in the vicinity of the dikes and benefited from their protection. For reinforcement,
the villagers would add compacted earth to the top and sides of the
dikes. This work usually began in October, right after the rainy season,
and had to be completed by the end of March. After reinforcement was

completed, the mandarins would direct the villagers to plant rows of bamboo on the riverside base of the dikes, to lessen the force of the water flow and to facilitate silt deposit.

When a dike broke, local mandarins were held responsible and punished with demotion of one or several grades—depending on their rank—if they had failed to predict or prevent the rupture. Occasionally, villagers could see signs that a dike was about to break, and could warn the authorities in time. Once a dike was destroyed at its base, the entire structure collapsed with a thunderous sound—like cannon fire—and water spread rapidly over the surrounding land. Even if a breach could be detected in time, repair work could not always prevent a collapse in stormy weather. The swollen river would sweep away the woven bamboo mats and poles from the sodden ground in which they were planted—a heart-breaking sight for the tired and cold villagers and mandarins, toiling under a threatening sky. When a rupture became imminent, a mandarin would have to rely on his military commander to keep the conscripted villagers from running away and to force them to continue working. Once a section broke, the water would begin to tear away part after part of the remaining dike.

In 1892, my great-grandfather was faced with the task of containing the might of the Red River in Thai Binh province. He spent days and nights on the dikes, braving the heavy rain, inspecting, supervising, praying to the river god, and exhorting the workers to redouble their efforts. His tireless work saved the province, the only one to escape unscathed in the general inundation of the delta. At the end of his life, my great-grandfather would look back and feel extremely proud of having saved so many lives in Thai Binh. The French high authorities commended Duong Lam for his courage and leadership, awarded him a gold medal, and made him a "knight" of the Dragon of Annam order. In addition, the emperor awarded him a blue robe made of the finest brocade. As a sign of my great-grandfather's ambivalent attitude toward the French, he accepted the gold medal but hung it in his pigsty in a gesture of contempt.

Three years later, Duong Lam was recalled to the viceroy's office to serve once again as his assistant. In 1897, the viceroy gave him the title of War Minister. It was only an honorific title, but it signaled that my great-grandfather was now just a few rungs from the top level in the mandarin hierarchy. Not long after this promotion, however, the French eliminated the function of viceroy, which had served as the last link between Tonkin and the court in Hue. The *résident supérieur* in Hanoi now assumed direct control. In the provinces, the mandarins lost the last shreds of autonomy and were reduced to mere figureheads. True power was now concentrated in the hands of French officials at all levels. After this happened, my great-grandfather transferred to the court in Hue, where he assumed the title of Minister for Public Works and, at the same time, fulfilled the function of Deputy Director of the Imperial Historical Records. The French annexation of Tonkin had distressed Duong Lam. So he welcomed the transfer, which, he thought, would give him the chance to take refuge in the last bastion of Vietnamese autonomy.

But the autonomy did not last long. After sweeping royal authority away in Tonkin, the French proceeded to emasculate the court in Hue. The emperor became only a figurehead. The royal decrees might bear his name, but the French were behind the decisions. In the case of my great-grandfather, they were the ones that approved his promotion to governor general, and they were the ones that told the emperor to grant him the title of Baron of Khanh Van. The court was powerless. The French now held the purse strings. Instead of controlling the country's treasury, the emperor received a monthly stipend for himself and his family. After pushing the anemic court to the side, the French set out to create a new and more modern government apparatus, with agencies like customs and management of state monopolies (of opium, salt, and alcohol), public works, agriculture, commerce, postal service, and communication. Vietnam was no longer a nation, but three distinct parts: the colony of Cochinchina and the protectorates of Annam and Tonkin. Then all three were merged with Laos and Cambodia to form the Union of Indochina. The French governor general, headquartered in Saigon, became the ruler of this forced union.

Although my great-grandfather's career was not immediately damaged by the French annexation, he viewed this turning point in his country's history as one of the saddest periods in his life. In the autobiographical poem he wrote for his family two years before his death to review his experiences and teach his descendants how to live by the same traditional values he had obeyed, he compared the situation in 1897 when the French swept away royal authority to the end of a chess game—with the Hue court checkmated—and to a withering flower about to die. For a man who admired his country's achievement and tradition, the annexation was a blow to national pride. He also took it as a blow to his own pride. In the same poem, he expressed his feeling of impotence in stopping the decline and chided himself for his failure.

But as much as he resented this foreign yoke, he had to suppress his hostility and maintain a facade of civility toward the French, with whom he corresponded in the traditional flowery language of the scholar and official, full of exaggerated courtesy ("You are like a star in the firmament") and humble references to himself ("I am but dust and ashes"). In truth, he did not dislike all the colonial officials he met, and seemed to have been friendly with some of them, such as the *résident* in Hung Yen Province, whom he asked to look after his oldest son before he left for his post in central Vietnam. For their part, the French also had an ambivalent attitude toward him. Most of the colonial officials he dealt with recognized his intelligence and leadership and were anxious not to alienate him. But because of the continuing opposition among many mandarins, they never completely relaxed their vigilance over him.

As my great-grandfather must have known when he decided to "engage" himself, this relationship with the French authorities—however ambivalent and reluctant—could tarnish his reputation not only during his lifetime, but also in the verdict of history. Through the good he accomplished, he managed to retain the respect of his contemporaries in a very difficult situation and at a time when the public was quick to condemn mandarins who collaborated with the French. My family still retains the text of an anonymous poem that was posted to the gate of Hoang Cao Khai, the last viceroy of Tonkin, on the occasion of one of his birthdays. Each year, on the viceroy's birthday, all the high-ranking mandarins had to troop to his residence to pay their respects. The poem's anonymous author took this opportunity to express his contempt and hatred for several of the officials present at the celebration, condemning them for their venality and cruelty, but praising Duong Lam and his brother Duong Khue for their filial piety and detachment from the unscrupulous activities of their colleagues. It was a tacit recognition that they had not abused their power.

As for the verdict of history, it remains critical. Although collaboration would become widespread over the eighty years of colonial rule, leaving few of the elite untouched, modern historians in general continue to condemn high-ranking mandarins of Duong Lam's generation for their association with the French. In my great-grandfather's case, there was an undercurrent of criticism that sometimes erupted into print after his death. He was usually attacked not for anything specific, but for pursuing power and prestige when he should have withdrawn from service.

My great-grandfather did not let his concern over his country's state of affairs or his anxiety over whether or not to serve keep him from living fully. He was a vigorous man who knew how to appreciate the good things in life. My parents remembered him as an intimidating figure and yet one with a laugh "so resonant it could be heard in the street," who enjoyed food, wine, and song, but in moderation, as dictated by Confucian rules of behavior. He had a good sense of humor and could laugh at himself. He was not demanding in his tastes and could easily adjust to whatever circumstances in which he found himself: He was just as content eating a humble meal as one full of delicacies, dressing in the finest brocades or in rough cotton. Of course, like all traditional scholars, my great-grandfather loved philosophy and literature, especially poetry, which he considered the most refined and accomplished of the art forms. Like other scholars, he enjoyed reciting and composing poems in the company of friends. On these occasions, wine would flow. He and his guests would drink cup after cup, to put themselves in a better mood to savor the beauty of the verses. These and other poems he wrote were mostly for the enjoyment of himself and his friends or family.

My great-grandfather also appreciated chess and a good card game, mostly for the social aspects. He also loved music and the company of female singers, whom he frequently hired to perform for him and his friends, or visited in their quarters. In the red-light district, singers would ply their clients with food and wine and entertain them with songs. But my great-grandfather's interest in the singers was connected to his love of poetry, since the songs were poems chanted to the accompaniment of musical instruments. He himself wrote several compositions for the singers, some of which he dedicated to those whose talent he appreciated the most, or those with whom he had carried on short liaisons.

My great-grandfather would marry four more times after the death of his first wife. Polygamy was then legal. It was considered natural for a man of his stature to take several consorts. The more he married the more it demonstrated his power and influence, and the magnetism of his achievements. His additional wives were widows or women without good marriage prospects. They became his secondary wives because they had no hope of doing better, or because they believed that being the secondary wife of a great man was better than being the chief wife of a man without a future. Between them, they produced twenty-five more children, giving him a total of thirty sons and daughters. (My great-grandfather was not the only man in the clan to take several wives. So many of my male relatives married so many women who produced so many children that, as their descendants multiplied, I would end up with perhaps one of the most complicated family networks in the world, with ties as tangled as a century-old vine. It is so complicated that my American husband, who holds a Ph.D. in political science, finds it impossible to unravel.)

The four wives were unhappy over his affairs with the singers, but were too afraid of him to complain vociferously. In general, they accepted these liaisons as part of their marriage to someone of his stature, and as a man's natural right. Duong Lam was kind to them, took good care of them, and gave them the dignity that they deserved. In the eyes of society at the time, this placed him beyond reproach. Toward his children, my great-grandfather was a loving but stern father, always insisting on correct conduct, although he was known to indulge them when they were small. In this, he followed the Confucian injunction that a mandarin should first learn to maintain strict discipline and order within his household before he could hope to master the art of ruling a country and an empire. In his strict adherence to Confucian ethics, especially those that governed the relationship between subject and emperor, and between a son and his parents, Duong Lam was also typical of his generation. Toward the throne, Duong Lam was loyal to a fault, questioning but never actively opposing its decisions, even when the Nguyen Dynasty was paralyzed by impotence in its twilight years. In his relationship with his parents, he never deviated from the dictates of filial duties, even at the expense of his flourishing career. Yet he would constantly chide himself for not doing enough to repay his debt to them.

While he was working in Hue, my great-grandfather received the news in February 1898 that his father was gravely ill. Duong Lam immediately requested a leave of absence to return home. Because of his high rank, the emperor alone had the authority to approve this request. But the emperor was on a spring tour, and the request languished at the Ministry of Administrative Affairs. The delay distressed my great-grandfather. Not being at his father's bedside was a serious infraction of filial piety, so every day Duong Lam felt like he was sitting on fire, but he had to suppress his impatience. Then, while he was still waiting for permission, his father died. He immediately submitted a new request, asking for a three-year leave of absence to observe the mourning period, although it would have been acceptable for him to return to work after one year. He knew he would risk his career by withdrawing for such a long period of time. He was getting on in years, and the court gave him no reassurance that it would reappoint him again to another high position when his mourning ended. He took the risk, not only because he believed it was his duty to mourn for three years, but also because he was demoralized by France's brazen grab for complete control of the country and did not want to stay "engaged." His father's death gave him an excuse to retreat from government service without his action being construed as political. The moment he got home, he prostrated before his father's coffin and begged for forgiveness, although he believed that his dereliction of duty was unpardonable and that he would carry his guilt with him until he died.

Withdrawal might have given my great-grandfather moral satisfaction, but it also burdened him with financial worries. At the time he left office, his household had mushroomed to thirty-one dependents. Duong Lam's only income came from rice fields he owned, but it was not enough to feed so many people. At the end of his three-year mourning period, my great-grandfather reluctantly returned to government service and was appointed governor general of the provinces of Binh Dinh and Phu Yen in central Vietnam, a significant assignment. He hesitated, not wanting to leave his elderly mother behind, but she urged him to accept the post. This position marked the highest point in my great-grandfather's career. A governor general was, in the mandarin hierarchy, equivalent to a cabinet minister. After the lean years of retirement, he now enjoyed a life of power and abundance. The French might have clipped the wings of the mandarins, but they left them the outward trappings of authority. At every meal, my great-grandfather was served "delicacies from the mountain and from the sea." Whenever he appeared in public, soldiers riding on elephants provided protection for his retinue, and his route was cleared of traffic. His arrival was heralded by criers and by attendants beating on large and small drums and gongs. According to family lore, the common people would withdraw indoors to avoid disturbing his passage. It was during his tenure here that he married his fifth wife, apparently the distant niece of one of the Nguyen emperors.

But Duong Lam's life was not all ceremony. Once again, he found himself in a sensitive military post, and had to lead expeditions against rebels in the mountain areas. For crushing a revolt in 1902, he was awarded a gold medal and made a "knight" of the Dragon of Annam order, for the second time. In the same year, the emperor also granted him the court title of *Thai tu thieu bao*, or Tutor to the Crown Prince, which now made him a mandarin of the highest grade in the realm. My great-grandfather would stay at this post for only two years. Again, the demands of filial piety, the desire to withdraw from a position in which he felt he was just a puppet of the French, as well as the fear that he could be entrapped by the lure of power, made him cut short his career. He resigned in 1902 when his mother died. He would return briefly to public life in 1907 to write manuals for the teaching of Chinese classics. Although this was a position far below those he had held, he assumed it with enthusiasm because it gave him a chance to help preserve the old learning that he revered. But in 1910, the French decreed that only one more round of imperial exams would be allowed, after which they would be abolished, and eliminated my great-grandfather's position. He retired in that year at age sixty. As a last gesture toward my great-grandfather in his twilight years, the court made him a Great Chancellor, giving him one of the highest honorific titles in the realm.

Duong Lam was now a man whose time had come and gone. Yet he continued to cling to the past. Like many other scholars of his generation, he could not accept Western civilization, believing that traditional Vietnamese learning and culture were superior. He refused to learn French and dismissed modern Vietnamese script as crude, a tool of foreigners to subvert the country. (On this point Duong Lam was right, because this writing system, using the Roman alphabet, had been invented by a French missionary to help spread Catholicism among the masses.) My great-grandfather could not see that the traditional learning he so loved had become an intellectual straightjacket, discouraging independent and progressive thinking with its insistence on repeating the thoughts of Confucius and his disciples.

My great-grandfather returned to his native village upon his retirement and took up residence in the house he had built in Van Dinh, which included an ancestral temple—a privilege granted only to mandarins of high rank. The residence also included separate living quarters and gardens for each of his four wives. The second wife, the most senior after the death of the first, had the nicest house and the best landscaped garden. The third, fourth, and fifth wife each had a smaller house that consisted of one room used both for dining and entertaining visitors, a bedroom, and a simple kitchen with an earthen floor toward the back, where meals were cooked over a fire fed with wood or straw. Each of Duong Lam's wives had at least two maids, one to do housework and the other to shop and prepare meals. The ancestral temple and houses were built with bricks and wood, in the traditional Chinese style of architecture. The residence was austere but stood out nonetheless among the more modest dwellings of the villagers, most of which were thatched huts. Duong Lam's residence and the one built by his older brother right next to it occupied a large area, which came to be called "Governors' Hamlet" by the people.

A large gate, topped with a drum tower, opened onto a paved courtyard. The ancestral temple, the most imposing building in Duong Lam's residence, spread along one side of the yard, flanked by two old camellias, and looked out on an inscribed brick-and-mortar screen that shielded it from evil spirits, and porcelain pots bearing azaleas arrayed on stands. The structure and decorations were intended to inspire reverence for the departed forebears. The temple's five compartments were separated by large columns of ironwood bearing plaques with gilded inscriptions and paved with porcelain tiles that felt cool to the feet. Each compartment was richly decorated with red-lacquered furniture enhanced with gilded carved designs. Halls adorned with the eight ancient weapons, flags, parasols, fans, screens, and tall vases led to the inner sanctum where the altar, an elaborately carved, red-lacquered and gilded table, sat behind a bronze urn and candelabras in the shape of cranes. It bore the ancestral tablets and other ritual objects. A door led to my great-grandfather's private quarters, which looked out on an inner courtyard.

My great-grandfather now began to lead the life of a retired scholar, not entirely that of a hermit, but certainly removed from the excitement of his past positions. He spent his days reading books from his library collection, writing poems, and entertaining a stream of visitors who came to chat, listen to him discourse on the classics, appreciate his poems, seek advice, play a game of cards, or simply pay their respects. As the most eminent man in the area, he was beseeched by the surrounding villages to preside over ceremonies and rituals. According to my family, the peasants had so much faith in his power that they even sought him out on one occasion to help drive a ghost away.

Like other Confucian scholars, my great-grandfather loved rituals, because rituals helped maintain harmony between mankind and the universe, because they linked the living to their ancestors, and also because they were part of the culture that he was trying hard to preserve. For him, the most important one each year was the commemoration of his father's death. The ceremony would begin at dawn when servants lit torches in the courtyard, put the food offerings in the temple, and sounded the drums and bells. As a band struck up ritual music, the worshipers would take turns kneeling and bowing in front of the altar. After the ceremony, a banquet would be served. My great-grandfather would not take part in the feasting, and would wait for relatives and guests to leave before retreating into his private quarters to eat a simple meal by himself, because on such an occasion, he, as a loyal son, was not supposed to be merry.

In their retirement, scholars like Duong Lam usually became teachers to pass on their learning. So my great-grandfather would give lessons to students in the local area who were preparing for the last round of imperial exams. He would also teach his youngest daughters still living at home. This was highly unusual, since families tended to neglect their daughters' education, preferring to focus resources on that of their sons. The lesson was the highlight of the day for his daughters. They would put on their finest clothes, which they kept as wrinkle-free as possible under their sleeping mats. Then they would troop to the ancestral temple to see their father. First they would serve him tea as part of his morning ritual, and then they would listen to his lessons. Under his tutelage, two of my great-aunts would become fine poets.

Although he had four living wives, my great-grandfather preferred to stay in his own private suite of rooms. He usually ate by himself, because by custom his secondary wives were not allowed to sit and eat with him as long as his eldest son—my grandfather—was alive. As the most senior male descendant from Duong Lam's first or principal spouse, my grandfather outranked Duong Lam's secondary wives in the family hierarchy in everything, so it would have been presumptuous for these women to take his rightful place at the dining table, even when he was not home. Though their inferior position was completely traditional, the secondary wives still resented it all their lives, long after such distinctions had become meaningless. When I interviewed Duong Lam's surviving daughter from his third wife in Montreal in 1993, I noticed that, although she was now in her nineties and respected as the matriarch of the clan, she still felt sensitive about the status of her mother and her siblings within the family.

Duong Lam's secondary wives and their children ate in their own houses, except in the late afternoon, when they dined together in a room specially set aside for this communal meal, which usually consisted of basic dishes made with fish, tofu, vegetables, clams, and shrimp. With over seventy people to feed, delicacies were not affordable, and meat was rarely served. At dinnertime, a servant would go down to the riverbank and sound the gong to summon everyone. Children and adults would hurry from wherever they were, afraid that if they showed up late, all the better food would be eaten by those who were more punctual. A better meal would be served to my great-grandfather, who ate alone, with his eldest son when he was visiting, with his guests, or sometimes with some of his smallest children whom he wanted to spoil.

In a poem he wrote to describe his life in retirement, my great-grand-father poked fun at its simplicity: an unchanging diet of rice and beans for breakfast, and fish and vegetables for lunch and dinner; a bamboo cot for a bed in the summer, set near the river to catch the cooling breeze; a tattered fur coat to ward off the chill in the winter; an occasional glass of wine; a bumpy cart for transportation; and a wooden cane for support when leading village processions on foot. Although his poem was exaggerated for effect, he wrote it not to complain, but to point out the dignity of rustic living and to express his pride at the austerity of his existence, which impressed people who used to know him in the days when he had so much more.

Outwardly my great-grandfather might have seemed content to live quietly in retirement. But deep down he still felt despondent over the French domination, the more so because he thought he and his peers had failed to find a solution for their nation's predicament. Taking stock of his life, he admitted that he had many questions but no answers. Looking at the generation waiting in the wings, however, he saw a glimmer of hope. He became persuaded by their arguments that the young should adopt French education so that they could help modernize the country, like the Japanese had done, and give it the required strength to expel the colonial masters. My great-grandfather had rejected this Western learning earlier, condemning it for reducing traditional culture "to ashes," but now he realized that it could offer a solution. He reluctantly embraced it. He also felt he had no choice, since the French had made traditional education obsolete.

As my great-grandfather got older, his thoughts began to turn toward death and the afterlife. Preparing for one's death was not considered macabre, and the Vietnamese used to buy their coffins in advance and even display them in their houses. Since the location of a grave could ensure the well-being of his descendants, my great-grandfather began to search for a proper site. As a man who believed in the world of spirits, he turned for guidance to the god of Tan Vien Mountain. This deity rarely descended from his holy place to talk to mortals but, out of consideration for my great-grandfather's position as a mandarin of the highest grade in the realm, the god responded on this occasion as he had before when Duong Lam prayed to him. He dictated a poem telling my great-grandfather to place his grave in the largest knoll among the sixty-four mounds that dotted Tao Khe, the village next to Van Dinh. As instructed, my great-grandfather visited Tao Khe and began to build a tomb there to reflect his vision of an ideal resting place, within a replica of the world—complete with a mountain in miniature, trees, shrubs, flowers, and water.

The tomb included a temple that contained statues of my great-grandfather, his first wife, the spirit of Tan Vien Mountain, and the mysterious monk in my family's legend. The temple was decorated with a drum and a stone gong, with statues of kneeling attendants, and with Duong Lam's writings inscribed into two wooden scrolls that were gilded and lacquered in red. The two scrolls expressed my great-grandfather's view of life and death. On one, he wrote that the human body trapped man in a web of desires from which only death could set him free. On the other, he wrote that, in death, man could finally leave all worldly belongings behind and go free. A small shrine was erected in front of the temple to house a tablet bearing my great-grandfather's philosophical reflections on life. A series of steps led down to a lower platform where Duong Lam's grave would be located, flanked by carved dragons and elephants. More steps led down to a half-moon pool surrounded with a low wall and decorated with carved unicorns and the miniature replica of a mountain. To complete the effect, my great-grandfather had pine trees and shrubs planted around the site.

Duong Lam fell gravely ill with cancer in 1920. He expressed his suffering in a poem, which read in part:

> I have been longing for death for a long time.
> What is the use of living, when I only cause so much
> Pain and trouble for my children.
> My body is still here, but my spirit is already gone.
> My skin hangs on my bones, and my flesh is weary.
> I will lie buried three meters deep in the ground forever
> Leaving behind my burnished loyalty.

Neither traditional herb doctors nor a French physician could halt the disease, and the end finally came on October 17, 1920. On that day, Duong Lam told his children and grandchildren gathered around his bed that he would leave them at five o'clock that afternoon. When the hour of death approached, they fell weeping to their knees, and bowed with their foreheads on the ground to pay their last respects. A poet to the very end, Duong Lam told them to stop crying and listen to his admonition:

Even if your tears flow profusely like a river
You cannot keep my spirit from flying away.

At exactly five o'clock, Duong Lam looked around at his children and grandchildren and said:

Throughout my life,
You have been unfailing in your filial duties.
Now I can leave without any regrets.

Then he clasped his hands together in a gesture of farewell and breathed his last.

The news was cabled to the court in Hue by the French *résident supérieur* of Tonkin, who requested that Emperor Khai Dinh grant my great-grandfather a posthumous noble title. The emperor signed a decree naming him "Baron of Khanh Van," a nonhereditary title. Sealed in a small casket, the decree was carried to Van Dinh by a royal delegation consisting of the Minister of Rites and six other high officials. Duong Lam's funeral was delayed for two weeks to wait for their arrival, and his coffin was placed in the ancestral temple. After a commemorative service with an elaborate procession, Duong Lam's body was carried to Tao Khe and laid to rest in the tomb he had carefully designed. After his death, this village began to worship my great-grandfather as its guardian spirit.

In building his tomb, my great-grandfather had truly believed that it would serve as his undisturbed resting place for a long time: The words "Here I will lie for ten thousand years" were inscribed on the entrance. While the tomb has survived, Duong Lam would scarcely recognize it today. When I first visited his tomb in October 1993, I discovered how close it had come to being obliterated by the Communist revolution that had swept through north Vietnam. There was no trace left of the temple, which had been demolished when revolutionary zeal reached its peak, and most of the stone carvings and statues had disappeared. A robber had dug a hole in the grave. Weeds were everywhere, sprouting even between the bricks covering the grave. The land around the tomb had been turned into rice fields, and the pine trees and other plantings were gone. What was left of the tomb was in a state of disrepair. For decades, Duong Lam's remaining descendants had been too afraid to come and take care of it. The Communist Party had classified them as the offspring of landlords and feudalists, "class enemies" of the local peasants. One nephew who did show up in the village for a visit was chased away by angry peasants. Fortunately, the peasants continued to believe that my great-grandfather, the former guardian spirit of their village, would punish them if they desecrated his resting place, so they did not dare to raze his tomb or dig up his remains.

By the time I visited Tao Khe, Vietnam had embarked on a policy of political, economic, and social reforms—a local version of *perestroika*—and things had changed in the village. Two cousins, Phi and Thai, had secured permission from the authorities to undertake the much-needed repairs at the tomb. In a complete reversal, instead of seeing Duong Lam's resting place as an undesirable remnant of the feudalist period, the village authorities now viewed it as an asset. With the shift in the villagers' attitude, Phi and Thai had no trouble finding workers to repair the tomb. Proving how well traditional beliefs had managed to survive even after four decades of communist rule, the workers told my cousins that they had agreed to work for pay, but they also hoped that my great-grandfather's spirit would bring them good fortune. The day I arrived, the repair was in full swing. After my cousins and I finished inspecting what had been done, we took a rubbing of the stone tablets that the workers had washed to remove the accumulated grime and dirt. We looked at the inscribed characters but could decipher only a few simple ones. Just as Duong Lam had feared, we had abandoned the old learning, and could no longer read what he had wanted to pass on to his descendants.

My great-grandfather left a legacy of pride among his descendants. Partly because the cult of ancestors forbids making unflattering remarks about one's forebears, and partly because they were still cowed by his status as a mandarin of the first rank in the empire, my relatives viewed any criticism of Duong Lam as sacrilegious. For decades, they basked in the reputation he left behind. Many were insufferable snobs even though they had no accomplishments of their own. The passage of time, several wars, and the communist revolution put an end to this delusion of grandeur. Today, relatives of my generation share a sense of pride in our ancestors, but among the generation that comes after us, no one really cares about Duong Lam or what he accomplished. To them, his time is ancient history.

In Van Dinh and the neighboring area, people are still aware that Duong Lam was a "big mandarin," but he is no longer worshiped as the guardian spirit of Tao Khe where he is buried. A few old-timers in Van Dinh still remember stories of Duong Lam they heard from their own parents. I ran into these old men and women when I visited my ancestral village in 1993. They remembered Duong Lam as a mandarin with *dao duc*, virtue and integrity, whose power protected the villagers and made them respected wherever they went.

As a mandarin, then, my great-grandfather left a good reputation. As a scholar, his writings, mostly in classical Chinese rather than in the more accessible Vietnamese characters, were well known to his contemporaries, but are no longer familiar to today's audience. As a poet, Duong Lam was admired, but was not as popular as his older brother Duong Khue. For the most part, Duong Lam's poetry was considered "serious" and too lofty for the public taste. Modern critics generally praise his poems as elegant and full of noble sentiments, but feel they lack the freshness, lyrical flow, and beauty of his brother's compositions. Marxist critics, who tend to be much harsher toward "feudalist" writers, criticize him for his failure to oppose the French openly, but concede that his poetry reflects the "spirit of the people" and a sense of patriotism.

Duong Khue had a life that illustrated the vagaries of serving as a mandarin and the importance of poetry in his culture. The low point of his career came when he was dismissed by the court and almost beheaded for taking two bars of silver from his provincial treasury to loan to an old friend, a poor scholar. The Council of Ministers recommended imprisonment followed by decapitation, but Emperor Tu Duc, who remembered Duong Khue, granted a pardon. Still, he dismissed Duong Khue from office, stripped him of all his titles, and sent him to an uninhabited region where he was put in charge of clearing land for cultivation. From a comfortable life, Duong Khue suddenly found himself transported into an isolated area, without basic amenities.

For a scholar who lived and breathed poetry, it was perhaps fitting that a poem eventually saved his career. Years after his disgrace, Duong Khue composed one of his most famous songs, in which he reflected on the capriciousness of life. It included a line in which he expressed his gratitude to the emperor for his clemency: "Though my crime was serious, the emperor showed his mercy." The lyrical song became extremely popular and eventually reached the court, where it was performed one day for the emperor himself. Moved by Duong Khue's gratitude, loyalty, and lack of bitterness for his punishment, Tu Duc recalled him to court in 1879. Duong Khue did not stay for long and subsequently resigned, discouraged as was his brother by the court's ineptitude in dealing with French aggression. He used his mother's illness as an excuse for resigning, to avoid being branded as an opponent of royal policy. The rest of my great-granduncle's career would be marked by summonses to service, resignations, followed by more summonses. But honors and promotions, even to the rank of cabinet minister, could not keep him in the government. In 1894 he retired for good, claiming ill health. He died eight years later, in 1902.

Duong Khue's career was perhaps less impressive than that of his younger brother, but he achieved greater literary fame. Many of his poems are well known even today. Readers can still relate to the emotions he described, and respond to his carefree spirit, his subtle and self-deprecating sense of humor, and his philosophy, which says that life is fleeting, everything is an illusion, and all efforts are futile. One should abandon oneself to the joy of living, for tomorrow everything will dissolve into nothing. True to this philosophy, Duong Khue sought escape in the company of female singers, whom he frequently visited. Yet his hedonistic quests were simply efforts to escape his own predicament of having to serve a court dominated by a foreign power.

After the death of Duong Lam and Duong Khue, the political, social, and cultural changes that had started during their lifetime began to gather speed and to eventually transform Vietnam in ways even greater than they had feared. Traditional scholars like them who had been hailed at the beginning of the French conquest as protectors of the country's traditions and culture would be ridiculed decades later as hidebound old fogies by younger Vietnamese anxious to modernize their country. And the very same traditions and customs that Duong Lam and Duong Khue wanted to preserve would be attacked as backward practices that should be thrown out the window.

2

Shut Gate and High Walls

Duong Tu Phan, my grandfather, was unhappy most of his life, dogged by a feeling that he never received the rewards that someone of his caliber deserved. He wanted to be a mandarin in the grand old tradition, but the colonial regime forced him to play a quite different role. He wanted to follow in Duong Lam's footsteps, but never achieved fame as a poet, nor had the opportunity to make the same kind of mark his father had. A dour man by nature, he became more taciturn as disappointment followed upon disappointment. While he controlled his family with a firm hand, he often felt powerless in the current of change that was slowly but surely transforming his country and society.

By this time, the French control of Vietnam had brought some bene-fits. Peasants were not revolting. Bandits had disappeared. Armed bands of rebels had been subdued. Indeed, with their superior firepower and their colonial army bulging with native recruits, the French were able to keep things so calm that they boasted of having brought *la paix française*, or "French peace," to Vietnam. It was an uneasy peace, but it was peace nevertheless. With the colonialists here to stay, the Vietnamese turned their thoughts from resisting to adapting to the new situation and improving their own personal lot. My grandfather, like-wise, resigned himself to living and working in the long shadow cast by these foreigners.

Phan was born in July 1874, a year after the first French attack on Hanoi, and grew up during their final conquest and pacification of Tonkin. As a testimony to the Vietnamese single-minded devotion to education, his focus on his studies never wavered, in spite of the unset-tled conditions of the time. As the oldest son of my great-grandfather's first wife, he carried the main hope of the family. He began well, pass-ing the master's degree in 1897, when he was twenty-three years old. But then things began to go wrong. In the old days, he would have obtained a post in the imperial bureaucracy right away, but no appoint-ment came through. While waiting for a government post, he was nom-inated to attend a newly established school that would teach him how to read and write the modern script. But, sharing his father's disdain for this system of writing, he did not bother to enroll. He was also select-ed to attend a special school set up by the French to train mandarins with more relevant skills, such as knowledge of French and the new administrative structure, regulations, and procedures. However, like his father, Phan believed that French was not worth learning, and that the French had nothing to teach Vietnamese scholars about how to govern. These decisions were mistakes that would eventually blight his career.

Instead, my grandfather went on to study the Chinese classics, in the hope of earning the doctorate degree. Although the old learning had become less and less relevant, he and other scholars of his generation clung to their dreams of achieving success through the imperial exams. In 1901, he was finally given a government post as education magistrate in Nam Dinh Province, but three days after his appointment, Phan requested a leave of absence to take the doctorate exam in Hue. It was granted, because the right of education magistrates to take time off for exams was still honored. According to my family, Phan turned in a stel-lar performance that should have earned him not just the doctorate but the second highest honor as well. One of his essays was so brilliant that the examiners read and reread it to savor his eloquent arguments and wonderful style. But in the course of doing this, they noticed a minor infraction that disqualified him. He returned to his post unhappy. This failure foreshadowed others that were to come.

A few months after returning to his post, Phan asked for a promotion. He wanted to become a district chief with the power that an education official did not have. Not only that, but he did not want a district in a poor, sparsely populated, pestilential mountain region. He wanted to stay in Nam Dinh, a large and important province, so he could spread his wings and show what he could do. Usually mandarins had to remain in a post for at least two years before getting a promotion. Phan's audacity in demanding a promotion before his time, and particularly in specifying a post in the desirable lowland, irritated the French. Nevertheless they initially granted his wish. In 1903, after having spent the required two years as education magistrate of My Loc, Phan was promoted administrator of the same district. Phan thought he was at the threshold of a brilliant career.

Instead, he languished. While other magistrates were promoted every two years, Phan remained in the rank of district magistrate for eighteen years. He saw men with less seniority, and sometimes without the required education, get promoted and even surpass him in rank. These men had nimbly adjusted to the time, learning to speak French and to get along well with their colonial superiors. Phan had bothered to do neither. The language gap naturally led to communication problems, but this was only part of the reason why the French never warmed to him. Unable to understand these foreigners and their culture, Phan always felt awkward with them, and this showed. The French *résidents* found him too formal, too rigid, and too uncommunicative and were predisposed to think badly of him and what he did.

Although their perception of Phan was colored by cultural differences, I can understand it when I look at the few pictures I have of my grandfather. In them, he appears stern, dry, and humorless. With high cheekbones, square jaw, mustache, and short goatee, he looks determined if not stubborn. His eyes are kind but tired, as if halfway through his life he was already fatigued. Whereas his father Duong Lam was an extrovert, with a zest for everything he did, Phan's personality was the opposite. His disappointments took the wind out of Phan's sail early, and he ended up moving through life in a rather detached and perfunctory way. The only thing he felt passionate about was his family, or more precisely his father and his sons.

The French province *résidents* who had so much power over mandarins like my grandfather existed only in the protectorates of Annam and Tonkin and not in the colony of Cochinchina. A *résident* held all administrative, legal, and political power within a province. The Vietnamese mandarins under his supervision served at his command and reported to him. These *résidents* came and went, rotating in and out at the end of their term of office, so during Phan's career he dealt with more than half a dozen. He got along with some better than others. The *résidents* were not all hardened colonialists, and a few were quite sympathetic to the Vietnamese. Some were genuinely interested in the welfare of the people and tried to rein in the corrupt mandarins under their supervision. But in general, *résidents* were in Vietnam to enforce colonial policies and to produce the results expected by the colonial regime. Even those with good intentions could not escape the system of which they were part.

My grandfather's dealings with some of his Vietnamese superiors were not much better than his relationships with the French. Proud of his learning and his lineage, he tended to look down on officials above him whom he believed were not as well educated and as well bred as he was. He never bothered to hide his contempt, and of course this attitude did nothing to help his career. He particularly despised a new breed of people who were emerging to displace traditional scholar-officials like himself. These were the French-speaking interpreters and clerks that the colonial administration had recruited to staff its bureaucracy. Usually, they were men with little or no education. Their only qualification was that they could speak French and knew how to ingratiate themselves. As the middlemen between the Vietnamese and the new French masters, these interpreters and clerks gained an influence that was totally out of proportion to their status. Many extorted bribes. Others used their knowledge of French laws and bureaucracy to acquire land at the expense of the peasants and to enrich themselves. A number eventually rose in rank and became important officials. Their arrogance did not sit well with the local people, who called them "houseboys" of the French behind their backs.

Not knowing the modern script was a problem for my grandfather. As fewer and fewer people learned Chinese characters, documents had to be written in Vietnamese, which would then be translated into French or, in Phan's case, transcribed into Chinese characters when they arrived at his office. To make up for his handicap, Phan had to hire a clerk who could translate the documents for him. During his career, whoever occupied that position became an indispensable member of my grandfather's staff. At one point in his early years as a mandarin, his assistant started to extort bribes from constituents who came to the office on business. In exchange for an illegal "fee," he would let the villagers in to see Phan, or he would make sure my grandfather saw and signed their documents. This kind of petty corruption was not uncommon, as underpaid clerks often resorted to it to survive. Indeed, bribery has survived under all sorts of regimes in modern Vietnam. But when this assistant became too aggressive, people started to lodge complaints against him, which reflected poorly on my grandfather. Unable to function without the clerk's service, Phan simply refused to believe any of the accusations.

As an enforcer of policies—many of which were unpopular—it was easy for a mandarin to attract resentment. While French officials were far away, and were rarely seen by the people, a mandarin was more visible. Besides, as judge and chief of police in his territory—arresting, trying, fining, and jailing people—a mandarin inevitably made enemies. Most of those he alienated never acted on their grudges, but some would look for ways to harm him, such as banding with more powerful and sophisticated enemies. My grandfather, no exception to this rule, was denounced for abuses of power in a number of letters sent to the French *résident* and *résident supérieur* in Hanoi. The letters were suspicious and probably fabricated, but nonetheless the Vietnamese province governor recommended my grandfather's transfer. In 1909, Phan was moved to Phu Tho District, Son Tay Province.

This province, located on the edge of the Red River Delta, controlled access to this large plain from the mountains to the west. From here, the ground rose gradually into the plateau region of Tonkin. Still nurturing the hope of making his mark in life, my grandfather did well in his new post and was recommended for a promotion. But the proposal was shelved in Hanoi. Later, my grandfather was transferred to Dong Quan District in Thai Binh, the same province that his own father had saved from inundation years before. Here he at first won praise from the *résident*, who called him "an excellent mandarin." But no promotion would come through then nor for the next eleven years. Phan ended up spending the longest stretch of his career in this district, and most of the major events of his life took place while he was here.

With his career and ambition blocked, my grandfather focused his full attention on his family. Outside his gates, those who sought to modernize the country were encouraging people to adopt Western education and customs. They attacked traditional learning and conservative values. But inside his household, Phan could stop the clock. He insisted on everyone staying in his or her place, and behaving as they had in his father's time. His anger was quick, and so was his punishment. Family members were afraid to disobey or even displease him. If a son did something that made Phan angry, he would banish him from his presence. Then, my grandmother would have to wait until he was in a good mood to cajole him into forgiving the guilty child. If he was pardoned, the son would put on a formal blue brocade robe, prostrate himself, and knock his head on the floor several times to beg for mercy.

My grandfather was especially demanding toward my grandmother. In the Confucian order, he was her lord and master, and he expected her to sacrifice her needs to his, and those of the family. He had married her when he was fifteen and she was only twelve years old. At that malleable age, Tran Tue Nam was easily molded to her husband's will. Her only mission in life, in his traditional view, was to take care of him, bring up the children well, and manage the household well. She accepted her duties with dignity and performed them to perfection. I suspect my grandmother had special qualities that enabled her to tolerate my grandfather's demands. Her portrait shows an attractive, noble, and kind face, not quite oval and not quite round, a high and large forehead, eyes that are large and direct, a small and well-shaped nose, and full lips. She appears to be an intelligent and aristocratic lady with a modest but self-assured presence.

She was the youngest daughter of viceroy Tran Luu Hue, who had brought her up in the strict Confucian manner. She knew all about the "three submissions," the code of conduct that kept a woman subservient to the most important men in her life: her father, husband, and oldest son. Perhaps no other doctrine in the world was as successful as Confucianism in convincing women that self-abnegation should be their highest aspiration. To my grandmother, it was perfectly natural to obey all my grandfather's wishes—good or bad, reasonable or unreasonable. She paid no attention to her own needs and tried to please my grandfather in every way—even if this meant having to be civil and generous with Ba Tre, my grandfather's second wife and favorite. She was younger and prettier, with a lovely white complexion, prized over the honey skin tone that most Vietnamese had. My grandfather was so taken with her that he spent most of his time in her company, and neglected my grandmother. Yet when Ba Tre fell ill after the birth of her baby, my grandmother—to please Phan —personally took care of her. Despite special care, the beloved second wife died a few months later. Knowing what a grievous loss this had been for my grandfather, my grandmother bought him another wife as a gift.

My grandfather was not only strict, but also difficult to please. Life with him was not easy for my grandmother and for my father and his siblings. Each morning, the first thing my grandmother had to do was to prepare his tea. After servants brought in the special tea set, my grandmother would brew each cup to perfection, neither too weak nor too strong. If the tea was not to his liking, Phan would get angry, and everyone in the room would quake like a leaf with fear. In the afternoon, another round of tea would be served after Phan's siesta. Since he usually awoke in a bad mood, everyone around him learned to expect a tongue-lashing at these times.

Whenever my grandmother was not home, one of my aunts would have to take her place for the tea ritual. It was a task none of my aunts was anxious to perform. So, whenever they could, they would ask one of their sisters-in-law to fill in for them. Surprisingly, although parents in those days often terrorized their children-in-law, my grandparents did not fit this mold, and always treated their daughters-in-law kindly. My mother still marvels at how gentle they were with her.

Everyone had to show respect to my grandfather at all times, since he was the great patriarch. If he was sitting, everyone in the room would have to stand respectfully in attendance. If my grandfather allowed a son to sit down in his presence, the son would have to sit to the side and not directly in front of him (a daughter would simply never be allowed to sit). This constant show of respect made every interaction formal, almost staged. My grandfather never relaxed with his children, not even at lunch and dinner, because these meals were just another ritual to perform, down to the half-bottle of French wine that had to be served in a special glass reserved only for him. While he ate with my grandmother, daughters and daughters-in-law would stand respectfully in attendance. In summer, a servant would pull on a rope to move a large woven flap back and forth—called a *pukka* fan—to relieve the heat. Sometimes, one of the children would use a feather fan to cool them down.

Once in a while, my grandfather would summon one of his children to share his meals. The one who had the honor would dread it. Whenever my father was called, he would eat whatever he was told to eat, even dishes that he hated. Nor was he allowed to speak unless spoken to. My grandfather enjoyed making his children talk, however, and so on these occasions he would ask my father questions. Being articulate, my father usually managed to please my grandfather with his verbal skill and clever answers. But some of his siblings, who were less adept, would get tongue-tied out of fear. Then my grandfather would scold them for letting "words get stuck in their throats." At other times, Phan would test his sons' quickness of mind by making up verses and asking them to respond on the spot with improvised verses of their own. Phan, of course, never tested his daughters this way, because women were not required to go out into the world and survive on their wits.

As in any traditional family, sons were the center of my grandfather's life. Their education and, with it, the dream of success, remained the lodestar. When his sons were small, my grandfather personally taught them at home, as he himself had been taught. Although the colonial authorities had begun offering free classes in French, even paying a monthly stipend to each student who enrolled, tradition-minded parents still refused to send their sons. They were adamant that the French classes would prepare them only to become lowly interpreters and clerks, and nothing more, while traditional education would fill their minds with real learning and prepare them to be mandarins. My father began to study classical Chinese at the age of five. Every day, my grandfather would give lessons to my father and his brothers before going to his office, once in the early morning and again in the afternoon after his siesta. Phan taught them how to read and write using the traditional primer. After Phan left for his office, my father and uncles would have to continue studying on their own. They were not allowed to go out and play until they had mastered their lessons. The next day, Phan would interrogate them. If they could not recite their lessons by heart—either because they had failed to memorize them or because they were so scared in his presence that they forgot what they had learned—Phan would hit them with a rattan switch.

Later, my grandfather hired a tutor. School lasted all year, except for the last week or so in the calendar, when the tutor went home to celebrate Tet with his family. There were no weekends, holidays, or vacations. Watching the tutor packing his bags to go home was the happiest sight during the year for my father and his brothers. The French put an end to this classical tradition. Knowing that only a drastic step would force the Vietnamese to assimilate French culture, the colonial authorities announced in 1910 that they would allow one last regional exam in 1915 for the master's degree, and one last metropolitan exam in Hue in 1919 for the doctorate degree. My great-grandfather and grandfather were upset, but there was nothing they could do to turn the tide. My grandfather now had to take stock of what this development would mean for his sons' future. Of his three oldest sons, only Tuong, the first-born, had mastered enough of the Chinese texts to have any hope of passing the exam. The other two, my father and my uncle Chinh, were so far behind they did not have the whisper of a chance. So my grandfather told Tuong to continue. He also realized that unless his younger sons obtained a French education, they would have no future at all.

My great-grandfather, too, had reached the same conclusion and, following the old tradition of seeking the best education at the best school or under the best teacher, he instructed Phan to send the two boys to Hanoi to get the best schooling the French could offer. My father and my uncle Chinh, aged twelve and thirteen, were packed off immediately. My father accepted the decision without a murmur. I can only guess at his fear at having to leave home and attend a foreign school with strangers, and his disappointment at having to give up the learning that still commanded respect in his family. Indeed, whenever he talked to me about his oldest brother Tuong, I sensed envy and awe for my uncle's doctorate degree obtained at the last imperial exam in Hue, feelings shared by many people in our clan. Although my father regretted having to abandon traditional education, my siblings and I thought the switch made him more modern and in tune with the times. Our uncle Tuong, who did not have to make the change, seemed to us old-fashioned and out of step. Our impression was reinforced by the traditional costume of turban, dark tunic, white pants, and slippers that our uncle—playing the role of the traditional scholar—would wear throughout his life.

Tuong was probably relieved that he did not have to start his education anew in his mid-teens. But at first things did not look too bright for him. In 1915, he took and passed the last exam for the master's degree. Unlike the old days, however, this degree did not open the door to a mandarin career for him. The French now recruited mandarins only from the special institute they had set up to train government officials. Tuong enrolled in the school, but he could not compete against students who had received a modern education and learned French. He failed to qualify. To a traditional scholar like my grandfather, the only acceptable career besides being a mandarin was farming. Commerce was becoming more respectable, but to Phan it still seemed unrefined for a gentleman to pursue. He rented a few acres of land in Van Dinh, and told Tuong to return there and grow rice for a living. My uncle dutifully moved to the village with his wife, the daughter of a mandarin. But not knowing a spade from a hoe, the two could not make a go of it. The task of managing and supervising rice planting fell to the women, but my aunt was unprepared for this kind of responsibility. Instead of walking to the rice fields to check on the workers, she would hire porters to carry her back and forth. Instead of feeding workers the typical fare of stewed fish to go with their rice at noon, she would feed them huge portions of stewed pork, a luxury many families could afford only a few times a year. My aunt also did not know how to control pilferage, a common problem with poor laborers. Kind and generous, she was a failure at farming. So rice growing was not a viable career option for my uncle, either.

My grandfather did not know what to do next with his oldest son. Fortunately, in 1919 my uncle Tuong journeyed to Hue for the last doctorate exam and passed. My great-grandfather and grandfather were mad with joy. They held a huge celebration in Van Dinh for Tuong when he triumphantly returned to the village in a traditional *tien si* procession, the last that Van Dinh was to see. The ceremony was also for my great-grandfather, who was marking his seventieth birthday. It lasted for several days. According to custom, every villager had to be invited and fed well. Families sometimes would go into debt or sell a part of their land just to finance these elaborate feasts, lest they lose face. For this occasion, my family had oxen, pigs, goats, and chickens slaughtered to feed a huge crowd each day. For the poorer villagers, who lived on two meals of rice and vegetables a day, a banquet like this was a welcome event. As they left, each of the guests received a package of sweet sticky rice and a portion of meat to take home and prolong their pleasure.

Earning the doctorate finally opened the door to a career for my uncle, as a low-level official in what was left of the royal court. Tuong eventually transferred to Tonkin, and rose to the position of governor general of Hai Duong Province. Because a governor general had the same rank as a cabinet minister, he became known to me and my siblings as "uncle minister." He had a successful but short career, and retired after the Viet Minh revolution in 1945. He was lucky to have squeezed through the gate before it was shut in 1919. Although Chinese characters continued to be used in official court documents until 1924, older students who had invested years in learning the Chinese classics and who could not— or chose not to—switch to modern education after 1919 now found themselves obsolete. They ended up trying to eke out a living as farmers, herb doctors, or fortune-tellers in their villages. Even before French policy made them marginal, these scholars had no love for the colonial regime. They yearned for the old days, clung to Confucian traditions, and remained loyal to the king and his court. In Thai Binh Province, an enclave of old learning, where Phan served as district magistrate, many traditional scholars with similar views supported exiles living across the border in China who were plotting to drive the French out by force.

Life in the district was comfortable but offered few diversions for my grandfather. In the district town, the only readily available form of entertainment was card games, which were traditionally a favorite pastime for many families. My grandfather liked to play with small stakes to make the games more exciting. His fondness for the cards, however, gave some French *résidents* the impression that he was a "big gambler" and probably contributed to their negative assessment of him. Whenever he could, he would sit down, cards in hand, in the company of senior clerks on his staff, canton chiefs, colleagues from neighboring districts, or visitors to the residence. Later, his favorite companions were his grown sons, whenever they came home for summer vacation from their studies in Hanoi. Once they became adults, Phan's attitude toward them mellowed. He now felt he could relax with them and indulge them without fear of spoiling them. Their return provided a break from the routine, and my grandfather made their stay an endless party of games and feasts. Each night, he would stay up late, until one or two o'clock in the morning, playing Chinese chess with one of them. At the end of the summer, it was hard for Phan to say goodbye; whenever the subject of his sons' departure came up, he would get angry. My grandmother would have to wait until he was in a good mood to talk him into letting them go. Then he would relent, and start worrying about how and where he could borrow enough money to send them back to Hanoi in time for the start of their school year.

My grandfather loved literature. Before traditional education was abolished, every once in a while he would hold literary seminars for students preparing for the imperial exams. He would critique their essays and poems and give small awards of writing paper or packets of tea to those he judged the best. When his sons were still living at home, he would read to them and discuss his favorite poems or tell them tales from classical literature. On the rare occasions when scholar friends dropped by to visit, my grandfather would sit and talk with them for hours about well-known poets and writers, while my father and his brothers stayed in the room to listen. This was how my father learned to appreciate classical literature. In his spare time, Phan would compose his own poems in the classical form. His most moving compositions were those in which he talked about his disappointment in life, yet his poems were never mired in despair. They retained a feeling of hope that things would get better, at least for his sons.

Orchestrating his sons' upbringing and education gave Phan's life a purpose, as did his focus on his father Duong Lam, who was then living in retirement. He took it upon himself to make Duong Lam's last years happy and comfortable and would spare neither money nor time. He would invite his father for extended stays in Dong Quan. Duong Lam would arrive with a large retinue. During his visit, Phan would organize chess or card games every evening to keep his father entertained. He would have the cooks prepare a large assortment of dishes for each meal, as well as special snacks throughout the day. To enliven things even more, my grandfather would hire *a dao* singers or *cheo* opera troupes to perform. In between visits, Phan would send a servant to Van Dinh at least once a month with a gift of fruit that had just come into season, or some special products from the local area. Besides these gestures of filial piety, my grandfather also shouldered the lion's share of Duong Lam's financial needs, after my great-grandfather retired from office and could not support his many wives and children on his pension alone. Phan would send a large portion of his salary home each month. Later on, when his younger half-brothers needed an education, he would take them into his own household and pay for all their expenses. He would go into debt to meet his obligations but would never complain to his father.

Family events and rituals helped fill my grandfather's life. Each year, he asked for so many leaves to attend weddings, engagements, birthdays, anniversaries of ancestors' deaths, funerals, and memorial ceremonies that some of the French *résidents* thought he was not serious about his job. The commemorations of the deaths of our ancestors were the most important. After Duong Lam passed away, the responsibility for holding these rituals fell to my grandfather. Phan did not go to the same lengths as Duong Lam had done when he was alive. There was no throng of worshipers, no fancy banquet, just my grandfather and his family paying their respects. At five o'clock in the morning, to the sound of music, my grandfather would kneel and bow in prayer in front of the altar to start the ceremony.

In 1913, the "French peace" in Thai Binh was shattered by a bomb that killed Nguyen Duy Han, the province governor general. Despite the tight surveillance—with nightly patrols by village watchmen and provincial troops and frequent inspections by the district magistrates— a group of anti-French exiles succeeded in smuggling the weapon from China to their accomplices in Thai Binh. The assassination was an isolated terrorist act and the perpetrators were quickly caught. Although it did not spark a popular uprising, the attack, coming on the heels of another one in Hanoi early in the same year, sent shock waves among the French. In his report to Hanoi, the province *résident* said he hoped the incident might jolt the mandarins into realizing that their fate had become tied to that of the colonial regime, and make them even more zealous in working for its survival. At the same time, he worried that it might have the reverse effect, making mandarins more afraid to show support for the French.

How the assassination affected my grandfather is difficult to judge. His performance appraisals remained as inconsistent as ever—but even when they were good, the praise was modest, and the criticism for lack of zeal seemed to grow starting in 1913. There could be several reasons for Phan's indifference. Unhappiness over the slow pace of his promotion and frustration over his lack of any real authority probably had more to do with his lassitude than fear of retaliation by radicals. But he may have also felt an increasing distaste for colonial policies and a growing reluctance to enforce them.

In the past, the court had trusted mandarins to govern their territories firmly and fairly, and gave them discretion within its guidelines. But with the French in power, all that changed. My grandfather and his Vietnamese superiors could not make any decision, even a minor one, on their own. Phan could not even issue a certificate commending a subordinate for a job well done, or give his staff time off, without approval. The French believed in a hands-on style of management. Phan had to inform them of everything that went on in his district, no matter how trivial. He was required to prepare a monthly report covering over ten topics outlined by the French—from the people's attitude toward the government, to the security situation (including every instance of robbery and burglary), to inspection tours of dikes, to taxes, education, health, the growing of rice and other crops, and public works projects. The French were most interested in the security situation, particularly any hint of opposition to colonial rule. They also paid attention to the sale of alcohol, salt, and opium, the tax on which made up a good part of the revenue.

Taxes financed the colonial government and the construction of roads, railroads, harbors, bridges, and drainage and irrigation networks. These projects benefited mostly the French colonists. Roads, railroads, and harbors helped the locals, but they were really intended to allow the settlers to carry the products from their plantations, and the coal and other raw materials from their mines, mostly to markets abroad. Drainage, improved irrigation, and clearing opened up vast tracts of land for rice and rubber cultivation, but all of the rubber plantations and most of the new rice fields became the property of the settlers.

The taxes on salt and alcohol, the two most widely used products, provided the largest revenue stream. Few Vietnamese smoked opium, so the tax on it was of little importance. But while people bought salt in large quantities for daily use, sending a steady flow of money into the national coffers, the consumption of alcohol had to be pushed to increase its tax receipt. Wine had always been a part of daily life, used in rituals and festivities, and as a gift. No ceremony could be held without it. In the past, peasants could make their own wine or buy it from fellow villagers. But now this was forbidden, and the alcohol monopoly was awarded to a couple of French firms with powerful connections in Paris. Higher alcohol sale and larger profit would please these firms and at the same time increase revenue for the local government. So the colonial authorities began to force each village to consume more than it normally would. Each had to purchase a quantity of alcohol in proportion to the number of its inhabitants. If it failed to buy its compulsory share, a village would be fined, because this would be sufficient proof that it had been making alcohol illegally for its rituals and festivities.

French *résidents* themselves were under pressure to sell alcohol and, in turn, pressured the mandarins. Failure to produce results could kill an official's chance for promotion. This was what happened to my grandfather when he was serving in Dong Quan. His district had eight cantons, but four of them were poor. The district consistently fell short of its alcohol quota. This failure was a black mark in Phan's record, contributing to his being held back in the same rank for over a decade. In the meantime, his colleagues in the other districts, who did not have as much seniority as he did, were promoted frequently because they could produce higher alcohol sales, either through local demand or more ruthless enforcement.

In 1920, Duong Lam died, but the sad event had a silver lining. The French *résident* in Thai Binh Province was sympathetic to Phan's loss. As a reward for his long years of service, this *résident* gave him a favorable appraisal that earned him a promotion to county magistrate, a higher and more prestigious rank. But the promotion was too little, too late, and failed to inspire Phan. While in his new post in Khoai Chau County, Hung Yen Province, my grandfather celebrated his fiftieth birthday—a significant milestone—in 1923. The Vietnamese traditionally did not mark their birthday every year, but only once in a decade, starting with the fiftieth one, to rejoice over the longevity already achieved, rather than to note the day of birth. For this happy and important affair, Phan's children and their spouses gathered at the residence to present their gifts and wishes. My grandfather asked permission to take the day off and to slaughter a calf for the celebration. The Hung Yen Province *résident*, perhaps unaware of the significance of the occasion, refused. Phan went ahead anyway, and had a photograph of himself taken in a formal brocade robe, surrounded by attendants carrying parasols, his children and their spouses, and his grandchildren. Since my great-grandfather had died shortly after celebrating his seventieth birthday in 1920, some relatives advised Phan against observing his own fiftieth, cautioning that it might bring him bad luck, as it had to Duong Lam. Perhaps Phan should have listened to them. He too did not survive long after this ceremony, and died three years later.

Duong Lam's death freed my grandfather from a main family burden: He was no longer obligated to support Duong Lam's wives and children. In a poor country like Vietnam, the margin of protection from want was quite thin. It usually disappeared with the death of the male head of household. Without the monthly subsidies from Phan and his younger brother, and without the pension my great-grandfather was getting, Duong Lam's widows now found themselves plunged into a life of near-poverty. Their only income came from the land Duong Lam had left. But after deducting expenses, the fields gave each widow and each child only twenty-five baskets of rice per year, not enough to survive on. Duong Lam's widows had to supplement their income by buying and selling things at the market or by other means. They could not even afford new clothes now. Sometimes, my grandfather or his younger brother—who had fared better than Phan and had advanced to the rank of province governor—would invite their half-siblings home and give them money or new clothes to replace the patched outfits they were wearing. Gradually, the villa in Thai Ha Ap and the rice fields that Duong Lam had left to his wives and children were sold to cover living expenses. The villa was bought by a rich merchant in Hanoi, as were other mandarin houses in this exclusive residential area. Eventually, Thai Ha Ap would become a weekend and vacation retreat for the very merchant class that the mandarins used to despise.

Two years after his promotion, my grandfather—tired, dissatisfied by a career that had only inched along, and probably also demoralized by his lack of authority and the unpopular policies he had to enforce—applied for retirement and a pension. His request was turned down, on the grounds that he was still in good health and could continue working for many more years. Without this income, he could not survive financially. He had to stay in office. In 1924, the French transferred him to Nghia Hung in Nam Dinh Province. He had not been particularly active, and they thought this county would suit him better. It was prosperous and stable, and did not demand vigorous management. Nam Dinh, bordered by the sea to the south, was one of the most important and richest regions in the Red River Delta. It had only two counties, so my grandfather in effect administered half of this province.

With each passing day, life became more and more pleasant with the introduction of modern conveniences as French and other Western companies expanded their markets globally. By 1920, people could buy more comfortable rickshaws with rubber wheels. Bicycles also became more common. By 1919 kerosene oil lamps started to replace candles in homes that could afford them. The French were using Vietnam as a market to absorb their products, and did little to stimulate local industries. Practically all manufactured goods, even basic products like soap and matches, were imported from France. Some of the goods were too unusual for some Vietnamese to appreciate or understand, like the gramophone that my grandfather bought. When they heard it for the first time, our peasant neighbors in Van Dinh thought that ghosts were talking from it.

As procedures for going to France were loosened in the 1920s, more and more Vietnamese began to go there to get the best education money could buy. These were usually the sons of affluent and well-connected families. My grandfather had little money, but this did not stop him from sending his favorite fifth son—quite an about-face for a man who had bitterly opposed Western education at the beginning of his life. My uncle Nam was already married, but at Phan's command, he left his wife behind and sailed for France. My oldest uncle Tuong was ordered to pay for all the expenses, but the money was wasted. No one in my family knows what my fifth uncle did in France, and whether he even bothered to enroll in any school. It is easy to imagine how difficult it must have been for someone like him to adjust in France—a man with a traditional upbringing, alone in a foreign country, one of a small handful of Vietnamese lost in a sea of alien Frenchmen. Fifth uncle wrote home just a few times, but soon after my grandfather's death, he died of osteomyelitis. His body was shipped back to Van Dinh for burial.

My grandfather could have spent the last years of his career peacefully in Nghia Hung. But in 1925, barely one year into his tenure there, he decided to transfer to what he thought would be a larger and more prestigious county. By the time he realized that the move was a mistake, it was too late. In declining health, he found the larger Xuan Truong county hard to administer, with frequent robberies and a dike that kept breaking. A tough and demanding *résident* presided over the province.

My grandfather found him overbearing and he, in turn, disliked Phan and criticized his performance harshly. Misunderstandings were so numerous that communication became almost impossible. Less than a year after he moved to Xuan Truong, the end began for Phan. It was painful, as though life wanted to inflict one more wound on an unhappy man. My grandfather fell ill with cancer of the throat, though no one knew what was wrong at the time.

Finally awarded a sick leave, Phan left for Hanoi to look for a cure, accompanied by my grandmother. My grandfather's third wife and her son, who was also ill, came with them. They moved into a vacant villa owned by Phan's sister, who had married the son of the last viceroy of Tonkin. My parents and my second uncle Chinh and his family also moved in to pool resources and help my grandparents meet expenses. With money tight, living together would eliminate the cost of keeping separate households. My parents remembered that year as one of family crisis. Death stalked the villa where they were staying. My oldest brother, whose birth my grandfather had celebrated so joyously only one year ago, was battling acute bronchitis. My parents struggled to keep from sinking into a deep depression, faced as they were with so much pain and the impending death of my oldest brother, my grandfather, and my father's stepbrother.

Sparing no expenses, the family asked the two best French doctors in Hanoi to treat my grandfather. Their fees were high and the imported Western medication expensive, but they were no more successful than the herb doctors. Knowing his end was near, Phan asked his family to take him back to Van Dinh, so he could die in his native village. Death came in June 1926. Phan was fifty-two years old. After my grandfather passed away, it was my oldest brother's turn. He went into convulsions and then death finally took him in one last spasm. After burying my grandfather, my grandmother remained in Van Dinh for a while. Then she began to spend time visiting her three oldest sons, now serving as mandarins in different provinces. Whenever she came to our house, my father would try to make her stay as happy as those his father had staged for Duong Lam.

Before she died, my grandmother had the satisfaction of seeing her oldest son, my uncle Tuong, promoted to the rank of province governor, and herself honored by the emperor. When a son reached this rank, his mother was awarded a title by the court, usually one that was two grades below that of the son. In this case, a province governor had the second highest mandarin grade in the kingdom, so my grandmother was given the fourth highest grade and the title of "Lady of the Fourth Rank." An impressive ceremony was held for this occasion, including a grand procession bearing the royal decree to Van Dinh. The ritual that followed was called "Worshiping a Living Being." (It was similar to those performed to honor deities.) The festivity was also a celebration of my grandmother's sixtieth birthday. For the occasion, she put on a formal brocade robe and hat, and sat on a chair on the porch of the ancestral temple. My oldest uncle knelt and read a poem he had composed for the occasion. Another senior relative knelt and presented my grandmother with his best wishes and a cup of wine. Then fruit was offered, along with more good wishes. All this was done to the sound of traditional music of string instruments, cymbals, trumpets, and drums. Finally, after a life of devotion to her family, my grandmother got the recognition she deserved. After the ceremony, a huge banquet was held for relatives, villagers, and the large crowd of guests who had come to pay their respects.

A painful illness took her life soon afterward, but my grandmother at least died happy, still glowing from her great honor. My grandfather, on the other hand, died feeling unrecognized and still smarting from the harsh criticism of his French *résident*—an unhappy ending for a frustrated life. Yet, where it counted most for him, his life was not a failure. Within his own family, behind his shut gate and high walls, he had succeeded in enforcing the traditional values he revered. As a son, Phan had fulfilled his obligations toward his father. And as a father, Phan instilled in his own sons a faith in education and—most important of all in his own view—an attachment to the values of loyalty and filial piety.

3

The Silk Merchant

Trinh Thi Hue, my maternal grandmother, stored her silk in six large wooden trunks—each the size of a piano—in the two rooms upstairs, toward the back of her house in Hanoi. The chests were protected by the Chinese god Quan Cong presiding on an altar set up in the outer room. They looked simple, but they contained the small fortune my grandmother had painstakingly accumulated since my grandfather's death. They gave her a livelihood, without which she would have fallen into a marginal existence. They allowed her to prosper and to earn respect at a time when wealth was beginning to confer status and prestige. The two upstairs rooms were like an inner sanctum: Only my grandmother and my oldest uncle's wife could go in and handle the delicate silk threads. Even in the middle of the day, these rooms were gloomy and mysterious. And with the god protecting their precious contents, there always seemed to be an uncanny presence. When my sister Thang was living at my grandmother's house, she always felt a chill going down her spine each time she was sent there to get herbs from the jars set on a table next to the altar, and she would leave as quickly as she could, afraid even to turn around and look back.

My grandmother had learned business skills from her mother, who had opened a shop buying and selling sugar. Her father had been involved with an armed resistance movement against the French. When that failed, he refused to work for the colonial government, relying instead on the income from his wife's shop to survive. Matrimony was every girl's destiny, so when she was still very young—probably in her early teens—my grandmother married Nguyen Nha, the son of a mandarin. Her father-in-law had something in common with her own father: He too had fought against the French. My grandfather did not oppose the French as his father had. Instead, he went to work for them, serving as district and then as county magistrate, but this does not mean that he approved of what they were doing to Vietnam. Concerned that imported French and Chinese products were displacing local goods and destroying the livelihood of many artisans, he and a small group of mandarins banded together to save local industries from extinction. They started a shop that sold only locally made products. But consumers who were not motivated by patriotism only wanted to get quality for their money, and preferred to buy nice imports over shoddy Vietnamese goods, so the shop could not turn a profit. After a few years of absorbing losses, my grandfather and his associates had to admit failure and closed down the business.

These activities represented the good side of my grandfather. His bad side was not so much personal failure as a reflection of the culture in which he lived. After her marriage, my grandmother moved with my grandfather from district to district, following his transfers from post to post. It was an uneventful life, but not one free from tragedy. Her first six pregnancies ended in miscarriages, though the two sons and four daughters to whom she gave birth later all survived. The quiet facade shattered when she found out that her husband had been carrying on with another woman whom he had installed in a nearby village. Taking mistresses was standard practice among men, and my grandmother had suspected that sooner or later my grandfather would fall into the same trap. Still, when the shoe finally dropped, she was shocked and hurt, finding it difficult to accept the social convention that allowed men to take several wives. She could not acquiesce to the situation, and tried to break up the relationship, to no avail.

Then, at age fifty-four, my grandfather died. At first, this looked like a disaster. My grandmother had no livelihood to support herself and her three small daughters—my mother and two sisters. However, though my grandmother probably did not view the situation this way, her husband's death set her free. For one thing, the emotional scar inflicted by my grandfather's extramarital relationship could now heal. She felt at peace for the first time in years. More important, by going out and earning her own living, she became mistress of her own destiny, no longer dependent on a man for survival. It is a tribute to her that she turned a tragedy into an opportunity for herself. At her husband's death, my grandmother considered her few options: She could do nothing and slowly chip away at her savings. This would not have kept her afloat for very long. She could remarry, becoming the secondary wife of some mandarin. But this option, even if it had been viable for someone her age, was unthinkable and totally unacceptable. For a woman of her stature and moral character, it would have been a shameful act of self-abasement and a violation of her loyalty to her husband and his memory.

Instead, she decided to take matters into her own hands. She went into business. To her, this seemed natural. She had part of the capital, and she had the skill. She saw no shame in being a merchant, even if she had been a mandarin's wife. Her own mother had owned a shop, and she felt it would not be amiss for her to do likewise.

It was a risky decision. If my grandmother had failed, she would have become destitute. She put all the money she had inherited from her parents into the silk business, but even that was not enough to get started, so she borrowed heavily from relatives to put together a capital of 20,000 piasters—a huge sum then, considering that houses on average were selling for only 300 or 400 piasters each. With so much money at stake, it was a big gamble. Yet my grandmother was not afraid, and plunged into the new venture with the sense of authority and confidence she brought to everything she did. She moved into the shop that she and my grandfather had bought earlier in Hanoi, located in the heart of the commercial area near the Hoan Kiem Lake. The store also served as a home for her and her children.

My grandmother did not have to hang a sign declaring she was in business. Word of mouth spread. Silk growers began bringing their threads to sell to her. Then, on market days—four times each month—weavers would come to her shop to examine the merchandise and to buy. Her ability to keep the silk in her big wooden chests was the source of her profits. She bought the threads from the producers as soon as they became available. These growers were peasant families living hand to mouth, who had to sell their goods right away so they could feed themselves. Weavers were in the same situation: They could not afford to store a lot of dead inventory and would buy silk only when they needed it.

Silk was a cottage industry, produced by families living in villages near Hanoi. Raising silkworms was usually a woman's occupation. It was technical and time-consuming. Chopping mulberry leaves and feeding the voracious worms when they were ready to spin their thread took a great deal of time. Then the growers had to know exactly when to remove the cocoons and plunge them into hot water to kill the larvae. If they did not do this in time, the larvae would turn into moths, chew their way out of the cocoons, and destroy the thread. After killing the larvae, the thread had to be gently pulled out of each cocoon and spun into skeins for weaving. The growers would bring their bundles, still damp from the processing, to my grandmother's shop, packaged carefully in bamboo tubes to protect the delicate fibers. My grandmother would gently poke through the coils to determine the quality of the silk, paying more for good threads and less for coarser ones or those with too many knots or defects. Once she bought the thread, my grandmother had to dry it and then store it in her big trunks upstairs until she could sell it. Mice were my grandmother's greatest fear: If they got in and chewed up the silk, they would wipe out her livelihood. This was why among my grandmother's few possessions the one she cherished the most was her sleek black cat, which was fed fresh fish each day. If the maid forgot to buy the fish or feed the cat, my grandmother would scold her for days.

The weavers who came to my grandmother's shop came from villages near Hanoi that specialized in making a variety of fabrics, from the finest brocades and satin-like materials to the less expensive ones. On market days, they and other merchants and traders would travel into Hanoi to buy and sell, clogging the streets in the commercial quarters. On those days, my grandmother would open her shop promptly at seven in the morning and the customers would come in an endless stream, keeping the family so busy that no one could break for lunch until two or three in the afternoon. The customers were savvy men and women, and liked to haggle over price. Once in a while, a weaver short on cash would plead with her to sell on credit, and my grandmother would accommodate, recording the sale in a register kept by one of my aunts. Other than that, there were no legal documents, as business was conducted on trust.

There were many cottage industries like silk production, centered in different villages in the Red River Delta. Villages would become known for a certain merchandise. Nghi Tam specialized in growing flowers and silkworms. Chuyen My was known for furniture and decorations inlaid with mother-of-pearl. Ngu Xa was famous for bronze objects, Dinh Cong for its gold- and silversmiths, and Bat Trang for its ceramics. Vong produced a type of rice snack made from young grains harvested in the fall when they were milky and sweet and then processed in a special way so that they remained chewy and fragrant. Products that came from the celebrated villages carried a special cachet, and consumers who bought these goods always knew they were getting quality for their money.

My grandmother was one of about five silk merchants on Hang Gai, which was typical of the business streets in what the French called the "native" district—as opposed to the section of town that they had transformed with colonial buildings. There were another thirty-five small streets like Hang Gai, each dominated by shops selling mostly one product. Hang Dao specialized in quality finished fabrics; Hang Non merchants sold hats; to buy sugar, people headed toward Hang Duong. Together, these streets formed the commercial heart of the city. The district went back to the thirteenth century, when artisans and merchants that lived there used to belong to guilds, similar to those in the European cities of the Middle Ages. Each guild consisted of families, usually from the same village, that had migrated into Hanoi, attracted by the opportunity to make money there. Each group of families brought with it a special skill in a handicraft or trade that they would pass along only to members of the guild. Each guild had its own temple where members could worship their patron deity.

The street on which my grandmother lived was lined with shops, one right next to the other, with no space between them. Across from her store, a small shrine had been erected to worship the spirit of a huge banyan tree there—ancient, mysterious, and forbidding—with a diameter that is at least three meters wide and countless creepers that hang from its branches. Joss sticks were constantly burning in the small incense urn. My grandmother's shop was a typical "tube" house that can still be found in the old commercial quarters of Hanoi. It was narrow but long, extending far into the back. The room opening out onto the street served as the shop. My grandmother would conduct her business there, and the wives of my two uncles had taken advantage of the space to set out a few counters and shelves where they displayed other merchandise: joss sticks, candles, golden votive paper, and pine sap that could be used as glue. My grandmother had encouraged them to do this so they could earn some extra money, but eventually lack of profit forced them to fold up their business.

Beyond sat the massive furniture—two long settees, a table, a cabinet, and a bed—of the kind that Vietnamese who could afford it loved to display, made with black hardwood and inlaid with mother-of-pearl. At night, my grandmother slept on the carved bed that she had bought after spending a whole month comparison shopping. Next came a room that was used as a storage area, followed by an open inner courtyard with the old well, two more rooms, another inner courtyard, and then the kitchen and servants' quarters. Upstairs, there were the two rooms where my grandmother stored her silk, and a couple of other rooms. My mother's two older brothers and their wives and children, who had moved in with my grandmother, occupied the inner rooms downstairs and upstairs. My mother and her younger sister slept on a plank bed near the shop counters. Compared with the official residences occupied by my father's side of the family, my grandmother's house was simple. Because of the close quarters, my mother remembers that, as a girl, she was constantly aware of the rhythm of life in the household: the hailing of peddlers and checking their goods, the chopping of firewood in a pit built into the tile floor of the kitchen, the preparation of food, cleaning up after meals, and other daily chores.

Even for someone with money like my grandmother, life in Hanoi had few amenities. My mother, who was seven when her family moved to Hang Gai in 1910, recalls growing up in a house that initially had neither running water nor electricity. At first, the only source of water for the neighborhood was the public tap down the street. Each day, maids would line up with their buckets. In the summer, waiting in the heat in the long queue, they would lose their patience and get into fights. Finally, my grandmother reluctantly opened her purse and had water piped into the house. There was no heat, either. In the damp, cold winters, everyone bundled up in bulky quilted jackets and tried to stay warm. Their skin would chafe and crack unless a special salve was applied. My mother remembers that her fingers and toes would get swollen every winter from the cold.

At first, there were only oil lamps at night. Electricity was available, but my grandmother was reluctant to have it brought into the house. She did not want to go through the expense, but she also feared that her neighbors would think she was showing off. On Hang Gai, the first family that did something new was always criticized for being pretentious or ostentatious. The merchant who lived across the street from my grandmother was the first one to buck the neighbors' disapproval, and defiantly had her house wired for electricity. After criticizing her for a while, everyone else followed suit, including my grandmother. The first woman on the block to trade her large hat with the cumbersome round brim and voluminous ribbon for an umbrella, and her slippers with the curved tips for Western shoes, was branded as a "Frenchman's wife"—the worst insult. Soon, other women would do likewise, and anyone who clung to the old fashion would be called a *nha que*, or rustic.

My maternal grandmother believed in a quiet and frugal life. While my father's side of the family liked to live grandly, even when they could not afford it, my grandmother—who could afford to live very well—chose not to. She did not entertain lavishly, because she did not hold an official position and so had no social obligations or status to maintain, but also because this kind of lifestyle did not appeal to her. For servants, she had a maid and a houseboy. My two uncles' wives did the cooking: basic dishes prepared over wood-burning braziers built into a brick platform. Each day, peddlers would pass through the neighborhood, selling everything needed for cooking—fresh vegetables, bean curd, fish, and ready-made steamed or fried pork patties. My aunts had to choose what they bought carefully, because my grandmother could not stand anything that was not just right. Spring onions had to be small and tender; bean curd had to puff up nicely when deep-fried (crusty on the outside but moist and soft on the inside); vegetables had to be young and fresh, not budding with flowers and ready to go to seed. My grandmother made sure the family had plenty to eat, but everything had to be simple and healthy. Perhaps this was why my grandmother lived until she was eighty-three, vigorous and clear in the head until the end.

Like others who had to earn every penny of their own living, my grandmother was obsessively thrifty. Whatever she bought—whether it was a head of cabbage or a house—had to be worth what she paid, and she did not mind spending the time to find exactly what she wanted at the price she thought was right. If it was time to buy fabric for clothes, my grandmother would set off by herself to make the rounds of the shops, going back and forth for days. She would check each piece of cloth carefully, turning it over and over to look for defects, before she would purchase it. There was no such thing as "impulse buying" for my grandmother.

If there was anything my grandmother disapproved of as much as ostentatious living it was frivolity. She forbade idle chatter, loud laughter, and noise. There was no music and no entertainment of any kind. My grandmother never took her children out to a play or to the opera. She allowed only one pastime—reading—and this was only because she could not decipher the modern script herself and mistook the novels my mother devoured for schoolbooks. The novels that my mother borrowed from relatives were a motley collection, ranging from translations of *The Three Musketeers, Gulliver's Travels,* and Chinese classics to Vietnamese literary masterpieces and modern fiction. Like many women and girls at the time, the one that my mother loved to read over and over again was *The Tale of Kieu,* a story in verse written by one of Vietnam's foremost poets about a woman from a good family who had to turn to prostitution but was eventually redeemed.

The only treats my grandmother allowed her children were the snacks bought from peddlers that circulated throughout the neighborhood. Each peddler had a schedule and a special cry to announce their merchandise. Just from the hour of day and the cry, my mother could tell what was being sold—roast peanuts kept warm inside a large tin box, sticky rice steamed with Chinese sausage, eel rice gruel, steamed *banh gio* buns kept hot under layers of banana leaves in baskets that the peddlers carried on top of their heads, cold and hot noodle dishes like *bun cha, bun thang,* and *pho.* My mother loved all the snacks, but one of her favorites was the *keo keo,* or pulled candy. This was a Chinese specialty. The candy had a white sugary crust and a filling made with peanuts. Depending on how much my mother wanted to buy, the vendor would pull out a section from the pliant mass kept under a piece of cloth. My grandmother never took her family to restaurants, which were mostly French or Chinese, because when the Vietnamese dined out they preferred to eat exotic food. She thought the prices were too high and the dishes too fancy for her taste.

Whenever my mother went out with my grandmother, it was to worship in a temple or pagoda. Once there, they would give alms to the beggars, a gesture to remind my mother that she should help those less fortunate. The only break in the long cycle of work was Tet, when my grandmother would close down her business for two weeks. But even Tet was a stay-at-home kind of celebration, punctuated only with visits to relatives' houses to present good wishes for the new year or excursions to temples and pagodas in Hanoi or the surrounding areas to pray. For the first three days of Tet my grandmother allowed one indulgence: card games. After that, she would put the cards away for the rest of the year. (After my mother married, her in-laws were appalled by her lack of knowledge of games of chance, and quickly remedied her education.)

In its frugality and modesty, my grandmother's life was a lot closer to that of most Vietnamese than the one led by my father's side of the family. It was also less restricted by the Confucian teachings that reigned in my father's household. My father's parents and grandparents were scholars for whom these teachings had almost the force of a religion. Their relationships with those around them—even their own children—were distant, separated by the wall of formality and rituals. Although my mother also grew up in a household with a clear and defined code of conduct, the atmosphere by comparison was more relaxed. In spite of my grandmother's strictness, relationships had a warmth that was stifled by rituals in my father's household.

My grandmother's religious practices were also closer to those of ordinary Vietnamese, not as heavily influenced by Confucian culture as in my father's family. To her, marking the deaths of her ancestors was important, but she did not elevate this to the level of worship in Duong Lam's household. The anniversaries of ancestors' deaths, along with Tet, were the highlights of the year for her as well. But no one had to don formal robes for the ceremony, and there was no band to provide ritual music. The offerings were also simpler than in Duong Lam's family. Instead of buying a lot of expensive shark's fins or bird's nests for some of the dishes, my grandmother would use substitutes, such as vegetables that were carved intricately or sliced into tiny strips. They were meant to deceive the palate, but those who ate them knew they were not tasting delicacies. In my father's family, most of this tedious food preparation would be done by a large domestic staff. In my mother's household, such help was not available, and she remembers having to stay up most of the night cutting, chopping, and cooking. Finally, everything would be ready. The altar would groan with boiled chicken, fruit, flowers, rice wine, and the special cakes and dishes. Relatives would be invited to pay respects and share the meal. Afterward they would burn votive products, to make sure our ancestors did not have to go without the creature comforts they had enjoyed in their previous lives, such as paper money, clothes, and shoes. Rich families usually burned a lot more: fancy cabinets and beds, rickshaws, and—later on—even televisions and refrigerators. But my grandmother did not believe in wasting money on lavish offerings.

To my grandmother, visiting the temples and pagodas to pray to Buddha and the pantheon of gods and goddesses was as important as worshiping her ancestors. My mother inherited this religious tradition from her, and while my father would never set foot in temples and pagodas, my mother would go there regularly. I still remember the many trips I made with her to these places of worship when growing up in Hanoi. I share her love of those shrines, where everything spoke of age and the passage of time: the worn steps, the moss-covered walls and gates, the rafters and statues darkened by incense smoke, the gilded and red-lacquered altars with their sheen softened by the years. Her obvious pleasure would infect me. We would arrive at the gate of a temple, give alms to the inevitable gaggle of beggars, buy fragrant flowers and joss sticks from the vendors lining the entrance, and then enter a world of quiet and serenity, where time seemed to stand still.

It was my mother who would keep up other traditions in our family. Except for ancestor worship and Tet, my father was indifferent to Vietnamese religious customs and festivals, viewing their celebration as a "woman's affair" and leaving it up to my mother to observe them or not. My mother would celebrate holidays to which my father hardly paid attention, such as the fifth month festival, all souls' day, Buddha's birthday, and the fall moon festival. She continued the ceremony of sending the Kitchen God back to heaven each year, a week before Tet. I learned to appreciate other aspects of our culture through my mother. While my father preferred the music of an *a dao* singing classical poems, my mother liked to go to see *cheo* operas that appealed to a broader popular audience, and sometimes took me with her when I was growing up in Hanoi. I can still picture myself as a child sitting on the edge of my seat so I could follow the action of the plays—usually woeful tales that made the grown-up women weep. I feel lucky my mother has a background different from that of my father. Instead of being linked only to the Confucian-influenced elite traditions, I grew up connected also to the mass culture.

Unlike my father's mother, who spent her life catering to her spouse, my silk merchant grandmother could—after her husband's death—organize her household to satisfy her own needs, rather than focus on pleasing him. She liked order and cleanliness, and there was a routine that everyone had to follow day in and day out: Every piece of furniture had to be dusted, and the floor swept and mopped. Preparing her herbal potion was another sacrosanct routine. To stay healthy, each day my grandmother would drink a brew made with six different herbs that had been simmered in a clay pot to produce exactly one small bowl of liquid. The herbs came from a traditional apothecary. After buying them, my grandmother would slice them and roast them in a pan, and then store them in jars in the room upstairs. Every day, she would take out a small amount of each to boil in three bowls of water. Whoever she assigned to prepare her potion would have to watch to make sure that it did not burn, or risk being scolded for several days in a row.

My grandmother did share two things in common with my father's parents: utter devotion to the family, and the love of and faith in education. Her children, grandchildren, and other relatives formed the center of her universe. For her, the greatest joy in life was to be with them. My grandmother was strict but also very kind. Even her scolding was not mean, just long, boring lectures. Like other Vietnamese, she did not show her affection with hugs and kisses or express it in words. But she indicated her love by taking good care of her children and grandchildren. She was generous with money whenever anyone needed help. She supported two of my uncles and their families, and bought a house in Hanoi for my parents, the only one they would ever own. My mother and her brothers and sisters inherited my grandmother's kind and quiet personality. Because of this, I became partial to my mother's siblings, and preferred them to many of the hypercritical relatives on my father's side.

As with my father's parents, education was extremely important to my grandmother, the one area where she did not mind spending money. At first, she hired a private tutor to teach all her children—including her daughters—Chinese characters, but when French teaching began to take hold, she immediately had them make the switch. As a merchant, my grandmother was not wedded to a Confucian scholar tradition that she felt she had to maintain at all costs. She was much more open-minded, and saw the value of a modern instruction much faster than did the conservative scholars and mandarins. She shared this progressive attitude with other merchants. At this time, while most scholars cried out against change, merchants were embracing modernization as a way to save Vietnam. It was they who provided critical financial support to various revolutionary movements, without which these groups would not have survived for as long as they did. As Vietnam moved further and further away from its old roots, the influence of the merchants would rise while that of the traditional scholars would diminish.

In giving my mother and her younger sister a modern schooling out-side the home, my grandmother was also ahead of many women in her generation. Other mothers believed that it was not necessary to teach daughters at all, and that if a girl knew how to read and write, she would use her knowledge to do only one thing: write secret love letters to boys. My grandmother did not agree, and sent my mother and her younger sister to the École Brieux, a school for girls the French had set up on Hang Cot Street, not far from the house. (By this time, my moth-er's older sisters had gotten married. Otherwise, my grandmother would have enrolled them too.) But my mother's promising education was cut short after she got married at age sixteen. My father made her quit because he was jealous of her reputation as an excellent student—even outshining him in this area—but also because he thought she should be a full-time housewife. Even if my father had been more reasonable, my mother could not have gone on with her studies because she started hav-ing children one after another, seventeen in all.

In showing so much independence, my grandmother was continuing in the indigenous tradition of Vietnamese women. Before Confucianism restricted what they could do, women would compete in exams or even lead armies. Some of the most famous military leaders were women. Two of the most famous poets were also women: Ba Huyen Thanh Quan wrote aristocratic, lyrical, and evocative poetry, while Ho Xuan Huong was her opposite, writing rebellious, witty, and earthy poems. This tra-ditional independence was so strong that Confucianism could not destroy it entirely. Among the merchants, in particular, there were many women like my grandmother. Together, they dominated commerce.

While my mother was busy at school, my grandmother grew richer and richer. She bought three choice properties in the commercial dis-trict, which she rented to Chinese merchants. One shop sold glassware; another one sold Chinese herbs; and the third sold sausages, roast ducks, roast pork strips, and roast suckling pigs. Whenever my mother went to these stores, she found the scene quaint. The Chinese men wore pigtails and robes that came down to their ankles, and their womenfolk hobbled around on bound feet. My mother would feel lucky and glad that she was not the daughter of a rich Chinese merchant, being sequestered in the shop that was also the home, and spending her youth bent over some intricate embroidery. The lucrative rent from these shops added to my grandmother's wealth and reputation as a savvy businesswoman. Perhaps because of her growing stature, my grandmother was not worried about my mother remaining single at the advanced age of sixteen. She knew that her money and the solid family background would attract a bidder for her daughter's hand sooner or later.

Besides her family's wealth, my mother offered other advantages as a prospective bride. She was considered a beauty. She had a smooth and white complexion, an oval face, large dark eyes, and a nose with a high ridge, not a flat one. Her teeth were lacquered to a rich and even black, another mark of beauty. Young women who dropped the time-consuming and bothersome practice of dying their teeth, applying layer after layer of lacquer and abstaining from solid food for a couple of days to avoid damaging the dye, were considered ugly. People would say, "These women think they've become modern, but they look terrible when they smile, showing their white teeth that look like those of a dog." My mother's delicate and refined figure with no curves was another advantage. But when parents looked for a wife for their son, physical appearance did not count as heavily as character, because the wife had to be submissive, well behaved, and diligent. In this respect, my mother also met the standards. The fact that she was doing well in school was taken as a good sign, for it meant that she obeyed her family's code of conduct, working hard and not wasting her time on frivolous pursuits.

The union between my mother and father happened without a hitch. A matchmaker told my father's parents about my mother, and the marriage was sealed. The day my paternal grandmother came to take a look at the prospective bride in the traditional *xem mat*—checkout—visit, my mother hid under a blanket in panic, so the only parts of her that my paternal grandmother saw were her two feet sticking out. My father, who was not consulted about the match, did not come along. My mother never caught a glimpse of him prior to her wedding. She learned what he looked like only from relatives who had seen him. They reassured her that he was tall—five feet five inches—and handsome, with a "high" nose, high cheekbones, and large eyes. They also told her that he was thin and not strong looking, but this too was encouraging because it showed that he was a scholar who worked with his brain rather than with his muscles.

As comforting to my mother was her mother's reassurance that her future husband and parents-in-law were kind people who would undoubtedly treat her well. So my mother did not feel alarmed about marrying someone she did not know. In fact, she felt proud about joining a prominent family. The wedding was a big affair, with four automobiles to take the bride's party back to Van Dinh. When they arrived at the gate of my grandfather's residence, my mother, woozy from the trip, was helped out of the car by her two bridesmaids, each of whom held a huge, round hat to shield my mother's face from view. My mother, decked out in gold jewelry, a brocade gown, and shoes embroidered with colored beads, only saw a patch of ground from under these hats. Then she saw a brazier filled with burning coal. She stepped over it to kill any back luck that might accompany her into her new household, and at the same time stepped into a different world. In her new family, she would find a more formal atmosphere and more rigid relationships, but she would also find protection and support.

My mother was lucky. When I was little, I wondered why so many Vietnamese girls wept bitterly before and on their wedding day. At first, I thought they cried from happiness, but as I grew older I realized that they cried from fear. They were leaving the protection of their families for a household of strangers, including their own husbands, and they would be at the mercy of these new relatives. Most of them ended being bullied by their mothers-in-law. Many were also badly treated by their husbands. To me the epitome of a union turned into misery was the marriage of one of my father's sisters. Her husband abandoned her to his mother's clutches in the native village while he pursued an education and a career. Later, he would abandon her for one mistress after another. Her mother-in-law turned my aunt into a maid without pay—shopping, cooking, cleaning, and waiting hand and foot on the old woman. One day, on her way back from the village market, the live fish she had bought jumped out of her basket onto the muddy bank of a pond she was passing. Terrified that her mother-in-law would make her life hell if she did not bring the fish home, she dove after it. In this struggle, my aunt was even more desperate than the fish, and she managed to catch it before it could swim away.

Besides prosperity and success, my silk merchant grandmother also enjoyed a long life. Even in her last days, she was blessed. If there was such a thing as a painless death, she had it. She fell one night when she tried to get out of bed, and drifted into a coma. A week later, she was gone. She was buried in Lang village near Hanoi. (Later the communist government had the tomb razed and the remains moved to Son Tay, to make room for a vegetable plot.) After she died, my oldest uncle's wife divided up the inheritance. According to Vietnamese custom, the sons got the largest part. One of the shops was kept for *huong hoa:* The rental income would be used to pay for expenses related to the upkeep of my grandfather's and grandmother's tombs and the ceremonies commemorating their deaths. The remaining two shops were split between my two uncles. The house on Hang Gai was sold and the proceeds divided among my mother and her sisters.

None of my grandmother's children followed her example and went into business, and her wealth did not survive long after her death. At first, my oldest uncle built up his inheritance into a fortune. His wife also came from a wealthy family and they bought several choice commercial properties together. My aunt-in-law was parsimonious and did not like to spend money on clothes. Once, a fortune-teller she consulted took a look at her shabby quilted jacket, and then told her with pity in his voice, "You're destined to be poor." Infuriated, she grabbed the fee she had put on a plate and stormed out. Later, his prediction turned out to be accurate. After the communists took over Hanoi, they seized her properties. She and the rest of her family were herded into the garage of her villa, leaving the rest of the house to several families of strangers. She died brokenhearted.

My second uncle also lost his wealth after 1954. Afraid that the communist government would condemn him as a bourgeois, he donated all his properties to the state. The communists also seized the house that my grandmother had bought for my mother and turned it into state property. The only person in my mother's family that did well after the communists took Hanoi was her oldest sister, whose husband supported the Viet Minh. The French had forced him into early retirement from his teaching job. He thought this was unjust, and his anger made him more open to the appeal of the Viet Minh. His oldest son also joined the Viet Minh, and later rose to become a deputy prime minister in charge of planning and development. Because of his position, but also because all the children and grandchildren had moved into the villa, leaving no room for other families, the communists did not force my aunt to share her house with strangers. My second aunt had married into a poor family. The inheritance she got was like a pinch of salt thrown into a vast ocean: It disappeared quickly. In a few decades, what my grandmother had worked so hard to build was gone.

When I asked my mother recently what she thought was the happiest period in her life, she answered without hesitation, "When I was young and living at home with grandma." I can understand why she felt this way. My grandmother gave her a secure, worry-free childhood, within a warm and supportive family, in an orderly and stable household. Like most people, my mother could never recapture her childhood innocence and happiness. Once she reached adulthood, her life became bittersweet. Her marriage had its periods of joy, but also its days of darkness and grief. Through it all, she could look back with nostalgia on those years with my grandmother, and wish she could be young again in the shop on Hang Gai Street.

4

French Veneer, Confucian Soul

As early morning broke over Hanoi, my father Duong Thieu Chi and his brother Chinh rolled out from under their mosquito net to get ready for their first day at the Collège Paul Bert. They wanted to get to school with plenty of time to spare. They dressed in their brand-new and unfamiliar Western shoes, which they put on backward, and their new Western shirts and khaki pants. It felt strange not to be putting on the silk pants, long robe, and wooden clogs they had been wearing just a few days before. It felt stranger still not to feel the weight of the long tufts of hair that used to hang down their backs. But they were pleased with their new appearance, which would help them fit in at school. They felt urbane and civilized. When they heard the first electric trolley clanking in the street, they rushed out and jumped onboard. The school gate was still closed when they arrived. They sat in the cool morning light and waited for hours.

Things had happened very fast for my father and uncle. Just a couple of weeks before, a servant had whisked them from Dong Quan in Thai Binh Province to their grandfather's villa in Thai Ha Ap outside of Hanoi. My father had stayed at the house before. After his grandfather Duong Lam moved to Van Dinh, my father would occasionally come with his mother to the villa. They would make the trip from the village and back on a rickshaw with metal wheels. It would take them a whole day to cover forty kilometers. The ride would jar every bone in my father's body, but he enjoyed the pastoral scenes en route. He passed by rice fields dotted with graves, some bearing stone carvings. In the distance, he could see the whitewashed village gates flanked by thick green bamboo groves. Once in a while, he could spot shacks nestled at the foot of tall trees offering refreshments and snacks. Now and then, he could glimpse clumps of vendors gathered at a small market. Depending on the season, the trees that he saw could be stripped of leaves, luxuriant with foliage, covered with flowers, or laden with fruit. The rice fields could be a rippling emerald green or golden sea, or barren with dry stalks of the harvested rice plants poking through the brown dirt.

Duong Lam's house in Thai Ha Ap was by now deserted and watched over by a caretaker. It seemed spooky to my father. Practically everyone who lived there said that the area was haunted. In 1788, thousands of Chinese soldiers had died on the Dong Da hillock nearby, in one of the most savage battles in Vietnamese history, when Emperor Quang Trung led his troops to Hanoi and routed the Chinese army. Quang Trung's campaign took place just before Tet and would later be invoked by the Viet Cong as a historical precedent, when they launched their own infamous Tet Offensive in 1968. A temple and a pagoda had been built on the Dong Da hillock, but they could not banish the souls of the dead Chinese. My great-grandfather's servants used to claim that at night they could see ghosts in pigtails sliding down the villa's roof and drinking basins filled with blood. Now my father and his brother were back again in the scary house. They would stay here while they applied for admission into the Collège Paul Bert. The day of their entrance exam, they boarded the trolley for Hanoi from the last stop outside of the city. The two boys were used to trains, but the tramway was a mode of transport they had not tried before. The big clanking iron vehicle that ran by itself, without being pulled by horses or oxen or propelled by steam, amazed them. They sat on wooden benches near the windows, and watched the landscape flow by.

Hanoi was their next shock. It was bigger, noisier, and awesome compared with the little province towns they knew. It was turning into a large and bustling city, acquiring a European flair with imposing, French-style buildings. Climbing the flight of steps and the long staircase in what looked to them like a cavernous *résidence supérieure* bureau, the two little country boys felt intimidated and disoriented. As they stopped outside the Primary Education Director's office, where they were scheduled to take their exam, they looked out the window at the beautiful multistoried Métropole Hotel across the street, and thought they had wandered into paradise. No such buildings had been erected in the country before. Even the Imperial Palace in Hue was tiny, a modest replica of the splendid and gigantic Forbidden City in Peking. In a country that used to despise commerce, glorify poverty as proof of moral probity and strength, and keep land ownership fragmented, there had been no concentration of wealth to produce imposing buildings, nor wealthy patrons to spur and sustain the creation of great works of art. My father wondered how human beings could build such magnificent edifices.

The entrance exam to the Collège Paul Bert was perfunctory. This school had been reserved for French children, but now it was enrolling native students as part of a new assimilation policy. After several revolts in 1908, Albert Sarraut, the new governor general, decided to implement some reforms to calm the restive natives. For the first time, he promised that Vietnam would be set free. But first, it would have to become civilized and learn how to govern itself under French tutelage. Until this happened, France would have to stay, to serve like a father to Vietnam, teaching it and bringing it gradually into the civilized world. In short, the Vietnamese would be given independence only when they became like the French. To many Vietnamese, the policy seemed like a step in the right direction. Families like mine that did not want to resort to violence to get rid of the foreigners welcomed the change. Without bloodshed, and after a period of peaceful evolution, their country would be free, they thought. By thus removing the prospect of eternal bondage, Sarraut made it easier for my family and others to accept French domination. As long as colonial rule was finite, they felt they could live with it. And if assimilation could speed Vietnam toward freedom, then getting a French education and absorbing Western culture was not only practical but also morally acceptable.

Although Sarraut opened more schools as part of these reforms, only the upper classes benefited from the new opportunities. Peasant children usually stopped after they finished the schooling available in the village. Their families could not afford to send them to nearby towns and then to Hanoi and Saigon to get a higher education. The upper classes, on the other hand, could pay the tuition and the expenses involved. When Sarraut opened the exclusive Collège Paul Bert in Hanoi and the Collège Chasseloup Laubat in Saigon to natives, the Vietnamese elite were the only ones to enroll their children. To increase attendance, the entrance exam to the first grade at the Collège Paul Bert was made easy. All that my father had to do was to answer in French whenever the Primary Education Director held an object in the air and asked, "What's this?" My father had learned enough French words from a tutor back in the province to identify correctly such things as a "matchbox." Both he and his brother passed and were admitted in 1912.

Before they could attend classes, they had to show proof that they met the age limit for the first grade. They had already invested several years learning Chinese. Now, at ages twelve and thirteen, they were too old. The only solution was to falsify their birth certificates. This was easily arranged. My grandfather did not understand that they could be admitted even if they came in under the age limit. So he had both their birth dates changed to 1903, to give them the exact age of nine. This created another problem. The two brothers could not have been born in the same year, only six months apart. My grandfather came up with another solution. He declared that my uncle was born from his first wife and my father from his second. The French accepted the explanation.

In their new Western clothes and haircuts, the two teenagers easily fit into the student body. Half of the pupils were natives from the emerging middle class: mandarins, government employees, landowners, and merchants. The richest among them preferred to board at the school. They were the envy of their Vietnamese classmates, because they could eat French food in the canteen, sleep in clean and comfortable dormitories, and wear handsome school uniforms. Their winter uniforms dazzled their friends the most: purple woolen jackets with shiny brass buttons. Every afternoon, they were served a snack of French bread and bananas, while their less well-off friends watched and drooled. The monthly tuition was two piasters for the primary grades. It rose gradually for the upper primary grades until it reached ten piasters, about a third of what most government officials took home in salary each month. Boarding cost twenty-five piasters per month, plus expenses for hot and cold weather uniforms and other items.

Poorer students like my father and uncle lived off campus and walked to school, taking the rickshaw only when it rained or when the tropical heat was unbearable. The two boys had almost no money. Every couple of years, my grandparents gave them a new set of clothes. They kept their woolen winter jackets—the most expensive of their school clothes—as long as possible, even after they had become threadbare and faded. Their shoes were reinforced with iron patches under the heels and along the sides to make them last longer. My grandparents gave them new ones only when the old ones could no longer hold together. In the summer, the two boys wore hats made of woven palm leaves decorated with a purple band, to shield their faces from the burning sun. These were much cheaper than the cloth hats. Although my father and uncle envied their wealthy classmates, they were not unhappy. They knew they were much better off than the students attending the non-French schools who were so poor they had to wear heavy and uncomfortable wooden clogs to school because they could not afford to buy shoes.

My father's wealthy classmates were part of a new social group: people who had made their money from land-ownership and commerce. Indeed, Vietnamese society was becoming more diverse, and the gap that separated the rich from the poor began to widen. In the past, the mandarins who were at the top of the social scale were not much better off materially than the peasants, artisans, and merchants they governed. All this changed with the introduction of a market and cash economy. Money now meant influence and power, and it was all right to earn lots of it. Commerce and business became not only respectable, but desirable for those who wanted to develop the country, provide employment, or raise revenue to finance political activities. This change in attitude was most prevalent in the south, where there were more economic opportunities and a less hidebound society, but even in conservative Tonkin things started to thaw. The prominent mandarin Hoang Trong Phu, the governor general of Ha Dong Province and the son of the last viceroy, did not think it was beneath him to start a kiln to revitalize blue and white porcelain production. Others quit their mandarin posts to take up commerce, something that would have been unthinkable in the past. Within my family's circle of acquaintances, a province judge resigned to open a shop.

Among the new breed of businessmen, the richest were entrepreneurs who had cleverly seen how they could make a fortune from the French presence: as contractors for the massive building projects, as suppliers of foodstuffs and other materials to the colonial army, and as distributors

of French imports and, later, fabrics produced by the local French textile mills. Others made their money by obtaining land concessions that
they turned into plantations of rice or other crops. Before the arrival of
the French, large land-ownership was rare, especially in Tonkin where
land was limited and mostly communally owned. Those who wanted to
build up their holdings had to do it gradually over the years, buying a
few hundred square meters at a time. Anyone who could piece together
six to seven acres was thought of as a big landowner. After the French
arrived, however, it became easier to accumulate land. In the south, the
first big landowners were those who got their properties by seizing the
rice fields of peasants who had fled their villages to escape the French
attacks. In the north, as village land became available for sale, people
who had money began to increase their holdings, sometimes through
unethical means—such as lending the poor peasants money at an usuri-
ous interest rate and then seizing their land when they could not repay.

But the biggest landowners owed their fortune to the French
drainage projects, which opened up vast tracts of land for cultivation.
While supporters of the French in the north could each get 100 acres at
the most, those in the south could each receive hundreds of acres. In
Tonkin, the new land was located in the narrow coastal region on the
edge of the Red River Delta. In the south, the new rice fields emerged
from the huge, unexploited, swampy, and sparsely populated Mekong
Delta. Because of the limited amount of new land, the number of
Vietnamese receiving land concessions in Tonkin could be counted on
one hand. In the south, the total was much higher, giving rise to a new
landowning class: the big absentee landlords with vast acreage who
lived in the towns and sent their children to French schools or to France
to study. They hired managers to take care of their estates, and—no
longer setting foot in the countryside—lost contact with their rural
roots.

At the Collège Paul Bert, my father and his brother now had to put
up with the indignity of attending classes with five- and six-year-old
French children. Some would still soil their pants once in a while.
Whenever this happened, they would try to keep the offending material from falling out by tying up their pants' legs with the strings of their
spinning tops. The odor would drive the Vietnamese sitting next to
them to distraction, but none dared—or knew how—to complain to the
French teacher. The French children were quick to understand that they
had a big natural advantage over their native classmates: They knew
they could talk to the teachers, who would side with them in any dis-

pute, out of affection and trust. They took full advantage of the situation to make the Vietnamese do what they wanted. If the Vietnamese balked, the French boys would run to the teachers and make up stories to get them punished. To avoid trouble, Vietnamese children learned to turn the other cheek.

My father and uncle quickly found out how costly it was to cross their French classmates. One day, they took their shiny new marbles to school. Their toys immediately attracted the attention of a boy named Mercier, whose aunt happened to be the class teacher. Mercier, of course, wanted the marbles, but my father and uncle were not ready to part with them. Upset, Mercier ran to his aunt with the story that the two boys had disturbed the students by "singing during class." The aunt confronted my father and uncle. When they could not defend themselves with the few words of French they knew, she immediately punished them with a detention for that coming Sunday. After this incident, my uncle—more clever and manipulative than my father—bought off Mercier by bribing him with a tamarind fruit. After that, they had no further trouble with him. This success taught my uncle a lesson on how to deal with powerful but corruptible enemies.

With their limited French, school was a real struggle for my father and his brother. They could not get help from anywhere. Private tutoring was out of the question because their parents could not afford it. The two teenagers managed as best they could. The only tool they had to make sense out of their school materials was a rudimentary French-Vietnamese dictionary. They learned to compensate for their handicap by memorizing everything. Their capacious memories, honed by years of learning Chinese primers by rote, saved them from abject failure. They did not understand what they were studying, but they could recite by heart that their "ancestors were Gauls" who "hung mistletoe boughs on New Year's." My father became the top student in his class. He was first in everything that he could learn by heart, but did not do as well in subjects like French dictation and composition. He did so well that he was allowed to skip a grade the next year. After that, his French improved and he became a star pupil, earning prizes and honors in every grade. When he finished his primary school, he had the great honor of being chosen as one of ten candidates for the *certificat d'études primaires* exam, which only the best students could take.

After that, my father moved on to the next level, the breeding ground of the future educated elite. Many of his classmates later became Vietnam's doctors, lawyers, engineers, and leading officials. But this was still years and years away, after the French decided to train more native professionals and to open up the middle and upper levels of government to the locals. My father was outstanding in every subject except English, which he hated. At the end of each level, there was an exam to be taken. Like his contemporaries, my father loved degrees and exams of all types and at all levels. He would take them even when they were not required for advancement, just for the fun of it. When he passed one at the end of the upper level—one of a handful of candidates that did at the time—my great-grandfather gave him a special honor. He made him ride in a rickshaw shaded by a large yellow parasol in the procession organized for his oldest brother Tuong, when the latter returned to Van Dinh in triumph after getting his doctorate degree. My great-grandfather also had a banner made for the occasion to proclaim my father's achievement, inscribed with Chinese characters that said, "Pioneer of European Learning." Armed with this degree, my father could have enrolled in the University of Hanoi—which was really just a vocational school to train teachers, administrators, and technicians. Unfortunately, because of the lie he had told earlier, he was now considered too young to be admitted. He was officially sixteen, while the minimum age for enrollment was eighteen.

His brother Chinh solved the problem by changing his birth certificate once again. At this time, Maurice Cognacq—the man who eventually became the most corrupt governor of Cochinchina—was the director of public education, with power over admissions. My uncle bribed Cognacq's secretary, an alcoholic Vietnamese. The clerk pretended to get drunk and spilled ink over the birth certificate my uncle had submitted with his application, making it illegible. Chinh was told to provide another one, and he presented a new one with the birth date now changed back to the correct year. But that was not the end of his problems. His graduation grades were too low to get him into the medical school, his first choice. So he bribed the same clerk to give Cognacq— an avid collector of antiques—a beautiful old Vietnamese vase. Cognacq waved the grade requirement, and my uncle was accepted. My father found out later that his brother was only one of several unqualified candidates that Cognacq had admitted in exchange for bribes.

With the option of attending the vocational school closed off, my father got married and returned to finish his high school. Again, he was the first in his class, outdistancing his classmates in every field and winning first prize for every subject. When he passed with honors the *brevet supérieur*, the first student in Vietnam to get this degree, he became famous, and newspapers carried articles about his achievement. He also became the darling of the school officials and teachers, one of whom told him that she could get him a teaching job with the salary of 100 piasters per month, an enormous sum for my father who was not only poor but also saddled with a wife. He was tempted, but my grandfather wanted him to continue studying in order to get into Hanoi's College of Law, the most prestigious institution in Indochina at the time. The high school director then offered to get my father, a scholarship to go to France. Such scholarships, along with simpler emigration procedures, were part of the colonial authorities' effort to encourage the Vietnamese to go to France to study. Later, when they realized that many of the students were going there to engage in political activities—rather than to get an education—the colonial regime would try to reduce their numbers. My father was sorely tempted by the prospect of an adventure in France, but had to turn down the offer because he did not want to leave my mother behind. In 1921, he graduated from high school and was now old enough for Hanoi University. As his father had wished, he enrolled in the school of law, which trained students to become functionaries. The choice made sense because, even at this time, government employment still offered the best salary and the highest prestige in the country.

My father moved into the dormitory, as required. After their wedding in 1919, my father had lived for about a year at his mother-in-law's house. This common practice was called *gui re*, roughly translated as "parking a bridegroom," to stress that the arrangement is temporary until the newlyweds could move in with the bridegroom's family, as dictated by custom. Then, when my father's younger brothers descended on Hanoi to go to school, my grandfather rented a house for them. My father went to stay with his brothers until he had to board at the university. Since there was not enough room, my mother continued to live at home and would see my father only briefly on Sunday during the school year.

The university was the only one for all of Indochina. Most students came from the three regions of Vietnam, but there were also students from Cambodia and Laos. The Vietnamese were divided. In the old days, the elite shared the same classical education and Confucian values. There was a unifying cultural thread. After the French broke up the country into three distinct regions, Tonkin, Annam, and Cochinchina began to drift apart. Of the three, Cochinchina was the most Westernized. It was ruled separately as a colony, under French law, and had more political freedom. It had the most economic potential and enjoyed the highest level of economic development, which gave rise to a much larger class of entrepreneurs, businessmen, and large landowners. The elite in Saigon was more French than anywhere else in the country; some even acquired French citizenship. Contacts between people of the three regions diminished, because it was no longer possible to circulate freely. Those that wanted to go from Annam or Tonkin to Cochinchina had to get a passport. Under this French policy of "divide and rule," natural regional differences became exacerbated and divisive.

The deepest division was between students from Tonkin and those from Cochinchina, who rarely socialized with one another. The ones from Annam usually remained neutral. Cambodians and Laotians did not want or bother to get involved. Tonkinese and Cochinchinese students had frequent fights, often over the slightest things, such as the cafeteria menu. All students had to live on campus, but everything was free, including the food. Each month, students selected one of their own to set up the menu for lunches and dinners to be prepared by the kitchen staff. When their turn came, students from each region would take the opportunity to ask for their favorite dishes. But those from the other regions would find them inedible. Tonkinese would criticize the Cochinchinese menu, and vice versa, and pretty soon the hotheaded youths among the two groups would come to blows. But the friction existed more among the young students than among those who were more mature. Many of these were already married, like my father, and others were low-level government functionaries who decided to go back to school. Regional differences could be overcome, and friendships developed, especially since students did share one thing in common: their elite class background. My father got to know some of his southern classmates, who later became colleagues and even lifelong friends.

Besides having his room and board paid, each student also received a small monthly stipend. After deducting expenses like books and breakfasts—which were not provided by the school cafeteria—and tips to the servants who cleaned the dorm, my father still had enough left of his subsidy to spend on rickshaw rides and entertainment. Compared with the province, Hanoi had richer possibilities. There was a cinema near the central lake. Hanoi also had two theaters: one offering northern *cheo* operas, and one specializing in *cai luong*, or reformed operas that originated in the south and were beginning to sweep the country.

There was also entertainment on campus. In the evening, music filled the air, as students played their favorite regional traditional instruments. One of the southern students who was a good *cai luong* singer and who later on became a province governor in Cochinchina would rehearse his music before performing at the local theater where he moonlighted as an actor. On Saturday nights the campus emptied, as students left to go home or to have a night out on the town. In their Western suits and bow ties, the students, especially those from the south, cut an elegant silhouette in Hanoi. Their classmates from the more conservative regions of Annam and Tonkin reverted to their Vietnamese costumes for the weekend. A few students would venture into Kham Thien—the red-light district of Hanoi—where traditional singers plied their trade, and where they could stay for the night. It is possible that my father might have acquired his lifelong passion for *a dao* singing from a few visits to this area during his university days. But the students' freedom was brief, and they had to return to the dorm by nine o'clock in the evening of the next day at the latest. Everyone tried to get back on time before the French supervisor made his rounds, to avoid being punished and confined to school the following weekend.

Another form of entertainment for the students was spectator sports such as soccer and bicycle racing, new to the country. Sports events existed in the old days, but consisted only of games such as wrestling, climbing up a greased pole, or demonstrations of martial arts during village festivals. The colonial government rarely acted without a political motive, and the introduction of Western sports was no exception. It was done to divert the young from dangerous political activities. Unaware of or unconcerned about the ultimate political aim, the young responded enthusiastically. A physical fitness fad developed, and many youths eagerly took up soccer, weight lifting, bicycling, and swimming.

My father sometimes watched soccer games and bicycle races but rarely went out with his friends to sports events or anything else. On weekends, he simply rushed home to be with his family—not with his wife, but with his brothers in the rented house. My mother would drop by on Sundays to see him. Even then, because of the lack of privacy and the prying eyes of my father's siblings, who were always ready to make fun of them, my parents were too shy to even talk to each other, let alone show any affection. They could spend time with each other only during the summer, when they went home to my grandfather's residence for vacation. My parents accepted this arrangement. My father was still in school, and they could not afford to live on their own. Besides, they did not have a passionate relationship, and did not feel they had to be with each other frequently.

Like other marriages at the time, theirs was a family rather than a personal affair. It was a union of two families of equal social standing and not a union of two individuals in love, and the main purpose was to procreate and perpetuate the lineage rather than to share a lifetime of love and companionship. My father had come close to getting married twice, but both times the intended bride died. By the time the matchmaker found my mother for him, my father was desperate, because he had already reached the advanced age of nineteen. He quickly accepted the idea of marrying my mother. Of course, even if he had objected, it would have done no good because his parents had already decided for him. The same was true for my mother. When her mother asked her what she thought, my mother said what every girl in the same situation would have said, "I'll sit wherever my parents tell me to sit." Though affection and companionship developed after they married, my parents' relationship was held together more by bonds of duty than of love.

By the time the young began to rebel against the tyranny of the family and search for individual freedom in the late 1920s, my parents and many of their peers were already locked in the kind of loveless, arranged marriages that these youths condemned. But my parents did not feel sorry that they had missed this social wave. Throughout their lives, they believed that unions based on *nghia*, or duty, which lasts a lifetime, were stronger than those based on love, which usually fades away. In their view, the youths of the next generations who married for love did not end up finding more happiness. Not only that, their marriages were more fragile because they were not sustained by *nghia*.

My parents were typical of their generation. They had their feet in both the old Vietnam that was disappearing and a new Vietnam that was only just taking shape, but their hearts were still with the old world. At school, they acquired a French education and a Western veneer, but at home they fell easily back into the rhythm and values of traditional family life. Despite my father's Western appearance, his soul remained very Confucian. Once back in my grandfather's residence, my father would take off his Western clothes, put on the traditional costume, and play the role of the filial son, deferring to his father in everything. Although the next generation would chafe under this kind of parental authority, my father felt no kinship with the new youthful rebellion. Instead, he was alarmed by the rising attacks against the old traditions and by the calls for more individual freedom at the expense of the family.

Indeed, the family—his own and his extended family of parents and siblings—was the center of his universe. Like his grandfather and father, he believed that his ultimate goal in life should be to protect it and ensure its survival. Throughout his career, this concern would always override other considerations. Within the extended family, his father stood at the apex in importance. Next came his mother and his oldest brother, the most direct male descendant who would perpetuate the cult of the ancestors and whose authority ranked second only to that of his father. After that came his wife and other male siblings. My mother did not resent her lack of importance within the family. She accepted that in her husband's household she was only a small cog in the Confucian wheel. My father was not as demanding as his father had been toward his wife. He paid more attention to her and showed more affection. He listened to her more and tried to please her more. But my mother knew her place and endured her low profile. She would develop a knack for acceptance that would astound me later. While some women were beginning to clamor for liberation from family tyranny, my mother just looked on all this agitation with curiosity and with disapproval.

While these debates were raging outside in newspapers and books—the main sources of radical ideas—my father buried himself in school work, studying morning, noon, and night. He felt he could not afford not to succeed, and pressured himself to finish school as quickly as possible so he could go out and find a job to support his family. In the summer, he would relax for a few weeks, and then would hit the books to cram for the *examen de passage*, the exam that would allow him to move on to the next level. Every night, he would study under his mosquito net with a small oil lamp. He got so little sleep toward the end of the summer that my mother would worry about his health. In his second year in law school, my mother gave birth to their first child, Luat—a daughter. The stress became so intense that my father began to develop an ulcer. Then, toward the end of the summer of that year, he came down with malaria. Instead of studying for the *examen de passage*, he lay in bed shivering and shaking. He was deadly sick for three weeks and, by the time the disease had run its course, was too exhausted to cram for the exam. Fortunately, he managed to pass anyway.

With Luat's birth, my mother moved in with my father's parents in Nghia Hung County, in Nam Dinh Province. At the end of his third year, my father had to pass the last hurdle, the formidable graduation exam. Just as he was getting ready for it, Luat was struck by tetanus. The beautiful little girl with the clear bright eyes was two years old, and just beginning to talk. To avoid worrying him at this crucial time, my mother and the rest of the family kept the news from him. Then, while he was in the middle of the exam, Luat went into convulsions and died. This news was also kept from him. Unaware of the tragedy, he made one last burst of effort and passed, becoming one of the first three students in Tonkin to graduate from the school of law. He learned of his daughter's death only when he went back to Nghia Hung with the news of his success. He grieved over the loss but remained stoic and did not reproach his parents and my mother for having kept him in the dark about her condition, accepting the explanation that there was nothing he could have done to save her and that they had acted in his—and the family's—best interest. As did my mother, he would bury the memory deep within himself. Decades later, when we talked about the circumstances of my sister's death for the first time, he would choke back tears and I would see that the pain was still there, even after all those years.

My father graduated in 1924—twelve long, hard years since the day he arrived in Hanoi, wearing his traditional robe and the long tuft of hair that bounced on his back. There was no triumphant return to Van Dinh for him. That custom had disappeared along with many others. But my grandfather held a big celebration at his residence. To give the place a festive air, he had a string of lights hung under the eaves and illuminated at night. A rich merchant sent a group of musicians to perform for the celebration, one of the first bands in the Red River Delta that could play French music. So when my grandfather prostrated himself in front of the ancestral altar to report the news of my father's graduation, they struck up not the traditional ritual music, but the *Marseillaise*, the French national anthem.

Perhaps it was fitting that my father's personal success was highlighted by the *Marseillaise*. At the time, France stood triumphant in Vietnam. There were currents of opposition, but the country was generally quiet, as though the people had resigned themselves to their fate. Pessimists even began to believe that, just as among the species, nations that were weak—like Vietnam—were destined to be dominated by those that were strong—like France. It was in this national mood of pessimism that my father began his career.

5

Taxes, Floods, and Robbers

My father received his first appointment in September 1924 as a *commis* trainee, fourth class, in the Finance Bureau in Hanoi, with a respectable salary of 100 piasters per month. He and my mother immediately moved into the city and rented a house. When he got his first month's pay, my father went out and bought a "dress for success" wardrobe: two pairs of shoes, a brand-new umbrella, and a couple of Western suits. He purchased a rickshaw with rubber wheels, and hired a puller to take him back and forth from his office. My father now began his career as a bureaucrat, with an uneventful daily routine that people referred to as "leaving home with an

umbrella in the morning, and coming home with it at night." My parents settled into a comfortable lifestyle, complete with a staff of servants
and a cook. For the first time since their marriage, they had a home of
their own, but they were still paying off my grandfather's debts and
sending money to my father's younger brother studying in France, so
they usually were broke by the end of the month.

My father's job was typical of the government positions available to
the Vietnamese. Higher level jobs were monopolized by the French.
The Vietnamese elite was, of course, unhappy with being kept bottled
up in lower positions, but it was a take-it-or-leave-it situation. Except
for the government, there was no other viable outlet for employment.
The finance office, headed by a Frenchman, had about five sections, each
staffed with four or five clerks. My father quickly mastered the paperwork routine that he found so boring that he would take as many days
off as he could get away with, often sending his rickshaw driver to the
office with a note saying he was sick. Yet he still managed to impress his
French boss with his efficiency.

The years my father spent as a bureaucrat—from 1924 to 1929—
were a period of dramatic economic expansion. Encouraged by the
promise of stability, cheap labor, economic privileges, and tax shelters,
French capitalists, newly recovered from World War I, invested heavily in the country. They put their money mainly into enterprises that
would produce raw materials for export, such as coal and rubber. By
1924, the investment had triggered a boom that benefited mostly
French firms. The expansion, however, came from the sweat of many.
Almost a third of the capital was poured into rubber plantations in
Cochinchina, which imported thousands of laborers from Tonkin and
Annam to tend the trees and gather the sap. The laborers were destitute
peasants who were dragooned into these plantations. Once there, they
found concentration camp-like conditions. However, they were bound
by contracts, and if they tried to escape and were caught, would be
viciously punished.

Housing was crude and built in muddy and swampy areas. Food was
inadequate and water was contaminated; malaria was rampant. The
back-breaking work began in the early morning hours, and did not stop
until after nightfall, most of it performed in the blistering heat or in the
drenching downpour of the monsoon season. Under these terrible conditions, it was not surprising that many laborers died. Their plight horrified their countrymen and came to symbolize the degradation of colonialism. It also shattered the myth of the *mission civilisatrice*. Even when

I was growing up three decades later, I still heard stories of their terrible suffering, long after the inhuman practices had stopped.

The year after my father started his job at the finance office, opposition to the French became more militant and more structured. Before, nationalist leaders had placed their faith in modern education to free their countrymen or their hope in French reforms. There were no organized political movements. When they saw how their faith in reforms had been misplaced, the new generation of leaders turned to armed resistance and political organization to achieve their aims. The most revolutionary and effective of these leaders was Ho Chi Minh. Ho had left the country in 1911, disillusioned by the failure of previous generations of activists to end colonialism and determined to find a new answer. He drifted to America and to England, but found no sympathetic ears or programs of action that he thought would bring a solution. He finally settled in Paris in 1919. At first he tried to appeal to the French government and other Western powers to help Vietnam. But after he was given the cold shoulder everywhere, a frustrated Ho concluded that the Vietnamese would have to win their freedom back themselves, not by pleading but by violence.

At this time, Russia was advocating the liberation of Asian colonies. This immediately caught Ho's attention and he left for Moscow in 1923 to obtain revolutionary training. Two years later, he made his way to the Chinese border, recruiting among the Vietnamese exiles and building his movement. Beginning from this date, the communist ideology would guide the Vietnamese fight for independence. Ho's movement would differ from those that preceded it in several important aspects: It would be national in scope; it would be a mass movement; it would have a social as well as a political agenda; and it would have links to the outside world via the communist movements in other countries, including France. It would also be sustained by the unshaken belief that history was on its side and that victory would be certain, because capitalism was on the decline and communism would triumph and usher in the millennium.

Communist agents began infiltrating Vietnam from China and by 1930 they had built up enough support to foment labor strikes and peasant demonstrations. In September, the communists launched their boldest protests in Nghe An and Ha Tinh, two of the poorest provinces in Annam. Peasants in several districts revolted and seized power. They formed "red villages," distributed the land they had seized, and ran these districts for three months. In their revolutionary zeal, they also attacked landlords, well-to-do families, and educated people. These attacks scared the middle class and, for the first time, gave them a frightening glimpse of what life would be like for them under communism. Accordingly, they threw their support behind French efforts to suppress this movement and restore order. The repression was brutal and effective. Thousands were arrested and deported to penal colonies, including practically the entire leadership of the Communist Party. By the end of 1931, it looked like this party was finished.

Mandarins whose districts were embroiled in protest marches got into trouble with the French, who held them responsible for the breakdown in public order. A friend of my father's lost his job in the aftermath of a demonstration in his district. He was dismissed from office for one year, and although he was reinstated later, the incident left a black mark in his dossier, and his career suffered. This period of disturbances made life difficult for the mandarins. If the communist red flag with the hammer and sickle was raised in a village, the local mandarin would be summoned by the *résident* and given a dressing-down. If communist leaflets were disseminated in his territory, the mandarin would be given a warning. Furthermore, the French security police would arrive to investigate and question him, and quite likely the province *résident* would begin to suspect his loyalty, competence, or both. Whenever an incident took place in a province, all the mandarins would receive a confidential memo telling them what had happened and ordering them to increase their vigilance.

It was at this time of political ferment that my father decided to switch from being a finance bureaucrat to being a mandarin. He was well regarded and well paid, but he felt restless in a job that he found devoid of challenge and social prestige. Looking back on his family tradition, he thought that unless he could become a mandarin, he would never measure up to his grandfather and father. Although radicals were condemning the mandarin system as obsolete, my father—and other men who shared his traditional background—continued to yearn to join its ranks. He decided to try his chances in the highly competitive exam that the French held each year to select just a handful of mandarins, and succeeded. The Finance Office tried to retain him with a big promotion and a substantial raise, but he turned them down and left Hanoi for the remote district of Hat Tri, in Phu Tho Province, to assume his new position. There he would begin the kind of life that his grandfather and father had led.

Located in the midlands of Tonkin, this large province is surrounded by hills and traversed by several rivers, including the upper reach of the Red River and its two large tributaries. One of them, the Clear River, ran through my father's district. These rivers provided a convenient way for the local people to carry forest products into the delta for sale, but also posed a threat, and had to be contained by a network of dikes. Due to the hilly terrain, there were not enough rice fields to even feed the small population of 300,000. But people survived by supplementing their diet with other crops, such as manioc, sugarcane, and sweet potatoes, and by earning extra income from selling forest products, such as lacquer varnish, wood pulp for paper, and leaves for roofing. The climate of the province was considered unhealthy because of its abrupt changes in temperatures and because of rampant malaria. Phu Tho was known as a "poisonous water" region, because of the belief that its water was the source of this dreaded disease.

With its hills and forests, Phu Tho throughout history had been a favorite hideout of rebels and bandits. My great-grandfather Duong Lam had battled bandits there when the province was still known under its old name of Hung Hoa. In 1930, the province was again a trouble spot, having just seen a courageous, but disastrously unsuccessful mutiny by Vietnamese soldiers in the colonial army. It was not the kind of post one would have chosen to begin a mandarin career, but my father accepted it when it was offered.

With the upsurge in violent protests, maintenance of political security was a much bigger responsibility for my father as a mandarin than it had been for my grandfather. Despite their no-holds-barred suppression of the 1930 uprisings, the French were afraid that they had not wiped out the troublemakers. When my father arrived in Phu Tho, mandarins in the province had received orders to heighten their vigilance, and had been told in no uncertain terms that they would be held responsible for any protest or anti-French activities in their territories. To keep track of outsiders who might try to infiltrate the province to disseminate propaganda and recruit sympathizers, each village chief had to maintain a list of strangers who passed through. Once in a while, the mandarins would conduct a surprise night patrol in the villages to see whether the watchmen were making their rounds and whether any suspect activities were taking place. Or they would drop in unannounced to check whether the village chief had kept his register up-to-date. In addition, each district magistrate had to maintain a top secret list of any political suspects in his territory, which he kept locked in his desk drawer.

With the communists busily trying to convert peasants, the

mandarins had to compete with them to win the allegiance of the people. They could no longer remain as distant authority figures who governed by wisdom and virtue. To force the magistrates to meet the people and forge closer ties with them, the French province *résident* required each mandarin to make weekly visits to the villages in his territory, in addition to the surprise inspection tours. My father could choose his own villages to visit, but after each trip, he had to file a report to the *résident*. Later, this practice was dropped, perhaps because the *résident* felt the communists and other nationalists were not a threat in his province. Still, my father thought these visits were useful in helping him run his district, so he continued to make his weekly rounds. They allowed him to stay on top of the local situation, uncover the villagers' needs and wishes, and build closer ties with the village leaders, the elite who could rally the peasants and help him carry out projects. Once he found out what the villagers needed, he did what he could to help. Besides satisfying his desire to do good, this tactic also had a practical aim: to win the support of the villagers, without which his work would be harder, since he no longer enjoyed the unquestioned authority mandarins had in the old days.

These village visits were not always easy to make, because of the hilly terrain and the lack of passable roads. My father owned a car, a sporty black Renault—a convertible with a sloping, pointed end that the Vietnamese called "a duck's behind"—that he had bought with a 200-piaster loan my mother had obtained for him. If he had to go to remote villages with no road big enough for his car, he would ride the pony that he kept in the stable at his residence. Sometimes he would spend days riding from one village to the next, feeling lonely as he crossed the vast Dong Mo grass plain on the back of his pony. When he could take the car, he cut quite a dashing figure, sitting in the back between two armed guards, while the chauffeur eased the shiny car— with its top down—along the country roads.

Although being a mandarin was hard work and paid less than the new job at the finance office would have given him, my father enjoyed it a lot more than the dull routine in Hanoi. What he liked most was being able to use the little power he had to help people. He knew he could not change the situation or influence policies, so he saw his role mainly as a buffer, shielding the peasants from the excesses of the colonial regime as best he could. The work could be frustrating, but it was never boring. No two days were alike, and every day brought different challenges. One aspect of a mandarin's job had not changed: He was still a jack-of-all-trades, and everything in his district was his responsibility. On days when he was not out visiting villages, he would take care of administrative matters and see petitioners. Even before the office opened, the courtyard would be thronged with people wanting to see him. His office was only across the quadrangle from the residence, so from our house my mother could see the crowd, and she would wonder whether my father would be able to handle the crush of business during the working hours. Somehow, though, he always managed to dispatch all the day's cases.

My father's work did not end at dusk. Many nights, he would have to take a detail of soldiers with him and rush out into the darkness to look for opium smugglers, or he might get a report that a group of peasants were gambling with the game of *soc dia*, guessing the combination of coins under an inverted bowl on a plate, and he would have to go and stop them. Other nights, he would receive a report of suspect activities or of a robbery in a village, and he would have to go and investigate on the spot. On nights when he was not out patrolling, pursuing criminals or opium smugglers, or breaking up gambling sessions, he would stay up until two or three o'clock in the morning to catch up on paperwork.

My father also had to serve as a judge for minor cases involving small fines and as an arbitrator for civil litigation. He would refer serious criminal cases to the province. But first, he would have to conduct an investigation and question the suspects, victims, and witnesses. My older brothers remember seeing prisoners being brought into the tribunal all trussed up. If the suspects refused to talk, my father would bang on the table and shout to intimidate them, or he would threaten them with physical punishment. A soldier standing nearby with a rattan switch would glare at the suspects and make them quake with fear. In fact, though some mandarins were quite ruthless with their interrogations, my father was too kindhearted to carry through with his threats. Usually he relied on his clever questioning and his thorough investigation to build up his cases. Then the suspect and the file would be transferred to the province.

My father had one assistant and three clerks to help him with the voluminous paperwork. Everything had to be documented, reported, and filed. The only way to relay all these documents up and down the administrative chain was to have someone carry it by hand. This job of *chay giay*—literally, "running with the paperwork"—was performed by three unarmed militiamen called the *linh le*, who were assigned to my father as orderlies. In the office, these militiamen were at the bottom of the totem pole—standing guard, fetching things for my father, even run-ning errands for my family—but when they carried official documents to a village they put on airs. As my father's personal attendants and repre-sentatives, they expected the villagers to show respect and, most impor-tant of all, to entertain them with a meal. Since peasants considered boiled chicken dipped in salt, pepper, and chopped lemon leaves a del-icacy, village notables would usually serve this dish to the linh lệ as proof of their hospitality.

To enforce the law in the whole district, my father could rely on only five or six armed militiamen. They were badly trained, and rarely if ever had to fire a shot during their whole military career. Once a year, they would report to the French province military commander, who would refresh their rusty skills with a session of target practice. This training did not make them feel any more comfortable with their firearms, and their hands would shake whenever they had to raise their rifles and take aim. My father thought they were more of a menace than a help. Whenever he took them in the car to pursue robbers, he would order them not to load their weapons, afraid that the bumpy ride over rough roads would make them discharge their rifles and kill someone. Ultimately, as security in the countryside deteriorated even more, the French would hand over its maintenance to their own secret police.

The rhythm of a mandarin's work remained unchanged, still dictated by the seasons, the cycle of rice growing, and the ebb and flow of vil-lage life. Each year was marked by three high points: the tax collection right after the fifth month's harvest, the high-water season with its threat of flooding in June—right on the heels of the tax season—and the insecure time around the lunar new year when thefts and robberies reached their peak. Of these, tax collection ranked at the top in terms of difficulty, especially since my father had only one month to collect the money and deposit it into the province treasury. As in the old imperial days, it was up to each village to distribute the taxes among its families, as long as it collected the correct amount. If the village was corrupt, the rich and powerful would conspire to lessen their own burdens and make their neighbors pay more than their fair share. Tax collection gave cor-rupt village officials an opportunity to pocket some of the money, and this could lead to charges and countercharges. Each year, dispute after dispute would erupt, and people with grievances about the tax distrib-ution or the collection itself would throng to my father's office to lodge complaints.

After the taxes were delivered, before he could catch his breath, my father would have to gear up to battle the threat of flooding during the monsoon season. Many nights, he would drop in on a village located near a critical section of the dike to make sure a watchman had been assigned to keep an eye on the water level. If the river became threatening, my father would leave his residence and literally live at the dike, like Duong Lam had in his time, to mobilize peasants and supervise the reinforcement work. Following the high-water season, things would more or less quiet down until the approach of Tet, when my father would have to increase his night-time patrols. Sometimes he would take a few armed militiamen to a distant village or to one that he knew had a security problem. Once there, they would walk around to check whether the watchman was doing his job. My father felt it was important for him to go on these patrols, to demonstrate to the people that he was concerned about their security. If he received a report in the middle of the night that a village had been robbed, he would rush to the scene, even if a storm was raging. He knew full well that by the time he arrived, the robbers would be gone, but he would do it anyway, just to show he cared. When he reached the crime scene, he would conduct a search, interrogate suspects, and make an arrest if he found enough incriminating evidence.

After slightly more than a year in Hat Tri, my father was promoted to Cam Khe, a larger district, also located in Phu Tho Province. The promotion was both good and bad. Of all the districts in the province, Cam Khe was the most difficult to run. The people were more stubborn than those in Hat Tri, and their village chiefs were not at all reticent about lodging complaints against their magistrate with the French *résident*. Another headache for my father was the presence of a French plantation that formed a world unto itself, and was outside his authority. Although they were living and working on Vietnamese soil, Europeans and their properties could be dealt with only by the French officials themselves. The original owner had obtained his property when the colonial authorities were making land concessions to settlers, in the belief that the string of plantations would form a barrier against the infiltration of armed bands into the unpacified delta. By the end of the nineteenth century, large French concessions dotted the midlands, growing cash crops like coffee, jute, tobacco, and tea. Most of the owners lived not on their plantations, but in Hanoi, and paid only an occasional visit.

The biggest security problem for my father in Cam Khe was not political agitation but cattle rustling. Since each peasant family owned only one buffalo or ox for ploughing, losing their cattle was almost a calamity. In Cam Khe, the problem was compounded by the fact that the Vietnamese foreman of the French plantation was an accomplice of the rustlers, and would let them hide the cattle there in the owner's absence. If the local mandarin was bold enough to enter, the foreman and his accomplices would confront them and resist a search. Afraid to create a clash, previous mandarins had been powerless to solve the problem. My father, however, figured out that if he could get the *résident* to back him in a search, he would be able to arrest the culprits. Just as he had hoped, the *résident* ordered the French province military commander to go with him. The foreman and his accomplices did not dare to put up a fight, and my father found two stolen buffaloes, which he seized as evidence. The foreman was arrested, taken to the province capital for trial, and executed. This frightened the rustlers and put a stop to their activities.

As time passed, my father discovered that being a district magistrate brought satisfaction as well as feelings of guilt. Like his father before him, he sometimes had to enforce policies that did not meet his own standard of fairness. The job he disliked the most was recruiting conscripted laborers to work on public projects in abominable conditions, although he was fortunate that during his career he had to do this only once: sending workers to build the road leading to Lao Kay near the border with Laos. This happened near Tet. To make up for having had to send them away from home at a time when families gathered together to celebrate the new year, my father paid them a special visit. He brought with him huge bamboo hampers filled with the treats that people usually ate at Tet to distribute to the workers. He had bought the food with his own money. It would be fair to say that my father was one of just a handful of mandarins who would show such concern for conscripted laborers.

But being a mandarin also had its rewards, wanted and unwanted. One of these was the constant stream of gifts that villages brought to our residence. This was an old custom that had persisted. In the old days when mandarins could barely survive on what the court paid them, these gifts were very helpful in keeping them afloat. They were not costly, but it meant a lot to the villagers to have them accepted. If a village held a feast, a sample of the food—nicely arranged in a round, red-lacquered box—would be conveyed to my father. After the harvest, village chiefs would send a basket of the new rice to my father as a gift. Even wild boar would be brought to our house. During his time in the provinces, special products of the areas he administered—such as pineapples, persimmons, and lychee nuts—would be delivered to his residence right after they came into season. Later, villages located on the coast would send him fish, some of which were so big that he did not know what to do with them. My father had a delicate taste when it came to food. He would not even touch anything that had garlic or onion, finding the odor too strong. The sight of the enormous dead fish staring at him with their glassy eyes made him feel nauseated, but he would hide his disgust and graciously thank the bearers for their villages' generosity.

My father's work earned him a promotion, and he was sent to Nam Dinh Province, a more desirable location. He would spend the largest part of his mandarin career here and would remember the province fondly. Several of his children—myself included—would be born here, and it was here that his own personal finances began to improve. By 1937, he had repaid the debts incurred by my grandfather, so now he and my mother could begin to save. The money would come in handy in 1945, when he was forced to retire after the Viet Minh came into power. The savings were made easier because my maternal grandmother was generous with cash gifts whenever a large and unexpected expense came up. For example, when a Frenchman put up his sideboard, china, silver, and glassware for sale before going back to his home country during the Great Depression, my father decided he would like to buy them for entertaining. My mother did not relish the thought of spending so much money, but did not object. She went home to talk to her mother, who gave her the large sum she needed.

Indeed, entertaining was my father's favorite way to relax from the demands of his job. He was very social, and loved company. Except for a few occasions, his guests were Vietnamese. He preferred to keep his interactions with the French to a minimum. He never socialized with the province *résident*, and his contacts with this official were always formal and work-related. In Phu Tho, a remote and isolated province, my father did not have frequent visitors; now, in Nam Dinh, he was closer to Hanoi. He began to have a lot of guests.

Many times during the year, several cars carrying my father's relatives and friends would begin to arrive at the start of a weekend. Sometimes they would bring a troupe of *cheo* opera singers, complete with costumes, for a performance. On other occasions, they came to play mah-jongg or cards. Once in a while, the Vietnamese province governor and mandarins from other areas would come and visit. To feed all these guests, my mother would have the kitchen staff slaughter a goat, pig, or calf, and roast it over an open pit. Without frequent cash infusions from my mother's family, my parents would not have been able to save anything. Between a growing family, a large servant staff, a stream of visitors, and frequent entertaining, there was little left from my father's pay by the end of the month.

As Western influence grew in Vietnam, those who could afford it began to copy the leisure life-style of the French, taking up dancing, going to nightclubs, and spending time at weekend retreats in the mountains or on the beach. Some went further, smoking opium and entering into liaisons with the hostesses they met in the dance halls. At one point, a cousin of my father's—whom we called Uncle Governor Mau— decided to build a cabin on the beach near Hai Hau, asking my father and several of his friends to contribute twenty piasters each for the construction. When the cabin was completed, Governor Mau held a house-warming party—a boisterous one, as he was a playboy and an opium addict. He had invited young women to keep his male guests company and to dance with them to Western music from a gramophone. None of the wives were asked to attend. There were also card games and opium smoking for those who could not get through the evening without it. Fortunately, my father was never attracted to this drug, preferring Vietnamese tobacco smoked through a water pipe. Governor Mau was the type of mandarin that was giving the whole system a bad name. He did not do anything that would hurt someone—such as arresting inno-cent people to extort money from their families—but according to rumors he was greedy and took a lot of bribes. In leading a dissolute life-style, my uncle had plenty of company within the elite. Their display of excess amidst the general poverty of the population provoked a number of journalists and novelists into condemning their hedonism as insensi-tive, if not immoral.

My mother did not share in the excitement of my father's life. She was a traditional stay-at-home wife, and my father, like other men at the time, never took her anywhere. Her world revolved around whatever official residence my family happened to occupy. My mother accepted her lot as normal. She did not complain, because her life was comfort-able and she never had to do any hard work. Her daily routine consist-ed of checking in on her children, making sure they were cleaned, fed, and clothed properly by the servants and taken to school and back by the orderlies; giving orders to the domestic staff and overseeing their work; and entertaining, if required. She had no friends. Except for the wives of my father's assistants, she had no other social company.

My mother started bearing children right after her marriage, practically one after another. After fourteen years of marriage, by the time she was thirty, she had gone through eleven childbirths. Her first two children had died tragically and then she suffered a couple of miscarriages. When she was pregnant with my brother Giu, she fainted in the courtyard. The doctor told her to abort, and warned her that she would die if she gave birth. But she said she could not kill her own child, and would take a chance on her own life. She was rewarded for that selfless act, for my brother was born healthy and my mother went on to have many more children. Understandably, she got tired of this endless cycle of pregnancies and births. There was no birth control available then, and although she tried abstinence as the only way to stop bearing children, it was not very effective. She continued to have babies and would give birth a total of seventeen times.

The only result of her abstention was that my father began an affair. He would have eventually, regardless of what was going on at home; it was simply part of the culture. But my mother's abstention drove him to do it sooner rather than later. His betrayal happened without any soul-searching or guilt on his part. To him, it was a man's birthright to wander. There were no sacred vows of fidelity at the marriage ceremony nor were there religious injunctions against adultery. Neither was there an emotional hurdle to overcome, because love did not exist between him and my mother. I suspect that, in this brief liaison as in subsequent ones, my father was out to satisfy his lust more than to look for love. Later in Hanoi, he did fall in love with a singer and would take her as his concubine.

His first affair took place while he was working in the midland province of Phu Tho. He was discreet about it, and my mother did not suspect anything until an acquaintance told her and suggested that she go into the province town to put an end to the liaison by *danh ghen*. In a *danh ghen*, a wife would find out where her husband was seeing his mistress and would go there to catch him *in flagrante delicto*, causing a terrible scene to make him lose face in front of his paramour and to frighten her off with verbal abuse or even by pulling her hair and hitting her. Although women generally accepted their husbands' affairs, rationalizing the infidelity with the saying "Under heaven, it is normal for a man to have a lot of women," they still felt angry and threatened when betrayed, and some would resort to *danh ghen* to vent their feelings. My mother decided to follow the acquaintance's advice, and that weekend, she quietly slipped into town to find out what was going on. But being a dignified, kind, and timid woman, she changed her mind once she reached the city, and turned around and left. She found this one and only attempt at *danh ghen* so distasteful that she never tried again.

Besides *danh ghen*, making life miserable for their unfaithful husbands was another favorite revenge for jealous wives. Mostly, they relied on verbal abuse. When their spouses came home late at night, they would chew them out to keep them from going to sleep. This tactic rarely worked, because usually the husbands were so tired after an evening of dalliance that they would quickly fall asleep, even with their wives' curses ringing in their ears. As far as my mother could find out, none of this did any good, so she simply resigned herself to the situation. She told herself that as long as my father did not neglect her and the children, and as long as he continued to treat her with affection and respect, she could live with his infidelities. Even to this day, in spite of the heartaches he caused throughout their married life, my mother still thinks of my father as a good husband who always fulfilled his duties to her.

Despite the fact that the district magistrates' wings had been badly clipped in the French regime, they were still the "king of the heap" in their districts, and our family was treated with respect by everyone. My brothers and sisters were so pampered by people inside and outside the household that they could have easily turned into spoiled brats. Servants would bend over backward to satisfy all their whims. If one of them broke down and cried over something, everyone would get anxious, afraid that my father would blame them. When my brothers and sisters were old enough to go to school, teachers and school officials let them do whatever they pleased, and gave them good grades even if they did not do any work. If they failed an exam, they would be allowed to take it again with answers already supplied, so all they had to do was to copy them into their own notebooks. Fortunately, my parents were not haughty and made sure that my siblings did not grow up thinking that it was their birthright to have others defer to them.

In our isolation, we hardly felt the effect of the Great Depression. While many districts were badly affected, the areas we moved to in succession were spared its worst impact. By 1931 the bottom had fallen out for the French enterprises. Raw materials and agricultural products such as rice and rubber, in which the French had invested heavily, were hard-hit by the plunge in commodities prices. French companies faltered and the ripple effect reached the native entrepreneurs, who were forced into bankruptcy; the workers in plantations, mines, and factories, who were thrown out of work; as well as the landlords and their tenant farmers, whose crop prices dropped. The Great Depression showed the

Vietnamese to what extent their country, once insular under emperors who restricted foreign trade, had become enmeshed in and sensitive to economic developments elsewhere in the world.

The districts my father ran did not have large rice and rubber planta-tions, mines, or factories, so he did not have to cope with high unem-ployment or masses of dispossessed peasants. At the height of this world-wide crisis, and until after it ended, my father was in Hai Hau. This dis-trict was prosperous and so the impact was cushioned. Hai Hau lay on rich alluvial soil on the seacoast. Villagers here enjoyed two bumper har-vests each year without fail, rather than the one harvest that people else-where struggled to produce. The yield per acre was also much higher because of the more fertile land. Life was easy. There was no threat of flooding, and there was no costly dike network to maintain. Besides rice, the villagers also produced salt, which they sold to the government, get-ting a nice sum of cash for each delivery. The sea provided another source of food and income. So, while the drop in the price of rice had an impact, the production of salt and the fishing allowed villagers to weather the crisis better than those in other areas of the country.

One of the side-effects of the Great Depression that my father had to deal with was the drop in the sale of rice wine. With their income reduced, fewer people in Tonkin could afford to buy the monopoly wine, and the sale of cheaper contraband grew. The monopoly protest-ed. The Fontaine distillery shareholders were powerful capitalists with much political clout, and they had the support of National Assembly deputies in Paris. The French government soon came under pressure, and it in turn put pressure on the governor general for Indochina. The mes-sage was then passed down the chain of command, and eventually the mandarins were told that they had to increase alcohol sales at all costs, on the grounds that the drop in sales was hurting the general budget rev-enue. Of course, the real objective was to pump more profits into the coffers of the monopoly. This was not the first or last time that the *colons*, backed by their powerful capitalist supporters in France, were able to influence colonial policy or to thwart reforms.

Every mandarin was told that he would be reprimanded, even pun-ished, if alcohol sales did not improve in his territory. At every meeting with the *résident*, my father and the county magistrate of Xuan Truong usually found themselves in hot water, because their two areas produced the most moonshine, had the liveliest trade in contraband wine, and therefore the lowest sales of monopoly alcohol. My father at first chose to ignore the order, but because Hai Hau was consistently at the bottom of the list for Nam Dinh Province, he was finally called into the *résident's* office and forced to sign a paper saying that he would accept punishment if he did not increase sales. Luckily, the French officials' warnings and reprimands were only for show, to get the *résident supérieur* and *résidents* off the hook and allow them to pretend they were taking action on behalf of the monopoly.

In his various posts, my father had never had to confront the communists, yet he knew where he stood with them. He understood that, as part of the colonial regime they vowed to destroy, he—like other mandarins—was guilty by association and a target in their eyes. Through the grapevine, he had heard stories of communist intimidation and retaliation, so he knew that he would have to be careful if he ever had to deal with them. He had also heard of the "red villages" in Annam and of the attacks there against middle-class people like himself, and realized that he would be denied a role, if not eliminated, in the society envisioned by the communists. Yet he also sympathized with them because he understood that they were fundamentally patriots who wanted to drive out the French. For the rest of his career in the colonial government, my father would feel torn between sympathy for the cause of national independence and repugnance for the violent social revolution advocated by the communists.

Among the mandarins, some shared my father's sympathy for the nationalistic side of the communists, while most simply hated and feared them at the same time. A few, however, had no qualms about suppressing them. Among the most notorious in this regard were two mandarins related to my family by marriage: Cung Dinh Van and Vi Van Dinh. Cung Dinh Van was a county magistrate in Son Tay Province who became infamous for his arrest and torture of communist suspects. His favorite interrogation technique was to wire his victims to the batteries of his car, and then start the engine to electrocute them and make them confess. An aunt of mine who had married into his clan was visiting his household one day when she heard the screams of agony of one of his victims. After the Viet Minh came into power, the communists got their revenge and Cung Dinh Van was executed.

My uncle Chinh had married one of Vi Van Dinh's daughters after his second wife died. Vi was, if not less violent than Cung Dinh Van, at least more subtle. He did not do things out of pure brutality, but always with an aim in mind. His father had been the absolute feudal lord of a county in Lang Son Province, and since this function was hereditary, Vi took it over after his father died. The French wanted to keep in Vi's good graces, so they gave him special treatment, and eventually made him governor general of three of the most important provinces in the Red River Delta in succession.

Like a feudal lord, Vi kept order by instilling fear among his people and treated the communists the same way he treated village officials who dared to disobey him or to upset things in his territory. He did not flinch from corporal punishment to maintain absolute control. He got away with this because he was so powerful and because the French did not want to challenge him. Of the many stories circulating about him, my family was not sure which ones were true. According to one, during a visit to a village, Vi was displeased with what the village chief had done and, as punishment, ordered the man to eat a weed that grew in the water until he became violently sick. There were also many stories about Vi's arresting and torturing revolutionaries, but my family could not confirm any of them. When the Viet Minh came into power, many people in Tonkin thought Vi would be executed. Yet, like the French before them, the communists saw him as a valuable ally and wooed him. He stayed in their zone, became an advisor to Ho Chi Minh's government, and remained a strong supporter of Ho's movement until the bitter end.

In 1937, my father's ambivalence toward the communists made him turn down his promotion to magistrate of Xuan Truong, the largest county in Nam Dinh Province, because he had heard rumors that it was a hotbed of communist activities. As a matter of fact, Xuan Truong was the native area of the man known under his assumed name of Truong Chinh, who would later become a hard-liner in the politburo of the Communist Party. My father did not want to be put in a position where he would have to help the French suppress the communists and their sympathizers in Xuan Truong, fearing that it would bring retaliation against him and his family, but also believing that it would be repugnant for him to denounce his own patriotic countrymen to the colonialists for arrest, imprisonment, torture, and even execution.

At this time, the communists were going through a period of renewal and were rebuilding their ranks. Their resurgence was made possible by events in France. As fascism grew in Europe, the Communist Party in France allied itself with the Socialists and the Radicals to form a united front against this new threat. The alliance, called the "People's Front," won the national election of 1936. The victory had a ripple effect in Vietnam, where thousands of revolutionaries were released from jail. Prison had hardened these people and made them more committed than ever to their cause. The moment they got out of jail, they went back into action. The Communist Party re-emerged, although Ho Chi Minh was still inactive and living in Moscow where he was out of favor with Stalin, who preferred other more ideologically militant leaders willing to put Vietnam in the vanguard of the communist revolution. Ho wanted to focus first on eliminating the French. Ho would not be able to restore contact with this party until 1940.

In 1938, my father was given another promotion as county magistrate of Nghia Hung, the same county his own father had run. This time, he accepted. He knew that he would not have to cope with the communists there, because most of the people in this prosperous county were Catholics who heartily disliked communists as godless people and were therefore not receptive to their appeals. But while his job went along smoothly, a personal tragedy struck. It was here that Mao, his second child, went mad. Before Mao was born, my paternal grandmother had a strange dream, in which she saw a large eagle fly into the house and lay an egg that fell on the floor and broke. Grandma thought the dream foretold both good and bad things. Mao was a beautiful girl, with an oval face, a porcelain-like complexion, dark almond eyes, a small straight nose, and nicely shaped lips. She was also extremely intelligent, and always placed at the top of every grade she attended. Then, while she was in high school, she suddenly began to neglect her studies, and her performance plummeted, plunging her to the bottom of her class. No one understood why.

That summer, she went home for vacation. Her behavior was strange. She would shut herself up in her room and weep. When my mother asked her why she was crying, she kept silent. My parents summoned a traditional doctor, who took her pulse and said that it was extremely weak. He told my parents not to send her back to school, and prescribed a lot of herbs that had no effect. Then Mao went crazy. In those days, Vietnamese still believed that mental illness was caused by evil spirits or by bad karma, for something wicked done in a previous life. Over the years, my mother, with my father's acquiescence, tried every treatment that she heard might chase away the malevolent spirit or dispel the unlucky karma and bring a cure. She would take Mao and pray for her at temples known for their supernatural power. I still remember when my mother hired a shaman in 1947 to conduct a three-day ceremony in our courtyard to exorcize the evil spirit from Mao. But nothing worked. Because of the Vietnamese belief that the crazy had been chosen by heaven to bear all their families' burdens, my parents drummed into us that we should be grateful to Mao and love her. Reluctant to put Mao in an institution, they cared for her at home where she was free to roam the house and the yard. I would live with her until I left for college in the United States.

By mid-1939, the colonial authorities began to crack down on the communists once again. The People's Front in France was fading, and after the Second World War began, the French Communist Party itself was dissolved by order of the new government, on the grounds that the party was opposing the war efforts. Several of its members were arrested and executed for sabotage. In Vietnam, the colonial authorities were more than happy to follow Paris's lead. Seeing the situation taking a turn for the worse, the communists hastily withdrew back into the shadows, but it was too late. Their networks were severely damaged, and several important leaders, as well as thousands of party members, were arrested. The beginning of World War II and the arrival of the Japanese occupation army would change the situation for both the French and the communists in Vietnam. It would also change our lives.

On the eve of World War II, the French had been in Vietnam for over sixty years. During that span of time, they had transformed the country. They had brought modernization. They had built cities, hospitals, roads, harbors, and railroads. They had developed the country's natural resources, exploiting mines, setting up plantations, draining land, and expanding agriculture, especially the production of rice. Yet, by being unwilling to share the benefits of these developments more equally with the local people and by refusing to restore independence to Vietnam, they would earn animosity instead of gratitude from the Vietnamese. As World War II brought dislocations and weakened the colonial regime, the Vietnamese would seize the opportunity to take up arms to drive them out of the country.

6

The Third Month in the Year of the Famine

It was nine o'clock in the morning of March 10, 1945. The day before, the Japanese occupation army had toppled the colonial government. My father had never thought the time would come when an Asian could strike down a Frenchman and get away with it; now he was watching a captain of the Japanese occupation army in Nam Dinh hit the deputy *résident* of the province over and over again on the head with the hilt of his sword. The French official lay crumpled on the floor, where the Japanese had thrown him with a deft judo move. Blood streaming down his face, he took the blows meekly, without a word of protest. My father and the province governor had been in the middle of a meeting when he burst into the room and, saying that the Japanese were pursuing him, begged my father and the governor to hide him. Before they could recover from the shock of seeing a frightened Frenchman pleading for help, the officer appeared suddenly in the doorway. The Japanese bowed to them very politely, and then went straight for the Frenchman. My father and the governor watched helplessly, horrified by the soldier's blows, but they dared not intervene. After his anger was spent, the Japanese pulled the Frenchman up and led him away. My father never saw the deputy *résident* again.

That incident was just one in a string of horrors in that nightmarish year of 1945. We first encountered the Japanese in 1943 after my father became assistant to the province governor. Their occupation army had arrived in 1940, but did not spread to the little county town where we were living. Now, they were right behind our house in Nam Dinh, the province capital. We could see their sentries guarding the barrack they had commandeered. We could see them marching in formation in the streets or riding in their military vehicles. They were unfriendly, inscrutable, and secretive, and did not flock to nightclubs or bars as the French had. They kept to themselves. As their occupation wore on and their requirements for supplies depleted food reserves, they became a heavy burden for the people to bear, and the initial curiosity, expectation, and admiration they evoked would turn into anger and hatred.

The Japanese presence began after Hitler had occupied France. Anxious to avoid defeat, the French government, headed by the collaborationist Henri-Philippe Pétain, decided to accept Japan's ultimatum and acquiesce to the occupation of Indochina. The terms also required Admiral Jean Decoux, the newly appointed governor general, to pay for the costs of occupation; to provide Japanese troops stationed in Indochina with transport, food supplies, and other materials, and not to interfere with their movement or with their use of airfields and naval bases to strike at neighboring countries. By being compliant, the French hoped Japan would let the colonial government stay in place, which was exactly what the Japanese, wanting to avoid the costs and complexities of an outright takeover, allowed it to do at first. Although the French retained control and escaped the internment meted out to Westerners living in other parts of Asia that the Japanese had taken over, they nonetheless felt humiliated at having to bow to the will of an oriental army and fretted about losing the respect of the local people.

The Vietnamese now had two sets of masters who competed for their allegiance. The Japanese tried to impress them with propaganda, cultural events, and exhibits about their military successes over the Western powers, appealing to Asian pride. They touted their slogan "Asia for the Asians," but paid only lip service to it. More interested in maintaining the status quo and preventing disturbances that would disrupt their military activities than in helping the Vietnamese achieve independence, they would turn a blind eye to French suppression of those Vietnamese who thought the opportunity had come for them to assail colonial rule. When they felt disturbances had become too disruptive or when the opposition was directed at them, the Japanese themselves would not hesitate to arrest dissidents and subject them to brutal interrogations. For their part, the French pursued a two-pronged policy. At the same time that Governor General Decoux tried to keep the local people quiescent with more schools and with promises of greater participation and more equality, he also suppressed opposition ruthlessly to show that, despite defeat in France and acquiescence to Japanese occupation, his government was still firmly in control and still capable of subduing Vietnamese challenges to its authority.

Like the rest of the population, my family at first felt ambivalent toward the Japanese. My parents and older brothers and sisters were impressed with their discipline and power, calling them *oai*, or awe-inspiring. At the same time, they were also afraid of the occupiers, having heard stories about how quick the Japanese were to punish and execute those they believed had disobeyed their wishes. Once, after my family had moved to Hanoi, I saw a soldier slap and kick a boy selling popsicles. After that, the nasty stories I had heard about the Japanese became more real to me and I would run back into the house whenever I saw them on our street. As Japanese occupation brought not independence but suffering, Vietnamese admiration would turn to hatred, and many people—my older sister Thang included—would refer to the occupiers as "Fascists" and "dwarf bandits." For the first few years, officials like my father had no direct contact with the Japanese. Following the March 1945 overthrow of the colonial regime, however, with the French no longer acting as a buffer, my father was thrust face to face with them. He found the officials he dealt with educated and courteous, but also ruthless in enforcing their demands for food and labor and callous to the impact these demands had on the Vietnamese.

The Japanese occupation turned our country into a war zone. Nam Dinh was an important town with a large textile mill, power plant, harbor, railway line, and a large army barrack that the Japanese had taken over, as well as distilleries supplying fuel for their transports. It became a target of American planes trying to knock out military and industrial sites and communication lines that the Japanese could be using. The attacks started in August 1942. The bombings became more frequent as the war went on, and by 1945 there was one day when my father counted twenty-seven runs on Nam Dinh. Shelters were dug in public places such as parks, and the wailing of sirens became a part of our lives.

My father's office and our house were located near the textile mill, a prime target. Whenever we heard the alarm, no matter what time of day or night or what weather, we would run to the shelter located in the yard of my father's office building, a couple of hundred yards away. Our bunker was just a trench dug into the ground, with a roof made with bamboo poles holding up a thick layer of dirt. It would not have saved us from a direct hit, but it was the best protection we had. Sometimes the sirens would wail in the middle of the night, and my parents and servants would wake all of us up and rush us to the shelter. One of the maids had the job of carrying my younger sister Loan, who was not yet a year old; another one was responsible for me, then about four years old. One day, before we could make it to the shelter, I heard the windows rattling from the bomb explosions. I put my hands on the panes, and the vibration I felt is one of my earliest memories of childhood. But the bombs were not just rattling windows, they were killing innocent people living close to the targets. Some days, dozens were killed. My father used to attend the victims' funerals, to offer comfort as an official representative of the government. During one of the services, he noticed that blood was still oozing out of the flimsy wooden caskets.

War brought shortages. With imports from France cut off, and so much food and materials going to the Japanese, goods became scarce. Prices shot up as speculators hoarded merchandise to make a killing, and inflation became frightful. The government began to issue ration coupons for rice, salt, and even matches. Sugar became a luxury, and once in a while each family would be allowed to buy one or two kilos. The rations for mandarins, high officials, rich merchants, industrialists, Frenchmen, and people with French citizenship were more generous. As a mandarin, my father received rations that were double those allocated to the lower-level government employees, and we were also allowed to buy milk, coffee, cigarettes, flour, and cloth. The government tried to encourage local production of consumer items, but because of lack of skill, equipment, and materials—the result of decades of keeping Vietnam dependent on French products—the goods were close to unusable: Cloth was too thick and rough, newsprint was brownish, lumpy, and flimsy.

In 1944, famine struck in Tonkin and north Annam. These regions had always been short of rice, and depended on supplies shipped from the south to survive. But Allied bombings of railway lines and attacks on shipping reduced the supplies to a trickle. Despite the severe shortage, the colonial government continued to force the peasants to deliver rice to meet Japanese and French requirements. Flooding had destroyed a large part of the October crop that year. Yet instead of relenting, the government raised the quantity of rice the peasants had to deliver. Warehouses were bulging with food stored for Japanese soldiers, while people died by the hundreds of thousands.

Conditions were appalling. Starving peasants flocked to the cities to beg for food that no one could spare. Rice was so scarce and so expensive that even middle-class families had to stretch out the small supplies they managed to get, eating two meals a day, one of which would be thin rice gruel cooked in a lot of water. The streets were littered with dying peasants, their bodies reduced to skin and bones. Every day, ox carts collected the dead for burial in mass graves. Nam Dinh, a populous city, was full of the dead and dying. At the height of the famine in the third lunar month of 1945, my mother saw carts piled with dead bodies passing by our house every morning, their bony legs dangling over the edge of the carts. My father often saw people collapsing in the street and dying before his very eyes. Peasants who could no longer feed their children tried to give them away, or just abandoned them in the streets of the city. These emaciated children would rummage through garbage piles for food scraps, or they would steal to survive. They would lie in wait and then snatch food packages from people as they left the markets or stores. This happened twice to my mother. At mealtimes, starving children would crowd in front of our house, hoping to get our leftovers when we finished. At first, when there were only a few, my parents gave them some food. This quickly attracted a bigger crowd than we could feed, however, so we stopped.

My family managed to survive with a lot of effort and careful planning. We had two meals a day, with one consisting of rice gruel or boiled taro roots. Once in a while, my mother would add some bread or a little meat. Yet she continued to set aside a little rice each day to contribute to the soup kitchen operated by a charity. Many families with a lot of children, like ours, began to let their servants go. But we kept ours, knowing that letting them go would be like handing them a death sentence. One day, a former maid whom we called U Mien—U being the peasant term for Mommy because she had been a nursemaid and a surrogate mother to my brother Luong—who had left to go home years earlier, showed up at our house to ask for help for her starving family. My parents gave her some rice that saved her, her son, and a nephew, but not her husband. In fact, the food killed him. Crazed with hunger, he cooked a pot of rice in secret and ate all of it at once. His stomach could not handle the sudden intake of solid food.

After eating everything that could be eaten—grass, leaves, roots, dogs, and rats—some people resorted to cannibalism. Parents with children, especially those that were plump, lived in fear of having them kidnapped and eaten. Whenever my father had to travel, he would avoid eating in restaurants or stalls along the way, because he could not be sure whether the meat he was served was rat meat or human flesh. Twice, reports of cannibalism reached him, and he had to go and conduct an investigation. In the first case, the murderer was caught calmly selling the surplus flesh that he could not consume. In the second, he found two crazed parents who had slaughtered their own child and eaten it. He had no choice but to arrest them, try them for murder, and put them in jail. Another grim task he faced was to punish starving peasants caught stealing rice grains in the fields before they matured. Unless he could stop them, there would be no harvest, and even more people would die. Exercising his power and authority in chaotic situations like these was a burden he found hard to bear.

The colonial government made no effort to deal with the famine, except to issue rice ration cards to the urban population to stretch out the supplies. The countryside was left to die. The Nam Dinh province government was helpless, and could do nothing for the starving. The only groups that tried to do something were the charitable organizations, which went from house to house to collect rice for soup kitchens. Their efforts were futile, however. The food collected was too meager to feed the growing number of starved people that kept flocking into the city. The death toll finally reached two million in Tonkin and north Annam. Every Vietnamese who survived this period still carries vivid memories of the nightmare that engulfed the country—of the countless dead that lined the streets and roads—and regards food as precious. I grew up under my mother's constant admonition to eat every grain of rice in my bowl.

In early 1945, as the tide of the war began to turn against them, the Japanese became worried that the Allies would land in Indochina.

France had been liberated, and General de Gaulle had sent envoys to southern China to prepare for a French return to its colony. The Allies were dropping agents into Tonkin. And in Vietnam itself, seeing that a Japanese defeat was certain, Governor General Decoux radioed Paris swearing his commitment to de Gaulle. In reply, de Gaulle instructed him to work with General Eugène Mordant, commander of the French forces in Indochina, to coordinate activities with the Allies and to protect French interests. The French, ever boastful and talkative, were incapable of keeping their preparations secret. The Japanese soon got wind of their activities and decided to crush them.

At 7 p.m. on March 9, 1945, Ambassador Matsumoto Shunichi presented an ultimatum to Decoux, demanding that the entire colonial administration, including the army, navy, police, and banks, be put under Japanese command. Decoux refused. An hour later, the Japanese struck. French troops put up a feeble resistance, and then the general staff surrendered. Out of 20,000 French soldiers, only a few thousand managed to escape to southern China. The rest were disarmed and interned. In that one night, the colonial regime collapsed. Decoux, General Mordant, and other high-ranking officials were arrested and put in jail.

The swift turn of events caught everyone by surprise. In Nam Dinh, after supper on March 9, the French province *résident* summoned the governor, my father, and the chief judge—the three top province officials— to his house for a meeting. The *résident* told them he had just received a confidential cable from Hanoi. He said, "The Japanese are attacking in Hanoi right now. I'm sure Nam Dinh will be next. And when this happens, there's no way we can resist. We should all flee—me, the deputy *résident*, and all of you. But before you leave, I want you to burn all the secret files in your offices." These files dealt with actions to be taken against the Japanese in concert with the Allies. After that, the *résident* handed out a pistol to each man. My father said, "Thank you, but I don't want it. I don't know how to use it."

After the meeting broke up, the province governor asked my father to go through the papers in the office and burn those that were incriminating, then he hurried back to his house where he hid in case the Japanese might be looking for him. My father found a clerk in the office and the two of them set to work. At 1 a.m. they heard gunfire. My father looked up and saw shadows passing across the window bamboo blinds. He thought the Japanese had come to arrest him, so he quietly slipped home. He gathered all of us and took us to hide in an adjacent park. As we were running, a bullet grazed the head of the maid carrying me. She was so frightened that she did not utter a sound, and just let blood trickle down her head and over me as we sat in the park. After the gunfire died down, my family returned home. When they turned on the light and saw the maid and me covered with blood, my parents thought both of us had been shot. It turned out most of the gunfire people heard that night came from firecrackers, big and small, that the Japanese, not wanting to waste their bullets, were exploding. In the still of the night, and in the general panic, everyone mistook the explosions for real gunfire.

The next morning, everyone woke up confused and wondering what the coup meant, and what would happen next. The situation was chaotic in the provinces, with the top French officials fleeing or in jail. It was the hour of humiliation for the French. Colonial rule had been predicated on the myth of the Europeans' cultural superiority and military might, now Vietnamese everywhere saw how quickly the French could be brought down from their lofty perch. Frenchmen were being beaten up in the streets. Japanese soldiers were going to French houses and taking their residents to jail. In Bac Giang Province, where my brother-in-law Hau was working, the Japanese raped the wives of the French officials, including the province *résident*'s wife, who was gang-raped. In government offices, French employees continued to show up for work, but they were now under Japanese control. They behaved meekly and avoided looking the Vietnamese in the eye. Suddenly, the French no longer looked so mighty to the Vietnamese.

To calm popular fear, the Japanese announced that they had no ambition to take over Vietnam, and that they would help the Vietnamese to recover their independence. The Japanese took over the top leadership positions, but left the administration intact and the lower French officials in place to avoid disruption. Two days after the coup, to show that they were serious about giving Vietnam back its freedom, the Japanese asked Emperor Bao Dai to set up an independent government. The emperor had been a puppet of the French, and now became a puppet of the Japanese. Bao Dai was only twelve years old when he was summoned back from France to inherit the throne at his father's death in 1925. As a minor, he was obliged to rule under a Council of Regents. Then in 1932, after spending ten years studying in France, he returned to assume full power. At first, he showed vigor and ambition for his reign and country, but he lacked the power to carry out his plans. Disillusioned, he withdrew to hunt, travel, and chase women.

The government that Bao Dai now set up at the request of the Japanese was independent in name only. In fact, it was totally powerless and incompetent. Everything about it harked back to the old Confucian days, from the names of its ministries to the revival of the position of viceroy for Tonkin. It could not ignite any enthusiasm among the people, who were looking for vigorous leadership to take the country into the future. It floundered even in the only one valuable job that it might have performed: coping with the widespread starvation.

In Nam Dinh, the Japanese handed the province administration to the governor, a man appointed by the new viceroy. The governor now replaced the French province *résident*, while my father assumed the function of the deputy province *résident*. Every day, Japanese officials would come in to press their demands. They wanted more rice, at a time when people were dying of famine. They demanded conscripted laborers to build a military base in Lac Thuy, a malaria-infested region in Ha Nam Province. The Japanese also demanded that the governor deliver province militiamen for them to take to the mountain area to help fight the Viet Minh, who had started a guerrilla war against the occupiers. The militia were ill-trained troops armed only with muskets, little more than cannon fodder. The Japanese also insisted that more land be converted to industrial crops, like jute, to meet their war needs. This conversion, started under the French, now had to be accelerated. The price for these crops was higher, but during the famine peasants who grew them could not fall back on the rice they usually planted to survive.

The Japanese officials viewed the province government as their agents, there to take care of their needs, thus freeing them from routine problems to deal with the big military picture. Every time they ran into some difficulty—no matter how trivial—they would come into the office and order the governor to find a solution. Whenever market vendors refused to sell them pork at the lower official price, for example, they would storm into the governor's office and demand that he force the merchants to comply. The one time the governor dared to resist one of their demands, the Japanese arrested him and jailed him in the guards' barracks under the pretext that they were putting him in "protective custody to keep him safe from Viet Minh assassins." My father helped to get him released the next day. In such a dicey situation, no one felt safe. My father thought he himself might be arrested any day.

My father's knowledge of Chinese characters now came in handy in dealing with the Japanese, who could not speak French, but could read Chinese. He began to communicate with them in writing. This helped him to get us out of Nam Dinh safely. The morning after the coup, he decided to evacuate us to the Vu Ban district town—ten to twelve kilometers away from Nam Dinh—and was able to get a pass for us from the Japanese commander.

With our things piled on an ox cart, my family set out on foot for Vu Ban. I was perched on the cart and my sister Loan was carried by a maid in one of two baskets suspended from a pole. The trip was like a journey through hell. Along the way, we saw corpses lining the road, victims of the famine. In Vu Ban, we shared a house with another family. There were no military or industrial targets here, so the Allied planes left the little town alone. Once in a while, my mother would go back for a day to check on my father and my sister Mao, who had both remained in Nam Dinh. Mao had resisted the move so fiercely, and it would have been such a job to drag her along and keep her from running away during the trip, that my parents decided to leave her behind. Each time my mother returned, she would find our courtyard littered with copper bullet shells that had been sprayed by the American planes. During the bombings and strafings, Mao would refuse to take shelter, and would wander around the yard laughing to herself. Somehow, she survived unharmed. After two weeks in Vu Ban, my family returned to Nam Dinh.

The only group that was opposing the Japanese and dealing seriously with the famine was the Viet Minh, short for League for the Independence of Vietnam, which had been set up by Ho Chi Minh in 1941 after his return to the region near the Chinese border. During Ho's absence from the scene, communist leaders in Vietnam had been focusing their energy and resources on fomenting a social revolution rather than on getting rid of the French. Ho was much more realistic. He knew there was no popular support yet for such a revolution. He made national liberation the top priority, and set up the Viet Minh as a broad-based coalition of middle-class, intellectual, and other patriotic people to fight the French. Communist leadership of the Viet Minh was firm, but kept well hidden, to avoid alarming those who had serious reservations about its ideology. The Viet Minh was supported by a host of popular associations for national salvation, each one covering one social group, such as women, teachers, peasants, youths, and old people. These associations helped to rally the masses for the fight against the French. They also allowed the communists to sink their roots in Vietnamese society.

Ho Chi Minh had a knack for looking at a situation and detecting his opportunity. After Normandy, he predicted the Japanese would lose, the

French would try to return to Indochina, and the Japanese would overthrow the French colonial regime to protect their army, and that in the
ensuing chaos, there would be a power vacuum that the Viet Minh
could fill. From his headquarters near the Chinese border, Ho began
launching guerrilla attacks against the Japanese: ambushing convoys, cutting roads, attacking isolated military posts. Within three months, the
Viet Minh controlled almost the entire mountain region. Alarmed, the
Japanese began to arrest and torture Viet Minh suspects. Since no other
groups in Vietnam had the courage to fight the Japanese, the Viet
Minh's daring attacks won them a lot of prestige among the people.
Rumors of their activities reached the cities, and young people began to
slip out into the mountains to join them.

Early on, Ho Chi Minh recognized that the Americans could be valuable allies. He contacted those operating in southern China and offered
to help locate downed Allied pilots and to provide intelligence about
Japanese troop movements. Since the Viet Minh was the only viable
group in Vietnam, his offer was accepted. Ho developed a close relationship with American officers of the Office of Strategic Services that
were parachuted into the Viet Minh zone to work with him. They gave
his movement little material support, but Ho was clever in exploiting
this connection and made it appear as though he had the backing of the
Allies. This gave the Viet Minh added prestige. From their mountain
base, the Viet Minh began to spread toward the delta, by combining
propaganda, political agitation, and intimidation of local officials. They
immediately saw that the famine was a ready-made chance for them to
win popular support.

At this time, desperate peasants were taking matters into their own
hands, storming granaries to take the rice. The Viet Minh moved in and
took over leadership of this spontaneous revolt, directing "rice strug-
gles" to break open warehouses and distributing food to the hungry.
This too earned them a lot of support. Local officials were too intimidated and also too powerless to retaliate. Those that dared to resist
were eliminated. On the eve of the Japanese surrender, the Viet Minh
had gained control of most of the countryside near Hanoi, and several
districts and counties near Hue.

In the province of Nam Dinh, Viet Minh agents in the countryside
spread propaganda leaflets and assassinated officials and village chiefs
who tried to collect taxes. Local administrators pleaded for help from
the governor's office. But whatever action the government contemplated
was immediately divulged to the Viet Minh, who had heavily infiltrated

the province administration. Their agents were everywhere: in the villages, districts, governor's office, and among the orderlies to the mandarins. The Japanese made arrests, but the Viet Minh continued to gather momentum in the southern part of the province. In the days before the
Viet Minh takeover, cadres led attacks and uprisings in districts like
Nam Truc, which my grandfather had run as a magistrate a few decades
earlier. The Viet Minh would break into depots, seize the stored rice,
and distribute it to the people. The peasants' resentment of the administration's fecklessness was now exploding, blasting the government to
pieces and propelling the Viet Minh to power.

Soon after hearing the news on August 11 that Japan was about to
surrender, the Viet Minh issued an order to the people to rise up and
seize power. General Vo Nguyen Giap, then a trusted lieutenant of Ho
Chi Minh, led a detachment of the Viet Minh army toward Hanoi.
Peasants in Tonkin and northern Annam took over their villages under
Viet Minh leadership. In the urban areas, with the power vacuum created by the Japanese surrender, euphoric rallies and demonstrations
erupted spontaneously in every city, as if a dam had broken. The Viet
Minh moved quickly to harness this emotion. Rallies and demonstrations became Viet Minh affairs, with red flags, banners, slogans, and
speeches calling on the population for support. People were so eager for
leadership, they responded enthusiastically.

Emperor Bao Dai and his government were helpless. Power simply
fell into the hands of the Viet Minh, usually at gigantic demonstrations.
On August 19, the Viet Minh took over Hanoi. My sister Thang happened to be in the city at that time. In Chi Linh Park, she witnessed the
storming of the office of the former French governor for Tonkin. She had
gone to the park to meet an old classmate who had joined the Viet
Minh. From where she stood, she saw her friend rushing forward from
the surging and screaming crowd. Timid, Thang did not join the mass of
protesters. Her heart pounding with excitement, she watched the beginning of the end for a government she considered a puppet of the "brutal
Japanese."

After the takeover of Hanoi, one city after another fell into Viet
Minh hands. Hue and Danang on the 23rd, and Saigon on the 25th. On
the 30th, Emperor Bao Dai abdicated at a ceremony in the imperial
palace and transferred power to the Viet Minh by handing over the symbols of his Mandate of Heaven: his gold sword with the ruby-encrusted
handle and his gold seal. Proclaiming his abdication, Bao Dai said that
he was happier becoming the citizen of a free country than he had been

as the king of an enslaved nation. The Viet Minh delegate declared the end of the monarchy. The imperial flag was lowered, and a Viet Minh banner hoisted in its place. Two days later, Ho Chi Minh appeared for the first time to his countrymen at a gigantic rally in Ba Dinh Square in Hanoi to proclaim that Vietnam was now an independent republic.

In the provinces of Tonkin, some mandarins did not want to give up. On the day the Viet Minh took over Hanoi, government forces in the provinces were still fighting them and arresting their agents. On order from the royal government, however, all the provinces had to surrender. During that day of August 19, we heard a few scattered gunshots in Nam Dinh. That scared us and we did not dare set foot outside the house all day. The next morning, a Viet Minh delegation from Hanoi arrived in the city. They drove straight to the governor's residence and demanded a transfer of power. He had to acquiesce. On the same day, a three-man Viet Minh delegation entered through the open gate of our residence. As they reached the middle of the yard, my father came out to meet them. He thought they had come to take him away for execution. They were very polite, however. The leader of the group introduced himself and reassured my father that nothing would happen to him. As the group turned around to leave, the leader added, "Sir, if you should need anything, let us know." The next day, the Viet Minh took over the city without a fight.

All over the country, the Viet Minh were emerging to seize power in similar scenes. The middle class was shocked and repelled to see who the Viet Minh followers were. To them, the Viet Minh were rough, tough-looking, and ignorant people, the great "unwashed" masses of peasants and workers. It was galling to think that these social inferiors would now hold power. When I asked my relatives and acquaintances to describe their reaction on first seeing Viet Minh followers in those days of 1945, they would say things like, "They looked like robbers" or "How could they run a government when their cadres included people like the barber who used to cut hair at the street corner near our house or the guy who had been caught stealing chickens earlier?"

The day after they seized power in Nam Dinh, the Viet Minh organized a large rally in front of city hall to fire up popular anger against the old regime and enthusiasm for the new. They asked the province governor to appear at the rally to give an address. It was a setup to humiliate him and repudiate what he represented. My father and his colleagues also went, as protocol required. The atmosphere was electrifying. The Bao Dai government had been so discredited by its subservience to the Japanese, and by its incompetence in dealing with the famine, that it was not hard to get people whipped up against it. The rally was full of ardent Viet Minh supporters. Some people in the crowd, however, had come out of curiosity and not necessarily out of support for the Viet Minh, whose agenda they did not yet fully understand. They had heard that there had been a coup, and wanted to come and see what the fuss was all about.

As the governor got up to speak from the podium, he looked down on the sea of people, stretching all the way to the old French sports club, with fluttering red flags and unfurled banners that the Viet Minh agents had handed out. My two teenaged brothers, Giu and Xuong, were in the crowd, drawn like everyone else into the heady swirl. For weeks now, the seething activities had been like a magnet, luring my brothers with their novelty and excitement. Without understanding what they were doing, they had taken to aping the Viet Minh support-ers: taking part in marches, writing slogans on banners they hung from our balcony until my father made them take them down, and singing songs like the one about "exterminating the Fascists and their running dogs." At this rally, Giu was in the back, near the sports club. Xuong was in the front rank, carrying a red flag with the yellow star. As soon as the governor uttered a few words, shouts of "Down with the gover-nor! Down with the governor!" erupted. The slogan was taken up by the throng, and swelled like thunder. Xuong ardently repeated the slogan, raising his left hand in a clenched fist, without understanding the mean-ing of what he was shouting. From his place in the rally, he could not see that his father was among the mandarins on the balcony. Seeing the mood of the crowd, my father and the other officials signaled to one another, and slipped away.

After they took over Nam Dinh, the Viet Minh set up a committee to run the province. At first, they left the province officials in place to achieve a smooth transition. My father continued working for about two weeks. He wanted to resign, but was afraid that quitting would brand him as a "reactionary." In spite of the courteous meeting at his residence, he—and his colleagues—were sure their days were now numbered. There was no rule of law. The Viet Minh had unlimited power, and could arrest and kill anyone they wanted. There was a secret police sta-tion near our house. One night, the Viet Minh came to arrest an agent— the most powerful under the French—and took him away for execution. In Nghia Hung County, where my father had just served, the Viet Minh executed a notable in front of the county magistrate's office. There were also stories of mandarins being killed in other provinces or taken away, never to be seen again. These arrests and executions frightened my parents. During the night, whenever they heard the sound of a car coming to a stop near the house, they would think that the Viet Minh had come for my father. Right after the takeover, my parents had sent me and all my siblings (except Mao) back to Hanoi to get us out of harm's way. We sailed out of Nam Dinh on a rented boat; with the constant bombing, traveling by train was too dangerous. My sister Thang's husband Hau accompanied us and would take care of us until our parents could complete the move.

Fortunately, the chairman of the Viet Minh committee in Nam Dinh was a courteous and moderate man. Many Viet Minh leaders came from middle-class intellectual backgrounds, some even from mandarin families. The committee chairman in Nam Dinh himself was the son of a traditional scholar. My father went to see him one day and asked to be allowed to quit. The chairman agreed and my father immediately slipped out of town and headed for Hanoi, where he was not well known and could more easily melt into the background. After he left, my mother and our domestic staff packed up all our belongings and sailed for Hanoi. One of the servants, however, chose to return to his home village. My family's mandarin background had earned us the stigma of "bad elements" in Viet Minh eyes, so this servant wisely decided that it was not a good idea to remain associated with us in any way. Instead of being a desirable job, working for us had become a liability. Dealing with all this was hard enough, but my mother also had to cope with my sister Mao, who struggled and refused to leave. My mother, who already had her hands full, did not feel up to dragging her along, so she left her with a relative. Later, after we got settled, my mother came back to get her.

In Hanoi, we moved into a house my mother had bought with money given to her by her mother. She would have preferred to buy a beautiful large villa located near the Thuyen Quang Lake, but grandma disapproved. Instead, she told my mother to buy a much more modest house on a street not far from the largest hospital in Hanoi. The house had two stories, with a spiral staircase leading to the second floor and a balcony overlooking the front garden. A round glass window let light through where the staircase began to turn. I used to look through the window into our neighbor's yard to observe the Chinese troops who came to occupy Hanoi in 1946. The space under the staircase was one of my hiding places when I played hide-and-seek with my sisters.

Hau, an agriculture expert, loved to experiment with growing exotic plants in our garden and to tend to the yard. With the famine still raging, Hau's skill was in great demand, so the Viet Minh let him keep his job in the Agriculture Department. He was the only one working in my family then. My father was now idle, with nothing to occupy him and no income. To keep from going crazy with boredom, he would visit friends, also made idle by the revolution. For a month or two, until our driver quit to join the Viet Minh army, he would make his rounds in our rickshaw. Looking at the way we lived, in a nice house with a staff of servants, riding in a private rickshaw, people would have thought we had unlimited resources.

This was far from the truth. Over the years, my mother had been buying gold on and off with savings from grandma's gifts and my father's pay. This investment now proved to be prescient. With galloping inflation, the gold was now worth ten times what she had paid for. My parents began to sell it little by little to meet our daily expenses. But with no income, our savings were quickly dwindling. To stretch out the money, my mother embarked on an austerity program. She cut down on food expenses. Stews became brine water with bits of meat floating in it. Then she decided she should try to earn some income by going into business. She only broke even in her first venture: buying and selling corn. In her next businesses, selling soap and then matches, she lost money. After an associate ran off with some of her capital, my mother gave up.

Besides worrying about taking care of our daily needs, my parents also worried about our future, which looked extremely bleak. Schools had been closed because of the war and the disturbances. No one knew when they would reopen. Even if we could get an education, the traditional career route for our family was now gone. The Viet Minh had destroyed the mandarin system, one of their prime targets in remaking Vietnamese society. Being a mandarin was no longer a viable career option for my two oldest brothers, so my father suggested they go into business. Two young men who lived across the street were planning to go from Hanoi to Lao Kay, near the border, to sell cooking grease and votive products. Tet was approaching, a time when people ritually burned paper money and paper household goods to send to their dead relatives. The two neighbors told Giu he could join them on this trip and make some profit.

The plan sounded good to my parents. Tre and Truc, the two neighbors, belonged to a family of merchants, were older, and seemed to know what they were doing. My mother sold an ounce of gold to buy the votive products and a few barrels of grease for Giu to resell in Lao

Kay. With transport still disrupted, Giu found only a night train. He left one evening, with my parents entertaining high expectations for the venture. Suddenly, at midnight, there was a knock on the front door and they heard Giu's voice. My mother jumped out of bed, opened the door, and found Giu standing outside. She said, "What happened? Why did you come back?" Giu said, "The train ride was rough, and I got tired and dizzy. Tre told me not to bother making it all the way to the border. He said he'd give me the money after Tet." Of course, Tre never did, and the investment was lost. My parents should have learned from this venture that if my pampered brother could not take the discomfort of a trip to the border, he would not be motivated to do anything rigorous for a living. Instead, my father now decided that Giu and Xuong should go back to Van Dinh and grow rice for a living. My father found a piece of land for sale but, unable to get the price reduced, he had to drop his plan of turning Giu and Xuong into farmers.

Then, events propelled my two brothers through some experiences they would never forget. The Viet Minh were now mobilizing everyone to do his or her share for a country in shambles, but also to become indoctrinated into their movement. The head of the Viet Minh committee on each block made sure everyone joined. The protective wall around our sheltered existence came tumbling down. My parents became members of the Parents'and Old People's Association, while my older siblings now found themselves thrust into a world of swirling revolutionary activities: rallies, marches, meetings, speeches, slogans, campaigns, and paramilitary training and duties. My brothers Luong and Tuan, eleven and ten years old, were in the Children's Association for National Salvation. My father was convinced that the main job for the children in the association was to keep tabs on what was happening in the neighborhood and report it to the Viet Minh. Xuong and Giu joined the Youth Association and were also drafted into the self-defense militia, along with their untrustworthy business partners Tre and Truc. For weapons, each militiaman had a spear, three meters in length, ending with a two-inch-long pointed tip. While my parents skipped their association meetings and Tuan and Luong were indifferent to their group's activities, Giu and Xuong thought everything the Viet Minh asked them to do was a lark. My parents resigned themselves to the situation, telling each other, "What can we do? These are the times in which we live." If they got too annoyed with Giu's and especially Xuong's zeal, they would console themselves with the thought that their sons were "too young to understand what they're doing."

As militiamen, Giu and Xuong had the responsibility of maintaining order and security in our neighborhood: standing guard in the street at night in shifts, walking up and down the block with their spears, and checking passers-by for identification papers. Whenever there was a rally, the militiamen were mobilized to attend. This was how on September 2, 1945, my brothers went to hear Ho Chi Minh in Ba Dinh Square when he proclaimed Vietnam an independent republic.

The square was filled with people. To underline the unity of the population behind the Viet Minh, the crowd included Hanoi residents, peasants from nearby villages, groups representing ethnic tribes, and delegations from various religious faiths. Among those in attendance were members of the American OSS delegation that had worked with Ho Chi Minh in his mountain base. When Ho appeared on the raised platform, he was greeted with the thunderous chant of *"Doc lap! Doc lap!"*—independence. My brothers were standing so far back in the crowd that they could not see the man who had been only a name and a mystical figure to his countrymen. When Ho began to speak, they could not hear him. But even if they could have, they would not have completely understood a speech that Ho started with sentences taken from the American Declaration of Independence to flatter the OSS delegation in attendance and, through them, perhaps win support from the United States.

For the French, Vietnamese independence was no better than Japanese rule. In Hanoi, soldiers who had been incarcerated by the Japanese in the old citadel remained imprisoned. French civilians became the targets of Vietnamese hostility. They lived in fear of pillaging and attacks. French housewives could not buy food in the market, because merchants were afraid to sell to them. Vietnamese who were sympathetic to the plight of the French had to help them in secret. We heard that Nguyen Huu Tri, the man who would later on become the governor of Tonkin, used to pass food over his fence to his French neighbors.

After those first exhilarating days of seizing power and shouting Vietnam's independence to an indifferent world, the Viet Minh began to tackle the more difficult job of governing a country on the brink of collapse. The situation was chaotic. The Japanese were still at large, with their army and their weapons. The French, emboldened by the Allies' victory and awaiting reinforcements from General de Gaulle, were spoiling to regain control. The Viet Minh did not even have access to the central bank, guarded by Japanese troops and still run by the French. Famine had not abated, so one of the things that my brothers had to do was to go around collecting rice to feed the hungry, as part of the "A Loving Handful of Rice" campaign, one of several launched by the new government. The Vietnamese had never seen mobilization on this scale before. My brothers and their colleagues in the Viet Minh youth association, each carrying a reed basket, would make their rounds, knocking on doors and asking for rice donations. Most people cooperated, partly out of sympathy and partly out of fear of antagonizing the Viet Minh. The youths from poor backgrounds were much more dedicated and zealous than my brothers. If someone refused, my brothers would turn around and leave, but the other youths would not give up and would insist until they got a donation.

To signal that a new era was dawning, the Viet Minh also embarked on an ambitious program of social reform, banning many social vices such as prostitution and opium smoking. In addition, they launched a campaign to teach people to read and write in order to combat the high illiteracy rate that Vietnamese generally condemned as a shameful legacy of French domination, and also to make it easier for their propaganda to reach the masses. Everyone, no matter how old, who could not read or write now had to attend classes. There was a poor quarter not far from our house. People here lived a life on the edge, in flimsy huts of straw and mud walls, at the foot of the dike near the Red River. The Viet Minh built a crude shed there, and began to give literacy classes for people in this neighborhood. My brothers were among the youths mobilized to teach these people the alphabet, chanting simple verses for the students to repeat. This was the first time that my brothers had to try and communicate with really poor and uneducated people. Giu and Xuong took this in stride, accepting it as another fun part of being in the revolution.

In those dizzying days, the country was seized by patriotic fervor. The young responded enthusiastically to every call to action. Up and down the country, thousands of youths were joining the Viet Minh, not simply because they had been drafted into it, as were my brothers Giu and Xuong, but deliberately, out of a sense of determination to help keep the hard-won and still fragile independence. In the south, young people joined the Vanguard Youths in droves, including my cousin Hien, who was then working in Saigon, and his wife. In the north, three more cousins would join the Viet Minh. Reflecting the division within our society at the time, however, three others would leave to join the rival anti-French Nationalist Party. Regardless of what their political affiliation was at the time, all eight were swept up in the great patriotic wave of 1945. Of these eight that responded to the call of revolution, half would die for their cause.

Among the cousins who joined the Viet Minh, the youngest was

Luc, one of my uncle Chinh's sons. Luc was the grandson of Vi Van Dinh, the feudal lord of the Tay (also known as Tho) minority. Both his father and mother came from two of the most prominent families in Tonkin, so Luc had an aristocratic upbringing. At first, he led a sheltered life and was apolitical like my brothers. He went to the Lycée Albert Sarraut, where he was an average student. In 1943, the *lycée* closed down because of the Allied bombings in Hanoi, and the students dispersed. Luc went to live with a sister in nearby Ha Dong to continue his schooling. The Vietnamese students at this school were quite different from the classmates Luc used to know at the *lycée*. For one thing, they came from a diverse social background, rather than from the mandarin and elite class alone. For another, they were more politically aware, and had a stronger social conscience. Many were sympathetic to the Viet Minh.

Some of Luc's new friends began to talk to him about this movement, telling him that the Viet Minh were patriotic and revolutionary people who wanted to expel the Japanese and French to free the country from slavery. They appealed to his emotions. Like the other youths at the time, the famine that was turning Tonkin into a hellhole horrified Luc and made him receptive to their arguments. For months, he had seen the emaciated and contorted corpses of the victims being carted away each morning to be dumped in mass graves, but had not connected these scenes of horror with the French and the Japanese. Now he was convinced that the famine was a deliberate French and Japanese ploy to keep the Vietnamese too hungry to fight back. He felt a strong surge of emotions, a burning hatred and an uncontrollable urge to act. He made up his mind to join the Viet Minh. But he kept his feelings secret from his sister and her family.

At school Luc was never maltreated by the French teachers. But he once experienced what it felt like to be part of a slave race. This happened at the Opera House in Hanoi where he had gone one day to attend a play performed by Vietnamese students about the defeat of the Mongol invasion of their country in the fourteenth century. When they heard that the play was a veiled attempt to arouse Vietnamese patriotic fervor against colonial domination, French students invaded the theater and disrupted the performance. The Vietnamese protested and a fistfight broke out. The French police was summoned. After arresting those they suspected were the Vietnamese ringleaders, they told the audience to leave in single file. But outside the entrance, the Vietnamese had to run the police gauntlet. Every time they saw a head with black hair passing by, the French police would bring down their nightsticks. Like everyone else, Luc had to walk out of the theater with his head lowered and take the blows. After this incident, Luc nurtured a resentment against the French, which made him receptive to the appeals of his classmates in Ha Dong.

Luc's friends began to pass to him clandestine newspapers and documents so he could learn about the Viet Minh and what it stood for. This education was part of the induction process. Luc would hide the documents under the planks of his bed and read them in secret. His sister and aunts found some of these papers—which it was a crime to possess—but not realizing how serious Luc was, they dismissed it as youthful folly. In fact, Luc did not know much about the Viet Minh, but the little he had seen and heard had fired his imagination. When he was still living in Hanoi, he had noticed evidence of the Viet Minh's bold activities in defiance of the French and Japanese. One day he saw the slogan "Long Live the Viet Minh," written over and over again until it covered the entire wall of the Quoc Tu Giam school. Another time, he saw an electric tram flying a Viet Minh flag running down the tracks without the Vietnamese policemen daring to stop it. Other exploits he did not witness, but heard about. Rumors were circulating in Hanoi about Viet Minh women shooting security police agents right in the center of the city and of Viet Minh guerrillas attacking Japanese troops and taking their weapons. He began to idealize the Viet Minh, imagining an idyllic liberated zone where people led a heroic life and did heroic deeds. Many others shared this romantic vision, including the famous composer Van Cao, who wrote a song describing the imaginary liberated zone. Luc knew the danger of joining the Viet Minh—the possibility of being arrested, jailed, tortured, and killed. This, too, contributed to the romantic allure of the movement. He had heard stories of Viet Minh agents dying under torture, because they refused to divulge information that would betray their comrades. Luc pictured himself dying courageously like the martyrs in the stories.

It was in Lang Son where his family was living that Luc made the jump into the Viet Minh base. He had returned home as they got ready to move and join his father, who had been promoted governor and transferred to another province. Lang Son was in the mountain region, close to the Viet Minh zone. Once he got home, Luc got in touch with friends who were already in the base. Shortly after that, the local Viet Minh contacted him and told him that he had been recruited for training. He kept his plan secret, so no one in his family knew he was leaving. He needed money for the trip, but did not have any. The day before he left, he stole some from a sister. He also left a few pieces of clothing with an acquaintance, so that he could walk out of his house without having to carry a bundle. The morning of his departure, he got up while it was still dark. Out in the courtyard, he bumped into a chamber pot and woke up his mother. He heard her sleepy voice asking, "Who's that?" He answered, "It's me, mom." She said, "Where are you going at this hour?" He lied, "I'm going to the bathroom." As he was making his way to the gate, he suddenly thought of his newly born sister. He turned around and went to her room to hold her for a while and kiss her goodbye. Then he went and collected his clothes and, without a glance backward, left for the Viet Minh zone. He knew he might never see his family again, but it did not matter. Running through his head were the lyrics of a song about the soldiers who left home to join the revolution without worrying whether they would ever make it back again.

In my own family, while Giu and Xuong went along with the Viet Minh because it was popular, my sister Thang and her husband Hau supported this movement out of personal conviction. In Thang's case, the decision was emotional. Among my siblings, Thang is perhaps the most morally pure person, someone with a very strong sense of what is right and wrong, and an unshakable sense of duty. She is compassionate, extremely straightforward, and unselfish. In her student days, her admiring classmates used to call her the reincarnation of Buddha. My parents were very proud of her because she was beautiful—with a kind and full face, a smooth complexion, a small and straight nose, and large eyes—as well as quiet, obedient, and diligent.

After she finished the grades available in the province, my parents sent her to school in Hanoi, where she moved in with my grandmother on Hang Gai street. My mother was the one who had the idea of sending her to school, breaking down my father's resistance with the argument that Thang would suffer without an education since modern men expected their wives to have a modicum of schooling, and that the family could not cling to old-fashioned ideas. My father finally relented but cautioned that they should keep an eye on Thang because "girls who go to school absorb bad outside influences. They read bad books, they go to bad movies, and they become bad." Thang worked hard and ranked first in her class year after year.

My parents did not expect much from Thang because girls who went to school were only supposed to get an education before they married and became housewives and mothers, and not to prepare for a career. Part of the curriculum was geared to giving them the skills needed to be housewives, including home economics, sewing, and embroidering. In my entire clan, Thang was one of only four girls of her generation who were allowed to continue past elementary school. After she finished the lower grades, Thang passed the entrance exam to the Dong Khanh school and was admitted. All the students had to board, so Thang moved into the dormitory. My mother bought her two long tunics, two pairs of white cotton pants, and a pair of sturdy shoes made of coconut fiber that would last for a long time. That was the extent of my sister's wardrobe for school. Thang did not mind, and even liked the shoes, which she found comfortable and easy to care for. In the winter, my mother added a maroon woolen jacket and a charcoal gray satin tunic to Thang's wardrobe.

Thang's classmates were from middle-class or affluent families. They were more demanding than my sister and would complain about dorm life. While they criticized the food at every meal, Thang just ate quietly her share of three bowls of rice. She did not envy or try to emulate their fashionable clothes or their more active social life. On Sundays, they would leave the campus as soon as they could, but Thang would stay and bury herself in her books. The only breaks in the routine for Thang were the monthly visit she paid to the Hang Gai shop while my grandmother was alive and the infrequent occasions when my mother came to the dorm to see her.

At school, Thang was a genius at math, and could solve any problem that was thrown at her, taking first prize in each of the four years she was at the Dong Khanh school. The only subject she did not excel in was literature. She read the novels assigned in class only because she had to, being utterly indifferent to them, and heartily disliked having to write essays critiquing them. She was even less interested in the romantic novels that were enthralling female readers, and never bothered to find out for herself what had made them so popular. In the summer, she went home, and spent a lot of her time tutoring her younger siblings. The year Thang finished her secondary school at Dong Khanh, my parents discussed what she should do next. They disliked the options: sending her to a coed high school or, as a last resort, enrolling her in a vocational course that could train her for a profession suitable for a woman. While they were still debating, Hau asked Thang to marry him. Or, more precisely, he had someone ask my father on his behalf.

There were many things in common between my sister and Hau. Like Thang, he was quiet, partly because he was hard-of-hearing. Like her, he was a person of strong principles, honest, and unmaterialistic. He shared her gift for math and took a lot of prizes in this subject. Like her, he also worked extremely hard, because he knew that getting an educa-tion was his only hope of escaping his poverty. He was rarely seen with-out a book and would read even while taking a bath—scooping up water out of a jar with a dipper and splashing himself with it with one hand, while holding the book with the other. Hau descended from man-darins and scholars, but his father did not follow the family tradition and became a merchant in Nam Dinh. Both of Hau's parents died early, and after their death, life had turned extremely hard.

In 1936, Hau started high school in Hanoi. He was such a bright stu-dent that he won a scholarship, which paid the tuition and gave him a small monthly allowance. This was the year when the country was seething with political activities. At the school there was an under-ground movement. Although he was interested, he did not get involved because he was afraid he might get arrested, and focused on his studies instead. After finishing high school, he enrolled in the college for agri-cultural engineers. This was not what he wanted to do in life, but it was the most practical option for him then. The school had just been set up and, to increase enrollment, it was waiving tuition and giving each student a monthly stipend of twenty-five piasters. After he graduated, Hau was sent to the provinces for a six-month on-the-job training ses-sion. One of the provinces was Nam Dinh, where he met my father, then running Nghia Hung County. His job was to encourage peasants to use new seeds, plant new crops, and adopt more modern methods. Like other officials, whenever he came to Nghia Hung, he would be invited to stay at our house.

Hau had met many mandarins, and had developed a general dislike for them. He found them haughty, corrupt, brutal, or all three. He was pleasantly surprised by my parents. He thought my father was kind and generous toward everyone, even toward the ordinary people who came to petition him in his office. They never discussed the dangerous topic of politics, but he sensed that my father was a man who deep down loved his country and his people. Hau also sympathized with my father's predicament of having to go along with the policies of those in power. As a government official himself, he knew that if my father tried to resist, he would bring retaliation on himself and his family. This retali-ation could take many forms: arrest and jail, torture and execution, demotion, or transfer to remote, malaria-ridden mountain regions. Hau was also surprised by my mother. The mandarin wives he had met were usually an insufferable lot, haughty and mean, but the few times he had contact with my mother he was impressed by her modesty and her soft-spoken manner.

Hau was now a person of some stature: an engineer with a decent job and a good future. He felt the time had come for him to look for a wife. Once he got to know my parents, he decided he wanted to be part of our family. He had never met my sister, though he had seen her from a distance, and thought that she appeared simple and modest. He concluded that ours was a "good" family—one that had status but had managed to retain decent values. He also saw that my father was a mandarin destined for higher positions, and knew it would not hurt to become connected with him.

Hau began to drop hints to relatives and acquaintances that he wanted to marry my sister. One of them volunteered to be a matchmaker and went to see my father. My parents were delighted since Thang had turned eighteen and might soon become too old to marry. So, one day, my father told Thang about the proposal. While he asked her what she thought, he made it clear that he believed Hau would make a good match. Thang did not know anything was going on and was taken aback. She protested that she did not want to get married, and asked for time to think things over. The next day, my father told her that he and my mother had made up their minds to accept the proposal, and Thang acquiesced out of filial duty. Yet while she resigned herself to the marriage, Thang also felt reassured by her parents' affection and respect for Hau and trusted that they had chosen the right man for her. Although she was not motivated by romantic love at the beginning, her marriage turned out to be one of the most successful in the family. She and her husband shared an exciting but hard life of idealism and revolution.

The wedding took place in 1944 during the Japanese occupation. As yet, Hau had nothing to do with the Viet Minh. He was now established in society, with a good future, a devoted wife, and a supportive family. He did not want to risk everything he had worked so hard for. It was not that he was completely happy with his job—far from it. Like other qualified Vietnamese, he was irked by the limitation imposed on native employees and by the inequity of the colonial system. In his agricultural service, the top jobs, such as regional director and the head of stations experimenting with new crops, always went to Frenchmen. Not all the French bosses were well qualified, and yet they were getting paid three or four times more than the locals who worked for them.

Also like a lot of other Vietnamese, Hau was irritated by the arrogance and racism of many of the *colons*, who believed that they were superior to the natives by the simple virtue of their skin color. They would call the Vietnamese names, dismiss them as a "dirty race," and attack them without being prosecuted. In one famous incident, a Vietnamese physician had his ear twisted in public by a *colon* when he objected to being called "an idiot" by the settler's friend. In another famous incident, the head of a political party in Saigon was kicked in public by a *colon*. Hau himself suffered a public humiliation at the hand of a settler. One day, he had an argument with a French policeman. The settler, who was just passing by in the street, stopped to intervene and slapped Hau in the face.

None of these irritations alone would have driven Hau to join the Viet Minh, whom he saw, like most middle-class Vietnamese, as uneducated and uncouth. It took a series of events to push him over the edge. The gruesome famine was a motivating factor. His changed perception of the Viet Minh once he had contact with some of their leaders was another. After the Viet Minh took over power in August 1945, Hau became an employee of the new government. At first, he was not enthusiastic about the revolution. He worried about his own future, wondering how long he would be able to keep his job, support his young wife, and help my parents. The example of my own family—how quickly we had gone from a comfortable life to a precarious one practically overnight—told him that he could look forward to the same fate under the Viet Minh. Then a former classmate of his, the famous poet Cu Huy Can, became the new Minister for Agriculture. Hau had always admired him as a man of high moral principles. Watching his old friend in action, Hau liked him even more. He approved of Can's choice of associates to help run the ministry: people who were sympathetic to the Viet Minh, naturally, but who also were qualified and had strong moral character. Hau thought this was an encouraging sign that the Viet Minh would recruit good people and that they were serious about making meaningful changes.

Through his former classmate, Hau met a few other top officials, and realized that the Viet Minh leaders were well-educated intellectuals, not the rabble-rousers he had thought. From long conversations with his poet friend about colonialism and Marxism, he became curious. His friend loaned him books to read so he could learn more. Hau found the writings of Marx too dense and too political. But he was taken by the works of Engels, and this discovery was the most important factor in his finally joining the Viet Minh. Engels's philosophy was so different from everything he had learned in schools. Hau was fascinated by the discourse on the laws of history, finding it objective and persuasive. Engels said that human societies evolved according to set laws. Once one understood these laws, one could foretell what the future would bring. Marxism had discovered these laws and could predict that in the future capitalism would be destroyed and capitalist exploitation of the poor and oppressed would end. From here, it was easy to infer that, by following the path of socialism, the Viet Minh—and therefore Vietnam—was catching the wave of history and riding to victory, because the end of capitalism would also bring the end of colonialism. To an agricultural engineer in famine-ravaged Vietnam in 1945, it was like finding a secret lifeline. Hau fell in love with the ideals of socialism: helping the poor, achieving social equality, and ushering in the communist utopia.

For Thang, the decision came from what she now calls two basic traditional values: compassion for the poor and loyalty to one's husband. The famine had horrified her. When her husband told her about the Viet Minh, she concluded that a movement that distributed food to the starving, tried to end the famine, promised to help the poor achieve equality, and wanted to get rid of the Japanese deserved her allegiance. Also, she felt she should support her husband in what he was doing, and so, without hesitation, she became a Viet Minh sympathizer. In those days of marches and rallies for independence, she would stand in the street and joyfully watch the people stream by.

The first priority of the newly established Viet Minh government was to relieve the famine and cope with the disastrous flood of the Red River Delta that took place in August. A campaign called "An Inch of Land Is an Inch of Gold" was launched to grow food on every piece of land everywhere. People, even those in urban areas, were urged to plant vegetables and crops that mature quickly, such as sweet potatoes, corn, and soya beans. Hau plunged into his work with zeal. He edited a newspaper called *An Inch of Land*, giving tips on how to grow food, a skill few Hanoi residents had. He would stay up late at night writing his articles, sprinkling his prose with recently introduced—and strange—revolutionary terms to give his articles the socialist flavor favored by the Viet Minh.

Before the Viet Minh could consolidate their power, the Allies imposed their own policy on Indochina. No country in the world had recognized Vietnamese independence, not even the Soviets. President Franklin Roosevelt had been sympathetic to giving Vietnam back its freedom, though under a trusteeship, but now he was gone from the scene. In the eyes of the Allies, Indochina was still a French colony.

With Japanese defeat imminent, a month before Tokyo surrendered, the Allies sketched plans to evacuate their prisoners of war held in Vietnam and disarm the Japanese army still stationed there. This was a task the Allied High Command knew the local French could not do on their own, because the Japanese had incarcerated and disarmed their soldiers. The Chinese government under Generalissimo Chiang Kai-shek was assigned to perform these duties in the north, while the British were sent into the south. These forces would set the stage for the French to return and retake their colony.

In Saigon, General Douglas Gracey, the British commander, found himself thrust into a chaotic situation, with the Viet Minh and their political rivals vying for popular allegiance and control, and the French trying to reassert their rule. After clashes occurred, General Gracey, who despised the natives and personally favored restoring the French to power, decided to ignore his official instructions to steer clear of local politics. He clamped down on the Vietnamese and released French soldiers from detention so they could help him enforce the martial law he had declared. The troops went further, ousting the Viet Minh from offices and then, together with angry French civilians, went on a rampage, ransacking numerous Vietnamese homes and shops and beating up the people they found. Enraged, the Viet Minh launched a general strike and a retaliatory attack. In the ensuing chaos, Vietnamese extremists invaded a French residential complex and murdered and kidnaped over 200 civilians. Not wishing to get further embroiled and wanting to withdraw British forces as soon as possible, London armed offshore French troops and transported them to Vietnam to restore order. The French forces then proceeded to reconquer the south, and the Viet Minh, powerless to stop their advance, retreated into the countryside to launch a guerrilla war that lasted until 1954.

The Chinese troops in the north were under the command of General Lu Han, the cousin of a powerful warlord who controlled Yunnan Province across the border of Vietnam. From the start, Lu Han had one thing in mind: to enrich himself at the expense of the Vietnamese. Although the Allies, and in particular the American commanders in China, wanted to send only a limited number of troops into Vietnam and to restrict their mission to disarming and repatriating the Japanese army, Lu Han brought close to 200,000, mostly his own soldiers. Of these, he stationed a division in the mountains of Laos to control the opium harvest. The Chinese began crossing the border into Vietnam at the end of August, and by September 9, their hordes arrived in Hanoi.

It was a day Vietnamese who witnessed their arrival and who thought they saw the specter of another long Chinese occupation, still recall vividly. All day and all through the night, the Chinese troops kept pouring into the city. They shocked everyone, including the Chinese community, which had organized a formal welcoming ceremony for them. What the population saw was not the disciplined and well-trained regular army of China but a warlord's own band of soldiers. The troops wore shoes of woven straw, cloth, or rubber cut out from tires, or even went barefoot. They had tattered uniforms, and looked hungry and thin. Each unit was accompanied by cooks laden with pots and pans, making a racket. Unlike the disciplined and imposing Japanese, the Chinese looked like they had just been scooped up from the streets, markets, and rice fields. With these ragtag soldiers swarming all over town, women—Vietnamese and French—were afraid to venture out into the streets.

General Lu Han arrived five days later and immediately installed himself in the luxurious former governor general's palace, while his troops were stationed in hospitals, barracks, and private homes that they commandeered. A detachment of about fifty marched into our house the day Lu Han's column poured into Hanoi. The soldiers' sudden appearance scared my mother, who was at home with just us children. (My father was visiting a friend.) One glance at the undisciplined soldiers was enough to convince my mother that anything could happen. She immediately sent Xuong to bring my father back to protect us from possible assault and, if possible, to communicate with the Chinese and get them to move. But there was nothing he could do to get rid of them. He told my mother, "I can't throw them out. We'll just have to live with this." Once again, my father put his knowledge of Chinese to good use. He could talk to the commanding officer in writing. The officer was impressed, and reined in his soldiers so that they were better behaved than those elsewhere. They did not steal any of our belongings, as they did throughout Hanoi. But they herded us upstairs and took over the ground floor. The peasant soldiers were not used to urban amenities, and at first Giu had to teach them how to turn on the electric lights and ceiling fans. They were so pleased that they would stand by the switches, turning them on and off and staring in wonder at the effect.

The Chinese left us alone. But we could hardly wait for them to depart. For one thing, the fifty or so soldiers in our house were full of lice, which carried a disease that began to infect and kill the local people. We lived in fear of catching this illness. The soldiers also had habits that we found revolting. There was garbage inside the house and outside in the yard. A sour smell of unwashed bodies lingered in the air. In the residence across the street from us, the Chinese dug a latrine in the front yard, and would relieve themselves in full view. After the first group departed, my mother thought that was the end of the occupation. She had the house scrubbed and disinfected, and the walls whitewashed with lime. But two days later, to our dismay, another group showed up.

The Chinese troops led such a hard life that we could not help but feel sorry for them. Their meals usually consisted of rice accompanied by a soup made of vegetables boiled in a lot of water. Sometimes the soup was just water mixed with a big handful of mashed peanuts. When they fell sick, they received no treatment. Besides the lice, the Chinese also brought cholera with them. If a soldier came down with this disease, his comrades would just abandon him to his terrible fate—either quarantined in a room spread with lime, left out in a courtyard, or thrown on the sidewalk to die. When one of the soldiers next door became seriously ill, he was carried outside and left without medication. Throughout the night, we could hear him groan. The next morning, he was dead. His comrades casually threw his corpse into the garbage cart that was making the rounds of the neighborhood. When one of the soldiers quartered in our house became sick, he crawled under our stairwell to keep out of sight, perhaps hoping his comrades would not banish him to the sidewalk. My parents were afraid he would die under our roof, but he recovered and left with his unit.

To a Tonkin still reeling under the famine, the Chinese troops were a scourge. The soldiers had to be not only housed, but fed. Every morning, the Vietnamese would watch with a heavy heart as a convoy of trucks laden with fruit and vegetables made their way from the markets of Hanoi to the Chinese barracks. Soldiers in the markets would brandish their worthless Chinese banknotes, pegged at an inflated rate of exchange to the Vietnamese currency, and demand to buy food. If the merchants refused, they would hit them or threaten to shoot. They also looted homes; when they left the country, their trucks would be piled high with furniture, drain pipes, bathtubs, vases, stools, chairs, and other pillaged items.

With his large occupation army, Lu Han could have easily gotten rid of Ho Chi Minh and installed his own protégés in his place. But he never did, and instead accepted a compromise worked out with Ho to include them in a coalition government. Rumors circulated that Ho knew of Lu Han's greed and had bought him off with a large gift of gold.

Some people said Ho gave him a complete opium-smoking set made with pure gold; others said it was an urn or a large statue. Everyone whispered that the gold had come from a campaign called "The Week of Gold" launched by the Viet Minh to collect funds for national defense a week after the Chinese had arrived. My brothers Giu and Xuong were among the swarm of people sent out to gather this precious metal. They went from house to house, knocking on doors and entering names and donations in a register. Most people felt compelled to give something, many out of patriotism, some out of fear. The campaign was extremely successful. In all, 370 kilos of gold, as well as 20 million piasters, were collected. According to some reports, two-thirds of this collection went to bribing Lu Han and buying Japanese and French weapons the Chinese had impounded.

With the Viet Minh hemmed in by the French and the British in the south and the Chinese in the north, other political rivals sprang up to jockey for power. Ho had to carry out a precarious balancing act. To give his government an aura of legitimacy, Ho invited former Emperor Bao Dai to become his advisor, decreed universal suffrage, and announced a general election for December 1945. This announcement met with an outcry from rival groups, which were afraid they would be outmaneuvered by the Viet Minh. To placate them, Ho promised that, regardless of the outcome, he would reserve a large bloc of seats in the national assembly for them. So, even before the votes were cast, it was apparent the results would be predetermined. Popular enthusiasm was high. However, since the people had never been exposed to this democratic technique, the election was easy to manipulate. In my neighborhood, old voters asked my brothers and their colleagues manning the polling station how to cast their ballots. My brothers would fill in the name for them and then, when the voting was over, they and their colleagues simply dumped the ballots in the trash without bothering to count them. After that, they made out a report saying that Ho Chi Minh, who was running for a seat, had won 99.9% of the vote. After the election, Ho had to share power with his rivals by giving them cabinet posts, but he cautiously kept the most important ones in Viet Minh hands.

Although Ho Chi Minh had cleverly neutralized Lu Han, the situation remained critical. The presence of Chinese troops revived the population's fear of Chinese domination and annexation. The French, too, were afraid that the Chinese had come to displace them and began negotiating for China's departure. In return for French concessions in China and in Vietnam, China finally agreed to make Lu Han withdraw. It also agreed, in complete disregard for the Vietnamese wish for independence, to let French troops return to relieve their departing soldiers and complete the job of disarming and repatriating the Japanese army. French ships immediately left Saigon for the north to reinforce troops already arrived in Hanoi. Although the Viet Minh and the people in the north were glad to see the rapacious Chinese finally depart, they were disturbed at the prospect of a restoration of French control. After dragging their feet, the Chinese finally left in the summer of 1946.

Ho Chi Minh realized that he was too weak to stop the French from coming back and that his best option was to negotiate. On March 6, 1946, he signed an agreement accepting the return of the French to relieve the departing Chinese, with the understanding that all French troops would leave Vietnam at the end of five years. In exchange, France agreed to recognize Vietnam as a free—rather than an independent—state within the French Union. The agreement was a bitter pill to swallow for Ho Chi Minh, but he believed it was the lesser of two evils. As Ho explained to his close associates, in the long run it would be better for Vietnam "to sniff French *merde* for five years than to smell Chinese dung for one thousand years." The March agreement was immediately denounced in Vietnam for allowing the French to return without a fight. Ho had to put all of his prestige behind it to secure popular acceptance.

Violations of the March 6 agreement immediately occurred, and the French began to renege on their promises, going as far as to create a separate state of Cochinchina in the south, effectively dismembering the country. A series of negotiations followed, but proved futile. Vietnam wanted to keep its territorial integrity and to remain independent of French control, while France was determined to pursue its separatist policy in the south and, at the same time, keep Vietnam firmly within the orbit of its colonial empire. As war became inevitable, both sides began to prepare for its outbreak. After repeated reinforcements with troops, tanks, armored personnel, planes, and ships, the French now had the decisive military edge. The Viet Minh, on the other hand, could deploy only a weak army to face this threat: Their ill-trained militia was armed mostly with swords, machetes, and spears, and their regular troops were equipped with a small stock of assorted weapons that they had seized from arsenals in the wake of the August Revolution or bought from the Chinese. The Viet Minh's only ace in the hole was the popular support they had managed to win.

The French were confident they could pacify the country quickly.

The French were confident they could pacify the country quickly. They landed troops in Danang, then sailed their ships into the port of Haiphong in November 1946 to reinforce troops already positioned there. They took over this city after shelling and bombarding it, destroying the native quarter and killing over a thousand civilians. It was obvious after this that Hanoi would be conquered next. With newly arrived troops, the French began to occupy some key positions in the city. A company of Legionnaires was even stationed in the Metropole Hotel, right across from Ho Chi Minh's office. In our neighborhood, other soldiers were poised, ready to strike. Hanoi became a checkerboard of areas controlled by the French and the Viet Minh. Tension mounted, the two sides glaring at each other sometimes from just across the street.

To cope with the imminent attack, the Viet Minh started to make preparations of their own. With the help of civilians, their militia worked feverishly to turn the most densely populated areas near the central lake and main square into a fortified zone. They dug up the streets, planted mines, built road blocks, and cut holes through the walls connecting the neighboring houses to facilitate troop movement. The plan was to force the French to take the city block by block. This would buy time and allow for the safe evacuation of the Viet Minh government and the main body of the army into the mountain base. An advance party was sent to ready the base for the move there. Rice and salt were stored in hidden depots in Hanoi to supply the troops and the civilians who had elected to stay behind. A couple of obsolete artillery pieces outside Hanoi were trained on the French positions in the city near one of its ancient gates. By the middle of December, most of the Viet Minh leaders and government staff had secretly withdrawn, leaving behind a force of ill-armed troops and militia—including my two oldest brothers—to pin down the French.

Hanoi was set for war.

7

The Head on the Roof

When war reached my doorstep, I was too little to understand what was going on, but not too little to sense that something terrible was happening and to feel afraid. The experience etched such powerful scenes in my memory that even now I can still see myself as a six-year-old child listening to the sound of gunfire, being yanked from my game and rushed to the shelter, imitating my adult relatives and raising my arms in surrender to the French, fleeing the smoldering ancestral village transported in a wicker basket, and looking back and seeing the severed head on the roof.

That day in 1947, my family and I lived through one of the most frightening experiences of our lives. My family had evacuated to Van Dinh weeks before, after my father had decided fighting was imminent. We packed up and left for what he believed would be a short stay. He thought that it would take the French just a few days to overcome the fledgling Viet Minh force; then things would be calm again, and we would be able to return home. My brothers Giu and Xuong did not go with us. They knew that there was going to be war and were eager to be part of the action. At this time, two of my sisters could not be evacuated—my older sister Mao and my younger sister Cuc, who was in the hospital with chronic osteomyelitis—so my parents agreed to let Giu and Xuong stay in Hanoi, in part to look after my sisters.

Before leaving, my parents gave my two brothers enough rice and money to last until we returned. If my parents could have guessed what would happen later, they would have ordered them to come along. After we departed, many neighbors also left, part of the first wave of refugees out of the city, and the streets became deserted. At night, my brothers felt exposed and uneasy, afraid of the robbers that were roaming in the increasingly empty city. For protection, Giu strung wire across the windows and doors. When a family next door that had not evacuated invited them to move in, my brothers eagerly accepted.

On the morning of December 19, 1946, the French issued an ultimatum, ordering the Viet Minh to throw down their arms and stop all preparations for war. The Viet Minh rejected it and, from their secret radio station hidden in a cave outside Hanoi, issued a call for national resistance with a succinct message: "The Fatherland is in danger. The hour of fighting has arrived. Let's sacrifice ourselves and fight till the last drop of blood. Let's annihilate the French colonialists! Let's fight to the finish!" The hour of war was secretly scheduled for eight o'clock that evening. That night, Vietnamese workers sabotaged the power station near the central lake. Suddenly, the whole city went dark. This was the signal for the Viet Minh offensive. Their few pieces of artillery opened fire on French positions, and scattered attacks against pockets of French control erupted. From his bed in a house near the outskirts of Hanoi, waiting for the evacuation to the Viet Minh base, my brother-in-law Hau listened to the gunfire and felt elated. Finally, the hour for Vietnam to wash away its humiliation had arrived, he thought. On that same night, fighting broke out in other cities throughout the country, marking the start of the national resistance war.

After the initial attacks in Hanoi, the Viet Minh told the residents to evacuate, and people began to pour out of the city. In all, about

100,000 people—two-thirds of the population—fled, streaming into
the countryside to look for shelter. The day after the outbreak of war,
on December 20, Ho Chi Minh issued an appeal for national resistance,
calling for sacrifices and predicting a long and hard struggle with certain victory at the end. Vietnamese responded en masse to this call to
arms. All over the country hundreds of thousands of people pulled up
stakes to trek into the Viet Minh zone to be part of the war against the
French, and youths volunteered in droves for the army. The flame of
nationalism never burned as bright in the hearts of the people, and the
Vietnamese never united as strongly behind the Viet Minh, as in those
first days and months of the resistance.

At the outset of hostilities, the French moved quickly to take over
key Viet Minh government agencies in Hanoi, but when they finally
stormed the buildings, they found out that most of the Viet Minh leadership had quietly slipped away. The French expected to seal off and
destroy Viet Minh forces in Hanoi within twenty-four hours, and
then—with new reinforcements slated to arrive at the end of the year—
push into the countryside to pacify Tonkin. But like the U.S. Marines
that would take over the city of Hue in the 1968 Tet Offensive, the
French discovered how slow and arduous house-to-house fighting could
be. Even after they managed to secure an area of town, scattered sniper
fire and occasional ambushes continued to harass them. The battle for
Hanoi lasted sixty days, a lot longer than the French had anticipated.
The Viet Minh strategy of pinning down their adversaries worked, and
bought them the time they needed to move their government and troops
into their mountain base.

The day after hostilities flared up, fighting reached my neighborhood. Suddenly, being in the militia was no longer just fun and games
for my brothers Giu and Xuong, no longer just marches and drills with
spears. Their militia unit buried its first casualty when French snipers
shot a squad leader as he climbed up a flagpole to display the Viet Minh
banner. Right after that incident, a messenger arrived with the news
that French troops stationed in the Lanessan Hospital near our house
were getting ready for an assault, supported with lots of tanks. The messenger told the militia unit to withdraw that night, under the cover of
darkness. But the French attack came before nightfall, with airplanes
and tanks strafing the Viet Minh troops' barracks near the dike. After
the bombardment, French paratroopers advanced into the neighborhood
from three directions, with fierce shouts of "*En avant!*" There was no
return fire from the Viet Minh regulars, who had secretly and hastily

withdrawn, leaving the militiamen to fend for themselves. The swift-
ness of the French arrival caught Giu and Xuong by surprise. When
they heard the footsteps of French soldiers approaching, my brothers at
least had the presence of mind to toss their incriminating spears over the
wall. If they had been caught with these weapons, they would have
been shot on the spot as Viet Minh suspects. Then Giu ran and hid
under the stairwell, while Xuong rushed out the back with Mao in tow
to hide in the garden. The French found them cowering in a corner of
the yard, and led them away. They put Xuong in jail, and when they
realized that Mao was crazy, let her go. She wandered in the street until
an acquaintance spotted her and took her to live with his family, sending her back home when my parents returned to Hanoi. Inexplicably, the
soldiers did not enter the house, and Giu and the neighbor's family were
spared.

That night, the Viet Minh sneaked back and opened fire on French
positions. No damage was done, but the attack angered the French. The
next day, they stormed back with German shepherds to search the
neighborhood. The streets echoed with the furious barking of the dogs,
the crunching of French boots, and the angry voices of the soldiers, who
were spoiling for retaliation. The older neighbor suggested to Giu that
it would be best for them to come out and surrender, and not wait for
the French to come in and shoot them. My brother agreed. When he
heard the soldiers at the gate, he came out of hiding and met them. In
fluent French, he said to the commander, "I'm a student at the Lycée
Albert Sarraut. I haven't been able to evacuate with my family. My
father's a mandarin." He thought this string of reassurances might calm
the jittery French. The commander listened attentively and scrutinized
him. Giu was wearing an old discarded military shirt that my mother
had bought for him dirt cheap in an open-air market. But this did not
arouse the commander's suspicion. He seemed persuaded. Suddenly, a
half-naked French soldier rushed in. He looked at Giu, took him for a
Viet Minh, and angrily swung his rifle butt at my brother's temple with
all his strength. The commander raised his arm in the nick of time to
ward off the blow, and instead of splitting Giu's skull—and perhaps
killing or at least blinding him—the rifle butt landed just above his left
eyebrow, cutting him and leaving a permanent scar.

The French took Giu and the neighbor by truck to the Lanessan
Hospital, then serving as a temporary detention center. From then on
until his release, Giu, like the other prisoners, was at the mercy of their
captors, and could live or die at their whim. Prisoners could be alive one

moment and dead the next—shot for being Viet Minh suspects or simply executed in revenge for those killed in Viet Minh attacks. And yet the French could show kindness as well, especially toward those with whom they could empathize, and this was how Giu—and my brother Xuong—survived their imprisonment. The first day he was at the detention center, Giu found out how precarious life could be. One by one the prisoners were interrogated. One of the prisoners, a Viet Minh security police officer, aroused the suspicion of the French. Right after they finished questioning him, they led him away, shoved him against a wall, and shot him in the mouth. When Giu's turn came, the interrogator told him to sit down, and then, pointing at the epaulets of his shirt, asked where his stars were. Giu said he was not a Viet Minh. He repeated the story that my mother had bought the shirt for him at an open-air market. In his youthful innocence, he showed no nervousness or fear. His guileless attitude, and especially his fluent French, delighted the officer. The Frenchman broke out laughing, and terminated the session.

That afternoon, the prisoners were herded into a truck and moved to the Hoa Lo Prison. Since no POW camp had been set up, the French army was holding its captives here temporarily. When food was distributed that day, Giu had his first taste of prison fare: mushy rice, half burned and half uncooked, which came with a salt tablet the size of an aspirin pill. Prisoners who had been captured the day before held out leaves or discarded cans to receive the food—makeshift utensils they had picked up when they were let out into the yard—but Giu had nothing. He was about to wave away his portion in disgust, when the prisoner next to him said, "Hold out your hands and take it. You can give it to me if you don't want it." So Giu cupped his hands and took the mush; to him it looked and felt like vomit. He could not force himself to eat that first day, and gave his portion to his cell mate. The man could not believe his luck. Prisoners were shackled to the two beds that flanked a concrete cistern in the middle of the cell. Whenever he got thirsty, Giu would drag himself to the tank to drink the revolting reddish water, scooping it up with a coconut shell that was also shared by all the cell mates. And yet despite the filth and the lack of food, my brother—who had occasionally suffered bouts of malaria and dysentery in the past—never fell ill during his imprisonment.

The day after his capture, Giu was assigned his first prison duty, working with a group of other prisoners to collect dead bodies from houses in an area that the French had cleared. After a day in prison, he had become a little more clever. As he went through the empty houses, he took a bowl and a pair of chopsticks, and some food supplies, mostly candies and sugar. Eaten in a bowl and with a pair of chopsticks, accompanied with sweets, the mushy rice became more palatable.

The day after this expedition, Giu and a number of POWs were led to a truck. As they clambered on board, they saw a pile of picks and shovels. Many of the POWs broke down and wept. An old man told my brother, "They're taking us to the Lanessan Hospital to bury French soldiers who've died from their wounds. Whenever their comrades die, the guards at the hospital would take it out on us. They won't give us any food or water today. They'll beat us with their rifle butts, and they'll find an excuse to kill at least one of us. Just yesterday, a POW was murdered at the hospital. We're crying, because we know we're going to have a rough time." When they arrived at the hospital, my brother immediately introduced himself to the guard. He thought he might be able to defuse the situation this way. Surprised and mollified, the sentry put him in charge of the digging detail. Encouraged by the soldier's amiable attitude, halfway through their digging, the POWs told Giu to go and ask for water. As the other prisoners watched anxiously, the Frenchman listened to Giu's request, thought about it for a few seconds and then said, "all right." The prisoners did not get anything to eat that day, but at least they got water to drink. They did not get beaten or killed, either. They left in good spirits and thanked my brother. On this and several other occasions, Giu would find himself thrust into the role of go-between and conciliator, defusing tension or cajoling the French into doing some small favors for him and his fellow inmates.

By the end of December, the area up to the central lake and the citadel had been secured, and the French began to shift their focus to the densely populated Vietnamese quarters. These commercial and residential streets were harder to clear, and would remain a stronghold of resistance for several weeks. The task of defending this area fell to a hodgepodge regiment that the Viet Minh patched together with regulars, militiamen, and secret policemen. Viet Minh propaganda celebrated the exploits of this unit, grandly called the Capital Regiment. It captured the imagination of the people and became a symbol of the heroism of the resistance. In fact, the Viet Minh, outnumbered and outgunned, were like grasshoppers kicking at elephants. Their soldiers would open fire on the French and then disappear inside houses whose walls had been pierced through to create a maze like a rabbit warren. In the streets, they built barricades—many of which they rigged with crude mines— to slow down the French half-tracks. The French would dispatch gangs of POWs to clear the barricades with their bare hands. My brothers had to do this so many times they became experts at it. They learned how to take apart each barricade carefully to avoid triggering the mines. And they got used to the deadly fire of the snipers and to the sudden death that occasionally struck those around them. Once, an old prisoner, who was standing right next to Giu, quietly collapsed like a deflated balloon from a sniper's bullet.

By the middle of February, the French had gradually pushed the Viet Minh position back to a smaller and smaller radius. With their food reserves and ammunition almost depleted, the Viet Minh forces decided to withdraw. Under the cover of darkness one night, they slipped away without alerting the French. In the battle for Hanoi, the French inflicted most of the damage, destroying homes in many parts of the city and killing several thousand civilians. With the city under control, French forces then fanned out to pacify the countryside.

Meanwhile in Van Dinh, my siblings and I had the time of our lives. To avoid the fighting, several aunts and uncles also moved to the village with their families. We all shared quarters within the residences built by my great-grandfather and great-granduncle. Although my uncle Trinh had decorated his suite of rooms with vases and urns, some made of beautiful green jade, and an impressive tiger-skin rug, my parents were nearly broke, so our quarters were not as grand. But my brothers and sisters and I did not mind our modest rooms; we were too busy enjoying ourselves to pay attention to how we lived. With so many cousins running loose in the two residences, Van Dinh became like a summer camp for us.

I was only six at the time, and things that worried my parents were beyond me. What preoccupied them the most was the fate of my brothers and sisters stuck in Hanoi. I was too young and too self-absorbed to care. Giu had always acted like a little tyrant with us, and we disliked having him around. Because he was the most senior male descendant, he could impose his will, demand instant compliance, and punish us whenever he thought we had disobeyed him. No matter how badly he treated us, my parents would not try to stop him. Giu was arbitrary and unpredictable, frequently changing his rules to fit his whims. Whenever he was around, we would feel tense and fearful.

With my oldest brother staying in Hanoi, there was no one to spoil our fun. There was no school for my five older brothers and sisters and other cousins, so I had plenty of companions for games. Our great-grandfather's residence became our big playground. The village outside the gate, with its open spaces, provided another great setting for games and adventures. My brothers and male cousins would roam from rice field to rice field looking for birds to shoot with their slingshots. Or they would fish and dredge for clams in the river behind the houses. They would not let me tag along, but within the confines of the compound, there was still plenty for me to explore. To my eyes, it appeared vast, with its many houses, large courtyards, and its mysterious and forbidding ancestral temple, which I was afraid to set foot in for fear of being caught by the ghosts of my ancestors. My older siblings had taken a lot of pleasure in frightening me and other smaller children with the ghost stories they had picked up from the servants, tales that seemed so real to me, especially at night. Van Dinh did not have electricity, and in the evening my parents would burn wicks soaked in dishes of oil. The flames cast yellow circles of light in the darkness and projected scary shadows on the walls. To conserve oil, the wicks were lit only for a short while, and then extinguished, plunging us in darkness. This lugubrious setting fed my febrile imagination, and I scared myself half to death with fantasies of ghostly encounters with my ancestors. The fact that the ghosts were related to me did not give me any comfort. At night, I wrapped myself tightly in my blanket, making sure my toes did not stick out for the ghosts to pull, and always woke up with relief to see that day had come.

The haunted ancestral temple was part of the charm of Van Dinh. In the beginning, my family and other relatives led a rather comfortable life, and everyone felt like they were on a prolonged vacation. We had enough to eat, and the adults spent their time playing cards. My mother had brought along a maid to fetch water from the river, to cook, and to run errands, and a nurse to take care of my younger sister Loan, so we more or less continued our middle-class existence. The rhythm of life in the village was so peaceful that Hanoi and its troubles seemed to belong almost to another country. The village presented an idyllic tableau. Men walked along the narrow pathways between the rice fields, on their way to tend their crops, their spades and hoes propped on their shoulders. Women dressed in brown clothes, their heads wrapped in black turbans or hidden beneath large conical hats, bent over the vegetables or walked to and fro, rhythmically swinging the bamboo baskets suspended at each end of their shoulder poles. Little boys herded water buffaloes, riding on the backs of the animals, or lay in the grass while their charges munched peacefully nearby. A lone heron pecked in the fields and then took off, spreading its large wings in the sunlight. Smoke rose lazily from hundreds of cooking fires into the afternoon sky, as the villagers settled in and waited for their meal. I remember the sounds of the village, too, so different from the noises of Hanoi: the occasional bark-ing of dogs, the crowing of roosters, the floating notes of flutes attached to kites, and the clinking of bowls in baskets—like tinkling music—as the women walked to and from the river where they washed their dish-es after meals.

Gradually, as the fighting in Hanoi dragged on, and the prospect for a quick return dimmed, the mood changed among my relatives, and gloom began to set in. My parents' savings dwindled, and toward the end of our stay in the village, we ran out of money. My father got a loan from a relative, and bought twenty barrels of rice: enough to feed us until we could return to Hanoi, he thought. We now had two meals a day instead of three and rustic dishes to go with our rice. My brothers and sisters and I did not notice the poor fare of vegetables and tiny crabs from the rice fields. We were always hungry, and just gobbled down whatever was served. Some days, my mother fed us only one meal of sticky rice mixed with mung beans, so dense, starchy, and hard to digest that we did not feel hungry for the rest of the day.

The only bad memory I carry from our stay in the village was the itching open sores that covered my body, the result of too many baths with polluted water fetched from the river. Soap would have prevent-ed these skin eruptions, but we did not have any, as there was a short-age of even basic items then. In the village, we learned to make do with whatever substitutes we could find. We boiled pods from the *bo ket* tree to make hair shampoo. We swirled *bo hon* nuts in water to produce a foaming mixture for washing our clothes. For my sores, my mother used a paste of blue dye. I walked around like a tribal warrior for a few days, but my skin did not heal. Then, my mother had a maid bathe me in water in which she had boiled leaves from the Indian lilac tree. The burning sensation made me jump. I felt like alcohol was being rubbed into my open sores. My body was stinging so bad that I struggled free and ran away screaming in pain. The maid grabbed me and, ignoring my cries, pushed me back into the pungent brew. At that same time, my younger sister Loan, who sported boils like tiny volcanoes on her head, was getting shampooed with the same innocent-looking water. She too was screaming and flailing against her tormentor. The cure worked, however, and we forgave our mother.

A few weeks after we left Hanoi, rumors reached us that the fighting in the city had been fierce, that a fire had raged in our neighborhood during the attack, and that a lot of people had been killed. My parents were stunned. As days passed with no word from my brothers, they grew increasingly worried. My father could not sleep at night. Whenever the thought crossed his mind that his children might have burned to death, he would break out in a sweat in the middle of the cold winter night. That Tet, the celebration for the new year was somber, for my parents at least. Instead of feasting on the many traditional delicacies, we had only a single *banh chung*—a rice cake wrapped in banana leaves—and some candies. My parents were despondent, but my siblings and I thought it was great fun.

At that time, Uncle Chinh decided to leave Van Dinh to take refuge in Bac Giang Province, where he had bought rice fields and an orange grove. Before leaving Van Dinh, Uncle Chinh told my father, "Why don't you and your family come with us? We don't have money, but we have the rice fields, and we'll have rice to eat. We'll share whatever the land can produce." But when my father mentioned this to my mother, she rejected the offer. She did not want to move further away from Hanoi, where my brothers and sisters might still be alive. It turned out to be a good decision, because Uncle Chinh got stuck in Bac Giang, which later on became a Viet Minh stronghold. He and his family endured a lot of hardships, and eventually paid dearly for opting to return to his land.

After Tet, my oldest sister Thang also left with her husband and infant son. Hau, now well settled in the Viet Minh mountain base, had come back to fetch his family. Their departure added to my parents' sense of loss. But they did not try to stop them. Toward the Viet Minh, my father and mother were as ambivalent as ever, objecting to their ideas for a social revolution but sympathizing with their struggle to recover national independence. Part of them felt that Thang and Hau were doing the right thing in moving to the Viet Minh zone. Also, in their old-fashioned way, they believed that it was Thang's duty as a wife to follow her husband wherever he happened to go. The night before Thang and Hau were due to leave, my mother prepared food for their journey: boiled rice pressed into dense balls and roasted sesame seeds. The day of their departure was cold and rainy. Thang bundled up her six-month-old son from the winter chill, and my mother daubed some ashes on the baby's forehead to protect him from the dangers of the journey. She also gave Thang a knife wrapped in a piece of cloth as a talisman to ward off accidents. Then Thang and her family boarded the boat docked at the river's edge behind our house and, as it floated away in the freezing morning rain, my sister wept and wondered whether she would ever see her parents and siblings again.

Not long after Thang left, the French arrived. We had heard rumors that the Viet Minh had finally abandoned Hanoi, and we knew that—with the capital secure in their hands—the French could now drive into the countryside to pacify the rest of Tonkin. But we did not know how swiftly they were advancing. We did not realize they were coming our way, that Van Dinh would be in their path, and that the war we had tried to avoid was about to engulf us. We were caught like fish in a net. In February 1947, the French advanced from Phu Ly and the Day River toward us. Even the few Viet Minh guerrillas in the village were unaware of this movement, and were caught by surprise like all of us. That morning, we heard the droning of airplanes in the distance, but did not suspect that an attack was about to take place. When the planes came nearer to the village, and their engine noise grew louder, my parents ordered everyone into the shelter that had been dug in the courtyard. In the panic, I was left behind in one of the rooms. I was so absorbed in my game that I did not notice the eerie silence after everyone had left. Suddenly I heard a strange sound, like the noise made by dry bamboo poles being dragged on the brick pathway, but louder and in angry bursts. At that moment, my brother Luong rushed into the room, pulled me by the arm and yelled: "Run, come with me quickly!"

As we huddled in the shelter with all the other relatives, I remember listening to one of the women chanting a Buddhist prayer. I did not understand the words, but the sound was soothing and hopeful. Suddenly, we saw the flowers of the Indian lilac trees near the house detach from the branches and swirl away, blown in a strong wind—like a colorful stream floating over our heads. I and the other children clapped our hands in delight and cried, "Look, how beautiful, like hundreds of butterflies!" We did not know that the French had set fire to some huts in the village, and that the blaze was creating a powerful draft that was tearing the delicate flowers off the trees. Then we heard the sound of boots on the brick pathway. Luong, who had gone out to see what was happening, came running back in panic with the startling news, "The French are here!" Everyone was incredulous. My father scolded him, "Don't be silly! It can't be true, it must be the Viet Minh. There's no way the French can be here so quickly." My brother insisted, "No, they're French, not Viet Minh. They have long noses and blue eyes!"

We were all frightened and crouched in the shelter. Then we heard footsteps in the courtyard and voices asking, *Où sont ils?* ("Where are they?") My father told my uncles, "If we stay here and they find us, they'll shoot us. Let's come out and meet them." They agreed and together clambered up, with their arms raised. My father said to the soldiers in French, "We are not Viet Minh guerrillas, we're civilians. We're law-abiding citizens." One of the soldiers said, "In that case, you've nothing to fear. You can all come out." So we all climbed out with our arms raised—men, women, and children—still unsure of what might happen next. The troops laughed when they saw the tiny children coming out with their arms raised in surrender. And they laughed even harder when they saw my younger sister Loan, who had her arms in the air while being carried by her maid. Their good humor did not calm anyone's fear. Their reputation for rape and pillage had preceded them, and my mother and the other women were expecting the worst.

The troops taking over the village that day belonged to the Foreign Legion. On the whole, they were more disciplined than those from the Expeditionary Corps, whose soldiers were recruited from Morocco and other French colonies in Africa. Vietnamese had never seen dark-skinned people before, and in general felt very uneasy in their presence, especially that of the black soldiers whose faces bore the criss-crossed scars of tribal rituals. Ignorance of these people and their culture bred fear, so though ordinary Vietnamese feared all French troops, they were most terrified of the Expeditionary Corps.

The Legionnaires began searching our residence, looking for Viet Minh and weapons. They slit our suitcases with their bayonets. Whatever they found that they liked, they would take, like cigarettes and cans of condensed milk, which they pried open with their bayonets. With a knot in her stomach, my mother watched them gulp down the thick and sweet milk hungrily. Hau had bought the milk at a black market on his way to Van Dinh and had given it to us as a gift when he came to fetch Thang and the baby a couple of weeks before. My mother had been saving it for resale, hoping to make a little money. But now, her capital was going down the throat of the Legionnaires. After looking all over the residence, the soldiers led my father and uncles away, and marched them to the dike—to be shot, we thought. My mother and aunts broke down and wept with despair. On the way, my father and uncles passed by my great-granduncle's residence, and saw a severed head stuck on one of the rooftops, with a cigarette dangling jauntily from its lips. The soldiers said mockingly, "*Savez-vous ce que c'est? C'est la tête d'un Viet Minh!*" ("Do you know what it is? It's the head of a Viet Minh!"). My father and uncles, who up to that point were still clinging to the small hope that their lives might be spared, now became convinced they were about to be executed. The decapitated man, it turned out, was actually not a Viet Minh, but the rickshaw puller for one of my aunts. As the French advanced into the village that morning, he had tried to flee by climbing over a wall in the residence. The soldiers took him for a Viet Minh, cut off his head, and displayed it to frighten the villagers.

When they reached the top of the dike, which also served as the main road in and out of the village, my father saw that it had been turned into a staging area crowded with French troops. Airplanes were circling overhead. The soldiers told my father and uncles to sit down and wait. Then they fetched their commander, a captain. With his life and his relatives' lives in the balance, my father summoned all his power of persuasion, explaining his family background and what he had done in the colonial administration. Fortunately, the captain was an educated and reasonable man, a graduate of the Saint Cyr Military Academy—the French equivalent of West Point—and my father was able to convince him that he was not dealing with the Viet Minh or their sympathizers. The captain said, "I'll let you go back to your house, but you'll have to stay there." Then he took them back and toured the ancestral temple. What he saw impressed him and convinced him even more that he was dealing with a mandarin family, and not with Viet Minh guerrillas. He made sure that the soldiers understand no harm should come to us, and even offered to take us back to Hanoi with his troops. But, fearful that we would get caught in the crossfire if the French column came under Viet Minh attack, my father turned down the invitation.

That night all my relatives gathered in the ancestral hall. The gate, doors, and windows were tightly shut. Suddenly, we heard pounding on the gate and, through slits in the doors, saw the glow of light from the fire in the village. When a servant opened the gate, a guerrilla rushed in with his old musket, and said he had to hide from the French. My relatives were terrified, and told him, "You can't stay here. The French have been through here, and they'll be back again. If you stay and they find you, they'll kill us all." In the dark of the night pulsating with the glow of the inferno raging in the village, he appeared to us like the messenger of death, and we stared at him in horror. Suddenly, he turned to leave, and ran toward the river behind the residence. Five minutes later, French soldiers arrived in hot pursuit, and started banging on our doors, shouting, "Come out, all of you!" They were in an angry and foul mood, because they said someone had just fired on their ambulance. The captain was with them, however, and when he recognized us he exclaimed, "*Ce sont les mêmes ce matin!*" ("It's the same people we had this morning!") We were allowed to go back inside, unharmed.

The village was engulfed in flames by this time; burning ashes were falling into our courtyard like a stream of flickering little stars and tongues of fire were leaping into the air and setting the night sky aglow. After heated arguments, my relatives concluded that it would be more dangerous to leave than to stay, so we just waited for morning to come. When it finally did, we found out that the French had left the village, and a calm of sorts had descended over Van Dinh. My relatives agreed that we had to leave. Now that the French were gone, the Viet Minh would surely come back, and they would say that we had sided with the French. We decided to go to Ngo Xa, a neighboring village, and then cross the river to Phung Xa, to relative safety. We hurriedly gathered as many belongings as we could carry and, leaving the precious barrels of rice behind, fled the smoldering village. My younger sister and I were too small to make the trip on foot, so a maid carried us in two wicker baskets slung over a bamboo shoulder pole. As we hurried out of Van Dinh, my parents told us not to look back. But I did, and that was when I saw, behind drifting wisps of smoke, the head on the roof with the cigarette in its lips.

After the French left, the Viet Minh regained control over Van Dinh, which they had used as a transit point for ferrying supplies such as salt into their mountain base. (They had kept their activities so secret that no one in my family knew.) After they retook the village, my family did not go back there again. Ngao, a faithful old servant of the clan, volunteered to stay behind to take care of my great-grandfather's residence and its ancestral temple. Later on, the Viet Minh had my great-grandfather's and my great-granduncle's residences razed to the ground. My parents believed that they had ordered the peasants to tear down these structures to get rid of what they viewed as vestiges of the feudalist class. It could be, however, that the Viet Minh had destroyed the buildings as part of the scorched-earth tactic ordered by Ho Chi Minh to slow down the French advance. No one knew where Ngao went after the houses were demolished until he reappeared in Hanoi later.

From Phung Xa, my family moved on to the small village of Ngoc Dong to put a little more distance between us and the fighting. For the next four months, we would live there as refugees. Cut off from sources of news and with no idea of what was going on, we thought the safest thing would be to stay put, until we could figure out whether it was safe to go back to Hanoi. We did not know how widespread the fighting was, or exactly where it was taking place, and were afraid that if we moved toward the city we might walk right into the eye of the storm. There were plenty of rumors about the war, but no hard facts, so we just stayed in one place, because we believed it was the prudent

thing to do. My siblings and I felt exhausted emotionally and physically by the brush with war, by the loss of the familiar surroundings of Van
Dinh, and by constant privations. Instead of living in a large and pleasant residence, we took refuge at the house of the village chief who was
kind enough to take us in as permanent guests. Although better than the
huts that the peasants lived in, it was still a simple structure with a
thatched roof and dirt floor.

Our family of nine shared one room. At night, we slept on beds that
were made of several hard planks stretched over two wobbly wood
benches. We ate a monotonous diet of rice and watery soups. Some
mornings, our craving for the crusty French bread and butter we used to
have for breakfast in Hanoi was unbearable. We cooked our meals over
a fire fed with straw and drank rainwater caught in a large vat. We took
baths in the little courtyard near the kitchen, with water that my parents had to pay a peasant woman to carry back to the house in buckets
from the river.

At this time, my parents still did not have any news of my brothers
and sisters in Hanoi. Added to this constant worry, they had to figure
out how to keep us fed from day to day. At that moment, our future
looked extremely bleak. Considering my parents' fear of the Viet Minh,
following them into the safe mountain zone was out of the question. And
yet we could not wander around as refugees for much longer, because we
were running out of the money my parents had borrowed from relatives.
The only alternative was to return to Hanoi. But at that point, my parents did not know whether it was safe to go back, or whether we even
had a house to go back to. If, however, we stayed in Ngoc Dong, the
war might overtake us again and force us to flee to another village, further and further away from our home.

The veil of gloom was partially lifted one day when word finally
reached us about my brothers and sisters. One of our relatives had made
her way to Hanoi and, on her return to the village to rejoin her family,
brought my parents some sketchy news. She said that my four siblings
were alive, and that Giu was living with my father's two older sisters,
whose family had not evacuated from the city. We also learned that
Cuc, my dying sister, had been moved by the French from Hanoi's best
hospital—now set aside for the French—to the less well-equipped Bao
Ho Hospital, reserved for the "natives." This hospital, however, was
located closer to my aunts' house so Giu could visit her frequently. My
parents wept with joy. If they had known what my two brothers had
survived, their happiness would have been even greater.

The relative's trip showed that it was now possible to return to

Hanoi with the help of someone who knew how to pick a safe way through the war zone. My father and mother talked things over. My mother said we should try to go back. Since she was worried sick over my brothers and sisters, especially about Cuc, she volunteered to go first. She promised that, if she made it, she would immediately send word to my father, so he could bring the rest of the family. In that chaotic situation, it would be safer for her than my father to go back, because as a man my father would attract the suspicion of both the French and the Viet Minh.

Thus, my mother, a woman who had led a sheltered existence most of her life, set out to travel through a war zone to rejoin her children and comfort her dying daughter. She left Ngoc Dong one day in April 1947. Her traveling party consisted of a guide and fifteen people, including some relatives of my father's: an aunt, a cousin, and her small children. My mother carried a tiny sum of money for the long journey—400 piasters in all—hidden in her hair braid, which she covered with a scarf. The cousin had a few thousand piasters, a gold necklace, and a gold bracelet, which she hid in secret pouches under her children's clothing. It was a dangerous trip. At any point, they could run into robbers who would strip them of their belongings, or the French, or the Viet Minh, who might arrest, and even shoot them. The robbers were on the lookout for city dwellers-turned-refugees, whom they knew usually carried valuables. The French could take the traveling party for a band of Viet Minh and shoot at them as they emerged from the Viet Minh-controlled zone. And the Viet Minh could capture them for deserting the revolution and attempting to go back into French-controlled territory. Not long before, the Viet Minh had caught one of my father's cousins who was returning to Hanoi and thrown him in a prison camp for a month, until his wife managed to get him freed.

The group traveled for several days on foot and by boat, through areas my mother did not recognize. Her body ached from the long hours of walking. At one point, they were stopped by French soldiers, well-armed and ready to shoot, but were let go. When they got near Hanoi, they ran into French soldiers who searched everyone in the party except my mother, for some unexplained reason. The soldiers took all the cash and valuables they found on the other refugees—including the money and gold my father's cousin had so carefully hidden—and calmly ignored the weeping of the children. The loss was a heavy blow for the refugees, who were down to their last resources, but they were lucky that they had not been summarily shot. They finally passed the last French checkpoint and entered the city without incident. Once inside, my mother found out to her dismay that she would need a *laissez-passer*—a safety pass—to circulate in the streets. Without it, she would run the risk of being arrested and jailed by the police. So she had to restrain her burning impatience to go across town to find my brothers and sisters.

After a couple of days at the home of a relative who lived nearby, my mother obtained the pass. She set out on foot, taking most of the day to reach the house of my father's two older sisters where she had heard Giu had been living since he was released by the French. A former classmate of Giu's had seen him being transported one day in a truck with other prisoners and had told his father. Then, this man, who would later on become the governor of Tonkin, had interceded with the French, who let Giu go. Giu was now working in a pharmacy, one of the few shops that were beginning to open their doors as more and more residents returned, to earn his own way.

My mother cried with relief when she saw him. Immediately, however, her mind turned to the fate of Xuong, Mao, and Cuc. My aunts reassured her that my other siblings were doing as well as could be expected under the circumstances. Xuong, independent and adventurous, was living by himself. Right after his arrest, he had to clear roadblocks and pick up rotten corpses for burial like the other prisoners. After only one week, he managed to win the trust of his captors. They assigned him to a prison gang detailed to clean a hospital, and then after three months they set him free. Being resourceful, Xuong managed to get himself hired by a French captain, serving as his orderly in exchange for room and board (including, to Xuong's delight, unlimited access to cigarettes and wine) and a small salary. When the captain left with his unit, Xuong, displaying his survival skill, found employment in a liquor store at a time when jobs were extremely scarce in a still moribund city. As for Mao, she was still living at the house of the acquaintance who had found her wandering in the street after French soldiers had let her go. My younger sister Cuc was also still at the hospital. Her disease, however, was reaching the final stage. It had eaten into her spine and paralyzed her. She was in constant pain, with pus oozing out of her inflamed backbone. I still remember what a stoic girl she was. Before she was hospitalized, once in a while I would drop into her room at our house in Hanoi for brief visits, and was amazed at how she never cried or complained. Since it was getting late, my mother did not dare to venture out in the deserted streets to visit Cuc. The next day my mother set out on foot to find her. She cried, filled with guilt and pity, when she saw her emaciated child on the hospital bed, being tended by the maid who had been by her side during the months our family was gone. In pain, Cuc just stared at her with sad eyes, and did not utter a sound.

Once settled in Hanoi, my mother sent word to my father that it was safe to return. Her message reached him one day in June, and he immediately rented a boat to take us back to Hanoi. We kept quiet about our plan to avoid alerting the Viet Minh. After traveling a day and a half, we landed at a village close to Hanoi where we disembarked and spent the night. The next morning, we set out on foot but did not get beyond the village market. A group of Viet Minh barred the way and would not less us pass. Luckily, the villager who had given us shelter knew these Viet Minh and got us through their checkpoint. As we entered Hanoi, we saw burned-out shells of houses, broken glass, twisted metal, crumbled walls, and collapsed roofs.

My mother and Giu were waiting when we reached my aunts' house. We cried, happy to be together again and relieved that we were all safe and that we had left behind the fighting in the countryside. I must have collapsed after the emotional reunion and slept for hours. I only remember waking up and finding myself in a nice bed, in a nice room, in a nice and cool house, and then being fed an edible meal for the first time in weeks. Since our old neighborhood was still deserted and insecure, my parents did not want to go back to our old home. We moved into a house owned by some acquaintances of my aunts who were still somewhere in the countryside.

At this time, the maid who had been at Cuc's bedside quit to marry a nurse she had met at the hospital. My mother began to keep permanent vigil over Cuc in the room that my sister shared with another patient. The hospital was almost empty, as most of the city's population was still gone. At night, it was deserted and disturbingly quiet. About a month after my mother moved in with her, Cuc was finally released from the disease that had tormented her for years. The night she died, my mother bathed her tenderly and carefully with a washcloth, making several trips to get water from a tap in the deserted yard, as an owl—the bird of death in Vietnamese belief—hooted in the dark. Then my mother put some fresh clothes on my sister and pulled down the mosquito netting over her bed. When all that was done, my mother went and sat down in a chair outside on the veranda and waited for morning to come. As dawn broke, she went looking for the nurse on duty and told her the news. The nurse had my sister moved to the hospital's mortuary. My mother asked that Cuc be placed in a private room there as a special favor. But when she returned later with the funerary clothes, she found my sister in a stuffy room with four or five grotesque corpses: people who had died alone, contorted in pain, without anyone to straighten out their limbs before rigor mortis set in. From that day onward, my mother became very afraid of dying alone, unattended—like the twisted corpses in that hellish room. Cuc was buried in a lot nearby; with the city still not completely secure, my parents did not dare to travel very far. Later on, after things returned to normal, she was disinterred and buried in a proper resting place in a cemetery.

With life not yet restored to normal, there were very few jobs available, and my father now faced the problem of finding employment to support his large family. To tide us over, my mother had to borrow a small sum of money from one of her sisters, a loan she did not know how she was going to pay back. Our life was hard, and we could barely afford food. My older brother Luong, who was only fourteen, shopped at an impromptu market that had sprung up in a safer area of town near the central lake, and cooked for the family. We ate mostly rice, corn, soup, and sometimes bean sprouts or bean curd, never meat. Once in a while, Giu or Xuong, who were still working at their jobs, would bring back a can of condensed milk as a special treat.

One day my father ran into Dr. Dang Huu Chi, an old friend, who had been appointed by the French as chairman of the Hoi Dong An Dan—Council to Calm and Resettle the Population—that was about to be created in Haiphong. Mr. Chi took my father to see some old French acquaintances such as Mr. Leroy, a former *résident* of Nam Dinh Province where my father had served. Mr. Leroy was now holding a high position in the recreated colonial administration, and was delighted to see my father, whose competence he admired. The government was desperately short of staff, and hired practically any former employee who made it back to Hanoi and showed up for work. Mr. Leroy offered my father the position of vice-chairman of the council in Haiphong, serving as assistant to Dr. Chi.

My father at first turned down the offer, fearing that if he took this post, the Viet Minh would retaliate and harm his older brother, who was still living in their zone. He asked Mr. Leroy to give him a lower position—even a clerical job would do. But Mr. Leroy said anything less than the post of vice-chairman of the Haiphong council would be beneath him and a waste of his talent. My father went to see Dr. Chi to talk things over and his friend persuaded him that my uncle would be all right. With no other viable alternative, my father reluctantly decided to take the offer, and went back to see Mr. Leroy. The next day, he left for Haiphong with Dr. Chi, while the rest of the family stayed in Hanoi until he could send for us. With this appointment, a new phase began for us: a generally happy period for me and my brothers and sisters, but a trying one for my father.

8

Into the Resistance Zone

The boat drifted in the misty rain, buffeted now and then by the gusts of cold air that Arctic currents sweeping down from Siberia across China had brought into Tonkin. Beneath the woven bamboo canopy, Thang hugged her six-month-old son, trying to keep him warm, and watched the banks slip by. Under the low and gray winter sky, the river looked like lead. Nothing was stirring as people and animals burrowed in their shelters to keep out of the bitter and penetrating winter cold and *crachin*—fine drizzle— that falls nonstop and shrouds Tonkin in a depressing mist from February to March. She and Hau were traveling northward into the resistance base, away from the war-torn delta. For a day and a night, the boat went through areas she had never seen before. They were not stopping anywhere to get provisions, so the pressed rice balls and roasted sesame seeds my mother had given them before their departure would have to last for this leg of the trip. After the long ride, they disembarked in Son Tay, where they changed boats, and continued on to Trung Ha. From there, they hired a horse-drawn cart and made their way to Phu Tho city, in the midlands province where my father had served as a district magistrate. Hau took them to the house of one of his relatives for a brief rest, where they bathed, changed clothes, and did their laundry, drying the wet clothes by a fire while the rain drenched the outside. The baby's diaper rash had gotten worse, but there was no medication for it. Whenever he got too cranky, Thang would nurse him to calm him down.

My sister's excitement about following the resistance now gave way to weariness. When Hau had asked her in Van Dinh to go with him into the Viet Bac mountain base, she had simply said, "Fine." The French were here, she thought, and they had to be driven out. Joining the resistance was the right thing to do. Her husband had decided to take part, and so she would just go with him and be part of it too. Victory or defeat—the outcome did not worry her. Fighting the French was something that had to be done, regardless of how it would end. She did not even bother to ask Hau what she could expect to find in the base, how they were going to get there, what they would do once they got there, and how long he thought they were going to stay. The journey turned out to be harder than she had imagined, and the baby's condition worried her, yet she did not complain. Hau had made the trip back and forth from the base to Van Dinh a couple of times, so he was used to the rigors of the journey. The Viet Minh had sabotaged railways and roads to slow down the French advance. The only way to get around was to travel by boat, cart, bicycle, or, most frequently, on foot. Trips that should have taken a day or two now took a week. Hau had become resigned to the inconveniences of travel, but the enthusiasm he had felt during the first days of the resistance was beginning to dampen. He tried to fight off weariness, sadness, and a nagging worry about the future. As the war spread and the scorched-earth tactic took its toll, he had seen settlements set ablaze, towns left in ruins, and frantic refugees streaming into the countryside to find shelter. The destruction and the suffering undermined his resolve. Also, the Viet Minh's weakness in the face of French military might made him wonder whether the resistance would survive.

From Phu Tho, my sister and her husband set off on foot for the next leg of the trip. They ate whatever they could buy in shacks along the way. Then they boarded another boat to cross into Tuyen Quang Province within the Viet Minh resistance zone. When they docked, Hau said, "We're almost there!" His words lifted the weariness off Thang's shoulders. Finally, she could look forward to settling down— having a roof over their heads and getting in from the endless rain and the cold that chilled her to the bone. They made their way to an old French coffee plantation, now under Viet Minh management. The cadre in charge welcomed them and told my sister, "You've made it all the way from Van Dinh, carrying your baby. That's quite a feat for a pampered mandarin's daughter." Thang smiled in reply. Marriage, motherhood, and war had not changed her, and often she still went through a whole day without saying a word. The manager put her family in a room of the old two-story villa with four other families that eventually would move into the forest base with her. This was malaria country. All the windows were covered with mesh screens to keep out the mosquitoes. By six in the evening, everyone would huddle indoors with the screens tightly shut. After dusk, other unwelcome visitors also appeared. Tigers would come down from the forest, leaving footprints the size of soup bowls around the coffee plants. Here, someone told Thang about a local remedy for the baby's diaper rash: a black paste that cured it right away although it left a sooty mess on his clothes. The cough that had been bothering him also went away, and he began nursing and sleeping.

Before war broke out, the Viet Minh had set up two bases in Tonkin, one in the northeast near the Chinese border and one south of the Red River Delta. The one in the northeast, called the Viet Bac, included six provinces spread over 10,000 square miles. The other one covered the hilly and jungly areas of Thanh Hoa, Nghe An, and Ha Tinh—the provinces bordering on the sea that my ancestors had crossed in their journey to Van Dinh. Other bases also existed in the central and southern parts of the country, but the Viet Bac was the best prepared and the most important. Throughout the war, it would serve as the nerve center of the resistance and as the seat of the Viet Minh government-in-exile. Ho Chi Minh and his key lieutenants would direct the war from here until the final climactic battle of Dien Bien Phu. The Viet Bac, in fact, covered the same ground favored by rebels and bandits over the centuries, because its mountainous terrain, limestone peaks and caves, and forested hills provided good cover and made the base easily defensible.

Beginning in March 1947, as French troops fanned out to pacify the

delta, Viet Minh agencies and their employees retreated into the Viet
Bac. At the same time, thousands of civilians also moved into the base,
choosing to live under the Viet Minh rather than under the French, or
simply trying to get as far as possible from the fighting in the delta.
Among the refugees was a contingent of intellectuals, writers, singers,
musicians, actors, and actresses who had trekked into the Viet Minh
zone to support the resistance. In the Viet Bac, government agencies
scattered in the forest to avoid detection, and would change locations
once in a while to throw the French off their track. The employees lived
in huts spread among the various hill tribes that inhabited the area,
whose languages, customs, and cultures shared little in common with
their own. The Viet Minh had successfully wooed these tribes very
early on. In fact, the mountain people provided the initial recruits for
the Viet Minh army, and one of their leaders, Chu Van Tan, rose to
become a famous general. Tribal support for the Viet Minh, though
widespread, was far from being total, however, and the French were
also able to recruit allies among these diverse groups.

Knowing that they would be cut off from supplies in the delta for a
long time, the Viet Minh had stockpiled rice, salt, and cloth in the base.
Before leaving the lowlands for the mountains, they had also dismantled
machinery they had taken from shops in the delta and reassembled the
equipment in the forest. Small factories sprang up in caves, and using
raw materials that had been painstakingly carried into the forest, produced soap, matches, cloth, paper, and a few other basic goods. Medical
equipment was also carted into the base, along with a small quantity of
weapons and ammunition. Makeshift workshops were set up to repair
weapons and produce a few small firearms. But with 30,000 soldiers
now to equip, General Vo Nguyen Giap—the Viet Minh commander—
did not have enough weapons for his men. The shortage was so acute
that several soldiers had to share a rifle. In some units, the ratio was
twelve men to a rifle.

Employees of the government-in-exile settled under the canopy of
trees in the forest. They sorely missed things they had taken for granted, such as electricity and running water. Everything was scarce, from
cloth to soap to matches. But at the beginning when enthusiasm was at
its peak and the hardships had not taken their toll, most of them did not
mind. Initially, they found that having their life reduced to the barest
necessities actually had its advantages. They felt liberated from the
material worries and personal ambitions that used to dog them in the
cities. They poked fun at their dramatic transformation from city residents to forest dwellers and laughed at themselves. Their biggest fanta-

sy was to visit Bac Can, the capital of the resistance, to stroll among its modest coffee shops, restaurants, bazaars, and bookstores, and to get light by simply flicking a switch and water by simply turning on a tap. Their only aspiration was to win the war quickly.

Thang and Hau would end up in the same primitive conditions. After a few months, as a French attack appeared imminent, they and the four other families that had settled down at the plantation retreated into the forest, about twenty kilometers away. The weather was unstable. One moment, the rain would soak them, and then the sun would come out and steam their wet clothes dry. The poor baby who was repeatedly turned into a soggy bundle became lifeless, his small body burning with fever. No one could tell Thang what was wrong with him and they had no medication. Fortunately, they found a Vietnamese who had been living in the forest for many years and had learned from the local Tho tribe how to use the various herbs that grew in the area. He gathered some bark and leaves, and boiled them to make an infusion. Each day, Thang would drink a huge bowl of the medicine, and pass it to the baby through her milk. The cure worked, and the baby recovered.

Thang and Hau and the other four families settled in a forest clearing, where they shared a long house on stilts—similar to those used by the Tho tribe—that had been built for them. A rickety ladder led up into the hut. They cooked their food in a small area located on the porch near the ladder, setting their pots over a fire in a three-by-three-foot bamboo frame with sides that were six inches tall and a bottom covered with a thick layer of packed dirt to insulate the bamboo floor from the flames. Chickens foraged and slept underneath the house. The hut and the narrow strip of land around it formed the only open space. Beyond the fringe was the forbidding forest, where boars, bears, and tigers roamed among the trees. At night, the ladder had to be pulled up to keep tigers from climbing in. Thang did not like the forest after dark. It seemed mysterious and menacing, its impenetrable mass pressing down on the tiny hut. In the daylight, the forest did not look so threatening and Thang would stand by a window, her baby in her arms, listening to the bird whose strange cry sounded like "*Bat co troi cot*," or "Catch her and tie her to a stake," or to the pleasant twinkling of bells that the local people strung around the necks of their buffaloes when they let them graze in the forest. Thang liked the rhythm of life here and enjoyed watching the people go about their business, tending to their animals and trees, or dropping seeds into holes in the soil fertilized with the ashes of the trees they had burned down to clear land for planting.

In that long house, Thang had her first taste of what the communists,

who secretly controlled the Viet Minh, called the collective, or communal, life. In the mountain base, everyone had to set aside their own
wants and learn to live in harmony with others. The common good of
the collective had priority over everything else. My sister, who never
paid much attention to her own needs, found the constant compromises
easy to accept. Thang's group of five families lived in a dormitory-like
setting and ate together. Each family's living space was confined to a
reed mat spread on the bamboo floor. Not even a curtain separated one
mat from the ones next to it. In another setting, the close quarters could
have created strains, but among these families bound by a common goal,
the arrangement seemed to encourage socializing and bantering. There
was much laughter, and the good humor that prevailed—as well as the
fact that they were sharing the hardships together—made the challenge
of their stay in the forest less formidable. Besides, they were then intoxicated with the dream of winning freedom for their country, and this initial enthusiasm allowed them to ignore their privations. It was a bond
Thang would remember for the rest of her life.

For bathing and washing, the families went down to the clear stream
that flowed nearby. The men had rigged up a series of bamboo tubes to
carry water from the stream into the hut for washing food and dishes
and for drinking and cooking. Each person had only one change of clothing. All the clothes were dyed either brown or indigo blue, to blend in
with the surroundings and make the wearers less visible to French airplanes. Hau's spare outfit was made by Thang, dyed and sewn with the
help of the women in the group. Sewing was not one of her skills, so the
pants and shirt were lopsided and lumpy. But Hau did not criticize her
clumsy work, and instead cherished his brown outfit. He wore it
throughout the war. Thang kept it for years after they returned to Hanoi
in 1954. Sometimes, in later years, she would take it out of the dresser
and examine it with misty eyes.

In that forest clearing, the four cadres and their wives would become
like a family to Thang, replacing the one she had left in Van Dinh. She
tends to look back on this phase with nostalgia now, and thinks of it as
the happiest period of her life in the resistance zone. One of the wives
was a graduate from Thang's secondary girl school in Hanoi. Of the five
women, only one was involved in Viet Minh activities. Revolution was
primarily seen as a man's work, and women tended to do things like
sewing flags and writing slogans on banners. A higher level of participation would be working in the Women's Association to encourage
women to support the resistance, but "supporting" usually meant stand-

ing behind husbands and sons, taking care of their families so the men could focus their attention and energy on the fight against the French, or serving as porters to carry weapons and supplies for the army.

The women who had small children spent all their time taking care of them, and were spared any work except cooking and cleaning up. If they were not summoned away, the men focused their energy on finding food to supplement the rice provided by the government. They cleared some land to grow vegetables and raise chickens for eggs. They also fished for shrimp in the stream, and foraged for wild bamboo shoots and edible leaves in the forest. Hau turned out to have a knack for locating the tender shoots, and was crowned champion bamboo shoot gatherer. The active part of each day was short. By six o'clock each family had to retire to their reed mats and pull down the nets to keep from being bit-ten by mosquitoes. But no one could be careful enough. In spite of all the precautions, Thang, Hau, and the baby all came down with malaria.

With thousands of displaced civilians, employees, and soldiers to feed, the Viet Minh faced the enormous task of producing enough food for everyone. Supplies from the delta were no longer available, because of the distance and also because this region—Tonkin's traditional food basket—was now under French control. To avert a crisis, the govern-ment urgently asked everyone—soldiers, government employees, teach-ers, students, civilians—to grow food and become self-sufficient. Producing food became part of the fight to liberate the country.

But the urban refugees did not know what to plant and how to grow it, especially since the soil and climate of the highlands and midlands were different from those with which they were familiar in the delta. Hau was one of a handful of people who had enough technical know-how to help. He became a consultant. Viet Minh agencies would ask him to come and give advice on what they could grow. Part of his job was to go to different regions to collect the best seeds, and then make the rounds of the government offices and towns to hand them out and teach the displaced people how to plant them. His job was also to teach peasants to grow new or better crops so they could produce more food. Throughout the resistance, food would remain as critical as weapons for the Viet Minh. When the French entered Viet Minh villages, they would destroy rice stockpiles or kill draft animals used for ploughing. When the rice ripened in the fields, they would launch operations to disrupt the harvest. So, with food remaining at the heart of the struggle for survival, Hau never tired of his work. Growing things for him took on a meaning that went beyond mere professional satisfaction. As he tramped across the Viet Minh zone, he felt like a true combatant in the fight for independence.

Traveling through the forest was not for the faint-hearted. Hau carried an old musket to protect himself against wild beasts. He only had to use it a couple of times, once when he scared off a bear. He was never attacked, but he knew of a cadre who got mauled and disfigured. Hau saw a tiger once, from a distance, but the animal left him alone. The forest teemed with fowl and wild boars, but being a poor shot, Hau never managed to bag one for dinner. Hau also carried a machete, which he used to hack his way through thick forest undergrowth. The dense foliage harbored another danger: snakes. There were king cobras and vipers, the most lethal of which was the small green snake that could kill a water buffalo with just one dose of its poison. Hau had a phobia about snakes, but had to forget his fear and forge ahead. Once in a while, he would see a snake crawling across the trail. He would stop and wait for it to disappear before continuing on his way. Snakes could be found in houses, too, and Hau once saw a huge black one chasing squealing rats in the rafters of a hut where he was staying. But *bo cho*, similar to ticks, were the worst affliction by far. They drove Hau crazy. They hid in his clothes and snuggled up in the moist and warm parts of his body, like his arm pits and the hollow of his back . Each bite made him jump with pain. The only way to kill them was to throw them into a fire.

As if these dangers and inconveniences were not enough, Hau had to worry about French airplanes as well. At the beginning of the war, the French had complete control of the skies. Knowing that the Viet Minh did not have the weapons to bring them down, French reconnaissance planes sometimes would descend to low altitudes to fire on people walking along a road or a dirt path in the Viet Minh zone if they suspected them of being cadres, porters, or guerrillas. Not being able to hear well, Hau could not tell when planes were approaching to take cover. The forest paths were well hidden by trees, but in the exposed lowlands he could be spotted by them. He got caught in so many strafings that he lost count. Once he was riding his bicycle along the top of a dike when an airplane appeared, firing on the road as it bore straight toward him. He jumped off his bike and instinctively raised his knapsack to his head as the only protection he had. But none of the bullets found its mark. Another time, he kept on pedaling until some guerrillas dashed out of nowhere, grabbed him, and pulled him into a bush. Afterward, they said he had to be an enemy agent who had deliberately stayed in the open to send a secret signal to the plane. They searched him to see whether he had anything that could send a signal—like a mirror—before they let him go.

Of all the attacks, he remembered best the airborne assault the French launched against the Viet Minh base in the autumn of 1947. The weather was favorable for their operation. The monsoon rains had ended and given way to the dry season, the interval before the cold set in and before the *crachin* began. With this huge operation, the French command thought it could wipe out the Viet Minh by capturing their leaders and destroying their regular army in one fell swoop. For a month, a 15,000-strong force consisting of ground troops, fighter planes, armored carriers, and shipborne battalions attacked the base in a huge pincer movement. At dawn on the first day of the operation, over a thousand paratroopers landed in Bac Can, the capital of the resistance, and two other key market towns, hoping to catch Viet Minh leaders by surprise. But the Viet Minh were clever enough not to congregate in the cities, and had instead scattered into different parts of the forest near the towns. They had also made preparations for a quick evacuation if necessary. Each site was located near trails that would allow escape in several directions. At the first hint of trouble, they would destroy sensitive documents and then leave quickly. Hau had gone to Bac Can the night before the French assault to visit an older brother employed in the Finance Ministry. The next morning he left on his bicycle. Not long after he was gone, the paratroopers began their attack. A few miles away, Hau could see the planes and parachutes that trailed beneath them like giant umbrellas. Most of the Viet Minh in the vicinity, including Hau's brother, escaped by following one of several trails radiating into the forested hills.

At the same time that planes were dropping troops, another column was making its way into the base on ships sailing up a tributary of the Red River. That evening, my sister was sitting in the hut, listening to the men hammering nails into a makeshift coffin to bury one of the cadres who had died, when they learned that the French had landed at Binh Ca, not far from their hideout. The group, now larger with the arrival of a few more men, hurriedly buried the cadre and fled. Before leaving, they plugged up their ears with cotton balls and tied up their sleeves and pant legs to keep the tiny forest leeches from crawling inside to suck their blood. They also smeared soap on their exposed ankles, so they could brush the leeches off quickly. Then, they plunged into the dark forest. A guide with a feeble light strapped to his head led them along narrow trails deeper into the forest. When Thang's arms began to ache from holding the baby, the guide took him into his. Once in a while, they would stop for a quick rest and to pick out the leeches clinging to their clothes and shoes.

The group walked silently for a long time. They must have covered several kilometers in the dark before they arrived in a mountain settlement that would serve as their temporary quarters for a while. They scattered into the huts of the local people, each family going into a different house. When Thang entered the hut assigned to her, she found her former teacher from the Dong Khanh school living there. A secret sympathizer in the days when she was teaching in Hanoi, she was now a leader in the Women's Association. The brief stay in this small settlement of huts spread among the trees was a pleasant respite. The days passed peacefully.

Thang's group did not know it at the time but Viet Minh troops had scored a victory of sorts at Binh Ca. A band of soldiers, dug into foxholes and armed only with two machine guns, fired on the French landing craft making their way up the Lo River, and then moved along the shore to fire at them again as they advanced further into Viet Minh territory. They managed to sink a craft or two and damage a couple of others. It was not much of a battle, but the Viet Minh mobilized their propaganda machine to turn this small encounter into a great fight and a resounding triumph. Well-known composers wrote songs to glorify what was now referred to as the "Lo River Victory," while poets, painters, and novelists did their part to praise the heroism of the Viet Minh fighters. At the same time, photographs of "victories" in other "battles"—including one of French nurses pleading for mercy when they were captured after their truck was blown up by a mine—were distributed among Viet Minh agencies. Doubts of being able to stand up to the French onslaught now gave way to hope that final victory was possible. In the gloomy forest, the news of these successes was like a bright ray of hope for Thang and Hau and their comrades. It helped them to believe that their sacrifices would not be in vain.

During the resistance, propaganda would play an important role in sustaining morale among Viet Minh supporters. With some of the country's best artists working for them, Viet Minh propaganda was very skillful. Music, in particular, would become the most effective tool in inspiring the peasants—the bulwark of the Viet Minh—and the soldiers who came from their ranks. Composers would write songs based on traditional folk music for traveling troupes to spread in the countryside and among the army units to reinforce hatred for the French and determination to continue the fight. Simple plays, some using the old *cheo* opera format, were also popular among the peasants and the soldiers. Theater troupes would go from village to village, and unit to unit, to perform skits and plays, in the tradition of the itinerant actors of the past.

After a brief stay in the small settlement, with the French operation still in full swing, Thang's group fled again. Every time they heard the rumor that the French were in the vicinity, they would move on. They lived on the run for as long as the attacks lasted. In early November, the French command finally called off the operation. The French had failed to capture the Viet Minh leadership and destroy their regular army, but managed to capture a number of towns, including Bac Can, and other key points. These were costly to hold, however, because they tied down troops in defensive enclaves. Between these pockets of enemy control, the Viet Minh continued to slip through. A few weeks later, toward the end of November, the French launched another large operation into Thai Nguyen and Tuyen Quang provinces, hoping to engage some of the Viet Minh's best units in set-piece battles and wipe them out. But the Viet Minh knew it would be suicidal for them to stand and fight against overwhelming odds, and simply melted away, allowing the French to capture some weapons and a few supply depots. Once the French left, the Viet Minh came back. This war without battle lines frustrated the French, who would keep looking for the one big conventional battle where they could smash the Viet Minh army once and for all.

It was to this Viet Minh army that my cousin Luc aspired to join when he sneaked out of his house in 1945. He was only sixteen years old. Like my sister Thang, he had no idea what he was getting himself into, and like her he was determined to take whatever came—not out of a sense of duty, but out of youthful bravado. When he got to the Viet Minh base, he finally had a taste of what it was really like. At home, he had plenty of rice to eat and tasty dishes to go with it. But here in the forest, in what was grandly called the Bac Son Military Training School, he had only two bowls of rice twice a day and some watery soup made with shreds of a banana tree trunk; on good days there were bits of pork. A few months after he joined, Luc came down with malaria, his first brush with this terrible disease. He did not know what had hit him. There was no medical care and no drugs at the makeshift school due to shortages after World War II and the Viet Minh's inability to produce their own in the base. Local tribesmen tried to treat him with traditional remedies, including a broth made with a wild boar's penis, but Luc stayed as sick as ever. When his condition got worse, his unit put him in a field hospital staffed with first-year medical students who knew nothing about health care. At first they mistakenly treated him for tuberculosis, but when he almost died, the staff decided to move him to a better hospital in Thai Nguyen. There, his disease was correctly diagnosed, and he received a treatment of quinine, which cured him. A few months later, he was sent to attend the Tran Quoc Tuan Military Academy.

This school had been set up in May 1946 to produce the officers that the Viet Minh badly needed. The training was unsophisticated and rudimentary, and was culled from French, Japanese, and Chinese manuals. It also included a heavy dose of political indoctrination. The aim was to turn out officers who not only knew basic combat tactics, but also were fervently committed to what the Viet Minh called their "just cause." As in every Viet Minh organization, real control was in the hands of a political cadre, a member of the Communist Party that had gone underground after the Viet Minh took power in August 1945. Most of the trainees were students—young, ardent, and impressionable. Life in the academy was no better than what Luc had experienced at the beginning. The Viet Minh at this time were receiving no support from the Soviet Union or the Chinese Communists, who were still battling their Kuomingtang foes. The Viet Minh army lacked everything— weapons, ammunition, clothes, shoes, and food. Luc was given an old musket and eight cartridges to use—not in training, but only in a combat situation. If he used up all eight bullets, he would not be resupplied. "Each bullet should kill an enemy soldier" was the slogan drilled into the recruits.

For food, the Viet Minh soldiers had to depend on the local population to survive. Each day, each family would put a handful of rice in a little jar. At the end of a week or a month, they would take the jar to the Viet Minh and contribute the rice to feed the army. Food was extremely scarce, and like before, Luc had two bowls of rice per meal and some watery soup. Sometimes, the meager ration was reduced to one gram of rice per day. Other times, no rice was available, and the trainees would have to dig up manioc, which was considered all right as a snack but a poor substitute for rice, or roots to eat.

At mealtime, the recruits would line up in ranks of six, and then sit down to eat six to a group. Before they began eating, one would be picked as the leader with the job of dishing out two bowls per person.

Another would be chosen for the next meal and so on to make sure that the food was shared equally. They made their own eating utensils, using bamboo trees that they sawed into sections, each of which is naturally separated into a sealed compartment. The ones near the root, each about five centimeters tall, served as bowls. Soup was served in a long section that had been cut in half lengthwise and made into a trough. Serving spoons and chopsticks were also fashioned out of bamboo. Bamboo was used to make other things, such as baskets for serving rice, knapsacks, and helmets. Canteens were nothing more than sections of bamboo carried on a string.

There were no uniforms for the recruits. Like soldiers in the entire Viet Minh army, they wore whatever they had managed to bring from home. Those that did not have shoes or could not afford to buy rubber sandals went barefoot, even in the depths of winter. As the Viet Minh got more organized, they would each receive one set of clothes. Once a month, they would pile up the clothes that needed patching, and local volunteers would come into the camp to pick them up for mending. In the summer, they would go down to the stream to bathe and wash their garments. Then they would set the clothes out to dry on rocks in the sun, while they hid stark naked in the bushes to avoid being seen by local people who might happen to pass through. While they waited, most of their lice also waited patiently for the clothes to dry; only a few got disturbed enough to crawl out onto the rocks. Whenever they bathed, they would post a sentry to keep watch and turn away people—especially young girls—heading in their direction, with the admonition, "You can't go that way because we're protecting a military secret." If he saw someone approach, the sentry was also supposed to give the alarm. But the early warning system was not fool-proof. One time, the guard left his post. Suddenly, Luc and his comrades heard the sound of women's voices. When they looked up, they saw a group of young girls on their way back from the market. In panic, Luc and his friends lowered themselves into the water, which was crystal-clear and only knee-deep, and lay down flat on their bellies. Speaking in their tribal dialect, the girls teased them, "What are you doing?" The trainees joked, "Can't you tell? We're looking for fish."

Another time, they were bathing naked late one summer afternoon when they saw General Vo Nguyen Giap, the Viet Minh commander, riding on a horse along the dirt path that was about two meters from the stream. Giap was behind another man, who wore a hat and a kerchief tied over the lower half of his face. Usually, Giap, as the supreme commander, would be at the head of a traveling party. But that afternoon, he was riding behind the other man and talking to him in a very deferential manner. The trainees guessed that the other man must be Ho Chi Minh himself. It was too late for them to take cover or to run away, so they all squatted down, with their hands cupped strategically over their genitals. In concert, they greeted the man who was now called Uncle Ho by everyone: "Good afternoon, Uncle!" Ho asked, "What are you doing?" And they replied, "We're taking a bath." The exchange, though brief and banal, was special to them; for the first time they had met the leader whom they revered as a man of integrity, totally committed to freeing his people and his country. The Viet Minh triumph would owe much to their success in turning Ho into a beloved figure among their followers, a man filled with virtue and patriotism who was at the same time like a benevolent family member.

The setting of the military academy was similar to the one in Thang's forest clearing. Luc and the other trainees lived in huts made with wood poles and bamboo and set on stilts. In the middle of each hut was the cooking area where a fire was kept going at all hours in a wood frame heavily lined with packed dirt. On cold days, the trainees liked to gather around this hearth to keep warm. At night, they would roast manioc roots by wrapping them in a thick layer of parchment and then burying them under the hot ashes. By the time the paper had burned away, the manioc would be cooked to the right degree of doneness. Whoever had sentry duty would snack on the manioc, and then before going out to stand guard he would put a few more tubers in the ashes so that the sentry relieving him would also have something to eat. Enjoying the hot manioc by the light of the dancing flames, as his comrades lay asleep on the floor around him, is one of many pleasant memories of the resistance for Luc. In winter, a sentry would also get the most precious possession the unit had: a lightly padded and quilted jacket, reserved only for those on guard duty.

Although they were living in a malaria-infested zone, Luc and his comrades had no mosquito netting, which was why so many recruits came down with the disease. In winter, they got covers that were either horse blankets—the warmest and the most coveted ones—or blankets woven with rush or jute. These as well as the quilted jackets had been collected by the government from the peasants—two of each per village—and distributed to the army. Luc's unit of ten had three blankets. At night, they had to give one to the sentry, leaving the remaining two to be shared by nine. To fit under the cover, they slept close to each other, on their sides, like nestled spoons. Whenever one of them wanted to turn over, he would shout, "Turn!" and everyone would move in unison. They took turns sleeping on the colder edges. This willingness to share allowed them to live in harmony. There was no distinction between recruits, foot soldiers, and officers. They all had the same daily food ration and the same stipend of about twenty cents per month, not even enough to buy cigarettes or Vietnamese tobacco. Everyone in Luc's unit loved to smoke, so they pooled their scant resources to buy the cigarettes or tobacco they craved.

They had not experienced their first combat, so war and its horrors were still unknowns. Even love, with its longings and distractions, did not intrude. Living far away from their own people, there were no opportunities for them to meet girls. The tribal girls living in the settlement a kilometer away from the forest school belonged to an alien culture and to them were "not the same kind." They viewed the girls simply as good friends, and taught them the new revolutionary songs and dances; in return, the girls would take them home and share with them whatever food they had. Any stirring they felt they quickly suppressed, afraid of getting the girls pregnant and themselves punished by the army. Visiting the girls was the social highlight for Luc and his comrades, and they would try to appear as presentable as circumstances allowed, which meant borrowing the best clothes they could find in their unit. Permission to visit the settlement came from their squad leader, who would say, for example, "Today, it's Luc's turn to go to the village. Minh, you have the best shirt, and Lam, you have the best pair of pants. You two loan your clothes to Luc to wear. He'll return them to you when he gets back tomorrow." The material and moral support of the local girls and their families helped ease life for Luc and the other trainees.

Luc's officer academy was located near Bac Can, the main target for the French attack in October 1947. The day French troops landed, Luc and his fellow trainees were performing a field operation about four kilometers away from the school when the news of the general attack reached his group. They were ordered to retreat to Chiem Hoa, and then to Ban Thi. The officer candidates were the future leaders of the army, so instead of throwing them into combat the Viet Minh command decided to preserve them for the long war to come. As it turned out, however, they bumped into a French column in Ban Thi. For the trainees who were closest to the enemy line, it was their first brush with war. Luc, however, was positioned too far away to be part of the action. After the exchange of fire, both sides withdrew because they were afraid of walk-ing into bigger trouble. Some time later, Luc's unit returned to the bat-tlefield to look for their dead and wounded. Afraid that the French might come back, they picked up their one dead and quickly left—miss-ing a soldier named Phong, who was hiding in a bush, his cheeks bleed-ing from a bullet that had pierced his mouth. After they were gone, the French also came back to look for their own dead and wounded. They were more thorough, and spent a long time searching, their men moving out in a widening arc. From his hiding place, Phong suddenly heard the French commander ordering one of the soldiers to go into the bush and see whether anyone was lying there. As the soldier parted the branches and leaves to check, he saw Phong crouching there with blood on his neck and shirt. Phong's eyes met the pair of blue eyes. The soldier froze, and the two men stared at each other for an instant. Then the soldier turned around and left, reporting, "There's no one in the bush." Later that night, Phong managed to crawl back to his unit and told the story of how he had been spared. The soldier's gesture surprised and moved everyone in the academy, and reminded them that not every Frenchman was a cruel brute. In making its tally later on, Luc's unit estimated that it had killed thirty-one French soldiers while losing one dead and one wounded.

After these operations, the Viet Minh government decided that the base was too dangerous for the dependents of cadres. Hau and his col-leagues had to pack up their families and take them out of the area. It was winter again and the journey was arduous. Thang bundled up her son, piling on all the clothes that he had, and covering his head with a cap and his tiny feet with socks, but it was impossible to stay warm.

She and her family would not have survived during this trip without the support of the hill tribes. In the forest, there were no inns and no restaurants, but wherever they went, they could always rely on these people to give them shelter and food. The accommodations were rustic and the food basic, but the tribes shared the little they had gladly. One man went out to catch a duck and made soup for Thang and her group, then gave the children four eggs he had been saving for his own family. This support and the solidarity within the Viet Minh movement rein-forced Thang's faith in the resistance. Instead of weakening her resolve, her stay in the base convinced her that the French would not be able to prevail in the face of so much determination and such a high morale. At this point, Thang only understood the overall goals of the Viet Minh but not the theoretical underpinnings of socialism. She knew that once independence was achieved, the "ruling clique" that was cooperating with the French would be overthrown. She thought they deserved to go, because they had done nothing for their country and their people. She was not perturbed by the fact that, when this happened, her father would lose his position. She was certain he would not be harmed; in fact, she thought that, since he was a patriot, he would be utilized by the Viet Minh, as were other former mandarins now serving in the resistance. The revolution wanted to get rid of the privileged class, not individuals like her father who made up this class, she believed.

Thang's group went through several provinces to reach Bac Giang, also in the midlands region. Here, Hau left Thang and the baby with the family of my uncle Chinh at their farm—a plantation that used to belong to a Frenchman—and returned to the mountain base. She said a sad good-bye to the rest of her group, who would scatter from here to find shelter wherever they could.

My uncle had bought his farm a long time ago, when he was a district magistrate in a nearby province. It included about 260 acres of rice fields, for which he paid a low price because the hilly terrain was not fertile and the crop yield was low. On this property, he had built a thatch house with several compartments, large enough to accommodate several relatives who had come to seek refuge. With my sister's arrival, the household now included over forty people. Besides the rice fields, my uncle also owned an orange grove that spread out over thirteen acres. Thanks to the large income from his properties, my uncle had no difficulty feeding everyone. He was generous, and did not mind having to support so many people. Of the rice fields, he kept only about nine acres to farm himself with the help of hired laborers, and rented out the rest in exchange for 10 percent of the crop. Compared with what some greedy landlords were collecting, his rent was reasonable and still left his tenant farmers with enough to survive. Besides the hired laborers, my uncle had a staff of servants who did household chores and helped him take care of his buffaloes, oxen, and hundreds of chickens, which he housed in a large shed. My uncle loved his farm, the cycle of planting and harvesting, and the sight of his orange trees in late fall when their branches would bend under the weight of the fruit. With all that the land and his labor was producing, he and his family led a comfortable life by local standards.

At this time, the Viet Minh were preaching unity and trying to recruit anyone who was willing to join their movement, regardless of class origin. In time, the communists would turn the old social order upside down, destroying the traditional elite and the middle class to put the workers and poor peasants on top. But for now, they could not afford to alienate people like my uncle. So, in spite of his background as a big landowner and a mandarin, the Viet Minh approached him. They invited him to serve as vice-chairman of the province committee of the Lien Viet, an organization they had set up to attract middle-class people and intellectuals into their ranks. My aunt, meanwhile, was recruited to serve as the head of the Women's Association for Region III, one of the fourteen regions into which the Viet Minh had divided Vietnam to facilitate command and mobilization of resources. My aunt and uncle immersed themselves in these activities, supporting the resistance as ardently as the poor peasants that the Viet Minh considered the core of their movement. Life under the Viet Minh, with its strict code of behavior, had changed my aunt and uncle. My aunt, the daughter of Vi Van Dinh, the feudal lord of the Tho tribe, had turned from a haughty aristocrat into a modest and solicitous leader. Meanwhile, my uncle, who had fathered two children out of wedlock, had ceased his womanizing.

For the first time since she left Van Dinh, Thang found herself among relatives. My uncle's family was very kind to her; there was plenty to eat, and servants to wait on everyone. Whenever he passed through the area on mission, or at Tet, Hau would pay his wife and son a visit. The normal rhythm was disrupted only by French sweep operations. Although the French did not once set foot in their village, and they heard gunfire only from afar, Thang and the villagers would flee whenever there was an operation, just to be safe. After the French left, Thang and the villagers would come back. Everywhere in the Viet Minh zone, this game of hide-and-seek was going on. More often than not, the French would find nothing in the villages but ducks, chickens, oxen, and buffaloes when they passed through. To their frustrated troops, it must have appeared like they were boxing against shadows.

With the dependents gone, Hau's office relocated to a clearing in the Tan Trao area, about thirty kilometers from Vinh Yen City. The site was chosen because it was in a sparsely populated and difficult to reach area, and provided good cover against detection. There were a few settlements nearby, but they were strung out several miles apart. The largest and the most "civilized" would be one with a couple of huts where Hau and his colleagues could buy a box of matches, a tinned biscuit or two, or a few bananas. Two tall mountain peaks rose on either side of the clearing. It was gloomy and damp under the canopy of trees. Tigers roamed at night. Inside their huts, with the ladders drawn up, sometimes they could hear the tigers' loud panting. Twice, the tigers broke through the pens to take their animals: a calf the first time, and a dog the second time—in broad daylight.

Hau's group of thirty people lived in three or four huts scattered among the trees, a short distance from one another, so that if a bomb should fall the entire office would not get wiped out. They received enough rice to eat, but there was no market where they could buy food, so they grew their own vegetables and raised chickens for eggs, their only source of protein besides the tiny fish they managed to catch once in a while in a stream.

With the help of his colleagues, Hau started a garden. Visitors marveled at the sight of row upon row of chapote vines climbing over stakes and fences in the middle of a wild forest. For water, the men dug wells or used the many clear streams that rushed through the mountain. Firewood was plentiful and they always kept a fire going. In winter, they burned logs from the lim hardwood trees, which produced intense heat and deep purple flames. The heat was so powerful that it would roast peanuts scattered around the fire. As far as medical care was concerned, they were on their own. After the first few painful attempts, Hau managed to master the art of giving injections to himself and others. When he traveled, he would take along a syringe, a supply of quinine for malaria, and a few aspirin tablets for headaches and colds.

The Viet Minh strove to retain the trappings of government within the zone that they controlled, so although they were located in the forest, far from each other, the scattered ministries and their offices tried to function like regular bureaucracies, with a daily schedule, meetings, and business trips. The routine, of course, was different from the one they used to have in the cities: There was little paperwork, trips were difficult to make, meetings were rare, and the cadres led a "collective life"—sleeping and eating together—instead of going home each day after work. In Hau's camp, a length of rail, salvaged from a sabotaged railway and suspended from a post, served as a bell marking events in the daily schedule. Wake-up calls were at 6 a.m., followed by breakfast. At 7 a.m., they started work. Mostly, they tended to their vegetables and animals. After lunch and a brief rest, they would return to their chores until dinner time. Hau spent most of his time traveling, reporting to his bosses about activities in the area he supervised, finding out whether there were any new plans to increase food output or any new techniques or seeds for him to disseminate, visiting people under his charge that were scattered in various settlements, or dropping in on villages to check on the planting or harvesting. Every month or so, he would give a class to students at the middle school specializing in agriculture, about two kilometers from where he lived. Hau discovered that fighting against foreign domination might be romantic in concept, but in practice it could be a dull routine. Only the prospect of achieving freedom made his daily grind worthwhile.

Once in a while, the political cadre assigned to Hau's office would conduct an education session: reviewing the current situation and discussing in general terms what the Viet Minh as a whole needed to do to achieve victory. The main goal of the seminar was to maintain morale. The analysis was usually optimistic. The cadre would talk about recent victories, the strengths and weaknesses of the revolution, and the successes and failures of the French. He would usually end with a statement of belief in the final victory and an exhortation to keep up the fight no matter what. No one dared voice any feeling of doubt or discouragement, to avoid harsh criticism from the political cadre, or from their own colleagues for a weakening of the will. This policy of enforcing high morale, combined with peer pressure and their isolation from other sources of news that could have given them a different picture of the war, allowed Hau and his comrades to keep from losing their resolve. There were moments of fatigue and dejection, but these would pass, and news of victories would pump up their enthusiasm again.

To avoid detection, Hau's agency moved five or six times. Gradually, as the liberated zone was enlarged and the Viet Minh became stronger, Hau and his colleagues began to edge toward more populated areas. There, they found more ample food supplies and had access to markets where they could buy what they needed. After four months, Hau thought that Thang and their son Lap were probably overstaying their welcome at Uncle Chinh's house, so he decided to take them to Ninh Binh Province to live with one of his brothers. Once more, they packed up and set off on foot. When they were close to Van Dinh, they decided to stop in to check on my family. They had had no news of us since they left. Thang eagerly looked forward to finding her parents and brothers and sisters, but when they got there, they found that we had moved elsewhere. No one knew where we were. Thinking that she would never find us again, my sister wept. After a few days' rest, they rented a boat to go to the village where Hau's brother was living. Hau's brother and his wife gave them a warm welcome and said that Thang and Lap could stay indefinitely. Once they were settled in, Hau immediately turned around and headed back to the mountain base, hundreds of miles away. That night, my sister cried herself to sleep. For the first time since she left home, she felt utterly alone. Her parents and siblings had disappeared. Her husband was now going to be much further away, and she did not know when she would see him again.

But Thang's nomadic life was not going to stop here. Once again, French attacks drove them away, into Thanh Hoa Province. When she had left Van Dinh, Lap was six months old. Now, he was close to three, and she was still living on the run. Another bitterly cold winter had arrived. Again, she bundled up her son and set out on foot this time with her brother-in-law's family. They traveled to Cau Bo, in Thanh Hoa Province, where Thang's brother-in-law decided to settle.

Thanh Hoa Province was part of the second Viet Minh base south of the Red River Delta. Throughout the war, this province remained relatively quiet, and was one of the most secure Viet Minh areas. The French were tied down in defending more strategic regions, such as the Red River and the Mekong deltas, or were busy trying to destroy the Viet Minh in the Viet Bac base, so they did not venture into Thanh Hoa except for occasional air strikes. Cau Bo had an open-air market, one of several that enterprising refugees had set up in the Viet Minh zone. These markets were just clusters of crude shops that sold goods smuggled from the French zones, usually items that were scarce in the resistance areas. Thang's brother-in-law and his wife opened a shop in the Cau Bo market. Thang now had to find a way to support herself and her child. With just a monthly rice ration and no salary, Hau had no money to send to his family. To pay for her expenses, Thang got a job packaging medicine for shipping. The medication was produced by an uncle of Hau's, who was a chemist, to sell to the Viet Minh army. Thang settled into a dull routine. She was glad she no longer had to be on the run, but she missed the excitement of life in the forest clearing. She wished she could be with her old friends, back in the Viet Bac base. Here in Cau Bo, commerce, not revolution, was the main activity, and it was hard to sustain the enthusiasm she had felt when she was among comrades heady with their ideals.

Later, the uncle closed down his pharmaceutical business, discouraged by the Viet Minh's high taxes, which took up to 80 percent of his profits. Thang followed her brother and sister-in-law and moved to a village where they built a hut near a stream and grew corn and vegetables in a small garden. It was good to be away from the bustle of the market settlement, but conditions were primitive: One night Lap got bitten on the foot by a rat. Even in this remote village, war remained a menace. Sometimes, a plane would come to bomb and strafe. Thang would scoop up her son and run to the riverbank, where they hid at the foot of a bamboo grove until the plane left. The hut they lived in was made with mud walls and a thatched roof, and was so flimsy it collapsed during a typhoon. In the driving rain and howling wind, so strong it almost sent her flying backward, Thang clutched her baby and crawled through rice fields to find shelter elsewhere. After what seemed like an eternity, they finally reached a neighbor's hut. But that hut too was in danger of collapsing, and the neighbor and his family were racing from corner to corner, trying to prop up the walls and the roof, which was leaking like a sieve. Thang and her baby sat on a pile of straw, wet and cold, and waited till the neighbors were free to tend to them. After experiencing firsthand what life was like for the peasants here and else-where, her sympathy for their plight grew even stronger. When the Viet Minh eventually took the land of the landlords to give to the poor peasants, Thang felt they were right to do so.

In 1950, the Agriculture Ministry set up an experimental station in Tan Phong, in Thanh Hoa Province. To be near his family, Hau asked to be transferred there as the head of the station, although this position was lower than the one he had in the Viet Bac. His request was grant-ed. Thang was elated to get the family back together again, and also to have a place of her own for the first time since she left Van Dinh, as they were given a hut to live in on the station grounds. Having his family next to him eased Hau's mind, since he no longer had to wonder day in and day out how they were doing far away. The greatest drawback to being in Tan Phong was the distance from the ministry headquarters. Whenever Hau had to go there to attend meetings, present reports, and get new instructions about food production, he would have to travel for hundreds of kilometers by bicycle and on foot. The job of the station was to develop better strains and better growing methods for staples like corn, sweet potatoes, and rice, and then disseminate them.

Hau was the head of the station, but he and his family did not enjoy any privileges. Their hut was made of bamboo and thatch, like the hous-ing built for the rest of the station's personnel of thirty. At mealtimes, Thang would go to the communal kitchen with a bamboo basket to get her family's share of steamed rice and salted fish. To these, she would add vegetables that Hau was growing or that she had bought at a near-by market, and a small bowl of anchovy or bean paste for extra protein. Life remained simple, but she felt happy being with her family and liv-ing once again among like-minded people who were doing their part for the resistance. And she loved to look out at the station's fields that spread over several acres of land.

Because of the threat of bombing, Thang did not want to send her son to the public school, which was located three or four kilometers away from their house. She started her own class to teach Lap and the children in the station. When Lap was six years old, however, she decided that the time had come for him to attend a regular school. Classes were held at night, to avoid bombings. Every day, at five o'clock, Thang would feed Lap, and then give him a storm lantern to light his way back from school, a stick to keep dogs at bay, and a book bag to carry. Then Lap would set off, following the riverbank and a mountain trail to get to school. During the class, whenever they heard the droning of an aircraft, the teacher would blow out the lantern, rekindling it only after the plane had left. When class was over, Lap would light his way home with his lantern, singing as loud as he could to drive away any ghosts that might be thinking of scaring him. At the time Lap was due to return, Thang would stand by the front door, anxiously peering in the direction in which he was coming. When she saw the tiny dot of light of the lantern on the riverbank, she would heave a sigh of relief. After he got home, she would feed him a hot drink made with a pinch of manioc flour boiled in water and sweetened with a bit of sugar, and then put him to bed.

The year that Hau transferred to Thanh Hoa, aid from the Soviet Union and Communist China started to arrive for the Viet Minh. The Viet Minh's most fragile period—when they were completely on their own, without resources, and were badly outgunned by the French—finally came to an end. The turn of fortune came after the Chinese Communists took over China in 1949. In that year in Hanoi, when he heard the news that Mao Tse-tung had won, my father feared that China would begin aiding the Viet Minh, and that the French might have a hard time keeping Tonkin. In January 1950, the Chinese recognized Ho Chi Minh as the rightful leader of Vietnam. The Soviets promptly followed suit. Soon both the Chinese and the Soviets began to send weapons and supplies across the border. The French tried to stop the flow, but were powerless to seal the long frontier. The steady stream of equipment disturbed the French, but they thought that it would take the ill-trained Viet Minh army a long time to digest all these new weapons. As always, the French badly underestimated their enemy. With Chinese help—through advisors and technicians dispatched over the border and through training classes held in China itself—Viet Minh personnel learned quickly. The machine guns, mortars, and antiaircraft weapons from his allies allowed General Vo Nguyen Giap to greatly expand his firepower. By the summer of 1950, he would have five well-armed and well-trained regular divisions, of 10,000 men each, equipped with machine guns, antiaircraft weapons, and field radios for communication and coordination, and supported with heavy mortars. His army had come a long way from the days when several men had to share a rifle.

Once he felt ready, Giap launched his offensive. In October 1950, at the end of the monsoon season, he attacked a string of border garrisons in the northeast that were manned by about 10,000 men. They fell one by one, triggering panicky evacuations of the troops. By the time it was all over, the French had suffered a stunning defeat. Of the soldiers deployed along the frontier, over half had been lost, most of them captured by the Viet Minh. In addition, thousands of rifles, machine guns, and mortars and hundreds of trucks were also lost, mostly abandoned in Lang Son. It was during this border campaign that my cousin Luc saw his first battles. After he graduated from the officer training school, Luc was assigned to the general command headquarters as a staff officer. Although his parents were working for the Viet Minh, his mandarin and landlord background nonetheless tainted him in the eyes of his Viet Minh commanders, and they did not trust someone like him to lead combat troops. Luc accepted this without complaint, confident that in time his worth would shine through and he would be recognized.

Luc had essentially a desk job, helping to plan operations and going into actual battles to assist with the execution, observe, and report back on what had gone right and what had gone wrong. His first assignment was to serve as a field radio operator for a platoon attacking a French post near the border. At this time, the combat units were usually better equipped than the staff officers with weapons and clothes that they had obtained from enemy supplies. Every infantryman fantasized about capturing a Colt .45, an ammunition belt with a holster for the pistol, and an American jacket, out of the belief that wearing this getup would make him look dashing and irresistible to the girls. With the vision of such booty dancing in his head, Luc was thrilled to get his first combat mission.

That night, before his unit went into action, Luc made an entry in his journal, noting the pale moonlight and recording his excitement and his indifference to death. He felt like the romantic lead in a war movie. But when it came, combat was anything but romantic. It was frightening, deadly, and chaotic. At ten o'clock, shrouded by mist and guided by the moon, his unit began its assault. Suddenly, deafening explosions rent the silence and bright flashes of light sliced through the darkness. Everyone, on both sides, was yelling. Bullets whizzed by Luc's head, and his dead or wounded comrades were collapsing next to him. He saw a close friend rush forward and then fall down, killed by a bullet. Luc lay flat on his back, scared out of his mind, trying to make himself as small a target as possible, but holding on to his field radio. In the middle of this chaos, a couple of soldiers crawled over to him and yelled over the din of the battle, "The platoon leader's been killed. No one's commanding us, and we can't go on." With trembling hands, Luc radioed the battalion commander, who ordered a retreat. The rest of the unit hastily withdrew. It was a defeat, and for Luc a rather humiliating experience. Marching back, he was haunted by the death of his friend and other comrades. He felt guilty and ashamed of his own behavior and, although he was still shaken by the brush with war, resolved to be braver next time, even if it meant putting his own life in danger.

Luc's next assignment was to join the offensive against the border garrisons, taking part in ambushes against the retreating French column. Each attack ended in a rout for the French, and remnants of their units fled for their lives into the hills where they hid, usually without food. After three or four days, all Luc's unit had to do to induce the famished soldiers to come out of hiding was to brandish a handful of rice. Since he could speak French, Luc was given the job of interrogating the POWs. There were so many that he had time only to ask each one for his name, rank, function, and serial number. The massive number of POWs simply overwhelmed his unit and the Viet Minh command. In an effort to cope, the army sent all the prisoners to Lang Son, the largest French logistics base in this border region, to be sorted out. So, Luc headed for Lang Son where he conducted the same cursory questioning.

Hardly able to feed their own troops, the Viet Minh now had to feed the thousands of prisoners as well. Used to a better diet, the POWs could barely survive on the food ration they got, although it was better than what the Viet Minh officers and soldiers themselves were getting. The lack of medication that plagued the Viet Minh army also wreaked havoc among the POWs, killing many. Later on, camps were set up along the border to house the POWs, but conditions remained primitive and took a heavy toll.

The capture of French supplies in Lang Son and elsewhere exceeded the wildest dreams of the Viet Minh. They now had tons of weapons to add to their arsenal. Luc received a Garand rifle as a reward for his part in the fighting. The Viet Minh also found themselves in the possession of hundreds of trucks and jeeps. In fact, very few of them could drive, so they put POWs to work ferrying them around. Lang Son was such a large logistics base that it had its own shoe factory to supply the French soldiers manning the string of posts along the border. The factory was located in a cave in the beautiful Tam Thanh Mountain. Noticing that Luc was still wearing a flimsy pair of shoes, his battalion commander said, "I'll tell the Logistics Unit to give you a coupon that you can take down to the factory and get a pair made." Armed with the piece of paper, Luc made his way to the cave, where he found four or five French cobblers busily cutting, sewing, and hammering as though nothing had changed. One of them took Luc's coupon. Luc said, "Please make it quick." The Frenchman nodded, and said amiably that the shoes would be ready in two days. When Luc returned, the Frenchman handed him a beautiful pair of leather shoes that had been buffed until they shone like mirrors. The military reversal had not destroyed the cobbler's professional pride in turning out first-quality products.

The French high command, however, was stunned and embarrassed by the defeat along the border. Until then, they had viewed the Viet Minh army with contempt, but with Giap's soldiers heading for the Red River Delta, there was panic in Hanoi and talk of evacuating French women and children. Some wealthy Vietnamese families moved to France just to be safe. In December 1950, the two top French officials in Vietnam, the high commissioner and the commanding general, were recalled and replaced by General Jean de Lattre de Tassigny, who now assumed both functions. General de Lattre, one of France's greatest soldiers, had complete freedom to direct the war as he saw fit. He lost no time in restoring French confidence. He jolted the army out of its stupor by ordering a shake-up of the French command, and canceled the evacuation of French families to stop the panic. De Lattre's firm leadership, along with the reinforcements and supplies that began to arrive, did wonders for French morale.

It was at around this time—when the French were noisily and aggressively trying to regain the initiative—that my sister Thang decided to pay her family a visit. She had been gone for four years now, and her longing to see her parents and siblings had grown even stronger. One day, a relative happened to pass through Tan Phong and ran into Thang. He told her that we had survived the fighting in the delta and were now living in Hanoi. Thang was deliriously happy and immediately made plans to visit us. She obtained permission from the Viet Minh authorities to leave their zone and found a group of women traders who agreed to take her to Hanoi and back. As she started out, her excitement gave way to anxiety, and she felt apprehensive during the entire trip, afraid that once she crossed into the French zone she might be arrested as a Viet Minh suspect. She ran into a mortar barrage just before she reached a market on the other side of the invisible dividing line, and then after seven days' traveling by boat and on foot, she made it to our house.

When she arrived, it was pandemonium. We had not had any news from her, but having heard how horrible life was in the resistance zone, we had assumed that she had died either from disease or hunger or had been killed in the fighting there. All the pain and anxiety of the past few years welled up. We broke down, crying but also smiling with relief through the tears. Then Thang sat down and talked with the grown-ups to catch up on the family's news. I just watched and listened from the edge of the circle. I had not been close to Thang. By the time I was three, she had gotten married, and when I was five and a half, she had her first baby. When she left to join the Viet Minh, I was only six, and my memory of her was quite dim. Now I was almost ten, and although I still loved her in a general way as my sister, I did not seek her company during her visit in Hanoi. In fact, I tried to keep out of her sight because I knew she would disapprove of my tomboy behavior. At this time, I was going through my wild phase, as though I knew that that was the only period in my life when I could act in this fashion. Once I reached puberty and became a little woman, I would have to settle down and learn to behave like a lady. I was cutting school regularly, running around with my male cousins, and trying to outdo them in everything we did—climbing trees, playing marbles, shooting with slingshots, wading in flooded streets after monsoon downpours, or fighting. My father started to call our raucous bunch "the pirates" and me "the pirate leader." My behavior discouraged him, but he was too busy with his work and his social life to bother with me, leaving it to my mother to mold me, and trusting that I would absorb the family values in time and turn genteel.

Thang downplayed the hardships of life in the resistance, not because she wanted to spare our parents the anguish, but because in her words, "it just wasn't a big deal." However, even the little she told was enough to distress our father and mother. Thang enjoyed being back in Hanoi, although she was dismayed by the large presence of French troops and their military equipment—what she called "the French machinery of oppression and terror." At this time, General de Lattre liked to impress the natives with his power and the majesty of his office. Whenever he moved about in the city, he would ride in a black sedan flying the French flag, accompanied by a motorcade and a loud siren. Still, neither de Lattre's display of power nor his French soldiers and weapons impressed Thang or made her lose heart. Instead, she tried to win her family over to the cause. During her stay, she would take every opportunity to try to talk my father into resigning from his post in the colonial government. She would tell him, "Don't work for the French— don't do anything for them. It's not a good idea for you to keep your job with them." To this, he would only say, "Look at all your young brothers and sisters. If I don't work and earn a salary, how am I going to feed them?" During one of these discussions, they heard the clattering of French trucks and half-tracks passing by in the street. My father gestured toward the window and said, "Besides, the French are so strong. Just look at them. How are we going to defeat them?" The word he chose, *minh,* or "we," is a term that denotes the ethnic and cultural bond Vietnamese feel with one another. By using it, he indicated that although he was working for the French he continued to identify with the Viet Minh, who were part of his own people. Thang said, "Don't be fooled by the French. They can make a lot of noise with their equipment, but in reality they're weak. They'll lose."

At this time, Xuong, my second oldest brother, had become an officer in the French colonial army. Thang thought this was wrong, and said to him, "Why don't you leave? Why should you fight for them? Youths like you should be patriotic and help their country." Embarrassed, Xuong only said, "Don't worry. I might be in their army, but I'm not going to do any fighting for them. Why should I die for them? If I get into a combat situation, I'll just turn around and run!" On their side, my parents did not criticize Thang about her decision to support the Viet Minh, nor did they attempt to talk her into abandoning the resistance and returning home to a life of comfort.

When the time came for Thang to leave, my parents tried to get her to stay longer. But when she insisted that she had to go back to her husband and son, my father accepted her decision with resignation, saying, "Yes, it's your duty to be with your own family." And then, just as suddenly as she had appeared back in our lives, Thang was gone. My parents did not know it at the time, but that was the last time they would see her. When she arrived in Hanoi in 1954 after the Viet Minh had taken over the city, we had fled to Saigon. And when she got to Saigon after the communist victory in 1975, my parents had fled to the United States and then to Paris.

In Thanh Hoa, Hau and Lap were happy to have her back. Everyone at the station was glad to see her again and besieged her with questions about Hanoi. After the first days of excitement following her return, she settled back into her routine. Instead of feeling depressed about being back to a life of hardships, Thang actually experienced a new sense of enthusiasm. The trip had satisfied her need to see her parents and sib-lings, and she was now at peace. Her determination to stay with the resistance until the end grew after her visit. Her firm resolve pleased Hau, and also surprised him a little. She had always accepted all the sac-rifices the resistance imposed, not only with stoicism, but even with good cheer. Still, there had been times when Hau wondered how much longer she could put up with the hardships. When she left, the idea had crossed his mind that once she had a taste of life in Hanoi she might have second thoughts about staying the course. After all, that was the kind of life she had grown up in. Even for him—someone who had known poverty and privations most of his life—the demands of the resistance had at times stretched his endurance. Inwardly he was very proud of his wife and admired her even more than before, but he told her only, "It's good that you didn't let yourself get swayed by things in Hanoi, and that you're as determined as ever." She felt pleased, understanding the tenderness and pride behind those words uttered by her quiet husband. In a culture where feelings were communicated sparingly even between spouses, she did not expect him to say more.

Thang and Hau would count among the hard-core Viet Minh fol-lowers who refused to give up no matter how rough things got. This staying power was due partly to their faith in the revolution, partly to a yearning to see their country free again, and partly to personal pride— a desire to prove to themselves and others that they could put up with the tough challenge until the very end. Giving up in midstream would have brought a sense of shame and guilt that they knew they could not live with. Others did not have their fortitude. At about the time Thang returned to Thanh Hoa, an increasing number of urban middle-class peo-ple were beginning to abandon the resistance. Life for the Vietnamese in the French-controlled zones had stabilized and, with so much money pouring in to keep the war going, was actually getting better. Meantime, in the Viet Minh areas, the fighting and the hardships had chipped away at the determination of the people who had flocked there with so much enthusiasm at the beginning of the war.

Those who lost heart, became disillusioned, or ran out of resources and could not earn a living in the depressed economy of the resistance areas started to move back to the French zone, dodging the Viet Minh along the way to avoid being arrested and accused of deserting the cause. This reverse migration was called the *dinh te* movement, from the pidgin pronunciation of the French word *rentrer*, or re-enter. From a trickle, it started to gather momentum as the war dragged on. The Viet Minh had abstained from making social revolution an overt goal to avoid alienating the middle class and intellectuals. Now as the defection grew, the Viet Minh concluded that unless they promised to implement a social trans-formation to give benefits to the workers and peasants—the core of their support—they would run the danger of losing these followers as well.

The Viet Minh signaled their shift to the left by declaring their sol-idarity with Communist China and the Soviet Union and putting them-selves openly in the socialist camp. Then, at a national congress in February 1951, they reinstituted the Communist Party, which they had disbanded in 1945 to attract the middle class, and declared that a social revolution would be carried out as soon as independence was achieved to benefit the poor. Although they gave their party the new and less threatening name of the Workers' Party, the communists made it clear that henceforth they would be in control. Middle-class people with mandarin ties like Hau and landlords like my uncle Chinh who remained in the Viet Minh were welcome to stay, but only in secondary roles. With the communists tightening their control, writers and artists in the Viet Minh began to see their creative freedom curtailed. Disillusioned, some abandoned the resistance. Among these was the composer Pham Duy, who had written some of the most memorable and popular songs for the Viet Minh.

With the *dinh te* movement picking up pace, faces familiar to us began to reappear in Hanoi, relatives and friends who had followed the Viet Minh into their base or who had simply fled deeper into the hinterland to escape the French push into the delta. After years of living in the vil-lages or in the mountains, they were disoriented by the city at first, but picked up the tempo of urban life quickly, as though they had never left. Among those who returned were my uncle Loc and his family. With no savings, no means of earning a livelihood, and no government subsidies to help them rebuild their life, they came to stay with us for a long time. My father not only had to feed and house them, but also had to find a job for my uncle so he could get back on his feet. After my father got him a position equivalent to what he had held before, my uncle and his fam-ily moved out.

It was also around this time that my father sent word to my uncle Chinh, the brother with whom he felt the closest, to move from Bac Giang back to Hanoi. Chinh turned him down, because some of his children were in the Viet Minh and he did not want to return without them, and also because he did not want to leave his farm. The Viet Minh were not talking about land reform or about destroying the landlords then, so he did not feel threatened. Besides, his family was respected and their support for the resistance appreciated. He did not want to go to Hanoi and start all over again. In a couple of years, however, his life would change drastically, for the worse.

The year 1950 was a turning point for us as well as for the Viet Minh. By the time Thang came to visit us, the arrival of the Cold War to Vietnam and the emergence of the Bao Dai government that was created in its wake had set in motion a chain of events that had dislodged my father from his position in Haiphong and forced us to move back to Hanoi, where my sister had found us.

9

Poison and Bribes

Half asleep and half awake, I heard muffled voices and the faint clanking of dishes. I opened my eyes and looked around the strange room. Sunlight was streaming through the open windows, with their shutters pushed outward. It took me a full minute to remember that I was in my new home in Haiphong. I got out of bed and found my way to the dark wood staircase. The steps felt cool under my bare feet. In the small dining room, I saw my family already gathered around the table, being served breakfast by an old man. My mother said, "Come and get something to eat." Before I could adjust myself to the new surroundings, the strange man put a chunk of French bread, crusty and warm, smeared with creamy French butter, on my plate. I could not believe my eyes. I had been craving this food for almost a year, and now it was sitting right in front of me. I grabbed the bread and took a big bite. The taste was wonderful, like something straight from heaven—just as I had imagined during all those months of deprivation.

We had arrived in Haiphong the night before, after taking a whole day to cover the distance of seventy-five miles by car from Hanoi. Since the sabotaged railway was still in shambles back then in 1947, a single highway served as the only link between the two cities. As we inched along, we felt not like we were moving to a new home but rather like we were taking part in a military operation. With security still a problem, the only sure way to make it from Hanoi to Haiphong and back alive was to travel with a military convoy. That day, our car was sandwiched between French army trucks and armored personnel carriers. The line of about fifty vehicles moved slowly, on the alert for Viet Minh ambushes and snipers. We did not know whether we would make it safely to Haiphong until we reached the city after nightfall. (It was not until the middle of 1949 that daytime traffic between Hanoi and Haiphong finally became secure, and vehicles could make the trip without military escort.)

My father had made the same trip on June 6, 1947, when he first went down to assume his new post and to find housing for us. The security situation was worse then, since Haiphong was just a French toehold in a Viet Minh sea. He did not dare bring us to join him. A few days after he arrived, the Hoi Dong An Dan, or Council to Calm and Resettle the Population, was set up to restore a semblance of government in Haiphong and the Maritime Zone that the French were retaking. This zone stretched from Haiphong through a couple of neighboring provinces all the way to the Hon Gai coal mine.

The role of this council, and of another similar one that had been set up in Hanoi, was ceremonial and bureaucratic, while the French continued to control the real levers of power, such as finance, military, and security matters. Dr. Dang Huu Chi, my father's best friend, chaired the council, and my father served as his deputy. As its name implied, the most important task for the council was to help resettle the refugees who were beginning to drift back to Haiphong. Welcoming centers were set up to help them get back on their feet and encourage others to return as well. My father would visit these centers to show his support, arrange temporary housing for the refugees whose houses had been destroyed in the French reconquest, and provide them with enough rice to eat until they could rebuild their homes. Other important tasks for the council were to maintain public health and restore administrative procedures such as the issuance of identity cards, commercial licenses, and building permits. Although the council had little authority, the Viet Minh viewed it as part and parcel of the French effort to re-establish their colonial regime. In their eyes, by lending a Vietnamese front and a degree of legitimacy to the French, the council members were collaborators of the worst kind.

Haiphong lies twenty kilometers inland from the sea, on the right bank of the Cam River, a branch of the Red River. Crisscrossed by six rivers and canals, it was originally a large fort, which the French turned into a port in the nineteenth century after spending a considerable amount of money and effort constructing a harbor capable of handling seagoing vessels. Haiphong did not offer the most ideal spot for a port, but it was the best location the French could find in the north's swampy and sandy coastline. The city quickly became the gateway into Tonkin and a major industrial center. Its most noticeable industry in colonial times was cement, produced by a subsidiary of Portland Cement. Through the port, the French exported rice, rubber, spices, coal, and minerals, and imported sugar, canned goods, wines, pharmaceuticals, paper, petroleum, steel, iron machinery, automobiles, and spare parts. Local merchants would buy the merchandise from French import firms and then resell it to consumers. The United States was one of the trading partners, buying rubber, and shipping vehicles, gasoline, and metals from Vietnam.

From the surrounding areas, Haiphong got a rich supply of seafood, but it had to import rice from the south. In normal times, rice could reach the city easily. But after the fighting started in 1946 this supply became tenuous and remained so until 1949, when the French managed to restore security. Even after the French left, Haiphong would remain the gateway to the north. During the period of American involvement, a significant amount of aid that the North Vietnamese received from their communist allies arrived through Haiphong. To choke off this flow, the Americans blockaded the port and mined the harbor.

Like Hanoi, Haiphong had a European flair. The main part of town, located near the harbor, boasted fine colonial-era buildings, including the city hall, the chamber of commerce, a theater, banks, hotels, villas, and business offices. This was the heart of the city, where the French held sway over political and economic life. Poor Vietnamese did not feel at home here, and would rarely set foot in the French section. Haiphong also has a distinctive Chinese flavor. Some twenty-five percent of its population was Chinese, attracted here by the city's importance as a trading center. The Chinese lived in their own quarter and, as elsewhere in Vietnam, served as middlemen for French enterprises. They controlled the part of the city's commerce not monopolized by the colonial settlers.

The Viet Minh took over the city on August 23, 1945. A year later, the French wrested it back, but they could not gain total control. Only three months before my father arrived in Haiphong, the Viet Minh had conducted a daring attack on the city. A company crossed one of the canals that flowed through Haiphong and damaged the cement and carpet factories, the customs office, the power plant, and the Cat Bi airport. This was their only major operation against the city, however. After that, the Viet Minh could not muster the forces and resources to stage another attack. They could resort only to acts of sabotage, such as destroying the pipes carrying water into the city or damaging the railway and forcing the French to post guards to keep the line secure. Inside the city, all the Viet Minh could do was to remind the population of their presence. They would plant their flags in various parts of town, hang banners carrying their slogans, or spread propaganda leaflets. Whenever this happened the French would randomly arrest young men they suspected of being the culprits, throw them in jail, and beat them up. My father would politely but firmly tell the French, "You can't arrest people like that without proof. For all we know, they're innocent." He would keep up this quiet protest until the arrests stopped. In remonstrating the French, my father was observing the mandarin code of conduct, which asked that officials be loyal and yet unafraid to point out government crimes to their superiors, and try to stop them to protect the people.

The French expeditionary forces were used as a police force to ferret out criminals or Viet Minh still holed up in the city. In this twilight zone, with law and order not yet fully restored, the French troops were as much a danger to the residents as the criminals who took advantage of the insecure conditions to rob. While going through houses to look for the Viet Minh, the soldiers would rape the women and young girls they found or take valuables. When my father heard of these abuses, he immediately went to see the French commander and said, "You must forbid your people to commit these criminal acts. You want to calm the people's fear and restore law and order in the city. But your soldiers are scaring the population and undermining their faith in our ability to get things back to normal." The commander began cracking down and punishing the guilty soldiers. Soon after that, the crimes stopped. My father was convinced that his pragmatic reasoning had persuaded the commander to act, and would count this among his accomplishments in Haiphong. However, even after the incidents halted, residents remained leery of soldiers in general, especially at night when many of them would get drunk and stagger around in the street, ready to get into a brawl or to chase any woman they came across. To be safe, people would not venture outside their homes after nightfall.

The eerie emptiness of Haiphong added to the sense of insecurity. With the streets deserted and most of the houses left vacant or in ruins, those who lived there felt very exposed. When my father arrived in Haiphong, there were less than 3000 people in the city, or only about five percent of the original population. Over a thousand had been killed in the fighting in 1946 when the French retook the city, and most of the rest had fled. Much of the housing had been destroyed. At first, my father stayed with Dr. Chi, but then he got his own living quarters in a somber, small villa on Ngo Nghe street. After we moved in with him, my siblings and I got such bad vibes from the place that we were convinced it was haunted. The stories we heard from neighbors confirmed our worst suspicions. The villa had been used by the French secret police at one point as a jail and interrogation center. Many people had been tortured and killed there. We always sensed a malevolent presence, as though the horrors that had happened here could not dissipate and continued to linger. The compartments in the back of the villa had been used as the torture chambers. We could feel the evil there, and I would set foot in that part of the house only if someone was with me. We scared ourselves so much that one night when my mother tapped my sister Yen's shoulder from behind, Yen—thinking that a ghost had touched her—fainted and began foaming at the mouth. One day a secret cache of weapons was discovered in an underground bunker, adding to the sinister mystery of the place.

It was in this villa that I thought I saw a ghost for the first time. It was the Vietnamese All Souls' Day, the time of year when the gates to the underworld open and souls can wander back to the realm of the living. Every family has to worship the dead and prepare meals for them, especially to placate the hungry ghosts who do not have any relatives to feed them. On that day, worshipers packed the temple next door. From our yard, we could hear the gongs and bells, and we could smell the incense drifting over our wall. My sisters Binh and Yen and I decided to have a cookout, not to eat but just for fun. We built a fire near the wall and were absorbed in keeping the fire going and watching some beans boiling in an old can. Suddenly, without speaking to one another, all three of us felt something horrible behind our backs. Our hair stood on end. In unison, we turned around and looked. In the darkened doorway leading into our house, we saw the figure of a man dressed in Vietnamese clothes—loose pants and loose shirt—that looked like prison garb. But his face was featureless, and his head looked like a giant egg perched on his neck. Our screams stuck in our throats. Together, we ran toward the back of the house to the kitchen where we found a maid. Our hearts were pounding and our eyes were wild with terror. Binh was the first one to recover her voice. She stammered out to the maid what we had seen. The maid was a Catholic and ghosts did not frighten her, especially when she had a crucifix around her neck and felt well protected. Just to be on the safe side, she grabbed an iron cleaver because this metal would frighten off the ghost, and set off. We followed her, still shaken from what we had seen. She cautiously searched the house, but found nothing.

Besides this maid, we had a couple of unusual characters as servants. With most of the city's population gone, it was difficult for my father to find domestics to help him with cooking and cleaning when he first arrived. So he hired whomever he could. He found three ex-convicts who had served twenty years or longer on the penal island of Poulo Condore, and took them in as servants. He was confident in his judgment of people and felt that he could trust these men who had paid for their crimes and had reformed. Besides, as he tended to do at times, my father decided to leave whatever happened next to fate. In spite of their past, they turned out to be more loyal than many servants we had had before. We never felt threatened, although they did look fierce. One had hollow cheeks, a jutting jaw, piercing eyes, stiff black hair, and tattoos on his sinewy arms.

The old man who worked as our cook was the most devoted. We heard stories that he had killed someone in revenge but we did not ask him questions about his past. He prepared sumptuous meals. My mother was puzzled by the amount of food he served each day, which far exceeded what he could have bought at the market with the budget she gave him. She thought he was using his own pay to feed us extra, so she told him, "There's no way you can feed us the way you do with the money I give you for the market, so you must be spending your own money. Please stop." The old man only said, "Please don't worry. That's just me. I can't bear to cook skimpy meals." It was only after he died that we learned that instead of shopping for expensive items like meat and seafood at the market, the cook would look for vendors selling illegally in the streets outside. He would take his time, taking the food in his hands, examining it carefully, and haggling over the price. When policemen arrived on their roaring motorcycles, and the vendors bolted to avoid getting arrested and fined—and their merchandise crushed by the vehicles—our cook calmly put the food in his basket and walked away without paying. Not long after he came to work for us, the old man came down with lung cancer. My parents put him in the hospital, and my father personally asked the doctors there to take special care of him. When he died, my parents gave him a decent burial. No relatives showed up for the funeral. As more refugees began to return, my parents found more conventional domestics, and let the remaining two ex-convicts go.

Outside Haiphong, fighting continued as the French pushed out of the city to enlarge their zone. At first, they took back the main roads, but the Viet Minh continued to control the villages strung along these communication arteries. In the next phase, the French launched operations into these villages to dislodge the Viet Minh. Back then, before Soviet and Communist Chinese aid arrived, the Viet Minh were still weak, giving the French the decisive military edge. To pacify a village, all the French had to do was to lob artillery shells and dispatch planes to drop a few bombs, and then send in their troops to follow up with a ground sweep. The Viet Minh would melt away without firing a single shot. At night, we could hear the boom of French artillery firing into the areas under "pacification." When they swept through the villages, soldiers from the French expeditionary forces would steal water buffaloes, which they would then resell. For the peasants, losing these draft animals was like losing their livelihood. It was difficult, if not impossible, for them to come up with enough money to replace the buffaloes, without which they could not plough their fields. Some local officials colluded with the troops. Although they knew the cattle had been stolen, they would let the soldiers resell it and split the proceeds with them. A buffalo could fetch thousands of piasters, so each operation could net those accomplices quite a bit of money.

When he got wind of all this, my father again went to see the French commanding general and said, "The peasants are suffering enough from this fighting. You can't allow your soldiers to make things worse for them. All this must stop." He also asked the commander to round up the stolen cattle, identify the rightful owners, and return the animals to them. In their operations, expeditionary troops also committed rapes and robberies as they had in Haiphong. When my father heard of these acts of depredation, he again protested to the French. As usual, he did not try to appeal to their moral values, but to their desire to defeat the Viet Minh. He reasoned simply that these crimes would alienate the people and push them into the arms of the Viet Minh. My parents believed that his argument persuaded the French to put an end to these abuses.

Without real authority, quietly protesting, trying to influence the French and mitigate against their army's excesses, and protecting the innocent people as best he could was all my father could do at this point. And yet, to the Viet Minh, he and other members of the council were marked men, enemies to be eliminated. Three months after my father assumed his post in Haiphong, the chairman of the Hanoi council was assassinated. He had a bodyguard, but a Viet Minh agent managed to shoot him while he was leaving his house for his office one morning. To replace him, the French appointed Dr. Chi. That left the chairmanship of the Haiphong council vacant, so they asked my father to take over. He accepted, becoming in effect mayor of Haiphong and governor of the Maritime Zone. He was willing to cooperate with the French, because to him they were the lesser of two evils. The communists, in his view, posed a bigger threat to the country in the long run. In the short term, he wanted to defeat the Viet Minh first. Then, with that menace out of the way, he would work for a peaceful transition to independence from France.

At least he committed himself to a course of action. He knew this was a path full of dangers, but he was willing to face whatever came. Around him, many people who would have been willing to collaborate with the French were afraid to make such a commitment. Frightened by the Hanoi chairman's assassination, they stood on the sidelines and waited for conditions to become more favorable. Along with other fence-sitters who were reluctant to commit themselves to either the Viet Minh or the French, they would form what the French called the *attentistes,* or those who wait. Vietnamese would describe them as *trum chan,* meaning people who lie in bed hidden under a blanket, unwilling to get up and take some action.

With Dr. Chi gone, we moved into the villa that he used to occupy, just around the corner from our old house. I was relieved. Although the house we had been living in was better than the one we had borrowed in Hanoi, I hated every moment I spent there. In my mind, I could see the scenes of torture that the neighbors said used to take place there and hear the screams of the victims. It was also in this house that my sister Mao suddenly turned against me. I had never been afraid of her; I always found her harmless and even amusing. She had little rhymes that she liked to recite; when I ran into her I would ask her to say one for me. After she finished, we would laugh loudly together. But our benign relationship changed suddenly. Mao used to try to run away from home at every opportunity; it was as if she thought that by escaping she could leave her affliction behind. Whenever this happened, someone would have to go look for her. When she was led back, she would laugh, pleased that she had eluded everyone in the house and gotten away. One day, as my mother was leaving to visit a friend, Mao quietly followed behind, planning to sneak out the gate after her. By chance, I happened to notice what she was up to, and yelled a warning to my mother. She turned around, scolded Mao, and led her back inside the house. Mao turned to me, her eyes wide with anger and madness. Suddenly, she fell on her knees and started to kowtow to me, saying over and over, "I beg you, don't do this to me again!" But her look remained wild. She scared me and I started to cry.

From then on, whenever Mao got into her periodic rages, she would go looking for me to beat up. In her mind, I had become her enemy. In her outbursts, she would chase me around the villa with superhuman energy until I cried out in terror and someone grabbed her. I was only six at the time, and did not understand why she was singling me out for persecution. Instead of seeking her out when I got bored with my other sisters to ask her questions and see what unusual answers she would come up with, or talk her into reciting her favorite funny rhymes, I learned to keep my distance from her.

So, it was with great relief, then, that I moved from the house that I associated with so many sinister things. The new villa was a two-story building, with a porch and a balcony. It was light and airy, unlike the old one. Shrubs and trees were everywhere, and flowers brightened the yard for many months during the year. I loved the large bushes of *hai duong* with their orange-red blossoms full of sweet nectar, and the *khe* trees with their arching branches and sour ridged fruit. There was also a little shrine in the yard that kept evil spirits away and made me feel safe. The air here always seemed serene and fragrant to me, and I felt I had left the world of darkness and emerged into a world of light. While we were living in this house, my sister Tuyet was born. She immediately became my parents' favorite and began to occupy a special space in their hearts that I could not. With her arrival, I got even less attention than before and felt more lost in the swarm of sons and daughters.

My parents had a hierarchy of affection. Of their children still at home, they lavished the most attention and love on Giu and Tuan, their first and youngest sons, and on Tuyet, the last born. Not counting Mao, among the seven middle children, they were partial to those they were proud of, like my older sisters Phu and Binh because they were beautiful, especially Binh, who had light-brown hair, hazel eyes, dimples, and a complexion as white as that of a European. My brothers Xuong and Luong, my sisters Yen and Loan, and I had neither looks nor brains, nor any accomplishment that could make my parents proud, and so they paid hardly any attention to us. Indeed, more often than not, the five of us felt we were merely tolerated. The fact that we could not make them love us as much as our other siblings made us feel inadequate. This shared bond drew Yen, Loan, and I together. They became my constant companions and confidants. Luong and Xuong spent most of their time at school in Hanoi, so I did not grow close to them. At least my mother paid some attention to me: She taught me how to read and write Vietnamese, she took me out with her on occasions, and she saw to it that I was clothed, fed, and educated adequately. My father, on the other hand, was so busy he rarely exchanged a few words with me. He would remain a distant figure until my late teens. I felt affectionate toward my mother, but toward my father, I felt filial respect and gratitude rather than love.

One day, my mother told my older sisters and me that a new school year was about to begin and that we would have to attend classes. Formal education had stopped for the children in my family for years now because of the war, so I never thought I would have to go to school. The news came as a shock. The French had not yet reopened the Henri Rivière school—the most elite in Haiphong—so my parents sent me and my sisters to another one not far from our house. My brothers, as befit their status as sons, were dispatched to the Lycée Albert Sarraut in Hanoi at considerable expense. Our school gave me a glimpse of what non-elite Vietnamese had to put up with. It had just been reopened and was barely functioning. The classrooms were bleak, textbooks were nonexistent, and the teachers looked malnourished and wore shabby clothes. The toilets were filthy, and I always got sick to my stomach when I had to use them. The school officials and teachers did not try to teach me and my sisters, and let us do whatever we wanted, out of fear that my father would be angry if we did not get our way. The first day,

I did not want to sit in my own classroom, among strangers, and asked to be allowed to attend the same class as my sister Yen. I was more inno-cent than arrogant; I simply missed my sister. After a quick consultation with school officials, the teachers let me make the switch. The grade was too advanced for me, so during the class I doodled, tried to talk to my sister, or wandered outside.

The students at my new school came from all sorts of backgrounds. Some were quite poor. My best friend Phuong was a year or two older. Unlike the other pupils, who were intimidated by my father's position and kept their distance, she sought me out. She treated me like an ordi-nary kid. She accepted me for what I was—a shy but curious seven-year-old—and not as the daughter of the most powerful Vietnamese in Haiphong. In our childish, unself-conscious way, we did not see the social gulf that separated us, and developed a warm friendship. She would never come to my house to visit—her parents would not let her—but she would take me to her modest home. It was located in one of the many alleys radiating from our street, where the manual workers who kept Haiphong's port and factories running huddled in their ram-shackle homes. Her house was tiny and dark and furnished very simply. A tap that jutted out over a concrete tank in the small courtyard pro-vided running water. In this courtyard the family would do all its wash-ing, scooping out water with a dipper and pouring it into basins—dif-ferent ones for food, clothes, hands, and faces. Sometimes, Phuong would ask me to share a meal. She was not self-conscious about her poverty, but her parents would apologize for the poor fare, usually rice with fried bean curd and boiled vegetables. Like Phuong, I did not pay attention to social trappings, and loved to visit her and eat with her family. I have never tasted fried bean curd that can match what they gave me on those occasions.

In the meantime, pacification was proceeding apace. One village would become secure, and then another. My father's power, in his capacity as the Maritime Zone governor, expanded as the French took over more territory. After they gained a toehold in the hostile country-side, the French would supply weapons to my father. He would set up a military outpost, recruit self-defense militia, and arm them to hang on to that small island of control. In the case of Catholic villages, he would give the weapons to the people themselves to keep the Viet Minh out. The Catholics were fanatic anticommunists, so my father knew that he could trust the villagers to use the weapons only against the Viet Minh—and not turn around and use them against the French and their allies.

At first, no province was completely secure. On average, each district would control ten to fifteen villages surrounding the main town. Beyond that belt, the land remained in Viet Minh hands. Gradually, the French would drive the Viet Minh further and further away to control whole provinces. As the Viet Minh became stronger, however, they began to push back. In outlying areas the *pourriture,* or rotting from within, would begin. Viet Minh cadres and guerrillas would filter back. Military posts in these areas would become isolated. At night, the self-defense militiamen would become prisoners in their own reinforced posts, afraid to go out on patrol. Outside, the Viet Minh—masters of the night—would come and go as they pleased.

Besides self-defense, the French also handed over the administrative reins to my father as soon as they took over a district or a province. He had complete authority to select the new leaders to run these pacified areas. The French did not interfere. Since he had won their trust, they felt they could afford to give him some leeway. With the freedom to appoint the heads of these pacified districts and provinces, my father had a golden opportunity to enrich himself—if he had wanted to. Corrupt officials could make a fortune by selling such positions to the highest bidders, and did so throughout French territory. Once in place, the province and district chiefs would earn back their bribes several times over by selling favors or extorting money. Rich men began to approach my father, offering tens of thousands of piasters—the equivalent to millions in later times—for each position of province chief, and slightly less for each position of district chief. But he turned them down. Instead, he went to Hanoi and invited men he knew to serve in his administration. To him, doing the moral thing was not only right, it was also good protection against heaven's wrath. Vietnamese folklore is full of stories of cruel or greedy people whose families are punished by violent or untimely deaths.

My father did not limit his appointments to his circle of former mandarins. He also sought out capable local leaders who had influence among the people. One of the issues my father faced was what titles to give these province and district officials. To call them by the old mandarin titles of province, county, and district magistrates would send the signal that the government was reverting back to an old and archaic system that had been thoroughly discredited in everyone's eyes during the 1945 famine and the August Revolution. So, together with the members of the council, he came up with the new titles of *tinh truong* and *quan truong,* or province and district chiefs. The new names conveyed the sense of change that he wanted to get across to the people.

In his appointments, my father had three basic considerations. First, he wanted loyal men he could trust. Second, he wanted courageous men who were not afraid of the Viet Minh and who he knew would not hesitate to plunge in and get things done. Third, he wanted capable men who could run their provinces or districts well. It was not easy to find people fitting the criteria, and it was even more difficult to persuade those who were qualified to serve. Some did not want to be tainted by an association with the French, and others were afraid of Viet Minh retaliation.

As pacification got into full gear, important officials began trooping through Haiphong to get a reading on the French military drive in the important Maritime Zone and to visit Tonkin's second largest city. Every week, my parents would hold receptions or dinners for the dignitaries and their entourage. Guests would drive up to our house in their shiny cars, and the VIP would more likely than not arrive in an official automobile with a fluttering flag and sometimes even an escort on motorcycles. During one reception, we heard a loud explosion down the street and then a single shot, causing a great commotion. Then we got the news that a Viet Minh agent had thrown a grenade at the neighborhood police station and had been shot dead. With that, the reception continued and the guests resumed their interrupted conversation.

For these official occasions, my siblings and I were herded upstairs, and told to stay away and keep out of sight. When my teachers asked me about what had been said and done at the reception or dinner, I did not know what to tell them. Like them, I felt like I was an outsider looking in. I had practically no interaction with my father—I rarely saw him, in fact—so I had nothing to tell my teachers or anyone else who wanted to know about him and what he was doing. To me, as to the rest of the people in Haiphong, he was just a figure of authority. At least they read about him in the papers or listened to his speeches. I was too young to even get a glimpse of him that way.

The year my family moved to Haiphong marked a turning point in French policy. Paris by this time had come to realize that it did not have the resources to defeat the Viet Minh. Other corners of its empire were in danger: Unrest was brewing in North Africa, and a revolt had erupted in Madagascar. Troops had to be dispatched to these places to maintain control. With her army spread so thin, France simply could not afford to deploy half a million or more soldiers in Vietnam to defeat the resistance. Furthermore, the increasing casualties and the prospect of an endless war with no victory in sight were demoralizing the army. Added to this, the cost of the war was growing, to the tune of $34 million a month. A military solution, then, would be out of the question. Negotiation looked like the only possible answer to a war that had already reached a stalemate just months after it had begun.

But negotiation was also problematic. The Viet Minh refused to change their basic demands: genuine independence and the return of Cochinchina as an integral part of Vietnam. To the French, these terms remained as unacceptable now as they had been at the start of the fighting. They began searching for someone to set up a government that would be an alternative to the Viet Minh, a government that could win the allegiance of the Vietnamese and, at the same time, one that France could manipulate into accepting terms that the Viet Minh would not. This was a policy built on the quicksand of illusion, since independence and territorial integrity were the aspirations of the majority of the population, and a government that was willing to live with anything less would find it impossible to win the broad support needed to defeat the Viet Minh. But to the French, who continued to think of independence as a dirty word, this seemed like their best course. From the beginning, former Emperor Bao Dai—who had abdicated after the August Revolution in 1945—looked like the most viable candidate for this thankless task. In early 1947, French emissaries began contacting the emperor living in exile in Hong Kong.

Many people in Vietnam supported Bao Dai. The emperor had shown that he was a nationalist. When he abdicated the throne in 1945, after the Viet Minh had seized power, he had proclaimed that he would rather be an ordinary citizen of a free country than the emperor of an enslaved nation. These words had won the sympathy of many people, including my father. He, too, was in favor of this "Bao Dai solution." He felt guilty siding with the French, and longed for the emperor's return as an answer to his prayers. In his fantasy, the emperor would gain independence from the French, and win so much popular support in the process that the Viet Minh would be reduced to a mere shell, no longer a threat to the normal order of things. My father could work for his government with a clear conscience. He would no longer appear to be a collaborator, but a nationalist on the same level with the Viet Minh.

It took the French until June 1948 to give Bao Dai the terms he deemed acceptable. Although he signed an initial agreement, the emperor became so disillusioned with its stipulations—its vague promise of independence and stubborn refusal to restore Cochinchina as a part of Vietnam—that he refused to return to the country. He thought he could not go back and face the people under the circumstances. In March

1949, the United States finally pressured France to give him a treaty he could go home with. Washington was casting a worried eye at the situation in Vietnam. The Cold War had begun, and the communists were gaining grounds in Europe and China. To the United States, the Viet Minh were part of this communist expansion and had to be checked. Like Paris, Washington thought Bao Dai was a good alternative to the Viet Minh and urged the French to be more accommodating to the emperor. In the 1949 treaty, Paris recognized Vietnam as an independent and unified state with Cochinchina as an integral part of its territory. There were many strings attached, however. Vietnam would have to remain within the French Union and France would continue to control Vietnam's foreign and military affairs. Powerless to wrest more from France, Bao Dai finally swallowed the bittersweet pill and flew home. The treaty failed to trigger the "psychological shock" that the French hoped for. It did not give the country enough independence to weaken popular support for the Viet Minh and rally the people behind the emperor, as the French soon discovered.

A new government with Bao Dai as Chief of State was created. This brought only cosmetic changes, however. The French remained firmly in charge. They still made all the major decisions, manipulating things from behind Vietnamese figureheads—from the emperor and his cabinet ministers on down. In Haiphong, the Council to Calm and Resettle the Population, which sounded provisional, was disbanded. My father formally assumed the titles of mayor and governor of the Maritime Zone, which gave the impression that he was now fully in charge, free of French fetters, as befit an official of an independent country. This was far from the truth, however, as his power did not get enlarged. The French retained control of political, financial, and military affairs. They gave him his budget and they directed him through two French advisors. Frustrated, my father would sometimes complain to my mother, "The French pretend to be my advisors, but they're really my inquisitors. When they come into my office, they don't give me advice. They interrogate me and tell me what to do." A typical article in a Haiphong newspaper at the time satirized the local government's lack of power, mocking that it was allowed to control only petty matters like regulating vendors who sold goods from "bamboo trays and bamboo baskets."

Three months after the treaty went into effect, the emperor made a triumphant visit to Haiphong toward the end of September 1949 to celebrate "independence." There was excitement among many noncommunists, who thought that Vietnam had reached a true milestone. Soon, however, they would become disillusioned. For this occasion, Bao Dai

flew to Cat Bi airport where my father met him at the head of a welcoming delegation of local notables and foreign dignitaries. Schools and
government offices were closed, and students and government workers
were sent into the street to swell the crowd and give the emperor a rousing welcome. Thousands lined the route from the airport into the city to
cheer him. My father, proud that the country had become independent,
banned the French tricolor and ordered that the crowd carry only the
yellow Vietnamese flag. The French were upset with him, and lodged
this slight in their minds.

My father led the emperor and the delegation to the official mayor's
residence for the raising of the flag ceremony. The French had just,
reluctantly, turned over this building—until now occupied by the top
colonial official in Haiphong—to my father. It was an emotional and
proud moment for my father when the Vietnamese flag unfurled as it
caught the breeze and fluttered in the wind. A snag marred the occasion,
however. Since there was no local band that he could use for the ceremony, my father had drafted a French military band to play the new
national anthem. Unfamiliar with the tune, the band ended it in mid-
song. My father and the delegation waited in vain for the musical climax. The unfinished anthem was like an echo of the incomplete independence that France finally condescended to give to Vietnam.

From our residence, the emperor and his motorcade proceeded to the
big main square, dominated by the large theater, to appear before the
people. My classmates and I were among the thousands that thronged
the Place du Théâtre Municipal to cheer the emperor and listen to his
speech. A sea of flags and banners filled the square. Expectations ran
high. People had a naive faith that independence would somehow work
miracles, and that security, employment, prosperity, and happiness
would descend like manna from heaven. Sprinkled among the banners
welcoming independence and expressing gratitude to the emperor were
a few urging Bao Dai to "come to the aid of local refugees," "release prisoners of war," and bring "warm clothes" and "plenty of food"—that is
to say, a decent standard of living—to Haiphong residents. When Bao
Dai appeared on the balcony to address the crowd, I shouted lustily
with everyone around me, "Long live the Emperor! Long live
Vietnamese independence!" When a teacher pointed out the figure of
my father on the balcony next to the emperor, I felt very proud, although
I knew he was not even aware that I was down in the square.

Unlike my father, I did not understand the political significance of
our move into the mayor's residence. I was simply impressed by the

grand quarters that suddenly became our home. The mansion, a colonial-style building, sat behind a wrought-iron fence on several acres of land. It occupied the grounds of an old temple that the French, in their insensitivity to Vietnamese culture, had razed. Two sentry boxes guarded the main and side gates. The yard, complete with a tennis court, was so large that my two inseparable sisters—Yen and Loan—and I felt like we were living in a park. No matter how much time we spent exploring it, we always felt we could never check out all its nooks and crannies. I remember most vividly the huge banyan trees with their creepers from which we loved to swing.

I remember also the balcony in the back of the residence, which led from the dining room. Once in a while, my father would have a French military band provide entertainment for a reception or dinner, and the guests would stand here and listen to the music. The front rooms looked out onto the large square that spread before the residence. From one of the windows, I used to watch elegant guests get out of their cars, or dragon dancers writhing their way to the front steps where my father waited to stuff a wad of money down the throat of the dragon as a gift for the new year. The only building next to the residence was the mayor's office building. Across from it stood the city hall, and on the other side of the street was the Henri Rivière, the elite school where my sisters and I were now enrolled. Curving around the square and across from it were beautiful colonial buildings and villas. Behind our house were the river and the port. Looking out from our windows, we felt as though we were in France and not in our own country. The only thing in our neighborhood that reminded me that I was still in Vietnam was a temple where I used to go and watch a shaman conduct her colorful worship.

Our household staff now included a chef who could cook Vietnamese, French, and Chinese dishes, several servants, and a chauffeur to drive the Citroën, my father's official car. My father also had two bodyguards who went everywhere with him, like shadows. And of course, there was the platoon of guards. They quickly identified me as someone still young enough for them to influence and yet old enough to act on their requests. They would talk me into taking prized cigarettes like Craven-A and 555 from the house for them to smoke, or treats from the pantry—things that they could never buy with their small salaries. With so many guests to entertain and so many official functions to hold, the house was always well stocked with cigarettes, liquor, wine, and other delectable things. I was unpredictable, however. I could be a foe as well as an accomplice for the guards, whom I liked to distract by throwing pebbles at their sentry boxes. One afternoon, I stole the rifle of a guard who had fallen asleep in the hot and steamy summer weather, and then ran to report him to the platoon commander. My mischief landed the poor guard in jail for three days.

In October 1949, Emperor Bao Dai returned to Haiphong for another visit. This time, he arrived on his motor yacht, named *Huong Giang* after the Perfume River in Hue. The ship created a sensation. There was a lot of rhetoric about how the yacht would be turned into a merchant vessel, the first in a fleet for an independent Vietnam. My family was invited on board for a private tour. Photographers were present for the occasion. I was allowed to come along, and marveled at the spit and polish of the ship and gawked at the Vietnamese sailors—a novelty. Of course, like all the early promises of this embryonic independence, the merchant navy never materialized. While the *Huong Giang* was in town, Bao Dai stayed at our residence. To make room for the august visitor, we moved from the main villa into the house toward the back. My siblings and I were so obedient that we stayed well out of sight, and never once had a glimpse of the emperor. After this visit, the city never saw Bao Dai again. Disillusioned and resentful of being used as a pawn and a puppet by the French, he would retreat to the central highlands to hunt and sulk.

With our move into the mayor's residence, I began the happiest and most carefree period of my life in north Vietnam. Except for trips to the beaches in the summer and an occasional outing, my world was confined to the house, its large yard, and school. Yet I did not yearn for a wider horizon, because to me the mayor's residence was a such special place that I never tired of being there. I did not make any close friends at school and did not feel I needed to; I had the company of Yen and Loan and that was enough. We did everything together: played games, explored the yard, invented an imaginary universe, and shared the same room. School was a lark. I never did any work, but each year would be deluged with honor prizes—armloads of books that I could not read or understand. All the students went out of their way to be nice to us because of who we were.

Life at our house was exciting. My father had to entertain lavishly and frequently. He had a chief of protocol to help plan each social function: receptions, small and large dinners, and *soirées dansantes* to mark the holidays and to entertain local or visiting dignitaries. Catering trucks would arrive bearing an array of dishes and pastries. The house would become festive with flowers and the large dining table would twinkle with silverware and crystal goblets. Elegant guests would throng the living and dining rooms, and the yard on summer evenings.

I thought my life would go on like that forever. But one day a terrible disease almost ended it. One morning, my sister Yen became sick. She complained about a headache and fatigue, ran a high fever, and could not eat. Two days later, I came down with the same symptoms. We thought we just had a common cold, but when our fever would not go down and Yen started to bleed, our doctor became alarmed. He took a closer look and diagnosed typhoid fever. A dose of penicillin would have cured us right away, but this antibiotic was not available in a Haiphong that was just beginning to recover from the fighting. We were rushed to the hospital. My mother wanted to stay and take care of us, but because of the danger of contagion, my father would not let her. He scolded her, "Look at all the children. If something happens to you, what would become of them?" A maid took her place and kept vigil over us.

Yen and I had a room to ourselves, a relative luxury. Other patients shared a long room with beds arranged in two rows. Most of them would die from lack of medication. At night, I could hear the groans and moans of these patients echoing into our room. Yen and I were very stoic. We just accepted our condition, and rarely complained. Gradually, we got worse. We took only liquids and had to be fed intravenously. We became so weak, we could not get out of bed. Our limbs atrophied. We began losing our hair. Yen was in worse shape than I, and started to become delirious. Her eyes became unfocused. When my mother came to visit us, she could not recognize her. I knew she was dying, and thought I would be next.

I had nothing to take my mind off my illness—no books, no radio, and of course no television. Fortunately, I was so drained that I would drift in and out of sleep. During the daytime when sunlight shone into our room, things did not look so bleak. Nurses would come and go, giving us so many injections that they ran out of fresh spots into which they could insert their syringes. We dreaded the huge needle for intravenous feeding, and Yen would cry at the sight of it whenever the nurse came in to change it. Whenever my mother or sister Phu came to visit, they appeared like a breath of life in death's chamber, and I would brighten up. I would feel invaded by an irrational and childish hope that somehow I would recover and go home and be with my family again. But at night, I was left alone with my own fears, and the hospital would turn more sinister. Whenever I awoke, I could hear more clearly in the quiet of the night the moans and groans coming from my sister's bed and from the room down the corridor. Once in a while, I could hear a sudden commotion and the wailing of a relative keeping vigil if a patient had died.

A British businessman who was acting as England's consul in Haiphong saved our lives. My father knew him, and he was a frequent visitor to our house. When he heard that Yen and I were dying from typhoid fever, he cabled Hong Kong for penicillin. When the drugs arrived by special courier one evening, he rushed to our house to deliver the precious medication. The drug snatched us back from the brink of death so quickly it seemed miraculous. We stayed in the hospital for a while longer and then were allowed to go home for a long convalescence. At the beginning, I could move about only by holding on to things and could eat only clear liquids. Although the disease had made my bowels paper-thin, I became obsessed with solid food and found even a banana tempting. At times, the urge to steal and eat something solid was almost too strong for me to resist. Fortunately, I managed not to give in.

At the time I recovered from my illness, Haiphong also started to prosper. With security restored, people from Hanoi and other provinces began to flock there to work. Most ended up in factories, at the docks, in the warehouses, and in the construction industry rebuilding houses and making improvements to the port's facilities. With the interior slowly returning to normal, the port once again became the trade hub of Tonkin.

Haiphong was a beehive of activity. The French had imposed a curfew from 11 p.m. to 7 a.m., but even before the curfew ended in the morning, people began moving about in the streets. Workers streamed from their hovels in alleys on foot or on bicycles. The sound of voices, laughter, and the noise of wooden clogs on the pavement echoed in the early morning. Soon they were drowned out by the noise of traffic—engines and horns honking in the crowded streets. Shops opened their doors, smoke belched from the big factories, and dockworkers loaded and unloaded ships at the wharves. The city kept going at night. While Hanoi was ready to retire for bed by eight o'clock, Haiphong's nightlife began at that hour. The brightly lit streets were so crowded and noisy people forgot they were still living in wartime. Eating establishments did a roaring business—from food stalls at curbside offering cheap meals cooked in woks sizzling over fires to expensive well-lit restaurants where a glass of orange juice cost the equivalent of a worker's day wages. But by eleven o'clock, all this had to wind down to comply with the curfew.

In December 1949, the municipal theater that had been under repair reopened. My father presided over the inauguration of this civic land-mark. Festooned arches were built in the streets leading up to the the-ater, and my father arrived at the head of a motorcade of dignitaries. Later I accompanied my parents to a performance at this theater, a play based on *The Tale of Kieu*. We sat in the box of honor, and although I was small, I was aware of everyone's deference—we were treated almost like royalty. My older brothers and sisters appreciated the flattering treat-ment more than I did. My older sister Phu in particular enjoyed her role as a sort of celebrity. My father often drafted her into service: to stand in for him at official ceremonies, such as inaugurating an office or flying in a newly arrived airplane. Newspapers frequently carried pictures in which she appeared, smiling her charming smile.

Starting in 1950, American officials began to appear among the many visiting dignitaries that my father had to host. By this time, the com-munists had won in China. The Soviet Union and China had recognized the government of Ho Chi Minh, and were sending him more and more aid. The United States, afraid that the French would lose the war, rec-ognized Bao Dai and provided aid for France to use in Vietnam. To jus-tify this aid, the American Joint Chiefs of Staff took the widespread fear of communist expansion and formulated it into what became known as the domino theory: If Vietnam fell, other countries in the region as well would fall to communism. This theory would turn into a dogma of American policy, and would be invoked again and again during the decades of U.S. involvement.

One day, my father brought a visiting American aid official home to stay with us. Before the guest's arrival in Haiphong, my father prepared a special welcome. He had arches entwined with green branches and fresh flowers built for the motorcade from the airport. He also had a dragon boat made ready so he could take the American on tours of the surrounding areas that were crisscrossed with waterways. When my brother Giu asked my father why he was going to such length with the American, my father said, "Unless we treat him right, we won't get any aid money." The French would go even further than my father to win the hearts of the visiting Americans, and were known on occasions to introduce them to beautiful women.

Beneath the social glitter lurked a lot of strain for my father. He had an uneasy relationship with the French. Unable to buck their power, he had to accept a lot of compromises, but he always stood firm on things that mattered to him. The French respected him for his ability to get things done and liked him because he was generally cooperative. At times, however, they became angry when he dug in his heels. Chinese businessmen made up another group of wealthy and powerful people who could give him headaches. They were used to buying influence with money, and tried to bribe him on many occasions. Once, a Chinese merchant asked him for permission to import votive goods. He refused, saying that he did not want to encourage poor and superstitious people to spend their meager wages on paper products to burn and send to their dead relatives in the other world. Trying to induce him to change his mind, the businessman brought an attaché case stuffed with cash to our house. My father politely turned him down and asked him to leave.

Another time, the Chinese asked for permission to open a six-month *kermesse,* a sort of combination trade fair and gambling festival. Besides stalls selling goods, it also had small gambling halls that brought enormous profits for their operators. My father still remembered vividly a *kermesse* in Hanoi years before, when many people killed themselves after incurring heavy gambling debts. He was afraid the same tragedy would strike Haiphong, a tragedy that the Viet Minh would be sure to exploit. He refused to issue a permit. The Chinese businessmen were stunned. They had bribed some powerful men—both French and Vietnamese, including the governor of Tonkin—and thought they would have easy sailing in Haiphong. They complained to the governor, who pressured my father hard. When he refused to change his mind, the governor sent a messenger to tell him that if the deal did not go through the Chinese would expose the fact that he had taken money from them. My father stood his ground. Seeing that their tactics had not worked, the Chinese decided to bribe my father as well. They came to our house carrying a briefcase containing a large amount of gold, but my father would not touch it. The *kermesse* never took place. The governor was furious.

In refusing the bribes, my father was observing the mandarin ethic that dictated that officials should keep their integrity. Besides, he felt that collaborating with the French was bad enough, and did not wish to make matters worse by ruining his personal reputation and family's honor. Also, he had seen many corrupt officials around him and feared becoming like them, where one bribe would lead to the next and the next until accepting payoffs turned into a habit. Last, my father believed that if he performed good deeds, he could induce heaven to protect him and his descendants from tragedy.

The pressure of all these conflicting interests and demands was draining for my father. Often, we would see him sitting in his study, in a deep frown, with his hands rubbing his forehead, as if trying to relieve a terrible headache. He told my mother, "A lot of people envy my position, but they only see the glamour. They don't know the problems that go with it. My job's like a shiny red pepper—on the outside, it looks delicious, but when you take a bite, it burns your mouth."

The Viet Minh, for their part, also made life difficult for my father. Their agents had infiltrated Haiphong by mingling with the returning refugees to recruit residents into their ranks and intimidate people who wanted to work for the French. To send a powerful message, they would resort to assassination. The attacks were daring. Of the twelve men who headed the various sections of the city, three were killed in their houses in the middle of the night; the fourth was murdered in broad daylight while sitting in his shop. The head of the secret police was shot in the stomach right in the middle of a crowded street one evening. In propaganda leaflets spread clandestinely by their agents, the Viet Minh usually claimed that those they had killed "owed a blood debt to the people"—that is to say, the officials had harmed the revolution. In the case of the security police chief, for example, the Viet Minh condemned him for his corruption and for hurting their movement. According to them, he had extorted money from returning refugees in exchange for getting them identity papers, and he had jailed and killed several Viet Minh cadres.

My father knew that he too was a marked man. When he first went to Haiphong to assume his post, the Viet Minh sent him a threatening letter. Although it conceded that he was a man of conscience who had done good things for the people, it also condemned him as a traitor and a collaborator. The Viet Minh tried to kill him three times. The first time, by pure chance, the French security police arrested a suspected Viet Minh agent and found a piece of paper on him containing an order in invisible ink instructing him to lie in wait for my father and shoot him when he emerged from our house. The second time, an armed Viet Minh agent managed to sneak into my father's office. But when the assassin saw him, he suddenly lost his nerve. Trembling, he handed over his pistol. After these incidents, my father knew he badly needed a bodyguard. None was available then, so he hired my brother Xuong, who had just moved down with us. Xuong used to accompany him, carrying a pistol in his holster and looking very proud and important. We used to laugh and say that he would not be much protection in a crisis. After schools reopened in Hanoi in 1948, Xuong went back to the *lycée*. More people had returned to Haiphong by then, so my father was able to find two professionals to take his place.

The last attempt against my father's life came not from a faceless assassin but from inside his own household. One of the servants had met and fallen in love with a peddler who was a Viet Minh agent. She gave him some poison to put in my father's drink or food. Somehow the French got wind of the plot and arrested the servant before he had the chance or decided to act. They threw him in jail and interrogated him with their usual brutal techniques. His mother came to see my mother, pleading for mercy, "Unless he gets out of jail, my son will die from the beatings." Feeling sorry for the servant and for the old woman, my mother talked to my father, saying that the servant had been very loyal up until now and that he had only accepted the poison to please the girlfriend with whom he was madly in love. My father agreed with my mother, and asked the French security officials to let the servant go. The French, nonplussed, said, "He planned to kill you, and yet you want us to release him?" But eventually, they acceded to my father's dogged requests and released the servant. My parents welcomed the news, believing that this good deed would be another mark in their favor— and ours—in heaven's eyes. (Needless to say, the servant was not rehired.)

Despite these plots against his life, my father carried on as normal. Among his official duties, the inspection tours were the most dangerous. Whenever he went to a village to check on things, explain a government policy, or motivate the peasants, he felt very exposed. A lone assassin hiding in a bamboo grove could easily shoot him while he made his way on foot into the village, or a sniper could plant a bullet in his head while he was giving his speech. Things were most dicey in the villages that had not been completely secured. My father could only hope that his karma and the good deeds he had performed would protect him from a violent and sudden death.

The attempts against my father's life took place in the first two years of his tenure in Haiphong, when Viet Minh policy against those they viewed as collaborators was implacable. In 1950, the Viet Minh switched tactics. Instead of trying to kill my father, they now decided to recruit him, as part of their new policy. They would continue to eliminate those officials they considered brutal, but they would try to convert those they thought had a feeling for the country and the people. After following my father closely, the Viet Minh special police in Haiphong concluded that, in spite of his mandarin background, my father was a patriot who was doing a lot to help the people and a nationalist who was yearning for independence. They also thought that he was a decent opponent. He was not resorting to underhanded and brutal tactics to fight them, such as inducing the French to make wholesale arrests in the hope of catching a few Viet Minh agents in the dragnet, or to torture and execute suspects. After he refused to issue a permit for the *kermesse*, they sent him a long letter, praising him for his integrity—comparing him to a lotus flower that was pure although its roots were sunk in mud—and asking him to "return to the fatherland." My father knew that the flattery was only a ploy to induce him to do the Viet Minh's bidding. Afraid that the letter might incriminate him in the eyes of the French, he burned it immediately.

When they got no response, the Viet Minh sent Ho, one of my cousins, to recruit my father. Ho had joined the Viet Minh in 1945. When they found out that he was related to my father, the Viet Minh transferred him from his military unit to the Haiphong special police. My family had lost touch with Ho, and we did not know that he was now a member of this revolutionary police. If Ho succeeded, the Viet Minh would have an invaluable operative planted in a sensitive position who could help their cause enormously.

While waiting for the chance to convert my father, Ho's other mission was to operate underground in Haiphong, under my father's unwitting protection, gathering information about French military operations, strategy, and tactics, and passing it along to the Viet Minh. Before contacting my father, Ho spent three months in a village near Haiphong, learning how to take secret pictures of documents. He was given Western clothes and taught how to behave and act like an urbane person—niceties he had forgotten while in the Viet Minh forest hideout. Then, when the Viet Minh thought he was ready, they dictated a letter for him to send to my father, appealing to family ties and explaining that he wanted to come to Haiphong and live with my father so he could continue his studies. My father was happy to hear from Ho, the son of a sister who had died young. He immediately wrote back, saying that he would take Ho into his household, enroll him in school, and then send him to France to study. The promise of an education in France alarmed the Viet Minh special police, who feared that Ho would not pass up such an opportunity and that once in France he would not come back. Rather than lose a cadre they had spent so much time training, they aborted Ho's mission. My father wondered why Ho never wrote back, but did not try to track him down after he lost contact. (My parents never found out about Ho's real intention. I learned of Ho's mission only when I saw him in Hanoi in 1995.)

The government that Bao Dai established after his return in 1949 set in motion my father's downfall. To consolidate his support among his core followers, a patchwork of religious sects and political parties, the emperor had divided power among them, giving each a piece of the pie. In Tonkin, the governorship had passed into the hands of Nguyen Huu Tri, a member of the Dai Viet Party, a noncommunist group mainly in the north. Through him, the Dai Viet began to gain power over Tonkin. Naturally, the Dai Viet wanted to place their own people in key positions to enrich the party's coffers and enlarge its influence. The governor knew my father and had nothing against him personally, but he had to place his party's interests over all, and this left my father vulnerable. He had enemies, people he had angered by refusing to be part of their web of corruption. He had lasted only because the French supported him, but now they began to pull back. My father had angered them at times with his stubborn and nationalistic attitude. Besides, they wanted to cooperate with the new governor, a man they believed would be effective in fighting the Viet Minh. Saving my father's career was not on their agenda. He was replaced by a Dai Viet Party member. But the governor was not heartless. Since my father was a friend, he gave him another job as general inspector for political and administrative affairs for all of Tonkin. Within a year, the new mayor had taken in enough money to buy an impressive villa.

Meanwhile, my family packed up and moved to Hanoi. My father left Haiphong as he had come, penniless. Few people believed in his integrity, however, since incorruptible officials almost did not exist. Rumors persisted that we left Haiphong loaded with gold, diamonds, and cash. Years later, when our house burned down in Saigon, people whispered that my mother, in a panic at the approaching fire, poured a bowl full of diamonds—spoils from our days in Haiphong—down the gutter in the hope of retrieving them later. Fantastic as the story was, everyone who heard it believed it.

10

The Fall of a Border Garrison

Mrs. Thong Ngoc, our landlady in Hanoi, lived upstairs, in a room in the back of the house overlooking the courtyard and the old *longan* tree. She had advanced asthma, so spent most of her time in bed. The room in which she had to confine herself was pleasant. She had decorated it with antique furniture and porcelain, and from her large bed in carved dark wood, she could survey her beautiful possessions. Even with all the fine furnishings, the room still felt like an invalid's chamber. Mrs. Thong Ngoc rarely set foot outside. Once in a while, a visitor would drop by, but that was all the company she had. The first time I spent an afternoon with her, she was so delighted that I would come back again and again. She gave me the attention I rarely got from my parents; I also saw quickly that her apartment was an ideal hiding place when I skipped school. She could not talk much and usually just listened to me or watched me play. I thought Mrs. Thong Ngoc did not have long to live, yet she hung on for years. What kept her going was the hope that her only son, who had joined the Viet Minh, would one day come back to see her. Although she had not heard from him since he left, she was sure he was alive. So, she was waiting patiently for the war to end and for him to return.

In being physically distant from the war and yet psychologically touched by it, Mrs. Thong Ngoc was like other middle class people in Hanoi. Like her, they carried on as if it did not exist. Deep down, however, it affected them deeply. The fighting might remain far away—raging in the rice paddies, in the remote hills, forests, and mountains—and the peasants who bore the brunt of the conflict might suffer and die out of sight and out of hearing, yet the war constantly impinged on the consciousness of Hanoi's middle class. There were frequent reminders, such as trucks full of armed soldiers and military vehicles clattering through the streets, news of victories or reverses, pictures of death and destruction in the daily papers. And when the Viet Minh moved closer to the city, as they did in late 1950, fear gripped the middle-class milieu. Besides, many families had relatives in the Viet Minh or in zones controlled by them, as we did, and once in a while they could not help but wonder how these relatives were bearing under French attacks. So, much as we and other families might have liked to, we could not banish the war from our thoughts.

We were living with Mrs. Thong Ngoc because when we returned to Hanoi in 1950, our house near the Lanessan Hospital was already rented out. Our new home was a two-story villa with a small front yard and a narrow garden that ran along both sides of the house. It was located at the corner of Gambetta Boulevard, near the central train station. Of all the places in the house, my favorite was the living room. It felt to me like a retreat into a serene, bygone time. In the summer, this room, dark and cool, became my favorite refuge from the blistering heat and harsh sunlight of Hanoi. Mrs. Thong Ngoc had decorated it the same way she had her own room, full of antique hardwood furniture, carved and inlaid with marble or mother-of-pearl. Wooden scrolls of different shapes and sizes bearing gilded Chinese characters hung on the walls. Big porcelain vases stood in niches on both sides of an arched doorway. At Tet, my mother put flowering cherry and plum branches in the vases, and narcissus bulbs heavy with fragrant white blossoms and long green leaves in bowls resting on carved wooden stands. Pleasant as it was, the villa was much smaller than the spacious residence we had enjoyed in Haiphong. Upstairs, besides the small apartment occupied by Mrs. Thong Ngoc, there were two bedrooms. My parents used one, and my brothers the other. My four sisters and I crowded into the large room behind the front part of the house.

It was while we were living in Mrs. Thong Ngoc's villa that my sister Phu got married. Considering my father's background and position at the time, it was a surprising union, hardly the sort of alliance between two families of equal social standing that ex-mandarins still prized. The groom's family was modest: The father-in-law was an elementary school teacher with a low salary.

Phu did not want to get married at age eighteen; she would have preferred to go on with her studies. She cried when my parents insisted, but her tears did not soften them. They thought she was too young to know what was good for her, and they thought they had found her a promising husband. A matchmaker, as usual, had initiated the proceedings, bringing the proposal from the groom's family, whom she knew. Since she was a relative, my parents trusted her assessment, believing that she had Phu's best interests in mind. The matchmaker said that the groom was an educated man, an engineer of public works with a solid job and a good salary who wanted to marry Phu out of love. He had been smitten with Phu the first time he saw her walk home from school. After that first chance meeting, he would wait for her outside our house, hoping to catch a glimpse of her.

Today, we might think of this as obsessive behavior, but all my sisters at some time had boys who were fixated with them, worshiping them from afar or, if they were bolder, trying to catch their attention by sending them passionate letters. My sisters would have mixed feelings about the unwanted attention, flattered, yet scared and repelled at times. In a sexually repressed society, where interaction between boys and girls was forbidden, this kind of fixation was considered a normal part of growing up for boys and for girls as well. So my parents were not alarmed by the bridegroom's obsession with Phu, nor were they concerned about the poverty of his family. They were looking for in-laws who would treat Phu kindly, especially since she would have to move in with them. The matchmaker reassured my parents: No need to fret, these were very decent people. My parents were persuaded. They did not investigate further.

The wedding was big, lasting a couple of days. After elaborate cere-monies, cars bedecked with flowers took Phu and her bridal party to her new home. While my parents rejoiced that they had managed to marry off another daughter—leaving only five to go—Phu was despondent. She cried on her wedding day. I will always remember the look of panic on her face when we left her at the end of the marriage ceremony, sit-ting by herself on the edge of her bridal bed. She seemed so lonely and afraid, with tears running down her cheeks—like someone awaiting her execution. That day marked the beginning of a hard life for her. Her new family, she discovered, had a dark history. Her father-in-law turned out to be an opium addict, and a daughter had committed suicide. Later, a son would shoot himself in the head in a bout of depression over losing his girlfriend. Phu's husband was selfish and possessive. Money was always in short supply and the family was burdened with debt. But tra-dition demanded that she should accept her lot without complaint, so she did. It was a matter of duty and honor for her to stay in the marriage, no matter how tough things got. Even if she had wanted to leave her husband, a divorce would have been impossible, legally and socially. It would have carried such a stigma that my parents would not have con-doned it, and Phu herself would have found it too much of a burden to carry. Phu would struggle the rest of her life.

For my father, Phu's wedding seemed to be part of a turn in his for-tune after he moved to Hanoi. Just when he thought that no one was standing up for him, Emperor Bao Dai intervened on his behalf. When he heard the news that my father had lost his post as mayor of Haiphong, the emperor summoned Nguyen De, his cabinet chief, and said, "This is unfair. Find him another position. Give him one that's prestigious but isn't too taxing. Get him a sinecure that'll pay him well and give him a comfortable living." Nguyen De, an old acquaintance of my father's from their university days, appointed him Vietnam's perma-nent representative to the Congress of the French Union located in Paris. This was a body created by France to give former colonies a voice, but no power. Just as Bao Dai had directed, it was a prestigious, high-ly paid, yet safe position, away from the instability and dangers of Vietnam—a job that a lot of people would have killed for. My father got ready to leave for France. But as he was about to do so, the politi-cal picture abruptly changed again.

General de Lattre de Tassigny had arrived as supreme commander for both civilian and military affairs, with complete authority to turn the situation around. To clear the deck in Tonkin, he swept aside political leaders he considered incompetent or corrupt. The Dai Viet Party had become hugely unpopular because of corruption and favoritism, and de Lattre directed the Vietnamese Prime Minister to dismiss all the party's members from the government. The governor of Tonkin, a member of this party, lost his job, and Dr. Dang Huu Chi became governor. Once again, Dr. Chi turned to my father for help. He pleaded with him, "Don't go to France. Stay and help me. I'll make you my second in command and put you in charge of all administrative and financial affairs." Out of friendship for Dr. Chi, my father took the offer and postponed his trip.

My father became in effect a deputy governor for Tonkin, at a time of drastic changes. At de Lattre's instruction, Dr. Chi launched into a housecleaning. He got rid of province chiefs who were members of the Dai Viet Party. He left the appointment of district chiefs and other mid-level officials in my father's hands. As he had promised, he turned over all administrative and financial matters to my father, who became his surrogate—running the day-to-day business of Tonkin, representing him on various councils, and presiding over the monthly meetings with the province chiefs. The governor had complete confidence in him and never questioned what he did. Preoccupied with his dealings with de Lattre, he would sign whatever decree my father put in front of him, and would go along with whatever decision my father had made. This job as the unofficial deputy governor would be the pinnacle of my father's career.

My father had been a philanderer, but his affairs had been discreet, such as the one with a teacher in Haiphong. My siblings and I were not aware of any of these. Now, he began to throw discretion overboard. He began to come home less and less often for dinner. Then, he returned later and later in the evening, usually past midnight. He explained that his official duties kept him away. My mother finally became suspicious and questioned our driver, who confessed that my father had been seeing a woman. Not any woman, but the most well-known *a dao* singer of Tonkin. Within the circle of ex-mandarins like my father who were still fascinated by this kind of music, she was the woman to possess. She had a honeyed voice and masterful singing technique. She frequently performed over Radio Hanoi. The singer's voice was her only asset. She was rather unattractive—plump and coarse—with a dark complexion that we associated with the toiling peasants. However, this did not matter to my father, who was bewitched by her voice and intoxicated with the triumph of being her lover. He enjoyed basking in the envy of his ex-mandarin colleagues.

The affair was the talk of Hanoi. A cousin of my father's gleefully asked my mother about it one day, savoring the pain he inflicted. My siblings and I were within earshot. We looked at each other, dumb-founded. We had idealized our father, and now we found out that he was no better than other men who routinely betrayed their wives. We withdrew silently, feeling crushed with shame. For my mother, this was the worst crisis in her marriage. She had ignored my father's previous liaisons, believing that they were only passing fancies, but this time she saw the obsession and recognized the danger to her and the family. My father could abandon us, or he might start diverting our resources into the singer's hands. My mother was humiliated by the openness of the affair. She heard the whispers and comments, and she sensed the pity of her friends as well as the jubilation of those jealous of her social status. She had bouts of depression and anger, but she was powerless against my father: She could not leave him, and she could not stop him. All she could do was to weep and beg him or hurl angry accusations at him. He was enthralled, however, and she could not shake him out of his infatuation. My siblings and I knew what she was going through, but we could do nothing except feel sorry for her. We pretended not to know, to avoid humiliating her further. To our father, none of us dared breathe a word. He remained the ultimate figure of authority, and we had no right to question what he did—no matter how awful. Besides, we mostly blamed the singer for our family crisis. We too accepted the double standard.

My family's crisis flared up right after the Viet Minh had given people in Hanoi another scare. This time, they pushed into the midlands, the region lying between their mountain base and the rich Red River Delta. It was an area of low hills, giving way to rice fields as the land became flatter, more densely populated, and richer than the mountain region. If they could capture this territory, they would have access to better resources to feed the growing demands of their war. They could also use it as a springboard to drive into the Red River Delta and push the French into the seas. But they had not counted on the new weapons that the Americans had given to de Lattre: napalm and heavy artillery. In the more open terrain, he could use them with deadly results against the Viet Minh if they attacked in large units. De Lattre's unflinching use of napalm, even in close combat where his own troops could get burned, would earn him the nickname of "fire general" among the delta peasants. After taking terrible casualties without achieving any significant gains, General Giap, the Viet Minh commander, decided to call off his offensive. Realizing that his troops were not yet ready for a frontal assault against a much stronger enemy, he withdrew them back into the mountain bases to rebuild the units and train new recruits. For the next two years, he would not risk his army in large unit combat where his soldiers would be exposed to deadly heavy weapons. He would revert to guerrilla warfare. If he attacked with his regular units, it was against only carefully selected targets.

By this time, the French had realized that they could not fight the war all by themselves. They simply did not have enough troops. The time had come for them to "yellowize," or Vietnamize the war. Part of de Lattre's mission was to build a native army. At first, the Vietnamese troops would man defensive positions and free the French forces to go on the offensive. Later, the French would turn the fighting over to them. America would bankroll this long-range effort, and was already paying a larger and larger share of the costs.

To begin building up this army, Emperor Bao Dai ordered the conscription of 60,000 men, to be trained in camps that as yet did not exist. It was left up to each region to determine how and where to find the bodies. Deputized by the Tonkin governor, my father flew to Saigon to meet with the prime minister, the governors of Annam and Cochinchina, and the defense minister, to figure out how to implement the draft and training. The most sensitive issue was how to explain the conscription to the population and motivate them to join the army. After all, why should Vietnamese want to risk their lives fighting other Vietnamese in order to keep the French in power? Together, my father and the officials labored over the wording of the announcement and of the propaganda leaflets that would be distributed throughout the villages under government control. They decided to tell the conscripts that they would not be fighting for the French, but against the Viet Minh to build a noncommunist Vietnam, although they could not define this in any compelling way. As usual, the village officials—the ones at the bottom of the totem pole—would have the thankless task of convincing the peasants that this was a goal worth fighting and dying for.

After he returned to Hanoi with fresh instructions, my father had eight weeks to build the two training camps—one located in Quang Yen Province and the other in Bac Ninh—for the thousands of conscripts who would soon be arriving en masse. He did not have enough funds to hire contractors, so he thought the fastest and cheapest way was to have these provinces mobilize the peasants, just as mandarins used to do in the old days to carry out large public works projects. Villages were asked to supply labor, bamboo, and thatch, and were told they would be adequately compensated. The province chiefs, however, pocketed most of the funds my father disbursed for the construction, making the villagers very angry. Other suppliers of materials like cement also complained about being shortchanged. Newspapers condemned the shenanigans, and my father took a lot of heat, although he had not personally profited from these wrongdoings.

Once the rudimentary camps were ready, my father again met with the province chiefs to discuss how to find up to 20,000 recruits for the camps. They agreed to give each province a quota to fill with youths chosen by lottery from a list of draft-age males. As it happened, the peasants—and not the middle class and the rich—were the only ones whose sons ended up on the provincial lists. After the meeting, my father read a speech at the Opera House to announce the draft policy and selection criteria. The popular reaction was resentful, but muted. In the countryside, the peasants were unhappy because they thought the conscription was simply a way to force their sons to die in place of the French. But no one dared to protest openly, because everyone knew de Lattre would not hesitate to crush any opposition. The secret police stood ready to arrest anyone who dared to sabotage the general's policy. Once the two training camps began to function, my father's responsibility ended.

After the initial flurry of operations against the Viet Minh, General de Lattre found himself in a stalemate. His plan had been to defend the Red River Delta while pushing into enemy territory—clearing out the Viet Minh and retaking control of villages in an oil-spot pacification drive, and driving inexorably into the Viet Minh mountain base. To protect the delta, he built a string of over 100 bunkers that stretched in an arc from east to west and southward toward the sea. From these posts, troops would conduct lightning strikes into the Viet Minh zone, supported by mobile units backed with tanks and heavy artillery. But the mountains, hills, and forests of the north slowed him down and his troops became mired in static defense. De Lattre's strategy failed to turn the tide of the war.

De Lattre's pacification of newly conquered territory was no more successful and permanent than his military gains. Try as he might to root out the Viet Minh behind his lines, he could not stop the *pourriture*. As soon as his mobile troops managed to clear an area, a village government would be set up and militia installed in a post to keep the Viet Minh out. Inevitably, after his troops pulled out, the enemy would sneak back. Within the delta itself, security was never complete. Guerrilla harassment and Viet Minh activities continued even in villages near Hanoi. At one point, de Lattre, in exasperation, wanted to create a secure belt around the city by razing several villages and forcing the peasants to move. When my father got wind of this, he went to see the Tonkin governor and said to his old friend, "You can't let de Lattre carry out his plan. Tens of thousands of people will suffer. Where will they go if their villages are razed to the ground?" Again, pleading was all my father could do—and hope that the French would listen. This time it worked. Dr. Chi got the general to abandon his draconian pacification scheme.

De Lattre was not the only military man tempted to lash out at the peasants out of frustration. In fact, *casser les nhac*, or peasant bashing, became practically a part of French operational routine, if not a pastime for many of the soldiers. Every time the Viet Minh fired upon or blew up a French vehicle, French troops would storm into the nearest village the next day to teach the peasants a lesson. Not knowing how to distinguish a Viet Minh from an innocent civilian, the French would punish the whole village, or they would make wholesale arrests and put the suspects in a prison camp. Then they would have Vietnamese officials come and sort out who the real Viet Minh were. This was not a foolproof process, and many innocent villagers ended up in jail. These highhanded tactics, along with the theft and rape committed by the Expeditionary Corps in the course of their operations, only deepened the resentment of the peasants and often turned them into Viet Minh sympathizers.

It was the job of province chiefs to consolidate the gains and make pacification work. After French troops cleared an area, the head of the province appointed officials to run the villages, keep the Viet Minh from coming back, and win the allegiance of the peasants. My father did not have direct responsibility for pacification. His job was to help the province chiefs hang on to what had been won, and keep the pacified area expanding. His other job was to staff the mobile propaganda teams, created by de Lattre, that went into newly pacified areas to win the hearts and minds of the distrustful and sullen peasants—by distributing gifts and medicine and trying to fraternize with the villagers. He usually recruited people such as ex-policemen, who would not be afraid to venture into these still insecure areas.

My father found pacification as frustrating as it had been in his days in Haiphong. The pacified villages assumed a schizophrenic character: During the day, government officials and militiamen were much in evidence, but at night, Viet Minh cadres and guerrillas would return. Since the propaganda teams kept moving from village to village, and never stayed long enough to win the peasants over, they had little effect. Under these circumstances, pacification was like holding sand in one's fingers. As the Viet Minh became stronger, the forts themselves came under attack, and many of the pacified villages fell back into their hands.

In November 1951, de Lattre, trying to recapture the military initiative, attacked Hoa Binh, sitting astride a major enemy supply route. French forces took the town, located among wooded hills, meeting hardly any resistance. Holding Hoa Binh was not as easy, however. General Giap counterattacked and soon had the town isolated. French airplanes and artillery, hampered by the wooded terrain, could not dislodge Giap's troops. Finding it increasingly difficult to resupply the town by road and river, the French decided to abandon it. The withdrawal was a repeat of the rout along the frontier in 1950, with weary French troops fighting their way out step by step through enemy lines and ambushes. Those who survived would refer to this battle as "the hell of Hoa Binh."

De Lattre did not live to see the debacle. About a month before the battle ended, he died of cancer in Paris. Before leaving Vietnam, the general indirectly had a hand in another turn in my father's career, when he appointed a new governor of Tonkin. Dr. Chi had died of tuberculosis less than a year after he took office, and de Lattre replaced him with Nguyen Van Tam, someone who was not afraid to kill, who would exact an eye for an eye. He and the Viet Minh were mortal enemies, with a blood debt between them: While he was in charge of Cai Lay district, he had viciously suppressed the Viet Minh. In retaliation, they killed two of his sons. Later, when he became special police chief of Saigon, he executed many people he suspected of being their agents. Instead of being repulsed by his violence, de Lattre admired his ruthlessness.

The new governor did not trust anyone and was manipulative, cunning, and dishonest. My father thought he was a dangerous man, and Tam for his part showed no support for my father. After a few months, de Lattre elevated Tam to the position of prime minister, one of many premiers who would come into and out of office through Vietnam's revolving-door politics. When de Lattre died, Emperor Bao Dai brought back Nguyen Huu Tri—his protégé—as governor of Tonkin, and the Dai Viet Party re-emerged to take over power. My father lost his position, and went back to the job Tri had given him in 1950 when he shunted him out of Haiphong—as inspector general for administrative and political affairs, with the added responsibility of overseeing financial expenditures for all of Tonkin.

In 1952, we moved out of Mrs. Thong Ngoc's house into a government-owned villa near the Opera House, located on a tree-shaded residential street. It was more quiet here than on Gambetta Boulevard. My
father and his staff of twenty occupied offices on the ground floor, and
our family had the entire upstairs. By Hanoi's standard, our quarters
were large and comfortable. Most important, they were also free. A
pebbled walkway, lined with flowering shrubs and bordered by a wall
covered with the branches of a huge bougainvillea, led into the villa,
and nicely landscaped yards surrounded the house. My sisters Binh, Yen,
Loan, Tuyet, and I—now forming a close band—had a lot more space
for games and for riding bicycles, which we borrowed from our brothers' friends whenever they came to visit.

We spent a couple of peaceful years in this villa. After the initial
shock and turmoil brought on by my father's affair, our family settled
down. My mother, who prized harmony above everything else, suppressed her own emotions to keep peace and resigned herself to the state
of things. The singer by now had become a de facto secondary wife. Her
relationship with my father, however, had turned routine, more marked
by a sense of duty on his part than passion. He still saw her regularly,
but the infatuation was gone. Since my mother's pain had lost its sharp
edge, my sisters and I could now talk to her about our resentment against
the singer and her intrusion into our family. My mother, although
pleased by our support and solidarity, would laugh at our tirades. She
would defend my father, "He's a good man. He's provided well for all of
us. It's just that he's so infatuated with that woman. If he were really
bad, he would've abandoned us for her." We did not know it at the
time, but my mother's accepting and even indifferent attitude was only
a front. Everyone who knew her marveled at her forbearance. No one
suspected how deep the hurt ran. It was only recently that I discovered
how much my mother still feels the pain of the affair. My father, for his
part, never felt contrite that he had taken a second wife; after all, he was
only exercising the prerogative that all Vietnamese men enjoyed.

Hanoi by this time had recovered from the fighting in 1946–47 and
was even prospering. War spending gave it an economic boost, although
it never experienced the boom that Saigon enjoyed. Profiteers found
plenty of opportunities to garner some of the millions of dollars that
were spilling into the country to feed the war. In our sheltered existence, my sisters and I were unaware of all these goings-on. Confined
within the boundaries of family and school as we were, the outside
world did not exist for us. School was now the École Sainte Marie, run
by French nuns. As we grew older, my mother was afraid that we

would become more open to bad influences, so she enrolled us in the best convent school in Hanoi, overcoming her fear that we would get converted to Catholicism. She had heard that discipline and surveillance were tight there—exactly what she was looking for to keep us in line.

In my case, her plan almost went awry. In fact, if it had not been for a stroke of luck, I would not have gotten into the school. Spoiled by my teachers in Haiphong, who allowed me to do whatever I pleased, I had learned nothing. Moving to Hanoi did not change my attitude toward school—I remained utterly unmotivated to learn. Every day, I would cut classes to visit Mrs. Thong Ngoc or wander in the streets with a couple of friends who also viewed school with boredom. I was nine years old when I applied to the convent school, which required an entrance exam. Although I failed miserably, no one told me that I had not passed, so on the first day of classes I followed my sisters to school. I waited patiently, but my name was not on the roll call; after all the students had filed into their classes, I was still standing in the yard. When the nuns came over and asked me, I replied that I had taken the exam and was supposed to be in class. Confused, the good sisters thought they had made a mistake with my record, and admitted me into the same grade as my eleven-year-old sister Yen, whose low exam scores had landed her there in the fourth grade.

At first I did poorly, and ended at the bottom of my class. One evening, when I heard Yen read a natural science lesson out loud, over and over, without being able to memorize it, I thought I would help by reciting the lesson with her and prompting her whenever she became stuck. When the teacher called on me the next day, I smoothly read the lesson back to her by heart, word for word, as I was supposed to. She looked surprised and gave me a perfect score. I was so pleased that I began to pay attention in class and to do my homework. The good grades I got made me think that learning could be fun. I climbed from the bottom to the middle of the class, earning the attention and affection of my teacher. By the third month, I had risen to the top where I stayed, pleasing my teacher and turning me into one of her favorite students. As in the old days, academic aptitude brought recognition and respect, so my classmates began to look up to me. I would remain a star pupil until I graduated from high school in Saigon. Yen, for her part, struggled that whole year, but did not resent my putting her in the shadow in school. She fell further and further behind me, and eventually dropped out to work as a secretary.

Since my father was no longer the deputy governor of Tonkin, my mother's social life had become less hectic, giving her more time to spend with my sisters and me. I was older now and had begun to show interest in things that she enjoyed doing, such as sewing, knitting, going to see Vietnamese operas or to worship at temples and pagodas, or visiting her sisters. My interest pleased her and she would take me along on some of her rounds. In her hierarchy of affection, I still ranked in the middle, but at least I no longer irked her with my tomboy behavior, which I had outgrown, and was even giving her a reason to be proud of me by doing well in school. I had become more thoughtful also and understood better the pain she had to endure from my father's infidelities. My affection for her grew, drawing me closer to her, and she responded by being more tender and giving me more attention.

Until 1954, our cocoon-like existence enveloped me and my siblings in a false sense of security. My brother Giu had gone to France to study. Giu was bright and capable, yet never did well in school. My father, thinking a change of environment and better instruction would do my brother some good, pulled some strings and got Giu permission to leave for France. My sisters and I could not wait for Giu to go, and rejoiced the day he departed: Finally, we were rid of our harsh and arbitrary brother. My other two brothers, Luong and Tuan, who were still at the Lycée Albert Sarraut, were apathetic teenagers, indifferent to the political and military questions of the day, and spent their leisure time hanging out with their friends—mostly playing mah-jongg and riding bicycles.

The war did not touch my second oldest brother Xuong, who had volunteered for the Regional Forces. He had always been restless and difficult to control. When he dropped out of school, my parents did not try to stop him, knowing it would be futile. He left home and then suddenly reappeared one day, wearing the uniform of an officer. My parents were surprised, but did not worry about him getting exposed to combat. They guessed that, being wily and clever, Xuong would never volunteer for any dangerous task and would manage to wriggle out of any risky assignment. After that, he came home only once in while. Whenever he did, no one in the family would take the trouble to ask him what he was doing in the army, knowing full well we would get only vague answers and jokes. We heard rumors that he had become a playboy, hanging out in dance halls and dating "taxi girls" or hostesses.

My father was the only one in our family who had any knowledge of what was going on in Tonkin, and my sisters and I rarely saw him. He came home more often now for dinner, but he ate with my mother and my brothers Luong and Tuan. We girls were still relegated to eating by ourselves. In my family, meals were served in two shifts: an early one for my sisters and me, and a later one for my brothers and parents. Eating with parents was a privilege reserved for sons. I did not resent this arrangement, accepting it as normal since it went without saying that daughters were inferior to sons. My sisters and I actually preferred eating separately, because we did not have to be on our best behavior; we could talk freely and be silly if we wanted to. Even if we had seen our father at dinnertime, he would not have said anything about the war. Once in a while he would confide in my mother, but he made it a point never to discuss his work with my brothers.

As inspector general for all of Tonkin, he served as the eyes and ears of the governor. His responsibility was to make sure that province and district chiefs were doing their jobs and to gauge the mood in the country-side. If a grievance was lodged against a provincial official, he would investigate and relay the results to the governor. Being a kind man, he usually softened his report of the wrongdoing so that the punishment would be a little less harsh. On the other hand, he would lavish praise on a good official and would urge the governor to give the man a promotion. But bad officials outnumbered good ones; the tendency to use government positions for personal gains was too ingrained. In the years he was inspector general, my father got a couple of province chiefs and several district chiefs dismissed for malfeasance. Again, his position gave him another excellent opportunity to get rich, because local officials knew he could make or break their careers. But he never accepted bribes, being as determined as ever to adhere to the old mandarin ethics and to protect his family's name. The governor nicknamed him "The Kind-Hearted Inspector."

It was dangerous work, and it got more and more risky as security worsened. Province and district officials were getting killed all over the country by mines and snipers. My father knew that the small detail of *bao an*, or civil guards, that the local officials assigned to protect him on his visits would have been useless against determined Viet Minh agents. Whenever he had to address a huge crowd, he wondered whether a bullet or a grenade would end his life. On occasions, when his work kept him in a province town overnight, he would be too anxious to sleep. And yet he did not curtail his tours.

By 1953, the Viet Minh had destroyed de Lattre's defense line and gained control of 60 percent of the Red River Delta. After dark, they held sway over even more people and territory. More and more military posts came under attack. Although the Viet Minh were not as strong in the rest of the country, the worsening situation in Tonkin, as well as the instability and incompetence of the Bao Dai regime, worried my father because he thought the French might depart out of discouragement and leave the Vietnamese government, which was no match for the Viet Minh, to fight on its own.

During six years of fighting, the peasants had been the backbone of the Viet Minh. Their sons fought for the Viet Minh. They provided the food that kept the government and army alive, an army that now numbered over a quarter million. They served as porters, hauling the tons of rice, arms, and ammunition to the battle sites, and carrying the wounded from the battlefields. And yet the long-suffering peasants had gotten nothing in return for their sacrifices. The Viet Minh had promised to give them land, but they had postponed land reform, out of fear that seizing the land of the rich to give to the poor would scare the middle and upper-middle classes and destroy the national unity they had to maintain to defeat the French. Now they felt they could delay no longer, especially since they were going to escalate their demands. They had to give the peasants some reward for their efforts; they would need even greater sacrifices for one big final offensive to break the stalemate and force the French to sue for peace.

Rather than begin by expropriating land, the Viet Minh asked landlords in 1952 to drastically reduce rent so the tenant farmers could keep a larger share of the crops and live a little better. My uncle Chinh's area happened to be the first one chosen to carry this out. In this first phase, landlords could choose whether or not to comply with the request. Most simply ignored it. My uncle, as a province leader of the Lien Viet Front, felt it was his duty to set an example. Not only did he reduce his rent, but to show his support for the revolution—and perhaps to secure protection as the political wind began to shift—he also donated about forty-five acres to the cadres to parcel out among some needy peasants. Among landlords, such a generous attitude was rare, but since my uncle had such a large property, he felt he could afford to part with some of his land.

In early 1953, with rent reduction making little headway, the Viet Minh turned the screws more tightly on the landlords. They were now required not only to reduce rent, but also to return to their tenant farmers the "excessive" rent they had collected over the years. The burden of proof was on the landlords to show that they had not overstated their rented acreage and that they had not collected more than their rightful share of the crops, going all the way back to the year they began leasing the land. Teams of zealous cadres were sent into villages from the outside to enforce the new policy. Not being native to the villages, they were not likely to protect the local landlords with whom they had no ties.

My uncle was confident that he would come out of the situation all right, because he thought he had done nothing wrong and also because he believed his support for the Viet Minh would earn him a fair treatment. So, he and his family calmly greeted the group of cadres who arrived at his house one day to go over his land deeds. Although these papers showed clearly that he had not exaggerated his acreage, the cadres said that he had. They did not bother to go out and survey the land, nor did they have any map to back up their claim. Their threatening demeanor and harsh accusations stunned my uncle, and, guessing that his protest would make the situation worse, he signed the papers they put in front of him, "confessing" his wrongdoing. The cadres told him that over sixteen years—from 1936 to 1952—he had collected a total of about eighty tons of paddy, or unmilled rice—more than his rightful share. Now he had to give all this back to his tenant farmers, each of whom would get a proportionate share depending on the excessive acreage they had rented and the number of years they had worked the land. My uncle felt as though he had been hit by a bolt of lightning. Little did he know that his nightmare had only begun.

Chinh did not have enough paddy in storage or enough savings to pay, and he told the cadres as much, again hoping that his position in the Viet Minh would earn him some leniency. The cadres, however, showed him no respect and accused him of being devious. They suspected that he was rich but was hiding his assets, as other landlords had done. So they came back to my uncle's house to look for assets that they could seize. They measured the rice in storage, bowl by bowl, to make sure he did not have more than he had claimed. They questioned him, his wife, and each of their children separately and relentlessly about the things they had in the house. In the end, the cadres' efforts were wasted. They found no hidden assets, so they took away all the rice my uncle had in storage, along with whatever things of value they could lay their hands on, such as draft animals.

My uncle and his family were devastated. They owed tens of millions of piasters in excessive rent, and they did not even have rice to eat. My aunt had managed to conceal one precious possession, a diamond ring she had received as a wedding gift from her mother. Now, she furtively asked a messenger to take the diamond ring to Hanoi and pass it to one of her cousins to sell. This cousin got in touch with my father and other sympathetic relatives, telling them about Uncle Chinh's plight. My father was heartbroken. He did not have a lot of money, so he contributed two ounces of gold. Altogether ten ounces of gold were collected from a couple of relatives and from the sale of the ring, and given to the messenger to take back to my aunt. At five o'clock one morning, when it was still dark, the messenger secretly left Hanoi with the gold sewn inside the hems of her blouse. On her return to my aunt's village, however, she gave my aunt only one ounce, keeping the other nine for herself. (My aunt did not know about the messenger's treachery until she saw her cousin in Hanoi after the war). My aunt was distressed by the small amount of gold, because it was not enough to pay even 1 percent of the excessive rent. So she used it to keep the family from starving.

Just as the Viet Minh wished, my uncle, his wife, and the six children still at home were now living the kind of life that destitute peasants had led for years. To stretch out the money obtained in Hanoi, the family ate very little, just watery rice soup and boiled vegetables once a day. My uncle was allowed to keep and farm four acres of land, which he and his family had to work themselves. Though he was getting old and his children were still small, the Viet Minh forbade him to hire anyone to help out. The work was made harder because his draft animals had been taken away. To plough, my uncle had to strap the blade to his shoulder and pull it through the hard soil. The little children would stomp on the clods of earth to break them up and prepare the ground for sowing. My uncle was still renting out land, but the property was no longer his to dispose of as he pleased. The law forbade him to take it back and sell it. And the crop from these fields, when it arrived, had to be used to pay down the excessive rent rather than to feed his family.

My uncle also faced the prospect of going to jail if he did not pay back his tenant farmers. Worse still, he would be branded as a "criminal" landlord, a much-feared classification that would stigmatize him and his entire family and make life hard for all his children, even those that had joined the Viet Minh. Their father's "criminal landlord" background would be dredged up constantly, thrown in their faces, and used to harass them and keep them down. Desperate, my uncle decided to go see the cadres and plead for permission to sell his orange grove—now reduced to a third of its original size after a sale made in 1947—in order to raise money for the rent. He talked about the contributions his family had made. He reminded them that he and his wife had been working for the Viet Minh for years, and several of his children were serving in the army. These were village cadres who knew him, so they listened with sympathy, and gave him the permission. At last, things seemed to be looking up. When he found a buyer who gave him a down payment of eight million piasters, he felt elated and thought there was light at the end of the tunnel. He took the money to the cadres right away, as proof of his good faith. He promised to come up with the remaining ten million piasters, and agreed to a deadline.

But things turned sour again. When the buyer's husband, a Viet Minh regiment commander, came back, he scotched the deal. As land reform was heating up, he was afraid to have anything to do with a landlord like my uncle. The wife demanded that Chinh return her down payment. Now, my uncle had two huge debts to repay—to the cadres and to the buyer. Fortunately, the fire-sale price he had put on the orange grove attracted a group of merchants from a neighboring area, who snapped it up. My uncle paid the rest of the excessive rent. He felt relieved, but his troubles were far from over. He now had only three million piasters left to pay the previous buyer, five million less than he needed. In panic, my aunt set out on foot, traveling for five days, going from relative to relative in the Viet Minh zone, to borrow money. But no one had much to spare. She managed to bring back one ounce of gold, equivalent to half a million Viet Minh piasters. It was not enough. The woman pressed charges against my uncle.

In the heated atmosphere at the time, my uncle found that his position in the Viet Minh and his family's loyalty and contributions to the cause meant nothing. As a landlord, he had become an outcast. No one wanted, or dared, to help him. The regiment commander was determined to get his money back, and pressed the cadres to arrest my uncle, saying, "Just throw him in jail. Force him to pay me back." Soon a letter arrived, telling my uncle that unless he came up with the money by a certain date, he would go to prison. My uncle saw he had nowhere to turn. The night before he was due to go to jail, he gave in to despair. He dragged a water jar to the middle of the kitchen, climbed on it and put his head through a noose he had hung from the rafter. My aunt found him before he could kill himself. The next day, the Viet Minh came to take him away to a security police station hidden in the hills. The policemen there were sympathetic. They knew he had done a lot for the Viet Minh. They gave him enough to eat. During the day, they would let him sit on a chair in their office instead of locking him up in a cell.

Back at home, the family was now so hungry that my aunt decided to send five of the seven children—ranging in age from eight to eighteen—to live with an older sister, an aunt, and an uncle in the Viet Minh zone. They left on foot, two by two for company, mutual protection, and comfort. The trip was arduous, taking them through forests and mountains. Along the way, one of the little girls drowned in a stream, but my uncle and his family would not find out about this until months later. Meanwhile, my aunt, now in her fifties, again left on foot to visit other relatives and beg them to help pay the debt and get my uncle out of jail. Finally, after several trips back and forth, she managed to put enough together, and after three months in prison, my uncle came home just before Tet. The family greeted the new year with nothing to eat, but they felt fortunate. At least my uncle was out of jail and they were together again.

Harsh as they were, these blows directed at landlords like my uncle did not amount to a full-blown land reform. The peasants still did not have what they most wanted: their own land. At last, in December 1953, the Communist Party launched land reform. The campaign would start in six pilot villages and then spread out to cover the entire Viet Minh zone. The purpose was not only to give land to the poor; it was also to destroy the power of the landlords and put the poor peasants in charge.

A massive campaign ensued to build popular support. My brother-in-law Hau and all my cousins in the Viet Minh had to attend classes continuously. It was drummed into everyone that giving land to the poor would liberate them from decades of oppression, and that freeing the country from the French would not be enough as long as the majority of the people were not freed from exploitation. Those from poor backgrounds—not surprisingly—supported land reform, but even some people from more privileged backgrounds supported it, like my brother-in-law Hau and my uncle Chinh's own children, because—in theory—the idea of giving land to the poor peasants was laudable. Who could argue against bringing economic equality and social justice for those peasants who had suffered so much? Of course no one at the time could predict the ramifications that land reform would have, or guess at the violence it would unleash. Not everyone approved of land reform when it was launched, but those that opposed it did not dare express their reservations.

As land reform began, outside cadres arrived in each of the pilot villages to execute the new policy. Their mission went beyond forcing the landlords to share land. They were also ordered to carry out a purge of village cadres. Up to now, anyone who wanted to fight the French had been welcome in the Viet Minh. In theory, only workers and poor peasants could become Communist Party members, but in the villages, the cadres in charge did not come from destitute backgrounds; many came from families of rich peasants or landlords. The Party now feared that because these cadres had ties to the landlords, they could not be trusted to carry out land reform with the firmness that it demanded. In fact, it was afraid that they might feel threatened by land reform and might sabotage it. So, the Party ordered the outside cadres to undermine the village leadership and—ultimately—to purge it of people whose loyalty to communist policies was questionable. In their place, the outside cadres would install militant poor peasants who, because they benefited from the land reform, could be counted on not to reverse the changes that it brought and to support the party with zeal. In this new climate, class background, rather than patriotism or contributions to the war effort, would become the measure of a person's worth within the Viet Minh.

For land reform to be effective, the poor peasants had to become politically aware, as the communists put it, and take part in it consciously. They had to "own" it. The problem was that, after generations of being dominated by the landlords, they were too cowed to turn against them, and they were also afraid of the cadres running the village. The first thing the outside cadres had to do, then, was to motivate the peasants and dispel their fear and timidity. After they arrived in a village, they linked up with the poorest of the poor peasants. They moved into their hovels, lived and worked alongside them to win their trust. Once they had become accepted, they would draw out the peasants' unhappiness over their wretched lives and their grievances against the landlords. Then, they told the poor that if they joined in the land reform, their problems would come to an end. By bringing the resentment of the poor to a fever pitch, they created a groundswell for land reform. Finally, together with the most militant of the peasants, they took over the village. They arrested landlords accused of having ruthlessly exploited and oppressed the poor, and sealed their assets. They tried the landlords in a kangaroo court, carefully staged to make it look like it was the will of the people. About a dozen poor peasants who had suffered the most and who harbored the deepest hatred of the landlords were chosen and coached in advance to denounce them at this trial. While these peasants took turns denouncing the landlords in front of this tribunal, other poor peasants planted in the audience would shout "Down with the landlord!" to reinforce the atmosphere of hostility. If the sentence was death, the landlords would be executed on the spot. If the sentence was imprisonment, they would be led away. The properties of landlords found guilty of crimes—including land, houses, draft animals, and tools—would be seized and distributed among the most needy peasants.

While land reform was unfolding in the test villages, the war with the French was about to turn decisively in the Viet Minh's favor. The final, climactic battle of Dien Bien Phu got under way. To focus on this confrontation, the communist party temporarily halted the test phase of land reform in March 1954. Whatever the results of land reform in terms of social justice, it was a stunning success as propaganda. News about it boosted the morale of troops and civilians throughout the Viet Minh areas. The peasants, now more than ever, believed in the Viet Minh promise that they and their families would get land and power once the war was won. They responded with superhuman sacrifices in the struggle to bring the French to their knees at Dien Bien Phu. My sister Thang saw the peasants in Thanh Hoa Province become energized and filled with ardor. Thousands of laborers left to carry rice and other supplies to Dien Bien Phu, filling the roads at night. Young able-bodied men in my brother-in-law Hau's station left to join these laborers who trekked on foot across 400 kilometers to reach the front. The trip would take a month, and yet the difficulties did not deter them or dim their enthusiasm. Everyone, those that went and those that stayed, felt excited, optimistic, and united in their determination to bring the war to victory.

Toward the end of 1953, General Henri Navarre, the new French commander for Indochina, had stationed 13,000 troops and created a major garrison at Dien Bien Phu, a village located in a valley bordering Laos. Among the reasons he gave for this operation, the most important was that he would use Dien Bien Phu as bait. He planned to draw the Viet Minh main force into a large battle where he could smash them once and for all. Navarre deployed his forces in the valley floor, but did not take control of the surrounding high ground. This would leave his troops vulnerable to artillery fire from the hills above, but Navarre believed the Viet Minh did not have the heavy weapons that could rain destruction on his men. Even if they did, he reasoned, it would be impossible for them to move this equipment over rugged and mountainous terrain and put it in position to inflict damage. Napalm, bombing, and strafing would knock out whatever they could put in place.

Back in France, the people were getting weary of the long war and especially of the cost in money and lives. Pressure mounted on the government to seek a negotiated settlement, especially because a crisis in Algeria was looming. There was indication that France would use the international conference to be held in Geneva in April 1954 to discuss Korea—where an armistice had taken effect—to try and negotiate an end to the war. For their own reasons, the Soviet Union and China wanted to settle the Vietnam issue. Both wished to project a peaceful image to enhance their worldwide position and influence. They pressured Ho Chi Minh to negotiate. Ho was afraid that unless the war came to an end, the United States might enter the fray. As the conference approached, the Viet Minh felt they had to deal the French a decisive military blow to drive a favorable bargain at Geneva. They decided to pick up Navarre's gauntlet and to give him the climactic confrontation he wanted at Dien Bien Phu.

Navarre had badly underestimated his enemy's capacity and tenacity. It is true that Dien Bien Phu was a logistical headache for the Viet Minh, located hundreds of kilometers away from their main supply sources. The terrain of high mountains and thick jungles was formidable. But their determination to fight and win was fierce. In three months, General Giap moved 50,000 soldiers and tons of heavy equipment to the area around Dien Bien Phu. Over the course of the battle, close to a million workers—men and women—labored to carry food and ammunition to the site, traveling on foot over steep and rugged terrain with heavy loads, through daily strafing and bombing. No one knows for sure how many were killed and wounded along the way. When the young men from my brother-in-law Hau's station came back from their trip to carry supplies to the front, he was shocked to see that their faces had been partially burned by napalm.

The laborers' and soldiers' heroic efforts have become part of the mythology of the resistance war. The most compelling image, along with that of young soldiers charging French positions, was of laborers pushing heavy artillery pieces up steep and slippery slopes inch by terrible inch, up and down the mountain sides and over the peaks, using nothing but ropes and their bare hands, clearing a path as they went. It was said that in one instance, when the heavy equipment was about to roll backward and crash in a ravine, a man threw himself down to block it, sacrificing his own body to save the precious artillery.

Through these herculean efforts, the Viet Minh managed to put a ring of artillery around Dien Bien Phu. The weapons were well camouflaged, protected by thick foliage, and defended by anti-aircraft guns.

Neither French artillery barrages nor air attacks could knock them out. After the Viet Minh took the two hillocks protecting the airfield—the only supply artery for the besieged fortress—and began to keep it under constant bombardment, the French positions were doomed. In despera-tion, France asked the United States to weigh in with air support to save Dien Bien Phu. The American military, after pondering the advan-tages and disadvantages of U.S. intervention, including the use of tacti-cal nuclear weapons, recommended against it. U.S. air support would not necessarily defeat the Viet Minh, the Pentagon concluded, and might lead to Soviet or more likely Chinese intervention, which in turn would necessitate sending in American ground troops. After the experi-ence in Korea, the specter of American boys fighting another Asian land war stirred no enthusiasm in Washington.

Of the accounts about the agony of Dien Bien Phu that I happened to read, I remember most vividly the reports and pictures in *Paris Match*, France's equivalent to *Life* magazine, though in a delayed fashion as the copies took a while to arrive in Hanoi. I was fascinated by a series of pic-tures showing a French officer trying to recruit volunteers from a small group of soldiers for an air drop into the besieged garrison as reinforce-ments. How could a man ask other men to jump into certain and useless death? I wondered.

On May 1, the Viet Minh began their final assault, and on May 8, Dien Bien Phu fell. The success of the Viet Minh evoked ambiguous feel-ings in their countrymen. Even people in our middle-class milieu in Hanoi were proud that Vietnamese had defeated a much stronger foreign army. The Viet Minh's determination, commitment, and courage impressed even the French. The colonial officials my father talked to in Hanoi were awed by their enemy's efforts in overcoming tremendous obstacles to win. During the Vietnam War, Americans in Saigon would express similar feelings of admiration for the Viet Cong, while bemoan-ing the lack of dedication on the part of their own Vietnamese allies.

The Viet Minh had taken heavy casualties and paid a terrible price for their victory at Dien Bien Phu, but they had dealt a fatal blow to the French military ambition in Vietnam. General Navarre himself called for a cease-fire. In Hanoi, there was panic. The middle class knew that the French were not winning the war, but they had never expected the Viet Minh to break the stalemate. They were lulled into believing that the breathing space they enjoyed would last for a long time. Dien Bien Phu shattered this illusion. After their defeat, the French began to fall back toward Hanoi, abandoning one province after another. Even a province as close as Nam Dinh, where I was born, was abandoned. Soon, the French controlled only Hanoi and Haiphong, and the route that linked the two cities. As the colonial forces withdrew, people who had thrown in their lot with the French fled in panic before the advancing Viet Minh, afraid to stay and face retaliation. In Hanoi, the French themselves began to give up hope. Their pessimism spread to their Vietnamese allies, who began to lose faith in them. At night, I thought I heard the sound of gunfire of the approaching Viet Minh echoing in the stillness. We felt a sense of impending doom.

Rumors began to fly in Hanoi that the French were about to negotiate with the Viet Minh, giving them all of Tonkin with the exception of Hanoi and Haiphong. Some wealthy people started to liquidate their assets and move south. By June, it became clear that France was going to forge a deal with the Viet Minh at Geneva. The Bao Dai government, angry that it had not been consulted, staged demonstrations to protest against the negotiation, but to no avail. On July 20, 1954, the Geneva Accords were signed. Hostilities would cease. Vietnam would be partitioned in half, with the Viet Minh taking over the north, down to the 17th Parallel. The French would withdraw to the south. In two years, national elections would be held to reunify the country under the government of either the north or the south. The French now had to admit that their policies had failed not only to win the war, but also to create a viable alternative to the Viet Minh. Emperor Bao Dai, the man they had chosen to lead, still had no credibility among the people. Pitted against Ho Chi Minh in the contest for popular allegiance, Bao Dai had proved to be no match. His government, a patchwork of political groups constantly squabbling among themselves for power, was still floundering in corruption and incompetence. His army was not only small but also unmotivated, as pitiful a fighting force as ever.

Neither the Viet Minh nor the Bao Dai's party were happy with the Geneva settlement. The Viet Minh did not want to give up the south where they controlled a large chunk of territory. But they had to accept the terms under pressure from their Soviet and Chinese allies, and also to preempt direct intervention by the United States. They consoled themselves with the thought that, in two years' time, their popularity as liberators would help them win the south back in the national elections. The Bao Dai side was unhappy that the French had given away the north to the Viet Minh without so much as a by-your-leave, and refused to sign the declaration calling for the elections in 1956.

The fall of Dien Bien Phu and the partition stunned my parents. Their anxiety spread to all of us. There was a quiet but palpable fear in our home. My father was adamant that we would not stay in Hanoi. He was sure the Viet Minh would retaliate. He would be a dead man, and, as his relatives, we all would be persecuted. My parents had many grim discussions to which we crowded around and listened. Where would we go? We did not have the resources to move to France or any other country, and it was doubtful whether any would accept us as refugees. The only possible destination was Saigon. My father believed this would be only a temporary shelter, because he thought that in two years the Viet Minh would win the election and take over the south as well and we would have to flee again, but we had few options. The other nagging question was, What would we do for a living? No job was waiting for my father in Saigon, and other than a little cash and the pieces of jewelry my mother had, we had no savings. "We'll face that when the time comes," my father said; "for now, let's just go south." I was then thirteen years of age, old enough to understand that we were staring calamity in the face.

Five days after the accord was signed in Geneva, my father put us on a plane bound for Saigon, intending to rejoin us in May 1955 when he finished his job of transferring his office from Hanoi to Haiphong, and then from Haiphong to Saigon. My twenty-year-old brother Luong had already gone south, drafted into the officer training school where he was undergoing basic training under French instructors. When Luong's name came up just as the battle for Dien Bien Phu was reaching its climax, my father could have intervened to get him a deferment, but he felt it would be inappropriate. As someone who had spearheaded the mobilization of enlisted men earlier, he thought he should set an example by not trying to save his own son. If he had, it would have looked like he was taking part in the draft evasion. Luong's officer class would be the last wave of youths to be dragged into the French effort to "Vietnamize" the war.

Looking back, Luong would feel resentful over my father's decision, which set him back for many years. The war was ending, and there was no need to make him interrupt his studies for a lost cause. My brother thought that my father's scruples about the draft merely showed his indifference to his middle son. He compared his lot with that of his younger brother Tuan, and saw another instance of favoritism. While my parents ignored Luong, they doted on Tuan, their youngest and brightest son. Ever since a fortune-teller predicted that Tuan would enjoy great success and become a cabinet minister, my father started to nickname him "the minister" and put a lot of hope in him. When it looked as if the French might lose in Tonkin, my father sent Tuan to Dalat, a mountain resort near Saigon, to study and to get him out of harm's way. But he did not send Luong. So, when my father did nothing to keep him out of the army, Luong would resent the favoritism even more. Meanwhile, Xuong had left the favoritism behind for an independent life in the colonial army. Now, after Geneva, he told my parents he would take care of himself. My parents, always indifferent to Xuong, the black sheep of the family, and trusting in his resourcefulness, took his word for it and did not worry. Xuong would move to Saigon with the Regional Forces.

During the few days before we left Hanoi for Saigon, we frantically tried to sell what we could in the open-air market that had spontaneously sprung up, where people like us were trying to unload the belongings they could not take along and also to raise some much-needed cash for the move to the south. For a couple of days, U Mien, our trusted old maid, would carry furniture, dishes, old clothes, shoes, bedding, pots, and pans to sell at this market. We were now the only family U Mien had, having lost her husband to famine in 1945 and her only son to suicide. U Mien felt torn by the move; part of her wanted to go south with us, and part of her also wanted to stay and welcome the Viet Minh whom she supported. Finally, she decided to leave with us. My mother also tried to sell the house that we owned, but everyone knew the communists would not allow private ownership, so no one wanted to buy a house only to lose it later. In the end, my mother just abandoned it, but she left a message with her brother Dinh that Thang should try to collect the rent as long as she could to supplement her income, if and when she returned to Hanoi. My father thought Viet Minh agents might try to stop us if we did not move quickly, so we packed and departed in a headlong rush without saying good-bye to relatives and friends. When an aunt came to visit a few days later, she was shocked to find us gone and my father living all alone in the big, empty house.

While we in Hanoi thought our world was crumbling around us, Thang and her Viet Minh colleagues exploded in celebration at the news of the victory at Dien Bien Phu. She would remember this as the most memorable moment of her life in the resistance. All around her, people burst out singing a song that had been composed just in case the Viet Minh won: "Our troops have liberated Dien Bien Phu . . . ." Nine years of fighting had left everyone in her area on the brink of exhaustion, and so for them peace came just in time. They were elated and, for the first time in years, looked to the future with hope. With peace, priva-tions and hardships would end, and the stress and worries that went with the war would disappear. My sister immediately began making plans to return to Hanoi. She could hardly contain her excitement at the prospect of being reunited with her parents, brothers, and sisters. She only regretted that her husband, who had gone to the Soviet Union to get some technical training, was not there to share her joy.

My father remained in Hanoi until two days before the Viet Minh arrived to take over in October 1954. He was still in charge of the finances of Tonkin while the government was winding down its busi-ness and moving to the south. No one was willing to take his place, so he felt it was his duty to stay behind. With many of its residents gone south, Hanoi became eerie. While the poor looked forward expectantly to Ho Chi Minh's arrival, the middle class fell prey to uncertainty and anxiety. Security deteriorated, and middle-class families huddled in their homes, with their doors locked, fearful of crime and the future. At night, Vietnamese army deserters would break into houses and rob peo-ple at gunpoint. Their victims would bang on pots and pans to summon help, but the few policemen who were still around were too frightened to do anything. Alone at night, my father, listening to these clanking sounds of alarm, felt frightened too.

The time finally came for him to move to Haiphong. This city was the last center of French control and would serve as the exit point for their troops from Tonkin. It was crowded with refugees awaiting pas-sage to the south, living in makeshift tents set up by the U.S. Naval Task Force, which had arrived for the evacuation. Most were from Catholic enclaves that had supported the French during the war. Among the naval personnel that arrived to move and care for the refugees, my father met Tom Dooley, the Catholic doctor who later on wrote a best-seller about his experience and spearheaded a controversial anticommunist cru-sade. In sending its ships to move the refugees south, the United States performed both a humanitarian service and an astute political maneuver, since the refugees provided a solid base of support for Ngo Dinh Diem, the American ally who had been appointed prime minister of what now became a noncommunist South Vietnam.

Toward the end of April 1955, a few days before the Viet Minh were due to take over Haiphong, my father closed down his office for good and flew to Saigon. The last image that he would take with him was the chaotic scene in Haiphong as French colonialism breathed its last in Tonkin. But mingled with this picture of the pitiful ending to almost eighty years of French rule were images that gave him hope: the face of a young American doctor and the towering hulls of U.S. Navy ships loaded with refugees bound for the south. He took the Americans' presence as a reassuring sign that a new and much more powerful player had arrived on the scene to be Vietnam's savior.

11

Sifting Through the Rubble

One morning in July 1954, we piled into the black and squat Citroën with our suitcases, crammed with as many things as we could carry, said good-bye to our father, who would rejoin us in Saigon later, and rode to the airport for the flight south. As our driver pulled out of the wrought-iron gate into the street, we turned around and took one last look at our home. We were sure that we would never come back. Once a communist government was in power in Hanoi, it would be unsafe for us to return, even for a visit. Sad as the parting was, none of us broke down and cried; we were too numbed by the sudden upheaval and too worried about how we were going to survive as refugees in Saigon. We left so quickly that we did not arrange in advance for a permanent place to stay in the south. Through my father's older sisters, who had moved to Saigon earlier, we got an invitation to spend our first night at the house of one of their acquaintances.

I do not remember anything about that flight to Saigon in the droning propeller plane. I was too airsick to pay attention. As we approached Saigon, I heard the other passengers exclaim about how beautiful the city looked at night from the air, illuminated by thousands of lights that shimmered like stars. Deposited by a vehicle in front of the Continental Hotel, with its terrace cafe that served as one of the favorite hangouts for the French downtown, we milled around on the sidewalk with our suitcases, tired and lost in a strange city, not knowing how to get to where we were supposed to go. A couple of Frenchmen looked at us and laughed, making sarcastic comments about our confusion. To them, we appeared like country bumpkins bewildered by the big city. I angrily stared at them, and they quieted down, ashamed of their callousness. We flagged a taxi and asked the driver to take us to the address my mother had. His accent sounded strange, and we could not make out what he said, while ours baffled him. Finally, we straightened things out. Our host family was already asleep in their darkened villa. After a few moments' hesitation, we rang the doorbell and banged on the gate, rousing them out of bed. They let us in and gave us reed mats, mosquito nets, and pillows. We wearily threw our suitcases down, spread the mats on the floor, strung up the mosquito nets, and quickly fell asleep.

In the early morning hours, I heard the cries of vendors, different from the familiar ones in Hanoi. I could not tell what food they were selling. The gate clanked, and I saw a maid buy freshly baked French baguettes from a peddler who pulled them out from under some cloth in the basket mounted on the back of his bicycle. At breakfast, the bread, still warm, was served spread with butter and sprinkled with sugar. This was my first introduction to the southern fondness for sweet things, one of the many differences between Saigon and Hanoi. My sisters and I ate ravenously, too hungry to bother with the customary decorum requiring women to "eat daintily like kittens." While we were busy munching the bread, the couple's oldest daughter asked us, "Why did you leave the north now that it's become independent?" We looked up, surprised by the sympathy for the Viet Minh that was obvious in her question. My mother replied that we left because the Viet Minh were communists and we did not want to live under their government, but the daughter disagreed with our view. She said that the Viet Minh were heroic people who had fought and made sacrifices to gain independence. Now that they had won liberty for half the land, we should have stayed to live as free people instead of going south, where we would have to continue to bow under the French. Although she did not pursue the subject, it was clear she did not approve of our decision to flee. This confrontation gave us the first clue that there were people in Saigon, even affluent ones, who harbored a deep sympathy for the Viet Minh. It came as a shock, because we had always thought that the south, ruled as a direct colony and as an integral part of France, was a bastion of French support. As it turned out, this young woman was a dedicated supporter of the Viet Minh who was about to follow through on her conviction. Shortly after we left her house, she gave up her comfortable life in Saigon and moved to Hanoi.

The next day, we moved to the apartment of my father's aunt, the one who had married the son of the last viceroy of Tonkin. This lady was then the matriarch of the clan, as my great-grandfather's most senior surviving offspring and also as a member of the grandest family in the north, and she commanded respect and obedience. In her home, we had to be on our best behavior, using the most respectful language and gestures. No matter how we really felt, we had to look and act cheerful to show that we appreciated her hospitality, but the first night in her apartment, my emotions got the better of me. I broke down and cried, overcome by the upheaval of the past few days and by our unstable life as refugees. I wept quietly, trying not to disturb my great-aunt, yet she noticed my tears. Instead of being annoyed with me, she asked me kindly whether I was upset because I found her hospitality wanting. I shook my head. She pressed me, "Then, why are you crying?" I wanted to say, "I want to go home. I want things to be like they were. I want my past life back." Instead, I just sobbed and did not say anything. Having lost her husband and two daughters in an airplane crash, she understood what it was like to suddenly have the ground cut out from under you. She looked at me, and I could see in her eyes that she knew how I felt.

None of us was comfortable in my great-aunt's home, so my mother got in touch with my father's older sisters, the same two aunts who had taken us in when my family returned to Hanoi in 1947. They were staying at the villa of an acquaintance on the outskirts of Saigon. The moment we heard they would give us shelter for a while, we packed up once again. Each of our moves was complicated by the fact that we had to cope with my sister Mao. What she wanted to do was either to stay put, with a finger in each ear to block out the world so she could better hear the imaginary people she was conversing with—talking out loud and laughing with them—or to wander off on her own journey, away from us, following the voices that echoed in her brain. We had to stay close to her during the trip.

The villa was a two-story building nestled in the middle of large old trees that shaded it from the sun—much harsher and hotter than in the north because of the proximity to the equator. Here we got our first glimpse of the southern countryside, with its rice fields and coconut trees swaying in the bright sunshine. Everything seemed to be on a larger scale. There was a feeling of space, of more land and more sky. There was also a feeling of languor in the countryside, of life slowed down in the fiercer tropical heat. In the south the peasants spoke in a dialect with gentler accents, rather than with the sharp and angular tones of northerners. They wore black instead of brown shirts and pants. They looked darker and shorter, the products of the ethnic mingling with Cambodians, who used to own the south until Vietnam annexed it in the eighteenth century.

After the hectic and emotional departure from Hanoi and depressing initial arrival in Saigon, the peace of the villa and its surroundings was like a balm for our frayed psyches. We felt like we were on vacation. During the day, we roamed the novel countryside, in many ways reminiscent of our homeland in the north, and yet so different. One of my cousins had a daughter my age, and she became my friend, interpreter with the peasants, and guide. Together we explored the groves full of exotic fruit trees such as mango, rambutan, and mangosteen. We took walks along the narrow paths between the rice fields with our arms outstretched to keep our balance, luxuriating in the greenness that enveloped us. We looked for fish in the small canal that flowed on the edge of the property. When we got hungry, we would buy from vendors the typical sticky southern snacks—many of them flavored with coconut milk and coconut shreds—that were so new to my palate. At mealtimes, my family savored the wonderful southern cuisine that was much richer and more flavorful than the bland northern cooking. We feasted on the natural wealth of the south we had heard so much about, the fish, shrimp, vegetables, and fruit. To the people in the north, squeezed into the Red River Delta, living on the edge of hunger, at the mercy of flooding and drought, slaving to coax food out of the soil, the south had always appeared a tropical cornucopia, a flat, vast, and fertile land where rice fields stretched to the horizon and where fish swam in abundance in the rivers and canals that crisscrossed the region. I, too, had shared this vision, and now I came close to living this fantasy. My only regret while at the villa was that it was a long way away from the Plain of Reeds, the most exotic region of the south. This swampy expanse in the monsoon season occupied the same place in the northern imagination as the West did in pioneer days for Americans. We pictured it as a new frontier, where free spirits, malcontents, or people fleeing oppression could survive on the wild rice and fish that it harbored.

This wonderful interlude did not last, because we had to move on. My mother planned to go to the mountain resort of Dalat where my father's brother had retired. However, since my father was still commuting from the north to visit us occasionally, my older aunt suggested that we remain in Saigon to give him a place to stay whenever he came to town. Housing had become extremely difficult to find, but our aunt referred us to an acquaintance who had rooms she was renting out to refugees. Our quarters turned out to be a garage, for which the owner—taking advantage of the tight market—extracted a large rent, in a small residence where we shared a bathroom and kitchen with two other families. After a few depressing months, my family found what we thought was going to be our permanent home, when my brother Xuong located a two-room house across from the army headquarters. We hurriedly moved in, after paying what to us was a large sum for a long-term lease.

Compared with Hanoi—the serene, green, and beautiful little town that I loved—Saigon, sprawling out over a larger area and harboring ten times more people, looked like a bustling metropolis. It exuded an energy that Hanoi did not have, but lacked the charm and sense of history that used to inspire Hanoi poets to write elegiac verses. Distances were greater, traffic was heavier and more noisy, the streets were more dusty, commerce was livelier, and life was more hectic. Saigon did have pleasant quarters—nice residential neighborhoods with large villas and the downtown section shaded with trees and lined with shops, cafes, hotels, restaurants, and imposing government buildings—but the rent in those areas was out of our reach. The downtown district was the most French and most elegant part of the city, and had earned Saigon the names of Pearl of the Orient and Paris of the East. When I toured this section for the first time in 1954, I was struck by its elegance and impressed with its expensive merchandise and establishments. Later, when I went to France, I realized that Saigon was a replica of a French provincial town transplanted to Asia.

Our new house was near Cholon, the exotic and teeming Chinese twin city of Saigon. It sat like a long and narrow cubicle, cheek by jowl with other similar nondescript buildings, in an alley. There was no front yard. From the alley, we could step right into the first room of the house. Beyond were a second room, the kitchen, bathroom, toilet, and a small yard. A concrete cistern, set against one side of the yard with a faucet jutting over it, gave us our water supply. My mother, my five sisters, two maids, and I crowded into this small space. I had been longing for our spacious home in Hanoi—and for our past lifestyle—since we set foot in Saigon. Now, realizing that I would have to put up with these barren surroundings for years to come depressed me and made me even more nostalgic. Instead of diminishing with the passage of time, my yearning for what I thought was my golden age would grow stronger, and my memory of the north would become more and more romanticized. Our house's other disadvantage was its location, far from everything, including our school, which stood at the other end of Saigon near the riverfront. Without a car, the most economical and fastest mean of transportation for us was the *cyclo may*, the noisy motorized rickshaw spewing dense black smoke that poisoned the air. We began to take it back and forth to the school. My older sister Yen, my younger sister Loan, and I would squeeze into a *cyclo may*, and off we would go—in our school uniforms of white blouses and navy blue skirts, choking in the dust and exhaust, our hair flying in the wind as the driver sped his way through the traffic. When we arrived, we would extract ourselves, our bodies sore from the tight squeeze and the long ride, and our legs numb. What a change from the leisurely one-block walk to our school in Hanoi along a tree-shaded avenue!

We discovered that the people of Saigon, far from welcoming us with open arms or at least with sympathy, resented us and the other refugees, of whom there were eventually close to one million. Some hated us for having abandoned the Viet Minh and fled to the south clinging to the French; others saw us as carpetbaggers who were going to steal their jobs and their rice bowls, or who were going to drive up the price of everything and make life difficult for everyone. The French policy of divide and rule had worked very well among a large segment of the Saigon population. Instead of seeing us as compatriots, many people thought of us as aliens: They called themselves Vietnamese (*nguoi Viet*) while calling us *Bac Ky*, or northerners. On a bus one day, a man angrily shouted at me to go back to the north where I belonged, while the other riders looked on. No one felt any urge to come to the defense of a girl of thirteen.

My mother had chosen Saint Paul, a French convent school, for us. On our first day there, the students greeted us with resentful stares and curses. My sisters and I were the only northerners in the school then, and we huddled together to give each other comfort, surrounded by hostile pupils. There were moments when I thought the students might attack us. But then the bell rang, and we filed into our classrooms where—under the watchful eyes of the nuns in starched white habits— the students did not dare utter an unfriendly word. Some of the students who were most hostile in those initial days later on became my friends, but during the first years I spent at Saint Paul, I thought of myself as an outsider. It was only toward the end that I began to feel completely integrated. I refused to let the hostility and rejection crush me, however. I set out to become one of the best students in the school and succeeded, earning the grudging respect of my southern classmates. Our refugee experience had taught me that nothing in life was permanent— we could be riding high one moment and thrown into the dust the next. Now, my success at Saint Paul taught me that if I did not give up in the face of difficulties, I could move ahead again.

Many northern refugees saw Ngo Dinh Diem as their protector in this tense situation. During the two years he spent at a Catholic seminary in the United States, Diem had met and impressed some influential people who became his supporters, including Cardinal Francis Spellman and Senator Mike Mansfield of the Foreign Relations Committee. Their backing, as well as the fact that Washington did not see another alternative, made him America's choice for leading South Vietnam. It was said that the prime minister's job was a position few people in their right mind wanted at the time. South Vietnam's economy, based mostly on agriculture, had been devastated by the war. Politically, the country was also in a state of chaos, with different groups that could challenge Diem for control. The Viet Minh continued to hold sway over large regions that had been their strongholds during the resistance. In addition, the two major religious sects, the Buddhist Hoa Hao and the synchretistic Cao Dai, controlled sizable areas that they had run autonomously by consent of the French, who hoped that this would keep their allegiance against the Viet Minh. Led by their own religious leaders, these sects—with millions of adherents concentrated in the Mekong Delta—were a distinctive product of the south, where people less bound by traditional religion flocked to their millenarian message. Another group, a gangster organization called the Binh Xuyen, dominated Saigon and Cholon. The Binh Xuyen did not have as many followers but were far richer. They controlled most of the commerce in Cholon and kept a stranglehold over prostitution, gambling, and the opium trade. Each of these three groups had their own private army, which the French had funded to encourage them to fight the Viet Minh. They were so powerful that no Bao Dai government could survive without their support.

It was to this drained and chaotic South Vietnam that Diem returned in 1954. He had earned a reputation, mainly among the urban middle class and intellectuals, as a man of integrity when he refused to cooperate with the French and resigned his position as Minister of the Interior in 1933. His new appointment was greeted with guarded optimism in these circles, but did not generate much enthusiasm among the rest of the population. Diem seemed a lonely figure. He was a Catholic in a mostly Buddhist country, a man from the central region trying to govern a people dominated by southerners living in the Mekong Delta, and an expatriate without a large internal following. He was also a prime minister without an army to back his power. The chief of staff, a general with French citizenship, rejected his authority and openly flouted his orders. In this situation, Diem recognized that the northern refugees—most of whom were fellow Catholics from the fanatic anticommunist bastions of Tonkin—were his most reliable source of support, and he immediately moved to take care of them. With the financial help of the United States, he began the massive—and successful—job of resettling these Catholic refugees in areas outside of Saigon and in the central highlands.

As the main source of support for Diem, the northern refugees, even non-Catholics like us, along with his compatriots from the central region, began to gain influence. Some of our relatives would later rise to prominence in the army and in the government. Vu Van Mau, the son-in-law of my clan matriarch and a lawyer trained in France, became foreign minister. With so many people from the northern and central parts of the country in its ranks, the Diem regime increasingly took on the look of a carpetbagger government, and the population in the south grew to dislike it more and more.

Although the backing of the refugees was important, it would not have kept Diem in power if the Americans had not thrown their support behind him. After the Korean War, the United States believed that it had to hold the line in South Vietnam to keep communism from expanding in Asia. To Washington, the Viet Minh were not nationalists but communist proxies for the Soviet Union and China. Convinced that

Diem was the hope for keeping the Viet Minh at bay, President Eisenhower did what it took to prop him up. This marked the beginning of American efforts to sustain one unpopular regime after another with economic and military assistance—and eventually with ground troops—in an effort to defeat what the United States viewed as international communist expansion. The leaders that Washington backed were usually not men who had earned their spurs from years of dedication and arduous service to their country, but politicians or military officers with little or no credibility and without broad popular appeal. Once in power, they squandered their chance to win the allegiance of the people by their incompetence, venality, or both.

With American aid so critical for survival, the mere threat of its termination was enough to make Emperor Bao Dai toe the line. Anxious to keep Diem in power, Washington made clear that it would cut off assistance if the renegade chief of staff—who was scheming to get rid of Diem—was not dismissed from office. Emperor Bao Dai, who had moved to the French Riviera where he spent his time gambling in the casinos and sailing his yacht, hurriedly fired the general and ordered him to France. With the army now under his control, Diem turned his attention to the religious sects and the gangster organization Binh Xuyen. He first broke up their alliance by promising to give them positions in his government and to integrate their troops wholesale into the national army, and by offering outright bribes. The policy paid off, and in January 1955 sect commanders began rallying to the government, bringing their units with them. By the time the sects and the Binh Xuyen realized they were cutting their own throats and decided to join forces again, it was too late. Against unfavorable odds, and against the Americans' advice, Diem decided to take them head-on. Fortunately for him, the French had ended their subsidies to these private armies, and these units—numbering close to 40,000—were beginning to fall apart.

The Binh Xuyen made money by running opium dens and brothels, including one said to be the largest in Asia. But their most lucrative source of income was the infamous Dai The Gioi, or Great World gambling casino, in Cholon. The name evoked the image of a glitzy establishment, so one day my mother, out of curiosity and also out of fondness for games of chance acquired since her marriage, decided to go see for herself. Curious, I asked to go along to check it out, and since my mother thought it was a respectable place she took me with her. The Great World sat behind high walls on a huge lot at the edge of town. We followed the patrons through one of two gates and then crossed a bare earth courtyard to reach one of about fifty buildings with tin roofs, set on a concrete floor. The buildings held over 200 gaming tables, made of wooden planks painted with numbers or characters. There was a separate structure reserved for the more well-heeled gamblers, set in the back. We did not expect to see a casino like Monte Carlo, but were disappointed to find a ramshackle and depressing place, thronged with people who looked like they could not afford to lose the little money they had. I could not figure out the games—some Western, some Chinese—nor could I understand the Chinese that the dealers were speaking among themselves. After my mother tried her luck unsuccessfully at the roulette table, we wandered around for a while, feeling lost in a rather alien milieu, and then left. Later I learned that a French journalist had described the Great World, run by Chinese from Macao, as a mass-production gambling hell, and that suicides were frequent among the poor gamblers, when they saw no way out of their crushing debts or when they realized that with their money gone they could no longer feed their families. Diem chose to attack the Binh Xuyen first; because of their unsavory activities, he had the solid backing of the people for this move. Everyone at the time wanted to see these lingering evils of the colonial era ended once and for all. When Diem banned opium sales and smoking, and had the confiscated pipes burned in a bonfire in the square in front of the largest market, the people of Saigon cheered.

Our alley was almost right in front of the command center of Diem's army, and not far from the Y Bridge where the Binh Xuyen had set up their own headquarters. We knew we would be caught in the middle of any fighting, so when rumors began to fly that the two sides were ready for a military showdown, my mother moved us to a cousin's house. The first attack took place at the end of March, after Diem ousted the Binh Xuyen police chief. But the French stopped the fighting and arranged a truce—to save their Binh Xuyen allies, according to rumors. The cease-fire was fragile, however, and the situation remained tense. Every time we heard talks of an imminent attack, we would pack up and go to our cousin's. After a few such false alarms and fruitless trips to avoid the fighting that failed to take place, my mother decided not to pay any more attention to the rumors. My father, who had finally joined us for good, felt things had calmed down enough for him to leave us by ourselves and fly to Dalat to visit his oldest brother. When fighting finally erupted on April 28, 1955, we were right in the middle of it.

That day, after the Binh Xuyen shelled his palace, Diem's army drove them toward Cholon, toward our area of town. It was right after lunch,

楊琳
雲湖先生遺像

Dương-Lâm
Biệt-hiệu
Vân-Hồ

Portrait of Duong Lam, Mai Elliott's great-grandfather, reproduced from *Van Dan Bao Giam* magazine, 1920.

Duong Lam's tomb (after repairs) (circa 1996).

Hung Hoa Citadel, which Duong Lam defended against Chinese and Vietnamese bandits in 1889. This Vietnamese drawing depicts a battle at the citadel in 1884 between French forces and Chinese Black Flag bandits.

Portrait of Duong Tu Phan, Mai's grandfather (circa 1923).

Portrait of Tran Tue Nam, Mai's grandmother (circa 1923).

Mai's father and mother, with her father's parents, his brothers and sisters, and nephews and nieces, in photo taken at Duong Tu Phan's official residence. Mai's grandfather and grandmother are in the last row, standing in the middle. Her mother is in the second to last row, standing right below her grandfather. Mai's father is in the second row, third from right. (Circa 1923).

Trinh Thi Hue's (Mai's maternal grandmother) shop on Hang Gai street in
Hanoi, now replaced by newer structure
(with grille). Photo taken in 1993.

Duong Thieu Chi, Mai's father,
wearing his ivory mandarin
insignia, early in his career as a
mandarin. Photo taken in the
1930s.

Mai's father and mother at the Haiphong airport, welcoming Prime Minister Nguyen Van Xuan and his French wife. Mai's father is in the second row, holding his hat. Prime Minister Xuan is the man in the trench coat, first row, far right. His French wife is the lady in the middle, holding bouquet of flowers. Mai's mother is in the second row, far right, behind Prime Minister Xuan. (Circa 1948–49).

Mai and members of her family at the mayor's official residence in Haiphong. In the first row, starting from the left: sister Loan, Uncle Tuong, Mai, and sister Binh. In the second row, first, second and third from the left: sister Phu, mother, and father. (Circa 1950).

Mai's brother Luong, photo taken in the 1950s.

Mai's sister Phu in hill tribe costume,
Hanoi 1950.

Mai and sister Yen, Saigon
circa 1960.

Mai's brother Giu in France, 1952.

Mai, seated third from right, graduation day, Saint Paul School, Saigon, 1960.

Mai, dressed for fashion show, the evening she met David Elliott, December 1961.

Mai, far right, at JFK's White House garden reception for foreign students, with her friends My Luong, far left, and Huong Mai, in the middle. (Circa 1961).

Mai, with bouffant hairdo, and David Elliott at their wedding banquet, Saigon, March 1964.

Mai working at the Rand office in Saigon. (Circa 1965).

David Elliott, with rented Citroen, in Saigon. (Circa 1966).

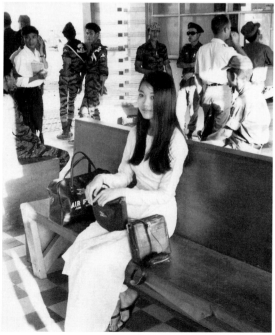

Mai, waiting for a helicopter ride at Can Tho Airport, after completing interviews with Viet Cong prisoners and defectors in this city. (Circa 1965). (Note South Vietnamese soldiers in the background with skull and cross-bones insignia).

Mai's uncle Chinh, with Ho Chi Minh, and the mandarin Vi Van Dinh, at the Lien Viet
National Congress, in Chiem Hoa, in 1951. Trinh is in the front row, seated, far left. Ho
is in the front row, seated, third from left. Vi Van Dinh is standing in the last row, third
from left.

Mai's father, in Saigon, in the
1960s.

Mai's mother, Nguyen Nhat An, in
Saigon, in the 1960s.

Mai and David Elliott, with her family in front of her parents' house in Saigon, Tet 1966.
First row: niece Lily. Second row: father, first from left; Mai, second from left; sister
Tuyet, third from left. Mai's mother is in the second row, far right. David is in the last
row, first from left.

Mai's father and niece Trang, on the deck of the USS Hancock, after being evacuated by helicopter from Saigon in April 1975, during Operation Frequent Wind. (Official photo, Operation Frequent Wind, U.S. Marines).

Mai's sister Thang, North Vietnam 1974.

Mai's brother-in-law Hau, in photo taken in 1993, standing in front of map of Cu Chi tunnel, near Saigon. Mai is standing in the middle, between Hong, the wife of her nephew Lap, and Hau.

Mai's cousin Luc, in front of display of the kind of rifle he obtained after participating in border campaign of 1950. Photo taken at Military Museum in Hanoi in 1993.

Mai's nephew-in-law Nam and his wife Lan (Mai's niece), Australia 1982.

Peasants in Van Dinh, whose families still remember Mai's great-grandfather Duong Lam. Photo taken in 1993.

Mai, in front of her grandfather Duong Tu Phan's tomb, after it underwent repairs. Photo taken in 1993.

and my mother and sisters were taking a siesta. I was reviewing my lessons and getting ready to go back to school for the second round of classes. In the quiet afternoon, with our shutters and doors closed to keep out the suffocating heat, we did not realize that the fighting was spreading our way. Suddenly, my brother Luong rushed in with a rifle slung on his shoulder. He told us that fighting had broken out and that he had hitched a ride home from the military academy the moment he got the news. Our neighborhood was now ringed with government troops, he said. He had managed to get through only because he was in uniform. We were stunned, but it was too late to leave—our area had been cordoned off. We sat in the shuttered house, straining our ears to hear the first bursts of gunfire. Then, from the small inner courtyard separating our two rooms from the kitchen and bathroom in the back, we saw smoke drifting over the rooftop. We rushed out into the alley to find neighbors all peering anxiously in the direction of the fire, which had been set by the Binh Xuyen to sow panic among the people. My brother said, "We must leave to get away from the fighting, and also in case the fire spreads here." The conflagration still seemed far away, but we fled anyway, leaving behind most of our money and all the jewelry that my mother had brought from Hanoi. At the last moment, as we rushed out the door, I grabbed my school satchel full of books and homework—rescuing what I instinctively recognized to be my best hope for the future.

The closest relative, an uncle, lived about two miles from our house, so we headed in that direction on foot. We did not see any Binh Xuyen, but Diem's soldiers were crouched behind trees, with fingers on the triggers, ready to open fire. Luong was with us, so the troops did not stop us or force us to go back to our house. We felt terribly exposed and expected shooting to break out at any moment. We were about to turn down one street when we came face to face with a group of foreign reporters. They stared at us without speaking. To them, we were just part of the story: refugees on the run. I looked at one journalist—a Frenchman, it turned out—and something in my eyes must have prompted him to raise his hand to stop us. "Don't go that way," he said, "they're fighting over there!" We silently made a detour to get to our uncle's house.

The fire raged for hours before burning itself out. The next day, Luong came back from a trip to our neighborhood with the news that our house and everything in it had been incinerated. He took Binh and me back with him through the military cordon to look through the rubble and salvage what we could. When we arrived, the destruction shocked us. Buildings on both sides of our alley had been reduced to piles of charred debris. The only thing left standing in our former home was the concrete water tank. Everything we owned was gone, including the irreplaceable mementoes of our life in the north: family pictures, documents, and souvenirs. Staring at the ruins, I felt devastated. I realized I had just lost everything, my past, present, and future. It was the lowest emotional point of my life.

We stood in the hot sun, looking at the mounds of burned wood, bricks, and tiles. Finding valuables in this debris with our bare hands seemed impossible, like looking for a needle in a haystack, but we had to try, because anything we could salvage would be of help to our family. My mother had kept all her valuables in an armoire in a corner of the inner room, so we decided to start there first, figuring out approximately where that corner would have been. We removed each piece of debris carefully, looking for diamonds, jade, and gold. As we worked under the hot sun, sweating profusely, and getting filthier every minute from the soot, we prayed that no looters or renegade soldiers would arrive to hurt us or take whatever we found.

I was the first to locate something, a gold pendant underneath some bricks and tiles. This gave us hope that there was more to be found, and we felt a new surge of energy. We worked our way outward from the corner. My sister spied some melted gold, and after hours of more hard work, we discovered two diamond earrings. Late in the afternoon, we called it quits and left, our bodies aching from the back-breaking work but feeling happy that our efforts had not been fruitless. When we got back and showed our mother the little we had found, she was heartbroken. She had not owned a lot of valuable jewelry, but what she had represented her life savings and had been intended to keep us going for a while. The news of my mother's loss started making the rounds among our relatives, and got inflated with each retelling to the point that the few pieces of lost jewelry turned into a huge bowlful of diamonds.

Of course, we were not the only family to suffer. The destruction turned out to be widespread, and thousands of homes and shops had burned down during the fighting. As for civilian casualties, no one knew the exact figure, but one estimate—probably on the low side—put the number at 500 killed and 1000 wounded. The Binh Xuyen headquarters was blown to pieces by mortar and artillery fire, and Bay Vien and what was left of his gang were driven out of the city.

When I returned to school a few days later, the headmistress proudly presented me with the equivalent of 1000 piasters—about $30—in small bills, which the school had collected from the students for us. My pride was deeply hurt. I did not want any money from people who had rejected me and my sisters, and I did not think that we had sunk to the point that we had to depend on their charity to survive. I politely but firmly refused to take the money. The headmistress insisted, so I had to accept it, but I felt very ashamed, as if I were a beggar receiving alms from people who despised me.

Two days after the fighting, my father caught a flight from Dalat to Saigon to look for us. As the plane circled over the city, he saw the extent of the calamity and told himself there was no way we could have escaped from it alive. From the airport, he took a taxi to my uncle's and was surprised to find us all there. My sister Binh's fiancé at this point had a little house near the racetrack, and he let us use it until we could find other accommodations. The house had neither electricity nor running water, and was so small that it felt like a cell with the nine of us, plus two maids and a cousin, jammed within its walls. Our cousin Bieu, a son of my uncle Chinh's, had fled from the turmoil of land reform and made his way to Haiphong to find my father and follow him south. Now my parents had one more teenager to feed, clothe, and educate. Bieu had left the north only because he could no longer stand the privations, and not because he hated or opposed the communists. In spite of what they had done to his family, his allegiance to the Hanoi government did not flag. We tired of his defense of the Viet Minh and used to wonder why he did not just return to the north and live under a regime he thought so wonderful.

After a few weeks, my father moved us to another house, located on a large and leafy street, which turned out to be a villa belonging to Empress Nam Phuong. Relatives of hers had occupied it, but had left. It now stood half-empty. We were allowed to live on the ground floor, while the upper floor, still full of the owner's furniture, was closed off. Suddenly we found ourselves living in comfort again, with electricity, running water, Western-style toilets, and separate servants' quarters. My father was now working in the Finance Ministry. Because of the dedication he had shown in the north—working until the last moment when Haiphong was handed over to the Viet Minh—the finance minister had rewarded him with the use of the villa and the position of manager of the accounting section. This was a step down for my father, but he was grateful to find employment. Diem and his brothers, on whom the prime minister relied heavily to run the country, did not trust people like my father who had occupied important positions in the north, suspecting them of belonging secretly to the Dai Viet Party that had run Tonkin. Still tenuous in his position, Diem was afraid that this party would regroup in the south and pose a challenge to his authority. When Nguyen Huu Tri, the former governor of Tonkin and a leader of the Dai Viet Party, suddenly died after his arrival in Saigon, rumors circulated that Diem's agents—or the agents of his Machiavellian brother Nhu—had shot Tri the moment he stepped off the plane at the airport. Tri's own family privately confirmed the rumors later, and this was the first inkling we had of the shape of things to come. My father, like other prominent northern officials, was relegated to an inferior and innocuous job that would not give him a power base. In my father's case, this suspicion was groundless. Not a joiner by nature, he had never belonged to any of the many parties that clogged the political scene, despising them as *xoi thit*, or "rice and meat," parties—that is, people who were concerned only with their own personal self-interests.

With my father working again and with a home of our own, some stability began to return to my family's life—but not for long. After eliminating the Binh Xuyen, Diem smashed the resistance of the other two religious sects, then turned to the next step in his plan to gain complete control over South Vietnam—which was to remove Bao Dai. The emperor gave him an opening by trying to fire Diem. In response, Diem and his brother Nhu instigated a movement to depose him and to set up a Republic of South Vietnam with Diem as its first president. Bao Dai offered an easy target, because of his personal conduct and the corruption of his government, and also because he had no support. To legitimize their plan, Diem and Nhu held a referendum in October 1955. Even without rigging the election, Diem probably would have landed a decisive victory, but the urge to claim a mandate was irresistible. Diem took 98 percent of the vote; according to reports, there were more ballots cast than registered voters. Before the balloting, propaganda against Bao Dai went into full swing, with marches to denounce the emperor and burn him in effigy. Newspapers, controlled by the government, trumpeted the venality of the emperor and his officials. Some of these former officials—including the ex-mayor of Saigon, who had long since retired—were arrested and thrown in jail on charges of corruption. In this atmosphere, even if people had any residual sympathy for Bao Dai, they did not dare to show it.

Like other government employees, my father was forced to campaign for Diem in the neighborhood near his office, going from block to block for the first time in his life like a lowly foot soldier. This canvassing brought home to him how far he had fallen from his position in the north, and he felt even more humiliated that he had to be part of the push for the referendum—which he considered a sham and a disloyal act toward the emperor—just to keep his job. For my father, who remained a Confucian at heart, loyalty was very important, especially the loyalty of a subject to his king. On election day, voters were given two ballots: one with the picture of Diem, and the other with the picture of Emperor Bao Dai. My father took along a sheet of paper and cast a blank ballot. The referendum left him with a lasting distaste for Diem and his regime.

With Bao Dai defeated, the government began seizing his assets and those of his relatives, including the villa where we were staying. We had to move once again, for the last time, to a little house a few blocks away, where my parents lived until 1975. Our new home was located in an alley, in the middle of a long block of similar houses that were attached to one another like a series of cubicles. Across stood another row of similar structures. The area was reclaimed swampy land; part of the swamp still existed where the buildings stopped. Directly behind the row across from ours was a workers' slum, where people lived in huts on stilts built over the swamp itself. Our house consisted of two rooms, a small courtyard with a water cistern, a kitchen, a squat toilet, and a bathroom—a typical Saigon *pho chet*, or attached one-story home. To give us a little more space, my parents added a loft with a small window. The loft, located right under the tile roof, became sweltering in the afternoon under the merciless sun. A hot-water heater and Western-style toilet were added many years later. I and my sisters Yen and Loan slept in the front room downstairs, which served as living room and dining room during the day. Our bed was right next to the dining table and chairs, and a credenza on which sat a radio and a record player. That was all the furniture that could fit in the little room. My father, mother, and youngest sister Tuyet occupied the room in the back, while my brother Luong and cousin Bieu had the loft upstairs. U Mien, her assistant Chi Sau, and my sister Mao slept on a bed and a cot in the kitchen. When I saw the house again in 1993 after a twenty-year absence, I could not believe that so many of us had managed to live in these tiny quarters for so long without tearing each other to pieces.

As the president of a newly created republic, Diem now set out to give the country the outward trappings of democracy. In fact, this was just window-dressing to placate the Americans, who thought democracy would be the right antidote against communism. There was a new constitution, but it gave Diem enormous powers. There was a National Assembly, but it was only a rubber stamp. Nor was there a meaningful political opposition. To gather power in his own hands and in the hands of his family, the president began to reorganize the country, turning it into his and his relatives' private fiefdom. All power, civilian and military, flowed from him and his family—a group of arrogant men who firmly believed that they had almost a divine right to rule the country for its own good. Central Vietnam was put under the unofficial control of Diem's younger brother Can, while his other brother Nhu served as an assistant president, crushing any opposition to the regime through his secret police and intelligence networks. Throughout Diem's rule, Nhu was the most feared person in the whole country. While the president was an ascetic, Nhu was an opium addict, and it was said in Saigon that he got his destructive ideas under the influence of the "brown fairy." To help run the country, Diem and his brothers created their own political party, the Can Lao, which came to dominate the government and the army.

Knowing that whoever controlled the army would hold real power, Diem did not want to appoint a military chief of staff. Although he finally gave in to American pressure, he played it safe by appointing Le Van Ty, a cautious, unimaginative, and pliant former captain in the French army. While the general was a nice man—my youngest sister Tuyet later married his only son—he was an ineffectual military commander. Ty's only accomplishment as chief of staff was that he did not make any enemies. The generals who finally deposed Diem viewed him affectionately as a benevolent but befuddled older brother, and spared him after their coup d'état. Even with the obedient Ty in charge, Diem was still paranoid about military treachery, so he staffed the army with senior officers loyal to him and his family and set up a complicated structure to dilute the power of the field commanders who had troops at their disposal. Yet all these measures failed to save the president in the end.

Against American advice, Diem pressured the French to speed up the withdrawal of their forces, even before his army had become strong enough to fight the invasion from the North that American experts were predicting. By April 1956, all French troops were gone and the French high command was abolished. South Vietnam was now completely independent and appeared to be back on its feet—with the sects eliminated, refugees resettled, physical damage of war under repair, land put back in cultivation, economy reviving with the influx of U.S. aid, and a stable and seemingly strong government in charge. Diem felt so secure, in fact, that he refused to hold the 1956 national elections called for by Geneva. Despite this, North Vietnam, distracted by its efforts to rebuild its shattered economy and receiving no backing from the Soviet Union and China, did not retaliate by invading the South, as the Americans had feared. If this had happened, Diem's army would have been unable to cope with the attacks and America would have had to weigh in with air and naval support. Diem's successful challenge of the North, and the progress he had accomplished in the South, made him very popular with the Americans. When he made a triumphant visit to the United States in early 1957, he was hailed as a hero by the Eisenhower administration, Congress, and the press.

Encouraged by Diem's leadership and success, America now poured money into the country to make him even more secure, politically, economically, and militarily. South Vietnam became the leading recipient of U.S. aid in Southeast Asia. My father at this time had joined the Finance Ministry's foreign aid section. In his new capacity, he began working with members of the American economic mission, called the U.S. Operations Mission (USOM). He spoke little English—now displacing French as the language one had to know to succeed—but the Americans either spoke some French or brought along their Vietnamese interpreters, so he was able to communicate. He began to attend tea parties and receptions at USOM, and got on famously with his American counterparts, whom he found straightforward and well-meaning. He had dealt with Americans from time to time before in the north, so he did not find them hard to adjust to. The fact that the Americans were here as allies, and not as colonial masters, made his relationship with them more comfortable. Also, in his mid-level position, he was now just a cog in the government machine like thousands of other employees, and no longer a visible and influential official—someone who could be criticized as a "tool of imperialism" or "puppet." The stigma was gone. Later, when the Vietnam War became destructive and the U.S. military presence overwhelming, cooperation with the Americans would be condemned by a large segment of the population, but by then, my father had retired from the government.

Since the Americans now had the key to power in South Vietnam, cultivating them became important for the ambitious. For us, however, the relatively small group of Americans in Saigon remained distant. Except for my father's official dealings with the few USOM representatives, my family, like most Vietnamese at this time, had no contact with these Americans. They lived apart in their own houses or apartment blocks and socialized among themselves.

Nevertheless, the rising influence of Americans was visible everywhere. They were reorganizing the government and training administrators to staff them, bringing goods into Vietnam to improve the standard of living, building roads and bridges, and creating an army in their own image. Their objective was ambitious. They wanted not only to build a government with a powerful army but also to create a society with a strong middle class as its core to fight communism. Of all the U.S. aid programs, the economic one was the most ingenious. It funded Vietnamese government expenditures while at the same time building up a middle class of civil servants, military officers, businessmen, and landowners, and supplying consumer goods to raise their standard of living. The aim was to make life so comfortable for this middle class—the most likely source of support for Diem—that they would resist communist appeals and stay loyal to him.

Consumer products had become scarce during the long years of war. With peace and stability restored and life returning to normal, people now wanted to buy things they had deferred, especially since American aid was putting more money in their pockets. With so much cash chasing so few goods, runaway inflation was a real danger. In stepped the American aid mission with a commodities import program that neatly solved this potential problem. The United States made dollars available to the government, which in turn sold them to importers at a rate that was almost a third of what the dollar was fetching on the international foreign exchange market. The goods brought in were, in essence, subsidized by American taxpayers. The government put the piasters it got from selling the dollars, as well as the duties it collected on the imported products, into a special fund to finance expenditures. So, in one stroke, the Americans gave us plenty of goods to buy, paid for our higher standard of living, averted inflation, and financed the lion's share of our national expenditures. Since the government, with its bloated bureaucracy and growing army, was the largest employer in the country, absorbing one out of every eight able-bodied males—mostly into the military—the Americans were in fact feeding and clothing many middle-class families, including my own. Being Saigon's main provider of revenue gave the Americans enormous power over the national budget. They had the final say on how the special fund could be spent. The running joke in Saigon was that unless *ong My*, or the Americans, "nodded their heads in approval," nothing could be done in South Vietnam.

Getting an import permit was like getting a license to print money. With it, an importer could buy goods at a third of their real value and resell them at a sizable profit. Or he could choose not to bother with the business himself and simply resell his permit for a hefty sum to a trader—usually a Chinese merchant—who in turn would do the importing. Such an enormous source of profit naturally brought out the greed in people, and there was a mad scramble to obtain import licenses among the middle class. Of course, only those who had the right political connections, were Diem loyalists, or contributed to Diem's party could get them. The importers, both real and phony, would become part of the nouveau riche in Saigon. Since the program was designed to create an artificial high standard of living among the urban middle class, most of the commodities that were brought in were consumer goods, even luxury ones, instead of agricultural or industrial equipment that would have stimulated real economic development. In fact, the flood of imports heavily damaged the few small industries that were still sputtering along. By far, textiles dominated the imports, and Saigon's main streets would become lined with shops selling luxury fabrics. My brother Luong's future mother-in-law was one of the people who got rich from importing textiles. Later she set up a small factory making aluminum utensils and bought a coffee plantation, becoming even richer in an economy fueled by American war spending.

While it was boosting the South Vietnamese economy, the United States was also building up an army to resist an invasion from North Vietnam. The frontal attacks envisaged in such a conventional invasion did not take place, however, and the army built to defend against them would find itself ill-suited for the guerrilla war that would later plague the South. For any army to function effectively, it needs to have a good officer corps, and in this respect the Vietnamese force was seriously lacking. American advisors had been appalled by the caliber of many of the senior officers they met, men who had started their military careers in the French period, during which they had served as subalterns without command authority. This had bred in them a reluctance to take charge and a desk-bound mentality. Having worked for foreign interests against their own people, some also displayed a remarkable lack of what the Americans called "a national feeling." The advisors also complained that they tended to be aloof from their men, disinterested in going on operations and sharing hardships with those they commanded, and prone to corruption, political intrigues, and influence peddling. To correct this weakness, the Americans started sending senior officers to the United States for training. But once there, these officers seemed more interested in shopping, sightseeing, and socializing than in learning how to properly command an army. Other officers learned well but did not apply their training when they returned, shrugging off the American way as inapplicable to Vietnam.

A number of junior officers were also selected for training in America. In 1956, my brother Luong, who had graduated from the Thu Duc military academy and was working in the logistics branch, left for a one-year course at the Aberdeen Proving Ground in Maryland. He learned how to maintain military vehicles, mainly cars and trucks, although this training did not seem to fit his job in Vietnam as manager of a weapons maintenance center. The organization and discipline of the U.S. Army impressed him and his three Vietnamese colleagues. The moment they arrived, they received their daily schedule for the whole year, which was then followed to the letter. Classes were well organized and supported with manuals—a novelty for my brother. At Thu Duc, there had been no written materials to go with the courses.

Luong loved his stay in the United States, and enjoyed the treatment he got everywhere. Even the local chamber of commerce honored him and his colleagues with a special dinner. At that time, the American people still believed wholeheartedly in upholding the United States as a shining beacon of freedom and democracy for the undeveloped world in the competition against communism. The hospitality my brother enjoyed was genuine, but also was a deliberate effort to win hearts and minds for the Free World. Luong believed that an unspoken objective of the trip was to expose him and his colleagues to the American way of life and democracy. In this, he thought the Americans succeeded, as he left deeply impressed with the United States. America got no tangible return from its investment in his technical training, because Luong switched to the military justice department shortly after his return, but got a public relations boost as my brother began to praise its system to relatives and friends.

Thanks to massive American aid, instead of floundering in Saigon as we had feared before leaving Hanoi, my father and other members of my family found steady jobs, and we started to rebuild our lives. My older sister Yen was with the American Military Assistance Advisory Group. This was plum employment, as working for the Americans paid much more handsomely than any Vietnamese private or government office. Like Luong, my brother Xuong had been integrated into the new South

Vietnamese army where he held the rank of captain. My sister Phu's husband worked as an engineer in the Public Works Ministry, while Binh's husband, an agricultural engineer trained in France and England, had a job at the U.S. aid mission. Even my parents' dream of an overseas education for their favorite sons, Giu and Tuan, remained possible. Before leaving Hanoi, my parents thought that they would have to recall Giu from his studies in France for lack of money, but he managed to find a series of French scholarships that allowed him to pursue his education. Meanwhile, Tuan, who had found a French scholarship of his own, had left for Paris. After our life stabilized, my parents' main preoccupation was my sister Thang, who remained in the North. For a while, we could communicate with her via an officially formatted postcard. But after the war broke out again, even this came to an end. Contacts between the two sides of the conflict brought suspicion, so we stopped writing. Tuan in Paris became the conduit of news, passing to us information he got from Thang, who had moved to Hanoi, or letting her know what was happening in Saigon.

We lived frugally. A large portion of my father's salary went to paying for food and other basic expenses, and after our tuition at the convent school there was little discretionary income left. Once in a while, a large expense would crop up unexpectedly, and my parents would appeal to Tuan. My brother could not bring himself to say no, even though he was barely surviving on his scholarship. Tuan would borrow money from his professor, a compassionate and wealthy English scientist, and send it home without telling us where he had gotten it. My parents just assumed that the money came from savings he had managed to set aside from his scholarship.

With such a tight budget, a lot of things remained beyond our reach. We did not own an automobile, and usually just window-shopped the stores brimming with colorful fabrics and other consumer goods, such as 18-karat-gold Omega or Bulova watches from Switzerland, which had become a big status symbol for many middle-class families. My wardrobe consisted of two *ao dai*, or long tunics, that I wore for school, since the nuns now allowed older students like me to abandon the white blouse and navy blue skirt for our traditional costume. Yet although we had enough to eat and a roof over our head, and could pursue our education at a good private school, my sisters and I at times resented our poverty and the occasional money crises, and failed to appreciate that this was one of the most peaceful periods of our lives. The countryside was secure, and we could travel without fear of ambushes or mines in the roads. We went on vacation every summer to the seashore or to the mountains, although our holidays were on the cheap. We stayed at government guest houses and brought along our own maid to cook our meals, or descended on our relatives. We traveled by train to the seaside town of Nha Trang with its whispering pines and white sand beaches, rode the bus to the mountain resort of Dalat with its lakes and waterfalls; or took the road to Blao with its hills dotted with tea bushes, located on the edge of the jungle in the central highlands, the region that would later on witness some of the bloodiest battles of the Vietnam War.

The trips gave us a chance to escape from our crowded house. Another form of escape was the movies. Occasionally, when he had won big at a mah-jongg game—his favorite pastime—my father would give us a generous sum of money to go to the cinema and to buy ice cream after the show. Then we would hail a taxi and ride grandly to a decent theater, sit in comfortable seats in the balcony, and then go to an ice cream parlor afterward. More often, we would get a smaller allowance from my mother, which meant getting the cheapest seats in a cheap cinema, and coming home without any treats. At this time, American films were displacing French movies. For the sake of the audience, few of whom could understand English, they were dubbed in French and carried Vietnamese subtitles. I fell in love with them. My taste was indiscriminate. I liked tragic stories that would make me cry, but I also enjoyed comedies and westerns. My favorite films were old ones like *Autant en emporte le vent* (*Gone With the Wind,*) as well as newer ones, like *Tant qu'il y aura des hommes* (*From Here to Eternity,*) and *A l'Est d'Eden* (*East of Eden.*) I also enjoyed Danny Kaye comedies, Westerns, and Doris Day movies—such as *Annie, Get Your Gun*—because they were unfailingly cheerful and had a lot of singing. I devoured *Ciné Revue*, a movie magazine, and wrote to fan clubs to obtain movie stars' pictures. Once in a while, I hit the jackpot, and photos would arrive, bearing the autographs of the stars, delighting me with the delusion that far away in glittering Hollywood, on the other side of the world, these famous actors and actresses had personally responded to my admiration.

As I got older, I started to have a crush on some of the American actors who appeared much more glamorous than the boys around me. In some ways, they were also more real. I had seen them in films so many times I felt like I knew them. The boys populating my world, on the other hand, were only figures moving facelessly in the background. Dating was an unknown custom then, and I was attending a school for girls only, so I had no chance to meet any boys, much less get to know them or fall in love. I had also had experiences that made leery of the men around me. From the time I reached fifteen, I started to draw unwanted attention. Girls my age—virgins beginning to awaken sexually—fascinated many men. How many got harassed is difficult to determine; girls who got victimized usually kept quiet because they felt ashamed and afraid of causing a scandal, which would harm their reputation. The most upsetting incident occurred when a relative tried to lure me into his room while we were vacationing at his house. Another time, a neighbor approached me and attempted to seduce me with the promise that he would marry me as his second wife. Both of these advances from people I knew left me livid with rage but also scared and ashamed. Because of this feeling of shame, and also because of Confucian prudishness that made sex, or anything approaching it, a taboo subject with my parents, I did not tell them about these incidents. So, I confided to my brother Luong. He became my protector. He discreetly intervened on my behalf with both of these men. Since he was a lieutenant and had access to firearms, his words inspired fear. The harassment never happened again, but, aware of my vulnerability, I decided to keep my distance—physically and psychologically—from men in general. Dreaming about the stars gave me a harmless and safe outlet for my adolescent longing.

Instead of abating with the passage of time, my fascination with things American grew. Like the rest of my compatriots, I started to think of America as paradise on earth: a country where people led fabulously rich and happy lives in beautiful homes, and where everyone could afford a car and a plethora of appliances that made daily routines convenient. The wealth of the United States boggled our minds, and we began to refer to big spenders as "people who throw money out the window like Americans." Hollywood movies reinforced this perception of America as the land of material comfort. So did the U.S. Information Agency, whose mission was to impress underdeveloped countries with American success. I would go to the USIA office, located in downtown Saigon, and spend hours reading its magazines.

Besides the movies, I also began to develop a fondness for American pop music. On his return from a second trip to the United States, where he had served as interpreter for a group of newly graduated officers who were touring America for three months, my brother Luong had brought back a stack of singles. I would listen raptly to songs like "Too Young" by Nat King Cole, "April Love" and "Writing Love Letters in the Sand" by Pat Boone, and "Diana" by Paul Anka. There were also singles by

Elvis Presley, The Platters, and even a record of cowboy songs such as "Cool Water." I liked them all. I would play the records over and over again, to the annoyance of my parents, who thought the music was dreadful, so I could make out the lyrics. No one else in my family liked the music as much as I did, not even Luong, who preferred French ballads like "La vie en rose" and "Un jour tu verras."

The simplicity of our life in Saigon had its positive side. Being thrown together in the tiny house allowed me to become closer to my father for the first time in my life. Living in two rooms instead of in a large villa, we bumped into one another all the time. Face-to-face encounters and interaction, rare in Hanoi, now became routine. I had the chance to see him and talk to him more often. Instead of eating separately with my mother and brother, my father started to share meals with us girls. It was while sitting around the dining table that we talked the most. I discovered that far from being the distant, intimidating, and stern man that I had thought—the typical authority figure of a patriarch in a traditional family like mine—my father was really a very warm and charming person. I found out that he was also a great raconteur, with a wonderful sense of humor. He would entertain us with stories about himself, his parents, and grandparents, and would tease my mother with funny stories about her. These mealtime conversations sparked my interest in my own roots, and led me to suggest to my father that he write our family's story. When he demurred, I made a mental note to do it myself one day. In the north, I used to do things out of fear, to avoid getting my father angry and bringing down the punishment that everyone said would surely come from him. Now I did things out of affection for him and to make him happy.

My father's much less exalted government position also allowed him to see his family more often. Now his job did not take up as much of his day, and as he lacked the power he used to have in the north, the social callers and the invitations to functions practically disappeared. His mistress, whom he had evacuated from Hanoi and installed in a small farm near Saigon, was also commanding less of his time. By now, the honeyed voice that once had held him spellbound was gone, and his attraction to her had vanished. Instead of an accomplished singer who beguiled him with her art, my father had on his hands a matronly harpy whose irascible company made every visit a chore. Yet my father's sense of duty and loyalty applied even to his extramarital affairs, and he remained attached to her until she died.

My parents coped remarkably well with their loss of social status. I

rarely saw my father lose his temper, and I did not hear my mother complain more often than she did in the north. The perks that used to come
with my father's position were only a memory. Instead of having an official car and driver at his disposal, my father now had to find a cab or a
cyclo to get back and forth from his office. Sometimes, when he had to
wait in the heat and sun for a long time, he would come home exhausted, and would have to lie down for a short rest. He was in his late
fifties, and seemed more frail. The ulcer that he had developed after our
move to Saigon became more severe and gave him more pain, but he
refused to see a doctor, afraid that cancer would be diagnosed. The fear
that he would die of this horrible disease, like his grandfather, father,
and younger brother, obsessed him.

Whereas our clan name, the Duong of Van Dinh, commanded respect
and instant recognition in the north, it meant nothing to people in the
south. Our lack of social and political standing had a silver lining, however. Relatives and acquaintances no longer besieged my father with
requests for jobs, loans, or other favors. Enemies were also fewer, and
my father no longer had to worry about backstabbing and intrigues
against him. Relatives who used to bad-mouth us behind our backs out
of jealousy, or who used to complain that my parents did not do enough
for them, now became nicer and less demanding. Our new life turned
out to be, in some ways, easier for my mother, who had more time for
herself with fewer children to worry about and without a large staff of
servants to run. She could visit more often with close relatives, the thing
she liked doing the most. Nor did she have to attend receptions and
other official functions, which she had always considered a chore.

In Hanoi, the wives of other officials used to call on my mother to
talk about the big social events and to gossip about the intrigues and
escapades of the rich and powerful. In Saigon, we were completely out
of the social loop, but this did not mean that we did not hear stories.
The rumor mill at this time was churning with unflattering anecdotes
about Diem and his family. People told these with a lot of relish, vent-
ing their resentment against a regime that had become entrenched and
repressive. Passing along damaging stories was their only means for getting back at the government. They did this cautiously, however, for
secret policemen were said to be everywhere. No one would talk freely
to people they did not know, in case they might get reported. Of Diem's
family, people hated Madame Nhu the most because she was arrogant
and brazen, had a sharp tongue, and showed no respect for anyone—the
opposite of the gracious and modest woman we idealized in our culture.

By this time, the goodwill Diem had earned during his first few years in office was evaporating. His family's repression, paranoia, and abuses of power and the corruption and oppression of his government had alienated even the middle class, which had benefited from his regime. Underneath its tranquil surface, South Vietnamese society began to feel a sense of unease.

For me as well, there was a deepening crisis beneath the calm exterior. I was reaching adolescence, and my life, which before I had found merely unpleasant, now seemed downright oppressive and intolerable. I often felt depressed, angry, and frustrated. My new state of mind puzzled and confused me. I was raised to be obedient, polite, pleasant—if not cheerful—in the presence of my parents, not to argue with them even when they were wrong, and always to feel grateful to them for having given me life and taken good care of me. But now, I often felt angry toward my parents for reasons I could not explain, and found it hard to be compliant and pleasant all the time. Once in a while, I would even argue with my mother, although I did this very politely. If I talked back more than once, however, she would get mad at me and tell me that I was insolent and lacked filial piety. I never dared argue with my father, because this would have been too serious an infraction to even contemplate. Having to suppress my emotions so much only deepened my depression and frustration.

When things got really bad, I could not do what an American teenager would have done—go to my room and shut the door—because I did not have a room of my own. There was no corner of the house where I could be alone, no yard or garden for me to escape to. I felt so oppressed I longed to break free and get away. I began to have two recurring nightmares. In one, I was standing in a narrow room, and suddenly the four walls would begin to close in and crush me. In the other, I was lying in a crib with bars and holding a balloon, and suddenly the balloon would begin to inflate and to suffocate me. I would wake up with my heart pounding and my chest heaving. In my crisis, I sought solace in religion. After years at convent schools, I had become a Catholic in spirit, attracted by the Church's teachings about God, redemption, and eternal bliss. But I was also drawn by the Latin mass, which I had frequently attended at school, with its elaborate rituals. The miracle of the Eucharist, the mysterious language, the Gregorian chants, and the incense made me feel as if I had been transported into a divine presence and was communing with God Himself. Buddhism, which I had not studied but had simply absorbed at home, had become less appealing to me because it offered no redemption or eternal bliss but only escape and oblivion, and also because I found its teaching of withdrawal from the world to escape the cycle of reincarnations too passive. Before classes started at school each day, I would go to the Carmelite cloister across the street and kneel in prayer in the cool, silent chapel— to shut out the world and all its troubles, and to give myself hope that God would hear my voice and deliver me.

Living with my mentally ill sister Mao added to my unhappiness. This arrangement had not bothered me before, but now I felt it was one more cross for me to bear. At least I was no longer deadly afraid of her and her outbursts. As I grew older, I had realized that she in fact was afraid of me. The incident in Haiphong had turned me, in her confused mind, into someone who had power over her. After our move to Saigon, I still felt sympathy for Mao, and I would once in a while talk with her and share my *Ciné Revue* magazine, which she enjoyed as much as I did. Sometimes, I would just sit with her, look at her, and mourn her transformation from a beautiful and bright girl into a wreck of a person. But now, after years of dealing with her, burnout started to set in. Like the rest of my family, I paid less and less attention to her, leaving her care entirely in the hands of U Mien. Despite my best intentions, I resented having to live with her. I hated it when nosy neighbors peered inside our house to get a glimpse of her. And I hated it when she escaped and we had to look for her and lead her back to the house, with the inevitable gaggle of neighbors following behind as if they were watching a freak show.

I knew the only way for me to escape from all this was to go overseas to study. America would be my first choice. Failing that, France would do nicely. But how would I get there? My parents certainly could not afford to send me. Even if they could, however, they would not have done it, because they wanted to marry me off. Having so many daughters, one of my parents' main worries had always been to find husbands for us all. And for each of us, they only had one ideal window of opportunity: when we were between seventeen and twenty. After that, we would be seen as too old. My three older sisters had gotten married before they were twenty, before finishing high school. Age was a pressing concern, but also the fear that some whiff of impropriety—possible in an age when contact between boys and girls was getting more and more frequent, and more and more casual—might torpedo our marriage prospects. So, as I was finishing high school, I contemplated my future and felt very uneasy. I definitely did not want to get married, because when I looked around me, I saw how unhappy a lot of women were. And yet no matter how dreadful their marriages became, these women had no choice but to stay with their husbands because, without any professional skills, they could not get a job and survive on their own. I made up my mind that I would not put myself in a situation of such dependency.

When matchmakers began paying visits, I got nervous. Marriages were then still arranged through the intermediary of friends or relatives who enjoyed playing the role of cupids. The first step toward a marriage was the *xem mat*, or "looking over ritual." The matchmaker—always a woman—would bring the prospective bridegroom to our house so he could take a look at me. After the usual greetings, my mother would call out, "Mai, please bring us some tea!" This was the signal for me to appear, dressed in the better of my two long tunics—my mother had seen to this. In the kitchen, I would take my time making tea—which I was horrible at—delaying it as long as I could. Impatient, my mother would call out again, "Mai, is the tea ready?" Tarrying any longer would make my mother angry, so I would carry my tea tray into the front room, with my eyes downcast, feeling very self-conscious, all the more so since I knew my tea was either too weak or too strong. To keep me in the room longer so the young man could get a good look, the matchmaker would seize one of my arms, and ask me questions. While the young man studied me, I had to keep my eyes downcast, so that the only part of him I saw was his shoes. After about five minutes or so, the matchmaker would release my arm and I would flee. I remember one time I saw two pair of shoes dangling from the chair, an inch or so off the ground. I felt relieved because I knew a young man so short would never propose marriage to someone as tall as I was.

Girls usually did not mind being *xem mat*, and actually felt flattered by the attention. If there was no *xem mat*, a girl would be considered *e chong*—"unsalable"—and no one wanted to end up with that reputation. The more often a girl got looked over, the better her prospects would become. I, on the other hand, would have loved to avoid the *xem mat* altogether, and felt relieved when no marriage proposal came forth. I had several things going against me: I was too tall for most Vietnamese men, and I was considered too smart. I had passed the first French baccalaureate degree with honors, and was about to take the second part. At this time, many men, and especially their mothers, did not like girls who were well educated, believing that they tended to be arrogant, demanding, and not submissive. Men did not want to be overshadowed by their wives, either physically or intellectually, so my prospects quickly disappeared. Also, I was not as attractive as my older sisters, all famous for their beauty. There were no boys I wanted to impress, so I made no effort to look alluring. I dressed plainly. I wore no makeup. My permed hair just sat on my head like a mass of ringlets. While my sister Yen would spend half an hour each morning fixing her hair, I would just run a comb through mine and be out the door. The prospective bridegrooms who came to look at me expecting to find a beauty must have left quite disappointed.

One day in 1960, I saw an announcement in a newspaper about an American scholarship. The U.S. economic mission was recruiting students about to finish high school to send to American colleges, as part of something called the Leadership Training Program. I immediately applied for this scholarship, along with about 500 other high school students, competing for the fifteen slots in the program. To my surprise—and my parents' dismay—I won one of the scholarships. My parents tried to talk me out of leaving, but my mind had been firmly made up, and since there were no marriage prospects for me anyway, they decided to let me go.

Before our departure, the aid mission put me and the other scholarship students in an intensive three-month English-language training. I was the only girl enrolled in one of the classes. At first, I felt shy and awkward being thrown in the same room with boys my age, but I discovered that they posed no threat and that being with them did not automatically bring emotional or sexual entanglement. They came from family backgrounds similar to mine, and I found them rather educated, friendly, funny, and very well behaved: Not once did they say or do anything that I would consider improper. Like me, they focused their attention and energy on the training, trying to learn as much as possible to ease their adjustment in America.

Our teacher, an energetic and matronly woman from New York, worked us like a drill sergeant. We slaved to imitate her heavy accent, trying to swallow the "t" sound in words like "bottle." Her English was nasal, but to me it sounded genuine, much better than the French-accented English I had learned in my convent school. The texts she used looked more up to date, quite different from the "Living English" lessons in my school that were full of archaic expressions like "mind your p's and q's" and "it rains cats and dogs." After three months, we got ready to go to America. In my college application I had chosen political science as my major, hoping it would open the door to a career as a diplomat in the

Foreign Affairs Ministry that would allow me to travel the world and learn about other cultures. Frankly, I did not expect the aid mission to respect my wish. I thought surely it would make me major in something more practical and useful for Vietnam, such as engineering. But to my surprise, just before we left Saigon, I learned that I had been enrolled in the School of Foreign Service at Georgetown University in Washington, D.C. I could already see myself as a diplomat residing in Paris, London, Rome, or Washington. My dream was coming true.

My friends and teachers did not share my enthusiasm for an American college education, and told me I was making a bad mistake. I should go to France—still the center of civilization in the world—instead of wasting my time in America, a cultural desert in their opinion. I just brushed aside their concerns and doubts. My parents, too, were depressed about my departure. A fortune-teller had told them that I would marry a foreigner, and they feared that I would marry an American and not come back to them. The prospect of finally getting away, going to the land of my dreams, and pursuing the education I wanted made me steel myself against their obvious dejection. Nevertheless, I began to feel sad at the prospect of being separated from my family for several years. The day I left in 1960, I asked my family not to go to the airport and see me off, because I knew it would make it very hard for me, but of course they did not listen. We all wept when we said goodbye, and my sisters hung on to my arm, reluctant to let me go. I finally wrenched myself free, half ran toward the airplane, climbed the stairs quickly, and entered the cabin without looking back. I found my cheerful Leadership Training Program colleagues already boisterously settling in their seats. In their company, my anxiety gave way to excitement. When the plane took off, we looked at each other and smiled. I was nineteen years of age, sailing to a strange land halfway around the world, my pulse racing in anticipation of a great adventure.

12

The New Mecca

Honolulu was my first stop on
American soil. Or more precisely,
the Honolulu airport. I did not see
anything terribly exotic. I had read
about Hawaii, so I expected to see
hula dancers in grass skirts and bras
made out of coconut husks when I
stepped off the plane; instead, I
spotted only a few people in loud
Hawaiian shirts and a couple of
tourists with leis around their
necks. But my disappointment lasted only a few seconds. I was glad to
just walk on firm ground and get
some fresh air. My head was grog-
gy from the motion sickness pills I
had been taking. Suddenly I saw a
gorgeous blonde who looked like a
familiar movie actress. Star-struck,
I rushed over and breathlessly asked

her in my hesitant English, "Are you Kim Novak?" She suppressed her surprise, laughed, and—guessing that a long answer in English would be difficult for me to decipher—said simply, "No. I'm not." I wished we could stay longer, but we had to file back onto the plane for the flight to San Francisco and then to our final destination, Washington, D.C. San Francisco was everything I had dreamed it to be, like a mirage on the shore of the shimmering bay. We walked up and down the hills and gawked. The buildings, the bridges—everything looked awesome to me, accustomed as I was to the smaller scale of Vietnam.

Washington, in the heat and humidity of summer, did not appear romantic like San Francisco. With its marble buildings, large monuments, and broad boulevards, it seemed more austere and formal. The architecture, though French, was different from that of the nineteenth-century colonial structures I had seen in Vietnam, and so did not look familiar to me. The overall design, with the broad boulevards and many *rond-points*, or traffic circles, had an echo, but the size of everything dwarfed what the French had erected in my homeland. My group of exchange students, four girls and eleven boys, took up residence in a vacated dormitory of American University. We would go through an orientation session before scattering to the colleges where the Leadership Training Program had enrolled us. For the first time, I had a room to myself. For the first time also, I was on my own, without parents and siblings at my elbow, and I luxuriated in my private space and my freedom. I was in the constant company of the boys in my group, but without the social opprobrium hanging over our daily interaction, neither I nor they found the situation awkward. Besides, I had gotten to know many of them in my English class in Saigon, and had become friends with them.

In those initial days, I did not feel homesick or lonely. My group gave me the company I needed: I had friends to laugh with and talk to in my native tongue. Together, we set out to explore our new bewildering environment, putting our brains and our inadequate knowledge of English together to figure out how to do the simplest things. If we made a mistake, we would chuckle at our gaffe. Even getting a drink from a fountain was baffling, until we figured out that we had to step on a pedal to make the water spurt out. In the cafeteria, we did not know what to order. "Hot dogs" mystified us when we saw them listed on the menu for the first time. We asked one another in jest, "Do you suppose that people here also eat dog meat like peasants in the Red River Delta?" But no matter what I got from the menu, I found it unappetizing. I was not unused to Western cuisine; the badly cooked cafeteria dishes, however, tasted quite different from the French food I had eaten in Vietnam. I could not force myself to eat the first two days, and lived mostly on fresh fruit and milk, which I sweetened with a lot of sugar to make it taste more like the condensed milk I used to have back home. After that, I adjusted to the fare, and found even the hot dogs palatable.

For our orientation, we attended lectures about life in the United States. But it was information overload. There was so much coming at us—new images, new sensations, and new facts—that we found it hard to digest and sort out everything. One day, we were taken to Capitol Hill to see democracy in action. We sat in the visitors' gallery and looked down at a half-empty Senate chamber, and listened to an endless series of speeches that we did not understand. A few of the senators looked like they were dozing off, and the one presiding over the session seemed as bored as we were. Our visit to the Capitol left us bemused; we told each other that there must be more to democracy than that.

At the end of orientation, we scattered to colleges like Notre Dame, Purdue, and Fordham, among others. I was the only one in the group enrolled at Georgetown. The School of Foreign Service was an anomaly at this all-male university. It had begun admitting women—grudgingly—in the forties. At the time I arrived, there were about 150 of us out of a student body of about 900. Many of the girls were enrolled in the Institute of Languages and Linguistics, one of the three parts of the school, to become teachers or, in the case of those dreaming of wider horizons, simultaneous translators at the United Nations. Those that were in the School of Foreign Service proper were getting trained for a career that offered them few opportunities. The State Department recruited mostly men to serve in its diplomatic ranks.

Because the administration was reluctant to let female students live in close proximity with the boys, about seventy of us were housed in the Meridian Hill Hotel for women on Sixteenth Street, three miles from campus. There, under the watchful eyes of four prefects, we occupied the entire seventh floor. The rest of the residents at the hotel, as far as I could make out, were elderly ladies or single women. I shared a small room with a homely and bespectacled girl from Illinois, with a beaked nose, thin and compressed lips, and eyes that seemed to protrude behind her glasses. At night, when she put on her hair rollers, and padded around in slippers and a bathrobe, she looked like an old woman. We each had a bed and a dresser with drawers. There was a toilet and a sink, but we had to trek down a long hallway to use the communal showers.

My roommate was quiet and shy. She had as much trouble as I had in making friends. It was the first time she had been away from home and from the Midwest, and she hated every minute of it. She felt terribly homesick and cried a lot. Having me as a roommate made things worse for her. She could not really talk to me about her problems. My English was poor, and my understanding of American culture and society even poorer, so I could not fully grasp what she was trying to tell me. She did not last the semester, and packed up and returned home in a matter of weeks. It surprised me to discover that Georgetown and in particular our girls' world at the Meridian Hotel were such a culture shock for my American roommate. I could adjust better than she could, because I did not expect to blend in, to belong, or to be accepted. She, on the other hand, thought she could just step in and feel at home. But she found that her straightforward and simple midwestern ways set her apart from the more sophisticated crowd at Georgetown. She was an outsider in her own land.

For me, the fact that I was like a martian in the middle of earthlings did not bother me. I knew my experience would be temporary. I would spend a couple of years, get an education, and then go back to my native land. I observed my quaint surroundings and the people that populated it like an anthropologist, and yet I did not feel like a complete stranger. I had been exposed to American pop culture, and I found it in Washington even at the Meridian. Some of the students' idols were also mine, such as Elvis Presley, Troy Donahue, Sandra Dee, and Pat Boone. I heard songs that I knew, such as "Love Me Tender," "It's Now or Never," and "Let Me Be Your Teddy Bear," when they blared from the open doors of the girls' rooms. In our love for this new culture, my floor mates and I did have something in common. They loved it because it was a welcome change from the sleepy fifties from which they had just emerged. I loved it because it spoke of individual freedom and a zest for life that were not part of my own tradition. So, in some ways, I identified with my American classmates and felt at home in their youthful milieu. The Meridian Hotel was not like the America I had seen in Hollywood movies. Rather than glamorous, glitzy, and fun, it was fifties drab, with plain, functional maple furniture in the rooms. But it did have amenities, like air conditioning, a beauty parlor, a gift shop, a drug-store, a doctor, a dentist, laundry and valet facilities, an indoor swim-ming pool and sun deck, and a Hot Shoppe Cafeteria. It felt strange to be living in a hotel, instead of on campus among the rest of the students. Nevertheless I still found the experience exciting. The Meridian was part of America, and it was different from what I had known in Vietnam, and for these reasons it was interesting to me.

The girls on my floor, with the exception of a student from New York, showed no interest in me, my background, or my culture. With few career opportunities open to them, their minds were focused on finding dates and, ultimately, husbands. I found them insular in their lack of interest about the world, but marveled at their energy and their sense of fun, and envied the freedom that they enjoyed in a culture with more relaxed social mores. Every morning, while I sat in the bus sent by Georgetown to take us to the campus, trying to fight off sleep, they would burst into cheerful songs, one after another, such as "Oh, What a Beautiful Morning" or "You Are My Sunshine," and they would sing and clap until we arrived at our destination. They went on dates and invited their boyfriends to the occasional parties that were held at the hotel under the college's official supervision. They had a sense of partic-ipation, and took part in many of the college activities, broadening their experience beyond the classroom and the dorm, unlike students in Vietnam, who continued to confine their world to school and home even after they entered the university.

I rarely took part in the social activities sponsored by the college, because I did not fit in and because I disliked the aura of organized fun. In this, I failed to understand their broader socialization purpose. I pre-ferred to spend my time with a group of Vietnamese students attending local colleges, and so missed the chance to reach beyond the familiar and enjoy a truly American college experience. There were only about fifty of these students scattered in the Washington-Virginia-Maryland area. But precisely because there were so few of us, we felt a special bond. I had met them through Huong Mai, the daughter of our Foreign Affairs Minister. She was also a student at Georgetown and lived on my floor. With her and the other Vietnamese, I could share Asian meals and, most important, talk in my native tongue.

For us expatriate students, the South Vietnamese embassy served as our social focal point. Each year, the ambassador would give receptions to commemorate national holidays. At this time, the ambassador was Madame Nhu's father, who probably would not have qualified as a diplomatic envoy to the most important capital of the world had he not been so well connected. While the ambassador was modest and digni-fied, his wife was much more pretentious. She decreed that only she could wear imperial yellow because she had royal blood. Unaware of this rule, I arrived at my first embassy function resplendent in an impe-rial yellow *ao dai* embroidered in silver thread with a writhing dragon— another imperial symbol. The ambassador's wife gave me an icy look, and one of the women who worked at the embassy took me aside to tell me I had committed a terrible gaffe. I felt annoyed rather than contrite. We no longer had a monarchy, and the ambassador's wife had no right to dictate what I could or could not wear. Besides, that was the nicest outfit I had, and I was not going to discard it just to please her. My own defiance surprised me; back home, I would have complied with her wish in deference to her age and social position.

The students, the small embassy staff, and the handful of Vietnamese employed at Voice of America formed our expatriate community. They were all hard-line anticommunists. Reflecting the favoritism of the Diem regime, most of them were Catholic, rewarded with overseas posting or studies abroad. Naturally, they supported Diem, but some did have misgivings about his nepotism and the coterie of flatterers who surrounded him. And except for the ambassador and his wife, everyone disliked the Nhus and feared that they were destroying the president. Eventually, however, even the ambassador would split with his own daughter and son-in-law, and resign over Diem's treatment of the Buddhists.

I, too, feared and disliked communism, although my rejection of it was tinged with an ambivalence that I did not stop to analyze. I had absorbed my parents' belief that the communists were *vo gia dinh, vo to quoc*—people without a family and without a nation—meaning that they were bent on destroying loyalty to the family and substituting it with loyalty to the Communist Party, and that they owed their allegiance not to the nation but to international communism. I had embraced my parents' opposition without questioning their assumptions. From the treatment of acquaintances and relatives like Uncle Trinh at the hands of the Viet Minh, my parents, and therefore I, also believed that the communists were cruel and coercive, and we opposed them on these grounds as well. Above all, however, it was the communists' perceived lack of respect for our two most cherished ideals, the family and the nation, that seemed to my parents and me the most egregious fault. Yet I also admired them, as did my parents, for their success in ending colonial rule, and thought of them as *gioi*, or talented and efficient. This admiration was not abstract, but had a personal dimension as well because of my respect for my sister Thang and her husband Hau. I did not try, however, to analyze why the Viet Minh had succeeded where other movements had failed, and why they were able to attract and keep people like my sister and her husband. I compartmentalized my feelings: admiration for Thang and Hau and the Viet Minh's victory on the one hand, and fear of communism as an ideology on the other, which was the more dominant of the two sentiments.

By chance, I found a family link within this expatriate community: The military attaché was married to the daughter of a cousin of mine. This discovery gave me a home away from home. At first, they invited me to their apartment out of a sense of duty, and I had the impression that her husband was not thrilled at having to fulfill an obligation. I thought I had to go, and did not feel any more enthusiastic at having to renew clan ties that I believed I had escaped. Once we got over our initial reluctance, my niece and I began to enjoy each other's company while her husband graciously put up with my presence. Once in a while, I would visit them, and they would cook Vietnamese food to give me a change from the cafeteria fare at the Meridian, using spaghetti to make dishes that called for rice noodles. Ethnic staples were not readily available then, so they got most of their ingredients at Chinese grocery stores in downtown Washington. In exchange for their hospitality, I would babysit their little boy on occasion. I did not have a television in my hotel room, so whenever I went to see them I would watch a lot of programs, more to familiarize myself with spoken English than to be entertained. My niece's favorite was *I Love Lucy*, and we also watched game shows. The contestants received prizes that seemed fabulous to me, like hi-fi equipment and household appliances—things that many people in Saigon could only dream of owning one day.

The program I remember best was the presidential debate between Richard Nixon and John F. Kennedy. The 1960 presidential campaign was then entering its final phase, with the Cold War casting a long shadow over the country and over the election. Kennedy cleverly exploited the country's post-Sputnik anxiety by accusing Eisenhower of having let a missile gap develop between the United States and the Soviet Union. Arriving in the middle of the campaign, and totally ignorant of its background, I wanted Nixon to win. He was an unflinching anticommunist, while JFK was a young man inexperienced in the hard realities of world affairs. (If I had heard Kennedy's speeches or read his writings, I would have found out that he was calling for a moral crusade against communism and that his rhetoric was quite tough.) I believed that Nixon, seasoned by the Cold War, would not let the tricky communists outmaneuver him. Furthermore, he had been hand-picked as a successor by President Eisenhower, who was one of my heroes. Not only had Ike led the Allies to victory against the forces of evil, but he had evacuated the noncommunist refugees from the North and had built a secure South Vietnam. In the debate, the only point that mattered to me was Nixon's hard-line stand on Quemoy and Matsu, the two small islands off Taiwan. While Americans saw a haggard Nixon, with bad makeup, on television, I saw a tough leader who would not cede an inch of land to the communists. By extension, I believed that he would not give up on South Vietnam.

Back then, few ordinary Americans even knew Vietnam by its name or where it was located. Even the opinion leaders—the reporters, editors, politicians, and academicians—knew little about it. Whenever I told people where I was from, they looked blank. After a while, I learned to explain that Vietnam was part of French Indochina. It was a marvel to me that the United States was committing itself to defend a place most of its people did not even know existed. I remember the time President Eisenhower was asked by a reporter why America was intervening in Indochina. Ike pondered the question for a while before replying that it was in America's best interests to be there because of all the tin that it had. I wondered whether a country that displayed so little knowledge of my own would be prepared to support it for very long, but I thought that having someone as hard-line as Nixon in the White House would help keep the United States on course in Vietnam.

The young President Kennedy overcame all my resistance to him on the day he took the oath of office. Standing hatless in the cold, his breath turning into white vapor as he spoke, he issued his ringing pledge that America would "pay any price, bear any burden, meet any hardship, support any friend, oppose any foe, to assure the survival and the success of liberty." I felt relieved; South Vietnam would surely be included in this worldwide embrace. At that moment, when Kennedy promised to set America on a new heroic course of defending freedom and helping "peoples in the huts and villages of half the globe" to "break the bonds of mass misery," the United States appeared noble to me. His was the rhetoric of an innocent, idealistic, but also arrogant era, when America believed that, with its immense resources, it could defend and nurture the whole world. Vietnam, of course, would shatter that illusion.

Now that I was persuaded of Kennedy's resolve to stand up to communism, I gave in to the charm and intellect of the new young and handsome president. Like most Americans, I was entirely caught up in the general adulation, and in the public relations and media frenzy over him and his beautiful wife. I became a big fan of the First Family, and in particular of Jacqueline Kennedy, whose bouffant hairdo I copied. The advisors that the president had assembled—the best and the brightest—impressed me to no end. With people of such caliber, especially Robert McNamara, whose press coverage made me believe that he was a man of immense talent, to carry the torch of freedom, I thought we had a chance to keep communism from overrunning the world. The future held so much promise then, for the Kennedy administration, America, and the Free World.

After my first year, I moved into an apartment with three other foreign students in a building that stood at the corner of P Street and Wisconsin Avenue. Except for My Luong, who was born in South Vietnam, my other two roommates came from quite different cultural backgrounds, but since they were outsiders in America like me I felt a special bond with them. Pin came from a wealthy Chinese family that owned a couple of large retail stores in Thailand. The third roommate was a moody young woman from Syria. Like my roommates, I began to discover dating. However, until I met David Elliott, who became my husband, I found dating neither as exciting nor as romantic as I thought it would be. I dated mainly to avoid loneliness, because my roommates were out constantly and busy with their own boyfriends. Dating for me, as for most Vietnamese female students, was a chaste affair. We knew we would return home one day and marry Vietnamese men who would expect us to be virgins on our wedding nights. If we were not, our husbands would repudiate us, and their families would cause a scandal over us being "damaged goods." Also, there was a cautionary tale about a Vietnamese girl at the University of Maryland getting pregnant by an American student she knew only by his first name, who disappeared right after he found out that she was expecting his child.

In the first year, however, I did not have a lot of free time to date, because I was struggling with my studies and needed every minute just to keep up with my reading. My English was so poor that I had to stop every twenty to thirty words to look up something in my English-French dictionary. Also, I found it hard to adjust to the American method of college teaching. In Saigon, I had studied by rote memory. I was not trained to think critically and analytically. Here, professors were more interested in how I analyzed the information I learned or gathered in the library rather than in how accurately I could regurgitate it back to them. I sweated over every term paper. Economics and finance were difficult, but Shakespeare plays, with their Elizabethan English, were the hardest for me to penetrate. My only solace was that I did better than many undergraduates who took these classes.

But most baffling of all to me was my American literature class. The young professor who taught it was obsessed with sexual themes, and saw sexual symbols in practically every paragraph of the works that we read. To him, Henry James in particular was loaded. He would get carried away and foam at the mouth in his excitement as he explained to us the hidden sexual meanings. Not having been raised on Freud, I wondered how anyone could read an innocuous descriptive passage and infer that it was only about intercourse. His frank talk about sex surprised and embarrassed me; to my astonishment, it also made many of my classmates uncomfortable. This professor, along with a few others that I had the misfortune of studying with, was part of a rather uneven faculty that had been recruited personally—at times brilliantly and at times disastrously—by Father Edmund A. Walsh, the school's founder, without the advice of a search committee.

I took many classes also attended by students from other schools at Georgetown, some of which were large, such as Western Civilization, with over 200 vying for seats. I enjoyed their size: In my Saigon high school, I could not hide; here, I could be anonymous, lost in the crowd. Some professors were outstanding, giving lectures that riveted my attention with their masterful interweaving of themes and facts; others were performers, and I found their style a refreshing change from the subdued approach favored by the nuns in my convent school. By my second year, my English had improved to the point that keeping up with my readings was much less of a chore. I also got used to the way the classes were taught. My term papers and exam essays began to draw favorable comments. The most effusive praise came from a history professor, who once asked our class to write a short essay on the meaning of democracy. My insight impressed him so much that he commented in the margin that I was the hope of democracy for my country. He was one of those idealists and optimists who believed then that if the American system of government could spread throughout the developing world, the problems that plagued us would be solved.

Not everything about Georgetown was alien to me. I had gone to a convent school where priests would come to conduct masses and teach catechism, so the sight of Jesuits in cassocks on campus was comfortably familiar, as was the gold cross crowning Loyola Hall, or the sound of an organ and a Gregorian choir coming from a chapel. Yet although it was clearly a Catholic university, Georgetown did not foist its religious creed on its non-Catholic students. The School of Foreign Service where I enrolled had a more secular aim. It trained students for a career in business and in particular in the State Department, and did this quite well. In my 1963 class, half of those graduates who chose to take the rigorous Foreign Service Entrance Examination succeeded, well over the national average of only about 27 percent.

A belief in the importance of international cooperation was one of the main tenets of the School of Foreign Service. In an age where conflicts could lead to nuclear destruction, this faith was understandable. Here, the United Nations was regarded with respect as the defender of peace around the globe, and also as a forum where the world's countries could get together and work with one another in a spirit of conciliation. (Later, however, when the newly created nations in Africa and Asia began to side with the Soviet Union against the United States at the UN, this international organization began to lose some of its appeal.) The school also nurtured a strong belief in mutual understanding. Somehow, it was thought, if all the countries could understand one another, they would set aside their conflicts, regardless of their clashing national interests. In this spirit, each year the school held a Diplomat's Ball, its main social event. Banners in foreign languages hung in the background. Many overseas students would dress in their native costumes and put on performances to showcase their countries' culture. At a time when the United States had not yet become deluged with immigrants from all over the world, we were looked on as representatives of our countries. I and my Vietnamese compatriots took this role quite seriously, and in general avoided doing things that could reflect badly on our homelands. If we got caught doing something embarrassing—usually out of lack of understanding of American customs—we would hide the fact that we were from Vietnam. When pressed, we would say that we were Chinese or Siamese.

Undergirding the School of Foreign Service and Georgetown itself was a belief in the inherent values of Western civilization. Graduates of Georgetown, armed with this learning, could help spread this civilization across the globe, where there existed only lesser cultures. Looking back now, people might say that Georgetown was a narrow-minded place, but it was really just reflecting its time. It certainly did not strike me as a limited environment, because it gave me a window on the world that I had not had back home. I enjoyed being there.

Occasional references to women in the yearbooks and in the university's official pronouncements aside, the School of Foreign Service remained a male world. The handful of female teachers that I met were usually foreign language instructors, not professors. The women working in administration, with the exception of the Dean of Women, did not hold positions of responsibility. Highlighting the sense that women were a decorative touch for the school, one of the major events of the year was the selection of a Miss Foreign Service, who was chosen for

her looks, rather than for her brains. Georgetown was also predomi-
nantly a white world. With the exception of a Chinese-American, the
minority students I met came from overseas. The only black student in
my class of 1963 was from Kenya.

The Leadership Training Program took good care of me from the day
I set foot on American soil until the day I left. The scholarship was not
overly generous, but was more than sufficient. The program paid for my
tuition and gave me a monthly stipend that covered my share of the
apartment rent, food, and other necessities. Because I led a frugal life and
budgeted carefully, I never fell short of money. I ate mainly rice and stir-
fry, rarely shopped for clothes, and did not spend much on entertainment. For me, a splurge was going to a Chinese restaurant with
Vietnamese friends to share a meal (there were no Vietnamese restaurants in Washington at that time). Once in a while, I would take a trip
with my compatriots to places such as Luray Caverns, Skyline Drive, or
Atlantic City. I felt content and did not think I was missing out on anything in life.

After a year, I still spent most of my time in the company of other
Vietnamese; my contacts with Americans were superficial. American
society seemed to me so difficult to penetrate. People were always polite
and pleasant, but there was a gap that I did not know how to bridge.
After a while, I stopped making the effort because the people I met,
with the exception of two fellow students, did not show any interest in
pursuing a relationship that went beyond greetings and a few words of
chitchat. I did not feel resentful at being shut out, since I knew any foreigners who tried to break into the culture and society of another country would have run into the same initial obstacles that I did, but I felt I
was standing on the fringe looking into America.

The two fellow American students who took enough interest in me
and my ethnic background to pursue a friendship seemed to me more
complex than the average young people around me. The first one was a
girl from New York who lived around the corner from me at the
Meridian Hill. She was quiet but full of angst and repressed anger. I
attracted her because I listened with sympathy, although I could not figure out why someone with so much going for her was so unhappy, and
told myself that many Vietnamese would give anything to be in her position—having a rich family and going to an elite university. She used to
show me her poems and her anguished paintings. Our friendship ended
when we moved out of the Meridian, partly because she realized that I
did not understand her neurosis, and partly because by this time I had

taken up with my group of Vietnamese friends and did not make an effort to stay in touch. The other was a girl I met in my second year, who lived with her parents in a comfortable Georgetown house. She was also troubled, by a broken romance, and wanted a sympathetic soul who would just listen. She was the only American who invited me to her home on a regular basis. I understood her unhappiness better, because in my culture, there had been many instances over the centuries of women who lost their minds over tragic love affairs.

Most of my socializing with Americans happened at large events organized specifically to win the goodwill of foreign students, especially those from developing countries like me. Our American hosts wanted to give us a good impression of the United States, as a way of fighting communist propaganda in the Third World, the battlefield between America and the Soviet bloc. So, a couple of times a year, especially at Thanksgiving and Christmas, I along with a group of foreign students on American scholarships, would be invited to a reception at one of the elegant Georgetown homes to be feted like important guests. Even the White House waded in to welcome foreign students with a huge garden party, to which I was invited—the social highlight of my stay at Georgetown. For this occasion, My Luong, Huong Mai, and I dressed in our best *ao dai* and trooped to the presidential mansion—Camelot's hallowed ground—where we crowded on the south lawn with other young students as excited as we were. Suddenly, news spread that President Kennedy would come out to give us a few words of greeting. With that, we all turned toward the south portico and pressed forward. A rope held us back. Then, JFK appeared, as handsome as he had looked in the countless pictures we had seen of him. He had just returned from a vacation. His face was tanned and his hair had turned sandy red from the sun. He walked briskly down the path, spotted My Luong—whose looks had helped make her Miss Foreign Service—and stopped to shake her hand and ask her where she was from. My Luong was so awed she could hardly speak. Then Kennedy moved on. When My Luong showed me her hand—the one that Kennedy had touched— I was green with envy.

Much as I might idealize America and its president, I saw things here that tarnished the United States for me. It was shortly after my arrival in Washington that I witnessed segregation for the first time. The Jim Crow line was across the Potomac, in Virginia. On my first foray into this southern territory, I saw many "Whites Only" signs. At gas stations, there were separate restrooms for whites and blacks. When I first had to face the choice of going into a toilet for "colored" or one for "whites only," I hesitated, not knowing how I fit in the racial configuration. But then I made up my mind that I belonged where the white man belonged, and not in some undesirable category. The French had tried this trick on my people, treating us as inferior and keeping us down. They used to call us "yellows" or even *cochons*—pigs—because they thought their white skin made them superior. But Dien Bien Phu had shown us that the white man was no master race and had no right to despise us. There was no way I was going to give in meekly. When I decided to defy the signs and went into the "whites only" restroom, I found that the women inside did not react, nor did the staff at a "whites only" restaurant at our next stop. As I discovered later, the signs were in fact directed at blacks, and not at other minorities. In general, the southern whites did not feel strongly about us Asians at the time because there were not enough of us to pose a threat.

Of course, this did not mean that I did not run into any incidents of discrimination. In Washington I was snubbed twice for my ethnicity. One late winter afternoon, as snow was falling and the temperature was dropping, I climbed into a bus and asked the white driver whether he was heading in my direction. Instead of answering me, he fixed me with a hostile stare and told me rudely to get off his bus, while the riders snickered. Another time, a shoe salesman refused to wait on me. The two minor incidents I experienced made me understand better the daily humiliation that blacks had to put up with, and my sympathy for their struggle for equality grew. One of the most exciting events I witnessed was the march on Washington, when Martin Luther King, Jr., delivered his inspiring "I have a dream" speech. I remember the grainy images of the throng stretching away from the Washington monument on our black and white television. In spite of the fact that I had not become a Catholic or joined any denomination, rarely went to church, and only prayed intermittently, I was deep down very religious. So, I responded not only to King's call for justice but also to the spiritual overtone of the message, and I identified with the civil rights activist himself. I would miss the most trying phase of the civil rights movement, but when I returned to the United States in 1968 after several years back in Vietnam, I had to marvel at the changed legal and psychological landscape I found. Compared with when I was at Georgetown, the lot of blacks—and, by extension, that of other minorities—had improved markedly. I would remain grateful to the blacks and whites in the civil rights movement, and for their allies in government, for the opportunities that they opened up and the better treatment they secured for minorities like mine.

The Kennedy era was marked by several Cold War confrontations, and the most dangerous one loomed with the Cuban missile crisis of October 1962. For a few days, we felt the world stood on the brink of nuclear annihilation. At Georgetown, many professors canceled classes. It seemed absurd to carry on as normal in those circumstances, when we might all be blasted into oblivion. I found the situation ironic: I thought I was getting away from war, but here I was, about to be vaporized in a nuclear holocaust. When the Soviets backed down in the confrontation and agreed to remove their nuclear missiles from Cuba, the news left me and everyone I knew limp with relief.

Compared with nuclear brinkmanship, the situation in Vietnam looked easier to deal with. In the fall of 1961, it began to require attention. The communist insurgency that would doom the Saigon regime and draw America into the quagmire had started in the fifties. After Geneva, hundreds of thousands of former Viet Minh moved to the North, but an unknown number also stayed behind to secretly prepare for the national elections slated for 1956 to reunify the two halves of Vietnam, working in villages that had been Viet Minh strongholds to keep the people's loyalty and allegiance intact. To wrest control over these areas, Diem sent in troops to establish his authority, driving these cadres underground. In 1956, he launched a campaign to root them out, arresting thousands of people, including those who had nothing to do with the Viet Minh. He succeeded in crippling their movement; even as he did so, he alienated many villagers and drove the remaining Viet Minh cadres into fighting back. By 1959, Hanoi had begun sending Viet Minh cadres and fighters who had regrouped to the North back to the South, infiltrating them along the Ho Chi Minh trail, a secret network of routes that meandered through the mountains and jungles of Laos, Cambodia, and Vietnam's central highlands. The Viet Minh—now called Viet Cong or Vietnamese Communists by the Saigon government—painstakingly rebuilt their movement and started to expand, feeding on the resentment and unhappiness of the peasants. In December 1960, a few months after I departed for the United States, Hanoi created the National Front for the Liberation of South Vietnam, and stepped up its assistance to the South. Viet Cong attacks grew in size and frequency.

After the Bay of Pigs and the Berlin Wall, Kennedy could not afford politically to let South Vietnam go. The common wisdom at the time insisted that if Vietnam fell, other countries would fall to communism as well. Kennedy decided to increase American aid to help Diem. The Saigon army would be beefed up with weapons and helicopters, and military advisors who were experts in counterinsurgency would arrive to train the troops. The United States would also ship barbed wire and shovels to Diem to build strategic hamlets. Peasants living in areas that were contested or under communist control would be relocated inside these fortified villages to deny the guerrillas support and allow Diem to expand his control. This program bred dissatisfaction among the peasants, who did not want to leave their homes and orchards—usually strung out along canals in the South—to be concentrated in these barren fortifications, far away from their ancestral graves, fields, and markets.

Convinced that the communists were using insurgency to undermine poor areas of the world, Kennedy wanted the United States to demonstrate in Vietnam that it knew how to deal with this form of warfare. Counterinsurgency became the mantra of the day, and the Special Forces—the romantic Green Berets—would be the new standard-bearers in this kind of shadowy war. Many would end up in Vietnam as advisors, living in the jungle with mountain tribes or in isolated outposts. For the few Americans who followed the news about Vietnam, the buildup in Saigon gave hope. At Georgetown, an American classmate of mine told me confidently that now, with so much support from the United States, the South Vietnamese would surely defeat the communists. I looked at him and said that it would take a lot more than that. He thought I was unduly pessimistic.

I was too young, however, to brood over the crisis in Vietnam and elsewhere, or to despair over the threat of nuclear holocaust. In December 1961, I met a young American and fell in love. I became preoccupied not with war and destruction, but with thoughts of him. Many women fantasize about meeting the man of their dreams one memorable evening, and in my case, the fantasy came true. One evening, I went to a Christmas party thrown by the Vietnamese embassy staff for expatriates in the Washington area. There would be live music and a fashion show of Vietnamese clothing to enliven the function. An all-Vietnamese affair was an unlikely place to meet American men, but two Vietnamese classmates of Dave's at the University of Virginia in Charlottesville had invited him to bring his guitar and sing a few American folk songs. I was standing in the hallway, wearing another one of my imperial yellow *ao dai* and waiting for my turn to appear in the fashion show, when this tall, gaunt, and bespectacled American walked up to me, introduced himself as David Elliott, and explained that he was a guest of Hung, who was also a friend of mine. That broke the ice and we began to make small talk.

His obvious interest and attention flattered me. His gentlemanly manner and his intellectual demeanor attracted me, coming as I did from a culture that admired men of good breeding and learning. When he appeared on stage to sing, I thought he was artistic as well. I had been dating a Vietnamese student, also an artistic man who liked to paint, although I was not in love with him. That evening I was not looking for another date; my attraction to Dave happened so quickly that it left me flushed with excitement. I felt physically drawn to him with an intensity, as well as a warmth and a tenderness, that I thought could mean only love. After the performance, we spent the whole evening dancing together. He only knew how to do the slow dance, so no matter what music was playing we bobbled to the same steps. I did not mind. I was oblivious to my surroundings, even to the stares and sarcastic comments of my male Vietnamese cohorts, who resented David monopolizing my company.

After that, he came up to see me as often as he could, whenever he had the time and could borrow his parents' car for the trip. The first time he took me out on a date, he asked me where I would like to go. Having hardly gone out anywhere other than to Vietnamese friends' places, to a few restaurants, or to the movies, I did not know what to tell him. I remembered a restaurant with live Hawaiian music where I had eaten with some friends, so we went there. It was only later, when I got to know him better, that he confessed to me that he hated Hawaiian music. I discovered after a few dates that he was as WASP as they came. He descended from Scottish-German stock. He had gone to prep school and then to Yale, where he sang in the Glee Club, the Whiffenpoofs, and the Duke's Men. In fact, his ambition had been to be an opera singer, but he had given it up quickly after he found out what it would take to break into the field. Music and books were the loves of his life. Dave's father had taught at Harvard and had run its government department, but was now retired and living on a farm near the Blue Ridge Mountains of Virginia. From there, he commuted into Washington to teach part-time at American University and consult for the State Department on occasion. As I knew Dave better, I found out that besides being as intelligent, creative, and kind as I had thought, he was also a generous spirit. He would always give people their due. If he criticized anyone, he would do it reluctantly and usually only for constructive reasons. His basic instinct is to help rather than to hurt.

Dave was already drawn toward things foreign, and was now studying for his doctorate in Latin American studies at the University of Virginia, with Brazil as his area of focus. His ambition was to join the State Department and deal with international affairs when he got his degree. This attraction to foreign cultures was part of what drew him to me. When we started going out together, we just wanted to spend time with each other, but because he lived in Charlottesville and did not have his own car, we managed to see each other only once a month. It was too early in our relationship to talk about marriage, but I realized that there were too many obstacles for it to happen. Inter-racial marriages were still taboo. I knew that marrying me would probably compromise his chances of a successful career, and I did not want to be the cause of that. I also knew that marrying him would upset my parents terribly, and that if I tried to return to Vietnam, I would be ostracized. Even in the Washington area, my compatriots disapproved strongly of my relationship with him. So, for the moment, we just enjoyed each other's company. There were times when I wondered whether our relationship would survive once I returned to Vietnam upon my graduation—as my scholarship and visa required—but I dismissed the thought, preferring not to dwell on it.

As our relationship grew, Dave told his parents about me. His mother Louise wanted to meet me. Full of trepidation, I went to his father's apartment at the La Salle building to see her on her next trip to Washington. She greeted me warmly and gave me a big hug. She was a beautiful lady with a natural elegance that did not need to be enhanced with stylish clothes and accessories, but what impressed me most about her was the spirituality that shone through, and her loving nature. In Mrs. Elliott, I saw where Dave got many of his fine qualities. She had bought me a winter coat as a present—exactly what I needed, as my old coat had worn out. That gesture demonstrated to me the special gift that she has of knowing what others need even before they themselves realize it, a gift I have seen her display many times since. We talked about my relationship with Dave. I confessed I did not know where it was going. The strain of the uncertainty that I had been suppressing broke through, and I cried. Tears came to her eyes, and she took me in her arms, saying that she understood how I felt. Then I said goodbye, thinking I might not see her again.

One day, however, Dave invited me to his parents' farm to meet his father, William Yandell Elliott, and older brother Ward, who was getting a law degree at the University of Virginia. I felt nervous about the meeting, wondering whether they would approve of me. Dave's father had been a legendary figure at Harvard, whose students included future leaders like JFK and Henry Kissinger. He was the model scholar-statesman and one of the pillars of the Eastern Establishment that was still dominating academia and the government during the Kennedy era, and had advised several presidents and secretaries of state. During World War II, he headed the Office of Civilian Requirements within the War Production Board and in this capacity practically served as the czar of the civilian economy. Earlier, he had fought near Verdun in World War I, where he was wounded in the leg. He liked to lean on a cane when walking. Although he had a collection of canes, his favorite was an old gnarled stick that he carried with him whenever he went out to tour the farm, with his German shepherd frisking around him.

Even an average American girl might have been challenged to hold her own at the Elliotts' dinner table. Dave's father, a giant of a man physically and intellectually, dominated the conversation, which was erudite. When he was not dazzling me with the power of his intellect, he was entertaining me with his stories. He was a wonderful raconteur, in the southern tradition from which he had come. He would talk about his days as a member of the Fugitives group of poets at Vanderbilt, or his time as a Rhodes scholar at Oxford, or his tenure at Harvard, or his war years in France, or his boulevardier and lost generation period in Paris after World War I, or all the famous men he had met. Intimidated, but also brought up to be nonassertive and quiet, I just listened. The next evening, my future father-in-law tried to draw me into the conversation. He picked a topic he thought would be familiar to me, and asked what I thought of Confucianism and in particular the Golden Mean. Having spent my life studying about the West, my knowledge of this philosophy, gleaned from bits and pieces from my own culture, was so superficial, and my English still so basic, that I could hardly come up with an intelligible, let alone learned, answer. He gently let me off the hook, and discoursed at great length about Confucius and other philosophers. I discovered that he had a wide-ranging intellect, and that he loved beauty, art, and thought in any culture.

Asians at this time tended to dismiss America as a young country with a short past, a parvenu nation in comparison with older countries with thousands of years of history. But as I learned more about Dave's family, I found that they had as interesting a background as mine. Their family tree included, among others, a whaling captain in Nantucket, pioneers who had opened up the West, people who had worked in the underground railroad to help escaped slaves flee to the North, and an officer who fought in the Civil War on the Union side and was incarcerated at Andersonville. Their forefathers in Tennessee, who had sided with the Union forces in the Civil War, used to keep vigil at night with rifles across their laps to protect their families against enraged Confederate sympathizers.

The legacy had bred into Dave's family a quiet fortitude of spirit and the ability to maintain grace under pressure. They could take most things as they came, but they were not passive by any means. Before the outbreak of World War II, Dave's father had bravely attacked fascism, receiving many threats for his stance. Dave's mother was less confrontational, but was just as tenacious in fighting for things she believed in. However, ready as they were to meet challenges, the Elliotts had a hard time accepting how serious Dave's relationship with me had become. They worried that Dave might get carried away and marry me; being loving parents, they wanted to stop him from doing something that he might regret later. First, they pointed out that we were too young to rush into marriage: I was only twenty years old, and Dave was twenty two, too young to make hasty decisions. Second, they worried about the future we would have. Interracial unions were still a crime in many states, considered miscegenation. Worse, perhaps, was that a marriage would surely destroy Dave's future at the State Department, which he and they had set their hearts upon. They feared that our children would have a difficult time. Seeing that we were both sensitive people, they doubted our marriage could survive so much strain.

Although his parents did not express their misgivings to me, I could sense that they were worried by his growing attachment to me. His father was the more concerned of the two; his mother, I thought, was torn between wanting to give Dave more support and protecting him. I still had at least two to three years of study—plenty of time to be with Dave—so I decided that there was no point in worrying about where our relationship might head and just to enjoy it. Our relationship actually grew more intense because of the uncertainty and also because of the knowledge that couples like us were frowned on in both our countries. (It was only after Dave proposed just before I was due to return to Vietnam, and I asked him what his parents thought, that he told me about their misgivings. Being loving and kind, however, they accepted me with open arms after we got married. Throughout the years, they have always been at my side, helping me, supporting me, and giving me the love that I needed. They have been like my own parents.)

In 1962, about a year after we met, Dave had to join the army that

McNamara was building up to create a "flexible response" to communist expansion. Having had two student deferments already, he would be unlikely to escape the draft this time. He decided to enlist, so he could get training in a technical field of his own choosing. He had to leave for basic training at Fort Jackson in North Carolina. The separation was hard on both of us. I knew it would be a long time before I could see him again. After basic training, he went to the Defense Institute of Languages in Monterey to study. He hoped he would be assigned to a Portuguese class, but instead he was sent to learn Vietnamese. With the U.S. army presence in Vietnam growing, the Pentagon wanted people in the field who could speak the native language. By the end of 1962, there were already over 12,000 advisors to train and advise Diem's army, and the U.S. command in the country had been upgraded and a four-star general put in charge. Vietnam had become such a hot spot that senior American officers vied to be there. "It's the only war we've got," as one general put it. But it had not become so dangerous that it was a place for a young draftee to avoid, so Dave, patriotic and anxious to do his duty like most Americans at the time and excited about witnessing history, actually looked forward to it.

I was about to graduate and return to Vietnam, when Dave called from Monterey to propose that we get married after he arrived in Saigon. We talked about the opposition of our families and of the difficulties we might encounter, but decided that we would just face things together. I had finished my studies and could get a job, and he would have his army pay, so we could survive in Saigon. After he finished with the army, he would return to the University of Virginia to get his doctorate and go into teaching. He realized now that this was what he wanted to do; on reflection, he did not really relish the idea of joining the State Department and making his way through its bureaucracy. Also, academia would offer a liberal and tolerant environment where I and our children could live comfortably. We got excited at the prospect of marriage and adventure in Saigon. As to the future, we did not really care.

By now, I knew that Dave was the man I wanted very much to marry, and decided that I could not let my parents' feelings stand in the way or forego my chance at happiness just to fulfill my filial duty. Besides, I feared that unless I married Dave, my parents would likely force me to take as a husband a man they selected for me when I returned home; my sisters Phu, Binh, and Yen were then stuck in unhappy marriages that my father and mother had arranged, and I did not want to end up like them.

But I dreaded breaking the news to my parents. I had not told them about Dave, believing there was no point in upsetting them if we were not going to marry. As I labored over my letter, I knew that they would be angry with me for marrying a foreigner and for being the first daughter to breach my family's tradition, usurping their prerogative by choosing my own husband. I pleaded with them to understand and to forgive me. I waited anxiously for the reply, and when it arrived, I tore open the envelope. I expected a lot of recrimination, but instead my parents were understanding, saying things like "we accept your decision because the world is different now and we have to change with the times," and "we don't want you to marry a foreigner, but it's your life to live as you see fit." Unaware of the emotional crisis into which my decision had thrown my parents, I cried with relief.

While my prospects brightened up that summer of 1963, back in Vietnam, the conflict had taken a turn that should have served as a warning to Washington. A major operation in Ap Bac planned by American advisors—and combining for the first time the lethal firepower of helicopters, fighter bombers, and artillery supplied by the United States—ended in defeat. The Viet Cong shot down five of the fifteen helicopters piloted by Americans that were ferrying Diem's troops into battle, killing three advisors. The South Vietnamese soldiers, under the command of officers handpicked by the president for their loyalty to him rather than for their battlefield courage, cowered under the fusillade and refused to attack the outnumbered enemy. For the Viet Cong, the battle marked a critical point in their insurgency. They learned that they could fight back and win against helicopter-borne assaults and that Saigon had not gained a decisive edge with this modern technique of warfare.

For the Americans, the defeat should have driven home that the main problem they faced with Diem's army was not lack of firepower but the lack of will to fight. McNamara had created a reporting system to track the progress of the war by using statistics that, by their nature, focused on factors that could be measured such as the number of enemy troops killed during ground operations or by air strikes, or the number of engagements initiated by Diem's army. His system, however, could not capture and measure intangibles like the poor morale and motivation of the South Vietnamese army, or Diem's lack of popular support—which in the end counted more than the tangible factors he tracked. The statistics he pondered with so much faith were actually flawed, manipulated by Saigon to make him think that things were better than they actually were. Misled by the rosy numbers, the Secretary of Defense thought, four months after the battle in Ap Bac, that the United States had turned the corner and that its job in Vietnam could be wrapped up by mid-1965. Later, as the Viet Cong showed great tenacity in the face of the tremendous firepower that was deployed against them, McNamara would begin to be intrigued by the intangible factors that were driving them to fight on with such courage, and he would order the Rand Corporation to conduct a study of the enemy motivation and morale. Tellingly, however, he never ordered a similar study about the South Vietnamese.

After three years at Georgetown, I got my bachelor's degree in the summer of 1963. My sadness at leaving the United States was tempered by the joy that I would see my family again and that Dave and I would be reunited in Saigon. When I disembarked that October, my relatives could hardly recognize me, with my bouffant hairdo lacquered firmly in place, my makeup, and my more stylish Western clothes. I was no longer the ugly duckling that they remembered. While my younger sisters Loan and Tuyet approved of my appearance with huge smiles, my parents—especially my father—were aghast because I epitomized what they viewed as the new, immodest Western look that the young in Saigon were beginning to copy.

Three years is a short span in a lifetime, but within that time much had happened to me and to South Vietnam. I had left as an unformed and unsophisticated teenager and now came back as a more mature and cosmopolitan woman. I had fled Saigon depressed, now I was returning as a happy prospective bride. When I left in 1960, the political scene seemed calm and stable, Diem was fully in control, and the war was still in its infancy. Now in 1963, Diem's regime was about to lose its grip. The streets were convulsing with protests and demonstrations, and the Viet Cong had grown in strength.

The truth was that the seeds of destruction were already being sown at the time of my departure. The shops, brimming with goods, did a brisk business. There was little inflation and exports were rising, and most people were well fed and well dressed. A constitution and a rule of law seemed to have brought stability. But appearances were deceptive. The economy was humming along only because of the large influx of U.S. aid, while Diem's family—or their underlings—subverted the laws of the land. Lulled by their peaceful life and deceived by heavy government news censorship, my family and most people in Saigon did not suspect that *pourriture* was already spreading in many areas of the country. The Viet Cong had begun to attack in larger and larger numbers, and to inflict bigger and bigger casualties on the government army. But in Saigon, blissfully unaware of the growth of their movement, people continued to dismiss them as a ragtag band that could be eliminated with American military assistance. No one had to pay a price as yet to defeat the Viet Cong: Thanks to American aid, there was no income tax to finance the war, nor had the sons of the middle class been drafted into battle, so a large segment of the population was able to ignore the insurgency.

When I left, people had already started to grumble more and more about Diem and his family, though no one felt angry or unhappy enough to want him removed from office. The country seemed stable, so people like my parents continued to tolerate him, in spite of his shortcomings. His favoritism toward Catholics disturbed my devoutly Buddhist mother, and Madame Nhu's antics irked her and my father terribly, but my parents felt that at least Diem was a capable man who, though he might be authoritarian and blind to the corruption around him, could maintain law and order and was not robbing the country and people to enrich himself—a man still head and shoulders above the other politicians waiting in the wings for a chance to take his place.

What pushed my father and my mother to finally join the clamor for Diem's removal was his repression of the Buddhists. The crisis began when the government forbade the Buddhists to fly their own flag in Hue for the celebration of Buddha's birthday. Since Catholics had previously been allowed to fly their own flags for their religious celebrations, the Buddhists resented this blatant discrimination. For years, the Buddhists had been fuming over what they perceived as preferential treatment of the Catholic minority who dominated the government, while they were relegated to the status of second-class citizens. Their anger now boiled over. Monks and their followers took to the streets of Hue in protest. The government responded by bringing in tanks to fire into the crowd, killing a number of demonstrators. The protests spread to other cities.

Instead of negotiating with the Buddhists to end the dispute peaceably, Diem, under the Nhus' prodding, decided to crush them. To dramatize the plight of his faithful, a monk, Thich Quang Duc, doused himself with gasoline and burned himself to death in the streets of Saigon. The pictures of this human torch, carried by the media in practically every country, convulsed South Vietnam and the world in shock, anger, and loathing. I was still in Washington when I saw the television broadcast of Thich Quang Duc's immolation. The image of the monk sitting calmly in the lotus position as flames engulfed him and of his charred body finally falling sideways would be seared in my memory. Vu Van Mau, the Foreign Minister and my clan matriarch's son-in-law, shaved his head in a gesture of solidarity with the monks and resigned. Tran Van Chuong, Madame Nhu's own father and the ambassador to Washington, also quit his position. Nguyen Tuong Tam, a famous writer, killed himself in protest. Popular opposition, amorphous and unorganized until that time, now coalesced around the Buddhist monks, who became the spearhead for a movement to depose Diem and his family.

In attacking Buddhism, Diem and Nhu struck at what the Vietnamese viewed as the heart of their culture and tradition. People like my mother, who had been apolitical before, now were galvanized into action. My mother was a typical Vietnamese Buddhist: She had her own altar at home, prayed every evening, and went to the pagodas on special holidays. Unlike Catholicism, Buddhism was not an organized creed, and unlike Catholic priests, Buddhist monks were not activist leaders. Now, however, the crisis was turning these monks into political firebrands. They gave rousing speeches to summon their faithful to come to the defense of Buddhism. Hundreds of thousands of followers like my mother responded to their call and thronged to the pagodas to pray and listen to the monks speak. Students and other opponents of Diem's regime also flocked to the Buddhist cause, using the movement as an outlet for their own frustration. Angered by what he perceived as a challenge to his family's power, Nhu sent Vietnam's Special Forces—trained and paid for by the United States—to raid the pagodas and arrest the monks. This only inflamed the Buddhists and reinforced their belief that their faith was in danger of being destroyed. They took to the streets in greater and greater numbers.

By the time I arrived in Saigon in October 1963, the city was seething with anger against Diem and his family. Even the military had turned against him. Faced with so much hostility, the president withdrew even more into his family circle and became increasingly isolated. To contain this growing opposition, Nhu relied even more on his secret police to intimidate people, but this just bred more discontent. It was a vicious circle. The Americans had already begun to waver in their support for Diem, fearing that his unpopularity was damaging the war against communism. At first, President Kennedy thought he could salvage the situation by pressuring Diem to carry out reforms and to get rid

of Nhu and his wife, the main targets of popular hatred. But Diem, out
of loyalty to his family and out of natural stubbornness, refused to listen.
In spite of the worsening situation, the Americans clung to him, afraid
that his forced removal would only upset the war against the Viet
Cong, although this was going badly too, with the communists practically taking over the Mekong Delta. Finally, when Diem's crackdown
on the Buddhists plunged the country into chaos, the United States
decided to replace him.

By this time, Saigon was full of rumors of the portents of Diem's
demise. According to our traditional belief, rulers govern only with the
approval or mandate of heaven. When a ruler violates this mandate,
heaven sends signs that he will be punished, usually natural disasters
like earthquakes or unnatural phenomena like roosters suddenly laying
eggs. Stories of ominous portents began to make the rounds of the city,
feeding the hope that a change of regime was in the cards. The heart of
the monk who had immolated himself was found intact after he burned
to death, and was ceremoniously carried to a pagoda where it attracted
thousands of worshipers. A rumor circulated that people had seen statues of the Virgin Mary shedding bloody tears. One day, I heard a commotion in our alley late in the morning. I ran out and noticed a crowd of
people peering into the sky and saying, "The sun is spinning! The sun is
spinning!" I looked up and saw—to my amazement—that the sun was
etched with a dark circle that was turning very fast. Perhaps there is a
scientific explanation for this strange phenomenon, but none of us could
think of one. Perhaps, induced by the hysteria, we were only imagining
things. We stood there, awed by what we witnessed. My neighbors
told one another that this could mean only one thing: Diem was going
to be overthrown.

I had never seen my mother in such a state of agitation. My father,
more rational and less emotional, did not listen to the monks or become
their follower. But he, too, had reached the conclusion that Diem had
become too much of a liability, and that the time had come for him to
go. In fact, a coup d'etat was being plotted at that moment. The generals behind it, knowing they would need the acquiescence of the United
States to succeed, approached the American embassy through a CIA
agent about getting rid of Diem. When Ambassador Henry Cabot
Lodge did not object, they attacked the presidential palace on
November 1, 1963.

That afternoon, our radio suddenly went dead and then started to
broadcast martial music, a sign that something was happening. Then the

coup was announced, and military commanders began to go on the air to express their allegiance to its leaders. At the presidential palace, Diem and Nhu tried to rally loyal officers to their side. When this failed, they escaped through a secret tunnel and went to Cholon, where they were captured by the coup leaders. In spite of American wishes, the generals did not spare Diem, and had him and Nhu shot on the way to their military headquarters. Madame Nhu, who was traveling overseas to drum up support at the time, escaped retribution. Soon afterward, the military junta arrested Diem's younger brother Can, the feudal lord of Central Vietnam, and subjected him to a lot of humiliation, to the delight of the people. They finally had him shot. Saigon newspapers carried a picture of him at the time of his execution: a forlorn blindfolded figure, with his head hanging down and his hands tied to a stake.

At the news of the coup, Saigon and other cities erupted in celebration. Soldiers taking part in the attacks were hailed as heroes, and middle-class girls, who would not have deigned to glance at them before, smiled at them and gave them flowers. The generals were greeted as saviors of the country. Ambassador Lodge became extremely popular and was made an honorary citizen of Vietnam. When he accepted this title, wearing a Vietnamese traditional blue brocade tunic and a turban, the people felt a surge of affection for him. Diem's hard-core supporters, especially Catholic refugees, never forgave him and Kennedy for Diem's death. At the time of Kennedy's assassination, many expressed satisfaction that Diem had reached beyond the grave to exact his revenge.

My mother was jubilant that Buddhism had been saved. Although she found the pictures of Diem's murder inside the personnel carrier disturbing, she understood the generals' decision to smash "the head of the snake" to prevent future trouble. My father felt sorry for Diem, but was not surprised that someone like him, who had created his government from an act of treachery, would end up perishing at the hand of traitors himself. No one in my family mourned Nhu's death. We thought that he had been felled by the storm he himself had sown. We did pity Can, especially when we saw the picture of him bound to the stake. After the initial euphoria faded, people began to wonder about the qualifications of the coup generals to lead the country. In a short time, these officers would confirm everyone's worst fears and plunge the country into chaos.

13

Just Cause

That morning, I was working a day shift, preparing a news report for the English-language broadcast by the government-owned Radio Saigon. The city was like a kettle that was boiling over. Buddhists and students were *xuong duong*— pouring into the streets—almost daily to protest against Nguyen Khanh, the general who had deposed the military junta that had replaced Diem and set himself up as the prime minister, demanding his resignation. The office was full, but it hardly hummed with purposeful work. Clerks and secretaries were idling their hours away until lunchtime: the men reading newspapers and sipping tepid tea from glasses stained brown by long usage; the women knitting, gossiping, or, if they were more industrious, pecking at their typewriter keyboards with a pencil so as not to chip their nail polish. Suddenly we heard shouts coming from the street. We listened and thought we could make out slogans amplified by bullhorns and taken up by what seemed like a large crowd. We rushed to the entrance and saw a thin line of policemen in white uniforms trying to hold back a mob of students. The protesters surged forward, overwhelming the police. A group stormed into the station and rushed upstairs to broadcast a statement denouncing General Khanh as a dictator. The rest milled at the entrance and in the hallway at the foot of the staircase. Outside, the crowd spread out to surround the building, located at a street corner, to keep people from entering and leaving.

The moment they saw the students converging toward the station, some of the clerks had left by the side street. These were seasoned veterans who had gone through coups, attempted coups, and demonstrations. They knew things could turn ugly. In those pre-television days, disgruntled factions or generals trying to overthrow the government usually made a beeline for the station so they could relay their message to the nation and rally support, and the government, not wanting to cede such a powerful tool to its opponents, would try to take it back. The staff would get caught in the cross fire. Not having the experience of those veterans, my colleagues and I did not size up the situation correctly. By the time we realized what could happen next, it had become too late to leave. We could only wait anxiously for events to unfold. We were not sure how the mob was going to treat us. Would they beat us up for being part of General Khanh's propaganda machine? We took encouragement that the protesters did not go on a rampage. They did not smash things or beat up anyone. After a while, the rumor seeped down to our floor that the student leaders had been thwarted. A technician had had the presence of mind to destroy a piece of equipment, making it impossible for them to go on the air.

By one o'clock, I was tired of waiting, and I was also getting hungry. I decided to leave. I told myself that if the mob threatened and blocked me, I would just return to my desk. The students looked surprised when they saw me—probably the only woman in Vietnam at that time with a Jacqueline Kennedy bouffant hairdo. I was also wearing a short dress with slits on the sides instead of the *ao dai* favored by the female staff at the station. Evidently, I did not look like someone who was part of General Khanh's oppressive regime, because when I told those barring the entrance that I wanted to go home, the crowd parted like the Red

Sea, and I walked out. Not long after I left, the protesters gave up and dispersed peacefully. When I came back to work a couple of days later, I found paratroopers camped out in the hallway, dispatched by the government to keep the students from storming the station again, where they would stay for about a week in a brief show of force.

Nguyen Khanh, the object of the students' wrath, was an ambitious and scheming general who had edged out the ruling military junta in a bloodless coup three months after Diem's overthrow. Although he was hugely unpopular in Vietnam, the Americans were supporting him. They had become uneasy over the government of General Duong Van Minh (not related to me) and other junta members, who had done nothing to stem the tide of communist attacks and were rumored to be moving toward negotiating with the Viet Cong and turning South Vietnam into a neutral state. Washington feared that accommodation and neutrality would merely be preludes to a communist takeover. President Lyndon B. Johnson, afraid of being accused of losing South Vietnam to the communists, was determined not to let this happen. In Khanh, the Americans thought they could find a more malleable tool: someone who would defer to Washington's wishes, bring stability, and focus on defeating the guerrillas. Khanh, however, turned out to be a vexing client for his patrons. He was interested only in hanging on to power by endless manipulation. To make him more palatable to his own people, the Americans tried to enhance his standing. Defense Secretary McNamara toured Vietnam with Khanh to shore up the general's image. But the more the Americans tried to build him up, the more the people despised him as a puppet.

No one I had met respected or trusted General Khanh. Even his appearance did not inspire confidence. He looked like a slightly rotund weasel, with a round, oily face, protruding eyes, and a goatee, grown at the urging of a fortune-teller who had advised him that it would elongate his short face (considered an ill omen). He had been a protégé of Diem and, soon after taking over, embarked on what a lot of people thought was an attempt to bring back the old regime. He ordered the killing of the officer who had shot Diem and Nhu, and he reappointed many officials linked to the Diem government. These actions alarmed the Buddhist leaders and their faithful. Suspecting that he was trying to restore the Catholics and Diemists to power, they organized rallies and marches to protest against him and demand his resignation. At their exhortation, thousands of students joined the demonstrations in massive *xuong duong* in major cities.

This prompted the Catholic supporters of Diem who blamed the Buddhists for his downfall and death to organize demonstrations of their own to check the growing influence of their religious rivals. These marches and countermarches paralyzed many areas of Saigon, including the one where Dave and I lived. From our balcony, we could watch long columns of people filing by, carrying banners and shouting slogans. Men assigned to maintain discipline walked along the column at regular intervals, as a sign to the residents that the rally would be peaceful and would not get out of hand. But whenever the rival groups met, the fragile discipline would break down. We saw angry Buddhist and Catholic youths racing down our street brandishing sticks. The hatred and distrust grew to the point that my family wondered whether a religious war would break out.

Meanwhile, the communists were steadily taking over large chunks of territory. The strategic hamlets, the key to Saigon's military strategy, had been reduced to shambles. Sometimes with the help of the Viet Cong, sometimes spontaneously, peasants who had been uprooted from their homes and orchards and forcibly relocated into these fortified villages rose up to destroy and burn down what they viewed as their concentration camps. Even Saigon ceased to be a safe sanctuary. Viet Cong terrorists set off bombs right in the city. But instead of closing ranks to face and stop the communists, we were battling one another.

The deadly religious rivalry was only part of the chaos that was engulfing the country. At the top, the generals were squabbling and jockeying for power. Rumors of coup d'etat swept through Saigon almost daily. In September 1964, one did take place, in spite of President Johnson's injunction to the generals not to rock an already leaky boat. As usual, the coup generals who conspired against Khanh drove their troops into Saigon and took over key installations, including, yet again, the radio station. But Khanh survived this coup with the help of the air force, which threatened to bomb the plotters if they did not give up.

I was hoping to leave my job at the radio station, and not only because of the anxiety of working there in the unstable political climate. I felt I was not getting anywhere in my work. No one had bothered to give me any training or, indeed, any guidance whatsoever, even though I was writing news that the station would broadcast. The indifference was typical of a government office where few people took pride in their jobs. From day one, I was on my own. Fortunately, I had grown up in the system, and I knew instinctively where the political boundaries were and what I could put on the air. Even though no one cared about my performance, I realized that if I crossed the line, I would get myself and the man who had hired me—a friend of a friend—into trouble. I patched together bits of bland news about what the government was doing, about decrees that had been signed, or how the Saigon troops had killed a lot of Viet Cong and captured a lot of weapons in attacks. I shied away from stories of attempted coups, military setbacks, or religious protests, unless I knew what slant I should put on these events from reports carried by the official press agency. The picture I presented was of a government devoted to the welfare of the people and pursuing the war with great success. Once or twice, I was even put on the air. After the short burst of music that introduced the news—the overture to *Carmen*—the red light would go on in the booth, and I would stumble through, stopping now and then to apologize very politely for my mistakes, and then gamely continuing on until I finished. The broadcast was aimed at foreign listeners inside and outside Vietnam, although, as far as I could gather, few listened to it, dismissing it as propaganda. The Vietnamese ignored it—even my family did not bother to catch it, because they could not understand English and also because they found the program boring.

Through the wife of an American officer my husband knew, I made contact with Professors John Donnell and Joseph Zasloff, who were conducting research for the Rand Corporation on the motivation and morale of the Viet Cong. They hired me to conduct interviews with communist prisoners and defectors, and I gladly gave up my position at the station. By this time, I had been married for several months. Dave had arrived in Saigon about four weeks after I had returned from Georgetown, as an SPC5—a sergeant—in the U.S. army. He had received a high security clearance for a job in signal intelligence, monitoring clandestine communist military radio communication. Immediately after he arrived, he stunned his commanders by applying to marry me, a native. First, they thought he had met a bar girl and lost his head. They tried to talk him out of it. Once they understood the situation better and knew we were serious, they took away Dave's top-level security clearance and made him spend his days watching over some local workmen painting the barracks at his base near the airport.

I too had to change career paths. I gave up my dream of becoming a Vietnamese diplomat, knowing my application to join the Foreign Affairs Ministry would not pass muster. The prejudice against a woman taking an American husband would have been too strong for me to overcome. In any case, I thought my stay in Saigon was going to be short, since I would be accompanying Dave back to the United States after his tour of duty to finish his doctorate degree. Like other overseas students newly returning home after a long stay abroad, I found it difficult to reacclimate myself to the social constraints, the lack of the rule of law, the corruption, the poverty, the poor sanitation, and the debilitating weather. The prospect of returning to the United States, even if only as the wife of a graduate student, seemed attractive, in spite of my misgivings about getting separated from my family. However, as I adapted, and as I got absorbed in my job with the Rand Corporation, I would find it hard to leave when the time came.

Dave and I had to run a gauntlet of obstacles thrown up by both the Vietnamese and the American authorities to discourage a marriage like ours. Dave had to get approval from both the U.S. army and embassy. One of the requirements was for me to go through an interview with the chaplain of his unit, more like an interrogation. The chaplain started out by asking a lot of questions about my background, to make sure that I was a respectable woman worthy of marrying an American G.I. He seemed surprised to hear that I had a degree from Georgetown University, and a bit disappointed. My background could not be used as a pretext to hold up the marriage. Then he switched tactics. He warned me about the social and cultural problems that could confront an interracial marriage back in the United States. When I appeared unswayed by this, he added, "Listen to me. I speak from firsthand experience. I know personally what inter-racial couples run into, because I myself am married to a Norwegian." I felt annoyed rather than amused at being patronized in this way, but I simply thanked him for his concern and advice.

We met several other bureaucratic impediments to our marriage, but they paled beside my family's objections. Back in Washington, reading the loving letter from home, I had had no inkling of the anguish that the news had inflicted on my parents, especially my father. When I returned home, I found out that he had been devastated and unable to sleep for days after he learned of my decision. However, I discovered with surprise that my mother, though very upset, had taken the whole thing much better. She had cast my horoscope years ago and knew beforehand that my husband would be a foreigner. She thought she could not prevent something decreed by fate, so she resigned herself to it. I also found out that, far from being reconciled to the marriage, my father would give anything to stop it. He and my mother had soothed me with reassuring words in order not to upset me just as I was getting ready to graduate.

My father was more distressed by the shame that my marriage to an American sergeant would bring to our family than by my breach of filial piety. He told me that only prostitutes and bar girls got involved with foreigners, and that if I married an American, everyone in Vietnam would take me for a whore. My relatives would despise me, and my family's honor would be stained. He also told me that by marrying beneath my station I would make him and my mother a laughingstock. In his mind, an American sergeant was no better than the orderlies he used to have at his beck and call in his mandarin office—to fetch him his pipe and bring him his tea. He could already imagine the sneers and snide remarks of his relatives and acquaintances. When I stood my ground, he pointed out that Westerners do not make loyal husbands, and warned me that Dave might abandon me later on in a strange land. Even that did not faze me, because I was sure of my choice and also because I believed that, should Dave and I divorce, I could survive on my own in America.

I tried to reassure my father that I was not making a mistake, but he remained skeptical until Dave showed up at our house, charming my family with his Vietnamese and impressing them with his erudition. My parents now saw that, although he was only a sergeant, he came from a patrician family. Roots, along with intellect, counted heavily in their eyes. Also, they were cheered by his prospect as a college professor, as well as by his scholarly and refined appearance. The American military personnel they had seen in the streets had struck them as beefy and coarse, "like fat, dumb Russian potato farmers," my father said. Feeling much better about the marriage, they accepted my decision, gave me their blessing, and sent out the wedding announcements and banquet invitations to all our relatives. Then they waited for the roof to cave in. The uproar exceeded their fears. The matriarch of the clan was outraged. How dare I bring dishonor on the name of the Duong clan? She pronounced that she would boycott the banquet. Everyone else in the clan said they would follow her example. My parents were crushed. They knew the relatives would be upset, but they had not expected them to be so heartless. By this time, I had become so emotionally drained that I no longer cared. The idea of a wedding banquet was my parents', anyway, not mine. I would have gladly done without all the fuss and bother. They had insisted on it, because without a formal banquet to publicly seal the union, everyone would say that my marriage was not legitimate and that I was only Dave's mistress.

The guest list started out very short. But then, relatives began to get curious about the American groom. My aunts and uncles, the generation below that of the rigid matriarch, were the most intrigued, and several of them accepted our invitation. With Dave being a foreigner and his family in America, we had to dispense with the traditional rituals. On the wedding day, Dave and I went to the office of the chief of police for District Two for the civil ceremony, conducted entirely in French in the belief that a Western language would sound more comprehensible to an American than Vietnamese. Fortunately, Dave had studied French and understood enough to say "Oui" at the right moment. With my "Oui," we were declared man and wife. That evening, we hailed a taxicab, a tiny Renault that looked like a frog on wheels, and rode to the Chinese restaurant for the wedding banquet. I put on the brocade *ao dai* I had made for the occasion and the fake diamond tiara that middle-class bridesmaids wore at this time. This was considered a modern touch, a variation on the pin that French bridesmaids wore to hold their wedding veil in place. To my surprise, the private dining room was full. All my relatives pressed around, wanting to meet Dave. He delighted them with his gentlemanly demeanor and behavior, and especially with his Vietnamese. My father had coached him on what to say to give thanks to the guests. When my husband rose to express his appreciation for their presence in elegant and flowery Vietnamese, they exploded in applause. To my parents' delight, the banquet turned out to be a huge success.

Dave and I rented an apartment on a busy street near a market, in a small two-story building belonging to an overseas Chinese. It had one room, a bathroom, and a balcony that served as a kitchen. Bare wooden furniture set off the main room into three areas: a few arm chairs near the door indicated that this was the space for receiving our guests; an armoire and a bed marked our sleeping quarters; and a table and two chairs delineated our dining area. A ceiling fan provided a little relief from Saigon's oppressive heat. Although the apartment was small, it was mine and Dave's, and so seemed special to me. An energetic and cheerful Chinese maid, introduced by the landlord, helped me out with the cleaning, shopping for food, and cooking.

We settled into a two-career couple routine, seeing each other only at dinner. With our combined salaries, we were affluent by local standards. With benefits like the cost of living allowance and extra pay for serving in a hardship post, Dave was earning about $700 a month, more than a Vietnamese cabinet minister. I was probably making the equivalent of about $60 working for Rand. Since I was not yet an American citizen, I got paid according to local salary scale. Later, once I got my U.S. citizenship, I would get compensated as an American, and my salary jumped to $500 a month. I was happy, married and holding an interesting job. Conditions in the country, however, had been going from bad to worse.

At the time of our wedding, Defense Secretary McNamara had toured Vietnam, and upon his return, had given President Johnson a grim assessment. He told LBJ that the Viet Cong had gained control over almost half of the country, that Saigon soldiers were deserting at an alarming rate, that the South Vietnamese government had no popular support, and that Khanh did not look like he could last. In retrospect, many people later on said that this would have been the point at which the United States should have recognized the daunting odds and disengaged, especially since vital American interests were not at stake. Instead, LBJ, believing that American credibility was on the line, made the fateful decision to get more deeply involved to save South Vietnam in spite of itself. The United States had to blunt Chinese expansion through proxies like Hanoi. If it failed, the communists would be encouraged to take over Southeast Asia. Instead of withdrawing American advisors from the South by the end of 1965, as President Kennedy had promised to do, Johnson sent more. He also intensified covert commando raids into the North and secretly sent American ships patrolling close to its shores to pinpoint its radar sites and map its coastal defenses.

By the summer of 1964, Johnson found himself in a crisis. Increased American aid had failed to improve the situation. Hanoi was pouring more troops and supplies into the South down the Ho Chi Minh trail. In neighboring Laos, the government seemed about to topple under communist pressure. The U.S. presidential election was coming up in a few months, and a disintegration would hurt his chances for securing his own mandate. He would have to escalate American involvement yet further to prevent a debacle. The idea of bombing North Vietnam to stop it from sending reinforcements into the South had been considered for some time. Now Johnson had plans drawn up for this contingency. To avoid provoking China, the bombing would be limited. A resolution was drafted in secret to secure congressional approval. Then in August, claiming that the North had attacked American ships in the Tonkin Gulf, LBJ went to Congress and got the resolution passed with only two dissenting votes. American planes roared over North Vietnam in a limited reprisal.

In Saigon, my family heaved a sigh of relief. My father said, "Finally, the Americans are striking at the head of the snake." Like the Americans, we thought this show of U.S. might would deter Hanoi and make it pause in its tracks. But the bombing did not scare Hanoi, and the flow of men and materiel did not abate. Not only that, the Viet Cong had the audacity to attack an American air base near Saigon. So Johnson escalated again. He secretly bombed Laos to hammer the Ho Chi Minh trail as it threaded its way through that country before vanishing under the jungle canopy of central Vietnam. Still the communists gained momentum. By December 1964, they began to attack with large contingents, not just with small guerrilla units. Throughout the country, their forces were on the move. They occupied Binh Gia, only forty miles from Saigon, for about a week, and then cut to pieces the seven crack battalions supported by tanks, heavy artillery, and helicopters flown by American pilots that came to the rescue. Five American advisors died in the battle.

This first large-scale operation, involving more than 1000 Viet Cong, stunned the Americans and alarmed the middle class. But worse was to come: Just before Christmas in 1964, Viet Cong agents penetrated the Brinks Hotel in Saigon, housing American officers, and planted a bomb that killed two and injured fifty-eight others. Now, it seemed, nowhere could be considered safe. Back in the United States, President Johnson, who had been elected as a "peace" candidate against the belligerent Barry Goldwater, had lost patience. He no longer wanted to wait for the South Vietnamese to get their act together and pursue the war vigorously; he would step in with more American power and do it for them. He ordered American dependents to leave South Vietnam in January 1965 to remove them from what he knew would be a fiercer theater of war.

My husband and I had been married for only nine months, and I did not want to be separated from him. Although I was an American dependent, I was not yet a U.S. citizen, and I was allowed to remain in Saigon. For a while, it did not look like we could stay for very long. In February 1965, the Viet Cong attacked the barracks for American advisors in Pleiku. American planes bombed a North Vietnamese barrack in retaliation. The Viet Cong attacked another base for American advisors a few days later. LBJ and his advisors decided to escalate the violence further. Henceforth, the bombing of the North would no longer be a tit-for-tat affair. Starting in March 1965, the bombing went on continuously. It would be expanded gradually in an attempt to exert more and more pressure on Hanoi and to salvage the situation in the South. With relatives still living in the North, we worried about their safety even as we approved of stronger American action. My father said, "I hope the United States won't flatten the dikes and starve the people, and I hope it won't drop nuclear bombs." General William C. Westmoreland, the new U.S. commander in Vietnam, worried that the Viet Cong would attack the American air base in Danang, and at his request, LBJ sent 3000 Marines to protect it.

The situation only grew worse. The communists seemed poised to sweep across the central provinces and cut the South in half. The Saigon government crumbled. A group of young officers pressured General Khanh to resign, and named Air Marshall Nguyen Cao Ky as prime minister and a general by the name of Nguyen Van Thieu as chief of state. If the communists had chosen to stage coordinated attacks throughout the country, they might have won the war and taken over the South then and there. My family, and the middle class in general, lost heart. Their thoughts turned to fleeing. Rich people began to sell off their assets and leave the country. Among the Catholics who had fled south in 1954, there were rumors that their priests were making arrangements with Australia and Ceylon to move their flocks there en masse. My father heard that Australia had offered to make an island off its coast available for the settlement of refugees. According to this rumor, the island was large and wild, and the refugees would have to clear it and make it habitable. My father said that if Australia would take him and the family, even though they were not part of the Catholic flock, they would go. They were desperate enough to do whatever it would take to survive on this formidable island. (We do not know whether there was any truth to this rumor.)

But when the Americans stepped in, my family's flight was postponed. Days after the Viet Cong overran the district capital of Dong Xoai, at the request of General Westmoreland, President Johnson ordered that 150,000 G.I.s be sent over as quickly as possible in the coming weeks to take over the fighting and stave off disaster. While Defense Secretary McNamara intended for the G.I.s only to turn the tide in Saigon's favor and induce Hanoi to talk peace—and to do so quickly—General Westmoreland's strategy aimed to win through a war of attrition. He planned to take on the North Vietnamese regular units that had infiltrated into the South—the core of the communist forces—in conventional attacks, and grind them down with his awesome firepower and superior technology, killing more soldiers than Hanoi could train and replace. Eventually, his attrition would decimate the enemy, and he would mop up what was left of the communist forces and achieve victory. While Americans took over the fighting, the South Vietnamese army, under the guidance of American advisors, would secure areas cleared of communists, pacify the countryside, and win the hearts and minds of the peasants over to the side of the government.

The plan sounded good. In an America proud of being the world's most powerful nation and still glowing from triumphs in Europe and Korea, there were few dissenting voices. But the war got out of control, miring the United States in a morass and wearing down the patience of the American public. Instead of giving up under the punishment meted out by the United States, as the Americans had expected, the communists simply refused to abandon a goal they had fought for so long to achieve. President Kennedy had said that if the war were to be won, it would have to be won by the South Vietnamese themselves. Now, President Johnson and his team decided that since the South Vietnamese would not or could not do it for themselves, American soldiers and power would do it for them. Their misjudgment would lead to tragedy.

For the middle class and my family, the G.I.s brought a bright ray of hope. We welcomed their landing. My father said, "We're incredibly lucky. We're such a small and weak country, and yet the Americans have decided to save us with their money and their own lives." And they were coming in huge waves. By the end of 1967, the number would come close to half a million. The sheer size of America's commitment staved off defeat for Saigon. The middle class shelved their plans to flee. As the Americans impatiently took over the war, they would settle back and watch, happy to let these big and burly foreigners—who seemed so much more anxious to win—do the dirty work for them. Many would devote their time and energy not to defeating the communists, but to raking in money from the huge American presence. In time, as this presence battered their society, many among the middle class would become disillusioned. Many would turn against them and demand that they leave, in the hope that their departure would end a bloody civil war and allow the South to become a neutral state, insulated from the Cold War power struggle. But many wished they would stay on for as long as necessary, no matter how many years the fighting would last.

In Saigon, we saw no evidence of the first Marine landing, except for photographs of Vietnamese girls draping garlands of flowers around the necks of the soldiers, which reassured us that they were really here. The next waves, though, flung the soldiers in a wider arc. By the time U.S. forces were in the hundreds of thousands, the Americans seemed to be everywhere. Along with the combat and support troops, there was also a huge influx of civilians to build harbors, bases, roads, and bridges. In Saigon, the Americans took over the best houses and the largest buildings, paying for leases that were exorbitant by local standards two to three years in advance and making the owners rich. But there was not enough housing to accommodate them, so they sparked a construction boom and a financial boon for contractors. Having so much money to spend, the Americans also started to take over the best bars, the best cafes, the best restaurants. Services sprang up practically overnight to cater to their many needs. Tu Do, the main commercial street in downtown Saigon, turned into an American quarter. Suddenly, gaudy souvenir shops, tailors, and bars displaced the sleepy stores selling things like imported French food, fabrics, and jewelry. Because the Americans were also generous employers, paying more and setting less stringent conditions, maids flocked to their bases and households. Middle-class families started to grumble about how hard it had become to find good domestic help: Maids would rather work for Americans, at several times the usual salary, plus Sundays off, an annual vacation, and better food to boot.

The city boomed, reaching a level of affluence that it had never known before, even while artillery shells and bombs were falling not far from its edges and B-52 strikes were rattling its glass windows. At key street corners, armed soldiers kept watch from behind sandbags. Military vehicles mingled with civilian traffic. But residents seemed oblivious. Life was so good for those who benefited from the money the United States was pouring in that, after the Americans went home, they would later refer to this period as the "golden age." Imports financed by American aid continued to arrive. Motorcycles clogged the streets, spewing carbon monoxide that slowly killed its old trees. Luxury goods became more widely available. My parents got a refrigerator and their first television set. Even telephones, once rare, became easier to obtain, thanks to the Americans who had upgraded our network. My parents could not afford a telephone, but my brothers Giu and Luong, the most affluent of my siblings, each had one. Unlike in the North, there were no acute wartime shortages and no rationing. Rice production was falling sharply as peasants fled their land, but the Americans replaced the lost supplies with imports. Besides the legal imports, we could get an incredible array of goods that were siphoned off from the bulging American warehouses and Post Exchanges (PXs) and sold on the street. At social gatherings, black market Johnnie Walker whisky flowed. From this time onward, Saigon residents would become attached to

American consumer products, clinging to their favorite brands like a marketer's dream come true. Years later, after the communists had taken over, we would get letters from relatives in Saigon listing precisely the goods they wanted us to ship back: Colgate toothpaste, Prell shampoo, Salem cigarettes, and so on.

The newly affluent class included many who stole without qualm from the Americans. Some of the goods available on the black market had been pilfered from the U.S. military bases. We heard that sometimes Vietnamese drivers would squirrel even large items like air conditioners and refrigerators out of these bases under a thick layer of rubbish. The Americans themselves were not immune to corruption, and some would accept bribes and turn the other way to let the Vietnamese carry out what they wanted. To the Vietnamese who got rich this way, taking from the Americans was not really wrong, first of all because they were foreigners and normal ethical principles need not be applied to them, and, second, because they had so much that they would not miss what they lost.

The upshot of billions of dollars circulating in a country the size of Texas was that people had more money to spend. Supply could not keep up with demand, and prices shot up. But although people grumbled about inflation, only those who were not benefiting financially from the war had a hard time making ends meet. The countryside and Saigon in particular became schizophrenic. At the bottom were the many peasants who were paying in lives and limbs lost, and in homes and fields destroyed by the war. At the top, life could not have been better for the corrupt officers and officials, for men and women working as clerks for the Americans, for building contractors, and for real estate owners. It was also good for those catering to the Americans' needs, from prostitutes who could earn more than the head of a government ministry, to tailors, to *cyclo* and taxi drivers taking free-spending G.I.s around town on their furloughs, to the maids toiling for them. Some Vietnamese, watching greed displacing traditional values, complained that the American presence had turned society upside-down. In the old days, the social order was expressed in the saying "scholars first, peasants second, artisans third, and merchants fourth." But now, according to these disillusioned traditionalists, this saying should be changed to "prostitutes first, *cyclo* drivers second, taxi drivers third, and maids fourth." Money, not intellectual achievements or social usefulness, had become the yardstick of success. This social upheaval finally turned some of these educated Vietnamese against the American intervention, although they

knew it was keeping the communists at bay. While my family was dismayed over the impact of the American presence on our society, they
accepted it as the price to pay to defeat the communists.

The tempo of life in Saigon quickened. The city seemed much noisier, dirtier, and more crowded. The young in particular lived hurriedly,
as though the good times would end too soon. To the dismay of their
elders, they started to imitate the freer lifestyle of the Americans.
Children of middle-class families attended "boom" parties, where they
listened to loud rock music and gyrated to the latest dance from
America. Or they crowded smoky nightclubs, where they could listen
to singers aping Johnny Mathis or Elvis Presley.

Side by side with this hedonism was the sad evidence of a crumbling
society. Thousands and thousands of peasants were flocking into Saigon
to escape the fighting in their villages. They eked out a living as best
they could. On the sidewalks, we could see maimed people dragging
themselves and begging for money. Street urchins—orphans or homeless
children called the "dust of life"—pestered pedestrians, begging, stealing, offering to shine shoes, or on occasions even pimping. Right in the
middle of downtown Saigon, I could see them sleeping on flattened
cardboard boxes under the eaves of buildings. Lean-tos appeared in
many areas, butting against the walls of villas or clogging stinking alleys
as refugees tried to put a roof over their heads. Garbage piled up in many
parts of the city. Near my parents' house, a huge mound attracted
swarms of flies and rats, as the slum behind their quarters swelled with
more and more people. Destitute adults and children rummaged through
it to find something they could salvage. Crime soared. In the street, we
clung to our purses so that youths on motorcycles would have trouble
snatching them from us. When we made our way through a crowded
market, we kept a lookout for pickpockets cutting our purses open with
razor blades. A lot of the middle class, including my family, accepted
this social disintegration as the inevitable consequence of war. But others began to feel that the price for fighting off communism was getting
too high, especially when they realized what American firepower was
doing to the countryside.

Our country seemed to have become a testing ground for American
armaments. In their impatience to win, the Americans were applying
their technological wizardry to improve old weapons and devise new
ones at what to us appeared like incredible speed. They used sensors
that could detect movement and even sniff the body odors of the communists as they trekked down the Ho Chi Minh trail; herbicides and

defoliants to clear jungles, mangrove swamps, and tree lines and to kill peasant crops that could go to feed the Viet Cong; converted DC3 transport planes each equipped with machine guns that could spew out 18,000 rounds a minute; B-52 strategic bombers, designed to carry nuclear warheads into the Soviet heartland but now called on to drop 37,000 pounds of bombs each, either on suspected enemy sites or in tactical support of American and Saigon troops; huge howitzers; smart rockets; and all sorts of bombs, including Daisy Cutters that could each mow down an area the size of a football field; cluster bombs with hundreds of pellets that ripped into human bodies; and napalm bombs that burned their victims.

All this firepower crushed the innocent peasants as well as the guerrillas who moved among them. Like the French before them, the Americans found it hard to separate the combatants from the civilians. It was impossible for them to bomb, shell, and defoliate with surgical precision. And when they swept through villages on foot, it was difficult to tell whom they should spare and whom they should punish. Relentless violence eventually drove one-fourth of the population in the countryside to flee from their villages. When my husband began to conduct research for the Rand Corporation after his discharge from the army, we would see strings of refugee huts, one after another, along the highway leading into the Mekong Delta as we drove from Saigon to our new office in the provincial town of My Tho. Thousands of the displaced drifted into the cities, where many of their daughters went to work as bar girls and prostitutes. The hard-line anticommunists, however, were not unduly alarmed by the sufferings visited upon the peasants. It was the cost of defeating the communists, they would say. Once in a while, though, the carnage would intrude. My parents would murmur, "So many are getting killed. How long is this going to go on?" And my mother would pray to Buddha to ease into nirvana the souls of the innocent dead.

But no one I knew remained disturbed for long. On the whole, however, the people in our circle of acquaintances just shut the death and destruction out of their minds. I too preferred not to think about it. At the beginning of the war, I was as much of a hardliner as any other middle-class Saigonese. I had been brought up to believe that the communists were evil incarnate and had to be wiped out, no matter what. And yet I did not hate all the communists; I respected many of the individuals who made up this group, people like Thang and Hau, who had sacrificed so much to kick out the French. It was in this frame of mind that

I started to work for the Rand Corporation in late 1964. As I interviewed Viet Cong for the research project, I began to see that there were many like my sister and her husband on the other side, who were not evil. They possessed some of the same admirable qualities. They were patriotic, self-sacrificing, determined, and courageous. They puzzled me. I started to ask why it was that our side could not evoke the same response and bring out the same qualities in people. After all, the people I interviewed, and my sister and her husband, were Vietnamese too—and yet they were behaving so differently. They were responding to something that touched them deeply.

That something, called a "just cause" by the men and women I talked to, was what our side had failed to provide. Their just cause was composed of nationalism—driving out the Americans, healing the gash that cut the fatherland in two, and reunifying it—and also a program that promised to bring the poor a better future. But the communists had more than a popular cause. They also had the organization and the discipline to channel the people's support toward victory. Gradually it dawned on me that it was not communist cleverness or trickery that was making us lose. We were losing because of ourselves, because we had been unable to come up with a system, an ideology, and a leadership that could tap these same qualities in the people, inspire them, and pull them together in the same direction to win the struggle. I realized that I could not blame those that fought on the other side for our own failure to offer a more attractive alternative. Although I did not come to embrace their beliefs, I began to view them less harshly and I stopped thinking that they ought to be exterminated.

My job at Rand was to administer a detailed questionnaire that the two professors had designed to elicit information about a whole range of topics—economic, social, political, and cultural. The objective of the study commissioned by the Defense Department—Rand's main client—was to determine who the Viet Cong were, what background they came from, what made them join, and what motivated them to stay in the guerrilla movement against such daunting odds. At this time, the Viet Cong were really faceless enemies to the Americans, and McNamara wanted to learn why their fighting and motivation were so much better than that of the troops on the Saigon side.

The Vietnamese leaders thought they knew and therefore did not feel the urge to find out. I, too, thought I knew, but the sum of my knowledge was really just an amalgam of prejudices. The first interview I did made me realize how ignorant I was. I arrived at the jail carrying what were to become my standard props: a pack of American cigarettes to put my interviewee at ease and break the ice, my questionnaire, a notebook, and a pen to jot down answers, follow-up questions, and my impressions at the end of the day. Later, I would add a portable tape recorder. I was nervous, unsure of how the session would go. I had believed that among the Viet Minh, educated people like Hau and Thang were the exception rather than the rule, and so fully expected to meet an ignorant and brutish worker or peasant, someone with "the head of a buffalo and the face of a horse," as we in the middle class used to describe the communist followers. In short, someone uncouth, stupid, and not quite human.

The jail officer was shocked to see me, a nicely dressed young woman coming to such a grim place to do such an unpleasant job. He no doubt expected a tough interrogator. But the Americans had sent me, so he was not going to ask any questions. His reaction seemed to say, "Nothing these Americans do can astonish me." He took me to a bare interrogation room. After a few minutes, the door opened, and in came a man briskly. His amazement lasted a bare couple of seconds. I greeted him and he nodded politely, then sat down and waited. I could tell he was putting himself on guard. He could see the situation: I was the classic "soft" touch, the sympathetic interrogator who came in to get information out of him after the tough jailers had done their questioning with threats, beating, perhaps even torture. I studied him. He was a dignified middle-aged man, with the authoritative demeanor of someone used to leading others. He did not look like an ignorant brute. I offered him a cigarette, which he refused—he did not want to touch something so American. As I started to read questions off my list, he began to relax.

Perhaps it was the nature of the questions—it was obvious that I was not after operational information and that I was not pressing for hard intelligence data that could betray his comrades. Perhaps it was me—my youth and my innocence. Instead of laughing at me and my sometimes naive follow-up questions, he took me seriously and answered patiently. He opened up and started to talk at great length about his life, his family, his village, and his experience in the Viet Minh and the Viet Cong. It was, I sensed, the first time since his capture that someone had treated him like a human being and expressed an interest in him as a person. Although he had not had an advanced formal education, he was articulate and eloquent. He understood so much more than I, with my American college degree, about the revolutionary forces that had driven people like him to fight. He understood far more the conditions and aspirations of the peasants than I, insulated all my life in the cities, in French schools, and then in an American college. He had my complete attention.

I too began to relax, and my natural curiosity took over. I asked so many follow-up questions that, at the end of the initial session, I had barely covered a few pages. I think it took me about a week to finish the questionnaire. I walked away from this first interview rattled by what I had learned. My subject had impressed me as a man with deep conviction and great courage; in fact, he had more integrity than anyone I had met in Saigon in a long time. He might be misguided from my point of view, but he believed utterly in his cause, to the point of devoting his entire life and putting up with incredible hardships to achieve it. He believed that the Viet Minh would free his country from foreign domination and reunify it under a regime that would bring social justice and equality to the poor. He looked at himself as proof: a poor peasant who had been elevated to a position of leadership. Of course, one interview could not change my views right away. But it did raise troubling questions in my mind. Who were the good guys and who were the bad guys? At one time, I thought I knew. Now, the situation no longer seemed so black and white.

I caught the professors' project at its tail end, as they were wrapping up their interview phase. Right after they completed their project in mid-December 1964, a new Rand team started to pursue a different twist on the topic of enemy morale: How the Viet Cong were bearing up under the impact of different types of American weapon systems and military operations. As the months went by after the G.I.s arrived in 1965 and the war intensified, the number of prisoners as well as defectors for us to interview grew by leaps and bounds. Most of the defectors had left for personal reasons, some because they had been harshly criticized for taking up with a girl out of wedlock, some out of sheer exhaustion from the unrelenting violence of the war. But some also left out of disillusionment, not over the aims of the Viet Cong, but over their tactics such as assassinating South Vietnamese officials and other people who opposed them. The Rand staff had expanded with the arrival of experts to conduct several new studies intended to help Washington measure how well it was waging war. I did interviews for the team assessing the impact of bombing on communist troops' morale. Another team measured the impact of defoliation. The Rand villa, formerly a quiet place, now became crowded with the addition of a dozen more interviewers, and the two largest upstairs rooms were turned into offices. When they were not out talking to prisoners or defectors, the interviewers would be at their desks transcribing their tapes. Manual typewriters rattled as secretaries put the translated transcriptions into final form for mimeographing.

I and the other interviewers started to make field trips to province jails and defection centers. All were depressing destinations, the defection centers more so than the jails. At least the prisoners, for the most part, still believed in their cause and hoped that their side would win one day. The defectors no longer had a cause to keep them going. After spilling their guts to the Saigon side and the Americans to ensure lenient treatment, they sat or wandered around aimlessly, waiting for the day when they would be released. To me, they all looked tired and anxious. They knew that they had not really bought safety for themselves by opting out of the war, for it still might claim them in a bombing or sweep operation. The Saigon side might draft them into its army as cannon fodder, or the Viet Cong might retaliate against them for their treason. Of these possibilities, the latter was the most likely. Later, many of the defectors would end up joining American-sponsored Province Reconnaissance Units or the Phoenix Program after these were set up to hunt down their own former comrades; some would do this out of self-preservation, others to strike back at those they felt had wronged them.

While I was working for Rand in Saigon, Dave completed his military tour of duty and had taken a job with Rand himself. His stay had made him intensely interested in Vietnam and the communist movement, so he deferred going back to graduate school in order to research in depth the evolution of the communist insurgency in Dinh Tuong Province—as a microcosm of the insurgency in the South—which required him to spend the week in My Tho in the delta. The extension of his stay allowed me to continue seeing my family, pursue my fascinating work for Rand, and build up our savings to pay for his graduate studies, so I happily went along with his decision. He had been commuting back and forth from the delta, rejoining me on the weekend in a villa that we were now renting. The commute was dangerous, because the one and only highway connecting the two cities was a death trap—mined in the night by the Viet Cong, cleared in the morning, and then mined again. He assured me that he was not running any risk and that he traveled only after the road had been cleared. Unconvinced, I decided to move to My Tho and put an end to this commute. So, one day, we loaded our belongings into a rented black Citroën and left Saigon.

On the highway with the sun beating down mercilessly in the early afternoon, our car broke down, right across from a brick kiln. Dave hailed a soldier on a motorcycle, one of the few vehicles racing down the road at a time of day when no one went outdoors who did not have to. The soldier almost fell off his bike when he saw Dave, but was kind enough to stop and pick him up. While my husband rushed off with him to summon help from the district town ahead, I sat waiting in the stifling car. I wondered who would get me first: Viet Cong guerrillas emerging from rice fields bordering the road, or a jeepload of soldiers driving down the highway. I should have worried instead about the brick kiln, which, as we found out later, was a Viet Cong snipers' nest. Perhaps it was too hot that day for even snipers to be abroad, because nothing happened. Dave finally arrived with a mechanic who brought the car back to life, and we motored on to our new home. I started working for my husband's project. I continued to do interviews, but now spent most of my time transcribing and translating those done by Dave's staff of three.

The occasional interviews I did were with defectors, to spare myself the visits to the jails, of which I had grown weary. While working for the Rand office in Saigon, I had made several trips to prisons like the Military Interrogation Center (MIC) and the National Interrogration Center (NIC). MIC was the grimmer of the two. Security was tight, with rows of concertina and barbed wire and guards at the entrance to keep out intruders. I always had the feeling there that I was secretly being observed. The interrogation rooms were small, dank, and gloomy, and I was never sure whether the dark stains I saw were bloodstains or something less sinister. Once, noticing a contraption on the ceiling that looked like it was part of a pulley, I pointed to it and asked my interviewee, "What's that?" After a moment's hesitation, he murmured, "That's to make us ride the airplane." I was staring at an instrument of torture that allowed a jailer to loop a rope through the ring, bind a prisoner's ankles and arms at a sharp angle behind his back, and then yank him off the ground. If the jailer exerted the pressure fully, he could pull the prisoner's arms and knees out of their sockets. Other, more defiant prisoners told me, unprompted, that they had been beaten or had had soapy water poured down their throats and noses; that they had been struck repeatedly on the palms of their feet; that they had been subjected to electric shocks. Other colleagues at Rand also heard similar stories from prisoners, so the tortures must have been prevalent. We guessed that these prisoners were hoping that we could do something to air their grievances and improve their treatment, believing that since we were working for the Americans we must have had some influence. We knew that the government would retaliate against us and our families if we protested or made the grievances public, so we just reported the stories we heard to the people at Rand. But neither they nor the American officials in Saigon could stop the mistreatment. Even the exposure in the American media of the "tiger cages"—where prisoners were chained in underground cells even after they became crippled, were denied food, and had lime thrown at them—and the resulting outcry in the United States could not put an end to the mistreatment.

With Hanoi sending more of its soldiers into the South, I and other interviewers began to find more prisoners who had infiltrated from the North. I noticed a difference in my interviews between guerrillas from the South and regulars from the North. Both believed in the same cause, but the North Vietnamese had come to it more easily, having been brought up in the system and constantly indoctrinated in it. The southern Viet Cong had to come to it and accepted it as part of a more conscious decision. After Tet 1968, when the war had turned really brutal and was grinding down the southern native forces, many peasants, tired of the Viet Cong demand for manpower and taxes and exhausted by the war, were not as ready as before to join and fight with the guerrillas. My husband and I would be gone by 1968, but when we came back in 1971–72 so Dave could study the communist movement further, he could see this impact of Tet in his research.

In that early period, some of the Viet Cong prisoners as well as defectors also joined out of dissatisfaction with the Saigon regime. Usually, what pushed them to acting on their sympathy for the communist side was the behavior of the government itself. In fact, at the beginning, Saigon was unwittingly the best ally the Viet Cong had in recruiting peasants. Landlords came back with soldiers to collect back rent at gunpoint; soldiers swept through villages stealing from and roughing up, even murdering peasants; artillery shells landed on the peasants' houses, maiming and killing their relatives; officials conscripted villagers to build strategic hamlets and then coerced them to move there. I remember one interview with a woman defector who gave me a graphic description of the construction of the strategic hamlet into which she and her family were eventually relocated. It reminded me of a scene from one of my history books, of a time when a Chinese emperor forced a multitude of peasants to erect the Great Wall with their bare hands. Incidents like these convinced the villagers that the Saigon government was "tyrannical," which angered them and made them receptive to the Viet Cong.

Talking to the peasants of the South who had made that jump of no return into the communist camp, I felt what my sister Thang had felt when she lived among the destitute villagers of the North: deep sympathy. I could understand why these southern farmers decided that they had to fight to get rid of a regime—backed by a foreign power—that treated them and their families this way. I could no longer bring myself to hate these Viet Cong. Also, as I looked at these peasants who had so little, I felt moved by their accounts of how the violence of war was impacting their already hard lives, in a way that impersonal reports in *Newsweek* and *Time* had not. I began to wonder whether it was right to ask the peasants to suffer so to keep communism at bay. How could communism be worse than what they were going through? One day, Martha Gellhorn, an American reporter, asked me to accompany her to a hospital and translate for her. On this visit, I saw for the first time what the weapons were doing to real human beings. I saw children and adults who had lost limbs. I saw eyes staring out of heads swathed in bloody bandages. I saw a woman who had been burned by a phosphorous bomb, with peeling skin showing pink and raw flesh underneath. I knew this was only a fraction of the toll in human misery. I left shaken and more convinced than before that it was unfair to make the peasants bear the brunt of the suffering to save my family and other middle-class families from a communist system they felt they could not live under.

The results of the Donnell and Zasloff study for Rand on Viet Cong motivation and morale were presented to Washington at the end of 1964. After hearing the briefing, Defense Secretary McNamara's top aide said, "If what you say is true, we're fighting on the wrong side." The United States was putting its money, power, and credibility on the line in a country where the side it was fighting against was determined and well motivated, while the side it was fighting for was venal and lacking in commitment. The observations drawn by the Rand research team were shared by many Americans in the field. Like the French before them, many American officers could not help feeling impressed by the motivation, tenacity, and bravery of the Viet Cong. A U.S. general even called the Viet Cong "the best enemy" America had faced in its history. But neither the Rand report nor the reservations of these officers and other American officials changed Washington's policy.

Besides giving me an insight into the morale and motivation of the Viet Cong guerrillas and the political forces at work in the countryside, the interviews also allowed me to see how the war was evolving. At the start of the insurgency, the guerrillas armed with obsolete weapons—muskets and World War II vintage rifles—attacked in small bands, striking at outposts, and ambushing Saigon troops. By 1959, with southerners who had regrouped to the North returning to reinforce their ranks, and with weapons from China infiltrated into the South, they began forming regional and main force units that would take on bigger targets and larger Saigon units. Then, as the Americans entered the combat with search-and-destroy operations and conventional frontal attacks, the battles grew bigger, bloodier, and fiercer, and the North Vietnamese regulars would take on the brunt of the fighting. As American firepower increased, the communists kept pace; by 1967 the Soviet Union had supplied them with automatic rifles, rockets, and big antiaircraft guns (toward the end of the war they would have tanks and surface-to-air missiles). Prisoners and defectors I talked to would describe fearsome B-52 strikes and the crushing force of the bomb explosions, attacks by napalm, assaults by helicopters armed with rapid-firing machine guns, battles when phosphorous flares lit up the sky, or the spraying of defoliants that made them sick.

Even though my interviews made me more sympathetic to the North Vietnamese and the guerrillas, I had not yet reached the point where I wanted the United States to pull out and settle the war peacefully. I feared that once the shield of American power was removed, the communists would sweep the hapless Saigon regime aside and my family would suffer, with nowhere else for them to run and hide. For me, their well-being still came first. I could not discard so easily the loyalty bred into me over a lifetime. I hated the war and I wanted peace, but a peace that would keep the communists from winning. I began to wish that the group of people dubbed the Third Force, who were neither pro-American nor procommunist, would succeed in rallying the people, preempting a communist victory, and bringing an end to the war, so that my family would be able to live as they had before, under a noncommunist government. I was the only person in my family to have this fantasy. My parents distrusted the Third Force, considering them dupes of the Viet Cong who would hand South Vietnam over to Hanoi once neutrality was achieved and the Americans had left. Dave thought the Third Force was in disarray, had no popular base, and no hope of achieving its aims.

As the war ground on, my family, like most of the middle class, continued to stay out of it, as we had before. Young Americans were being drafted and sent to over to fight and die on our behalf. But the Saigon government, afraid of antagonizing the middle class, which formed its main base of support, had not yet seen fit to institute a general mobilization. No one in my immediate family had been killed or wounded in active duty. Even after general mobilization was decreed in the wake of the Tet Offensive in 1968, middle-class families like mine could wrangle desk jobs for their sons called up by the draft to keep them out of combat. My brother Luong, for example, who was still in the army, had desk jobs in the ordnance branch and then in a military tribunal and spent his time mostly in the safety of cities like Nha Trang and Saigon. Among my brothers, Giu was the one who came the closest to any fighting in this period—as a civilian rather than as a military man, however.

Fresh back from his studies in France, Giu got a job managing South Vietnam's only cement works in the remote town of Ha Tien, near Ca Mau at the tip of the country. Ha Tien was a showcase, one of the few industrial complexes that the country could boast during the war. Unfortunately, it also sat on the edge of a major Viet Cong infiltration route. From their sanctuary in Cambodia, the communists were funneling arms and supplies in transit toward the U Minh Forest, one of their most formidable bases in the South. The trans-shipment point was a reinforced stronghold buried in the hills a few kilometers from the cement works. When Giu first went down to the factory site, the area was still insecure. A forest of indigo plants covered it as far as the eye could see. Viet Cong guerrillas operated freely.

Gradually, a large swath of indigo plants was cleared and the forest was pushed back. The factory and the district town grew. Vietnamese Rangers were stationed in the forest and security improved, only to deteriorate again after the overthrow of President Diem. The situation finally stabilized with the arrival of the G.I.s, whose presence freed the Saigon army to conduct operations in areas like Ha Tien. Fearful that their retreat toward Ca Mau would be blocked, the Viet Cong regional forces withdrew, leaving the guerrillas behind to conduct occasional small attacks. Three American advisors arrived in the district town, part of the contingent of officers that the U.S. command was inserting into the South Vietnamese army chain of command to stiffen its backbone and improve its performance. They lived separately from the Vietnamese military district chief whom they advised and his staff, and tried to re-create as best they could a slice of suburban America in this remote corner: Between the three of them, they shared two Jeeps, a refrigerator, an air conditioner, and a generator—incredible luxuries to the locals—that had been brought down by air.

The Americans also brought other technical marvels: sensors planted in the border region to detect motion and even the body odors of the Viet Cong, radar, and rifles equipped with infrared night vision—which the Viet Cong learned to foil by smearing mud over their bodies. The Americans also brought awesome firepower. Anytime they thought they detected Viet Cong troop movement, they would radio for "harass-ment and interdiction shelling." They also could call in air support. Most awesome of all, they could summon B-52 strikes. My brother remembers well the time when these strategic bombers attacked. After some Saigon troops got pinned down trying to clear out a Viet Cong battalion that had massed in their hilly stronghold, the American advi-sor called for fighter jet support. But the bombing and strafing had no effect on the communists, who were well entrenched inside their caves. Finally, the Americans brought in a B-52 strike to rain bombs on the hillside. The caves collapsed under the powerful explosions, burying the communists alive. The local people said that for days afterward they could hear the cries of the Viet Cong dying in their mountain graves. In Ha Tien, as in many areas of the country, the war settled into a stale-mate, with neither side able to deliver the knockout punch. In spite of the resources and firepower they threw into the fray, the Americans could not tip the balance decisively in Saigon's favor, either in Ha Tien or elsewhere.

But the huge American commitment did blunt the communist drive and buy time for Saigon. Instead of using that time wisely to consolidate the gains against the Viet Cong, however, the generals were squander-ing it in endless squabbles. By this time, they had monopolized power in Vietnam. The only faction that could have challenged them—the Buddhists—had been squashed for good. In September 1967, a sem-blance of stability returned. General Thieu finally outmaneuvered his rival Ky and became president in an election held at the urging of President Johnson. The election produced a surprise for the Americans: A candidate who advocated an end to the war got the second largest number of votes. Thieu quickly had him thrown in jail for five years. The new government did not gain in stature or popularity. Yet it did not matter, because Thieu had the support of the Americans, who at this point were backing him by default, to avoid making a bad situation worse. And he could buy loyalty from his key commanders through a growing web of corruption. Province and district chiefs could buy their posts, rake in money by diverting funds or trafficking in military sup-plies—and in some cases even smuggling drugs—pay their kickbacks to those above, and still make a fortune. My father, watching the shenani-gans of the generals and officials, would shake his head in disgust and tell me, "With leaders like these, I'm not at all surprised that we're not making any headway against the Viet Cong. It must be terribly frus-trating for the Americans to be the patrons of such greedy idiots. One of these days, the Americans will have enough and they'll pack up and go home, leaving us to fend for ourselves." My father, however, was speaking in anger, for he thought the Americans would not leave until they had won.

It was not surprising to anyone that many of the foot soldiers were not willing to die for a regime with such cynical leaders, a regime that talked about democracy and clean government but never acted on its promises. They saw no point in trying to win the goodwill of the peasants for a regime in which they themselves did not believe. Often, when they went on operation, they stole from the villagers. (Once, Giu saw soldiers coming back from a sweep pulling an ox at the back of an armored personnel carrier.) Other problems that plagued an unmotivated army were a high desertion rate and, after general mobilization came into force, widespread draft dodging. As a military prosecutor, my brother Luong saw a long parade of people who tried to get out of the fighting. By this time, through hard work, Luong had embarked on a new career. After going to school part-time while serving in the ordnance branch of the army, he had obtained a law degree, which allowed him to switch to the military tribunal, the harshest in the land—at least for those without the connection or the money to obtain a favorable outcome from the presiding judge. It tried criminal cases involving the military, as well as civilian cases that fell under the broad rubrics of "disturbing order and security," "treason," and "hoarding and speculation."

After a few months serving as a military prosecutor drawing a small government salary, my brother decided to get out of the army and set up a private practice to make more money, defending the accused in the same military tribunal where he had served as a prosecutor. He found clients quickly, as the military tribunal had a heavy docket. They mirrored the times: from deserters, draft dodgers, and people charged with trading with or working for the communists to political activists accused of disturbing order and security or of treason. Some of these clients had powerful connections or were rich, and usually prearranged the outcome of their trials. They hired Luong as their defense lawyer only to maintain the facade that justice was being exercised; yet my brother, and his colleagues in the legal profession, did not question the charade, shrugging it off as the way things were in Saigon. Fortunately, in his private practice, Luong had opportunities to help people who did not have the wherewithal to engineer their verdict and for whom the trials were real, such as deserters and draft dodgers from impoverished families. He did not seek them out or become their champion, but for those who came to him for help, he would argue their cases for free and, since their guilt was evident, try to get them a reduced sentence.

By the end of 1967, the statistics looked favorable to the Americans. Slightly more than half a million G.I.s had arrived to fight in Vietnam. Planes had been pounding both the North and South, and had dropped a million and a half tons of bombs. The body count had been favorable for General Westmoreland's troops, and in conventional battles where he could use helicopters and B-52s, such as at Ia Drang, the kill ratio had been encouraging. Yet although he seemed to be winning most of the battles, Westmoreland had reached only a stalemate. He had arrived at this plateau after paying a stiff price: 15,000 G.I.s had died between 1965 and 1967. The communists continued to hang tough, believing that no matter how bad a drubbing they could get, time was on their side. Simply by not losing, they would win in the end. They were right. Back in the United States, the higher taxes to finance the added military expenditures, the accelerated draft to recruit soldiers for Vietnam, and the mounting casualties all eroded support for the war. Public patience began to wear thin. More and more, the American people started to question the wisdom of sacrificing American lives for communist lives, no matter how good the kill ratio, to defend a cause that appeared to them increasingly dubious. To shore up support, LBJ summoned Westmoreland home to tell the public that the enemy was on the ropes and that light could be seen at the end of the tunnel. But soon after Westmoreland uttered that optimistic prediction, the Viet Cong made a mockery of it with the Tet Offensive.

My husband and I happened to be in Saigon when this happened. After two years in My Tho, we decided that it was time for us to return to the United States so Dave could finish his doctorate and prepare for the future and a more permanent job. His stay in Vietnam and his research for Rand had changed his area of interest from Brazil to Asia, and he now wanted to get a Ph.D. in comparative government focusing on Vietnam and China. Both of these countries had gone through and were still experiencing tremendous upheavals (the Cultural Revolution had begun in China at this time), and he wanted to understand more about the causes and dynamics of their revolutions, and the changes they had wrought. Asia fascinated him intellectually, but it also held him emotionally because of me, my family, and all the Vietnamese he had befriended. He already spoke Vietnamese fluently, but had never studied Chinese, so he thought he should spend six months in Taiwan (China was still a closed country at the time) immersing himself in an intensive Chinese-language course as a preparation for switching his aca-demic focus to Asia.

It was difficult for us to tear away and leave Vietnam, but Dave's study had been interrupted for four years already while he worked in Saigon and My Tho. War and revolution is the human experience at its most intense and dramatic, and the conflict here was no exception. Terrible as it was, it held us in thrall, especially since our own countries and our own people were the combatants. It was not our life here that made us reluctant to leave. Our stay in the provincial town was simply tolerable: I had no relatives here, we knew few people, and there was little for us to do but read in our spare time. Here, as in Saigon, people acted hostile toward me whenever they saw me in public places with Dave. They treated me with contempt, either because they took me for a prostitute or a bar girl or because they abhorred my marrying an American. Rather, it was our fascinating work and the dramatic events in Vietnam that were the lure. Each interview gave us more insight into the communist movement that was thwarting American power, as did each trip Dave made into the countryside; each day brought fresh devel-opments to Vietnam, making us feel as if we were watching history unfold. Unlike the American soldiers, however, our lives were never in real danger, and we did not have to witness the terrors that they expe-rienced, and which gave them a very different perspective on Vietnam. They lived a war; we lived an adventure. Dave was more reluctant to leave than I, because he wanted to see how things would unfold in Vietnam and also because he thought he still had much more to learn about the communist movement there. I was more practical, and feared that the longer Dave stayed away from academia the harder it would be for him to resume his studies. I wanted us to go back to America and start building our future as soon as possible, even if this meant another long separation from my family. Like me, Dave left changed by what he had seen in Vietnam. He had arrived believing that America was doing the right thing in defending South Vietnam against communist conquest. But the destruction troubled him, and he could see that the United States was hurting rather than helping the very people it had come to rescue, and that its strategy was not working. He left My Tho with many questions about the American involvement, but without any idea as to what the solution ought to be.

A few months after getting settled in Taichung, then a quiet town in central Taiwan, we came back to visit my family for Tet. Both sides in the war had agreed to a truce for the holiday and to silence their guns so that the people could usher in the new year in peace. Everything seemed normal. My parents prepared for a traditional celebration. Since they could not accommodate us in their tiny house, my husband and I got permission to stay at the Rand villa on Pasteur Street, which served as both office and living quarters for the American staff. The U.S. embassy and the presidential palace were located nearby.

No one had any inkling the communists were massing their forces for a huge coordinated offensive throughout the country. There was much concern about Khe Sanh, where American troops were under siege, and which some had been calling another Dien Bien Phu. But it turned out that Khe Sanh was only a diversionary move; what the communists had in mind was an entirely different historical precedent. They were going to stage not another Dien Bien Phu, but Emperor Quang Trung's Tet offensive in the eighteenth century—when he attacked the invading Ch'ing troops by surprise, slaughtered them, marched triumphant into the capital of Hanoi, and then proceeded to free the country from Chinese domination.

During the night of January 30, 1968, Dave and I were sound asleep near the window that looked in the direction of the American embassy. Suddenly, we heard gunfire. Our first thought was, "Someone's attacking the presidential palace. It must be another coup d'etat." Because of the curfew, we could not go out into the street to check. We listened for a while, and then went back to sleep. The next morning, we learned that we had heard the Viet Cong attack the embassy. It was hardly the only major target, though certainly the most visible and the most significant in the eyes of the American public and the world. The Viet Cong had also struck at the presidential palace, the Joint General Staff and Navy headquarters, the radio station—where they were thwarted before they could broadcast an appeal to the people to rise up and overthrow the Saigon regime—police posts, and army barracks, among others. Not only that, the Viet Cong had also staged assaults in more than a hundred cities and towns, up and down the coast, all over the country.

Militarily, the Viet Cong's attacks in Saigon were little more than pinpricks. The downtown area returned to normal quickly. In terms of their effect on morale and public opinion, however, they were potent. The Viet Cong had struck not just remote villages, but the very heart of the capital city. As soon as it was safe to circulate in the street, we went to visit my parents. Their initial shock had worn off, and they were relieved that the attacks had been scattered and small. Still, they were apprehensive. They feared that the communists might fire rockets into the city, and even more they feared that Viet Cong agents would go through the neighborhood to look for people employed in the South Vietnamese government and kill them. My parents had heard rumors that this had happened in a quarter on the edge of town after the Viet Cong penetrated it. They kept their front door locked and the window that looked out into the alley tightly shut.

My parents were right to have been concerned. During the offensive, the Viet Cong captured and held the city of Hue for twenty-five days. Before they took over the city, the communists had prepared for elimination a list of government officials, military officers, and civilians who were hostile to their side or were collaborating closely with Saigon. When they occupied Hue, the communists went from house to house rounding up those mentioned on their list. After the Viet Cong withdrew, some 3000 bodies would be discovered in mass graves; many had been shot, beaten to death, or buried alive. It was news like this that terrified the middle class and hardened their attitude toward the Viet Cong. To them, a prolonged war seemed more attractive than a peace that could get them slaughtered. The battle for Hue turned the former imperial capital into a city of mourning. Both sides inflicted suffering on the residents. After they took back the city, Saigon assassination teams came in to kill those who had collaborated with the Viet Cong during their brief occupation, throwing the corpses into some of the same mass graves that had held the victims of the communists. The Americans reduced parts of the city to rubble with their furious air and artillery strikes. In all, death claimed 5000 communist soldiers, 400 Saigon troops, and 150 U.S. Marines.

The Marines' house-to-house battle for Hue was only one of the many searing images of Tet. The ruins of Ben Tre—a town flattened by the Americans in an attempt to "save" it—were another. But the most gruesome was the television footage of General Loan, the head of the police, executing a Viet Cong prisoner in the street of Saigon. The picture of him calmly firing his pistol point-blank into the temple of the prisoner confirmed in the minds of millions of people around the world the brutality of the Saigon regime. Tet took a terrible toll on the Americans, the Viet Cong, and the South Vietnamese army. By March, 2000 G.I.s and 4000 South Vietnamese soldiers had died, but the communists had suffered the heaviest casualties, losing a total of 50,000 soldiers. The offensive decimated the southern Viet Cong, who had carried out the brunt of the attacks. More and more North Vietnamese would funnel south to take their places.

Before the offensive, the communist leadership exhorted their troops to go into combat with the prediction that victory was at hand, that they were about to liberate their countrymen in the South, and that the unhappy southern people would rise up and overthrow the Saigon government when the attacks occurred. They did not explain that the other, and more realistic, aim was to inflict terrible casualties and show the Americans that their only alternative was to begin peace talks, because unless they were willing to commit even more resources and men and to fight for a long time, they could not overwhelm an enemy who still had plenty of power left after years of relentless American pounding.

While the middle class in Vietnam had recovered from the shock of Tet, and actually was feeling even more reassured by the power of the Americans, who had quickly driven the communists from the towns and cities and decimated them in the countryside, Tet shocked the American people, who had been fed optimistic official reports that the end of the war was in sight. When the press reported that General Westmoreland asked for a reinforcement of over 200,000 troops, it caused an uproar. The war seemed to have become a bottomless pit, draining American money and lives. Dissidence grew, not only among the public but also in Congress itself. The conflict threatened to tear the country as well as LBJ's party apart. Senator Eugene McCarthy, advocating peace, challenged LBJ for the Democratic nomination, and nearly won in New Hampshire. Robert Kennedy, also a peace advocate, declared he would challenge LBJ for the nomination as well. Polls showed that LBJ had lost his credibility and public support. In this climate, Westmoreland's request prompted a wholesale reassessment of American commitment. The choice was either to escalate further and further, take more and more casualties, and sink more and more money into the war, or start withdrawal. LBJ chose to disengage. On March 31, 1968, he declared that he would suspend air strikes in the heartland of the Red River Delta and open peace negotiations, and announced that he would not seek the presidential nomination.

Dave and I had returned to Taiwan in February 1968, and we were in Taichung when we heard the stunning news. I remember listening to the broadcast crackling with static over the Voice of America, sitting up in bed trying to keep warm under the electric blanket that we had bought at the local American PX so we would not freeze in our unheated rented house. My first thought was that there was finally hope for peace. My second thought, however, was for my family. The South Vietnamese government was doomed. It would not topple right away, but it was clear that the halt in bombings and start of negotiation were the first steps toward that dreaded day when America would pull up

stakes and go home, as my parents had feared whenever they got pessimistic. If Saigon had failed to win with so much support from the most
powerful country on earth, how could it prevail without it? Lying in
bed in Taichung, I could feel my family's anguish. Yet I could also feel
the jubilation of my sister Thang and other people in the North where
the bombs would stop falling. And I could feel the hope of the peasants
in the South whose lives had been mangled by the war. Once again, I
felt torn between concern for my parents, and my siblings and their families in Saigon, and my wish to see the war come to an end.

Shortly before the fall semester started at Cornell, my husband and I
moved to Ithaca. Even this remote area, where the sun rarely shines and
winter lasts nine months out of the year, was embroiled in the turmoil
sweeping across America. The campus, reflecting the disunity in the
country at large, was rent between hawks and doves. Many faculty
members demanded peace, but others said that the United States should
get even tougher. Among our friends, a large number were passionately
against the war, including a couple of Vietnamese students we knew. In
November 1968, after we had settled into our new home on a hillside
next to a stream, Richard Nixon was elected president.

Nixon had campaigned on a pledge to end war and win peace. What
he had in mind, however, was not to bring real peace, but to continue
the war with Saigon as the surrogate. He would withdraw American
troops and bring them home, while continuing to aid and arm Saigon,
and support it with advisors and his fleet of B-52s. He would deny victory to the communists, and he would threaten them with annihilation
to bring them to settle on his own terms at the negotiation in Paris. He
began by ordering a secret bombing campaign against communist sanc-
tuaries in Cambodia in March 1969. Then, operating on a parallel track,
he announced in July 1969 that he would begin withdrawing American
troops. From now on, Saigon would take over the fighting. The war
would be "Vietnamized."

The next year, he expanded the theater of war and ordered a joint
South Vietnamese-American invasion of the two communist bases across
the border in Cambodia, as part of his "fight and talk" strategy. His aim
was to intimidate the communists, to show that he might just annihilate
them if they did not heel. In Saigon, my family's admiration for Nixon
grew. They were still glowing with admiration for him when I visited
them on my return to Saigon in 1971. "What a tricky man," they would
say to me with sincere respect, and they would add approvingly, "He's
not afraid to use power. He's as scheming as the Chinese Communists."

The invasion sparked large, angry protests in America. Nixon had promised that peace was in sight; instead, he was expanding the war. Like their brethren elsewhere, many students at Cornell were outraged. Friends of ours decided to go to Washington and lobby for an end to the war, and they asked me to go with them. I demurred at first, but finally relented. I decided that the cost to my native land and its people had gotten high enough, and that the time had arrived for me to ask the Americans to take their arsenal with them and get out, and stop the spiraling violence—regardless of how the situation would sort itself out in Vietnam. The time had come for me to stop agonizing. With that, I finally broke free of the grip of my family interests and turned decisively toward the larger good of my homeland.

The two years I spent at Cornell had given me a different perspective. It was, of course, easier for me to contemplate a North Vietnamese victory than it was for someone in Saigon who would have to live under the communist regime. Nonetheless, I felt I could now look at the possible outcome more objectively. Up until now, I had been afraid of a communist victory—and therefore of peace—because I had accepted without question the prediction that there would be a wholesale slaughter of people like my family if the communists took over. American and South Vietnamese officials and hard-line anticommunists often talked about the bloodbath that had occurred in the North after the Viet Minh took over in 1954. I had not done any research to find out whether this had really taken place and to determine how plausible the prediction of a similar outcome in the South was. At Cornell, for the first time, I could research this precedent.

What I found out indicated that no bloodbath had occurred after 1954. True, there had been a bloody land reform during which thousands were killed. But this reform had been used to purge the Communist Party cadres as much as to destroy the landlords as a class, victimizing the party's own almost as much as the landowners. I started to link what I had read to the experience of our own relatives who had stayed behind in the North in that period. None of them had been killed. True, Uncle Chinh had died, but of cancer, the same disease that had taken my grandfather, my great-grandfather, and several other family members. I found the massacre in Hue troubling; yet I was not certain how much of it was the work only of the Viet Cong. Some said that many of the victims had been killed by bombing and shelling during the American offensive, and that the retreating communists had simply buried them in mass graves. For months, I mulled over the possibility of my family being wiped out; I finally came to the conclusion, however, that they would survive should the communists win. Life would be hard for them; still, they would make it. (On both scores, I would turn out to be right. Of my immediate relatives, no one was killed by the communists after they took over the South, but life was even bleaker than I had imagined.) I decided to join my Cornell friends and lobby for peace, although I suspected that it would ultimately lead to a communist victory.

I left for Washington unsure of how much I could accomplish. I hated confrontation, and did not relish the thought of exchanging arguments with hostile members of Congress. Having been brought up to respect authority, I also felt reluctant to question men who were my elders and who held power as well. Besides, I was young, I was a woman, and I was an Asian—at a time when all three were serious handicaps. I suspected that the men I was supposed to convert would not take me seriously. Also, coming from Vietnam where the people had no influence over their government, I felt cynical about what the exercise could accomplish. My American peers had no such qualms and no such doubts. Unlike me, they had grown up believing that as citizens they had the right to make themselves heard, and to try and change the policies with which they disagreed strongly. To me, they seemed naively confident about their power. At one time, they might have been as reluctant as I to question authority. But now, the leadership—the "Establishment"— had lost so much credibility that it no longer commanded the respect it had once held over the young. On Capitol Hill, my American colleagues moved with confidence while I felt uneasy. Our group did not want to spend time talking to the doves; we wanted to focus on the hawks. We went knocking on doors, and were received politely but coolly. I felt encouraged. Then we split up to lobby as many hawks as we could.

My target was a congressman from California. I was ushered into his office. We shook hands and he invited me to sit down. I could tell, however, that he was itching for a fight and to put me in my place. He listened to my arguments with a quiet assurance bordering on arrogance. I could see that I was not getting anywhere with my arguments about the futility of the war, and the damage that America was doing to its reputation by trying to defend a corrupt government in Saigon. So I switched tactics, and started talking about the plight of the people back in Vietnam who were caught in the war. But try as I might, I could see I was not reaching him; his mind was made up. Coming as he did from a generation that firmly believed that America could do no wrong, he rejected any suggestion that the United States could be committing any bad deeds in Vietnam. America was bombing and killing only the communists; its defoliation was not hurting the peasants, because only communist crops were destroyed; and so on. Our arguments became more heated. In my anger, I began to lose my reticence in the face of an authority figure. But I also started to lose my cool. In a very uncharacteristic and rude manner, I got up without thanking him, walked out, and even slammed the door.

Most of our group left Washington happy and convinced that we had made some headway. I did not share this assessment. Instead, I concluded from my brief foray that it would be near impossible to change American policies. The war would have to be settled by Vietnamese, on the ground back in Vietnam, and not by people like me wandering the halls of Congress. But the growing opposition among students like those from Cornell and the American public at large, and even within the Establishment, had a cumulative effect. Nixon realized that the American people's patience was fraying, and that the "fight and talk" strategy could be sustained only for a limited time. In the four years in which Nixon directed the war effort, another 20,000 G.I.s had died, bringing the total to over 50,000. Now he had no choice but to keep winding down the American presence in Vietnam. He had already begun secret talks with Hanoi, bypassing the more intransigent Saigon and southern Viet Cong sides, and he now stepped up his efforts to reach an agreement. In 1973, he finally fulfilled his pledge to bring the boys home. On March 29, after eight years of direct involvement, the last American G.I.s left Vietnam.

14

Short Peace, Long War

On a cold, blustery, and rainy afternoon in October 1954, the French flag was lowered for the last time over the citadel in Hanoi. Two noncommissioned officers folded the wet banner and handed it over to the general presiding over the ceremony, who in turn passed it to the commander of the citadel. As the band played the *Marseillaise*, the tears of the officers and soldiers mingled with the drops of cold rain drenching their faces. That night, the bulk of French forces withdrew, leaving only two infantry battalions in the quiet city. It had been seventy-five years since the colonial troops took over Hanoi. The next day, Viet Minh units, converging from five directions, reached the outskirts of the city where they had many supporters. The soldiers sat proudly in their trucks, their bared bayonets fixed to the tip of their rifles. Red Viet Minh flags with the yellow star fluttered from every house. People jammed both sides of the roads, and surrounded the trucks, screaming with excitement and cheering the troops. The adulation made the shy soldiers smile. On the final day of the handover, the last French battalions withdrew across the Long Bien bridge leading into the city. Hanoi was now completely in the hands of the Viet Minh.

The next day, October 10, the five Viet Minh columns entered the heart of the city itself. The unit, built from the remnants of the regiment that had fought in Hanoi during the first days of the war, had the honor of spearheading the triumphant entry. They streamed into the streets of the native commercial quarters where some of them had fought house-to-house until driven out by the French in 1946. Then the other four Viet Minh columns rolled in. The quiet city suddenly came to life. The streets echoed with the deafening sound of drums, exploding firecrackers, and cheers. From prominent buildings, large portraits of Ho Chi Minh looked down on the jubilant crowd. A sea of people carrying flags and flowers engulfed the soldiers. Then the mass of people converged toward the citadel to witness the raising of the Viet Minh flag. The general in charge of the takeover read a message from Ho Chi Minh asking for unity and cooperation to overcome the new challenges and make Hanoi prosper.

The joyous and festive welcoming in Hanoi did not happen spontaneously. An advance party of cadres had arrived days before to prepare for the takeover, mobilizing the jittery middle-class residents to turn out in force and welcome the Viet Minh troops and government. CIA-sponsored propaganda and sabotage activities in Hanoi before the takeover had demoralized the people and intensified their fears of life under communism. Trung, a Viet Minh cadre who would later marry my cousin Thuc, was part of this group. The prospect of taking over the prize of the North after years of incredible struggle left him giddy with excitement, and he threw himself into his task with youthful zeal. He tirelessly made the rounds, talking to the residents, calming their fears, and promising that the government would respect their rights and would not interfere in their life. Once he and his colleagues thought they had the people reassured, they turned to making the city look festive for this important celebration. They hung Ho's portraits, planted flags, strung banners, and painted slogans; Trung himself climbed up on the largest department store and proudly wrote "Long Live an Independent and Peaceful Vietnam" in huge letters on its façade.

The work that Trung and other cadres performed among the residents paid off. At a time when most middle-class people wanted to believe that everything would turn out all right, the comforting words persuaded many to give the Viet Minh the benefit of the doubt. Others decided to show support to be on the good side of the new government. On the day the troops arrived, Hanoi residents turned out in their best clothes, carrying bouquets of flowers, and waving flags to greet the soldiers. Years later, my relatives in Hanoi still remember the stunning transformation of the city's mood—thanks to the Viet Minh's organizational skill—from apprehension to enthusiasm and joy.

After the city had been secured by the troops and the groundwork for a massive celebration had been completed by the cadres, Ho Chi Minh, his fellow members in the Central Committee of the Communist Party, and his government made a triumphant return to Hanoi on November 1, 1954. Once again, the city put on a jubilant face. Thousands of people streamed toward the same square from which Ho had read his declaration of independence in 1945. But although this was a proud moment for Ho and his lieutenants, their joy was overshadowed by the knowledge that they still had formidable tasks ahead of them: rebuilding a shattered economy in the North and reclaiming the South, which Geneva had snatched away from them just as they were about to grasp it. Already the Americans had shown that they were not going to simply hand over this region to Ho; even in the North itself, CIA agents had been active, trying to disrupt the takeover. For Ho and his lieutenants, assuming control over the North would prove to be easier than governing it and developing it to ease the people's life after a long struggle. In Hanoi, things did not begin to function smoothly until at least a year later. But compared with what they had endured to win, the difficulties of peace did not seem so formidable to the Viet Minh and their supporters like my sister Thang. They simply relished their victory, and reveled in the peace.

Thang returned to Hanoi toward the end of 1954. Unlike the earlier trip when she had to sneak out of the Viet Minh zone, dodging the French and their agents, she proudly traveled across the land that she felt was once again hers and her compatriots'. She took her two children to stay with one of her husband's relatives and went out to look for the rest of her family, full of anticipation about a happy reunion. Not knowing where we were, she went to see Uncle Dinh, my mother's older brother, and found out that we had moved to Saigon. Uncle Dinh's wife gave her the message that my mother had left asking Thang to look after the rented house for as long as possible. How could we have fled, Thang wondered, right at the moment when the resistance culminated in victory and independence? She decided that anti-Viet Minh propaganda had probably scared us away. Her disappointment was eased by the holiday mood of the city, and finally the celebration carried her along. The excitement of being back in Hanoi after years of absence took over. She set out to rediscover the city and introduce Lap, her oldest son, to its sights and amenities. After growing up in a village that had neither running water nor electricity, the little boy thought he had stumbled into wonderland. Everything seemed gloriously civilized and modern to him. Even simple things that he had not seen before, such as rubber bands, fascinated him. Old-time residents might think that the city had fallen into a kind of depression and that goods had become scarce, but to Thang and her Viet Minh colleagues Hanoi appeared like a bustling metropolis, bursting with merchandise. Lap gorged himself on the delicacies of Hanoi: fresh milk, bread, and the snacks that vendors sold throughout the day. He got to know the cry of each vendor and what each one sold. Whenever he heard the clicking of two pieces of wood, he knew that the wonton soup merchant had arrived in his neighborhood, and he would beg his mom to buy him a bowl.

If life in the new Hanoi seemed luxurious to those who had put the hardships of their struggle behind them, the middle-class families that had not fled South were soon to taste their own privations. Among my relatives, the most prescient was Uncle Dinh, who guessed early on how far things were going to change. Right after the takeover, former colonial administration officials were retained to ensure a smooth transition, so my uncle was allowed to keep his job, but only after undergoing an education. He was sent to a village near Hanoi to live among the peasants and learn the value and redemption of manual labor. At this time, land reform had resumed in earnest, and Uncle Dinh attended trials where he saw landlords being persecuted and executed. What he witnessed frightened him. Realizing that the Viet Minh were out to get all people with money, he donated his properties to the state, including his own house, as soon as he returned to Hanoi, in the hope of buying lenient treatment. In recognition of his "enlightenment," the government allowed him and his family to stay in his house, but reduced their living space to four square meters per person—giving them about twenty-four square meters in all—and took over the ground floor for a kindergarten. Later, it closed the kindergarten, and moved other families into my uncle's residence, bringing the total to eight, including those of two of his children. Each family squeezed into a single room. When I came back to visit in 1993, there were forty people living in the house. Between them, they had to share one bathroom, one toilet, and one kitchen.

While my uncle and his family felt discouraged, people who were arriving in Hanoi to staff the new administration were relieved to find accommodation for themselves and their families. My sister Thang approved of this kind of housing arrangement the government was making all over Hanoi for its cadres. "It's only fair" was her reaction. "If you have a big house and you don't need all the space, it's only natural that you should share with people who need it." Having lived among the poor peasants and seen how they suffered, she felt no sympathy for the rich or for the landlords. To her, they were people who had profited from the labor of the workers and peasants, and they were exploiters and oppressors no less than the French colonialists. As she explained to me years later, "After we liberated the North from the colonialists, we had to move to the next step and liberate the poor from the enslavement of the rich."

In another prescient move, as soon as he returned to Hanoi from his stint in the countryside, Uncle Dinh also donated to the government the gold he had hoarded as a hedge against inflation and for emergencies. He guessed that it would be only a matter of time before the communists stripped the middle class of its gold, to impoverish it and take away its economic power, so he decided to give it up willingly beforehand, hoping to buy leniency and better treatment for his family. As Uncle Dinh had surmised, the government soon began to force middle-class residents to sell at requisition prices the gold they had saved to the state. Every family had to report how much it had; under-reporting was a crime. The pressure to comply was relentless. The cadres questioned them, cajoling and threatening in turn; they also questioned their relatives and acquaintances to ferret out all the gold.

Uncle Dinh's donation to the state even before the government started to ban private ownership of assets bought him peace but not complete protection. Not long after it took over Hanoi, the government asked him to retire, on the ground that his health was failing. Unable to support his family on the tiny retiree's pension he received, he gradually sold off his hardwood furniture and any personal belongings that had value simply to survive. Still, he had made a good move. When the communists later embarked on a full-scale effort to destroy the middle class and private ownership, my uncle escaped the harassment—he had nothing left for the government to take away. Because of his "enlightenment," his children were allowed to attend the university on a scholarship and to find jobs in the middle rungs of the vast communist bureaucracy, where they were tolerated but not favored.

Ironically, while Uncle Dinh, who had contributed nothing to the war against the French, survived the communists' drive to remake society, Uncle Chinh, who had labored for the Viet Minh, did not fare as well. When the land reform movement reached Uncle Chinh's area, he suffered greatly. By releasing and encouraging the hatred of the have-nots against the haves, land reform would be more vicious than anything he and his family had seen before. It created an atmosphere of fear, in which everyone was afraid to be implicated and no one dared to protest unjust accusations and persecutions by the land reform teams, which had unlimited authority to do whatever they saw fit in the countryside, so much so that peasants coined the saying, "Even Heaven has to bow to the power of the Team." In this situation, only one man—Ho Chi Minh himself—could step in to save anyone. Reluctant to undermine land reform, Ho rarely intervened, but in at least two cases that my relatives knew of, he stepped in discreetly; both involved Uncle Chinh's family. Ho had met my uncle at the 1951 Lien Viet Front national congress, an occasion for which Chinh had walked for 300 kilometers to reach the conference site at Chiem Hoa, in Tuyen Quang Province. A picture taken on this occasion shows him sitting cross-legged on the ground, not far from Ho. Other notables in the Lien Viet Front leadership also appeared in the picture, including the mandarin Vi Van Dinh, my uncle's father-in-law.

Ho prized Vi's collaboration, without which the Tay minority living in the sensitive border provinces of Lang Son and Cao Bang would not have supported the Viet Minh during the war. Vi stuck by the Viet Minh until the very end, returning to Hanoi after the victory against the French. In this period, with the communists trying to consolidate their rule, keeping Vi's support and through him the allegiance of the Tay remained crucial. Furthermore, several members of Vi's family held prominent positions in the government. This was a family Ho did not want to hurt. During the land reform, Ho made sure that Vi and his relatives would not be touched

Even for Ho, this was not easy, because Vi had run his province, Thai Binh, with an iron fist when he was its mandarin governor, and many peasants wanted to bring him back for denunciation and trial. Ho never came out publicly and defended Vi, although he kept him under his wing, tucked away safely in Hanoi, where no one could get at him. The

people of Thai Binh were angry and disappointed, but—out of deference
to Ho—bowed to his decision. They accepted the explanation, relayed
to them unofficially, that Vi should be spared, because he had made up
for his past misdeeds by joining the Viet Minh and securing the support
of the Tay minority in the vital border region.

Among Vi's relatives in the Viet Minh, my uncle was the only one
who was vulnerable. Unlike Vi, he was living in the countryside, where
he would be a prime target for any peasants seeking to vent their resentment on the landlords. One evening, a large group of them came to his
house and took him to the village school. There, in the flickering light
of torches, they tied him to a chair and made him sit facing his audience.
The mood was hostile, but a lot less virulent and less violent than a vil-
lage-wide denunciation would have been. Perhaps because most of these
peasants knew Chinh personally, the mass psychology that leads to hysteria was not at work that night. Only one woman stepped forward to
denounce him. Next, the land reform team, made up of cadres from the
outside and the village's most militant poor peasants, summoned my
uncle to confront the entire village in a trial. My uncle knew what this
meant. He would be forced to kneel on a raised earth platform built at
the foot of the hill, with his head bowed. His accusers would take turns
stepping up to the platform to denounce him, violently pushing his head
from side to side, or jabbing at his forehead with their pointed fingers
for emphasis. The mood would be ugly. The villagers would shout
"Down with landlord Chinh!" and scream for his punishment. If he was
found guilty of "blood debts" toward the people, he would be executed; if not, he would be taken away and put in jail. At the very least, he
would have his assets confiscated and he would face abject poverty.

The night before my uncle was due to appear at this trial, the deputy
chairman of the province suddenly arrived at his house. She told him,
"Show me the paper that you've received asking you to go to this meeting." When he gave it to her, she took it, and handed him another paper
saying, "You don't have to go anywhere tomorrow. If someone comes to
get you, just show this paper I'm giving you." Then she left. She must
have worked behind the scenes furiously that night, because no one came
to take him away the next day. Later, my uncle's family heard that he
had been saved from this trial by Ho himself. Evidently, Ho had summoned a trusted high-level cadre and dispatched him to the village to
watch out for Uncle Chinh. When he heard of the impending trial, this
cadre contacted the deputy chairman, who rushed to my uncle's defense.

In theory, my uncle should not have been touched at all. Under the land reform policy, he should have been classified as a resistance land-lord, that is, someone who had worked for the Viet Minh, and he should have been spared. But a movement motivated by hatred and resentment proved impossible to control. Once unleashed in the villages, there was no way to focus on only the "right" targets, and many inno-cent victims were consumed. At least this is the explanation that many people in the North offer, and one that my uncle's relatives publicly accept. The excesses of the land reform, my cousins would say, should be laid at the feet of the local teams, and should not be blamed on the leadership—and certainly not on Ho Chi Minh himself. Ho's vision of an egalitarian society was a noble one, these cousins say, but land reform was mismanaged and abused by the cadres who carried it out. Privately, however, I have heard that my cousins are divided. Some are still angry and bitter over what the land reform did to their family, but are reluc-tant or afraid to say so. Others accept what happened as the unfortunate consequence of a massive campaign that got out of control, and even feel that what happened to their father was a lot less painful than what other big landlords had to endure, thanks to Ho's intervention. Besides, they argue, the mistakes were corrected later, so there is no cause to complain now. Because Ho is still an untouchable icon, people in Vietnam are reluctant to say anything that might cast doubt on his lega-cy. When pressed, they would not question Ho's goal of distributing land to the poor, saying that it was laudable, and they would blame instead the land reform teams for the excesses and especially the teams' Chinese communist advisors for having pushed the Vietnamese to adopt the brutal land reform tactics that China had used against its own land-lords.

If the purpose of land reform had been simply to redistribute land, the communists could have easily taken it from the landlords and given it to the deserving poor, and this kind of trial—in fact, ritualized abuse—would have been unnecessary. But land reform was about more than land. Its aim was also to crush the landlords as a class by destroy-ing the traditional social, political, and psychological hold they had held over the peasants for decades. So, although my uncle escaped being arrested, tried, jailed, and perhaps even executed, he could not avoid the consequences of being a landlord. Uncle Chinh and his family were now subjected to constant harassment and humiliation. Even little chil-dren could insult them and hit them at will. In fact, the urchins in the village were the worst tormentors. Every time my uncle came out of his house, children would throw stones at him. Whenever anyone of any age insulted him or hit him, he had to bow his head and say, "Please, I beg you to spare me," addressing them as *ong* or *ba*, "sir" or "ma'am,'" to acknowledge that they were superior to him, and referring to himself as *con*, "insignificant person," to indicate his lowly status. Later, when my family heard of Uncle Chinh's persecution, they were horrified by the unfairness and harshness of the treatment and depressed over Uncle Chinh's public humiliation, saying things like, "To think that a high-ranking mandarin like him would fall as low as this, pulling his own plough and being insulted by peasants."

My uncle might have been a kind and reasonable landlord; still, the peasants felt that he had exploited their labor—at least they began to think this way once the cadres had indoctrinated them into believing that he had—so now they took their anger out on him. Landlords were made the scapegoats for the harsh life of the poor peasants. In my uncle's village, people persecuted him with zeal to show how ardently they supported land reform and to be in the good graces of the militant peasants now holding power. Others who had envied his wealth and his influence now took pleasure in humiliating him.

In this hysteria, even people Uncle Chinh knew well avoided him, not out of hatred but out of fear that they might be accused of being his allies and denounced. To show sympathy to a landlord and his family was to undermine land reform; even the teachers at my cousins' school were afraid to give them any attention, ignoring them and refusing to review and grade their work. Their classmates either shunned or harassed them. Villagers who were sympathetic to my uncle's family dared show their kindness only when they were sure no one could see them. Once, an old neighbor softly called my aunt to the fence after nightfall and furtively gave her a bowl of rice to feed one of her children who had fallen sick.

Now my uncle's house—the last asset of any value he had left—was seized by the village cadres. He and his family moved to a hut on a hillside, stuck in the middle of nowhere. They lived by themselves, isolated like lepers. Each night, a detail of young and tough militiamen would come to check and make sure that they were all home. The youths—unthinking, insensitive, and easily influenced by the cadres—would appear suddenly, sometimes at midnight, sometimes at one or two o'clock in the morning, pound on the door, and shout, "Where are that son of a bitch Chinh and his bitch of a wife? Come out here, all of you. We want to make a check." Then my uncle and his family would tumble out of the hut, fall on their knees, and beg for mercy, as the militiamen brandished their weapons. This ritual went on for months, after that, they were quarantined in the village, forbidden to leave.

Fortunately, my uncle's status as a resistance landlord entitled him to receive some land to farm. The cadres gave him about four acres to till, so that his family would not starve to death, but the land was poor and scattered on a hillside, a plot here, a plot there. After the heavy taxes they had to pay, there was little rice left for my uncle, aunt, and the children, including those that had been sent back by relatives who could no longer care for them. Their life became desperate, every day an agony of hunger. My aunt and uncle could not bear to watch their two youngest daughters Thuc and Hoa starve, so they decided to take them secretly to live with relatives in Hanoi. The plan was for my aunt to make two separate trips, taking with her one daughter at a time. The first try ended in failure. After walking for forty kilometers without running into any guards, my aunt and Thuc encountered a militiaman on the road, who arrested them. Desperation drove my uncle and aunt to try again. This time, they succeeded, and Thuc and Hoa were each left in the care of a relative in Hanoi. The same desperation drove Bieu, one of their sons, to flee to Hanoi and then to Haiphong where he found my father just before the Viet Minh took over the city.

As though all this punishment was not enough, the cadres taxed my uncle excessively to torment him further. His land could produce only one harvest per year during the rainy season, but the cadres made him pay taxes on two crops—like the rest of the villagers, who could get two harvests from better situated land. In the spring of 1955, cadres arrived to collect the tax months before my uncle had any income from his land, so he was unable to pay. The cadres arrested my aunt and strapped her to a pole in the middle of the yard, saying, "If his wife gets hurt, that s.o.b. Chinh will come up with the money to save her." My aunt was fifty-seven years old at the time, but this did not stop the cadres. They kept her tied up day and night, with nothing to eat. Fire ants bit her feet until they became red and swollen. Her children watched in anguish. There was nothing they could do, except sneak her scraps of food. Getting help from relatives was again the only recourse, so Phi, the older of the two boys, secretly left for Hanoi to beg for money. Finally, he returned with it, and my uncle gave it to the cadres. My aunt was released after three days of torment.

My aunt and uncle managed to keep going because they felt they had to, for the sake of their young children. After his attempted suicide, my uncle never again gave in so totally to despair. As they surveyed the wreck of their lives, they could take comfort in a few things. Thuc and Hoa were now living safely and comfortably with relatives in Hanoi. Their older children who had joined the army and the government ear-lier had not been punished along with their landlord father, and still had their jobs. Cam, Phi, and Thai, the three teenage children still liv-ing at home, were bearing up as well as could be expected under the cir-cumstances. Also, my aunt and uncle still had each other, and each other's support. Perhaps, like other Vietnamese who met misfortune, my aunt and uncle fell back on the belief that "heaven has eyes"— is just— and would rescue them from their predicament, and that good times always follow bad times. Perhaps, also, the hatred and anger they felt toward the cadres kept them going: They would not give their tormen-tors the satisfaction of seeing them destroyed.

My uncle was not the only person who received punishment instead of reward for his work for the resistance. As it spread from Viet Minh strongholds to regions that had just come under the communist govern-ment, land reform would take on a new dimension. Landlords would not be the only targets. The Communist Party would turn on itself and eat its own. The cadres in these villages were among the most hardy and the most persistent during the war, because they had had to operate right under the noses of the French. Their casualties had been high. Yet the Party now began to question the loyalty of those who survived, sus-pecting that they had avoided arrest and death only because they were really agents planted by the French. Moreover, the Party suspected that some survivors were also allies of the landlords by reason of their own class backgrounds, and would undermine land reform. Others were con-sidered corrupt or too tepid in carrying out the Party's orders. Most seri-ously, since the Americans and President Diem were advocating an inva-sion of the North, the Party feared that these cadres had come under the control of the CIA and would act as fifth columnists for the United States. Intelligence reports and sabotage acts by CIA agents during the transition period from French to Viet Minh control fed this paranoia. The Party concluded that at least eighty percent of the cadres in these villages could not be trusted, and decided to use land reform as an oppor-tunity to get rid of them. The land reform teams were told not only to destroy the landlords and redistribute their property, but also to purge the village Party leadership of unreliable cadres.

The land reform teams themselves were under a lot of pressure. The timetable was short, and they had to make things happen quickly. The drastic approach demanded by the top leaders led them to lean toward radical measures, and, competing with each other for results, they often labeled villagers as landlords and cadres as enemy agents indiscriminately at times. It is not known how many landlords and cadres accused of working for the enemy were executed, but the most objective and credible study, by Professor Edwin E. Moise of Clemson University, put the figure of landlord executions at around 5000; no estimate has surfaced for the number of cadres killed. In addition to the executions, however, there were also suicides, and no tabulation exists for these. In some villages, landlords and even members of their families killed themselves out of fear of persecution after witnessing the execution of fellow landowners. Most of the suicides were committed by cadres dismissed from office, who chose to take their own lives rather than face their disgrace and the prospect of imprisonment in some remote labor camp. For these cadres, the cruelest blow was the betrayal of the Party they had served so faithfully even during the darkest days of the resistance.

In some villages, the search for enemy agents within the Party's own ranks took on the atmosphere of a witch-hunt. A cadre who was denounced as an enemy agent would be persecuted as badly as a criminal landlord, dragged out to face the angry villagers and forced to confess. If he refused, the villagers would say that he was obstinate, and his crime would be compounded. Sometimes the accused would in turn denounce others to win leniency. These, in turn, would denounce more innocent cadres. Those that came under suspicion would get arrested and sent to labor camps. If their crimes were considered serious, they could face execution. This persecution decimated the Party in the countryside. Later, Ho Chi Minh would compare the Party to a man who used a knife to cut off his own hand.

In the place of the veteran cadres who were thrown out, the Party brought in militant peasants to run the villages. In a reverse form of class prejudice, the more destitute a peasant, the more worthy he or she appeared in the eyes of the Party. In one village, a beggar who had been sleeping under a banyan tree suddenly became anointed as a leader. Poor peasants who could neither read nor write, and who had no leadership skills, were given power. The more vehemently a poor peasant denounced or falsely accused landlords and cadres, the more he or she was trusted. During land reform, the poor peasant women were the harshest accusers of the landlords, and now many were rewarded with leadership positions. As women, they had had to put up with not only poverty but discrimination, so their unhappiness was even more acute than that of their menfolk. The cadres found them more receptive to their indoctrination and, knowing that their stories of mistreatment would ring more true to their fellow villagers, egged them on to denounce the landlords. Peasant women in Tonkin had honed their talent for curses and insults, since verbal abuse was the most potent weapon they had with which to defend themselves. During land reform, they were the shrillest accusers and often emphasized their words by slapping or jabbing a landlord's head with their fingers. Naturally, these new cadres did not enjoy the respect of their fellow villagers, who referred to them as "dogs jumping out of bushes," because they had sat on the sidelines and done nothing for the resistance, but were suddenly emerging to enjoy the spoils. Party leadership began to flounder, since the new cadres had no idea how to run their villages. When my uncle Chinh fell into disgrace during the land reform, he and his family would find that these militants were the harshest and the most unreasonable.

Not everyone assigned to a land reform team was a zealot. About half of the team members were army veterans from poor peasant backgrounds, and they tended to be ardent supporters of land reform. But among the remaining half, many were government officials, mostly from middle-class or intellectual backgrounds, who had been dragooned into service. After nine years of fighting the French, all these officials wanted to do was move back to the cities and settle down in a comfortable job. They had no desire to face the rigors of land reform. They had no choice, however. The Party intended this process to bring these officials closer to the poor, to help them understand them better, sympathize with their plight more, and heighten their commitment to the socialist revolution. My brother-in-law Hau was one of those officials. He spent three months in a village in Thanh Hoa Province living with a dirt-poor family. He thought that his time was wasted, because he already knew how the most wretched peasants lived and how much they needed help to improve their lot. Hau attended the mass trial of a landlord who was spared from execution. My brother-in-law did not believe that all landlords were bad, or that all poor peasants were innocent victims, and so came to the trial with an open mind, reserving judgment until he could hear the accusations. Hau thought that some of the stories of mistreatment by the landlord sounded true, but others struck him as overblown in an effort to impugn guilt. Hau noticed, however, that the peasant audience believed all the stories and that their anger grew with each telling. He did not dare to question some of the accusations, however, afraid that the villagers and his own team would denounce him for defending a landlord and haul him out for trial as well.

Land reform did have its ardent advocates, not only among the poor who benefited but also among those who sympathized with their lot. Thang was one of these. When it spread through the area where she was living in Thanh Hoa Province, she went a couple of times to observe peasants denounce landlords. To her, the trials seemed fair. She witnessed a lot of cursing and angry denunciation, but saw no physical abuse of the landlords. Some were found guilty only of exploiting their tenant farmers, while others were convicted of more serious offenses; none, however, was condemned arbitrarily or charged with crimes they had not committed. What she observed did not distress her. She thought the landlords deserved what they got. Sitting in the audience and listening to the stories that the peasants told of how they had been ruthlessly exploited and maltreated, her heart went out to them. She did not question whether the stories were true, having accepted without reservation the explanation that the poor were destitute only because the landlords had robbed them, and not perhaps because of some other reasons. Thang thought it was about time the poor who toiled away in the fields could enjoy the fruits of their own labor, without it being snatched away by the rich—who did nothing but "sit in nice houses eating from gold bowls" and rake in the crops that their tenants produced. Although later she would deplore the mistakes and excesses of the campaign, in her view, the fact alone that it ended oppression of the poor by the rich amply justified it. She also believed that the government more than made up for its mistakes later, and that it addressed the wrongs of land reform. In the case of Uncle Chinh's family, his children were allowed to attend the university—one even went to study in the Soviet Union—and to get good jobs.

The admission of errors took place in late 1956, and by early 1957 the government began to take steps to reverse its mistakes. Land reform was halted, but by this time the campaign had rolled over most of North Vietnam, leaving only a few mountain areas untouched. The turmoil within its own ranks, the disunity in the countryside that land reform had unleashed, and the fear of alienating people in South Vietnam who were watching developments in the North finally drove the Party to face up to its errors. Ho Chi Minh himself spoke out against the mistakes and promised that they would be corrected. Cadres falsely accused would be reinstated and their rights restored. People wrongly classified as landlords would be exonerated. To calm the furor, Ho announced the demotion of top leaders responsible for land reform, but this step was largely cosmetic, as these men continued to hold crucial positions in the

Party. As tension and confusion reigned in the countryside, Ho appealed for calm and unity. In the provinces, Party leaders asked people to refrain from taking revenge. The first thing the Party did was to release cadres who had been wrongly convicted. In the provinces, leaders staged cere-monies to welcome them back and proclaim their innocence. Their files were burned. Next, the government tried to make up for their unfair treatment, giving them free medical care to restore their health and granting their children priority for training and jobs. To these cadres, not surprisingly, these gestures were not enough. They wanted more than their honor restored—they wanted their old positions back and the assets that had been taken away from them returned. This sparked an acrimonious feud between them and the militants who had taken their jobs and their properties. In the end, many of the cadres were reinstat-ed to their old positions, but by then some had become too embittered to accept.

Protests began to erupt spontaneously. In Hanoi, groups of families that had been wronged gathered in front of Ho Chi Minh's residence and at the headquarters of the Communist Party to submit petitions and demand answers. In a tense mass meeting with the families who had suf-fered in the land reform, General Vo Nguyen Giap himself, one of the most popular and respected leaders, had to be dispatched to address the crowd and calm its wrath.

In the villages, the pent-up resentment and anger of those that had suffered boiled over. Violent clashes broke out between them and those who had denounced them and destroyed their lives and their families. Rectifying errors was easier said than done. The most tricky job was to return the property that had been seized and distributed to the poor. In the end, through much persuasion and patience, the cadres managed to get the poor to give back some of what they had received, but the result left all parties aggrieved. The poor were mad that they had to return the assets that they had been told were rightfully theirs. The landlords and the wealthy got back only some of their possessions. Often, they found that their houses and belongings had been damaged. The tension demor-alized the village cadres, and many of them wanted to give up and quit. In the end, not all the wrongs were or even could be righted. The dead, for one, could not be brought back to life. No matter how elaborate the ceremonies to honor their memories were in that year of 1957, the sim-ple fact remained that their lives had been snuffed out unjustly.

For my uncle Chinh the correction of mistakes came only after his death. When he came down with cancer, the village cadres allowed his wife to take him to the province capital, eighteen kilometers away, for treatment. They reached it on foot after two days on the road. Halfway there, my uncle felt too exhausted to go on. They stopped at a house and asked for shelter. The owner, recognizing them as landlords, slammed the door in their faces. At the hospital, the physician who examined my uncle was the first person in an official position, since land reform began, to show him kindness: He referred Chinh to a hospital in Hanoi to get better care, instead of sending him home simply because he was a landlord undeserving of any special consideration. With the doctor's permission, my aunt and uncle boarded a train for Hanoi. Unfortunately, Chinh's cancer was incurable and he died two weeks after he checked into the hospital there. When my father finally heard the news, he was devastated and told cousin Bieu, who was living with us, "You should never forget what the communists have done to your father." Bieu said "Yes" in such a perfunctory manner that it seemed he did not think the communists were responsible for his father's death.

When the government embarked on rectifying the errors of land reform, Uncle Chinh's family applied for and received a document that reclassified him as a notable who had worked for the resistance. My aunt thought that although this acknowledgment of his contribution did not make up for the wrongs, it at least restored his honor. Most important of all, the new designation removed the political onus that could blight their children's lives and careers. The reclassification also meant that his relatives could now reclaim their assets. With this paper in hand, my aunt and Phi went back to the province to get the rest of the required documents. With the correction of mistakes in full swing, the mood in the province changed. Cadres who would have shunned them in the past helped speed up the paperwork. When my aunt and Phi thanked them and said goodbye, the two top leaders in the province told them, "Please understand our position. It was the atmosphere at the time. We had to keep our distance from you." Phi and his mother accepted this apology, because they understood the incredible pressure that had been brought to bear on everyone during the land reform, and the dilemma of people who wanted to help but were afraid to. After collecting the last batch of documents that absolved my uncle, my aunt donated her land to the state. Then, she and Phi said goodbye to the village that had been a hell for their family. The only belongings they had left were an iron pot and a torn mosquito net, which they took with them. Phi still has the pot, which he has kept as a souvenir.

My uncle might have been officially absolved by the government, yet the social stigma of being a landlord under a communist system lingered on; the vilification of landlords had been too deeply stamped in the mind of the population to disappear with an official pronouncement. Years later, when Phi visited the national museum in Hanoi with his classmates, they saw an enlarged photograph showing his father at a 1951 Lien Viet meeting presided over by Ho during the resistance. Phi proudly pointed out his father to his friends. But they did not believe him. "Come on," they said, "your father was a landlord. How could he have had anything to do with Uncle Ho?"

In Hanoi, my aunt, Cam, Phi, and Thai moved in with Lang, an older sister who had returned to the city with her two children. My aunt's two youngest daughters rejoined them. All nine crammed into a single room that had been rented from the owner of the villa. Later, the government seized this residence, and the family ended up living there practically free. Thanks to having lost everything, they now qualified for the classification of "urban poor," a desirable category that not only shielded them from harassment but even entitled them to some benefits. In 1957, there were still private enterprises in Hanoi, so Phi was able to find work. After going to his high school classes in the morning, he would do accounting for four paper merchants in the afternoon. In the evening, he would tutor a couple of pupils in their homes. He earned enough to support his mother and his siblings.

But the North was about to shed the last remaining traces of a capitalist and free-market system and move to a full-blown socialist one. In the countryside, the peasants had to give up the land that they had received only a few years before, keeping only small private plots to farm on their own. All means of production—as the communists call it—that is, all land, draft animals, and tools, became concentrated in cooperatives in the countryside. Everything now belonged to the state, and the villagers worked not for themselves but for the cooperatives. In exchange, the peasants were assured of a stable income—a safety net that few of them had enjoyed before—and had access to consumer goods made available by the state at subsidized prices. Peasants had the choice of joining the cooperatives or remaining outside. Most accepted the new system as a way for them to achieve economic security, and decided to become members. The few who opted to stay independent quickly found out how difficult it was to survive. With the state controlling the distribution of basic products and their trade, it became harder for these villagers to sell their rice in markets in the towns and cities, nor could they buy the materials they needed for farming or purchase the consumer goods and basic staples that now required coupons issued by the state. In the end, virtually every household in the countryside joined a cooperative.

In setting up the cooperatives, the Communist Party wanted not only to control production and distribution of food but also to improve yields by grouping small plots together to achieve economy of scale and using better growing methods, better irrigation, and better labor management. The surplus produced by these advanced techniques would then be used to fund the development of heavy industry. The unrelenting demands of the war in the South, however, combined with the bombing, doomed this plan. At first, the cooperatives gave the peasants a better life, but the war chipped away at their gains. Men entered the army, depriving them of able hands to do farm work, and, as the state took more and more of peasants' crops to feed the army, their income dropped. Once again, the burden of the war fell heavily on the villagers' shoulders. And once again, they rose to the challenge, making enormous sacrifices for the cause. But as the war wore on, the peasants began to spend more time on their private plots of land—growing produce to sell in the markets to earn some needed extra cash—and to devote less labor to the cooperatives that, by the early 1970s, had lost their allure. The cooperatives suffered from the classic problem of a socialist economy: The state had removed an incentive for hard work by paying peasants according to their needs, not according to their labor. The peasants, ever practical, figured out quickly that working harder would not translate into more cash in their pockets, and saw no point in slaving away for the cooperative. This would eventually lead to the demise of the entire cooperative system, and to economic reforms that would reopen the country to private enterprise and outside investments.

All this was still far away when the communists first embarked on reforming the North. The economic makeover did not stop with cooperatives in the countryside. In towns and cities like Hanoi, the government went about smashing owners of private enterprises and the middle class and seizing their properties. In the Party's view, everyone who engaged in private commerce was a parasite, a cheater, and an exploiter of the labor of others. By this time, the ranks of entrepreneurs and the middle class—which had never been huge to begin with—had dwindled to only a few thousand, as many families, fearful of communist intolerance, had already moved to the South. Those that stayed now not only saw their assets taken away, but were condemned as decadent, and their past dealings with foreigners held up as proof that they were agents of imperialists. It was at this time that Thang decided to get rid of our house by donating it to the government, or, as the euphemism went, "placing it under state management." She felt neither remorse nor regret, because owning things was not important to her; besides, she thought the house was no longer ours, since Aunt Dinh considered it as collateral for a large loan my mother had been unable to repay before we left for Saigon.

All over Hanoi and other towns, most of the rich and the middle class donated their businesses, factories, houses, inventories, gold, and other assets to the state to avoid suspicion that they opposed government policy. By the time it was all over, the communists had managed to reduce everyone to the same condition, and in a country where most people barely eked out a living, this meant pulling everyone down to subsistence level. Life became uniformly drab. Everyone dressed in the same nondescript style: uniforms for cadres, and black trousers and white blouses for the women. The *ao dai* women used to wear disappeared, frowned upon because it used three times as much fabric as a simple blouse. Until Vietnam embraced the free market several decades later, the government would religiously enforce this economic equality. Anyone who showed signs of material advancement would draw suspicion. People who could still afford a small indulgence now and then had to do it in secret to avoid being berated for extravagance. When they ate chicken, they would cut it up with shears, instead of chopping it on a cutting board, to avoid making the thudding sounds that would alert their neighbors. The feathers and remains were thrown out at night in a public garbage dump. Anyone building a new house would attract the police, who would question where the money and building materials had come from and probably make the owner tear it down.

Once they had gathered all economic power in their hands, the communists ran the country in the same manner the Soviets did, by central planning. This was the same heavy-handed, bureaucratic system that finally destroyed the Eastern bloc's economy and led to the fall of communism. Starting in 1960, bureaucrats in Hanoi began dictating what, where, and how much would be produced in every industry. Working for the state instead of for themselves, people lost incentive to produce. The economy became stagnant. Shortages became a way of life, getting more acute as the war went on. To control access to scarce commodities, but also to enforce equality, the government introduced rationing. People had to buy goods such as rice, sugar, meat, cooking oil, and cloth at state-owned stores with coupons. They could buy them from vendors in the market, but would have to pay up to five times more. Only those who managed to save, couples with two good incomes or high-ranking cadres with large enough salaries, could afford to do the latter.

The rationing spread the shortages more or less evenly throughout the population, but kept everyone barely fed and clothed. In general, each adult was entitled to thirteen kilograms of rice per month, about half a kilo of meat per month, half a liter of fish sauce, and half a kilo of sugar. In addition, every year each person got four meters of cloth and two sets of underwear. Government rice was often moldy or rancid, and mixed with small pebbles or husks. Nevertheless, long queues would start at three o'clock in the morning—no matter how bad the weather— when rice shipments arrived in the stores. Meat came from poor cuts and was laced with a lot of fat. High-quality goods in the stores never got into the hands of the consumers. The sales staff usually snapped them up for themselves, their relatives, and their friends, or people whom they were courting for special favors.

My sister Thang, who could get by with very little, did not find this rationing too onerous. She accepted this as a logical and fair way to deal with the inevitable shortages. When fighting started again in the South, and especially after the Americans began to bomb the North, she considered that enduring rationing was her way of contributing to the war. "Everything had to go to the front," she explained years later, "We could not afford to let the soldiers lack rice and other basic things." She and her husband would cheerfully waive their rights to household items that became available for distribution in their offices. When a shipment of things like sewing needles, washing basins, and thermos bottles arrived, the office would hold a meeting and sell them to those who needed them or wanted them the most, at subsidized prices. Since he was among the top leaders in the office, Hau could have insisted on getting the merchandise, but he usually passed up the opportunity. Like Thang, he was too preoccupied with the war against the Americans and building a socialist system to care. Also, he wanted to set the example of how a model cadre should behave, always sacrificing his needs for the sake of others and the common good.

Thang and Hau ended up living in the most cramped and poor quarters—foregoing a nicer apartment so another cadre could have it—wearing patched clothes, and not eating enough. But they were oblivious to their privations. (Their children were not. They remember being constantly hungry because the rations were so small.) Lap, my sister's oldest son, confirmed for me in 1993, "My parents led an incredibly hard life, but they didn't think that they did. They were happy. They had a good marriage, and shared a cause they believed in with their hearts and souls—a mission that absorbed them totally. The only thing that nagged at my mother once in a while was being cut off from her own parents, brothers, and sisters."

But all the measures taken by the government did not create a truly classless society. Although not as glaring or as large as in the old days, inequalities continued to exist. The most pronounced gap was between the top Party and government leaders—the new privileged class—and the masses. These cadres and their families lived better, with large houses to themselves and more than adequate supplies of everything. They received more and better rice and meat, delivered discreetly to their residences, and they wore clothes of better quality. Even in death, they fared better, and got buried in a separate cemetery. None of these perquisites, though, came close to the luxuries enjoyed by their counterparts in the South who were getting wealthy from wartime speculation and siphoning off American aid.

Monotonous, drab, and controlled as life was under the communists, it nonetheless had its compensations. Everyone enjoyed a safety net and people felt a sense of economic security. The state met their basic needs of housing, food, health care, and education—free or in return for a small payment. As long as they refrained from doing anything that could be construed as opposing the Party and the state, their life was taken care of. Competition, ambition, and envy were not absent, but did not exist to the same destructive degree as in other societies. Acquisition and self-interest did not consume people as they do now. There was nothing valuable to buy, except food items from vendors in the market, and no big gains or big money to be made. Joining the Party and being recognized as a hero of the working class represented the biggest dream to which anyone could aspire. This made it easy for people in the North to pull together when the war started again. They largely suffered privations to the same degree, and no big differences existed to drive them apart. Some people in the North now look back on this period with nostalgia, as a time when everyone shared alike, supported one another, and reached beyond themselves and their families to build a community. My sister remembers that society as healthier: People were kind to one another, dedicated themselves to their work and the war, and enjoyed a life safe from crime, and children did not fall prey to bad influences.

Lap recalls that complicated life and career choices did not exist for youths like him. There was only one road to follow: study, work in a job assigned to them by the state, and serve in the war. He and his friends enthusiastically jumped into every campaign that the Party and government dreamed up, whether it was calisthenics, manual projects, going into the mountains to help the hill tribes, or joining the army. Their only reward was praise from the Party and the adulation of the people. When the war came, it consumed everything and everyone. There was no time to sit and moan, and no other alternative but to see it to the end. To Lap, the sacrifices and demands of the war seemed natural and not too unreasonable. Everyone accepted them as the price to pay to achieve the ultimate goals: driving the Americans out of the country and reunifying North and South. In 1993, I asked Lap whether he and his friends were ever frightened by the ferocity of the war and the possibility of getting killed. He said, "You know, we were like people caught in a swift current. It swept us along. We did not know how powerful it was. If we had sat on the bank of the stream and looked down, we would have seen how strong that current was and felt scared. But we did not have that opportunity, or that luxury."

The deep reservoir of fervent patriotism helped the government keep the war effort on course. But it also helped that it had complete control over information, and told people only what it wanted them to know. Anything that could sow doubts about the system, Party, or war was banned. The state had a total grip over everything: radio, newspapers, books, poetry, music, and painting. It kept people ignorant of the rest of the world, holding up the socialist countries as paradise on earth while constantly disparaging the noncommunist camp. After land reform, artists were briefly encouraged to express themselves freely, but this flirtation with intellectual freedom ended quickly when some writers began publishing works that were highly critical of the Party. Dozens of authors who had taken up the Communist Party's urging to speak their minds were arrested, prosecuted, and banished to labor camps. Even those who escaped imprisonment ended up living in a kind of limbo, prohibited from publishing their works and shunned by everyone. After this, all artists had to toe the Party line. The population became so ill-informed that later some people would say that they were like frogs sitting at the bottom of a well and believing that the patch of sky they saw was the whole universe. Thang, however, did not mind this intellectual straightjacket. She believed that releasing only positive information was necessary to cultivate a healthy attitude among the people and to help them keep their commitment throughout the war.

To maintain the faith, the cadres held regular meetings and study sessions to disseminate the Party thinking and policies, not just to Party members but also to people working in offices, factories, and the army. It was not enough to attend these meetings passively; everyone had to participate and show they had absorbed the contents. Discussion was allowed, but only as long as the underlying ideas did not deviate from the Party line, so people learned to hide their true feelings and thoughts in order to avoid black marks in their dossiers, which were reviewed every six months. Even outside their homes and places of work, people had to be careful, because the secret police watched over their actions, ready to pounce to maintain security and deter antigovernment activities. There were also meetings to review attitude and performance at work, called self-criticism meetings, where people had to bring up their own errors, criticize themselves, and listen to the criticism of their colleagues. These self-criticism sessions kept people from stepping out of line, as did the neighborhood committees where they lived. The committees kept close tabs on everyone, not only to help those that might be in need, but also to watch for signs of unapproved behavior. In a culture that imposes constraints on the individual and stresses social harmony over personal liberty, many people did not see the system as stifling. Those that believed in it thought that it produced a safer, more egalitarian, and more harmonious society where people put aside their differences to work for the common good. As time went by, most people, especially the young that grew up in it, would come to view it as normal. They accepted it, because they had no knowledge of other systems.

As a worker in the Ministry of Agriculture, Thang became part of the state mechanism and had to attend similar study sessions and meetings. To her, the study sessions gave her the opportunity to learn new policies, while the criticism meetings allowed her to improve herself. While most people disliked the criticism meetings, Thang actually looked forward to them. As she observed later, "There's nothing to be afraid of. What's wrong with looking for your own mistakes and trying to correct them? Besides, only bad people fear these meetings, because they know that what they've done will be looked at and criticized." Thang, naturally, rarely got criticized, and when she did, it was for something minor. Her coworkers would usually scratch their heads and say, "Well, what can we criticize Thang for today?" My sister's class background was too much for her to overcome, however. In spite of her self-sacrificing attitude and her near-spotless record, she was never recruited into the Party—the ultimate club—which selected members only after a long period of observation and a careful investigation of their backgrounds. Induction followed after a rigorous education on the Party's ideology, organization, and discipline.

The end of the resistance brought a new beginning for my sister. After the war, the government encouraged women to study, work, and contribute to society. Thang saw the opportunity to break out of the traditional role of mother and wife that my parents had envisioned for her. She enrolled in a school to learn about agriculture in 1955 and afterward started work in the Agriculture Ministry. In 1965, she entered the university to get more training. By this time, she had four children. Lap, the oldest, was in school in Hanoi and living with a relative, but she still had three to take care of—the youngest two were only four and six years old. Knowing she could not study full-time and also take care of them, she sent Hoa, the second oldest, to her husband, who by now had gone back to Thanh Hoa to take charge of experimenting with growing cotton, and put Hoach and Hien, the youngest two, in a state-run nursery, while she moved into a dormitory. Once every couple of weeks, Thang would walk twelve kilometers to visit her two youngest children. This went on for two years, until she finished her training and returned to the Ministry of Agriculture to work. Thang thought there was nothing wrong with this arrangement, but her children felt abandoned. They remember vividly the loneliness of these years, and how much they missed being with their family. Once, when her mother left after a brief visit, Hien followed her all the way back to her dorm, jumping into a bush to hide whenever Thang turned around. (Thang and Hau would not be reunited until 1969. When my parents later heard of their long separation, they took it as evidence that the communists had deliberately broken up Thang's family to focus their loyalty on the Party. But this is not the case, as Thang's family has remained extremely close.)

Once my sister broke out of the confines of her family, she became highly active. She held a full-time job, attended study sessions and criticism meetings, took part in collective activities in her office, and at night volunteered to teach colleagues who had been forced to interrupt their studies during the resistance. Thang never felt guilty that her family, which had been the center of her life, now took the back seat; there simply were not enough hours in the day for work, revolution, and children as well. She credited the socialist system for making it possible for her to devote less time to her family and still have everything turn out all right. As they grew up, she did not need to supervise Hoach and Hien closely, because the schools and the community fostered and reinforced their positive behavior. She never had to worry about what they might be up to, or who they might be spending time with, in her absence. She knew that she could neglect household chores because they would pitch in and do whatever was needed around the house. No job was too big or too small for them. The schools had taught them to be selfless and useful to others, and conditioned them to perform physical work—making them take part in manual labor activities and sending them to the villages to help the peasants. Hien remembers carrying heavy loads of bricks at construction sites, transplanting rice shoots—wiping off the leeches that clung to her legs with her bare hands—harvesting crops, and lugging big bundles of rice stalks on her back. One of her brother Hoach's most vivid memories of his school years was of himself and his classmates bent over building projects or working in the rice paddies with the peasants. "It seems like I spent my youth with my butt pointing toward the sky," he recalled in 1993. The same socialist system that nurtured positive behavior in her children also provided Thang with a support network that took other family burdens off her shoulders. She did not have to spend hours standing in line at state stores to buy basic staples, because her colleagues at work would take turns collecting coupons and making purchases for her and other workers in the office. During the week, a communal kitchen in her apartment bloc provided her and her children with food, so all she had to do was to send Hien down to get their dinner.

Thang had not been a political person before, but as she experienced life under socialism and studied its principles, she became a true believer. It seemed like a logical progression for her: She already believed in the goals of socialism and approved of how it had transformed society, bringing equality and creating a web of "humane relationships" between people. The political lessons she received fascinated her, and because she tended to embrace the things she believed in wholeheartedly, she did not question that her education could be one-sided. She eagerly took in what she learned and earnestly tried to contribute what she could to making the socialist system work. In 1993, Thang would say to me, "Socialism is a good system. It creates a decent society and encourages people to get along with one another and to support one another." On this same occasion, her daughter Hien would marvel at her total commitment and zeal in this period, "My mother was captivated by the revolution at that time—it was as if it was coursing in her blood." When the war and the bombing intensified, my sister became even more absorbed in the struggle than before. Like other people in the North, she felt a sense of mission to stand firm against pressure.

The bombing of the North began in August 1964. By March 1965, it became a permanent policy, as President Johnson cast about for a way to prevent the Viet Cong from overrunning a shaky Saigon regime. Its scope was expanded. Now it was intended not only to block the stream of arms, supplies, and troops from reaching the South, but also to destroy the economy of the North, demoralize its people, and break its will to fight. As the flow continued and Hanoi showed no sign of buckling under pressure, President Johnson would escalate the bombing again and again, hoping to find that threshold of pain that would make the North cry for mercy and sue for peace. Even after Secretary of Defense McNamara had lost faith in the effectiveness of the bombing in the fall of 1966, Johnson would keep up the air attacks.

The list of targets kept growing. At first, the raids focused on troop staging areas, rail lines, roads, bridges, airfields, and weapons and oil storage sites. Later, the bombing spread to targets such as factories and power plants. The regions hit also kept expanding, from the area near the demarcation line at the 17th Parallel to the Red River Delta, the heartland of the North. Right after the bombing began in February 1965, the government ordered people to evacuate from Hanoi. Schools and most of the offices dispersed into the countryside. No one felt particularly alarmed, and simply accepted this as part of the sacrifice they had to make to win the war. But as President Johnson kept Hanoi off-limits to bombing to avoid provoking the Chinese communists into intervening directly in the war, people began to drift back. After three waves of evacuation, induced by intensified bombing, half of the population would still remain in Hanoi.

Once again, most of my relatives dispersed. Students and staff of Lap's university, a total of over 3000 people, moved into a forest in the midlands, cutting down timber to build their own lecture halls, dining rooms, and dormitories. They ate rice mixed with other staples such as corn to stretch out the meager supply. The clothes they wore had been patched over and over so many times that the original cloth was barely visible. They had no entertainment. In spite of the abject conditions in which they lived and worked, Lap and his fellow students kept up their studies. Then the draft caught up with him. Mobilization had begun in 1965, after the United States landed troops in the South, and by 1968 was expanded to send replacements for Viet Cong units decimated during the Tet Offensive; and the pace would keep up until the end of the war in 1975. Lap's name came up in January 1969, and he had to report for military duty. Instead of being dispatched to the South, he was assigned to teach at a military medical school, where he spent the remainder of the war. Many of his classmates were not as lucky. Lap heard later that for every ten students from his university that went South, braving diseases and bombs along the Ho Chi Minh trail, only two or three returned—the same rate of casualty suffered by all draftees. Yet the sense of mission, fed by deep patriotism reinforced with a lot of propaganda, led students to accept the possibility of death on the battlefield with equanimity. Over the course of the war, about half a million men from the North would perish. Families that had sons killed in the war would be called a "dead hero's family." The designation was an honor with few benefits attached—once a year, at Tet, the family would receive some gifts and a small sum of money. But to these families and their neighbors, the honor was not hollow; it represented a worthy achievement.

Constant propaganda helped the people to look on the army with affection and pride. To the population, the war was a good battle fought for a deserving cause, a sentiment akin to that felt by Americans during World War II. Troops were well received everywhere, as civilians appreciated their enormous sacrifices. When soldiers left for the front, a village would stage a big ceremony to send off their young sons to the sound of drums and amidst a lot of flag waving. Once the youths left, their families usually would not hear from them again unless they returned. Even if they died, their relatives might not get notified due to bad communication. Most families gave up hope that their loved ones had survived. The bodies of thousands of soldiers who fell in battle were never recovered. When they died, their comrades would bury them hastily somewhere in the jungle, then the survivors would link up with other units to fight on. These units might be wiped out in turn. Nobody would know where the dead lay. In all of Vietnam, at least a million people are still listed as missing in action.

In 1968, after the Tet Offensive failed, the spirit of determination flagged. The tremendous burst of effort and the huge sacrifice in men and resources brought not victory, but a setback. The Americans and the South Vietnamese army inflicted enormous casualties on the Viet Cong and pushed them out of large swatches of territory they had controlled. The war now looked like it would go on for a long, long time, and morale sagged. Ho Chi Minh's death in 1969 dealt another psychological blow. But indoctrination, mobilization, and appeals to patriotism once again restored the spirit of defiance and determination, especially when the Americans stopped the bombing, agreed to negotiate for a peace settlement, and started to withdraw their troops. In 1972, the

North was once again able to mobilize for the Spring Offensive. This outpouring of resources brought gains in the Mekong Delta, but also a furious retaliation by President Nixon, who blasted many targets in the North with B-52s and mined its rivers, estuaries, and the Haiphong harbor to choke off supplies from the USSR and China. The morale of people in hard-hit cities such as Hanoi and Haiphong was sorely tested by the fierce bombardment and also by the worsening food shortages. But by then, the Americans were already going home. People in the North knew that no matter how unbearable conditions could become, victory would eventually be theirs.

During the three and half years of almost daily bombing under President Johnson, American planes flew thousands of sorties and dropped a million tons of explosives, rockets, and missiles on the North. But except for the area near the demarcation line, they were under presidential order not to attack indiscriminately. Johnson did not want to inflict heavy civilian casualties, afraid that this would bring worldwide condemnation and compel the Chinese to send troops to help their North Vietnamese allies. President Nixon, who had secured detente with the Soviet Union and China, was less bound by this consideration, yet even he had to be careful not to push the Soviets and the Chinese too far, and not to provoke a backlash at home and throughout the world. In a country as jam-packed with people as the North, however, few targets were located far enough from civilians. Accidents were unavoidable, since roads, bridges, rail lines and yards, and factories tended to be located in populated areas. Over 100,000 civilians were estimated to have been killed during the height of the bombing. Many people have said that this rate of casualty was small for a country of 18 million, but this is scant consolation for the families of the victims.

Thang and Hau were much less afraid of the Americans than they were of the French, who could attack on the ground as well as from the air, sweeping in unexpectedly with troops to catch you in a dragnet. Their view of the bombing was colored by the fact that they never had to live through it. By the time the bombing escalated and planes started to bomb targets near Hanoi, Hau had gone back to Thanh Hoa and Thang was studying at the university, which had evacuated into the countryside. Later, they would live on a crop station in the midland region, which was not threatened by planes. "Nobody in the North was afraid of the American planes, not even of the B-52 bombers," my sister would tell me later. "Offices, schools, factories—we all dispersed into the countryside and carried on as normal. The bombing made life tense for us, but it was not a big problem." It was true that the air strikes failed to bring the North to a standstill. Hundreds of thousands of laborers were repairing roads, bridges, and railways as fast as they were damaged to keep supplies rolling. Aid from communist allies kept pouring in.

My relatives still look back on this assistance with gratitude. Soldiers in the army like my nephew Lap and cousin Luc remember food-stuffs that made their diet more nourishing, such as dry noodles and veg-etables, and canned meat. All the equipment they used came from what they used to call "the brother countries." Civilians remember the rice and consumer goods that China sent over in generous quantities. Still, official relations between Hanoi and its allies were not always smooth. When Vietnam sided with Beijing and criticized Moscow for moving away from orthodox communism, it pulled back home all its cadres who were getting trained in the Soviet Union. Hau, who had been sent there from his position in Thanh Hoa to get an advanced degree in agriculture, had to leave, even though he was close to presenting his dissertation the-sis. During the Cultural Revolution, the Chinese interfered with the shipment of Soviet supplies crossing their country on the way to Vietnam. And when the Soviet Union and China chose detente with Washington, Hanoi was outraged. Notwithstanding the talk of social-ist solidarity, each country in the alliance was pursuing its own selfish interests. Because they wanted to see the North mired in war and weak-ened for as long as possible, the Chinese told Hanoi to proceed slowly, sticking to guerrilla action and not pushing for quick victory. Because they were afraid that they might get drawn into a nuclear confrontation with the Americans, the Soviets, on the other hand, told Hanoi to sue for peace. They predicted that if it persisted in fighting a powerful enemy like the United States, the North would be reduced to destitu-tion. To the chagrin of Moscow and Beijing, Hanoi would ignore their advice and pursue its own course.

Hanoi would be proved right in the end, but in the meantime, its people had to brave the might of the United States as the war escalat-ed. Among my relatives, Luc had the worst time. He was stationed from 1965 to 1972 in a free-strike zone, across from the demarcation line between North and South, with an anti-aircraft regiment assigned to protect the town of Vinh Linh. Ironically, this assignment may have saved his life. He was almost sent South to fight, where he probably would have died in combat. At the last moment, the order was rescind-ed, thanks to his suspect class background. His commanders were afraid that, as the son of a landlord, he would take the opportunity to defect or, worse still, pass vital military information to the enemy. In the area near Vinh Linh, American planes could attack at will—everything was fair game, and nothing was placed off-limits. American jet fighters carrying unspent ordnance would jettison their bombs and rockets there before returning to their aircraft carriers in the South China Sea. When Johnson and later Nixon unleashed B-52 bombers over the North, it was to hammer this region. Even when the bombs stopped falling over the North's heartland in 1968, with Johnson's order to start peace negotiations, they would keep dropping here. For seven and a half years, except for brief halts to observe Christmas and Tet, Luc lived with bombs and shells exploding around him.

Even without the airborne bombings, Vinh Linh, a staging area for troops and supplies moving into the South, would have been one of the hardest-hit towns. South Vietnamese artillery lobbed over shells randomly, day and night. Luc thought he would go deaf from the constant explosion. There were days when he counted seven raids by B-52 bombers. He and his unit had to live in bunkers and move about in trenches. The bunkers were shielded by an A-frame roof, but could not protect them from direct hits. Once, when one of the bunkers was struck, Luc went over to inspect the damage. What he saw made him shudder. The bunker had become a gaping hole, and the platoon that had lived there had simply disappeared, pulverized into the dirt. Luc did not even see bits of flesh or bone fragments lying in the churned-up ground. The only evidence he found that men had lived there was a few wallets with their family photos still intact.

Life in the trenches would have been trying enough even without the bombing and shelling. Dust and mud were Luc's constant companions. For food, he ate rice that had gotten moldy from long storage in jungle sheds and C rations. It got to the point where he could not look at a C-ration without feeling nauseated. His teeth got bad, and he suffered from constipation, among other health problems. He yearned for fresh fruit and vegetables. The material craving was not as hard to bear as the psychological tension of living in the shadow of death and destruction, and the stress of being away from his wife and six-year-old son. Each morning, he would wonder whether he would live to see the sun set. He would wish that the deafening barrages of bombs and shells would cease so he could have some peace and quiet. And he would long to be home with his family.

Yet Luc and the other men accepted the hardships as normal wartime conditions, and at any rate did not dare to object. There was nothing they could do but grin and bear it. What kept them going more than anything was the determination not to let the Americans have their way. Luc would tell me later, "The United States is a rich and powerful country. It could afford to drop a lot more bombs on our heads than the French could. The war near the 17th Parallel was incredibly fierce—a hundred times worse than anything we had gone through during the resistance against the French. The Americans were pounding and hammering us, but we couldn't let them bring us down to our knees."

Luc and his comrades were not just passively sitting in their trenches, however. His regiment shot down eighty-six U.S. planes. Luc himself scored a personal success when he directed an attack against a South Vietnamese post at Doc Mieu, just across the demarcation line, using an anti-aircraft gun. The first shell went too far, but the second and third did the job. The gasoline tank behind the post caught fire, and the flames spread to the ammunition depot, making it explode like fireworks.

The same determination that kept Luc and his comrades going also prevailed in other parts of the North. At the Thai Nguyen steel mill, the North's only such complex, Trung—the youth who had gone into Hanoi as part of the advance party of cadres to reassure its residents before the arrival of Viet Minh troops in 1954, and who was now an engineer trained in the Soviet Union—endured repeated bombings along with his co-workers. The bombardment started in 1966 when industrial sites became targets, with the first wave of attacks taking place in November of that year. In March 1967, jet fighters carried out about fifty strikes on the mill in the space of two weeks. The steel complex was well protected with surface-to-air missiles and anti-aircraft guns. Planes that eluded these would meet a hail of gunfire from plant workers manning machine guns and rifles. The jet fighters, two to five operating in tandem, had a predictable schedule. They usually appeared at ten o'clock in the morning and two o'clock in the afternoon, when the slanting sunlight blinded the shooters on the ground. The planes would swoop down inside the sun shaft, drop bombs and rockets, and then bank upward. The workers knew when to stop work and take up position with their weapons to wait for the aircraft. Most pilots preferred to stay at high altitude, and missed their target. But some were daredevils who would swoop down low to drop their bombs. The workers shot down several planes and captured a pilot, whom they handed over to the army. The complex sustained heavy damage, but survived. Like others who lived through this trying period, Trung looks back on it with pride and a sort of nostalgia. He recalls the satisfaction of rising to a great challenge, defying the most powerful nation on earth. Today he misses the support, spirit of determination, and sense of mission that everyone shared at the time.

Of all the American bombs, Trung thought the huge Daisy Cutters, which contained 15,000 pounds of explosives each, were the most dangerous. Not only could they blow people to bits, but the shock waves they created could asphyxiate, or simply crush the life out of you. When Trung helped pick up victims for burial, he found the corpses completely limp, as though all their bones had been shattered. "The bodies felt like they were made of rubber," he recalled in 1995. The cluster bombs were also horrible; Trung buried several victims whose bodies had been shredded by their sharp pellets.

My cousin An, one of Uncle Dinh's daughters, was another relative who knew what it was like to live under constant bombardment. She had been assigned to teach in Nghe An, another hard-hit province. Six months' pregnant, she was terrified by the bombing day and night. She left her post and went home to her father's house in Hanoi to wait for the baby's arrival. She and her husband traveled on foot through the jungle, skirting the open roads and walking at night to avoid the bombings. Even so, they often had to run and take shelter from the planes. Once in a while, they managed to hitch a ride on a train. It took them a month to cover 300 kilometers. To commemorate this trip, they named their daughter Truong Chinh, or Long March. After leaving An at Uncle Dinh's home, her husband bicycled back to his post in Nghe An.

An felt safer in Hanoi, where there was frequent wailing of air-raid alerts, but at least not constant bombardment. The city remained off-limits to American planes, but no one considered it safe. Stray bombs sometimes fell into the streets, and everyone suspected that the Americans could reverse their policy and start bombing the city at any moment. Every house had a shelter of some sort—from a stairwell to a real brick and mortar construction—like the one in An's backyard. Whenever jet fighters approached, sirens would go off and everyone would hurry to a shelter. Hanoi's streets were lined with concrete shells with manhole covers set into the pavement, each large enough to accommodate one person. At my old elementary school, the École Sainte Marie, there was a large shelter dug under the front porch of the old chapel.

In December 1972, B-52s appeared over Hanoi for the first time. President Nixon had used these bombers to attack military targets in the

North in March, but the scope and ferocity of the December bombing would far surpass anything the North had seen before. This time, Nixon had a more ambitious purpose: He wanted to leave the North prostrate for years and buy time for the Saigon government to survive after American troops went home. He would throw B-52s against nonmilitary targets, to inflict as much agony as possible among the population. For eleven days, except for a pause to observe Christmas, the entire fleet of available B-52s and jet fighters hammered North Vietnam. Hanoi's vicinity suffered the brunt of the attacks, which took place mostly at night. Throughout the night, waves of between forty and seventy-two bombers each time rained explosives on their targets, mostly railyards, power plants, communication centers, and storage areas on the city's periphery, but from an altitude of seven miles, "collateral damage" was inevitable. A hospital got hit, along with the Kham Thien section of Hanoi, a densely populated area near the Hang Co train station.

As the bombers approached, the streets reverberated with the frightening message from loudspeakers, "B-52s approaching to carpet bomb. Everyone to the shelter." Tracer bullets from anti-aircraft guns, like the one mounted on the rooftop right above my cousin Lang's apartment, would light up the darkness. Flaming wrecks of B-52s hit by surface-to-air missiles fell from the sky. Hiding in the stairwell, Lang could feel the ground and the building shake, and she was certain that the house would collapse and bury her and her family alive. Even inside the stairwell, the force of the explosions pummeled her chest, so that she thought she was going to suffocate. Lang survived, but one of my nephews, who lived near the Yen Phu power plant, did not. He was hiding under the stairwell when one of the B-52 bombs intended for Yen Phu exploded close by. The pressure from the explosion asphyxiated him. His family found him still standing, holding on to the handlebars of his bicycle. He had taken it—his most precious possession—with him into hiding to protect it from harm. As the B-52s ranged further afield, Trung had never witnessed anything as awesome as when the bombers struck the thermal power plant, the railyard, and other targets in Thai Nguyen. It was night, and the planes flew so high in the sky that he could not hear their engines. Suddenly, the ground trembled as though shaken by an earthquake. The detonations came so close to one another that Trung could not tell one explosion apart from the next. The flashes from the bombs looked like a river of fire that flowed for several kilometers.

For days, the waves of bombers kept coming. People in Hanoi had no idea when the bombings would stop. Few expected to survive. Each time Lang ran into someone she knew, she would think it might be the last time. After the first night of bombing, my cousin Thuc went out into the street and saw the torso of a victim floating in the lake near her house, whose legs had been blown away, and his insides torn. A woman, probably a relative, was trying to pull the corpse ashore with a tree branch. When Lang returned to the Kham Thien area where she ran a fabric stall, she found the area devastated. She saw a corpse lying in the street, with his guts spilling out of his body, still holding onto his supper—a piece of bread stuffed with cold meat the color of his dead flesh. From that day on, the mere sight of cold meat would make Lang's stomach churn. At her stall, relatives of the dead crowded around her, demanding to buy cloth to wrap the corpses for burial. She sold so much fabric that her arms began to ache from cutting it. Not all the dead could be recovered from the rubble of the multistory buildings. Chemicals were sprayed to mask the stench of decomposing bodies, but it remained overpowering, and would waft all the way to the Nga Tu So intersection on the outskirts of Hanoi. Thuc remembers that for a long time after the bombings she would smell the nauseating odor the moment she entered this intersection. Even today, she can still smell it in her nostrils.

(When Thang and Hau moved to the Institute for Agricultural Science in Van Dien near Hanoi after the war, they found a wasteland. Bomb craters pockmarked the ground and weeds grew everywhere. They met people who had lost relatives in the bombing and those who had been wounded. One woman had been burned from head to toe. These encounters made them realize how fortunate they had been to have escaped the fury of the bombings.)

The December bombing killed and wounded over 2000 civilians in Hanoi, and another 300 in Haiphong. Considering the tonnage of explosives that were dropped, this rate of casualties was considered low. Also, U.S. policy was to inflict psychological anguish rather than kill innocent people, although no one in the North at the time would have believed this. To the residents of Kham Thien, where about 200 were killed, the death toll did not seem minor. In their eyes, the killing was deliberate. Each year, on the anniversary of the destruction of their quarters, families that lost relatives in the bombing light candles and joss sticks to commemorate the dead. With the passage of time, the anger and resentment has dissipated. After years of economic hardship, the residents of Hanoi in 1993 were eager for the Americans to return, as investors rather than as foes, to help develop their country and ease their own lives, and were ready to bury the antagonistic past.

The United States also suffered losses in the attacks, in aircraft and in pilots killed and captured. Surface-to-air missiles downed at least fifteen B-52s. The wreckage of one now sits in the courtyard of the military museum in Hanoi. The unleashing of strategic bombers against nonmilitary targets, coming on the heels of National Security Advisor Henry Kissinger's announcement that "peace is at hand," stunned and repelled the world and caused an uproar in the United States. But it mollified President Thieu of South Vietnam. Fearful that the departure of the Americans would leave him vulnerable, he had done all he could to scuttle the agreement that Kissinger had worked out in Paris. Now he felt he could hold out no longer. The Americans had given him massive military aid to ensure his survival and ravaged the North to buy him time. In any case, it was clear that the Americans had had enough of "mortgaging" their foreign policy "to the defense of one country," as Kissinger put it. They were going home. After more arm-twisting by Washington, Thieu signed the Paris peace agreement in 1973. Nixon declared that the United States had achieved peace with honor. The American pilots who had been captured and incarcerated were released as part of the agreement. Over the North, there was finally peace in the sky.

With the war still going on in the South and siphoning off resources, reconstruction proceeded very slowly. Thang and Hau continued to live as before, putting up with lack of food and other shortages. In the winter, they still wore the same quilted jackets that had been patched over and over. But they gamely carried on. When the tanks crashed into Thieu's presidential palace in 1975 and brought the war to an end, they rejoiced. They knew that at last their struggle was over. After thirty years of warfare, the chain of events that took them into the Viet Minh zone had finally led to victory.

15

Flying into the Unknown

One night in April 1975, the phone rang in our house in Ithaca, New York. I had been asleep, but hearing the voice of my brother Giu thousands of miles away in Saigon, I woke up instantly.

Saigon was falling apart at the seams, and the communists were closing in for the final assault. I had been trying to call my family in vain for days; the circuits had been jammed. Now, with Giu on the line, I had all kinds of questions I wanted to ask. I knew we could not waste precious seconds. Before anything happened to the fragile connection, I shouted over horrible static, "What's everybody planning to do? Do you want to stay or leave?" I could hardly make out the answer,

"Di—*di het*" ("We all want to leave—everyone in the family"). I said, "I'll do everything I can to get you out. But expect to have a hard time resettling in America." He answered, "Just get us out. We'll worry about surviving later." Then Giu's voice was cut off. That was all the time he could get at the post office for the call. Outside the booth, as he told me later, the line of people anxious to contact relatives overseas and ask for evacuation help snaked through the entrance and spilled into the street. If he had tried to call me just seven days later, it would have been impossible. By then the entire Saigon government and army had fallen apart and no one bothered to show up to run the post office.

That was how the war ended, in a massive disintegration. There was no climactic battle like Dien Bien Phu, no courageous last stand. The house of cards collapsed faster than anyone could have imagined. I certainly had not expected the sudden debacle. Just two years before, when I had gone home for a visit, Saigon had looked strong. True, American troops had left, but Saigon now had over a million men in its army, and over two billion dollars' worth of weapons that President Nixon and Henry Kissinger had funneled to President Thieu. The arms were the sugar coating to induce Thieu to swallow the bitter pill of U.S. withdrawal and sign the Paris Accords. The agreement had not solved any of the basic problems. It left the two armed camps in South Vietnam in place. It did not settle the question of how they would carve out power and share it peacefully. Kissinger knew that fighting would resume and had predicted privately that Saigon would fall two years after the Americans left. But the mood Dave and I found on our visit in 1973 was not as downbeat. My relatives certainly did not believe that the communists could defeat Saigon so quickly. Like me, they suspected deep down that the communists would win sooner or later. But for now, looking at the balance of forces, they were optimistic. They told me South Vietnam was strong enough to keep the communists at bay for a long time, especially since Washington was continuing to provide military and economic aid. Their assessment persuaded me. I felt glad for them— at least their lives would not be disrupted by a communist victory in the near future. I left for the United States thinking that the roof was not going to come down any time soon, and that I would have plenty of occasions to come back for more visits.

It was true that the communists were relatively weak then. They had not recovered from the losses they suffered in the spring offensive in 1972, when massive American bombings inflicted heavy casualties on their troops and turned the tide of battle. Their army was now only one-fourth the size of Thieu's army, and it was exhausted. The territory they controlled in the South was a patchwork of marginal and sparsely populated areas. With the North's economy depleted by the war, and its Chinese and Soviet allies cutting their military aid, the communist leadership was split. Some wanted to keep up the pressure in the South. Others wanted to pull back and devote more of the North's meager resources to rebuilding the economy, and this faction prevailed for a while. So, while they licked their wounds, rebuilt their forces, and tried to put their economic house in order, the communists in the South stayed relatively quiet.

Not long after our 1973 visit, the interlude of calm came to an end. President Thieu was the one who took the initiative. Pressing his military advantage, he went on the offensive and pushed the communists out of a quarter of the territory they controlled, mostly in the region near Saigon and in the rich Mekong Delta. But this success would turn out to have a disastrous cost, as his army became overextended and immobilized in defending static positions. Beginning in 1974, with Soviet military aid once again picking up, the communists began to prepare for a final offensive. Battalions of laborers built a highway, slicing through dense jungles and formidable mountains, from the North to the Mekong Delta. Trucks would start rolling down this route to channel troops and weapons into the South. They also built an oil pipeline stretching for 3000 miles and reaching all the way to Loc Ninh, about seventy-five miles northwest of Saigon, and a radio network that would allow their commanders to talk directly to Hanoi.

By this time, economic and political problems were already unraveling Saigon. My brother Giu is convinced that even if the communists had not made their final push in 1975, the regime would have collapsed on its own a year or two later. When they left, the Americans had taken their dollars with them. The economy dried up. Jobs disappeared. The first people to feel the pinch were those who had depended on the G.I.s for a living: bar girls, bar and restaurant owners, and others catering to their needs such as tailors and barbers. Others who suffered included workers at U.S. bases, and those employed by American construction companies that had been building roads up and down the length of the country. In all, two million people—30 percent of the workforce—were thrown out of work. In the second half of 1973, inflation rose drastically, eroding income even more. This time, the ripple originated with the Yom Kippur war and the Arab oil embargo, which led to a fourfold increase in the price of gasoline. The cost of oil and other commodities that the South had to import, such as rice, then shot up. With every dollar in economic aid that Washington continued to provide, Saigon could only import fifty cents' worth of goods. To reflect its declining value, the currency had to be devalued almost monthly. This only made imports more expensive and inflation worse. The vast majority of the people had a harder and harder time making ends meet.

The Thieu government made some attempts to cope with the crisis. But lack of planning and sheer incompetence, combined with factors it could not control, such as worldwide inflation and the continuing disruption and instability caused by the war, doomed its efforts. Except for a few feeble initiatives, such as hiring workers to sweep the streets and clean the gutters of Saigon, the government had no strategy to cope with the worsening situation. Instead, it pinned all its hopes on foreign investments and especially on the prospect of striking oil off the coast of Vung Tau. But the continued fighting made foreign investors leery, and although oil was discovered, it was too little, too late. A sense of doom infected Saigon.

In this crisis, those who suffered the most were the foot soldiers, all from poor backgrounds, who had to bear the brunt of the fighting while well-connected families shielded their own sons from the war. Considering that they had little to gain and everything to lose in this war, the soldiers' morale had been surprisingly high, and they had fought on occasion with a lot of courage. Now, however, they were getting demoralized—by the corruption and indifference of their leaders and by the frightful inflation that had eroded the value of their pitiful pay to the point that they had only one-third of what they would have needed to support their families at a subsistence level. In the past, their wives could find petty jobs to add to the family income. Now those jobs were gone. Waste and corruption were also undermining their fighting capability, as vital supplies were siphoned off and even sold to the communists, and equipment left to deteriorate. The malfeasance reached the highest levels of government. General Nguyen Vinh Nghi, the army commander in the Mekong Delta who was later dismissed for corruption, pilfered tens of thousands of small arms and sold most of the equipment to the Viet Cong. Some senior officers were even pocketing their units' payroll.

Government corruption had been endemic and brazen. Bribery was the grease that kept everything running. Even getting a passport and exit visa required bribing the powerful. The daughter of one wealthy family was said to have paid President Thieu's special assistant for national security six million piasters, which were delivered to him stuffed in a suitcase in exchange for a passport and exit visa to France. Government positions that could provide opportunities for graft, such as district and province chiefs, were up for sale through the prime minister's office or Thieu's own political party. Those that paid huge sums of money to get these positions could count on getting their investment back several times over through corruption and extortion. As long as there were plenty of dollars sloshing around and life remained comfortable, popular anger was muted, but when conditions worsened and people had to struggle to feed themselves and their families, they became less tolerant of corruption and more resentful of the rich and powerful who were profiting from the war.

The corruption had become so widespread that even those who would normally shy away from doing anything that might undermine Saigon and bolster the communists were moved to action. A group of Catholic priests—usually the staunchest supporters of Saigon and the most ardent anticommunists—publicly indicted Thieu and his family as corrupt and accused Thieu and his prime minister of involvement in heroin traffic. They also demanded that Thieu's wife be prosecuted for corruption. Thieu knew he could not ignore this movement, so he responded by firing two division commanders for selling rice to the Viet Cong and dismissing three of his four region commanders. In addition, he forced four of his cabinet ministers to resign. But this hardly scratched the surface, and left top officials like Thieu himself, General Dang Van Quang, and Prime Minister Tran Thien Khiem and their wives untouched. They continued to make their fortunes in real estate and other business deals.

In these difficult conditions, some people in my family fared better than others. Giu and his wife did the best. Giu's salary as a middle-level bureaucrat would have given them only a comfortable lifestyle, but Nguyet, his wife, was a shrewd woman who was making a great deal of money. Nguyet was tight-lipped about her family background and her activities, but the rumors we picked up claimed that she was making money from arranging business deals using her access to President Thieu, to whom she was related, and getting a cut for each one she helped secure government approval. Giu, however, told us that she had gotten rich from savvy investments in businesses like a pharmaceutical company. Nguyet kept her distance from us, and refused to assume her responsibilities as the wife of the eldest son, such as attending clan gatherings and organizing family festivities. Her aloofness annoyed my parents, although, out of deference to Giu, they never complained to him about her abdicating her duties.

My brother Luong had prospered in his private law practice, defending rich Chinese merchants in Cholon against charges of wartime speculation and other economic crimes. Thu, Luong's wife, got along well with my family and took part cheerfully in the clan and family functions, which meant a lot to my parents. Yet although they were going out of their way to be helpful and nice, Luong and Thu never got the attention and appreciation from my parents that they deserved. In their old-fashioned way, my parents continued to look up to Giu and Nguyet as the most senior members of the family and to defer to them. My other siblings and I disliked this bias, but my parents were too old-fashioned to shake this traditional attachment to family hierarchy.

Xuong, my other brother, had never found his niche in life, and had bounced from job to job. It seemed that he preferred to keep moving, to answer the call of some adventure—no one knew what. As the black sheep of the family, Xuong did not want us to pry into what he did. He kept us at a distance, by hiding behind an outrageous sense of humor that was uproariously funny but also at times inappropriate. Every question would be deflected with a sarcastic or exaggerated answer. But now, perhaps with age, he had begun to settle down. He found a job with the American Defense Attaché Office, which had stayed behind to provide logistics to the Vietnamese army. With his salary and the income that Hao, his wife, was getting from her work at an American oil firm, he and his family managed to get by.

My four sisters were not faring as well. Phu's husband's salary as an engineer in the Public Works Ministry was not enough to support his family of six children, so Phu spent most of her time trying to push business deals through the bureaucracy in the hope of getting a commission, but without access to powerful people, her efforts usually floundered. My other sister Binh was also struggling. Lu, her husband, an agricultural engineer trained in England and France, had quit his job to start a farm near Saigon to raise chickens for a living, but lost his capital when an epidemic wiped out his flock. Fortunately, Binh found a job working for Chase Manhattan Bank, and her salary kept them afloat. My sister Yen should have fared better but did not. Do, her husband, who was working as an engineer in a government-owned sugar refinery, had amassed huge savings. Being extremely parsimonious, however, he kept Yen and their children on a shoestring budget, feeding them and clothing them just barely enough. Yen had to work as a seamstress, doing piecework, to earn a little extra money. My sister Tuyet, who was married to Tuan, the only son of General Le Van Ty, the former Chief of Staff under President Diem, was teaching primary school in Cholon to supplement her husband's small salary as a lieutenant in the army. She and Tuan shared a villa with her mother-in-law, saving rent money that would have taken a large portion of their income. Tuyet had married Tuan out of love, but now the marriage was getting frayed by his gambling and drinking. At one point she left and returned to my parents' house full of anger and despair, but for the sake of the children, and because of the social stigma attached to any woman who left her husband, she went back to him.

My father was now retired, and with only about 6000 piasters per month in pension payment—$12 at the market exchange rate—he and my mother would have found it impossible to survive if they were not getting help from my brothers Giu and Luong. Giu bought the house they lived in when the government put it on the market, and gave them money to fix it up. He also gave them a large subsidy each month, as did Luong. Whenever I stayed in Saigon, I would also chip in with a gift each month, although my husband was still in graduate school and we were living on his fellowship. With all this monetary help, my parents had a comfortable life, free of the financial worries that were plaguing so many other people in Saigon.

Even those with jobs found it harder and harder to stretch their salaries and feed their families. Giu tried to help the workers at his cement works. Unable to get them raises from a tightfisted board, he gave them food subsidies, and he asked those he knew were the hardest hit to put in overtime so he could pay them extra. The meal stipends and overtime pay ended up costing his budget more than the regular salaries, but the enterprise was making good money and he could afford to keep his subsidies going. Higher prices overseas had forced a drop in imported cement, leaving his enterprise a bigger share of the market and allowing it to make huge profits. In other industries, businesses were suffering. Factories faced warehouses bulging with unsold goods, and had to lay off their employees—adding to the ranks of the unemployed.

While the communists recovered and made plans to renew military action in the South, the situation in Saigon went from bad to worse in 1974. The fall of Richard Nixon was a blow to Thieu. He had counted on Nixon to deliver military aid and to come to his rescue with renewed bombings should the communists start to gain the upper hand. Now the mood in America shifted. Weary of the war, the United States was determined to put its obsession with Vietnam behind and move on to other priorities. The Pentagon, feeling it had fallen behind the Soviets in arms buildup, preferred to spend resources on weapons instead of pouring it into Saigon. A new Congress, responsive to the public mood, was less willing to dispense taxpayers' money to the generals in Saigon. Even before Nixon was forced out of office, Congress voted to ban all bombing in Indochina, to make sure America would not again be drawn back into the conflict. Then it began to scale back the annual military aid to Saigon. President Ford, not wanting to be saddled with "Nixon's war," was not prepared to bail out Thieu and his cronies.

In a bid to extract more aid from Washington, Saigon claimed it was facing a severe shortage of ammunition and limited the use of ordnance across the board. This restriction had a demoralizing impact on the South Vietnamese army. The soldiers had learned to fight the war the American way—dependent on helicopters for mobility, close support of airplanes and artillery, and the unlimited use of ammunition. In Ha Tien, for example, at the height of the American involvement, the artillery unit could fire its two huge cannons to its heart's content. At the least sign of communist activity, it would open up. A ferocious artillery barrage would precede each infantry operation, to clear the ground before the troops waded in. The concrete ammunition depot was always brimming with about 800 shells, and the moment a hundred or two were expended, planes would replace the supplies the next day. Now the random shelling to harass the communists, or interdiction fire, was cut back to four rounds a day. When the troops went on operation, only twenty-five shells could be fired to support them. Now, if there was a sound in the night, it might be an animal stepping on a twig, the soldiers could not instinctively react with a hail of bullets.

Forced to fight a poor man's war—using ammunition sparingly and fighting it out on foot, as the Viet Cong had done for years—Saigon's soldiers felt hobbled. Because of the fuel shortage, they could no longer hop into helicopters or trucks to get to their target area or to respond to a sudden communist attack somewhere. Even without the shortage, many of the helicopters and planes would not have been able to take to the air to provide support because of poor maintenance or lack of spare parts. No doubt the aid cutback forced Saigon to economize, but the measures taken were extreme and ill-considered. When the Pentagon sent its own logistics expert to assess Saigon's needs in 1974, he reported that South Vietnam still had huge stockpiles of ammunition, and that much of its gasoline was being diverted into the black market. Even as its army began to fall apart in March 1975, Saigon still had two-thirds of the ammunition supplied by Washington during the massive buildup prior to the signing of the Paris agreement. Unfortunately, this ammunition was stored near Saigon and not available to field soldiers and officers.

The cut in aid made Thieu's position precarious. As long as he could extract bountiful aid from Washington, the generals left him alone. But now, his usefulness was gone. Precisely because his position had weakened, Thieu became even more reluctant to clean house to win the popular support he needed to defeat the communists. He clung even more to officers whom he could trust, although they were incompetent or dishonest—or both. And the more he felt threatened, the less he tolerated opposition. The more he cracked down on dissidents, the more unpopular he became. It was a vicious circle, and he grew more and more isolated. Opposition to Thieu continued to intensify, fed by discontent over the economic crisis and also by war weariness. Even among the middle and upper middle class, among people who had the most to lose in a communist victory, more and more voices were rising to protest Thieu's belligerence and intransigence. The yearning for peace grew, even among some Catholics. Encouraged by the Vatican's 1973 endorsement of a policy of accommodation with the communists, a small group of Catholic priests came out in favor of peace. They joined their demand with that of Buddhist leaders, who had been their bitter political opponents in the past. Although most Catholics remained hawkish, this call for an end to the war from among their own ranks was significant.

Thieu refused to listen to these voices, dismissing those who demanded a negotiated settlement as "communist sympathizers" and "communist dupes." He grimly pressed on with his military solution, confident that if he faltered the United States would re-enter the war to keep the communists from winning. This illusion persisted almost until the very end; he and his group simply could not bring themselves to believe that America would not return. Thinking the United States had invested too much blood and too much money in Vietnam to simply walk away, they kept waiting for the cavalry to come to the rescue. The Americans themselves had created this dependency, which permeated not only the top leadership, but all levels of government. No one took the initiative to do anything, and no one was held accountable for not taking action. Passing the buck became a favorite pastime for everyone, from the militia in the outpost to the ministers in Thieu's government. At the most critical times, when Saigon's survival hung in the balance, Thieu would press his closest advisors for comments on a policy he was contemplating. Used to letting the Americans plan and execute for them, these advisors would be at a loss as to what to do, and would keep silent or defer to Thieu's judgment.

It was against this backdrop of economic crisis, political malaise, and demoralization in Saigon that Hanoi put together its plan for a 1975 spring offensive. Hanoi's immediate aim was not to try to take over all of South Vietnam, but to be ready to exploit military advantages as they emerged, and to set the stage for an all-out assault in 1976. First, the communists attacked Phuoc Long, an unimportant province forty-five miles northwest of Saigon, in December 1974. The attack was a test to see whether the United States would re-enter the war and support the South Vietnamese army with the massive B-52 bombings that had saved Saigon several times in the past. When Washington did not respond, the communists knew they would have only Saigon to worry about from then on. Saigon did not have B-52s, and when it did get planes in the air, its pilots preferred to drop bombs from a height of 10,000 feet to avoid getting shot down, making the bombs more of a hazard for their own troops than for the enemy. The communists took Phuoc Long in the first week of January 1975.

The fall of Phuoc Long was a psychological blow for Saigon and a boost for Hanoi, which began a massive troop buildup to attack the two northernmost areas of South Vietnam, called Military Regions I and II. In February 1975, General Van Tien Dung, the newly appointed commander of communist forces in the South, arrived from the North to direct the offensive. He set up his field headquarters west of the small town of Ban Me Thuot, the first target for his campaign, located 150 miles north of Saigon. On March 10, the assault began and, less than a week later, the town fell. The day after the communists attacked Ban Me Thuot, Thieu met with his three closest advisors to discuss a strategy he called *dau be dit to*, or "small head, big ass." Thieu told the prime minister, the chairman of the Joint General Staff, and his national security advisor not to breathe a word of what he was going to do to the Americans. All three kept their word. (Later his aides delicately translated this earthy description into English as "light at the top, heavy at the bottom," to explain that, indeed, Thieu had a strategy when he ordered the retreat.)

Thieu explained to the other three generals that the army was stretched too thin, and that the time had come to abandon the marginal territories in the two northern regions, in effect shrinking the "head."

These were hilly and jungle areas that were poor in resources, sparsely populated, and a drain on Saigon's treasury. To Thieu, they had little value. The troops now being deployed to defend them would be moved south to defend the heart (or "bottom") of South Vietnam—the region around Saigon and the rich Mekong Delta—and to drive the communists out of the pockets they controlled there. In the two northern regions, only coastal enclaves would be held to protect the offshore oil fields. For Thieu, who had adamantly opposed giving up any land to the communists, this strategy was a major departure. Yet his advisors did not ask any questions or raise any objections. Without careful planning and without thinking through the implications of his strategy, Thieu decided to begin pulling back into a truncated South Vietnam.

The withdrawal was the beginning of the end. It started with the abandonment of the towns of Kontum and Pleiku—once a huge American logistics base in the central highlands. There was no master plan for the evacuation. Thieu simply told the general in charge that he would have four days to complete the retreat. The general quickly flew out, leaving subordinates to improvise. Chaos set in immediately. As regular troops pulled out of Pleiku, the militia also abandoned their posts and left. At the airport, most of the pilots had flown out with their families, and scores of planes were abandoned without anyone to operate them. Frightened civilians and the families of the soldiers also fled, becoming hopelessly mixed in with the withdrawing troops. As the line snaked toward a town on the coast, more people joined it. The convoy, now swollen to 100,000 people, was ambushed and shelled by the communists at a downed bridge and attacked by dissident tribesmen who had been fighting for autonomy from Saigon. The casualties turned the column into what people in Saigon called "the convoy of tears."

What was supposed to be a limited and tactical retreat turned into a rout and set in motion Saigon's debacle. Like an epidemic, the panic spread. Towns and provinces were abandoned without a fight. Thieu and his generals were powerless to stop this momentum. Saigon had allowed soldiers to bring their relatives with them wherever they were stationed, mainly in the hope that they would fight harder to protect their families. But now this policy backfired. As the communists advanced, Saigon's troops had only one thing in mind: to get their families out before it was too late. Each time the communists attacked a town, officers and soldiers would leave their posts, throw down their arms, and run home to get their families out of danger. Panic-stricken civilians would join the retreating columns, and the mass of humanity would dash headlong down the coast trying to find the next safe enclave.

After Hue, the proud former imperial capital, was abandoned, this mass of refugees descended toward Danang. As its population swelled from one and a half to two million, the city disintegrated into anarchy. Army stragglers sowed terror among the frightened residents. When the news spread that the communists were about to attack, thousands tried to leave. Panicking soldiers and civilians converged toward the two airfields. When planes and helicopters landed to pick up Americans and their Vietnamese employees, the mob stormed the aircraft. The last flight out of Danang was the most harrowing, called by an American journalist onboard "the flight out of hell." Armed soldiers charged on board, trampling women and children. As the plane took off, they clung to the hatch, wheel wells, wings, and landing gear. Many were crushed when the plane took off or lost their grip and fell to their death after the aircraft was airborne. Elsewhere, remnants of Thieu's divisions battled with civilians to get into fishing boats and put out to sea.

Up and down the coast of the two military regions north of Saigon, similar scenes of violence and panic were taking place. In all, over two million people were on the move, toward what they hoped would be a secure haven. Numbed by the disaster and worried about their own survival, the leaders in Saigon did nothing to help the refugees. Instead of dealing with the crisis, Thieu and his cabinet focused all their efforts on getting more aid out of Washington and pressuring Americans to bomb the communists. Again, they looked to Washington for an answer, not to themselves.

As his northern territory crumbled, the only option left for Thieu was to shrink back to the region around Saigon and to the Mekong Delta. But he had only six divisions left to defend Saigon and the rest of his "big bottom." In a matter of weeks, his regular forces had dwindled from 300,000 to 90,000 soldiers, or six divisions. He had also lost a billion dollars' worth of equipment—either destroyed in the fighting or simply left behind. Half of his planes and helicopters had been abandoned. Arrayed against him were over 300,000 communist troops, or eighteen divisions, supported by tanks and even heat-seeking anti-aircraft missiles.

Hanoi was as surprised as Thieu and the Americans by the speed of its success. As Thieu's army collapsed, the communists saw their opportunity and moved with lightning speed to take over the whole country. After the stunning fall of Danang into their hands at the end of March, they decided that rather than wait until 1976 they would push forward their timetable and move right away to strike the final blow. With nothing to stop them, they poured troops and supplies into the South, via highways and through newly opened sea lanes and newly captured airfields. Two more combat divisions rolled toward the South. Saigon's air force did little to stop this open movement of men and materiel, afraid of losing planes to the surface-to-air missiles that their foes had in their arsenal. The communists now had to race against nature. The monsoon season loomed on the horizon. Soon the heavy rains would bog them down in water and mud. With that in mind, they decided to launch their offensive against Saigon on April 29, before the rains came in May.

Until the communists took over Danang at the end of March, the Saigon middle class was in denial. They thought that the United States would surely come back, landing Marines in Danang as it had done in 1965, and turn the tide. Some even clung to the illusion that the retreat was only an American ploy to draw the communist army into a trap. Even while Saigon's defenses crumbled, there were reports that huge American transport planes were still landing at the airport, disgorging brand new howitzers still glistening with lubricants, and powerful tanks. People who heard this thought that the Americans were surely preparing an enormously unpleasant surprise for the communists. "There's no way the Americans can leave," these people reassured one another. "We've plenty of oil deposits that the Americans want. Besides, the Americans have invested too much money here to just walk away." Even after President Ford declared that as far as America was concerned the war was over, these optimists refused to believe him. "It's just another American ploy to lull the Viet Cong into a false sense of security," they would say.

At first, government censorship kept people in the dark about the true extent of the disaster. Later, as Thieu became too preoccupied with his own survival and overwhelmed by events, the press became more daring. Newspapers began to run detailed accounts of the rout. But events were unfolding so fast that the local press, with its limited resources, could not keep up. Everyone was bewildered, caught in a web of conflicting rumors and news. Different people came up with different scenarios of what might happen next, but as the debacle became clear, only the most diehard optimists continued to cling to the illusion that the Americans would come back. Most imagined that a coalition government would have to be formed, to give the communists a share of power and placate them into ordering a cease-fire. Very few understood that the communists were about to vanquish Thieu completely. Usually the foreign community, with its access to sources of news outside the country, was better informed, but even it had a hard time sorting out fact from fiction. The French, in particular, had delusions about forging a last-minute cease-fire agreement and a coalition government for the South. If they succeeded, they thought, France would displace the United States and once again become the dominant foreign power in Saigon, mediating between the two sides. Giu, the only person in my family who had good contacts among the French, was hopelessly misled by their optimistic reading of the situation.

When Ban Me Thuot fell to the communists, Giu was in Singapore attending a technical exposition. The television and press reports in Singapore predicted that Saigon would fall—not right away, but in one or two years. The first thing Giu did when he returned was to make the rounds of the French and Japanese embassies—where he also had con-tacts—to get a bearing on the situation. Believing that they could bro-ker an agreement between Saigon and the communists, the French told Giu to relax because he had at least six months to leave the country, if it came to that. They said, "Look, President Giscard d'Estaing has told us not to evacuate any of the ten thousand French people still in Saigon. Don't worry, in six months, if necessary, we'll help you get out. But, just to be safe, you should get your wife and children out now." The Japanese diplomat Giu contacted said something similar, which reas-sured him that the French assessment of the situation was accurate.

These rounds convinced Giu that Nguyet should take the children and leave. He told his wife to go first; he would find a way to join them later. It was now getting even more difficult to get permission to go abroad. The price for a passport had shot up to $3000. Nguyet hesitat-ed, but he urged her, "Never mind how much it costs. Just get out with the two kids." Since April 1 the Americans had begun evacuating cer-tain Vietnamese and moving them to Guam—secretly, they thought, although everyone in Saigon knew about these "black" flights. Saigon newspapers had run articles describing refugees living in tents, painting a dismal picture of them surviving on the charity of the Americans. Some even predicted that these refugees would be summarily kicked out and shipped back to Saigon once things calmed down. But to my brother, Guam was an alternative worth considering. He told his wife, "If you don't want to pay that much money, why don't you leave with the evac-uees?" But she said, "Our children are small. I don't want them to live miserably as refugees. I'd rather leave legally, on an Air France or Air Vietnam flight."

The secret evacuation had created a buzz of anxiety. Something must be afoot, a lot of people concluded, if the Americans were taking such a drastic step. Perhaps a fierce battle would take place before Saigon and the communists could come to a settlement. Many people thought of the disintegration of Danang and shuddered. If fighting broke out, Saigon would probably degenerate into anarchy and violence, as Danang had. So they thought it would be best to take some precautions—to get out and then come back later after things had sorted themselves out and a coalition government had formed. Thus, fleeing, and not stopping the communists, became the preoccupation of the middle class. When they met, the only questions on their lips were, "Are you going? When and how?" They anxiously traded tips and rumors about ways to get out.

Those who could afford the bribes were packing into the commercial airlines that were still serving Tan Son Nhut airport. There, affluent people mobbed the ticket counters, brandishing wads of dollars and piasters. Villas were shuttered as their owners departed hurriedly without trying to sell their properties. The luxury goods they could not take along appeared in the black market for sale. Others without the cash to pay their way out of the country tried to find other means of escape. My brother Luong was approached by a group of friends who wanted him to chip in money to rent a boat for an escape by sea. The going price for a seaworthy vessel had escalated to $10,000. Luong thought about the dangers of such a journey in a flimsy boat over rough seas and declined the offer. Worried about an uncertain future, both those who planned to flee as well as those who decided to stay began to hoard gold, pushing its price to over $700 an ounce. They also hoarded dollars, and the demand for the greenbacks was so brisk that the black market rate almost doubled. For those without connections and money, the only hope of getting out was through the American evacuation.

Washington had been debating when and how fast to evacuate the Americans still in Saigon, and whether to evacuate any Vietnamese. With the economy in recession, and unemployment reaching eight percent, it was not enthusiastic about opening the gates and letting Asian refugees flood into the country. Congress and the Ford administration wanted to focus only on getting the remaining Americans in Saigon out to safety. Even after the fall of Danang, Graham Martin, the U.S. Ambassador at the time, continued to stall the evacuation, refusing to acknowledge the communist military threat and still wanting to protect

Thieu. Afraid that any hint of Americans leaving en masse would under-mine an already shaky Thieu and topple him, Martin dragged his feet, under the pretext that an evacuation would trigger panic in Saigon and turn the people and soldiers against the Americans. Nonetheless, by the middle of March, a task force in Washington began quietly to plan for such an eventual departure, and drew up several options—from a sea lift out of the port of Vung Tau northeast of Saigon to an airlift using large transport planes out of Tan Son Nhut airport, and, as a last resort a full helicopter airlift to American warships anchored off Vietnam's territor-ial limit. U.S. army personnel would be flown in to provide protection.

Although there was supposed to be no evacuation of the Vietnamese, the American Defense Attaché Office (DAO) and the CIA on their own were quietly getting some Vietnamese out, beginning in April, a few hundred per day. At first, these were only high-risk Vietnamese—those deemed in most danger if the communists won—such as DAO's and CIA's own employees. American firms were also evacuating their Vietnamese staff and the latter's dependents using chartered planes. This was how my sister Binh and her family got out, through Chase Manhattan bank. There was little advance warning. The order to leave usually came unexpectedly, and the families did not have much time to get ready. The instruction was for them to travel light, so they depart-ed with little more than carry-on bags stuffed with a few changes of clothes. In Binh's case, her oldest son Minh was not home when the order came for them to go to a pickup point for a ride to Tan Son Nhut airport to board a plane bound for the Philippines. They had no choice but to leave without him, hoping he would somehow manage to get out later with my family. My brother Xuong and two of his children also managed to get out, evacuated by the DAO. At the last minute, he could not contact his wife and oldest son, so he left without them. Before departing for the Philippines, he promised my parents that he would come back to get them, the rest of our family, and his wife and son.

My parents put a lot of faith in Xuong's promise. But once outside the country he could not turn around and come back. Hoping against hope, most of my family gathered at my parents' house waiting for him to return and whisk them away. Everyone was tense and anxious, as the situation had gone from bad to worse. The communists were advancing, while Saigon was paralyzed with incompetence and internal squabbles. By the beginning of April, the leaders themselves were bailing out. President Thieu shipped his household goods and personal fortune out of the country, as did General Tran Thien Khiem, who had resigned as prime minister. By the third week in April, the debacle in South Vietnam convinced Washington that Saigon was doomed, and that no amount of American aid or bombing could save an incompetent and cor-rupt leadership incapable of rallying its own people and army. Not wanting to throw good money after bad, Congress rejected President Ford's request for more aid for Saigon. But while Ford made the gesture of asking for more money—which he knew Congress would not approve—he ignored Thieu's plea for B-52 bombings.

Now that Thieu had lost his touch with Washington, his usefulness evaporated. His enemies began to plot against him more actively than before. To save his own position, Thieu spent as much time fending off his political rivals as in dealing with the military crisis. The air was thick with rumors of impending coups d'etat. The population was angry, but felt powerless. In frustration, soldiers in Thieu's home province razed his family's ancestral graves to show their hatred and contempt. Yet despite the growing opposition and mounting popular anger, Thieu stood firm because Ambassador Martin, afraid of making an unstable sit-uation worse, refused to withdraw his support. The embassy told the plotters bluntly not to overthrow Thieu, and promised to take care of them and their families in America if they stayed quiet. The offer was too good to risk, so they did not make any move.

By April 21, when Xuan Loc, a town only thirty-six miles from Saigon, fell to the communists, the end seemed near. Now there was no denying that Thieu was finished. Reluctantly, Ambassador Martin told Thieu the time had come for him to leave. That evening, Thieu resigned, reading a rambling, tearful speech on television. Politicians anxious to negotiate a cease-fire with the communists and save Saigon wanted him out of the way, and he flew to Taiwan a few days later. General Duong Van Minh, whom the French believed could work out a political arrangement with the communists, took over as president. But it was too late for negotiations. Minh offered an olive branch to the communists; Hanoi, however, suspected that this latest peace overture was just a ruse by Saigon to gain time for rallying its forces. In any case, Hanoi was too close to its objective to take time out and talk. It pressed on with the offensive. Minh appealed to his army, asking them to keep their morale and their ranks intact to defend what was left of South Vietnam. But this, too, was too late. The whole structure was collapsing around him. At that moment, the anti-communists appeared for what they were: a conglomeration of tightly knit families motivated solely by a hatred and fear of communism and held together only by the glue of American power. When that glue dissolved, the group disintegrated into its individual parts—families now concerned with saving themselves. They had never had a larger vision of what South Vietnam should be or why one should fight for it. My relatives were no different.

The collapse frightened my family. After the fall of Xuan Loc, my brother Luong came home one day to discuss the grave situation with my father. "The communists are about to win and they'll drench the South in a sea of blood," he predicted. Since Luong knew many people in the government and in the army, his assessment shook my father. They decided that the family should try to leave at all costs, before it was too late. Fear of getting caught in a massive communist reprisal changed my father. He became short-tempered, always on edge. Like other people who had fled from the North in 1954, my father and brother were absolutely sure that the communists would settle scores with them when they arrived. Their fear was partly fed by years of propaganda predicting a bloodbath if Hanoi won, and partly by the reports of the 1968 Tet Offensive massacre in Hue. They also remembered the Viet Minh reprisals that had occurred in the North prior to 1954, and the attempt on my father's life by communist agents in Haiphong. My father was now seventy-five years old, but he remained convinced that the communists would not spare him because of his age. The stark choices my father saw were either to stay and face imprisonment—or even execution—or to flee into the unknown and try to survive somehow in exile. My mother was in a quandary. She wanted to stay and be reunited with my sister Thang, and she thought my father, who had the flu, was too ill to travel. When she told him that she did not wish to flee, he lost his temper and shouted at her. She broke down and cried. In the end, she yielded to his desire to leave.

By this time, the American embassy had been running its own secret flights out of Tan Son Nhut airport for about two weeks. At first, embassy officials were selective in choosing which Vietnamese to evacuate, but gradually, the selection criteria was thrown overboard, and anyone who was able to get an American sponsor could leave. Bar girls, chauffeurs, cooks, gardeners working for the Americans—all hardly high-risk Vietnamese—were evacuated. After the fall of Xuan Loc, the pace of evacuation quickened, and thousands of Vietnamese a day were leaving on black flights, which had become the talk of Saigon. My father had given up on Xuong, and decided to contact me in the United States to see whether I could somehow get the family out on one of these planes.

In that April of 1975, my husband and I were living in Ithaca, where Dave was finishing his Ph.D. at Cornell University. For weeks, we watched the television footage of the rout in South Vietnam, transfixed by the panic, the chaos, and the unbelievable suffering. The pace of events stunned us. The communists were sweeping Saigon's army aside with the ease of someone splitting bamboo with a razor-sharp machete, as the Vietnamese saying goes. Hue, Danang, Nha Trang—towns that held so much of my country's history and my own fond memories of vacations on pristine beaches and visits with friends and relatives—fell, one after another. One week, reports would say that Saigon was going to hold the line stretching from this town to that town, but the next week events would make a mockery of the prediction. Toward the end, experts were predicting that the South would survive in a shrunken form, reduced to two regions: the one around the capital and the Mekong Delta. After that, there was talk of a coalition government under Duong Van Minh, but then, suddenly, the communists were on the doorstep of Saigon and were getting their artillery into position to shell the city. As a warning, five large rockets slammed into Saigon.

Following the swift events, I felt pity for my countrymen caught in the fighting and the anarchy, anguish over the death and destruction, fear that more pain would come before the conflict ceased, but, at times, also hope that perhaps the war was coming to a head and would soon end. The changing predictions in the media of how the situation would resolve itself plunged me into gloom one week and hope the next. The prospect that South Vietnam would continue to fight in a truncated state depressed me, because this meant that the war could go on for many more years. The possibility of a coalition government lifted my spirits; I thought this would be the best outcome as it would allow for a peaceful, quick solution to the war. Finally, the thought that the communists could bring Saigon to its knees and then proceed to take over what was left of the South filled me with dread; I saw the city pulverized and its residents killed by the thousands. This nightmare scenario seemed the most plausible, as I watched the situation from thousands of miles away. When it finally unfolded, the denouement turned out to be more benign, and a lot swifter, than I had imagined.

The specter of my family being blown up along with Saigon made me lose sleep. As the media reported that more and more Vietnamese were fleeing, I wondered what plans my family was making. I repeatedly tried to call Saigon, but each time I could not get through because thousands of anxious people were calling and jamming the circuits. Then, a cousin of Dave's who was working in Washington, D.C., passed me the news that if my family called me from Saigon collect, they could get through. I immediately rushed out to send a cable; in the chaos, my family never got it. It was only when my father asked Giu to call me that I finally spoke to my family members.

I boldly promised Giu that I would get everyone out, but I did not know how to begin setting things in motion. Washington was still saying there would be no mass evacuation of Vietnamese from Saigon, although it had issued a parole for Vietnamese dependents of Americans residing in Vietnam itself by the middle of April. I did not know it then, but the guideline meant nothing in Saigon, where Americans simply evacuated whomever they wanted, claiming family relationship whether or not there was one. If I had known that to leave Saigon a Vietnamese simply had to get an American to put him or her on an evacuation list, I would have contacted American friends in Saigon to put my family on a flight.

I took another approach, the best one I could think of. Although I knew my family did not qualify under the parole, I decided to write to the State Department anyway, in the hope of placing their names on a roster in case a broader evacuation did take place. In my letter, I listed all my relatives except for Mao, who had died after a long struggle with tuberculosis. I racked my brain, trying to remember all the names of my nieces and nephews. I was afraid to leave any of them out. It was not an easy task, since there were so many—some born after my last visit to Saigon. Then, for good measure, I attached Xeroxed copies of my marriage and naturalization certificates to prove that I was an American citizen and could legitimately ask for help in evacuating my dependents. In my letter, I also mentioned that I had worked for the Rand Corporation on a project for the Defense Department. There had been talk about including high-risk Vietnamese in an evacuation, to protect them from communist retaliation. I thought my association with Rand, although innocuous as far as Pentagon projects went, might get my family included in this category. I sent the whole packet to the State Department, suspecting that my request would simply be ignored or would disappear in the maw of Foggy Bottom.

Without an evacuation, the only other alternative for extricating my family was to fly them out on a commercial plane. I trusted that they would somehow manage to get the necessary passports and exit visas to leave the country. I counted the names of my relatives, forty adults and children in all. How was I going to pay for the plane tickets and to feed them after they arrived, when we had no savings? Dave was a penniless graduate student, barely surviving on his G.I. bill stipend and his fellowship at Cornell. I was earning less than four dollars an hour working part-time at the university. I called Dave's mother at her farm in Virginia to talk about my problem. Louise—kind, always ready to lend a helping hand—told me to go on with my plan, saying, "Don't worry about anything. Just get them out to safety. They can come and live with us on the farm. We'll plant a lot of potatoes!"

I was reassured, but before I could get my family onto a commercial plane, I would have to obtain permission to bring them to the United States. I had no idea how to get this done quickly; the usual procedure could take years. On April 24, I heard that the parole had been broadened and that dependents of American citizens and of Vietnamese living in the United States could now get in without going through the normal lengthy formalities. I found out that I could go to the nearest Immigration and Naturalization Office and file a petition. With a couple of Vietnamese students in Ithaca who were also trying to evacuate their families, I drove to Buffalo in an ancient car belonging to one of them.

In Buffalo, it took me the longest in the group to complete the paperwork, since I had to file a separate petition for my father, my mother, and each of my siblings and their spouses, for a total of sixteen. Also, for each brother and sister, I had to list his or her children—twenty-four names in all. I had thought about the television footage showing thousands of people pressing around the fence of the American embassy in Saigon hoping to be evacuated, and wondered how my relatives were going to battle their way inside to complete their visa formalities. The procedure required that all my relatives—including children, regardless of age—would have to present themselves at the embassy for screening. They would have to show proof that they were related to me. I decided the only hope was for the embassy to contact my relatives directly and somehow arrange to get this done. In my letter to the State Department, I had listed the phone numbers of my brothers Luong and Giu and my sister Tuyet, the only ones with telephones. Now, I listed the phone numbers again in my petitions, just to be safe. I thanked heaven that I had kept the phone numbers in my address book all those years.

The date was April 25. I did not know that Saigon was going to fall only five days later, but I knew I was racing against the clock. As I handed my petitions to the INS clerk, I asked her how long it would take for my request to be approved. She said the petitions would be rushed to

Washington immediately, but she was not sure when they would be reviewed. The other students and I left, feeling hopeless and dejected. We knew the chances were slim. I told myself that at least I had done what I could. We drove back in silence, too depressed even to make small talk. I tried to chase away the thought that even if my relatives survived the onslaught on Saigon, I would probably not see them for a long time, if ever. Everything was now in the hands of fate. There was nothing I could do but watch the end unfold and hope for my family's safety. (As it turned out, none of the other students' families got out in the last-minute evacuation.)

In Saigon, the mood had become even more desperate. Those Vietnamese who were anxious to leave would approach any Americans they saw on the street and plead for help. The newspapers carried poignant ads by Vietnamese women seeking foreign husbands so they could leave. A Vietnamese senator approached an American reporter and offered his daughter in marriage, so that the reporter could evacuate the entire family. The reporter turned down the offer—he was already married. By April 26, the communists had moved even closer. Bien Hoa, a town fifteen miles from Saigon, and its air base had fallen. South Vietnamese army stragglers were looting and burning it, and refugees were streaming toward Saigon, overwhelming the checkpoints that had been set up to filter out communist infiltrators. With nothing between them and Saigon, communist forces moved to its perimeter, isolating it and cutting its supply and retreat routes. Now the communists were only five miles from the center of town. In the evening of April 28, communists flying captured planes bombed the Vietnamese air base at Tan Son Nhut; then in the early morning hours of the next day, mortars, rockets, and artillery shells began falling on Tan Son Nhut, one round every sixty to ninety seconds. The shelling focused on the flight line and on fuel and ammunition depots. One jet fuel tank caught fire, sending up a thick column of black smoke. Despair descended over Saigon.

At this hour when the survival of their regime was on the line, none of the political and military leaders had the stomach for a last stand. It was everyone for himself. Those leaders who had not already fled now scrambled to get out. The CIA flew Nguyen Khac Binh, the chief of police, to the Philippines. Other high-ranking Vietnamese flocked to the American embassy, hoping to be evacuated. General Cao Van Vien, the head of the Joint General Staff, sneaked into the embassy through a back entrance and wrangled a helicopter ride to the airport. General Dang Van Quang, national security advisor to Thieu, pushed his way through the sea of Vietnamese mobbing the embassy and was let in by a Marine guard at the order of the CIA station chief. Others were less circumspect. Some armed senior officers showed up at the DAO compound—where the secret flights were being carried out—and demanded to be flown out of the country. Air Marshal Ky, who had called those leaving cowards and traitors (but who had evacuated his family to Guam) flew out in his own helicopter, taking General Ngo Quang Truong, the commander of what was once Military Region I, with him. There were scattered individual acts of defiance and courage, like the few pilots who flew their last missions against the communists. But no one was left to give orders. The whole command structure had collapsed as the Joint General Staff personnel abandoned their posts and fled.

On April 28, the same day the communist shells began landing on Tan Son Nhut airport, my petition to the INS was approved and the State Department—acting on either my letter or a manifest supplied by the INS—sent a cable to the American embassy in Saigon requesting my family's evacuation. I was never notified, so I had no idea what was happening to them. That night, an American-speaking Vietnamese telephoned my brother Luong at his home, and told him to gather everybody at a villa on Truong Minh Giang Street, to catch a ride to the airport. It was a stroke of luck that Luong was there. His family had moved in with my parents, waiting for Xuong to come back and get them out. Luong's wife Thu was pregnant with their last child, and in the crowded house, it was hard for her to rest. Finally, she got so tired that they decided to return home and get some sleep. The night they got back, the phone rang. It was another stroke of luck that in the final days the embassy had decided to focus on evacuating what it called "deserving" Vietnamese, instead of the horde of "cooks" and "bottle washers"—as Ambassador Martin put it—who had been flown out earlier. On instructions from Martin, an embassy official made up a list of 2000 names. As the final evacuation got under way, embassy personnel called these chosen ones and told them to gather at various designated sites for a ride to the airport.

Because of the curfew, Luong had to wait until the next morning, April 29, to rush back to my parents' and let everyone know that they should gather at the collection point at one o'clock that afternoon. Luong had been told by the American official to make a list of people in the family who were going to be evacuated. The instruction left him in a quandary, because the government had decreed that draft-age males, active duty soldiers, and civil servants could not leave. Phu's husband

Phung was a government employee, and Quan, one of her sons, was in the army. The American had warned Luong that even if just one of the people forbidden to leave was on the family list, the whole group might be turned back at the airport checkpoint by Vietnamese policemen. Afraid of jeopardizing the rest of the family, Luong made the painful decision to leave Phung and Quan out. (In fact, they would have been waved through, because the Americans had bribed the security personnel at the airport, but Luong could not know this.) When the bus came to the villa, Phung and Quan were barred from boarding. They said goodbye to Phu and the other children. Everyone in my family wept as the bus pulled away, leaving father and son standing forlorn on the sidewalk.

On that day, war tore my family apart once again. The Saturday gatherings at my parents' house, when many of my siblings would show up to share favorite dishes, talk, and laughter, would become a thing of the past. My sister Yen was not in the group. She had decided not to leave without her husband Do. A longtime sympathizer of the communists, since his student days when he had briefly joined the Viet Minh in 1945, he had been won over by their appeals to his patriotism and their secret overtures for him to stay and help the country rebuild. Yen was torn, but in the end decided to remain loyal to her husband, although he had at times been abusive. Tuyet's husband Tuan was also absent. He too had decided to remain behind and to leave later with their youngest daughter and his mother on a commercial flight. General Duong Van Minh, the new president, had urged the old lady not to flee as a refugee, and had promised to issue her a passport so she could depart with dignity in a few days. Tuyet was pregnant, and had her hands full with their two other daughters, aged five and three, so her husband volunteered to take the youngest girl, who was a year old, with him. He promised to rejoin her in Paris.

Two of my nephews were also not in the group. My sister Binh's oldest son Minh was not at my parents', and did not hear about the departure. When he got there later, he found the place eerily empty. Another nephew, Tuan, Xuong's oldest son, was in the army, stationed outside Saigon. He too missed the bus. Giu, who had brought my parents to the villa, did not join them. After weeks of waiting, his wife and their two children had finally gotten their passports and tickets, and had driven to the airport early that morning. A couple of hours later, they suddenly reappeared at the house; their flight had been delayed. Giu felt he should stay and make sure that Nguyet and the children got out. He thought he could find a way to leave later. He did not feel in a hurry. The French had told him there was plenty of time. After all these tear-ful good-byes, my family departed with a heavy heart. They felt numbed, rather than relieved.

As it turned out, they got out just before the door slammed shut. April 29 was the final evacuation day. The CIA had intercepted infor-mation indicating that the communists were about to unleash an artillery barrage. Perhaps that intelligence report, combined with other devel-opments, persuaded Washington to push Martin to get all the Americans out by nightfall. Since the road to the port of Vung Tau was blocked, making a sea lift impossible, and since the runways across from the DAO compound had become unusable with debris and jettisoned ordnance and wing tanks abandoned by Vietnamese pilots when they scrambled their planes, Washington went for the last resort: a full heli-copter airlift. Besides the Americans, the airlift would evacuate Vietnamese dependents of U.S. citizens and high-risk Vietnamese that had by then been allowed to enter the United States. At the embassy, the destruction of files went into high gear. From the ashes spewed forth by the incinerator, observant Vietnamese could tell that the Americans were burning their sensitive documents and getting ready to pull out. That afternoon, Vu Van Mau, the new prime minister and for-mer foreign minister under Diem, asked all Americans to leave at once.

On the bus, driven by an American, my relatives were unaware of these developments, but they were anxious enough. To them, the ride seemed to last an eternity. Through windows covered with wire screens that the Americans had added to keep Viet Cong agents from throwing grenades into the bus, they took one last look at the congested street leading to the airport. To them, the heavy traffic seemed normal, but they did not know that an undercurrent of panic was sweeping thou-sands of people in Saigon as they looked for an escape route. At the air-port checkpoint, sullen Vietnamese soldiers peered at the lucky refugees and said to Luong, "If the Americans don't come and get you out, we'll come in and shoot you later." They were resentful that these people were escaping, leaving them to face the communists and probably to die in the fighting. Luong knew their threat was not idle. Once inside, they passed by the residential quarters of Vietnamese pilots, and saw suit-cases littering the ground, abandoned by the airmen and their families before fleeing.

The bus deposited them at DAO. Hundreds of people were already crowding the bowling alley that served as a holding room, sweating out the nerve-wracking vigil. The Americans in charge themselves did not have details of the evacuation, and could tell them only that they would be flown out that night. They waited and waited. There was nothing to eat. Later that night, my relatives were taken to the airfield. Suddenly, rockets began slamming into the ground. The explosions seemed very close. The few American Marines in charge shouted to everyone to lie down in a trench nearby, and threatened to shoot anyone who could cause panic among the refugees by getting up and trying to run away. About thirty yards away, something burst into flames. But then the bombardment stopped, and the fire died down. Encouraged by the presence of the American officials, they remained hopeful. Surely, they thought, these Americans were not going to be abandoned by their government.

Then, in the morning, like an answer to their silent prayers, my family heard loud thudding sounds in the sky. They looked out and saw six Sea Knight helicopters coming in to land like giant insects. Americans and Vietnamese on the ground broke into applause and cheered madly, delirious with relief. Marines jumped out of each helicopter and then fanned out. As they disembarked, the refugees waiting in line were waved on board. They scurried across the tarmac and clambered in through the open hatch. As soon as it filled up, the helicopter took off to deposit them on one of the American ships waiting offshore. My family was only two rows away from being picked up when more rockets fell in the airport. A pall of smoke hung in the air, and my family—their hearts pounding in their chests and their eyes riveted on the hovering aircraft—wondered whether more rockets would slam down right where they were and blow them to bits. Then another helicopter landed, and my family dashed toward the chopper with its engine running and its rotors churning up a ferocious draft. The powerful 90 mile-per-hour blast almost blew my father backward. He paused on the tarmac, trying to stay on his feet, barely able to breathe because of congestion and his advanced emphysema. The precious seconds were ticking away, and he had to get on board or be left behind. Luong lowered himself, hoisted my father on his back, and raced to the Sea Knight.

As soon as it was full, the helicopter lifted off and banked toward the sea. As the air rushed past her, Tuyet peered through the open door at the land below. It looked green and peaceful from the air, then she saw the gently undulating sea. Aboard the aircraft, my relatives felt nothing, just numbness and exhaustion. The Sea Knight landed on the deck of the USS *Hancock* and disgorged the refugees. An official military photographer snapped a picture of my father leading Trang, Tuyet's five-year-old daughter, by the hand. Ever a proud man, he had put on his best suit that day. He might be a refugee, but he was not going to look like one. The picture shows a dignified man, haggard but not frightened or broken by the tragedy, looking straight at the photographer's lens. At his side, the little girl is beaming with happiness, enjoying her adventure. The contrast between my father's and Trang's expressions makes the picture such a classic that it has been reproduced in several books on the Vietnam War.

On April 29, the CIA began evacuating its personnel by helicopter from their buildings downtown. When the radio that afternoon began to broadcast reports that the Americans were plucking out their last remaining personnel, the dam broke. Those who were desperate to flee jammed the streets, creating chaos and confusion. Nam, who would later marry one of Phu's daughters in Australia, was with an uncle when they saw helicopters landing on the rooftops of high-rises occupied by Americans, so they raced to a building that they knew belonged to the CIA. They found a huge crowd already surrounding the building, clamoring to get in. It was utter chaos. Women and children were getting crushed and crying in anguish. American soldiers barred the gate, spraying those who tried to clamber over the fence with a stinging chemical. Nam and his uncle climbed into the building, ignoring the spray that burned their eyes. They raced up ten flights of stairs to get to the roof. Suitcases, shoes, clothes, and Vietnamese money littered the staircase. Americans in civilian clothes were surrounded by Vietnamese soldiers, officers, and other people who had managed to get to the roof. Some of the soldiers and officers were firing their pistols wildly in the air; others threatened to shoot down the helicopters if they did not land.

Helicopters from Air America, the CIA's own airline, were coming in, but they were unable to load. Every time a helicopter touched down, the Americans would try to rush on board, but the crowd would bar their way. The helicopter would take off. Then the Americans would radio the pilot, and the helicopter would circle back and try another landing. But each time, the frantic Vietnamese would hold the Americans back, knowing full well that if all the Americans left, the helicopters would not come back again. Finally, the Americans worked out a deal with the Vietnamese. They told the officers, "You must get organized. We'll evacuate everyone on this roof, but we must have some order to get this done." The officers agreed. They picked out some youths to set up a cordon by linking arms to hold back the crowd, creating a space so the helicopters could land and load in an orderly fashion. The first helicopter landed without incident. But before the Americans could get in, a Vietnamese teenager rushed the helicopter. The crew pulled him onboard; one of the Americans climbed in after him. The helicopter immediately took off before other Vietnamese could mob it.

Watching this, Nam's uncle said to him, "There's no way the Americans will evacuate everyone here. There are just too many people. The next time a helicopter lands, let's try to get onboard." The same thought was evidently flashing through the minds of the young men holding back the crowd. As the second helicopter came in, amid the deafening sound of its rotors and the powerful draft, Nam rushed for it, following on the heels of two Americans who had hurriedly climbed in. At the same moment, the other youths also broke ranks and stormed the aircraft. Seeing the onrushing crowd, the helicopter quickly took off. Mad with frenzy, without a second thought, Nam hung on to one of the skids. As the plane lifted up into the air, Nam felt a heavy weight dragging around his waist. Looking down he saw a young man clinging to him, and further below, another youth was hanging onto that one. He looked across and saw three youths dangling from the other skid. He also saw the ground heaving hundreds of feet below him. Looking up, he saw the blue eyes of an American peering at him. But the American, horrified, made no move to pull him on board. The pilot circled back and as the helicopter hovered over the roof, Nam let go. He tumbled to the rooftop and landed on top of the two youths who had been clinging to him. He crawled away unharmed, while the other two lay dazed. The three hanging onto the second skid had fallen nearby.

Then the wait continued. But the pilots, knowing that the situation was impossible, did not come back. Nam heard the Vietnamese officers tell each other, "Let's hold one of the Americans as hostage to force the helicopters to come back and get us." But no one had the stomach to follow through. After a while, the remaining Americans left the building, probably to find another way to get out. After waiting for another half-hour, Nam knew it was hopeless. With his uncle, he left to look for his family. When he got home they told him they had been in another building across the street, and had watched with horror as he dangled from the helicopter.

When Nam had rushed off with his uncle, his father had gathered his mother and his nine brothers and sisters and driven to the Vietnamese General Staff headquarters where he worked, hoping to get aboard one of the Vietnamese helicopters he had seen landing and tak-ing off there. At the gate, however, paratroopers and rangers barred the way, threatening to shoot if he tried to get through. The soldiers were unruly, feeling betrayed by their commanders who had deserted and fled. They now had nothing but contempt for staff officers like Nam's father, viewing them as cowards only interested in saving their own skins. With this escape route barred, Nam's father drove to one of the American high-rises, which turned out to be across the street from the one where Nam was. While they waited for helicopters that never came, they saw Nam—with his telltale long hair—almost plunge to his death. Frightened, Nam's father decided after they got home that it was too dangerous to try to flee with the mob; he would try to find another way out later.

The USS *Hancock*, to which my family flew, was an enormous aircraft carrier that could accommodate up to 5000 people. It was already jammed, but more refugees were still arriving. When Vietnamese pilots, evacuating themselves or bringing their families, left their heli-copters on the fly deck, American sailors pushed the machines overboard to make room for the ship's own choppers. My relatives watched in awe as these million-dollar aircraft were dropped in the ocean. How rich the Americans were—they thought—to casually throw away such expen-sive machines! That night, April 30, they heard the news that Saigon had surrendered. The communists had won. Everyone was stunned—no one had thought the end would come so quickly. People broke down and cried. Most of them had left behind family members, whom they expect-ed never to see again.

Aboard the *Hancock*, my family was jammed in with thousands of other refugees. It was crowded and hot, but orderly. The Americans were well organized and had things running smoothly. Feeding so many people must have been a big challenge, but the ship's crew handled it well. The only problem was the long lines. It took four hours to get something to eat. By the time my relatives finished one meal, they would have to queue up again for the next. Tuyet and Luong's wife Thu were pregnant, and could not stand in line for long, so Luong and other rela-tives would bring back extra portions for them. Another problem among the refugees was security. Tuyet had to watch like a hawk the bag in which she had packed some jewelry and jade statues that her mother-in-law had thrust into her hands at the last minute, to help ease her reset-tlement in Paris with the two little girls. With so many people on-board, there was not enough water for bathing. Since the trip was supposed to last only twenty-four hours, the refugees were told not to shower in spite of the terrible heat. In fact, the ship was circling to wait for more refugees, and the trip dragged out to two days.

Back in Saigon, the frantic evacuation continued, a race against the clock before communist gunners unleashed their barrage. Some of the choppers were fired on by angry South Vietnamese soldiers, but none took a direct hit. Communist surface-to-air missiles locked on the choppers, but did not open fire. At that point, Hanoi just wanted to let the Americans get out once and for all. As the Americans pulled out, looters began breaking into their buildings: the CIA residential quarters, the American warehouse near Newport Bridge, the recreation compound at the embassy, the ambassador's own residence, and finally the embassy itself. Into the early morning hours of April 30, helicopters were still landing on the roof of the embassy to evacuate the last Americans remaining there. In the courtyard, hundreds of Vietnamese who had been promised evacuation were still anxiously waiting in vain to be plucked out. Then, finally, at about four o'clock in the morning, President Ford ordered Ambassador Martin to leave on the next chopper that arrived. Still weak from a bout of pneumonia, the ambassador wearily climbed onboard and was lifted out of Saigon in the early dawn. When the last helicopter came to the embassy at about eight o'clock on the morning of April 30, the remaining eleven Marines hurled tear gas grenades down the elevator shafts to keep desperate Vietnamese from surging after them to the rooftop, and then scrambled onboard. America's unhappy and unwise involvement had at last come to an end.

When it was all over, the tally indicated that during April 1975 the American DAO and the embassy evacuated over 65,000 people. Of these, about 7000 were taken out during the last eighteen hours of the war in the largest helicopter airlift in history, involving seventy aircraft flying over 600 sorties. Another 6000 were evacuated by barge on the final day. Of the total of 65,000, some 7000 were Americans living in Vietnam, and the remaining 58,000 were Vietnamese. Hundreds if not thousands of Vietnamese who could face severe communist retaliation were left behind.

Back in Washington, a controversy arose over whether President Ford had exceeded his legal authority in using the American armed forces to evacuate the Vietnamese at the last moment without a clear congressional mandate. Ford felt he had done the right thing to save these Vietnamese from communist execution. (The evacuation was not a tragedy for all the refugees. For some it was also an opportunity to leave problems behind and begin life afresh in America. I heard of an unhappily married woman who walked to the dock, got on the barge, and left without her husband. I am sure she did not shed many tears.)

As pictures of the final evacuation flashed across the globe, people all over the world were transfixed by the scene of frenzy at the American embassy. But away from the madhouse there, a calm of sorts prevailed as Saigon's four million residents waited in apprehension for the communists. They were already on the way. At 5:30 on the morning of April 30, even before the last U.S. Marines left the embassy, Tank Brigade 203 was rumbling toward Saigon.

16

The Spoils of Victory

After waiting in vain for the helicopters to return, Nam gave up and left to find his family. But most of those on the rooftop doggedly kept vigil, searching the sky for the dark speck and straining to hear the sound of rotor blades signaling that deliverance was on the way. Nam had never set foot in an American building before, let alone one occupied by the CIA whose hand Vietnamese thought they saw everywhere, pulling strings from behind the scenes to manipulate the generals and politicians. Curious about how they had lived, Nam wandered through the floors on his way out to take a look. The amenities astounded him. Every apartment was well appointed with fine furniture, fancy lights, a refrigerator, and air conditioning—average American creature comforts but unaffordable luxuries for most of the locals. Even while panic-stricken people on the roof were battling each other to get on the helicopters, poor families living nearby had pushed their way in and occupied the apartments. Through open doorways, Nam saw them relaxing in the air-conditioned living rooms, drinking beer and eating ham, chocolate, and other goodies they had found in the refrigerators. Men in undershirts and shorts that had turned dingy with wear wandered among the apartments, every one of which had been occupied.

Then the horde of looters arrived. They stormed into the building, overwhelming the squatters, and stripped the rooms of everything they could carry off, such as furniture, light fixtures, pictures, and fans. Some tried to haul away a couple of refrigerators, but—discovering that they were too heavy and too big for the narrow flights of stairs—pushed them to the window and heaved them into the street. Others tossed foam mattresses into the courtyard. It took them only a few minutes to turn the building into a shambles. Those that were mechanically adept dismantled air conditioners and carried them off. Outside the building, others gutted the cars that had belonged to the CIA, removing the tires, spare parts, and the seats, which they took back to their houses to use as furniture. Nam saw a family of seven straining to push an enormous Ford automobile home. They did not have the key to it, but could not pass up such a find. On the sidewalk, people were scurrying away from the building with their arms full of booty. He stayed and watched, riveted. He knew that this was a part of history that he would never witness again in his lifetime, and he did not want to miss anything.

Later that night, Nam returned to the building and climbed to the rooftop, now deserted. He looked out toward the outskirts of town. Fires were burning eerily miles away where some units of Saigon's army were battling in vain to stop the advancing communist columns, and he could hear the sound of gunfire and the echoes of helicopter gunships attacking Viet Cong positions. At intervals, American helicopters broke the silence over the city, making their last flights to the embassy. The death throes of Saigon and of South Vietnam, Nam thought. Feeling sad but also resigned to the inevitable communist victory and his being stuck in Saigon, he made his way down the stairs. Walking past the apartments taken over by squatter families, he could hear now and then the hum of an air conditioner. Several apartments had been stripped of their doors. In some of these, the occupants had pushed refrigerators into the doorway to block intruders.

At eleven o'clock that night, communist shelling began. Nam's house was located near the airport and the paratrooper barracks, the main targets of attack. The shells landed and burst with a terrifying din—a noise familiar to peasants, but jarring to Nam and most people in Saigon. The war that had been fought mostly in the countryside had arrived virtually at his doorstep. The shelling lasted for about half an hour, halted, and then resumed. Nam's family huddled in the lower floor of their house. Devout Catholic refugees from North Vietnam, they began to mumble prayers. Their lives had never seemed so precarious. In the morning, during a lull in the shelling, they decided to move in with a friend in the neighborhood. This house had four stories and was sturdy enough to protect them against artillery shells and rockets. Nam made several trips, taking his family members over one by one on the back seat of his motorcycle. As he was getting ready to make one last trip with his mother, they heard small arms fire and loud explosions. She said, "Let's not go right now. Let's wait for a while." After about fifteen minutes, the firing stopped, and they rushed out. A short distance away, they saw corpses lying in the street. Most of the victims were soldiers, but there was also one civilian whose head had been cleanly sliced off by a piece of shrapnel. Nam shuddered at the sight. If he and his mother had left earlier, they would have been caught in the same carnage.

That same morning, in downtown Saigon, my sister Yen was returning home when an airplane started to strafe near the dock area. People scurried for cover. Yen broke out in a run, thinking, "The attack's begun, and my four children are at home by themselves." People were shouting at her, "Are you crazy? Do you want to get killed? Take shelter!" But she kept running. She did not feel afraid. The one thought on her mind was to get home to protect her children. When she arrived, she rushed up three flights of stairs and shouted out their names. She found the apartment empty. Wild with worry, she ran downstairs, and found them huddled for cover under the staircase with her husband and some neighbors. She squeezed in. From their shelter, they could hear thunderous explosions. As they waited for the artillery shells and rockets that would soon be raining destruction and death on Saigon, they told each other that they and the city were doomed. So when they heard that General Duong Van Minh had surrendered at 10:20 that morning, they were limp with relief. They felt like they had been taken from the guillotine just as the blade was about to come down.

By capitulating and averting a fiery attack, General Minh earned the gratitude of many people in Saigon. Many of Yen's neighbors said that he had saved their lives. Others, however, felt bitter. To them, the general had presented Saigon on a platter to the communists. Some believed that Minh, whose brother was a Viet Cong general, had conspired with Hanoi. In the house of their acquaintance, Nam and his family also caught Minh's speech on the radio. As the general ordered the Saigon army to lay down its arms and to give up without a fight, they listened in shock. With that, the guns fell silent. So Nam's family took their leave and started for home. Suddenly, down the street, there was a big commotion: "The Viet Cong are coming!" From the direction of the barracks, they saw soldiers running pell-mell. The paratroopers stopped only long enough to throw down their weapons and take off their uniforms, stripping down to their underwear. In front of Nam's house, the ground was strewn with discarded uniforms, boots, grenades, and firearms. The scene that Nam witnessed in his neighborhood was also unfolding all over town. At the order to surrender, panic had struck the entire army, which simply disintegrated. Discarded weapons littered the streets, yet no one bothered to pick them up.

As if by magic, many of Nam's neighbors produced Viet Cong flags and hung them from their houses to welcome the victors. He realized they must have made these flags in secret, to be ready for this eventuality. Some rushed into the street to sing and dance with joy. Most of the residents, however, hid inside their houses, feeling apprehensive and uncertain. Those who had worked for the Saigon regime in important positions set about feverishly to erase the traces of their pasts. Nam's father pulled out documents, medals, uniforms, and other incriminating items and burned them in a bonfire in the backyard. He took out his pistol, removed the firing pin, and gave the gun to Nam, telling him to throw it away. Then, for good measure, he grabbed Nam, pinned him to the floor, and cut off the long hair that his son had grown to copy the American rock stars whose songs he adored. Nam cried, not so much over the loss of his hair, but over what he believed was the end of a freedom he cherished. He knew that the austere communists would not allow him to listen to what they considered decadent music or to follow a way of life that they thought was dissolute.

At this point, Nam could not sort out his emotions. On the one hand, he feared and disliked communism and mourned the passing of a society and a system that he knew and found tolerable—and in many ways even pleasant—although at times terribly corrupt. On the other hand, he also admired the victors out of nationalistic pride. These were Vietnamese, like him, who had managed to defeat the most powerful nation on earth. He took personal satisfaction in their victory. It was as if, by winning, they had washed away his own hurt. He remembered the blue eyes of the American staring at him through the door of the helicopter; he had made no effort to pull him onboard and save him. Maybe the American was paralyzed by the horrifying sight, or perhaps he was afraid that he would be pulled to his own death. But Nam believed that the American was simply indifferent to his plight. He felt betrayed. The United States had let down not only South Vietnam but also him personally. He was bitter, angry, and resentful. Through the communist victory, he felt that he had somehow exacted a measure of revenge.

In the grip of these conflicting emotions, Nam went out to watch the arrival of troops from North Vietnam. They looked like they were in their mid-teens, with the sallow complexion of people who had spent months in the jungle. They did not storm in like belligerent conquerors, but marched like they were in a military parade. Perhaps the communist leaders had ordered this disciplined entry to reassure the population of their peaceful intentions. Still, the takeover was not entirely smooth. In some neighborhoods, remnants of the Saigon army had fired on the soldiers. There had been scattered casualties. Perhaps that was why Nam thought he saw fear in the eyes of the young troops: They may have been wondering whether they would become meaningless casualties in the first hours of peace. Looking at this long column of children, Nam's neighbors could not believe their eyes. Some said, "They're so young, and yet they've managed to defeat the South." Nam, too, stared in disbelief. The sight of armed children marching as victors into Saigon would remain stamped in his memory.

At the news of the surrender, people in the North and those in the South that had fought and supported the revolution exploded in celebration, overjoyed that the peace for which they had yearned and the victory for which they had fought had finally arrived. To my sister Thang and her family in Hanoi, the capitulation marked a happy beginning. But to middle-class Saigon residents, it was a calamity. From the balcony of her apartment, Yen could see some of her neighbors rushing around, trying to escape the communists. A man she knew raced by on his scooter with his wife and children. One of her neighbors came up and whispered, "Do you want to leave? It's still possible. All you have to do is go to the dock and get on a barge." Yen thought of the refugees who had fallen off these barges and drowned during the evacuation in Danang, and said, "No, that's too risky. Besides, I've decided to stay with my husband." In the first weeks after the communists' arrival, many people were still attempting to leave the country. Subordinates of Nam's father, confused and frightened, came to his house to discuss escape plans. They told him, "The Viet Cong haven't taken complete control of the Mekong Delta. Let's go there. We can find a boat and sail to the American Seventh Fleet." However, by this time Nam's father had lost heart and could not even contemplate such a dangerous move. My brother Giu also toyed with the idea of going to the delta to find a way out, but dropped it in the end, afraid of the anarchy that he might encounter along the way and of the possibility of getting captured by communist guerrillas. Others took the chance and managed to flee before communist control tightened.

On the morning of April 30, the North Vietnamese columns entered Saigon as if sauntering into an empty house. The victors' arrival was spearheaded by three tanks that raced toward the presidential palace to take it over. The crews, newly arrived from the North, did not know their way around town. With only a map to guide them, they got lost and had to ask for directions from two startled South Vietnamese. After a few false turns, they managed to get to the palace. They found it undefended, its grounds deserted, and its wrought-iron gate closed. The first tank knocked down the gate, and the other two followed close behind. The leader of the first tank leapt out and rushed inside with the Viet Cong flag. He saw General Minh, his aides, and members of his cabinet waiting for the arrival of the "other side" to hand over the reins of government. The officer asked how he could get to the roof, and one of the aides showed him the way. Reaching the top of the building, he ran to the flagpoles and hoisted the banner from the highest one to proclaim victory. The time was fifteen minutes past noon. Then more camouflaged tanks and trucks full of soldiers began pouring in, accompanied by youths on motorcycles who showed them the way, cheering and shouting, "Liberation, liberation!"

With the old police and army falling apart, social order started to break down. To control the city, all the communists had were their advance columns. Profiting from this power vacuum, prisoners broke out of jail. Armed soldiers robbed people at gunpoint. Looters ransacked businesses, empty homes, and American buildings. Yen saw a soldier hold up a man riding a motorcycle at gunpoint, stripping him of his money and other valuables. Afterward, she lived in fear that rogue soldiers would rob her family. From her balcony, she had a front-row view of the looting that went on downtown. In the morning, she saw crowds converge on the Brinks building that had housed apartments for American officers. It took them until late afternoon to empty it of every item it had. The pillage was good-natured, like a street festival. Even ordinarily law-abiding people joined the action. Somehow, the usual stigma of taking other people's possessions did not seem to apply to things that no longer belonged to anyone. The teenager living next door to Yen hauled back a swivel chair and an armload of canned food. Neighbors were urging one another to go and take part in the fun. One woman told Yen, "Come on, what are you waiting for? Go and get things before they're all gone." Another called up to her, saying that crowds had broken into the Khanh Hoi warehouse to loot, and urged her to get her share. Yen just laughed at these cheerful invitations. To her stealing was wrong, no matter what the circumstances were.

For a while, to safeguard my parents' modest house in the alley off Cong Ly Street, Yen would go back every day to check on things. The first time she returned, the deserted house looked desolate and depressing. She went through the drawers and found family photos that my parents had left behind in their haste to flee. Looking at faces she thought she would never see again, she felt very alone. She bundled up the pictures to take back to her apartment as souvenirs. My parents had told her to let cousin Bieu and his family move in if they needed to, and to stay there as long as they could, so she did not remove anything else.

Amid chaotic scenes of looting, prison breakouts, and frightened residents rushing around looking for a way to flee, more and more communist troops rolled in. At first, people felt apprehensive. But then crowds started to converge toward the boulevard in front of the old presidential palace to welcome the victors, mingle with them, or just to take a look, out of curiosity, at the troops that had vanquished a regime backed by American power. In a wild swing of emotion, many people, elated over the peaceful takeover, now hailed the newcomers as saviors coming in to usher in a new era, washing away the garbage of the past. The middle-class people were not as rhapsodic. Most were simply relieved that a final bloody assault had not occurred and that at least the war was over. Those living in working-class neighborhoods, their hopes and expectations raised, were the most excited. At last, they thought, their lot would improve. The new regime, the champion of the poor and downtrodden, would see to that. They hung the new flag from their houses and poured into the street to sing and dance. But the rejoicing was marred by ugly incidents. In practically every quarter of town, tough characters rushed into the homes of people against whom they harbored grudges and abused them. Others tried to bully their neighbors by masquerading as Viet Cong cadres, firing their weapons in the air. Still others acted as "hunting dogs," denouncing their friends, acquaintances, and colleagues to the new government to curry favor. Saigon residents would refer to all those who took advantage of the confusion as the "April 30 gang" or simply as "the opportunists," and would come to despise, loathe, and fear them with a passion.

The Viet Cong soldiers, meanwhile, became the toast of the town. People had expected the worst from them, but instead of the brutal troops painted by Saigon's propaganda, residents found them disciplined and polite. In their relief, many people felt buoyed by hope and filled with affection, and would stop the soldiers in the street to talk to them, curious and anxious to get to know them better. Many, like Nam, felt a nationalistic pride in their victory. Looking at the troops' spartan life-style and naive honesty, they also came to view the soldiers as selfless revolutionaries with unquestionable integrity. Right after they took over the city, soldiers fanned out in groups of two or three to visit families and earn the goodwill of the population. The residents received them warmly. Many invited them to stay and share meals. Once again, residents of working-class neighborhoods were the most hospitable, and went to great lengths to show their appreciation, killing chickens and ducks to regale their liberators.

The students at the Buddhist university in particular—many of whom had been jailed by President Thieu for their opposition to the war and to him personally—felt energized by the arrival of peace and eager to help usher in a new and better order. Nevertheless, for the middle class, the appearance of victorious peasants was a bitter pill to swallow. As if to rub salt into a raw wound, their foes turned out to be not a sophisticated army, all spit and polish, but a force of undernourished peasant youths wearing ill-fitting uniforms, pith helmets, and rubber sandals, goggling at Saigon's tall buildings, large villas, and wide boulevards. In other words, country bumpkins with little education. For their part, the soldiers could not believe that their enemy had given up the fight so easily. Whenever people came up to them to talk, the soldiers would ask with wonder in their voices, "You've got so much here, such marvelous things, such riches. Why didn't you fight harder to keep all this?"

Of the two groups, the soldiers handled the culture clash with a lot more ease than their middle-class opponents. They were unselfconscious about their lack of sophistication, and carried on as if they were still living in their jungle bivouacs or in their villages in the Red River Delta. When they first got to the old presidential palace, the soldiers quar-

tered there immediately removed their sandals and waded into the fountain to wash the dust off their faces, hands, and feet. They did not know
that the fountain was for decoration only; to them, it was just a good
source of fresh water. Instead of using the toilets, they dug latrines in
the garden. They built fires in the yard to cook their meals, and they
hung their wash on the wrought-iron fence to dry. Others billeted in
American buildings took down windows and chopped them up into firewood. In the following months, middle-class Saigonese would regale
one another with outrageous tales about the country ways of the troops
from the North, like the story of the soldier who put a fishing line down
a toilet because he thought that it was a small pond, or the one who got
scared and ran away when the door to an elevator suddenly opened.
Although the Saigon middle class made fun of their conquerors, deep
down they felt ashamed that they had been defeated by such yokels.
They could not understand that, in the end, commitment to a cause and
willingness to accept sacrifices in order to achieve victory meant more
than all the sophistication of Saigon's army and its American weaponry.

With the victory, the small number of cadres and guerrillas that had
operated underground appeared to take over government offices and city
quarters. When they emerged, they turned out to be the people one
least suspected of working for the communists. The woman who ran one
of the shops on Yen's street was a secret agent, married to a high-ranking Viet Cong cadre operating in War Zone D near Saigon. Later, this
woman would become one of the leaders in the neighborhood. She told
Yen about her husband, and how she used to make repeated trips into
the war zone to bring supplies and information. Getting to know people like this underground cadre opened Yen's eyes. For the first time,
those she used to call Viet Cong (but now had to refer to as revolutionaries or liberators) ceased to be caricatures in Saigon government propaganda and appeared in flesh and blood. They turned out to be normal
human beings, with strengths and foibles like everyone else. The cadres
rarely boasted about their pasts; they were simply too preoccupied with
the present to think about what they had done. But once in a while,
they would reminisce about the war. Two of the women cadres in Yen's
Workers' Union had been guerrillas operating near Saigon, planting
mines and booby traps of grenades. Many times, they were attacked by
American helicopter gunships. "There was nothing I hated worse than
the helicopters," one of them said to Yen. "They'd circle around and
around right over my head, and then they'd point their guns down and
keep firing and firing at me."

With the end of the war, the tangled web of relationships between the communist and noncommunist sides was revealed to its full complexity. People found out that practically everyone in their circle of acquaintances had relatives in the communist ranks. My family was not the only one with siblings, uncles, aunts, cousins, nieces, and nephews on the opposite side of the fence. Our situation was the rule, rather than an exception. Even generals in the former Saigon regime had communist relatives, including Prime Minister Tran Thien Khiem and General Duong Van Minh. My brother Giu found out that two of his wife's aunts with mysterious whereabouts were married to important Viet Cong cadres. But the relatives who arrived with the communists paid little attention to family ties: None of my relatives on the winning side did anything to help those on the losing side who now came under scrutiny. There was nothing they could have done to change the situation anyway. Trying to help would only have exposed them and their own families needlessly to suspicion and perhaps even punishment. Besides, at the beginning at least, they themselves believed that a short stint at *hoc tap*—indoctrination—would not only be harmless but allow their southern relatives, who had been so steeped in the Saigon regime's political culture, to rectify their thinking and become better citizens. After all, they themselves had regularly gone through many *hoc tap* sessions to learn about this and that policy, and had not found them oppressive. So, despite their connection to influential cadres, most of my family members who had worked for the Saigon regime could not escape from being sent away for indoctrination.

With the country at peace and no longer divided into two enemy states, travel to the north and south became possible for the first time in decades. This free flow had a tremendous psychological impact. For people who during French colonial days had to have a passport to go from one region to another, and who were kept apart by the demilitarized zone during the Vietnam War, it was exhilarating to be able to circulate freely from one end of the country to another. Reunification made the population feel as one again. Families could be reunited, and ties that had been severed were re-established. With roads safe from war, each year, relatives from Ha Tinh, the province from which my ancestors fled over a century ago, now travel to Van Dinh, my family's native village, to worship at an ancestral temple built for all five branches of my clan. They are joined by other relatives who come in from Hanoi. When I go back to Vietnam now, I can visit relatives stretching from near the Chinese border to Hanoi, Ha Tinh, and Saigon.

The communists, focusing on their drive to victory, had not worked out a blueprint on what to do once they won, but they moved quickly to cement their control. The first leaders to arrive in Saigon to install a temporary government were men who had directed the final campaign. One of them was Le Duc Tho, the negotiator at the Paris peace talks who had shared the Nobel peace prize with Henry Kissinger and a member of the Politburo. On May 1, they set up a military committee to govern Saigon until complete security could be restored. To Saigon residents, the first signs were encouraging. The new leaders proclaimed a policy of reconciliation with former foes. No retaliation took place, even against the former Saigon army. The widely predicted bloodbath failed to materialize. The only crackdown was against criminals. Those caught in the act were swiftly brought to public trial, condemned to death, and executed on the spot. In my parents' old neighborhood, my nephew Minh witnessed the trial and execution of two criminals. After the cadre read out the sentence, he asked whether anyone in the audience had any objection. No one breathed a word, and the culprits were shot right then and there. This draconian justice worked, and crime immediately dropped. The tough approach, combined with the initial goodwill of Saigon residents, allowed the government to restore order quickly. Also, people were tired of the turmoil and wanted nothing more than to see life return to normal. In this atmosphere, no one tried to challenge the new authority. Everyone did as they were told.

But normalcy was not what it used to be. Things had begun to change right after liberation. First, Saigon got a new name: Ho Chi Minh City, which even the most sympathetic residents hated. New flags flew over the buildings. New plaques appeared on government ministries and offices. Newspapers, movies, and music all changed as the government stepped up its efforts to destroy the old culture and impose a new one—the same purposeful, but restricted and politicized culture that had stifled creativity in the North. New ways of organizing and controlling the population took effect. Saigon residents were taken aback by the level of government intrusion. First, the cadres visited every family in the city to take a political census, largely to ferret out the people most likely to oppose the government. At this early stage, the communists were paranoid about sabotage, and in particular about secret agents planted by the Americans to overthrow their regime. In this, they shared a belief with the middle class: that the Americans would not give up the South so easily and would scheme to get it back. Another purpose of the census was to find out who among the residents could be used to help the cadres carry out government orders and policies.

Like everyone else in her neighborhood, Yen had to give detailed information not only on herself, her husband, and her children, but also on her close relatives. Yen's family report did not look good. Most of her family were living abroad, and, worse still, many had fled with the Americans. To be safe, she did not list me, afraid that my marriage to an American would make her situation difficult. The report for Do, her husband, looked a lot better, with many relatives in the revolution, including his oldest brother, who had joined the Viet Minh in 1945. After they finished confessing about their families, Yen and Do had to submit detailed accounts about themselves. From these, the cadres would decide how to group them. Do had been in charge of technical operations in the sugar mill, which earned him the classification of tech-nician—a neutral one, because it implied that he had not been involved in the management and exploitation of workers. Yen had labored as a seamstress to supplement their income; now, this job, taken up in des-peration, gave her an advantage. It prompted the cadres to list her as a worker—a trustworthy and respected figure in the eyes of the govern-ment. In spite of her family ties, these classifications earned her and her husband peace. Do did not have to report for political indoctrination, and Yen escaped harassment.

My nephew Minh had a harder time because of his family. After lib-eration, he had moved back to his parents' farm, living by himself on the forsaken place. Just to be safe, he had burned the letter of recommenda-tion from Chase Manhattan that had done him no good anyway during the last hours of the evacuation. At first, no one bothered him, and he did not feel afraid. But then his neighbors denounced him, telling the local cadres that his family had fled with the Americans. The cadres summoned him to their office. They could not understand why he had not left with his family, and suspected that he was a secret agent plant-ed by the United States. They wanted to know where his orders were coming from, asking him over and over, "Who's giving you secret instructions?" They did not detain him, but every week they would ask him to return to answer more questions. They made him write a report on his background twelve times, a trick to trip him up. Any inconsis-tency would have been taken as a sign that he was lying.

After about a month of this, his case went to the District Re-educa-tion Committee, which decided who should be interned for indoctrina-tion. The cadres there were members of the secret police. Stepping into their office, Minh saw that they were all armed. A dossier on his father lay on the table. They said, "We know everything there's to know about your family. So, don't try to lie. If you tell the truth, the revolution will be lenient with you." Minh protested, "I've nothing to hide." They questioned him more, but then let him go. They did not call him back again, although they kept an eye on him. Some nights he would look up to see an agent standing at his window, watching him. After a while, the cadres seized the farm. Minh volunteered for the Vanguard Youth Corps and left the village. Years later, after things had loosened up, he got to know two of the village cadres who used to question him about his background. When he asked them why they had given him such a hard time, they said, "We had to. We had no choice. Your family had sided with the Americans and had fled with them." Minh would tell me in 1995, "You know, once I got to know these people, I found out that they're nice and normal—like you and me. They were harsh only because they had to carry out a harsh policy."

The Vanguard Youth Corps, as its name implies, went where others would be afraid to tread. It got involved in projects fit for prison work gangs. The government used it to rebuild roads and bridges and to clear new land for cultivation—priorities for a country recovering from the devastation of war. In a system that glorified manual labor, membership in the corps was like a badge of honor. The graduates inspired trust—after all, they had proven their mettle and dedication in incredible hardships. For Minh, the corps was a logical choice. It gave him a way to dispel the cloud of suspicion that had been hanging over his head, an opportunity to establish his credentials with the new regime. It also gave him food and shelter, at a time when he had lost his farm and could not find work in a sinking economy. After joining, Minh trekked to Ban Me Thuot in the central highlands—the scene of the first attack that had led to the fall of Saigon—to build a bridge and a road. Living and working conditions were primitive, and the work was backbreaking. It was also dangerous, with unexploded ordnance still littering the landscape, ready to detonate at the touch of a shovel or the pressure of a foot. He and his comrades were housed in huts set in the jungle. Their food was mostly rice and fish sauce, and soup that had nothing in it but salt and water. But at least they got enough to eat. At night, they slept on the log floor. Diseases were prevalent, especially malaria.

During the day, the corps members cut down trees and worked on the road and the bridge. The most dangerous job was to roll logs down the hillside. From above, workers would lower a log down slowly with ropes. Below, another group would plant stakes in the ground to keep it from crashing downhill. In this manner, the lumber would be moved slowly, one at a time, a yard or so at a time, toward the site of the new bridge. One day, while Minh was laboring below planting the stakes, the workers above let go of a log too soon. It rolled and crushed Minh's hands. Medical care was so primitive that Minh could not get an X-ray to see whether any bones had been broken. Neither could he get medication for the pain. He just put up with it and waited for it to subside. With characteristic good humor, Minh described the incident to me in 1995: "After my hands got crushed, they looked as flat as a sheet of paper. But the next day, they swelled back to their normal size." The new bridge spanned a creek whose water reached only to knee level when the project began, but no corps of engineers had studied it beforehand. In the monsoon season, the creek turned into a raging torrent. The log bridge that Minh and his comrades had almost killed themselves building was washed away. This project was typical of the disorganization and lack of planning after the war, due to a shortage of engineers and the numerous priorities that taxed the resources of the government.

Discouraged by the hard work and poor living conditions, Minh resigned and returned to Saigon. But his stint in the corps gave him the credentials he needed to find work with a state-run enterprise, carrying and lifting heavy bags and boxes of supplies. At this time, to encourage the clearing of new land for cultivation, the state gave each enterprise a piece of land to farm. The income from the land would go to the enterprise. Minh's company obtained a couple of acres in the Plain of Reeds. Each year, each worker had to spend ten days working on this land. It was an honor to go. But the workers saw no benefit in this for themselves and made only half-hearted efforts when they got there.

Yet Minh volunteered to go to this bleak area for two years. His manager had promised to send him back to school if he put in such a long stint. His friends told him he was a fool to take this cadre at his word. "You'll never come back. You'll get stuck there, and you'll rot there," they told him. Minh brushed them aside and left, determined to see this through. He moved into the hut that was going to be his home for two long years. The work was arduous. Minh had to clear the brush off the land. Most of the time, he was wading in muck; once he was bitten by a venomous snake. Another hazard put an end to his stay. He stepped on a razor-sharp piece of bomb shrapnel. It sliced through his foot and left a deep gash. Without proper medication, the wound got infected and his foot got so painfully swollen that Minh could barely walk. Finally, he asked for permission to return to Saigon. (My nephew had been lucky. The piece of shrapnel could have been a live bomb. In countless villages, an unknown number of peasants were getting maimed and killed by the lethal legacy of the war as they tried to put their land back into cultivation.)

The government was not allowing people to receive money or supplies from abroad, so teenagers like Minh, left without family support, had to do what they could to survive. He became a stevedore in the port of Saigon. He worked there for two years, loading and unloading heavy bags of cement by carrying them on his back. Then his life took a turn for the better. He got a job with a state agency that was making an inventory of military supplies left behind by the Americans and the old Saigon army to see what could be salvaged as scrap metal. The head cadre, a man with only a grade-school education, took a liking to him because he was bright and had a lot of good ideas.

As part of his job, Minh visited every base and warehouse from the tip of Ca Mau to the former demilitarized zone. He found huge stockpiles of tank and airplane spare parts still in unopened crates. He found ammunition piled up to the ceiling in depots. His discovery made him shake his head in amazement. The old Saigon government was always screaming that the Americans were abandoning it and cutting off aid and materiel, yet here was this mountain of supplies. Eventually, as government control loosened up, Minh would go into business for himself, buying and reselling scrap metal. In a country awash with old military equipment, but with a shortage of steel and iron, he had a steady source and many customers. Then, when the building boom hit Saigon in the early 1990s, his business took off.

In the old days before peace, every family was an island, devoting time and energy only to its members. Now everyone had to reach out and get involved with their community or the collective. Participation was supposed to be voluntary, but no one dared to refuse. Every Saturday and Sunday, residents had to help clean up their streets. They also had to take part in a labor project. Many Saigonese were mobilized to build a canal near Saigon. Once a week, they had to spend a whole day, working from morning to dusk, at the canal site. Everyone chafed at having to go out on a weekend and wade in the mud. They saw no glory in these manual tasks, only drudgery. Also, by this time, the cadres' contempt for the middle class—whom they viewed as selfish and morally corrupt— had dispelled the goodwill that people originally had toward the new government. So, those drafted for the job dragged their feet and tried to do only the bare minimum.

These communal projects were just one of the many facets of life that had been imported from the North. Another was the network of popular associations and residents' organizations that drew everyone into the fold—for control, for indoctrination, but also for mutual help and support. Like all the residents in her neighborhood, Yen had to join a cell, which was simply a source of free labor for the cadres and a tool to help them execute government policies. At first, before the security police became functional, when her turn came, she had to stand guard at night for two to three hours at a stretch to keep watch in her neighborhood. Then she got a new responsibility, selling bread to her neighbors. Every morning at four o'clock, she would join a couple of her cell colleagues collecting fresh loaves at the bakery. By six, Yen was sitting at a table in the street, ready to sell to neighbors so they could have their breakfast before they left for work. Rationing had been introduced, and each time she sold a loaf, she had to mark the sale in the buyer's coupon book. Yen had this job until the bakeries ran out of flour and had to shut down. Then she got the responsibility of selling foodstuffs at the local state store. The hours were long and unpredictable. Whenever merchandise arrived, she had to go and help with the sale. Sometimes a supply of fish would arrive at ten o'clock in the evening, and someone would summon her to deal with the crowd that was already lining up to snap up the food. Sometimes she had to spend the night at the store to keep an eye on the merchandise. Yet as a "volunteer," Yen received no compensation for her labor.

Besides helping in the cell, my sister also had to perform chores for the Workers' Union and the Women's Association. As a former seamstress and a woman, she had to join both. She had less and less time for herself and her family. On top of all this, she had to go to an endless series of meetings. At first, these took place every night, and no one dared to skip them. There, she had to sit and listen while the cadres praised the government and its policies and condemned the former "puppet" regime and the American "imperialists." Or they would talk about all the good things the revolution had accomplished, such as freeing women from oppression and making them equal to men. The job of the cadres was not just to lecture, but also to find out what the residents thought. To discover the real attitude of the people in the neighborhood, the cadres asked each one to pick an issue that had struck him or her the most and write a report on it. Yen wrote on the liberation of women. To her, this was a topic that carried the least political baggage. She said simply that the liberation of women had a personal meaning for her, because it allowed her to get out of the kitchen and go out into the world. The cadres accepted her report without comment.

Initially, the cadres were native southerners. These were hardened revolutionaries; many had fought in the heavily bombed and shelled area called the Iron Triangle by the Americans. In the glow of the first weeks of peace, when the new government tried to be conciliatory and to gain the people's goodwill, Saigon residents found these cadres—who had not been exposed to decades of communist indoctrination like those in the North—not only admirable but also reasonable and flexible. Also, Saigonese could identify with them more because they were fellow southerners. Later, after the country was formally reunified under one communist government in June 1976—with Hanoi as the capital—more and more cadres were sent from the north to the south. They were also true believers, but were a different breed: more rigid, more narrow-minded, more prone to parrot the Party line and believe everything the state told them. Many were poor peasants with little education. By now, with Saigon under control, these cadres did not feel they had to hide their contempt for the middle class and referred to them all indiscriminately as "puppets" of the Americans. At first, the middle class was too cowed to protest, but after a year, they became bolder and less afraid, and loudly objected. The cadres had to soften their approach and to drop the hateful term. "We're all Vietnamese," they now declared, "let's stop this distinction and division." Even among the cadres, those that were better educated felt discouraged by their ignorant colleagues. One of them said to Yen, "It's awful. Some of these people can barely read."

Not all the cadres were ignorant country folk. Among the first officials from the North to arrive in Saigon was Am, a doctor who had married Thinh, one of Uncle Chinh's daughters, and who had accompanied military units into the central highlands during the last months of the war. By this time, our cousin Bieu had moved into my parents' old home. When Am first met Bieu, his brother-in-law, at this two-room house, he was astounded that Bieu could live in such splendid privacy, having the whole place for himself and his family, without having to share it with at least one or two more households. (With so much housing stock left behind by the Americans and Vietnamese who had fled, the communists did not force the middle class to share their living quarters with other families, as they had done in Hanoi.) My brother-in-law Hau also arrived some time later to take a look at the cash crop industry in the south, in his capacity as head of his agricultural research institute. Wishful-thinking relatives, seeing him move around in a chauffeur-driven car, immediately told each other that he was an important cadre who could intervene and help them out if they ever fell into trouble with the new regime. That, of course, was far from the truth, as Hau was only a tech-nician with no political power. My cousin Hien, who had disappeared to join the Viet Minh in 1945, also showed up in Saigon, as the tech-nician in charge of raising rice production for the south by clearing more land for cultivation and adopting better growing methods. This first trickle of cadres from the north would become a flood, and gradually would displace the native southern communists. Eventually, northerners would end up holding most of the reins of power in Saigon, creating resentment among the southern population. This wholesale transfer of government and army personnel would change the character of the city.

Surrounded by the riches of the south, the newcomers from the north quickly gave in to temptation. Saigon residents became scornful when soldiers who had impressed them with their integrity right after the takeover began to loot abandoned private homes and businesses, taking anything of value with them when they headed back north. Then, as more and more cadres arrived in Saigon to staff the new government, they, too, became acquisitive. The north, with its bare shelves and severe shortages, had little to offer in the way of goods. But the south was still brimming with the consumer products that had been imported over the decades with generous American aid, items that northerners did not even know existed and had not even dreamed of, and now coveted. Even native southern cadres who moved to Saigon to staff the new administration alongside their northern comrades could not resist the lure of money. At first, Saigonese thought that the government, army, and police personnel would be impervious to bribes. But they quickly found out that, through the proper intermediary, they could buy their way out of any jam. Just as in the old days, with the right sum of money, they could bypass regulations, get some official documents, or avoid harassment—and later on even get on a boat to flee the country while secret policemen looked the other way. Those Saigon residents who still had plenty of gold and dollars, the unofficial legal tender, were all too willing to give cadres, policemen, and officers the money they needed to buy to their hearts' content and to acquire a more comfortable life-style.

Psychologically, cadres and soldiers alike were ready to give in to temptation. They reasoned that after making sacrifices and putting up with hardships for decades, they deserved to take it easy and to enjoy the fruits of their long and hard struggle. They thought they would be fools not to, especially when most of their colleagues and even some leaders were grabbing real estate, gold, and dollars right and left. Old-time true revolutionaries like Hau would manage to keep their integrity and dedication, but they would be in the minority. (The cynicism would lead some northerners to tell me in 1993, "Do you know who the real losers in this war are? They're not the supporters of the old Saigon regime. The real losers are the families who sacrificed their sons so that the revolution would win. They're getting empty honors, and nothing else, while the cadres are getting rich." With this everyone-for-himself attitude, the communist system would start to weaken. Instead of "everything for the Party and for the state," the new thinking became "the Party and the state be damned." It is no wonder that the young people nowadays, even sons and daughters of Party officials, are disenchanted. The cadres are no longer models of integrity, dedication, and selflessness, but corrupt officials.)

When I talked about this change in attitude with an acquaintance in Hanoi in 1995, he explained to me, "During the war, we had a cause and an ideal to sustain us. We fought nobly. We accepted incredible sacrifices. But once the war ended, we lost our sense of mission—our moral compass. Even our soldiers became thieves in Saigon. They started to steal, taking even light bulbs and electric fuses back to the north." As the corruption spread, Saigon residents grumbled that the revolution that had promised to usher in a new era of clean and just government had become as venal as the old regime it had attacked. Yen's husband Do was one of those who became disenchanted. After the takeover, well-trained technicians like Do and my brother Giu were sought after. The communist cadres, long on political training and short on technical knowledge, did not know how to keep factories like the sugar mill and the cement plant going. A cadre came to see Do right after the takeover and persuaded him to stay on as an advisor. At this time, Do was still fired up with nationalism and the desire to help the country get back on its feet. He was also impressed with the top leaders coming from Hanoi. While many of the rank-and-file cadres were incompetent, the people at the top were bright and savvy. That first Tet, he had the chance to meet the minister of industry, who had arrived in Saigon on an inspection tour. The minister, courteous and extremely solicitous, appealed to the technicians' professional pride and especially to their nationalism and emotions. He talked to them about the needs of the country, and how they could help the nation prosper and make life better for all the people.

But the initial glow quickly faded. Do became frustrated with the cadres assigned to the mill and with the new staff. A man with an explosive temper, he could not tolerate their incompetence. He would scream in their faces and tell them that they were stupid, that they were fit only for herding buffaloes and horses and not for running a mill. The first real blow for Do came with the conversion of the currency. It wiped out his savings. For a man who pinched pennies and half-starved his family in order to pile up millions in the bank, it was a loss from which he could not recover. Watching the cumulation of his lifelong efforts evaporate into nothing, he felt devastated. He said that he had saved his money in order to send his children abroad for study. Now, this dream was finished. Not only that, because of Yen's family ties, it had become apparent that they would not even have a chance to study in meaningful fields at the university and to have jobs that would utilize their talent—privileges reserved only for children of families with a sterling political background. He felt responsible for having destroyed their future, and he berated himself for his decision to stay behind, forcing his family to do likewise. He became despondent.

Eventually, he became shaky—his head jerked uncontrollably from side to side, and his hands trembled. He resigned from his job, but the mill management would not let him go. They tried to induce him to stay, and offered to admit him into the Communist Party. But he was not interested. He told them, "I'm old and feeble now. I can't contribute much. Besides, all my life I've never joined any party. I'm not going to change now." Determined to leave, he kept pressing for retirement. Finally, he asked for an examination by a council of doctors, who confirmed his medical condition and stated emphatically that he could not carry on. He was allowed to retire. In his last years, he became so bitter and disillusioned that he would not set foot outside his apartment. A heavy smoker, he died of lung cancer a few years ago.

The currency conversion happened suddenly, to catch everyone off guard and prevent people from subverting it. Its purpose was to wipe out the savings of the middle and upper middle class, and therefore reduce them to the level of the poor in order to achieve economic equality. Late one night, the cadre in charge of the neighborhood summoned Yen and other cell members and told them to visit each household and list the people living there, even those who were only temporary residents. He said this had to be done right away, although he did not tell them why. There were over ninety families for them to check. Most residents cooperated, but some would glare at Yen and refuse to give her a complete list. It took her until one o'clock in the morning to finish her rounds. She handed in the lists and went home, still puzzled by the whole thing. The next morning, like a thunderbolt, there was an announcement that the government would take the old currency out of circulation, and that each household was entitled to exchange a fixed sum of money based on the number of people living there. The ratio was 500 piasters of the old currency for one piaster of the new one. If a household had more money than it was allowed to exchange, the rest would be worthless.

In the neighborhood, people were in an uproar. But there was nothing they could do but line up at the exchange site to turn in their old money for the new. Several people carried large bags stuffed with bills, yet no one gave them a second look. Some got so mad that they started to toss their surplus money on the ground. Even criminals did not bother to show up to rob the long line of people. One of Yen's neighbors joked, "I've never seen Saigon so secure. Here we are, standing in line with tons of money, but no one's trying to grab it from us." In the end, each household could get at most 200 piasters in new money—actually a big sum considering how much each piaster could buy—even if the number of people living in it entitled them to more. Some residents, however, still managed to get more than the maximum allowed, through secret bargaining with the cadres in charge.

This conversion was only the first volley in the campaign to enforce economic equality. Subsequently, there were more exchanges—to the point that even if Yen could recover all of her husband's original savings from the bank now, they would be worth next to nothing. The conversions impoverished those foolish enough to keep their savings in local currency, but not those who had been clever enough to keep most of their assets in gold and dollars. Gold never lost its popularity, and remained the currency of choice for transactions like buying passage on a boat to flee the country. It became even more popular when galloping inflation eroded the value of paper money. Even now, with inflation tamed, people still prefer to buy and sell major assets like land and houses with gold, rather than with Ho Chi Minh banknotes. The dollar, too, remained attractive as the unofficial legal tender.

The next move for the government was to smash businessmen and entrepreneurs. This happened in two waves. At first, the big capitalists were targeted. The biggest of them all—Hoang Kim Quy, who had been known as the king of iron and steel—was arrested and sentenced to twenty years in jail, because he had provided the barbed wire used by the Saigon army. The second wave came in 1978 and focused on merchants. To prevent businessmen from dispersing their goods, the crackdown came like a bolt out of the blue. Cholon, the Chinese section of Saigon, was the hardest hit. Commerce had been its lifeblood, and practically every family there was engaged in it. Workers were mobilized as foot soldiers in this "anti-bourgeois" campaign, because they would not be inclined to feel sympathetic toward people more privileged than they. Young people were also recruited for this purpose, because they were most likely to carry out orders without hesitation.

As a dock worker, my nephew Minh got the tap on the shoulder to go into action. Accompanied by the cadres, he and his colleagues fanned out and invaded every shop and place of business to make an exhaustive inventory of the merchandise. Nothing escaped their vigilance. They would find everything—even valuables hidden inside pillows. Every item—soap, shoes, sunglasses, nuts, and bolts—went on the list. Nothing was too big or too small. Then all the items were seized and the businesses shut down. What the cadres had not counted on was the utter indifference of the workers and youths to both sides in this campaign. Their attitude was, "Pox on both your houses." The foot soldiers had no sympathy for the merchants, but neither did they have any sympathy for the state. When the cadres asked them to move the seized items to a collection point, they would casually drop things on the ground, damaging or destroying them in the process, or they would pile them up in the open under the monsoon rain. They would tell each other, "We're not getting anything out of this. Everything's going to the state anyway. So, who cares?"

Vietnamese merchants such as Mrs. An, a friend of Giu's wife and the owner of a large business, did not fare any better. In the sweep to convert the south to socialism, she became a target. One day, she received a notice asking her to attend a neighborhood meeting for business owners. At the meeting, a cadre got up and started to condemn the merchants, calling them exploiters, and threatening them. Then he passed out a form for each business owner to sign, voluntarily surrendering all his or her assets to the state. She signed. While she was at the meeting, a group of about thirty people led by a cadre arrived at her house. For two days, they systematically searched her residence. They did not miss anything that she might have used to hide her valuables. They overturned her potted plants and sifted through the dirt. They dumped out her bags of charcoal. They checked lamps and lamp shades. They opened up light switches. They slashed her mattresses. They checked the drain pipes and the garbage. They left her house in complete shambles, but found nothing. Before this happened, she had gotten rid of personal possessions she thought might get her into trouble, such as books and music tapes dating from pre-liberation days. In the end, she was allowed to stay in her house, but the government seized all her other assets.

In Yen's area, the campaign was not as harsh or intense. The merchants here were small shop owners, whose businesses could not compare in size and wealth to those of the Chinese or to that of Mrs. An.
For this campaign, the cadres summoned all the cells in my sister's neighborhood. Yen and the other inventory takers had to go to every store and
make an exhaustive list of the merchandise. They never went alone, but
always in teams of three. Knowing the others might be watching, each
one felt compelled to do a thorough job. For over a month, they visited
all the shops and listed every single item of merchandise, down to each
and every pair of costume earrings.

After they lost their businesses, the merchants had to face a second
hurdle. Those classified as criminals who owed a blood debt to the people—for having aided the former Saigon regime in the war or for having
ruthlessly exploited their workers—were kicked out of their homes and
sent to a New Economic Zone, where they were given a piece of land,
a hut with no walls, doors, or windows, a rice subsidy to tide them over
until they could harvest their crop, mosquito nets, and blankets. Then
the government seized their houses. This created panic among the merchants, many of whom started to flee the country, swelling the number
of boat people taking to the sea. Others were able to bribe the cadres
who had the power to decide who could stay in Saigon and who would
have to resettle in a New Economic Zone. When I returned to Saigon
in 1993, an acquaintance pointed out to me the house of one of the
cadres involved in the campaign who had gotten very rich from bribes.
This cadre and her husband later on became too grasping and corrupt for
the government to ignore. In one of the periodic clean-up campaigns,
usually window-dressing affairs that catch only the smaller fish, the
government indicted them and took away their assets.

By the time it finished smashing the merchants, the government had
taken over some of the choicest real estate in Saigon. These properties,
along with those seized earlier from those that had fled the country,
gave the government a huge holding of land and houses to parcel out to
its cadres. This distribution would give rise to yet more corruption and
lead to bitter squabbles over who got what. In other parts of the south,
wholesale transfer of residential properties into the hands of the state
and then to the cadres was also taking place. Although the new system
was supposed to be egalitarian, with no one much better off than their
neighbors, many cadres now seemed to live like kings, ensconced in the
fine homes of businessmen who had been sent to the New Economic
Zones or those of affluent residents who had fled.

With commerce killed off, downtown Saigon took on a sad and

abandoned look. Shuttered stores lined the streets. Here and there, a few businesses continued to operate, such as hotels, cafes, and restaurants. But they were no longer privately owned. They were state enterprises run by bureaucrats. Their clients came from the small community of foreigners, the ranks of cadres who had gotten fat from bribes, or those middle-class residents who still had plenty of gold. No one else had the money to patronize them. Besides commerce and industry, the state also took over food production. It pressed peasants to join cooperatives in April 1978 and to deliver their surplus crops to the government at official prices. This was the biggest economic blunder of the postwar period. Unlike farmers in the north whose villages had known a more communal tradition, the peasants in the south, descendants of pioneering settlers in what had once been Cambodian land, were much more independent and individualistic. Also, life in the Mekong Delta was not harsh like that in the Red River Delta, and the safety net that the cooperatives offered did not appeal to southern peasants, who could be self-sufficient. The southern farmers, resentful at being forced into cooperatives and angry at having to deliver their crops to the government at an artificial, low price, caused food supplies to plummet. To control food distribution, the government set up checkpoints to curb private trade in commodities. As in the north, rationing and coupon books were introduced, and how much in basic staples each family could buy depended on the number and age of people officially registered with the police as part of their household. This householding system had a security purpose as well: It allowed the police to keep track of who belonged where and who was doing what in the neighborhood.

The heavy-handed state control that clamped down over the economy brought disastrous results. With peace, the standard of living declined, rather than rose. Shortages became serious. Part of the problem was due to the embargo that the United States had imposed—out of resentment against a former foe, but mostly out of anger at Hanoi's stubborn refusal to help clarify the status of those Americans listed as missing in action. When all of America's friends followed its lead, Vietnam became isolated. The embargo restricted Vietnam's foreign trade and denied the country access to Western aid and investments and international credit. Even with international help, it would have been difficult to get the country back on its feet. Without it, the task became herculean. The economy shriveled. The embargo caused a lot of damage, cutting off materials and spare parts to factories that had been built with American know-how and forcing them to shut down. It also choked off mundane supplies like flour, and bakeries that used to churn out the wonderful French baguettes had to close their doors. In 1993, during my first visit back home, the embargo was still in force, although Hanoi had been cooperating in the search for American MIAs. Vietnamese were puzzled by its long duration and harshness. They would say, "Why are we being singled out for punishment for so long? There were thousands of Americans missing in action in Germany and Korea after those wars, but the United States did not take revenge against them. Why us?"

The year 1979 was a severe strain on the new Vietnamese regime. War had erupted again. The year before, in the area bordering Cambodia, the Khmer Rouge were shelling Vietnamese villages and crossing over to massacre peasants. The brazen attacks pulled the people together and for a while diverted their attention from their own distress. Popular anger boiled over, stoked by newspaper articles and exhibits of photos showing Khmer Rouge atrocities. The young in particular were outraged and many volunteered for the army. Minh and his friends rushed to the recruitment center to enlist. But while his friends were accepted, Minh found himself rejected. Being in the army was a privilege, reserved only for those whose background was acceptable. Because his family had fled to America, his was not.

Unable to prevail upon the Khmer Rouge to stop their attacks, the Vietnamese army invaded Cambodia in December 1978, and drove into the capital of Phnom Penh practically unchecked. Minh's friends who took part in the operation would tell him later on that they had won every battle they had fought. With Cambodia under its control, Vietnam ousted the Khmer Rouge and installed its own protégés. Vietnam got no credit for ending the reign of terror of the Khmer Rouge, during which over one million Cambodians had been murdered. Instead, it was condemned for having invaded a neighbor. It became the world's pariah. My relatives in Saigon and Hanoi still chafe at the feeling that Vietnam was not acknowledged for putting an end to the atrocities, which no other country in the world had tried to stop. Continuing Khmer Rouge resistance kept Vietnam bogged down in a quagmire. It finally withdrew in 1989. The official tally put its casualties at 25,000 dead and 100,000 wounded.

The negative reaction did not stop at verbal brickbats. Thailand and China armed the Khmer Rouge to keep the Vietnamese tied down. And China invaded the North to teach Vietnam a lesson in February 1979. Because it now viewed Vietnam as a Soviet ally, and because of its rapprochement with China, the United States did not react. The quickness with which the Chinese had come across the frontier reminded the Vietnamese of how vulnerable they were to the colossus north of them. The fear of being invaded and overwhelmed by the more numerous Chinese stirred once again. A cousin of mine who lived in Lang Son recalled how he woke up one morning, looked out his window, and saw a horde of Chinese soldiers already ensconced in his street. However, the Chinese army, which had not fought a war in decades, performed poorly. Instead of teaching the Vietnamese a lesson, the Chinese got a bloody nose. Suffering heavy casualties and humiliating reverses, but unwilling to admit failure, they haughtily declared that they had achieved their aim and withdrew. Yet their brief foray had created havoc in border towns like Lang Son. Vietnamese who saw the destruction claimed that the Chinese army had devastated the area. My brother-in-law Hau, after a trip to the border region, would shake his head in amazement at the brutal tactics of the Chinese and say, "The Chinese are a lot more destructive than the Americans. In all the years that the Americans dropped bombs on us, they never leveled an entire region, but the Chinese did."

Without American aid, it was natural that the standard of living in the South would drop to the level that its resources could support, but Vietnam's isolation, combined with the draining war with Cambodia and then with China, a series of bad harvests, and the failure of the cooperatives, plunged life into a depth of misery that was beyond all expectations. In 1979, the economy hit bottom. According to rumors about that period, rather than selling to the state, angry peasants in the South fed their surplus rice to their pigs or even, in some instances, burned it to show their resentment—aggravating the food crisis. All my relatives told me that 1979 ranks as one of the worst years in their lives. There was a frightful shortage of rice, to the point that people had to eat *bo bo*, a tough grain normally fed to horses. In a country that had once easily been able to feed itself, malnutrition became rampant. There were reports of famine in some areas. Even government workers, with steady jobs and steady incomes, had trouble feeding their families. In the space of just four years, Vietnam became destitute, and its per capita income sank to the second lowest in the world. The communists had won the war, but they were losing the peace.

Not just food, but everything else became scarce. Consumer goods disappeared. Even common things like toothpaste and soap were hard to find. Hospitals ran low on supplies; common drugs such as aspirin became almost as precious as gold. Morale—which had not been high to begin with—plunged to an all-time low. With their expectations dashed, people became demoralized and sullen. Vietnamese refugees in America, watching their homeland sink deeper and deeper into agony, felt hopeful that the U.S. policy of economic and political isolation would impoverish the country to the point that the people would rise up and overthrow the government. Some refugee friends and acquaintances used to say to me, "Let's strangle those communists until they croak."

The communists did not croak, but they did make many concessions to avert disaster, and while the people of Vietnam suffered terribly, they did not revolt. The dark malaise and the economic collapse, which stood in stark contrast to neighboring Asian countries that were booming, forced the government to reconsider its policies. Also, as the economy sank, people started to take things in their own hands to survive, breaking down the fence that the state had erected around their livelihood. They began to wheel and deal, and private trade, which the communists had not succeeded in choking off completely, expanded. This spontaneous breaking away and the positive results of a few cautious reforms led the government to begin loosening its stranglehold over the economy in 1979. The next year, the government, in a tacit admission that its cooperative policy had failed, moved to give the peasants more freedom. In the end, instead of just tinkering with a dying system, the government decided to unshackle the economy from socialist dogma, allow the free market to operate once again, scrap the cooperatives, and throw open the country's door to foreign investments. It was 1989, the year when communist regimes were falling all over Eastern Europe. Even true believers like my sister Thang and her husband—shocked by the disintegration of the Soviet Union, long upheld as the apotheosis of socialism, and by the news of popular uprisings toppling one communist government after another—recognized that there was no way socialist policies that had failed so miserably in Eastern Europe could succeed in a much poorer place like Vietnam. The problems besetting the country, they realized, represented not aberration but a fatal flaw built into the system itself.

As Vietnam withdrew from Cambodia and changed course, the foreign embargo began to crack. Global competition was pushing countries to pursue opportunities wherever they could find them, so America's friends broke ranks and rushed into Vietnam. By 1994, when President Clinton finally ended this policy, the United States was one of the last major holdouts. As could be expected, the people in the South—still entrepreneurial and still steeped in their freewheeling capitalist past— were the ones who knew how to take full advantage of the reform. It was in the South, an area not at all bound to or blinded by the ortho doxy of socialism, that the market economy really took flight. Eventually, the South's stunning transformation into a vibrant region, and the visible benefits of the open market, would prompt the rest of the country to plunge into the same waters. With the state giving up its control over many aspects of the economy, with private commerce allowed to flourish, and with foreign money flooding in, the country emerged from its darkness. Farmers regained their incentive and initia tive. Food became plentiful once again. Shortages disappeared as shops brimmed with goods, and rationing was abandoned.

But no one could have foreseen this evolution when the war ended in 1975. At that time, the system and the ideology that the Viet Minh had adapted from the Soviet Union and China—which had succeeded in winning an arduous war against foreign domination—seemed unassail able. But peace turned out to contain the seeds of change. In the end, the North, which tried to recast the South into its own socialist image, was itself transformed.

All of this was in the future, however, when my brother Giu entered the re-education camp, where he was to be cleansed of his capitalist ideas and his "puppet" thoughts.

17

The Hours of Gold and Jade

Giu was sitting at a crowded table loaded with plates of food and bottles of beer and soft drinks. Next to him, a pretty young woman was smiling shyly, holding up what was clearly one of her proudest possessions: a picture of Ho Chi Minh. The occasion was a dinner party to mark the transfer of the Ha Tien cement works to the new communist management. No one would have guessed that the people chatting and joking at this congenial gathering would, just two weeks before, have willingly tried to kill and maim one another. The pretty girl had been a communist guerrilla, and the picture of Ho appeared on a commendation she had received for her exploits.

Giu could remember how, not long ago, the dead bodies of Viet Cong guerrillas had been displayed near the factory as war trophies. Yet from the time they took control, the communists had been so friendly and full of goodwill that my brother was glad to let bygones be bygones. "We're all Vietnamese," they said, "The war's behind us now. Let's join hands to rebuild our country." This was how war was sup-posed to end—with both sides shaking hands and professing brother-hood. In this atmosphere, breaking bread with his old enemies seemed the natural thing to do. So, when the pretty girl guerrilla was intro-duced by the cadre presiding over the banquet, Giu joined in the applause, and admired her Ho Chi Minh commendation when she passed it to him.

My brother never imagined that he would be rubbing shoulders with the communists. He had thought that he would be long gone before they appeared, but the shocking collapse of Saigon had spoiled his plan to escape. In the first days after the surrender, he did not dwell on this momentous turn of events, too preoccupied with the fate of his wife and children to worry about his own. He had heard that the airport had been shelled heavily and many aircraft had been shot down. Giu had no idea whether his family had made it out alive. As he ran around Saigon, trying to get some news, he passed a Cessna dangling among the electric wires—either shot down or brought down by engine failure or an empty fuel tank. He was haunted by visions of his family plunging to a fiery death. Finally, a relative phoned with the news that their flight had taken off without incident. Relieved, his first instinct was to flee and rejoin his wife and children in France. But he knew the risks of such a move were enormous, and he reluctantly gave up the idea.

As the realization that he might not see his family again hit home, he fell into a deep depression. Then, after a few days, he began to think about what he should do, now that he was stuck in Saigon. He decided to go back to work at his headquarters office, to stay busy and keep him-self from brooding over his own situation. He found that the entire staff of 200 had reported for duty. Uncertain about what would happen next, they too had chosen to keep the office running as normal. Although my brother did not know what the communists were going to do, he expected the worst. Throughout Vietnamese history, the victors had usually hunted down the vanquished and taken wholesale reprisals, partly out of revenge, but also to make sure their former foes would not regroup and pose a challenge again. From all the brutal stories he had heard about the communists over the years, Giu thought that they would surely put previous victors to shame.

But nothing happened. When three former underground cadres— low-key, friendly southerners—showed up at the headquarters, they simply assembled the staff and announced that the new revolutionary government was now in charge. They were polite and deferential to Giu, and asked him to preside over the meeting, in his capacity as gen- eral manager. When they finished speaking, they turned to him and said, "Would you like to add anything?" My brother said no, and the meeting broke up. The cadres left and did not come back. In the absence of new instructions, Giu ran things as he had done before. Ten days later, another group of southern cadres, officially dispatched by the newly created government—a temporary administration until formal reunification—arrived at the office. The cadres had the staff submit thorough reports on themselves and their families going back to their grandparents, and listing every location where they had lived and every- thing they had done. Giu omitted many things about his family to avoid making his situation worse: He wrote only that his father had worked in finance—skipping all the important positions he had held in the North—and he did not say that he belonged to the Duong clan of Van Dinh, afraid that this would label him as someone related to "big feu- dalists." He worried about how the cadres would react, but to his aston- ishment, they asked him to remain in his post. Realizing that they lacked the technical skill to manage the cement works themselves, the cadres also asked the rest of the staff to continue as before. Giu and his col- leagues felt relieved: They were going to keep their jobs and feed them- selves and their families. Cautiously optimistic, they commenced to think that perhaps the national reconciliation that the communists had proclaimed was for real.

To complete the takeover of the enterprise, the new managers asked Giu and two engineers to go with them to the factory in Ha Tien. They traveled in a jeep. The cadres wore Viet Cong pith helmets and sandals cut out of rubber tires, just like the bad guys in propaganda posters and cartoons. Life is weird, Giu thought. A few weeks ago, he would have flown to Ha Tien to avoid the mines and ambushes that used to make the road a death trap. But here he was, driving merrily along a stretch of road that he had seen only from the air before, chauffeured by Viet Cong officers. Peace needed getting used to. He saw no jets streaking by, no military trucks clattering along loaded with soldiers. Sometimes they would pass a burned-out tank or an abandoned helicopter resting in the rice fields, and the guerrillas they saw along the road were not out to attack him, but simply manning makeshift checkpoints. They made a great point of stopping all travelers to look at their papers. One of the officers joked, "What do these guys think they're doing? They can't even read!" Giu had not expected the people he considered dour ideologues to have a sense of humor. Surprised, he burst out laughing with the other passengers. In Ha Tien, the atmosphere remained friendly. The communists did not bring up the past, although their secret agents knew full well what the management had done during the war to keep their side at bay. The handing over went smoothly. To mark the historic occasion, the plant manager held a banquet, inviting local civilian and military leaders to join the guests of honor.

Two days later, word reached Ha Tien that former Saigon officials, from the rank of manager and up, would have to report to the former National Assembly building, with all their old identity papers, for further instructions. Giu and other officials like him did not give the announcement a second thought. Once they got this formality over with, they expected to resume their life as normal. Giu hitched a ride back to Saigon with the officers who had brought him down to Ha Tien. At the meeting, Giu took his seat among former Saigon officials crowding the old assembly chambers. A cadre strode to the podium and explained the policies of the new government, but there were no denunciations, no punitive policies announced. In that month of May, Saigon was in a festive mood, with one major celebration after another. First came May Day, then Ho Chi Minh's birthday, then the celebration of the communist final victory. In that holiday atmosphere, it hardly seemed to anyone that anything sinister was waiting to happen. A few weeks later, in the middle of June, the government-controlled radio and newspapers announced that former Saigon civilian and military officials should present themselves once more at a number of high schools, this time for what was called re-education.

It was, in fact, a massive internment program, designed to isolate former Saigon officials so that they could not mount any organized resistance, serve as lightning rods around which other malcontents could coalesce, or—most important of all—go to work for the CIA. At the beginning, the incarceration also had another purpose: to indoctrinate them and convert them into supporters of the new regime. Each official was told to bring along a blanket, mosquito net, and sufficient money to last for a month. The phrase "one month" fooled people, as it was meant to. Everyone said to himself, "Well, this means I'm going to be gone only four weeks. That's not such a long time. I'll be back before I know it." Reassured (but also afraid of getting arrested for not showing up), nearly everyone reported as summoned. Later, when they protested and demanded to go home after four weeks, the cadres replied, "Who told you that you'll only be gone a month? We said only that you should bring along money for four weeks, because we thought we might not get organized quickly enough at the beginning to feed you adequately."

When Giu arrived at the Trung Vuong high school, he recognized many of those standing in line, including some former bank presidents, deputy cabinet ministers, and ministers. They seemed surprised to see each other, and greeted one another by asking, "What? You're still here? You didn't flee?" Late in the afternoon, a cadre appeared and told them to go home. People were disappointed. They had hoped to get the formality over with—to wipe their slates clean—so they could put their past behind them and begin their life anew. They were also scared that, if they went back to their houses, the police might think that they had dodged the order and put them in jail. The former manager of the Industrial Development Bank desperately pleaded with the cadre, "I had a very important job in the puppet government. You must take me for re-education." The cadre said, "Oh yeah, tell me how important you were. How many people did you oppress?" Trying to impress, the man said, "I oppressed one thousand people." But the cadres sent them all home.

The next day, newspapers announced that former officials had to present themselves at another high school. Again, they all trooped to the new site. The treatment was formal and polite throughout the proceeding. No one searched their bags or confiscated what they had brought along. No one insulted them. After lining up to give their names, dates of birth, and the offices where they had worked to cadres sitting at a couple of desks, they were ushered into different rooms. Lunch and dinner were catered by some of the best known restaurants in town, and served on tables set with porcelain plates. While the guards outside sat down in the dirt to eat their small ration of poor quality rice, the former Saigon officials inside sat down to meals of fluffy white rice and chicken stir-fried with cabbage. That night, the cadres came in to check on them, as solicitous as the proprietors of a hotel. They said, "Please push the tables aside to make room for your reed mats. Do you think you can go to sleep like this, right on the floor? Do you think you'll feel cold in the night? Have you gotten enough mats and mosquito nets?" All the former officials felt their tension evaporate. Not only had there been no bloodbath, but here they were, being handled with care and respect. Re-education seemed to be a breeze.

The next morning, a cadre came in with a piece of paper. He said, "I'm going to read out some names. If you hear yours, come up here and stand to my right." Giu heard the names of some people he knew, like the official claiming he had oppressed a thousand people. Then the cadre said, "Those whose names I've read, please come into this room. The rest can go back to your places." A while later, a truck showed up to take the others away. Then came an announcement, "You can all go home now." Those who were spared protested, saying that their neighborhood police would think that they had evaded education, so the cadre said, "All right, I'll give each of you a document that you can show to the police." Giu took the piece of paper and went home. My brother decided to return to work. The job gave him a measure of protection: Because he was accountable to an official organization that assumed responsibility for his actions, the local police had left him alone, instead of harassing him, as they did other former officials without an office to vouch for them. A couple of weeks later, however, as another wave of re-education was launched, Giu and seven other holdovers from the old regime at the cement works were told to report for indoctrination. Again, they gathered at a high school. At 10:00 p.m. a truck came to pick them up. It took them and another group of internees to a camp located in a former orphanage near Saigon. There, the driver handed them over to the camp authorities. No formal list changed hands; the driver just told the cadre how many he had brought. The cadre counted them one by one as they filed in, and then the truck took off. It was July 18, 1975, less than three months after the fall of Saigon.

The camp housed over 2000 internees, all but a handful of whom were men. The next morning, Giu saw several relatives who had been brought here, including Phung, my sister Phu's husband. For Giu, life at the camp was bearable at first. The government tried to live up to its claim that the detainees were here not for imprisonment but for political education, so the treatment was not as severe as Giu had feared. For about a year, my brother continued to get paid for a job he no longer held at the cement works, and like the other internees, he got a stipend to spend as he pleased at a canteen run by an enterprising Chinese. The shop also sold eggs, condensed milk, coffee, ramen noodles, and pens. In an ironic twist, for former officials who had not held jobs under the new government as Giu had, living in the camp was actually less stressful than living outside, because here they escaped the constant harassment of their local police and cadres. For the first month, they had to attend an indoctrination class every day, but they did not have to do any demanding manual work. Occasionally they were given a batch of newspapers, which they had to read and comment on. Other than that, their leisure time was their own. Some played chess or dominoes. Some made pictures, combs, hair pins, or toys to send home to their wives and children, using bits of wood and aluminum they salvaged around the camp. Some read books they borrowed from the camp library, which was stocked only with publications about the revolution. With several relatives among the inmates, my brother did not feel too lonely or depressed. As a precaution, they visited each other only once in a while, and hid the fact that they were related—pretending to be casual acquaintances—afraid that the cadres would start questioning them separately about each other and uncover things about their families that they had not revealed. Giu found the son and son-in-law of a cousin, who did not bear the last name Duong and who were young enough and removed enough not to know a great deal about him, and spent a lot of time in their company. After supper, they would sometimes take long walks along the dirt roads that meandered through the camp. Once safely out of earshot, they would curse the communists and try to outdo each other in hurling insults at their tormentors.

The camp, located on a hill, was spartan but clean. It had no running water, only wells equipped with electric pumps, courtesy of American aid. Wide, well-maintained dirt roads ran between its structures and along its perimeter. The camp had several buildings, each supervised by a cadre. The internees in each building were divided into cells, with ten cells forming a company. Each cell had a leader and a secretary, detainees who had been picked out by the cadre to coordinate activities and pressure the other inmates into obeying orders. The food was basic: soup and rice. Lunch and dinner were provided by the same Chinese businessman, free of charge. At mealtimes, a cell would send two internees down to get its ration. If they wanted to, the detainees could buy extra food and breakfast at the canteen. There were no beds; the internees had each brought a mosquito net and a reed mat. At night they spread out their mats on the floor, strung up their mosquito nets, and slept with their bags of worldly goods next to their heads.

Conditions were primitive but at least control was lax. Regulations did not allow the internees to run loose between buildings and between rooms, but at night, after roll call, they would go back and forth to visit people they knew. As long as they returned to their rooms by nine o'clock and got under their mosquito nets on time, the cadres turned a blind eye. At the beginning, the detainees were not forced to do manual work. The cadres encouraged each cell to grow vegetables for extra food. Some of the internees had brought along seeds, such as cabbage, bok choy, spinach, and squash. These were the more farsighted ones. They suspected that once in the camp they might never get out, and they knew that one day they would run out of the food and money they had brought along and would have to find a way to supplement their prison diet. They immediately started to dig and hoe, and soon they had neat rows of produce growing, along with the sweet potatoes that had been planted by the orphans who used to live there.

Giu had no vegetable seeds and very little money. Naively believing that he was going to be gone only a month, he had not packed anything of value in his small bag. His colleagues from the cement works were more clever; they had brought with them valuables like watches and gold jewelry, which they would sell to the Chinese merchant for extra cash when they needed to. One group made up of ex-ministers and deputy ministers came with a lot of cash and valuables and lived like kings. They despised the food provided by the camp and ate most of their meals at the canteen, treating themselves to hot rice and egg noodle soups. With scraps of lumber they found lying around, they made a table and some chairs. In the morning, they would gather around the table, smoke the expensive filter cigarettes they bought from the Chinese, and drink fresh-brewed coffee flavored with condensed milk. In the spartan camp, they still looked like the men of means they had once been.

Life in Giu's camp was not as brutal as that in the Soviet gulags or Chinese communist prisons, or even other camps tucked in isolated or primitive areas in Vietnam. Giu's location near Saigon ensured better treatment, because if the conditions had been outrageous, word might leak out to the international community and bring condemnation on the new government. But even so, living conditions here—in what could be called the best camp of them all—bordered on the intolerable. Food was deficient and medical care was minimal. The prisoners were not beaten or tortured, but that did not lessen the mental anguish they suffered. The internees had been gathered up and dumped here by pure government fiat, not for any specific crimes, but simply because they had worked for the former Saigon regime. None of them had gone through a trial, and so had not had the chance—or the satisfaction—of defending themselves in court. Sentences were not passed until a year later, in August 1976, so at the beginning, the detainees had no idea how long they would have to languish in the camp.

Many thought they would rot there. Some became despondent. One inmate killed himself by swallowing Mercurochrome. Another went into a deep depression. Seeing that he had stopped eating and was becoming emaciated, Giu tried to bring him out of his despair. He said, "Don't punish yourself. There's nothing you can do but wait this out. You must cheer up and keep your health—if you don't, you'll become a terrible burden to your family when you get out." The young man listened to my brother and got well again. He left two years before Giu did. Giu was telling himself the same things. After the first four weeks, Giu realized that he would be interned for a long time, but he nurtured the hope that he would get out eventually, and was determined to survive no matter how long his imprisonment lasted. During the years he spent in prison, my brother never allowed himself completely to lose his spirit and hope or let himself go to seed. Other prisoners also bore up well under the strain; Giu heard of only four deaths among the political inmates—one from suicide, one from falling off a roof he was repairing, and two from disease.

It was the sense of uncertainty that kept the internees on edge. Isolation added to their burden: They worried constantly about how their families were getting along outside in the vastly changed landscape of the south and felt guilty for having deserted them. Looking into the future, they saw little to cheer them up. Even if they could get out, they knew that they could never resume the lives and careers they had enjoyed before, because the communists would never trust them. Their education and training would simply be wasted. Those with children still in Vietnam feared for their futures as well, knowing that they would be tainted by association. Giu, at least, had learned through relatives in Saigon that his wife and children had made it to Paris and were doing fine, and he could feel reassured about their welfare.

The absence of brutality did not mean that the prisoners were not living in fear. They had to watch what they said and did, to avoid missteps that would prolong their stay or land them in a real jail, where conditions would be much worse. The cadres might look the other way when it came to violations of camp regulations, but they would crack down hard on anything they considered political opposition. An inadvertent comment would be enough to cause trouble. Informers—called "antennas"—recruited from among the internees with the promise of early release, kept their eyes and ears peeled for any signs of resistance, no matter how small. One man was reported to the cadres for joking, "I'd rather flee to Guam, die, and be a ghost there, than stay here and be a citizen of Vietnam." After sentences were pronounced for all prisoners in June 1976, this man was detained for several more years beyond his original term. A cousin of my father's got into trouble when an antenna overheard him and a group of older friends, in an idle conversation, making fun of a Soviet marshal who had been featured in a newspaper article. Some time later, with no warning, a truck suddenly showed up to take them to the infamous Chi Hoa prison. Giu learned to keep his thoughts to himself and be constantly on his guard.

The political intimidation carried over into the daily indoctrination sessions. Each morning, the internees lined up and marched to the auditorium, where they took their places on benches made of planks and tree stumps. The lecturing cadre launched into one of the nine re-education topics, condemning the crimes of the former Saigon regime and its American backers and praising the patriotic achievements of the revolution, which was held up as the proud heir to Vietnam's tradition of driving out foreign aggressors. If the subject was complex, a lecture could take two to three days. The "students" were expected to take notes.

When they finished a topic, the cadres assigned questions for the cells to discuss. They might ask, "Why do we believe that the American imperialists were the aggressors?" or "The American imperialists failed miserably in Vietnam. What do you think were the main reasons why they lost their war of aggression?" An inmate, designated as the cell secretary, took careful notes of who said what during the discussion, or who held back and said nothing, and then handed in the report to the cadre. If the cadre felt unhappy with any internee's answers or lack of participation, he would call him into the office and question him sharply. After the discussion, each internee had to write a report summarizing what he had heard in the lecture.

One purpose of the cell discussions and the reports was to force the inmates to reveal their counterrevolutionary thoughts and deeds. When the cadres posed the question, "The puppet regime committed many crimes against the people and had many blood debts. What crimes did you yourself commit?" everyone had to confess to something because, in the eyes of the government, every official was complicit in the criminal activities of the former regime. No one was allowed to evade this exercise, since confession was prelude to conversion. The communists believed that once these officials recognized that what they had thought and done in the past was wrong, they would become open to the new dogma. Then the officials would make peace with the new system and would no longer pose a threat to the political order.

My brother had not personally done anything that could be called a crime. True, he had given moral support to the troops who protected his

cement works, giving presents to the wounded and money to the soldiers' widows and orphans. This was hardly a felony, but he had to pay
lip service to this exercise and find a criminal angle to his activities. So
he said that he had encouraged the troops to fight against the revolution,
and that he had produced cement that was used to build concrete
bunkers for the Saigon army. He knew that confessing to these minor
crimes would satisfy the cadres' requirement without giving the authorities cause to punish him even more severely.

At the end of the series of lectures, Giu, like all the other prisoners,
had to submit a personal report, giving details about himself and his relatives, including grandparents, aunts, and uncles. Giu kept his report to
a few pages, giving as little information as he thought he could get away
with about his past and about relatives who might be liabilities, and
made a copy—in case he was asked to repeat the exercise. Others submitted reports that were thirty to forty pages long, and did not keep
copies. Sure enough, the prisoners were told to submit a second report.
Using his copy, Giu gave the same information, but changed it just
enough to make it look like the report had been rewritten afresh. This
way, he managed to avoid trouble.

The majority of the detainees were too afraid to protest against the
force-feeding of ideology, giving the cadres the impression that their
charges were receptive to the indoctrination, but this was far from the
truth. Giu always listened and retained enough to write reports and
answer questions, but he had too critical a mind—honed from years of
studying and living in France—to accept the cadres' simplistic lectures,
overblown claims about the achievements of the communists, or insistence on painting everything in black and white. He knew that the
Americans were not always bad, that the Saigon regime was not always
cowardly and venal, and that the communists were not always noble.
Like his fellow prisoners, Giu could parrot "marching with resolve and
speed toward socialism," but he did this only to stay out of trouble.
While Thang, who believed in socialism as if it were religious dogma,
studied its ideology with immense interest and accepted what she heard
on faith, Giu closed his mind to whatever the communists said out of
hatred for what they were doing to him, to the point of refusing to give
them credit where credit might be due.

At the end of the series of lectures, the cadres declared that the
detainees had completed their education, and the indoctrination
stopped. The internees had nothing to occupy themselves, so they spent
their leisure time reading, making handicrafts, working in their

vegetable patches, or sleeping. The indoctrination failed to convert Giu and his fellow detainees. In fact, the prolonged incarceration would turn them into implacable foes. At the end of the war, people like my brother had been willing to forgive and forget, but after months and years of increasingly harsh imprisonment, they came to hate their jailers with a passion. Their anger and resentment would be shared by their relatives, swelling the ranks of those who bitterly opposed the communist regime. By not following through with their initial policy of reconciliation, the communists missed a great chance for ending the divisions of the war and for harnessing the energy and talent of educated people to rebuild the country.

Over the first twelve months, about one-fourth of the camp's inmates, including my brother-in-law Phung, whose former government job was considered not important enough to warrant longer incarceration, were released in several batches. These discharges were designed to defuse the anger of the prisoners' families. If, as one conservative estimate has it, some 100,000 persons were incarcerated for a long time (and thousands more for a shorter period), this meant that when families and friends of those detained were included, the re-education process victimized at least one million people. In many cities, protest sprung up, demanding that the former officials be allowed to go home. By freeing some detainees, the communists were also trying to placate international critics, who were condemning them for holding so many political prisoners without trial. These releases raised the hope of the internees, who thought that if they just played the game and pretended to go along, they too would soon be set free. Some of those who got out were released for not purely political reasons. Rumors were rife that they had actually bribed their way out. My brother heard that the former bank manager who claimed that he had "oppressed a thousand people" got out by offering a Vespa scooter to one of the cadres. Among those let go were Giu's seven colleagues from the cement works, whose wives had found go-betweens who managed to grease the right palms. Looking back, Giu thinks that he, too, could have cut short his own internment with a few bribes.

About a year after Giu entered the camp, life there abruptly changed. Following national reunification in June 1976, the communists did away with the temporary government that had run the South since victory, replacing it with one central government based in Hanoi. The lenient attitude toward the detainees, favored by the native southerners, was replaced with a harsher policy, and the former Saigon officials were now officially sentenced to long jail terms. One day in August, the cadres summoned the internees to the auditorium to hear the resolution passed by the new National Assembly, the first one to be elected in a country-wide vote. This resolution, designed to put a veneer of legality on the internment program, said that those who had been sentenced would spend three years in re-education counting from the day they entered the camp, but that if they made good progress, they could be released sooner.

The cadres read the names of those who had been sentenced. Of the 1700 prisoners left in the camp, only 200, including my brother, did not hear their names in the roll call. A cadre later told Giu, "Yours and the cases of the others like you will be dealt with in a couple of months." Although Giu was never told how long he would be incarcerated, he did not care: To him, sentences were meaningless in a system where the communists could detain people like him as long as they pleased without regard to any laws. After prison terms were announced, members of the secret police arrived from the North to run the camp, replacing the previous administrators. Afraid that the political detainees who had been condemned to long jail stays might try to escape, the new cadres took several precautions. They moved these prisoners to one side of the camp and surrounded their buildings with chest-high concertina wire. Every evening, they lined them up and counted them as they filed back into their rooms. Roaming after dinner was forbidden. The regimen got harsher, and the Chinese merchant was told to close down his shop and leave. Early each morning, the prisoners had to line up and then march, shovels in hands, to do demanding manual work. My brother and the rest of the detainees were herded to the opposite side of the camp and prohibited from communicating with the other group. For the first time, Giu felt really alone. All his relatives, former military officers, had been sentenced. He was now completely cut off from them. Giu's group, however, was more leniently treated than the one under sentence. He could still move about freely in his part of the camp, and although he also had to do manual work, it was less strenuous.

At the end of August 1976, in another conciliatory gesture, the communists allowed relatives to visit the prisoners for the first time since they were interned. The camp was in a holiday mood. Cars streamed in from the direction of Saigon, carrying well-dressed visitors for an emotional and joyful reunion. An uncle of Giu's wife came with my sister Yen and about ten other relatives, bringing money and food. But the cheerful atmosphere was short-lived. One night, the sound of trucks woke Giu up. He heard footsteps and loud voices. The next morning, he learned that the trucks had come to pick up the sentenced prisoners and transfer them to camps in the North, where they would be even more isolated and subjected to more intolerable conditions. For about a month, these trucks came and went, until all the detainees on the other side of the camp were gone.

Giu expected his turn to come soon. One day, the cadres told him to pack up for transfer, but when the trucks were loaded, his name was not on the list. That was as close as my brother would come to going to the North. In the end, about 150 political prisoners would remain in the camp. Giu does not know why he was left behind. Possibly the cadres in Hanoi who engineered the prisoner moves might have been overwhelmed by the sheer number of cases and might have overlooked his file. He remembers that when the cadres called out names for transfer the first time, they mentioned three of the four detainees who had died, suggesting that the Interior Ministry in Hanoi could not keep track of all the prisoners. Then again, they may have picked names in a deliberately arbitrary manner to keep prisoners on edge, unsure of whether or when they would be transferred. This could explain why my brother and other high-ranking officials were spared while our cousin and the two nephews, who had merely served as army doctors, were sent north. Perhaps the communists were keeping cases they viewed as less severe, like my brother's, in the South for release so that they could display their clemency. Or perhaps the cadres decided to be lenient because Giu had many relatives who had toiled for the revolution for decades.

With most of the detainees gone, the communists moved drug addicts and women accused of various crimes into the camp, raising the population to over 5000. Giu and the political prisoners were nervous about living with such hard cases, but the cadres kept the addicts and criminals separate, behind barbed wire. They moved my brother and the other political detainees to the kitchen area and assigned them to help the staff cook for the whole camp. This turned out to be better for Giu and his colleagues. They slept on plank beds rather than on the floor. Being close to the source of food, they got more to eat. The atmosphere in the kitchen area was pleasant. The cadre in charge, a northerner with a middle-school education, was kind and treated Giu and the other political prisoners with respect.

For my brother, working in the kitchen was a far cry from running one of the country's largest industrial complexes and making billions of piasters in profit. But he tried not to mourn his former life or his loss of status. The past was the past, he told himself. Now he learned how to crush garlic, wash and chop hundreds of pounds of vegetables daily, make stir fries, and cook rice. One of his duties was raising chickens and pigs, and he became an expert at bathing the pigs, cooking their rice bran, and feeding them. He took pleasure in watching the chickens multiply and the pigs grow fat.

In 1979, Giu had been in jail for over three years. He had not been living, he felt, only surviving. The prolongation of his imprisonment without any official explanation did not surprise him, as he had become convinced of communist treachery. He resigned himself, suppressing his frustration and his anger, to avoid putting himself under more stress. Around him, many of his fellow political prisoners were still clinging to the hope that soon the United States would force the communists to take them to Vung Tau to board ships bound for America, where they would be given a house, a car, lots of money, and free education for their children. Their fantasy about freedom and a life of plenty in the United States grew as the atmosphere in the camp became harsher with the arrival of the addicts and criminals, and as they began to lose many of the small liberties they had enjoyed. The only thing that cheered my brother up was knowing that his wife and children, who had moved to America in August 1976, were doing well there.

One night in March, Giu and his colleagues were told to pack up. At eight o'clock, they were handcuffed, loaded on trucks, and taken to a camp in Xuyen Moc. With his wrist tied to that of another political prisoner, Giu thought the communists were treating him like a common criminal, and this violation of his dignity angered him. After he simmered down, he began worrying about what it would be like for him in Xuyen Moc. This new camp was located in the middle of a forest at the base of a hill covered with dense and thorny plants, making its floor impenetrable. As my brother had feared, conditions in this prison—which it clearly was, as it held common criminals as well as political detainees—were grim, and life was strictly regimented. In the morning, following calisthenics, the prisoners lined up and marched to a forest clearing to dig and hoe for four hours, tending sweet potatoes and corn under the watchful eyes of the armed guards. After lunch and a brief fifteen-minute rest, they returned for another four hours of work. When it rained, the work site turned into a muddy swamp. The cadres called this daily stint the "eight precious hours of gold and jade," hewing to the communist dogma that manual work was glorious. At each meal, Giu got one bowl of rice and salted boiled vegetables, but prisoners could add to this diet with supplies they got from relatives. Each night, between supper and bedtime, he and about four friends would steam rice and fry sausage or stew dry shrimp, using tin cans they set over three bricks. At nine o'clock, they had to get into bed, and a police officer locked the door to the building for the night.

It was easy to hate the guards and the cadres. Yet at times Giu could not help but feel sorry for his jailers. Most of them lived under conditions little better than the prisoners. With all the food they got from home, my brother and his friends actually had a better diet than the cadres and guards, mostly peasants whose families in the North could not afford to send them anything. They were so poor that it was easy for the prisoners to bribe them: A bag of cheap candies from Saigon and a cup of hot tea would be enough to induce them to relax the rules a little. A guard approached my brother and a group of his friends one day and whispered, "Can you spare an envelope and a stamp for me? I'd like to write to my mother. I haven't sent her a letter since I got here." Then he confided, "My situation's not that much different from yours. In the North, I was taken to a train station I'd never heard of, and after that I was put on a bus which took me here. I've been in this camp for a year, and all I know is this corner of the jungle. I haven't been anywhere else." Like the prisoners, the jailers had been dumped here and forgotten. Unlike their charges, the cadres' and guards' day did not end with supper but with an evening meeting to review their performance and their attitude. This was an acrimonious bout of accusations and criticisms, rather than a friendly get-together. The jailers, too, had to guard their words and their actions, and it seemed to my brother that they were as much victims of the government as he was.

Although life in the camp was bleak, the prison authorities restrained from physical and verbal abuse, in compliance with the re-education policy that the government had proclaimed. Conditions in other camps, according to former prisoners, were a lot worse. The internees have described beatings, rampant malnutrition, and denial of medical care that left them broken physically and psychologically. Yet even without torture or starvation, Giu saw the loss of freedom and the anxieties of prison life take a severe toll on his fellow prisoners. Some of the detainees fell into deep depression. Others were so consumed with worries about their wives and children that they were in a constant state of anxiety. Some could not sleep for months. One man Giu knew did everything he could to tire himself out so he could get some sleep. He worked like a dog every day, digging and hoeing, planting sweet potatoes, lugging buckets of water from the stream to irrigate the plants—but nothing worked. A few, stressed beyond endurance, suffered strokes that left them partially paralyzed. Even though my brother knew his wife and children were safe in America, he wondered whether he would ever be able to see them and share a life with them. He was depressed by the feeling that his children were growing up far away, probably turning into strangers. Yet he fought to keep his spirits high and his hopes alive.

One morning, about two months after my brother arrived in the camp, he and eleven other prisoners in his building were pulled out of the morning lineup. The cadre gave them fifteen minutes to pack up. Then he told them to follow him. They thought that perhaps they were going to be taken to a harsher camp; instead, they were led into an office to complete paperwork for their release. The cadres in the office gave each prisoner a form to sign, pledging to obey the laws set down by the state and the Party once they returned home, as well as the rules and regulations in their neighborhood, and then told them to line up to obtain their discharge papers. The formalities seemed interminable to Giu, who felt like he was on pins and needles, afraid that the cadres might change their minds.

Finally, Giu and the other prisoners were loaded onto a truck with

tainees had
dines, they
lle, did not
the top, he
by yard, he
irs. As the
ghway, his
something
ould break
up. Maybe
the release.
to another
g back on

about an
gon, some

to home, and preferred to go the rest of the way on their own, rather than stay on the truck and face the possibility that it might take them to another camp. Giu decided to stay put. Finally, at around 10 p.m., the truck stopped at a traffic light near his house, and he got off. He practically ran home. His sister-in-law, who had moved into his house with her family, almost had a heart attack when she opened the door and saw him. The first thing he did was to wash his hair, take a bath, get rid of his prison outfit, and put on some old clothes. Then he went to bed. But he could not sleep. The foam mattress felt strange—too soft, too comfortable, unlike the lumpy logs he had gotten used to. Also, the excitement of being home pumped him up and kept him wide awake the whole night.

But he was not really free. As his discharge document stated, for the first month he was put under the supervision of the local police, who were supposed to continue his "re-education." They kept close tabs on his whereabouts. They gave him a log, and each day he had to jot down where he went and what he did. At the end of every week, he had to submit this record for their review and signature. Every evening, a policeman would plant himself at his house and wait until he returned to question him about what he had been up to that day. My brother suspected that the policeman was taking advantage of his vulnerable situation to harass him and extort money, but he was afraid to offer a bribe. Not every policeman and cadre was corruptible, and not every harassment a prelude to a bribe, so if he guessed wrong, he could be arrested and charged with "attempting to corrupt cadres," as had happened to some people in Saigon who tried to buy favors. He needed a go-between to approach the police on his behalf, but he did not know who to ask. Giu also faced the possibility of being expelled from Saigon and sent to a New Economic Zone. His stay in the city was contingent upon the approval of the authorities. A month after he returned home, he had to apply for an extension. If it was denied, he would have to leave. When the deadline drew near, he nervously went to the city office and submitted an application. He immediately ran into problems. The cadre who took his document said that Giu's file was not in order and made him redo his application. Then the next time, he said that Giu needed additional documents. Again, Giu wondered whether a bribe would get things moving, but did not dare to offer any money. At that time the authorities were trying to push as many people out of Saigon as possible to reduce the population, which had swollen during the war, to a level that would not tax the city's infrastructure. Anyone who was unemployed had to leave. The only way for Giu to secure a permanent stay in Saigon—and end the regular treks to the city office to get an extension—was to find a job. But for a former political prisoner, trying to find work in a depressed economy was close to impossible. Fortunately for my brother, he was able to find a job that required education and language ability in the translation section of the Culture Ministry. He joined a large staff that included many former political prisoners and a number of cadres who had studied in the Eastern bloc. Their job was to translate into Vietnamese technical manuals for machinery that had come from the United States and other countries. The job was a godsend. It allowed my brother to stay in the city permanently and to obtain the coveted residency card.

Things turned out well for Giu in the translation office. His salary was modest, but he was surviving better than many people. He received a bonus for performance every month, and he earned more by moon-lighting as the director of an evening foreign language school that he and a group of ex-prisoners had started. To their surprise, it became a roar-ing success. The English classes were by far the most popular: Entire families would show up for classes together, from small children to grandparents. These students, it turned out, were would-be escapees who wanted to have the rudiments of English under their belts before they made their journey—they hoped—to America.

Yet the satisfaction of doing constructive tasks, instead of languish-ing in prison, did not cheer my brother up. In fact, he got more depressed. He had migraine attacks every day. More and more, he thought of fleeing the country, not only to rejoin his family, but also to get away from the communists. He saw no future for himself in Vietnam, and he did not want to continue working for a regime he hated. So, in 1980, he decided to leave. Giu's timing was bad; the government had started to crack down. For a while, under pressure from China, it had allowed overseas Chinese to leave unofficially. Hundreds of thousands would jump at the chance and would eventually resettle in the United States. In Saigon, traffickers in refugees—Chinese living in Cholon—sprang up to organize these trips at exorbitant fees. With the govern-ment turning the other way, the flow of escapees turned into a flood. Vietnamese who could get in with the organizers would masquerade as overseas Chinese and leave.

At the same time, thousands of small, leaky boats were also taking to the sea, carrying Vietnamese anxious to escape communist rule and the dire economic situation. No one knows how many died of exposure or drowning when their rickety boats capsized or were attacked by Thai pirates, but the number of refugees who ended up as food in the bellies of fish—as the Vietnamese put it—must have reached tens of thousands. Refugee camps from Thailand to Indonesia had been receiving the boat people, but the ceaseless flow swelled and overtaxed the camps, creating a crisis. Some countries like Thailand, Singapore, and Malaysia started to push the new arrivals back out to sea. The tidal wave of refugees and the tragic casualties prompted a chorus of international protest. Under pressure, the Vietnamese government ended the unofficially sanctioned departures and passed a law prohibiting people from fleeing the country. Those that were caught would be jailed for one to three years, and traffickers could get five-year prison terms. Former political prisoners who tried to flee and got caught would face a minimum sentence of three years in jail.

The law did not staunch the flow, though it slowed it down. With such a heavy demand for their services, and with profits remaining high, traffickers continued to stay in business. But without the unofficial government blessing, the departures had become much more dangerous. It was precisely at this point that my brother, feeling he could wait no longer, decided to leave. Mrs. An, his wife Nguyet's former business partner, made the necessary arrangements for him and gave him the gold he needed to secure passage on a boat. This sixty-two-year-old, very religious and kind lady, who had been like an aunt to Nguyet, felt she owed it to my brother. Nguyet not only had sunk a great deal of money in her business to make it a success but also had done her family many favors while she was living in Saigon. Through the family of an acquaintance who had made it to America, Mrs. An found a smuggling organization. The cloak-and-dagger operation would have made the CIA proud. Many people had been cheated by unscrupulous traffickers who took their advance payment without getting them out of the country, so now the accepted method was for the refugee's family to hand over the gold only after their relative reached safety. Giu worked out an arrangement with Mrs. An. Once out, he would send back a note under an assumed name giving her a coded message; this would be the signal for her to pay. With the price of passage and the promise of payment agreed upon, Giu received instructions on what to do on the appointed day.

At five o'clock one morning, he left the house and headed to the bus station designated by a man acting as his contact with the smugglers. He carried no baggage and no identification papers, just some cash to pay for expenses during the trip. He did not know the identity of his contact, nor did he know his itinerary. If he got caught, he would not be able to divulge any information to the police. Instead of going straight to the embarkation point for the ocean voyage, the smugglers would take him there in a roundabout way, with several stops at safe houses. For each leg of the trip, a different guide would take over. All through the journey, absolute secrecy would have to be maintained, to avoid alerting the police and the militia, and also any locals who might join in uninvited. Often, these gate-crashers would make the trip even more perilous: stretching water and food supplies, and loading down the flimsy vessel so that it barely could stay afloat.

The bus station was full of policemen, some working under cover, and informers, because it was the departure point for escape routes along the sea, especially toward Ca Mau at the tip of the country. Following his instructions, Giu went to a shabby cafe and waited nervously for someone to contact him. He knew he stood out among the traders, peasants, and workers who thronged the station. He had put on some simple clothes and had removed his glasses, but he was sure that anyone who saw him could tell right away that he was a former Saigon official trying to flee the country. A man suddenly appeared and greeted him like they were old friends. He told Giu to wait while he went to get bus tickets. He came back dejected and said that the bus they were supposed to take was sold out. Before leaving, he whispered to my brother that a woman wearing a flowery blouse and a plaid scarf wound around her head would come by. When he saw her, Giu should try to follow her at a distance and do everything that she did. After a while, the woman showed up. But Giu lost her among the huge crowd. Feeling more and more nervous about the whole situation, he gave up and went back to Mrs. An's house, where he had been staying to prepare for the trip. A few days later, he decided to try once more. Again, he contacted a trafficker to make arrangements.

This time, he managed to get on a bus. As it pulled away, he heaved a sigh of relief, but this was only the first of many hurdles. At every checkpoint along the way, the bus had to stop. Policemen boarded it to inspect the traders and their merchandise and collect taxes, as circulation of goods outside state channels had been allowed to resume. Giu waited nervously while the police moved among the passengers, afraid that they might guess that he was a would-be escapee and nab him. He sat still, trying not to fidget and attract attention, and looked away.

At eight o'clock that night, the bus arrived in Ca Mau. Giu had been traveling for fourteen hours without food. The snacks offered by vendors at the various stops had looked so unsanitary that he decided not to eat and run the risk of getting an upset stomach, or even worse, diarrhea, dysentery, or food poisoning. There were about six escapees scattered among the bus passengers. At the station, a man appeared and told them to follow him. They walked as fast as they could in the dark. Without his glasses, Giu stumbled after the others. Then they broke up into two groups. Giu and two other escapees were taken to the house of the smuggling ringleader. It was gloomy inside, and my brother had trouble making out anything. The leader—a woman—looked up surprised when she saw them enter. She said, "Why did you come down? I've sent word asking you to postpone the trip. It's gotten too dangerous around here. The police are on the alert. Just yesterday, they caught two groups." Her reaction made my brother only more nervous and scared. "You must find a way to get me out," he said. "I'm a marked man now. I haven't shown up for work. This is a tip-off that I've fled. My bosses must have informed the police. They must be looking for me. If I return to Saigon, I'll be arrested." The woman thought for a while and said, "I'll try to get you out with a group organized by a Catholic priest."

The next morning at six o'clock, she sent my brother off with a guide and another escapee, a sixteen-year-old boy. In the evening, they reached a safe house, where the guide hid my brother and the teenager for a couple of days. It was a large hut, built right on the bank of a river. The host family was kind and discreet, but the stay seemed terribly long. Giu felt anxious the whole time, afraid that word of their presence might leak out. Then finally one morning the traveling party set out again. Everyone in this area went barefoot, so my brother did the same. After the recent rain, the dirt road was slippery. Giu felt like he was walking through an oil slick. Every once in a while, they came to a bridge that was just a log thrown across a canal. Giu's muddy feet kept slipping, so he got down on all fours and crawled across. His guide looked on in horror, knowing that this would tip off the locals, who could scamper easily across even with the heavy loads they normally carried. He muttered under his breath, "You're like a stone tied around my neck."

After what seemed like an eternity, the group arrived at another house. That evening, Giu could not sleep, worrying that the police might burst in at any moment, tipped off about his party's whereabouts. In the middle of the night, the guide woke them up and took them to a sampan. When they reached a village near the mouth of the river, Giu could hear ocean waves lapping against the shore in the distance. He knew he was close to the embarkation point and that the hour of his deliverance was near. For the first time, he felt hopeful. After a while, the small boat docked at an islet. The guide told Giu and the teenager to crawl into a bush near a canal and wait.

Right away, mosquitoes swarmed over him. Giu felt like he was being eaten alive, but he did not dare to slap and crush them, afraid that in the stillness of the night the sound might carry over the water and attract the attention of peasants out looking for fish. He could hear them talking and wading in the shallow water. He was also afraid that if he crushed the mosquitoes, the smell of blood would attract even more. He tried to wave them away as best he could. After about twenty minutes of agony, a small child appeared at his side and whispered, "Uncle, please follow me." Relieved, he crawled out of his hiding place. The moon was shining its shimmering light over the puddles of rainwater in the road, making it hard for Giu to see the uneven ground, and he stumbled along, tripping and sliding. Finally, they arrived at another house where they spent the night. From here, a sampan would take him to a "big fish"—a boat large enough to carry refugees out to sea.

Early the next morning it began to pour. Giu looked anxiously at the sky and prayed that it would clear, but the rain became heavier and fell nonstop. Late that afternoon, the guide told him that a storm had blown into the area. It lasted for several days and brought howling wind and pelting rain. In the distance, Giu could hear the waves crashing against the shore. He knew that no boat would dare to go out in this kind of weather. His heart sank. On the fifth day, the guide told him and the teenager that they would have to turn around and go back to Saigon. The teenager took the news cheerfully; he was only leaving because his parents had forced him to flee, now he could return to his girlfriend. Giu was sick with worry, believing that he would be arrested and put in jail the moment he showed up in Saigon.

The return trip was just as roundabout, slow, and risky. Giu was jumpy during the entire journey. The smugglers that took him back remained very cautious, because the police and militia were on the look-out for escapees turning around after their attempt had failed. Giu's luck continued to hold, and he made it back without any hitches. When he got back to his house, he learned that the neighborhood police had been snooping around asking questions, after his office reported him missing from work. This frightened him, and he moved in with another relative. He remembers how fear dominated his life from then on, and how each day all he could think of was evading the police. He knew he would have to leave, and leave quickly, and thoughts of fleeing obsessed him. He made several more attempts, each filled with as much suspense as the first one—hiding in safe houses, listening with terror to the barking of dogs, and waiting for the chance to get on a boat—but each time his trip had to be aborted. He grew more frustrated and more desperate.

On his fifth try, he managed to get to Ca Mau. Like the first time, he took a roundabout way to get there. Finally, one evening he made it to a "big fish"—just a large canoe, about two meters wide and twelve meters long, equipped with an engine. Elated, Giu thought he was about to leave the country, never to return. He thanked the woman rowing the sampan taxi, emptied his pockets and gave her all the money he had and, shaking with excitement and fear, squeezed in among the ten escapees who were already crowding the bench on his side of the canoe; on the opposite bench, he saw another ten. Right away, Giu felt his feet getting wet. He looked down and saw oil slicks floating on the water's surface—leaks from cracked barrels of reserve diesel fuel. As more water seeped in, the escapees were asked to help bail out the canoe to keep it from sinking. Giu worried that the flimsy vessel might not be able to withstand the ocean voyage, but there was no turning back now, so he brushed his fear aside. The engine began to sputter and the canoe started down the stream toward the sea; Giu shouted with excitement. Suddenly, he saw the hulk of a large boat filled with firewood looming in the dark and blocking the way. The canoe veered to the side of the narrow waterway, and got stuck among the submerged indigo plants. While the crew was frantically trying to free the boat, policemen arrived. As they led Giu and the other escapees away, one of them said, "You should thank us for this. The revolution's doing you a favor. It's saved your lives. You would never have made it in this rickety boat."

Giu and the others were taken to a detention center near a small town, from where, my brother believed, he would be transferred to the harsh labor camp nearby to serve a long jail sentence. He felt anxious and depressed, wondering whether he would be able to withstand another prolonged imprisonment. Two weeks later, however, the leader of the smuggling ring bribed the police and Giu was freed. Feeling elated and nervous, my brother left immediately, before anything would happen to put him back in prison, and took a bus to Saigon.

If my brother had made it out to sea, he might have ended up in the belly of a fish. Or he might have experienced what Nam went through. Shortly after the fall of Saigon, Nam's youthful idealism quickly evaporated in the reality of life under communism. First, his father was incarcerated for re-education just a couple of days after the takeover and subsequently sent to the North, where he would languish for many years.

Then, one night, the neighborhood police summoned Nam to the station at two o'clock in the morning and ordered him to write a report on himself. They slapped him, accused him of lying, and made him redo his report over and over again. Humiliated and angry, Nam realized that no matter how patriotic and idealistic he was, no matter how ready to work for the good of the country, in the eyes of the communists he was not someone to be trusted, let alone used in any meaningful capacity. A few weeks later, professors from Hanoi arrived to reorganize the university in Saigon. They did away with the law school where Nam was enrolled and replaced it with a school of economics. Nam was reassigned to agricultural economics, but the teaching was so highly political that he spent more time studying Marxism-Leninism than economics or agriculture. He graduated in 1977, but already disillusioned, saw no future for himself and decided to flee.

He tried and failed nine times. In 1978, on the tenth attempt, he and a group of relatives made it out to sea. The night before, they had endured a nerve-wracking vigil, waiting for three hours in the dark for the tide to rise. At eleven o'clock, they finally lifted anchor and sailed into the stormy night. Swells made many of the passengers violently sick, but the sturdy fishing boat, piloted by an experienced captain and his assistant and powered by a good diesel engine, pushed on through the waves. There was an ample supply of fresh water and food onboard for the fifty-two passengers, nine of whom were related to Nam. After the storm died down, the weather stayed calm. During the day, the refugees would bake in the hot sun; as darkness fell and the fog descended, they would freeze. Women and children slept at night in the hold where they could stay warm, but young men like Nam had to lie on deck where the dense mist chilled them to the bone. Nam would sneak up and sleep next to the engine to keep warm. There was no privacy onboard. When he had to relieve himself, Nam would go to one end of the boat and cling to two ropes as he did his business over the heaving ocean. It was not easy. A man once fell into the water and had to be rescued.

One night, Nam thought he heard voices rising over the water. The sound was eerie, like hundreds of people whispering in the fog, and he felt a chill going down his spine. The next day, the captain said that they had just sailed past an area of the ocean where perhaps thousands of refugees had perished. Later, one of Nam's brothers would disappear into the ocean without a trace. Sometimes Nam wonders whether his brother has joined the chorus of ghosts over that patch of the sea.

After three nights on the open ocean, Nam and his fellow travelers saw a bright glow on the horizon one evening. They knew they were approaching a city. The next morning, the boat dropped anchor, but it was greeted by soldiers—Malaysians, it turned out—who threatened to shoot anyone coming ashore onto their country. They gave the refugees some food and water, showed them how to get to Singapore, and told them to leave. Five days later, the boat made land and docked again on the Malaysian coast. The area was so wild and inhospitable that they knew they would never be able to survive there. Disappointed, they got back on the boat.

Then one evening they saw the bright glow of Singapore in the distance, beckoning like a beacon of hope. A patrol boat approached and its captain told the refugees he would come back to take them ashore. The refugees shouted with joy, but they waited in vain. At one o'clock in the morning, a large ship arrived and towed them back out to the open ocean. Before cutting their boat loose, an officer on board warned them that he would blow them out of the water if they tried to dock in Singapore. Drifting on the ocean once more, the refugees were beginning to give up hope when a Dutch ship supplying food to oil drilling rigs off Malaysia picked them up. The captain took them aboard to shower and get a meal, while he cabled Amsterdam to obtain asylum for them. For the first time since he left his country, Nam thought he was treated like a human being, and felt revived. When his request was turned down, the captain gave the refugees provisions and a map, and showed them how to get to an island lying in Malaysian waters that he knew was taking in refugees. Nam and his group eventually arrived in Pulau Tengha, which had received some 1200 boat people from Vietnam.

The island had not as yet been overrun with refugees, and Nam found life there relaxing. He spent his time building rudimentary roads and houses and helping the United Nations refugee group establish personal files for the boat people; in his spare time, he went down to the beach to swim or read. Although there were moments when he felt like he was on vacation, he still faced the prospect of finding a country that would take him in for permanent settlement. Most refugees wanted to go to the United States, but Nam, still feeling rejected and rueful over events in Saigon in 1975, did not want to be a ward of the Americans. About two weeks after he got to the island, Australians arrived and announced that their country was ready and willing to take any refugees who wanted to settle there. While the Americans made their procedures cumbersome and prolonged the waiting period to discourage applicants, the Australians' formalities were speedy. Nam was touched by their warm welcome, and decided to apply for resettlement there. In July, after about a month on the island, Nam flew to Sydney where he met and married my niece Lan. The rest of his family eventually emigrated to Australia, joining over 100,000 refugees who had made their homes there.

Back in Saigon, Giu found himself in limbo. Although he was glad he had escaped jail, the fear of being on the run again took over. His residency card had been revoked, and he could not move back into his house. No one else was likely to take him in, because they could run into trouble too. He stayed briefly with Mrs. An and her family, but her husband and children, afraid that his presence would implicate them, insisted that he move elsewhere, so Mrs. An found him a place in the apartment of a woman who had good connections among the police and cadres. He could spend the night safely there. During the day, my brother wandered around, visiting relatives and eating at street stalls, at Yen's place, or at Mrs. An's house. Giu lived in anxiety, knowing he could be arrested at any moment. His old translation office was passing the word around that, should he return to Saigon, it was willing to take him back and get him a residency card. But Giu was afraid to contact them—he could not be sure the offer was not a trap laid by the police.

A year later, Giu found a couple of people willing to act as go-betweens with the police and help him get a residency card. It cost him more than an ounce of gold to grease the palms of police officers in his old neighborhood and in the district and city offices, but now he could move back into his house. Mrs. An, who had financed the cost of getting his residency card, gave him money to live on. Although his life was bearable, he felt he was wasting it away. He had nothing constructive to do with his time, and he had been separated from his wife and children for close to ten years.

Having tried five times to flee and failing each time, he decided to find a way to get out legally instead. When he was released from political detention in 1979, he had written to my brother Tuan in Paris, who put in a request for him. The French embassy was willing to start the paperwork, but the Vietnamese government would not accept his application to emigrate, even to a friendly country like France. Giu's technical skills, which had allowed him to find a job in the translation office, turned into a liability in this situation. So many trained professionals had left that Vietnam now barred people like Giu from leaving the country. By 1983, Vietnam had worked out an orderly departure arrangement with a number of countries to allow for the reunion of spouses, and parents and children, separated in the wake of the war, and to put an end to the chaotic and dangerous escapes by boat people. Under this humanitarian program, Giu's wife could have applied for him to rejoin her in America, but she had decided to start a new life without him, so she demurred. My mother in Paris stepped in to get Giu out, and her application for reunion with her son was quickly approved by the French. In Saigon, through a family connection, Giu's application to leave the country this time was accepted for consideration.

Because of the government's many obstacles to emigration, and the bureaucratic delays created by the number of applications, things moved at a snail's pace. In 1985, the government relaxed many rules, the pace of approval speeded up, and more and more people were allowed to emigrate. By this time, Giu's age worked to his advantage: He was now almost sixty years old, no longer a man in the prime of his life that the government wanted to keep. Still, it was not until June 1989 that he was issued a passport, and not until January of 1990 that he could actually get a seat on one of the few commercial flights from Vietnam. Onboard the plane, he felt drained, but also excited and relieved; he was going to be reunited with his mother and siblings, and he was finally leaving a life filled with fear and frustration. But he also felt anxious, wondering how he was going to support himself in France, what the future would bring, and how he was going to rejoin his children in America. When he arrived in Paris, my mother and my sister Tuyet had not seen him for fifteen years; my brother Tuan and my sister Loan had not seen him for about thirty years. Then, his daughter Lily flew over to see him. He cried when he saw her—out of happiness and out of grief over the lost years. She was only eleven when she fled Saigon, now she was a computer specialist managing a staff of programmers. Giu was happy to be in France, but his goal was really to go to America and be, if not with Nguyet, at least with his children. His wife finally relented, and applied for him to come over. He flew to California in 1992, and was finally reunited with Duc, his son, who was now a student at UCLA. The shock of finding an adult replacing the five-year-old boy he had last seen in Saigon in 1975, and the emotion of being with his own family again, overwhelmed him. Giu had feared that his children had become estranged from him; the reunions, however, reassured him that the strong family ties had held. Instead of rejecting him, Lily and Duc welcomed him back into their life and seemed even more loving than before. Giu moved in with Nguyet, but they could not rebuild a relationship that had been severed for seventeen years, so after a few months, he went to live with Lily and her family.

I too saw my brother again for the first time since I visited Saigon in 1973. I had expected to see a man broken by prison and years of living in limbo. To my surprise, I found him in good health and in good spirits. Restored by his stay in France, he appeared younger than his sixty years. He was slim, but not emaciated, and his posture remained straight, unbowed by the time in jail. He still looked pretty much like the dignified executive he used to be. His mind was sharp. The hard times had not destroyed him physically or mentally, but it seemed to me they had changed him into a different man. In the old days, he struck me as dour, stern, and uncommunicative, and I found him hard to approach. Now, he was more outgoing. He talked and laughed easily; I felt I could get close to him and know him better. There was also a quiet zest for life that I had not seen before. Having once lost his liberty, he seemed to savor each day of freedom.

Giu's release from prison camp and his reunion with us healed a painful wound left by the legacy of the war. As the echoes of what the French set in motion and what the Cold War wrought have faded away, my family has rediscovered normalcy. Over a hundred years have passed since the days my great-grandfather Duong Lam tried to hold his citadel against French attacks in the Red River Delta. In that span, Vietnam and our family have gone through trials and transformations that Duong Lam could scarcely have imagined. Yet, like Vietnam, we have survived, scarred, but not broken, and determined to forge ahead and to look to the future with optimism. Giu's departure did not sever our links with Vietnam and its history. Many of our relatives are still there, taking part in the new era that has dawned for the country. We have reason to hope that, in the new world order unmarred by warring ideologies, they will be able to pursue their life untouched by armed conflict and revolution. Only time will tell.

Epilogue: Across the Four Seas

After a short stay at the Guam refugee receiving center in May 1975, my family flew to Camp Pendleton, a Marine base in California, for processing and resettlement. There, among a sea of tents and Quonset huts, they found relatives who had evacuated from Saigon earlier. The first arrivals had settled in, but these natives of the tropics found southern California's spring weather, chilled by mist from the nearby ocean, too cold. Their Marine-issue jackets hung loosely from their tiny frames. After the euphoria of family reunion and the relief of getting to America, my sisters Phu and Tuyet began to worry about the husbands and children they had left behind. Every day, they would check the log of newly arrived refugees. For Phu, as the days passed, hope gradually gave way to despair. She cried a lot, and became bitter toward my brother Luong, blaming him for her husband and son getting stuck in Saigon. Tuyet remained optimistic, clinging to the hope of finding her husband Tuan in Paris. She thought he might have gotten out on a last commercial flight. My brother Xuong (whose wife Hao was with my parents) likewise wondered whether his oldest son had made it out before Saigon fell. But my brother and two sisters had to put their anxiety aside and deal with a more immediate concern: Along with all the refugees, they had to choose whether to resettle in the United States or go somewhere else.

No matter where they decided to move, the future looked cloudy. Except for Binh, who had been flown to New York with her family and had been given a job at Chase Manhattan Bank, none of them knew how they were going to survive and support their own families. All I could offer my relatives was either to join me in Ithaca or to live with my parents-in-law on their farm in Virginia until they could find jobs. Neither choice looked good to them. My husband and I could not provide much financial support; he was still in graduate school, and I was working part-time and expecting our first child. Neither Ithaca nor Virginia had many jobs to offer. In the end, my parents, brothers, and sisters decided not to move to either place. But wherever they settled, my siblings resolved to work at any job that was available and do whatever it would take to give their sons and daughters the education they needed to get ahead. This deep-rooted belief that education opens doors, which they shared with other Vietnamese refugees, would pave the way for their children to succeed in their adopted lands.

Luong's wife Thu had family members in Canada, so he made up his mind to move there. Phu had two sons in Australia, and this seemed like a logical place for her to go. Through the Catholic Relief Service, one of the charitable organizations that were helping resettle refugees, Xuong and his family got sponsored by a family in Huntington Beach, California, and moved in with them. My father, longing to be in a culture with which he was familiar, decided to go to Paris, where my sister Loan and brother Tuan were living. While at Pendleton, he had fallen ill and had spent a few days in the base hospital, where his inability to talk to the doctors or nurses left him utterly frustrated. In France, he thought, he could at least communicate with people, and he had many relatives there among the large Vietnamese expatriate community. Tuyet, who was expecting a child and still hoping to find her husband in Paris, decided to go with my parents. In spite of the marital problems she and Tuan had weathered in Saigon, he was still her husband and the father of her children, and she wanted to be reunited with him.

So, the day arrived when my family scattered around the world. My parents could hardly bear the thought of seeing the family break up, but they were stoic, and tried to accept what fate had brought their way. They exacted promises from their sons and daughters to stay in touch and make an effort to visit them in Paris. Tuyet, who was close to Phu, was disconsolate at her move to Australia. Phu tried to cheer her up: "Don't be sad. Australia isn't so far away. We'll see each other again." But she was wrong. That was the last time anyone in my family saw

Phu, who died suddenly in 1984. (Eventually, my siblings would be reunited with their children and spouses, with the exception of Tuyet. Her husband Tuan spent over ten years in a re-education camp in the North, and after his release, he preferred to remain in Saigon where he started a new family, after Tuyet herself remarried.)

As they had resolved to do, my siblings took any job they could find to survive. In Montreal, Luong went to work at a plastics factory, mixing resins, until he found a job in the city government. In California, Xuong began working at a hotel, while his wife Hao started assembling electronics components in a factory; they became self-sufficient so quickly that they never had to resort to welfare. In Australia, Phu took a job as a cleaning lady until she got a position in the post office. (My nephew Nam went back to school and, after taking a series of jobs, became a real estate agent.) Tuyet, in Paris, also started out as a cleaning lady for an office, and eventually found a position in a government agency. Other refugees around them were also taking odd jobs—pumping gasoline, waiting on tables—just to get by. They were driven by their traditional work ethic, but also by the opportunities they saw around them. They realized that once they got acclimated, they could move on to better jobs and get ahead.

Even I was amazed at how well my relatives adapted. After Dave finished his dissertation, it took him a year to find a teaching position at a private college in California: With the glut of Ph.D.s, academic jobs had become scarce while competition had grown fiercer. We bought a fixer-upper house in a modest section of town in 1977, and tried to survive on Dave's small salary. My brother Xuong and his son Dung came to visit us a few months after we arrived, in Dung's brand-new sports car, which he had bought with the money he had earned working at two jobs while going to school. They were shocked to see how we lived, making our home in a run-down house, owning a stereo system that dated back to 1966, and driving an old Maverick without air conditioning. They had always thought that I, married to an American, was rich. Looking at the sports car and their cheerful demeanor, I felt pleased with how easily they had taken to an American life-style and managed to prosper.

Other refugees in California were also taking advantage of the opportunities available to them. Often, everyone in the family who could work did so. Pooling their money, they soon could begin to buy things, lured by the cornucopia of consumer goods but also intent on competing with their compatriots. In the United States, every refugee started with a clean slate, ex-general and ex-clerk alike, as their social positions back in Vietnam no longer meant anything in the new country. Status now came from what kind of car you drove and, later, what kind of house you lived in. Whenever Dave and I went to Garden Grove, which had become known as Little Saigon for its concentration of refugees, our Maverick looked like a wreck next to the Mercedes, BMW, Audi, and Honda cars in the parking lots of the mini-malls filled with Vietnamese shops.

My brother Giu, who arrived in the United States seventeen years later, had an easier time than those who fled here in 1975. He did not have to take any job just to survive. His own family had settled in, and could provide him with housing and financial support. Nevertheless, as soon as he came to California in 1992, he looked for employment so he could be independent, but mainly to stay busy. When he discovered that his age, lack of English, and outmoded engineering skills made it impossible for him to find a professional job, he decided to spend his time studying English, updating his electrical engineering skills, and reading. His greatest challenge, like that of other refugees who rejoined their families after having been separated from them in 1975, was to fit in with wives and children who had lived on their own for years. Although Giu could not renew his relationship with his wife, he had little trouble re-establishing the bonds with his children. The closeness he had forged with them when they were in Saigon drew them back to him; also, his Westernized outlook made it easier for him to relate to his Americanized son and daughter. Many other refugees, coming from more traditional backgrounds, could not step back into their families as easily, unable to reconcile themselves to the independence their wives and children had achieved in America and to let go of their past role as sole providers and undisputed authority figures.

After Lily gave birth to her daughter in 1997, Giu began taking care of his granddaughter full-time. He seems content to lead a placid life after years of turmoil, and whenever I ask him how he is getting along, he says that he is just glad to have escaped from a life of fear under the communists. He no longer hates them as he did when he first arrived in America, but he swears he will not go back to Vietnam as long as they remain in power. My family members who fled in 1975 continue to distrust the communists as Giu does and, except for my sister Binh, who has made several trips to Vietnam, have no desire to go back. Toward America, Giu and my family members in exile feel no hatred. While many refugees remained bitter for many years about what they viewed as America's abandonment of South Vietnam, my parents and my siblings believed that the United States had the right to pursue its own national interest and to abandon a hopeless cause, and so did not blame the Americans for the loss. Instead, they condemned the Saigon regime for having squandered the time America had bought for the noncommunist side.

Since Vietnam has become to them a hostile land, my family members—except for my mother—do not long to return, and this has induced them to try and make their new countries home. The large refugee communities in America, Canada, France, and Australia have eased their resettlement: They can live in close proximity to people of their own kind, eat traditional foods, and shop in stores selling familiar merchandise. Also, all my siblings went to French schools, and their Western education made it easier for them to adapt. Yet, like other immigrants, they sometimes still feel that they do not completely belong and that they are strangers looking in, suspended between their old and their new countries. Although some, like my brothers Luong and Giu, and my nephew Nam, wish that they could have meaningful careers (neither Luong nor Nam had the money to go back to law school and become attorneys), they try to console themselves with the thought that they are fortunate enough to live in free countries and have jobs that allow them to support their families. They place their hopes in their children and are content to watch them blossom.

Back in 1975, I worried the most about my parents: old people, set in their ways, suddenly thrust into a new environment. In fact, my father found he was in his element in Paris, enjoying French culture and delighting in visits with old friends and relatives. He was happy to have escaped from the communists, and the problems of exile—such as cramming into my brother Tuan's apartment and lacking money—seemed a small price to pay for his freedom. My mother, on the other hand, spoke little French and found Paris baffling. She had not wanted to leave Saigon, and now demanded to go back. She went into depression and cried a lot. She finally resigned herself to living in France, but she never adjusted completely, and is still torn between staying and going back to her own culture.

While my mother, as well as many older refugees, had a hard time accepting exile, the younger ones embraced the culture of their host countries and quickly acclimated. Those who left Saigon when they were small children—like many of my nephews and nieces—before they had absorbed the language and culture of Vietnam, were like empty vessels, eagerly drawing in what they heard and saw. They became French, Canadians, Australians, and Americans, and had only a limited interest in Vietnam—in other words, they became typical assimilated second-generation immigrants. Even when they grew older, Vietnam would remain in their eyes a foreign country, perhaps one they would be interested in visiting, but not a place they yearned to live in. Most did not even want to take the time to learn more about the old country; they were too busy with their lives and careers, too caught up in enjoying their material success. Older refugees tried to keep traditions alive, but they found it hard to interest the young, most of whom were seduced by the more alluring Western culture surrounding them. Perhaps at some point, my nephews and nieces and other young refugees will stop and look at themselves, and wonder about their Vietnamese heritage.

I hope our twenty-two-year-old son Bryan will do the same. Living in a culture that pays little heed to traditions and constantly seeks the new, he has shown only limited curiosity about my family and Vietnam, or about the history of Dave's family. His interest in his dual backgrounds has grown in the last two years, but he is still at the stage where he wants to create his own space and establish his own identity.

Unlike some second-generation immigrants, I do not believe I have to choose between my legacies, one to the exclusion of the other. I view myself as a mixture of Vietnamese, French, and American cultural strains and feel comfortable moving in all three countries. Yet, underneath the French and American layers, I remain Vietnamese at the core and, as I grow older, I feel the pull of my heritage and an urge to return to my roots. Perhaps I am like a traveler who, having explored the world, is ready to go home and sit by the hearth. This desire to return to the source—to use the Vietnamese phrase—is what drove me to write this book.

After taking five years off from work to raise Bryan, I decided to take a job in 1982 with a bank in Los Angeles, where I ultimately became a vice president of marketing. I enjoyed the glamour and the responsibilities of an important corporate job, but as the years passed, my interest waned. Ever since I was a teenager, I had wanted to become an author. The idea of writing my family's story had germinated while I was still living in Saigon. When my father died in 1979, my yearning to pursue this interest grew. In 1993, I decided to quit my job and devote myself to the book, emboldened by the economic security of Dave's full professorship at his college and a grant from the National Endowment for the Humanities.

After stops in Montreal and Paris to interview relatives, I flew to Vietnam, to renew ties with my sisters Thang and Yen and with other relatives and to conduct research for my book. I felt anxious before I left, unsure of how they would receive me after decades of absence. I also hoped that the return to a Vietnam now at peace would finally dispel the images of war that had haunted me since I left in 1973, so that I could take back with me to California the certainty that the sorrows I knew were really of the past. As I spied the green Vietnamese country-side beneath the fuselage, I was overwhelmed with emotion, and memories of battles and deaths flashed through my mind. When my plane taxied on the runway at Tan Son Nhut airport, I looked out the window for the jet fighters that used to park behind the concrete embankments, but they were gone. Gone, too, were the sandbags and the soldiers toting M-16 rifles. I felt disoriented. Throughout my stay in the South, I would have to constantly adjust my memory of war to the reality of peace. My second shock was seeing communist immigration officials and guards in Soviet-style uniforms. For the rest of my visit, I would be surprised again and again by reminders—such as red flags and street and building names—that the Viet Cong were no longer at the gate clamoring to get in, but very much in charge.

My sister Yen was waiting for me at the airport. It took me a full minute to recognize her and she me, after twenty years. We embraced and held hands, looking at each other, too moved to speak. During the drive into the city, I felt even more lost. Saigon had changed in those twenty years; houses now stood where there had been empty lots . The traffic was heavy, and I saw the normal scenes of a big city life, unmarred by signs of war. I felt happy, but could not communicate my feelings to Yen, for whom peace had become routine and unremarkable. As our car approached a gate, one of its doors suddenly swung open, and I saw Thang running to push the other one to the side. I had been invited to stay here, in Lap's house, where my sister was now living with Hau. Thang had become seriously ill with kidney stones in 1989, and Lap had moved her and Hau to Saigon, where the warmer climate had revived her, as he had hoped. Lap had been transferred to Saigon earlier to work in a hospital, and he was followed by his sisters Hoa and Hien, who arrived to work in the agriculture office—part of the wave of personnel that the new government had sent south to staff its administration.

I jumped out of the car and called Thang's name in a voice cracking with emotion. She grabbed and squeezed my arms, in the traditional way of showing affection, and smiled through tears. Forty years, two wars, and a revolution, and yet the family bonds had held, I thought. Thang had the thick figure of a woman past middle age, and her hair was gray—no longer the young and willowy sister I had last seen in 1950. She was radiantly happy, surrounded by her children and grandchildren, and she seemed more talkative than I remembered. I was happy, too, that she had finally found serenity after such a hard life.

That evening, I could not go to sleep in Lap's house. I was excited about being back in Saigon, and my mind was racing with thoughts about my family, and about the war and the peace. The night was very quiet. The ground was not shaking from the explosion of bombs falling on the edge of Saigon. As I listened, I heard, not the boom of distant cannons, but the sound of rain falling outside and the intermittent deep-throated call of a bullfrog.

Hau arrived a couple of days later from the Mekong Delta, where he had gone to advise some local agricultural experts, although he was now officially retired. I knew who he was the moment I saw him: He looked like the emaciated person I had seen in old pictures, although, of course, his face was now lined and his hair gray. He smiled in greeting, teased me affectionately about my weight (heavy in comparison to most Vietnamese), and then brought out a bottle of his homemade liquor and we clinked glasses. I had feared that he might consider me an ideological stray for marrying an American, but I knew now that he had accepted me into the fold.

I had to coax Thang and Hau—and, later, my other relatives in Vietnam—to reminisce about the war, which had become distant to them. They preferred to focus on the present and on the opportunity to improve their lives, as the economy took off with the influx of foreign capital. When I could talk them into remembering the war, they would marvel at its ferocity and their luck in surviving its violence. Those who had fought on the side of the communists were at times nostalgic, recalling the noble sense of mission and the solidarity of purpose of those bygone days. Although they had suffered, they saw no point in dwelling on the past and nursing their resentment against those that had fought on the other side. Those who had been on the losing side were nostalgic for the old days but reconciled to the new state of things and trying to make the best of it.

Between intensive interviews with Thang and Hau, I visited Yen in her apartment. Her husband's death of lung cancer a couple of months before left her both sad and relieved. She felt a hole in her life now, although she was glad she no longer had to cope with an irascible hus-band who used to find fault with everything she did. She took comfort in the fact that he had lived long enough to see his family's fortune improve with Vietnam's economic transformation. Looking out from her balcony, the same one from which she had watched looters in April 1975, she pointed out to me the buildings that would soon be torn down to be replaced by shopping arcades, hotels, and office and apart-ment complexes. To her, these projects were signs of renewal. She thought she and her children were going through a personal renewal as well. Her family background that she had feared would hinder her daughter and her three sons was no longer an insurmountable handicap. Thi, her daughter, had graduated from the university as a pediatrician. Anh, her oldest son, had gone back to school to get an MBA while working for an English expatriates' club as a manager. Quang, her sec-ond son, was working as a technician in a factory and planned to enter the university to get an engineering degree. Trung, her youngest son, was finishing high school.

Minh, my nephew, was another relative whose life had taken a turn for the better. I remembered him as a teenager, but he was now a suc-cessful scrap-metal dealer, married, with two children, and living in comfort. He, too, had gone back to school to get a degree in business management. (In 1998, Minh flew his family to Houston, where his par-ents and siblings had settled, believing his children would have the chance to get a superior education there.)

Outside Saigon, I saw other signs of renewal. Driving to the seaport of Vung Tau, I did not see refugee huts lining the road, but new brick houses rising in the distance. In the Iron Triangle of Cu Chi, bombed, shelled, and defoliated, nature had taken over, and saplings were turn-ing into mature trees and obliterating many of the craters. Passing by a cemetery with 10,000 headstones marking the tombs of Viet Cong who had fallen in battle, I knew that the scars of war were still there, but no longer haunting the living.

After two weeks in Saigon, I flew to Hanoi. The city had changed little during the forty years I was gone. The communists had left it as they had found it, while they concentrated on rebuilding the country-side, and then on fighting the United States. Crowded and dilapidated, Hanoi was no longer the romantic city I remembered; yet, with its many lakes, tree-lined streets, old commercial quarters, and colonial-era build-ings, it retained a lot of its charm. Here too there was a sense of renew-al, and public buildings were being repaired and repainted.

To my surprise, my relatives in the North, whom I had not met or could scarcely remember, welcomed me warmly. Cousin Phi took me to visit his family, still living in the one-room apartment into which he had moved in 1956, although he had added a loft. Over several emotional days, he told me about Uncle Chinh's last years, hardly able to suppress the pain he still felt, although taking care not to level any accusations against the government's handling of land reform. Luc, now retired from the army and working for a small travel agency, told me his life story with pride and a sense of humor, although he also steered clear of any criticism of the government. He seemed happy, spending his time squiring French tourists to the old Dien Bien Phu battle site, and American visitors down the highway that runs along the coast to Saigon, passing by the Vinh Linh area where he used to fire at American planes. To me, he exemplified the let-bygones-be-bygones spirit of the Vietnamese, rubbing shoulders with people from countries he had once fought.

I had no trouble finding Uncle Dinh, still living in the same house. I remembered accompanying my mother to visit him and his wife in happier days, and I wept with sadness when I saw him, a thin, old man, sitting in the dark, dingy room that the communists had allowed him to keep. I had hoped that Uncle Dinh could tell me how to find my grandmother's grave, but his mind was gone; he had no idea who I was. Nor could his daughter An help me. I felt like my grandmother had disappeared without a trace. One morning, I went to Hang Gai street to look for something that could connect me to my grandmother. The silk shop she owned had been replaced by a store with a metal grille, but the old banyan tree and the small shrine at which she worshiped were still standing, and Hang Gai looked like it had not changed much since the days she lived there. I did not know where my sister Cuc was buried, so I went one day to the hospital where she had died, as a way of paying homage to her memory. I walked in the courtyard, but I could not make myself go in to wander along the corridors and look for the room where she might have breathed her last. Even after these decades, I still could not reconcile myself to her painful death.

One early morning, as the sun was just beginning to burn off the mist, Phi and his wife Thu drove me to Van Dinh. I had forgotten some of the customs for visiting ancestral graves, but Phi—although he had grown up under communism—had not. Phi's retention of tradition struck me, as did the religious revival I saw around me. Temples that had been shuttered for decades had reopened their doors, and people thronged their halls, burning incense and praying, or consulting fortune-tellers. We visited Duong Lam's grave in Tao Khe village first, and Phi carefully laid out the offerings of fruit and flowers, and lit joss sticks and candles. No one from the village showed up to drive us away or to threaten us, as they would have at the height of the revolution. I prayed silently to Duong Lam, as the incense smoke curled in the air, above the weeds that had grown profusely over his resting place, feeling happy that I could finally pay my personal respects.

We continued on with the tour, and Phi took me to the tomb of Duong Lam's wife, and then to those of my grandparents. My emotions welled up and I wept at Phan's grave, grieving over the years that had kept me away and the indignities that had been visited on his memory by peasants showing contempt for the feudalist past. Phan's restored tomb, by chance, now sits on land that belongs to a relative in the area, a new migrant who had retraced the steps of Duong Lam's ancestors several centuries ago from Ha Tinh to Van Dinh. She joined relatives belonging to another branch of the Duong clan still living in the village. Once a year, she and they hold a ceremony to honor the spirits of all the deceased Duong, and my cousins from Hanoi would travel back to Van Dinh to partake in the ritual and banquet. That day, between cups of hot tea, she and her husband—like other Vietnamese I met on my trip—told me how delighted they were that I had not forgotten my ancestral land. Their warm welcome made me feel that I still belonged.

In Van Dinh, all I could find of Duong Lam's and Duong Khue's residences was a stone gate, with carved inscriptions made almost smooth by the passage of time. The buildings themselves had been razed by the Viet Minh after my family and other relatives had fled from the village, including the ancestral hall that used to scare me as a child when my family took refuge here in 1947. Twenty families now lived on the ground where I had played games, and as I stood in the hot sun looking at the mossy roofs of their homes, I knew I could never recapture those magical days among the halls and gardens of my great-grandfather's residence. Yet visiting the graves and standing on the soil that my ancestors once trod gave me a sense of connection to my roots in a way that the family stories I had heard, and the research I had done, did not.

On the way back to Hanoi, I thought about my pilgrimage and wondered whether the monk who had wrenched us from rural poverty over a century ago would say that we are still enjoying success. For him, and for my ancestors, success meant fame as scholars and power as mandarins of the emperor. Now, my relatives are professionals, holding well-paying jobs and enjoying material comforts beyond the monk's imagination.

By the yardstick of his time, they have fallen short of his predictions: They are not steeped in ancient learning, nor do they have the prestige that Duong Lam enjoyed. Still, by today's different standards, I believe they are as successful as their forebears had been.

As my plane took off one fall morning from Hanoi, I looked out of my window and felt a sense of peace and closure. I had renewed family bonds unbroken by time and war, and I had reconnected with my roots and my native soil. I had seen my relatives put the past behind them and move on, stirred once again by hope rather than by fear of bullets and bombs. I had seen Vietnam, the land of two million war dead, become once again the land of the living. And I was taking back with me not the deafening explosions of weapons, but the gentle sound of the monsoon rain.

Bibliography

Ban Nghien Cuu Lich Su Ha Nam Ninh. *So thao lich su dang bo Nam Dinh* (1945-1954) (Preliminary History of the Party Chapter in Nam Dinh, 1945-1954). Nam Dinh (?): Xi nghiep in Ha Nam Ninh, 1976.

Beresford, Melanie. *Vietnam: Politics, Economics and Society*. London and New York: Pinter Publishers, 1988.

Bo Quoc Phong. *Lich su cuoc khang chien chong thuc dan Phap, 1945-1954* (History of the Resistance Against French Colonialism, 1945-1954). 4 vols. Hanoi: Nha xuat ban Quan Doi Nhan Dan, 1985-1990.

Bodard, Lucien. *The Quicksand War: Prelude to Vietnam*. Boston: Little, Brown, 1967.

Bui Diem, with David Chanoff. *In the Jaws of History*. Boston: Houghton Mifflin, 1987.

Butler, David. *The Fall of Saigon*. New York: Simon and Schuster, 1985.

Buttinger, Joseph. *The Smaller Dragon: A Political History of Vietnam*. New York: Praeger, 1958.

———. *Vietnam: A Dragon Embattled*. New York: Praeger, 1967.

Chesneaux, Jean. *Contribution à l'histoire de la nation viêtnamienne*. Paris: Editions Sociales, 1955.

Chu Thien, *But nghien* (Brush and Ink Slab). Saigon: Nha xuat ban Do Chieu, 1968.

———. *Nha Nho* (The Confucian Scholars). Saigon: Nha xuat ban Do Chieu, 1968.

Clodfelter, Mark. *The Limits of Air Power: The American Bombing of North Vietnam.* New York: Free Press, 1989.

Devillers, Philippe. *Histoire du Vietnam de 1940 à 1952.* Paris: Editions du seuil, 1952.

Doan Ke Thien. *Co-tich va thang canh Ha Noi* (Stories and Sites of Hanoi). Hanoi: Tien Bo, 1959.

Doan Them. *Nhung ngay chua quen* (Days Still Not Forgotten). 2 vols. Vol. 1: Saigon: Nam Chi Tung Thu, 1967; vol. 2: Saigon: Pham Quang Khai Publishers, 1969.

Duiker, William J. *The Communist Road to Power.* Boulder: Westview Press, 1981.

———. *Vietnam Since the Fall of Saigon.* Athens: Ohio University Center for International Studies, Center for Southeast Asian Studies, 1985.

Duong Thieu Tong. *Tam trang Duong Khue, Duong Lam* (The State of Mind of Duong Khue and Duong Lam). Vietnam: Van Hoc, 1995.

Elliott, David W. P. "Revolutionary Re-integration: A Comparison of the Foundation of Post-Liberation Political Systems in North Vietnam and China." Ph.D. dissertation, Cornell University, 1976.

———, ed. *The Third Indochina Conflict.* Boulder: Westview Press, 1981.

Fall, Bernard. *Street Without Joy.* Harrisburg, Pa.: Stackpole Press, 1961.

Fforde, Adam, and Stefan de Vylder. *From Plan to Market: The Economic Transition in Vietnam.* Boulder: Westview Press, 1996.

50 Years of Activities of the Communist Party of Vietnam. Hanoi: Foreign Languages Publishing House, 1980.

Hai Phong, lich su khang chien chong thuc dan Phap xam luoc (Haiphong: History of the Resistance Against French Colonialist Invaders). Hanoi: Nha xuat ban Quan Doi Nhan Dan, 1986.

Halberstam, David. *The Making of a Quagmire.* New York: Random House, 1965.

———. *The Best and the Brightest.* New York: Fawcett Crest, 1969.

Hammer, Ellen J. *The Struggle for Indochina.* Stanford: Stanford University Press, 1954.

Hickey, Gerald. "The Vietnamese Village Through Time and War,"

The Vietnam Forum, no. 10, Summer-Fall 1989. New Haven: Yale Center for International and Area Studies, Council on Southeast Asia Studies.

Hoang Ngoc Phach et al. *Tho van Nguyen Khuyen* (The Literature of Nguyen Khuyen). Hanoi: Nha xuat ban Van Hoc, 1971.

Hoang Van Chi. *From Colonialism to Communism: A Case History of North Vietnam*. New York: Praeger, 1964.

Hoi Dong Lich Su Hai Phong. *Luoc khao duong pho Hai Phong* (Summary Examination of the Streets in the City of Haiphong). Haiphong: Nha xuat ban Hai Phong, 1993.

Hue-Tam Ho Tai. *Radicalism and the Origins of the Vietnamese Revolution*. Cambridge, Mass.: Harvard University Press, 1992.

Huynh Kim Khanh. *Vietnamese Communism, 1925-1945*. Ithaca: Cornell University Press, 1982.

Huynh Van Tong. *Lich su bao chi Viet Nam* (History of Vietnamese Journalism). Saigon: Tri Dang, 1973.

Jamieson, Neil. *Understanding Vietnam*. Berkeley: University of California Press, 1993.

Karnow, Stanley. *Vietnam: A History*. New York: Viking, 1983.

Kolko, Gabriel. *Anatomy of a War: Vietnam, the United States, and the Modern Historical Experience*. The New Press, 1994.

Lam Giang and Vu Ky. *Giang luan ve Nguyen Khuyen* (Dissertation on Nguyen Khuyen). Saigon: Tan Viet, 1960.

Le Thanh Khoi. *Le Viêt-Nam, histoire et civilisation*. Paris: Les Editions de Minuit, 1955.

Ljunggren, Borje, ed. *The Challenge of Reform in Indochina*. Cambridge, Mass.: Harvard Institute for International Development, Harvard University, 1993.

Luro, E. *Le pays d'Annam*. Paris: Ernest Leroux, 1897.

Marr, David G. *Vietnamese Anti-Colonialism, 1885-1925*. Berkeley: University of California Press, 1971.

———. *Vietnamese Tradition on Trial, 1920-1945*. Berkeley: University of California Press, 1981.

———. *Vietnam 1945: The Quest for Power*. Berkeley: University of California Press, 1995.

Marr, David G., and Christine White, eds. *Postwar Vietnam: Dilemmas in Socialist Development*. Ithaca: Cornell University Southeast Asia Program, 1988.

Moise, Edwin E. *Land Reform in China and North Vietnam: Consolidating the Revolution at the Village Level*. Chapel Hill: University of North Carolina Press, 1983.

Ngo Tat To. *Leu chong* (The Tent and the Writing Couch). Saigon: Mai Linh, 1958.

Nguyen Anh Tuan. *South Vietnam: Trial and Experience*. Athens, Ohio, 1987.

Nguyen Ba Trac. *Hoang-Viet giap ty nien bieu* (Imperial Vietnam Year by Year). Saigon: Bo Quoc-Gia Giao-Duc, 1963.

Nguyen Cao Ky. *How We Lost the Vietnam War*. New York: Stein and Day, 1976.

Nguyen Duy Dien and Bang Phong. *Duong Khue, tieu su, tu tuong, van tho, phe binh* (Duong Khue: Biography, Thoughts, Writings, and Critiques). Saigon: Khai Tri, 1960.

Nguyen Hien Le. *Bay ngay trong Dong-Thap-Muoi* (Seven Days in the Plain of Reeds). Saigon: Tri Dang, 1970.

―――. *Hoi Ky* (Memoir). Ho Chi Minh City: Nha xuat ban van hoc, 1993.

―――. *Dong Kinh Nghia Thuc* (The Free School of Dong Kinh). Saigon: La Boi, 1956.

Nguyen Phut Tan. *A Modern History of Vietnam*. Saigon: Khai Tri, 1964.

Nguyen Thai. *Is South Vietnam Viable?* Manila: Carmelo & Bauermann, 1962.

Nguyen Thi Chan Quynh. *"Loi xua xe ngua. . ."* ("The Tracks Left by the Horse-drawn Carriage. . ."). Paris: An Tiem, 1995.

Nguyen Tien Hung and Jerrold L. Schecter. *The Palace File*. New York: Harper and Row, 1986.

Nguyen Tran. *Cong va toi, hoi ky lich su chinh tri mien Nam Viet Nam, 1945-1975* (Contributions and Crimes: Memoirs on the Political History of South Vietnam, 1945-1975). Los Alamitos, California: Xuan Thu, 1992.

Nguyen Trieu Dan. *A Vietnamese Family Chronicle: Twelve Generations on the Banks of the Hat River*. Jefferson, N.C.: McFarland, 1991.

Nguyen Vy. *Tuan, chang trai nuoc Viet, chung tich thoi dai tu 1900 den 1970* (Tuan, a Son of Vietnam: Witness of the Period from 1900 to 1970). 2 vols. Saigon: published by the author, 1969.

O'Ballance, Edgar. *The Indo-China War 1945-1954: A Study in Guerrilla Warfare*. London: Faber & Faber, 1964.

Oberdorfer, Don. *Tet!* New York: Doubleday, 1971.

Patti, Archimedes L. A. *Why Viet-Nam? Prelude to America's Albatross*. Berkeley: University of California Press, 1980.

The Pentagon Papers: The Defense Department History of United States Decision Making on Vietnam. 4 vols. Boston: Beacon Press, 1971.

Pham Cao Duong. *Vietnamese Peasants Under French Domination, 1861-1945.* Berkeley: Center for South and Southeast Asia Studies, University of California, 1985.

Pham Duy. *Hoi Ky, Thoi cach mang khang chien.* (Memoirs: The Resistance Period). Garden Grove, Calif.: Pham Duy Cuong, 1989.

Pham Quang Giai. *Trai cai tao* (The Re-education Camp). Houston: Liviko Printing, 1985.

Plamenatz, John. *German Marxism & Russian Communism.* New York: Harper & Row, 1954.

Porter, Gareth, "Imperialism and Social Structure in Twentieth Century Vietnam." Ph.D. dissertation, Cornell University, 1976.

————. *The Politics of Democratic Socialism.* Ithaca: Cornell University Press, 1993.

Rosie, George, *The British in Vietnam: How the Twenty-five Year War Began.* London: Panther Books, 1970.

Salisbury, Harrison. *Behind the Lines—Hanoi.* New York: Harper & Row, 1967.

Schriner, Alfred. *Les institutions annamites.* Vol. 1. Saigon: Claude & Cie, 1900.

Scigliano, Robert. *South Vietnam: Nation Under Stress.* Boston: Houghton Mifflin, 1963.

Shaplen, Robert. *The Lost Revolution, The U.S. in Vietnam, 1946-1966.* New York: Harper & Row, 1966.

————. *The Road from War.* New York: Harper & Row, 1970.

Shapley, Deborah. *Promise and Power: The Life and Times of McNamara.* Boston: Little, Brown, 1993.

Simpson, Howard R. *Tiger in the Barbed Wire.* New York: Kodansha International, 1992.

Snepp, Frank. *Decent Interval: An Insider's Account of Saigon's Indecent End Told by the CIA's Chief Strategy Analyst in Vietnam.* New York: Random House, 1977.

So Van Hoa va Thong Tin Hanoi. *Thang Long, Dong Do, Ha Noi* (The City of the Rising Dragon, the Eastern Capital, and Hanoi). Hanoi: So Van Hoa Thong Tin Ha Noi, 1991.

Spector, Ronald H. *Advice and Support: The Early Years of the U.S. Army in Vietnam, 1941-1960.* New York: The Free Press, 1985.

————. *After Tet: The Bloodiest Year in Vietnam.* New York: The Free Press, 1993.

Szulc, Tad. *The Illusion of Peace: Foreign Policy in the Nixon Years.* New York: Viking, 1978.

Terzani, Tiziano. *Giai Phong: The Fall and Liberation of Saigon*. New York: St. Martin's Press, 1976.

Thach Lam. *Ha-Noi bam sau pho phuong* (Hanoi and Its Thirty-six Streets). Saigon: Doi Nay, 1970.

Thanh Tin. *Hoa Xuyen Tuyet* (The Snow Bells). Irvine, Calif.: Nhan Quyen, 1991.

―――. *Mat That* (The True Face). Irvine, Calif.: Saigon Press, 1993.

Tran Huy Lieu et al., eds. *Cach Mang Thang Tam: Tong khoi nghia o Ha Noi va cac dia phuong* (The August Revolution: General Insurrection in Hanoi and Various Localities). 2 vols. Hanoi: Su Hoc, 1960.

Tran Phuong, ed. *Cach mang ruong dat o Viet-nam* (The Land Revolution in Vietnam). Hanoi: Nha xuat ban Khoa Hoc Xa Hoi, 1968.

Tran Van Giap, ed. *Luoc truyen cac tac gia Viet-Nam* (Reviews of Vietnamese Authors). Vol. 1. Hanoi: Nha xuat ban Khoa Hoc Xa Hoi, 1971.

Truong Nhu Tang with David Chanoff and Doan Van Toai. *Viet Cong Memoir: An Inside Account of the Vietnam War and Its Aftermath*. Orlando, Fla.: Harcourt Brace Jovanovich, 1985.

Vien Mac-Lenin. *Lich su Dang Cong San Viet Nam (tom tat)* (History of the Communist Party of Vietnam—A Summary). Hanoi: Nha Xuat Ban Su That, 1985.

Warner, David. *The Last Confucian*. New York: Macmillan, 1963.

White, Christine. "Agrarian Reform and National Liberation in the Vietnamese Revolution: 1920-1957." Ph.D. dissertation, Cornell University, 1981.

Woodside, Alexander B. *Community and Revolution in Modern Vietnam*. Boston: Houghton Mifflin, 1976.

Young, Marilyn B. *The Vietnam Wars, 1945-1990*. New York: Harper Collins, 1991.

Zasloff, Joseph, ed. *Postwar Indochina: Old Enemies and New Allies*. Foreign Service Institute, U.S. Department of State, 1988.

Index

A NOTE ON THE TYPE

The Sacred Willow is set in Deepdene,
a font designed by Frederic Goudy.
Goudy drew the font, named after his
house in Marlborough, New York, in
1927; the digitized version used here
was issued by Lanston Monotype.

Design and composition was by Adam B.
Bohannon; Helen Mules handled
production.